MALT
WHISKY
YEARBOOK
2024

Slàinte!

First published in Great Britain in 2023 by
MagDig Media Limited

© MagDig Media Limited 2023

ISBN 978-1-7394492-0-9

MagDig Media Limited
1 Brassey Road
Old Potts Way, Shrewsbury
Shropshire SY3 7FA
ENGLAND

E-mail: info@maltwhiskyyearbook.com
www.maltwhiskyyearbook.com

Contents

Introduction

Since the new millenium, the world of whisky has become increasingly more diversified and complex. In Malt Whisky Yearbook 2024, I asked six Whisky Hall of Fame inductees about their views on the state of whisky and got some fascinating comments. In the book you will also find articles discussing everything from intricacies of production and how whisky could be more inclusive to why Australia has risen to the top as a producer and the possible challenges to whisky´s world domination.

And as usual there is the thoroughly revised and updated section on Scottish malt whisky distilleries; the chapter on distilleries from the rest of the world has been expanded; The Whisky Year That Was provides a summary of all the significant events during the year. You will also find a chapter about independent bottlers and suggestions on where to find more information about whisky in social media. Finally, the latest statistics answers your questions on production and consumption.

Thank you for buying Malt Whisky Yearbook 2024 - I wish you a pleasant read!

Acknowledgements

First of all I wish to thank the writers who have shared their great specialist knowledge on the subject in a brilliant and entertaining way – Andrew Derbidge, Joel Harrison, Johanne McInnis, Neil Ridley, Kristiane Sherry and Ian Wisniewski. A special thanks goes to Ian who put in a lot of effort nosing, tasting and writing notes for this year´s independent bottlings. I am also deeply grateful to Stefan van Eycken and Philippe Jugé for their valuable input on Japanese and French distilleries.

The following persons have also made important photographic or editorial contributions and I am grateful to all of them:

Asa Abraham, Iain Allan, David Allen, Andre de Almeida, Alasdair Anderson, Russel Anderson, Nuno Antunes, Andrew Ballantyne, Fred Baumgärtner, Connor Beattie, Richard Beattie, Kirsteen Beeston, Blake Belluschi, Marilena Bidaine, Stewart Bowman, Thomas Boyd, Ross Bremner, Keith Brian, Katie O´Brien, Mike Brisebois, Andrew Brown, Angela Brown, Amy Brownlee, Gordon Bruce, Mark Brunton, Brendan Buckley, Erin Bullard, Neil Bulloch, Roselyn Burnett, Kerry Campbell, Daniel Cant, Rob Carpenter, Oliver Chilton, Jonathan Christie, David Clark, Suzanne Clark, Maria Coelho, Francis Conlon, Mairi Corbett, Georgie Crawford, Tori Currie, Ewa Czernecka, Steven Dalgarno, Stephen Davies, Alasdair Day, Paul Dempsey, Lucy Donaldson, Kenny Douglas, Alex Driver, Lukasz Dynowiak, Michael Elliot, Simon Erlanger, Wendy Espie, Graham Eunson, James Evans, David Ferguson, Allan Findlay, Robert Fleming, Paddy Fletcher, John Fordyce, George Forsyth, Leah Forsyth, Callum Fraser, Kathrin Furst, Gillian Gibson, Colin Gordon, Tomer Goren, Olivia Gould, Gemma Grierson, Andre Haberecht, Gary Haggart, Adam Hannett, Soichiro Harada, Mike Hayward, Islay Heads, Kieran Healey-Ryder, Euan Henderson, Kara Hepburn, Erik Hirschfeld, Peter Holroyd, Dánial Hoydal, Fraser Hughes, Robbie Hughes, Samantha Isac, Sandy Jamieson, Paul John, Rebecca Kean, Murray Kerr, Ekaterina Kolesnik, Andrew Laing, Cara Laing, Mark Lancaster, Wendy Lei, Richard Lin, Jamie Lockhart, Ian Logan, Alistair Longwell, Daniel Lumsden, Barry Macaffer, Iain McAlister, Brian MacAulay, Alistair McDonald, John MacDonald, Fiona McFadyen, John MacFarlane, Sandy Macintyre, Matt McKay, Sarah McKeeman, Connal Mackenzie, John MacKenzie, Jaclyn McKie, Julia Mackillop, Paul Mclean, Kevin MacPherson, Ian McWilliam, Patrick Maguire, Martin Markvardsen, Chris Maybin, Kwanele Mdluli, Eilidh Mellis, Charles Metcalfe, Gary Mills, Andrew Millsopp, Alison Milne, Carol More, Peter Moser, Jamie Muir, Louise Mulholland, Paul Mundie, Cristina Munoz, Neil Murphy, Kim Møller-Elshøj, Ulric Nijs, Ingemar Nordblom, Catherine Oag, Ian Palmer, Becky Paskin, Marc Pendlebury, Bruce Perry, Lauren Plumpton, Colin Poppy, Gemma Porter, Struan Grant Ralph, Malcolm Rennie, Ian Renwick, James Roberts, Joseph Sammons, Ernst Scheiner, Lila Serenelli, Andrew Shand, Sam Simmons, Sukhinder Singh, Greig Stables, Piotr Stachura, Kenneth Stephen, Paul Stephenson, Grant Sutherland, Stephen Symington, Jota Tanaka, Eddie Thom, Phil Thompson, Julie Trujillo, Kaitlyn Tsai, David Turner, Sandrine Tyrbas de Chamberet, Perry Unger, Andrew Waite, Stewart Walker, Leon Webb, Iain Weir, Susan Williamson, Anthony Wills, Alan Winchester, Jamie Winfield, Kristoffer Wittström, Rebecca Wood, Jason Yankelowitz, Allison Young and Derek Younie.

Finally, to my wife Pernilla and our daughter Alice, thank you for your patience and your love!

Ingvar Ronde
Editor
Malt Whisky Yearbook

The best known Australian whisky internationally is Starward

Australia
– the new whisky powerhouse!

by Andrew Derbidge

The opening of new distilleries in Australia
in the past 20 years is unparalleled in the whisky industry.
When the first Malt Whisky Yearbook was published in 2005 there
were five – now there are more than a hundred. Andrew Derbidge tells
the story of how it all started and what we can expect in the future.

———

For anyone wanting to understand or explore the story of Australian whisky, the challenge is not knowing where to start, but when. You could be forgiven for thinking that Australian whisky didn't exist until 2014. For that was the year that Sullivans Cove won World's Best Single Malt at the World Whiskies Awards and indelibly thrust Australian whisky as a category into the collective conscience of the international whisky community. But to think that the 2014 award came unexpectedly out of the blue – as many international commentators did at the time – is to ignore the 25 years of history and growth in the Australian whisky industry that occurred before then. And the 130 years of history and development that came before that.

If one was to present the history of Australian whisky in a movie franchise, it would likely comprise of five films or episodes, with the fifth episode currently wrapping production as we go to print. Not unlike the sequencing of the Star Wars films, most people were introduced to the story at Episode Four. Indeed, "A New Hope" is an apt descriptor: Its story starts in 1989 and its heroes were the likes of Brian Poke, Robert Hosken, and the more famous name, Bill Lark. These people are often termed the pioneers or founders of the modern Australian industry, as it was their actions that started a renaissance or re-birth after the Australian whisky industry had fallen entirely silent in the early 1980's.

It is not the intention of this piece to delve too deeply into Australian whisky's preceding episodes, but it would be remiss not to give them a cursory nod here for context. If we stick with the film

Bill Lark, a pioneer of the modern Australian whisky industry

analogy, Episode One covers the period of early European settlement and the production of spirit (initially rum, although whisky eventually followed) that laid the foundations for an industry. Episode Two tackles the period from the mid-19th century to 1920 and tells the story of the first large-scale distilleries that took on distilling on a commercial scale with commercial intentions, particularly in Victoria. They created a huge, vibrant and successful industry, with production levels and sales vastly exceeding the volume of Scotch being consumed in Australia – a situation helped significantly by protectionist excise tariffs that made imported Scotch a more expensive choice for consumers.

Episode Three starts happily enough in the late 1920's and initially covers the climb to the local industry's zenith in the early 1960's. However, its second act charts the sad and rapid decline to the 1980's when the industry fell silent, eventually dying.

Plenty of successful Australian whisky brands were introduced in the 1920's and 30's, most of them blended malts. That said, grain whisky was also being produced, particularly with the construction of the DCL-owned Corio distillery in 1929, which distilled both malt and grain in pot and column stills respectively. Corio launched several brands, including the all-conquering Corio's 5 Star Whisky in 1956 that sold over eight million bottles locally and overseas in its first four years. By 1960, locally-made blended whisky ruled the roost as DCL slowly merged with or bought out various competing malt distilleries and their brands, and then strategically downplayed or discontinued their products.

However, the removal of import tariffs in the mid-1960's changed the landscape irreversibly, and imported Scotch suddenly became a more affordable and appealing option to consumers. DCL – the pre-cursor to today's Diageo – owned both the country's largest distillery and all of its Corio-labelled brands. But it was cheaper, convenient, and more corporately strategic to import their own Scotch brands than to endeavour to make good whisky locally. Popular folklore has it that Corio's last 10 years were spent deliberately making an inferior whisky that would aid sales of DCL's more exotic Scotch brands. Corio eventually closed in 1980, and the last remaining Australian distillery, Gilbeys, followed suit in 1985. And thus the scene was set for a new hope.

The intricacies of production

To fully understand Australian whisky, it's important to appreciate four key aspects of production, particularly when comparing it to the Scotch industry. (A comparison, it must be said, that is becoming increasingly irrelevant, although the framework around Scotch clearly informs most whisky drinkers' knowledge and points of reference).

Firstly, the minimum age for spirit to legally be called whisky is only two years, not three.

Secondly, the Australian climate presents a very different environment for maturation. Hotter temperatures across the country and low humidity in the southern states and inland regions generally promote faster maturation times, and the vast majority of Australian whisky is released to market at between two and seven years old. The small handful of distilleries that have been around long enough to have older stock may dabble in older releases, but it is extremely rare to encounter whiskies with age statements – let alone age statements in the double digits. Generally speaking, either the angels will have been too greedy by then, or the wood will have overpowered the spirit.

The third aspect to appreciate is the whisky industry's reliance on the local wine industry and, until recently, a tendency amongst the smaller distillers to employ small-cask maturation. For the majority of distilleries, it is neither viable nor practical to stretch out for 200 litre ex-bourbon casks from the USA, when there is such a bountiful supply of cheaper casks on their doorstep from the vibrant wine industry. Ex-fortifieds are particularly popular, with most distilleries filling into ex-port and ex-apera casks. Ex-chardonnay and ex-red wine casks also feature prominently. The majority of the casks are French oak. For reasons of scale, economics, and to drive faster maturation times, many distilleries have their casks re-coopered into smaller 100 litre barrels. Between 2014-2021, many of the smaller start-up distilleries also embarked on filling 20 and 50 litre casks, bringing quite dark and seemingly "ready" whiskies to market at just two years old.

However, courtesy of the hot summers, dry conditions, and the tannins leaching out from the ex-wine French oak casks, many of these releases were hot, tannic, over-oaked, yet under-matured – doing the local scene and reputations no favours. Lessons have been learned; many distilleries are now investing in or sourcing American oak casks, moving to larger barrels, and planning their maturation more carefully.

The fourth aspect of production to appreciate is a tendency amongst distillers to only bottle and market single casks. Driven initially by their small scale and the accompanying economic necessities, this became tradition for many distillers, even after they'd subsequently grown in size and status. Until 2019, you could count on one hand the number of distilleries that vatted multiple casks together to create consistent house styles or higher-volume releases. Larger players have since entered the scene more recently with a view to creating more consistent and scalable "core-range" products, but single cask releases remain the norm for the small to mid-sized distilleries.

Since the early days of the new era, peat has been on the menu, although those that produce peated whisky typically source their peated malt from Scotland. Australia does actually have tiny peat reserves in very small and isolated locations around the country, although no producer capable (or willing) to take on the challenge of peating the barley via a traditional malting process. Instead, what has emerged more recently is a process of "post-smoking". Pioneered by Lark and now adopted to good effect elsewhere (Limeburners and Iniquity being two good examples), already-malted barley is re-wetted with water and then placed in a smoking box. Local peat is then burned in the box, thus infusing phenols and a soft smokiness to the grain.

The current state of play

For the period from the industry's re-birth until 2014, the vast majority of Australia's operating distilleries were small-scale operations that were effectively hobbies or passion projects being run on the side.

Financed hand-to-mouth or subsidised by the owners' main profession, production levels at most distilleries were extremely small, typically 3,000

The whisky producers have relied heavily on casks from Australian vineyards

– 10,000 litres per annum. The industry enjoyed no economies of scale; sales and routes-to-market were limited; and the result was a product that typically sold for anywhere between A$160-$350 and usually in a 500ml bottle.

This at a time when staple Scottish malts like Glenfiddich 12 year old retailed for $55. As good as some of the spirit was, the industry had a hard time convincing whisky drinkers to buy local when the extra premium was so high.

And so to Episode 5: The Sullivans Cove award in 2014 set in motion a series of events and changes in the Australian industry that few foresaw at the time. The first was an explosion of new distilleries being established as plenty of entities moved to jump on the bandwagon. At the time of the award, there were no more than 20 operating malt whisky distilleries in the country. Just 10 years later, that number is now 130, and a further 15-20 distilleries are making whisk(e)y from other grains and mixed mashbills.

The second change was a sudden injection of capital as big business entered the room. For the first time since the 1920's, commercially-minded companies were establishing distilleries or investing in them for large scale production. Diageo arguably started the run when their subsidiary, Distill Ventures, invested in Starward in 2015.

Bill and Lyn Lark had started to sell out of their business in 2013; by 2015 it was effectively owned by a venture capital group. Long-standing companies with interests and proven pedigree in other drinks categories (chiefly wine, fortifieds, brandy, and even soft drinks) built new distilleries or re-purposed old wine-spirit facilities and began distilling malt on a larger scale, backed by significant capital and already-established infrastructure.

Examples included Morris, Cambourne (from Angoves Wine Makers), and 23rd Street (from Bickfords). These players subsequently entered the market three or four years later with new releases that were attractively priced, forcing a much-needed price correction across the board. By the early 2020's, we saw something that hadn't been seen for almost 80 years – healthy competition.

In looking to the future of what the Australian whisky landscape might look like, the foundations have actually been laid in just the last five years. An undeniable aspect will be the return and rise of blends.

The celebrated renaissance period from, say, 1992 to 2017 was almost entirely a single-malt story. This changed in 2018 when Starward launched its Two Fold release – a two-component blend comprising Starward malt with a column-distilled grain whisky

from wheat. Priced at just $65 in a 700ml bottle, it was a genuine game-changer and set a new price point previously unheard of in Australia.

Other large distilleries have since emerged with a raison d'être to produce scalable, bulk quantities of grain and malt spirit entirely for the purpose of blending. Examples include the likes of the Tarac and Ostra distilling operations. Tarac is notable in that it produces malt whisky, yet via continuous distillation in a column still.

In the single malt stakes, other large-scale distilleries have recently been established and laid down stock; others are well developed in the planning stages. Callington Mill upped the stakes in Tasmania with its size and scale; it has a capacity of over 400,000 litres of pure alcohol if firing on all cylinders. Similarly, Coopers – Australia's largest, independent, family-owned brewer and beer company – announced plans in 2022 to enter the whisky market with a new A$50m distillery, visitor centre, and micro-brewery. After three decades of being almost exclusively a small scale, "craft" industry that, by necessity, looked inwards, Australian whisky now has players looking outwards and scaling for the international market.

So what is Australian whisky?

The one thing, however, that you cannot do with Australian whisky is pigeonhole it. As a category, it defies a simple, catch-all definition; there is no single word, phrase, or styling that can adequately capture it. Notwithstanding that Australia is a huge island continent with an enormous spectrum of different terroirs and production techniques being employed across the land, it is an industry where almost anything goes.

Unlike Scotch and the strict constraints put on it by the SWA, Australian whisky is relatively unshackled by restrictions and regulations. Many distillers rejoice in the freedom and innovation this affords with regard to their choice of grains, fermentation methods, still-types, distillation techniques, maturation, use of different casks (both in size and wood species), and product nomenclature.

For example, unlike their Scottish and Irish counterparts, Australian distillers are not obliged to do their own mashing or produce their own wash. Many distilleries thus outsource their wash production to nearby commercial breweries.

This freedom is, however, a two-edged sword. By 2023, some in the industry were starting to question if stronger definitions and regulation was required after several examples of misleading labelling and marketing. Noise was generated when one well-

Established as late as in 2007, Overeem Whisky can still be considered one of the precursors of Australian whisky

known producer started selling a single malt made at one distillery under the established brand name of a different distillery (not a long way removed from Scotland's Cardhu Pure Malt controversy in 2003).

Another issue has been "distilleries" that were still under construction or didn't have mature spirit ready, selling sourced single malt distilled elsewhere, but selling it labelled as their own product under the name of their distillery. Despite such controversies, there is no industry body with sufficient funding, government backing, or "teeth" to do much in the way of enforcement or redress. And in the absence of a more rigid set of definitions and rules around such practices, which many distillers don't want to see introduced, for fear of it stifling "innovation", there often isn't actually much to enforce.

What all this does mean, however, is that the Australian whisky appellation covers a vast array of styles, flavours, and production techniques. The category's strength, and arguably its appeal, is its diversity.

That said, there has been a narrative more recently to condense and categorise Australian whisky releases into one of two camps, and two terms have emerged in common lexicon: A whisky is said to be either "spirit-driven" or "oak-driven". In truth, these are euphemisms. The former typically describes the releases that are lighter in style (dare we say, more Scotch-like) where the malt, spirit, and oak are more balanced, harmonious, and you can taste the distillate.

The latter describes the releases that are typically matured in ex-wine / ex-fortified casks, where the oak dominates the spirit and contributes heavily to the majority of the flavour – often producing one-dimensional, albeit tasty whiskies. They are full-bodied and intensely-flavoured; often ridiculously dark in colour. When done well, they can be truly delicious; other examples occasionally fall into the trap of being too dry and tannic, or they simply come across as highly-alcoholic fortifieds. Nonetheless, they have their fans.

Notwithstanding the increasing tally of awards, medals, and trophies that the Australian distillers are coming home with each year from the various international spirits shows and awards programs, one of the frustrations of the industry has been gaining all those accolades and visibility, but not having sufficient stock to make meaningful inroads into overseas markets.

That is, at last, beginning to turn. It's been over 40 years since Australian wine burst into export markets and made huge splashes overseas. Perhaps Australian whisky is now not too far behind.

Andrew Derbidge wears several hats in the industry: He is the Chairman of the Australian branch of The Scotch Malt Whisky Society and has been one of its directors since 2005. He is also a part-time writer contributing to numerous media, and the man behind the award-winning whisky blog, Whisky and Wisdom. He has been writing about Australian whisky since 2003.

Whisky Evolution

- are you ready for the next frontier?

by Johanne McInnis

Something is cooking
in the traditional business of whisky.
There is a willingness to explore new possibilities
on how to embrace our favourite tipple. Old traditions are being
challenged and Johanne McInnis feels it´s nothing less
than a paradigm shift.

To be honest I am not a Star Trek fan so never understood any of the Mr. Spock references or jokes about how Captain Kirk made: Every. Single. Word. Its. Own. Sentence. However, what I do appreciate is how their franchise, which began in 1966, is not only alive and doing well but is a striving billion dollar industry 57 years later. Part of that success might be due to the fact they still consistently create new, often controversial but pioneering story lines that still respect the theme of every TV and movie spin off: "The final frontier, a continuing mission to explore strange new worlds; to seek out new life and civilizations; to boldly go where no man has gone before!".

I am ashamed to admit that prior to 2020, I spent the better part of a few years writing and boldly complaining about how the whisky category was close to reaching the pinnacle of its popularity. It was painful to witness: Brands tripling production or going from 6 to upwards of 36 core range bottlings. The daily emails introducing new distilleries dumping their products into the market faster then the Campbeltown whisky boom of the mid 19th century and finally, having less whisky stocks available at skyrocketing prices so out of control they have become unreachable to whisky imbibers.

I lamented that the past was doomed and we were about to repeat the 1980's Whisky Loch because the whisky conglomerate was turning into a fast cash, massive over produced/low quality bandwagon that was on the verge of crashing. In 2019, of course, that

Bars all over the world offer new ways to enjoy your favourite whisky   (Photo: Our Whisky Foundation, Jo Hanley)

Becky Paskin - founder of OurWhisky Foundation and Mike Brisebois who founded The Whisky Explorer Corporation

would be completed in the style of an epic Hollywood explosion of Highland Park 40 year old bottles careening in slow motion toward the camera on Tik Tok.

Everything changed when COVID arrived and made us sit still, evaluate and pivot. We shifted to online tastings while brand ambassadors and industry people were forced to present themselves and their products in new ways.

That was likely the point where my opinion about the state of whisky also considerably changed. I went from feeling like the end of an era was near to the realization that we were actually moving at warp speed into the unknown. So in late 2022 as the "stay 6 feet apart" signs came down and the "business as usual" ones started going back up again I watched in wonder as the whisky phoenix rose from the pandemic ashes.

But for some the old saying of: "If it ain't broke, don't fix it" stood firm. So when the wheels of change were set in motion, those exceedingly uncomfortable with the kick at the status quo took a defensive stance against others willing to explore the different possibilities.

The truth of the matter is, my friends, when a good idea builds and gains momentum there is no way of truly destroying the energy it is creating – thankfully that is simply the law of physics. Evolution will ultimately collapse the current antiquated, stagnant and divisive state of the whisky category which will be devastating to those who choose to hang on to those old days – can you say Blackberry?

Meanwhile I continued to embrace this huge paradigm shift, the cynicism leaving me completely and in its place emerged a level of excitement that I hadn't sincerely experienced in the last decade. My post COVID mission somehow became to seek out the people creating this new whisky frontier. I have since experienced opportunities that not only challenge old traditions but clearly demonstrate how these fresh concepts are triggering key individuals and institutions to quickly adapt to the rapid changing environment. The groundwork laid out this past year alone not only promoted but elevated the mindset and creation of inclusive friendly places for anyone to enjoy whisky, regardless of their level of expertise or demographic.

Stereotypical perceptions

I first started reading Becky Paskin's material in 2013 while she was The Spirits Business Editor. In 2015 when she joined Scotchwhisky as a founding editor, she sensed the imbalance of the representation of whisky industry females and the discouraging attitude toward women who drank it. Even with her long list of accolades and General Certificate in Distilling, her knowledge was often questioned and undermined.

This made her grasp how invisible and diminished many other women in the industry also felt and firmly planted a seed. Three years later she and Georgie Bell launched a social media movement called *OurWhisky* with the mission to challenge stereotypical perceptions of whisky drinker advertisements, predominantly depicted by cis white men. By omitting women from marketing campaigns, they were not only influencing what the public's idea was of a whisky drinker but dissuading anyone else from sitting at that table.

The concept immediately took flight with support from both the industry and the public. As 2019 drew to a close, Becky had more time to transform the movement into something even more impactful and began researching what was or wasn't working in various spirit industries.

She asked women what initiatives they felt would benefit them most and the answer was a mentorship program. She took that vision to Millie Milliken, past managing editor of Imbibe UK magazine, who had recently created a different program for another organization. Together they collaborated and the *OurWhisky Foundation* went live in March of 2022.

It still campaigns for greater visibility of women and underrepresented individuals in advertising and marketing but also stands on three core pillars that support, recognize and empower women in the whisky industry through a unique global mentorship program that matches applicants with free mentors who help them reach their goals.

Over 150 women from all over the globe have been through the program so far with many acquiring promotions, new jobs and even setting up their own businesses. The launch of their next unparalleled project came in 2023 – *The Modern Face of Whisky*. Due to the lack of inclusive pictures depicting whisky drinkers and most publications rarely having budgets, there was very little imagery showing people of colour and the female population was mostly portrayed scantily dressed or pregnant.

Becky and Millie took the idea to as many whisky producers as possible for support. It was also important that they have diversity behind the camera too so they enlisted the tremendously talented Australian photographer Jo Hanley to curate their first collection. Within a week of the free stock photo library going live it had over three million views and 20,000 downloads.

What they have initiated in less than 5 years is a massive step forward for equality and inclusivity in the global whisky realm thanks to their mentors, supporters and corporate sponsorships. Every single success is proof they are on the right track, not only for the underrepresented but for the future of whisky. David Vitale, one of their mentors recently stated that the impact of the *OurWhisky Foundation* is going to be multi-generational. Becky and Millie are banking on that.

Let´s open up over whisky

The UK is not the only part of the world where this transformation is taking hold. Sweden has extremely restrictive laws that prohibit alcohol advertising and unlike other demographics, there isn't much data available about the female whisky drinking population since so few attend whisky events or festivals.

High Coast Distillery's brand ambassador Sarah Larrson recalled a discussion where a man told her: "It was useless to try and bring women into the equation because, simply stated, it was part of a man's DNA to drink whisky and women were only meant to drink wine".

That conversation cemented her determination to change that narrative and over a cup of coffee with

Susan Stenström and Sara Larsson from
Let´s Open Up Over Whisky

The Cairn Distillery in the Cairngorms National Park

fellow brand ambassador James McCallum the *Let's Open up Over Whisky* idea was born.

Later in the summer of 2021 a group of industry suppliers came together in unison to start breaking down that stereotypical whisky consumer image. Their mission: Provide whisky education and training that will encourage respectful conversations for him, her and everyone.

One of the ways they hope to effectuate that change is through their unique whisky scholarship competition. Every year they accept nominations from women who are interested in making the whisky community more inclusive and award the scholarship to two people who get to experience a full week's stay at the High Coast Distillery in Sweden and also travel to Scotland for 4 nights to visit three different distilleries.

Albeit in its infancy, the *Let's Open up Over Whisky* team has a 5 year plan and are fully committed to create an equal and inclusive whisky community by forging forward on the difficult journey ahead.

In the end what they hope to create is a place where gender doesn't define who chooses to enjoy drinking whisky.

Whisky distillery of the future

Ardnahoe is but one of the modern distilleries recently built on Islay that I visited in 2019 and for the stunning view of the Jura Paps alone, I will go again. Until then I hadn't realized that most of the my distillery tours had one thing in common; I only went once because they all have the same guided wander through a historical old building explaining the entire process followed by a tasting then the opportunity to buy a bottle from the gift shop.

When visiting new modern distilleries, I often came away feeling like they tried to ride on the coattails of an 1800's yarn made up by an outsourced marketing team. So when the leading example of exceptional quality whiskies, Gordon & MacPhail, decided to take the plunge and design the whisky distillery of the future I was a little skeptical.

Four generations of the Urquhart family have been producing whisky through the perfect art of maturation and balancing casks. In 1993 they bought and restored the Benromach distillery with the goal to gain distillation knowledge by replicating the old Speyside whisky styles of the past.

I interviewed Richard Urquhart in 2014 and he expressed how they consider themselves stewards for the next generation knowing full well the present whiskies sitting in the warehouses would be enjoyed by their children and grandchildren.

The Cairn distillery is the fruit of the Urquhart's family dream that not only breaks away from the traditional past but continues their stewardship commitment into the future.

Nestled in the northern part of the Cairngorms National Park near Grantown-on-Spey, it is the furthest thing from the typical looking Scottish distillery. The buildings are rounded and made with an unusual combination of steel, stone and wood that harmonize perfectly with its inspiring natural surroundings. The roof, void of pagodas, is turfed with native plant species. The planning phase revolved around choosing a place where the distillery would fully integrate, becoming a part of the local community and surroundings.

Although the first whiskies distilled on site won't be ready to taste until the 2030's, visitors can be fully immersed in a variety of wide multi-sensory experiences. Through the environmental partnerships they have with the National Park, people can learn how they are recreating the Aspen corridor or hike some of the extensive nature trails.

The distillery also features local seasonal ingredients at their bistro as well as unique collaborations with the area's musicians, artists or chefs. As the Cairn continues to push the boundaries of what a modern distillery should be, its people slowly move forward creating a new kind of whisky history.

A new way of presenting whisky

Mike Brisebois is a Canadian who has never really filled any whisky mold and is often described as a genuinely driven geek who has always wanted to simply create unforgettable whisky experiences.

Like many of us he was introduced to Scotch when he received a bottle as a gift which naturally progressed to buying books and a lot more whisky. Then during a discussion with his wife she put forward the idea of the possibility of creating a community where different bottlings could be purchased and shared.

That opened the door for Mike to start a local whisky club which then steered him into his first job with a national whisky distributor. While most brand ambassadors poured whiskies behind the tables at festivals, Mike was renting a bus and borrowing a mansion that faced the ocean to taste an exceptional bottle of whisky with some very surprised but happy whisky geeks.

Simply said – Mike garners a large following because he has a reputation of not only knowing his whisky community but thoroughly understanding them.

Like everyone else, COVID gave pause but for Mike it ignited a new vision so when he parted ways with the company, he decided he would put his grand scheme in place. He wanted to capture what

he felt was missing in today's whisky culture. He wanted to change the way it is presented through a balance of education, passionate connections with people, stories and most of all fun.

With that, *The Whisky Explorer Corporation* was born. Mike doesn't do anything small so it came as no surprise that his first revolutionary project was overtaking Ottawa, our nation's capital, by storm in February of 2023 when he hosted a 3 day outdoor whisky extravaganza that embraced Canada's winter at its best – *Whisky Wonderland.*

Sold out crowds came in droves to take part which was unprecedented for any first year show. 2024 will once again bring *Whisky Wonderland* to Ottawa but his long term plan is to take it on a 5000km coast to coast tour.

But Mike doesn't just stop there as he's in the process of working on a new digital consumer driven whisky magazine that will be published in October of 2023, organizing a cross-cultural panel of judges for a different style of whisky awards in 2024, the creation of adult style whisky summer camps for 2025 and so much more.

The last thing he said to me as we closed down the interview was: "I've discovered my true purpose is to redefine what whisky is all about". His vision and ideas are grandiose but so is Mike's passion and will to get it done.

Being at the forefront of monumental change is never easy but when you have people like the ones listed above who are tomorrow's relentless, hard-working visionaries, anything is possible.

And with that, I'll reiterate where I first started, here we stand at the beginning of the next evolution and I've introduced you to just a few of the people blazing forward with the mission to explore this strange new world, and bring whisky boldly where it has never gone before – into the next whisky frontier.

Johanne McInnis, also known as the Whiskylassie, is a retired Canadian Whisky Awards Judge. She is a freelance spirits writer who mostly focuses on whisky and has contributed to various publications and websites such as Whisky Magazine, Cask & Still and Distiller. Johanne is a strong advocate for change in the spirits industry and currently serves as a mentor for the next generation of its women. She is looking forward to hosting masterclasses and Scottish whisky tours once again in 2024 and is currently in the process of writing her first whisky book.

Will single malt whisky be able to stand up to the challenge from other spirits?

The Succession Conundrum

by Neil Ridley

Over six centuries Scotch whisky has built
its reputation, although often challenged by other spirits.
In recent years, single malts (also from other countries) have pinnacled
to become the most sought-after spirit. Can the category protect
its glittering, global crown from the pretenders to the throne?

"Life's not 'knights on horseback': it's a number on a piece of paper and a fight for a knife in the mud."

All hail the realities of a thorough business dressing down: brutally, yet honestly spewed out by the late Logan Roy; the unscrupulous, power-hungry Scottish-born media mogul, in possession of a moral compass so fractured that his words both terrified his employees and simultaneously empowered his children to unspeakable ends.

If you're unfamiliar with Succession, Roy, (played masterfully and with utter menace by Brian Cox) his family, or their ungodly and bitter relationship, which saw his children repeatedly stab one another in the back failing to take over from him as the CEO of the fictional corporation, Waystar Royco, then you should consider addressing your viewing habits. Of course, the fictional Roys are wild caricatures of the worst human traits in many respects, but their relationship is a fascinating one, which got me thinking about the hierarchy in the family of global dark spirits and their 'pecking order' from the consumer's perspective.

There's little doubt in my mind that single malt whiskies, particularly those from Scotland and Japan, represent the pinnacle of the spirits world: the Logan Roy, if you will, both in traditional prestige and high-end value. However, like Roy's young, dynamic and highly ambitious offspring, the pretenders to this spirited throne are circling, sensing blood.

In 2022, sales of rum surpassed £1bn in the UK, meaning that for the first time ever the spirit now accounts for a bigger market share than Scotch. Similarly, global sales of super premium tequila have risen dramatically in the same time period: in the US alone, they are up nearly 20%, compared to a 2.5% fall in demand for premium Scotch. This groundswell in consumer confidence towards rum and tequila – particularly driven by a younger, more progressive and dynamic audience, is unlikely to cause the complete, untimely demise of Scotch whisky. However it is cause for concern across the industry.

So, like one of those expensive fictional therapists you often see in TV dramas such as Succession, I wanted to test this theory out, across some of the sharpest minds in drinks: from whisky itself, to those eyeing up the prize in both the tequila and rum sectors. I wanted to find out their inner thoughts about what whisky, particularly single malt, can learn from its competitors to adapt and succeed in the future. Unlike the Roys, can a harmonious and happy balance ultimately be found amongst such an ambitious, dysfunctional family of spirits?

The challengers

Firstly though, where do whisky producers see the main competition coming from – particularly single malt – in terms of these newly emerging premium spirit categories?

"Rum most immediately," thinks Angus MacRaild, independent whisky bottler, writer, and now co-founder of the recently announced Kythe whisky distillery in Perthshire.

"Then perhaps Armagnac and Cognac in the longer term. All of these other spirits are problematic in their own ways for the whisky drinker. The problems that Scotch whisky has are often the ones it makes for itself, which is about an imbalanced quality-to-price ratio. Ultimately, as drinkers educate themselves they'll look around, but if their first love is Scotch whisky, they'll often find their way back there," he continues.

"Single Malt is a global phenomenon, which has enjoyed a remarkable renaissance since 2000," continues Kieran Healey-Ryder, Head of Communica-

tions for Whyte & Mackay. "What we make speaks perfectly to the consumer demand for a highly crafted product, storied proposition, beautifully presented. Yet, what it took to stand out in 2000, would not stand out today, which is why it is an incredibly exciting time now – and a real moment for the maker. Competition is important, as it challenges us as makers, but inspiration is borderless."

I also wanted to see where some of the more global outliers in whisky making felt the competition was coming from. Step up Max Vaughan, founder of White Peak in Derbyshire, England and more further afield, Tomáš Mačuga from Slovakia's Nestville distillery, which has begun to make numerous European fans for its innovative approach to mash bills and cask maturation.

"I think any other category that invites consumers to appreciate the spirit neat i.e. can be appreciated for flavour on its own, is a potential competitor to the broad single malt category," explains Vaughan, whose Wire Works single malt is really lighting up the palates of whisky consumers and industry figures across the UK and Europe.

"But as an emerging single malt whisky brand, I see this competition as an opportunity. If consumers are increasingly enjoying a wider range of spirits, it suggests on average they will be more discerning about their single malt whisky choices, and a competitive landscape is something we've always factored into our plans."

For Tomáš, it's a similar view.

"It is true that the popularity of premium spirits in the rum, tequila and brandy categories is on the rise, but whisky still maintains its market position and sales in Europe. This could be best described and represented by a 'sine wave': where the popularity of some spirit categories accelerates as others drop. There are some years when rum and tequila outperform whisky and vice versa. Our whisky's advantage is in its versatility and adjustability, as well as the use of different grain varieties for the base spirit."

A view from the competitors

To turn the debate on its head somewhat, I thought it would be interesting to ask some of the producers of these perceived throne-challenging spirits – both aged rum and tequila, what it was they admired most about the whisky category, particularly Scotch, its global appeal and desirability.

"What I admire most is the integrity of the category," points out Richard Seale, Master Distiller & Blender at Foursquare rum in Barbados, a distillery, which has, over the past few years, been a guiding light in the super premumisation of rum, away from the wild west of the past and into a more regulated heritage-led future.

"Scotch attracts high value both at retail and secondary markets. People trust the contents. It has intrinsic value which comes from artisanal production and long maturation. The debate about age and preference is irrelevant: a long matured Scotch (or rum) has real intrinsic value. This is objective truth. Contrast with gin or vodka. These products have perceived value. They can be mass produced on an industrial scale. Paying more for one vodka over another is pure perception."

For Briac Dessertenne, co-founder of Cuba's Eminente rum (owned by the LVMH group, which also includes both Ardbeg and Glenmorangie single malts in its premium spirits portfolio,) his admiration comes from both the raw materials as well as the people behind the spirit.

"First, there are the roots of this category, e.g. the barley: it is a hard and relatively expensive cereal to grow, that needs careful attention and dedication. Then there is the know-how embedded in the region, the sharing of expertise from one generation to the next, something that we can definitely relate to in Cuban rum, with more than 150 years of rum making history on the island."

Over in super premium, 'Anejo' aged tequila – a category making apparent gains in the drinks cabinets of many whisky drinkers, especially in the US, it's a similar viewpoint shared by one of the key players.

"I think that beyond the mastery of the ageing process, single malt has demonstrated that terroir and the hand of the maker in a particular distillery both matter a lot and are worth paying a premium price for," believes Charles Dos Santos, Business Acceleration VP for Pernod Ricard's 'House of Tequila': home to the Altos, Avión Reserva and Olmeca brands.

"I believe its success is partly due to a growing un-

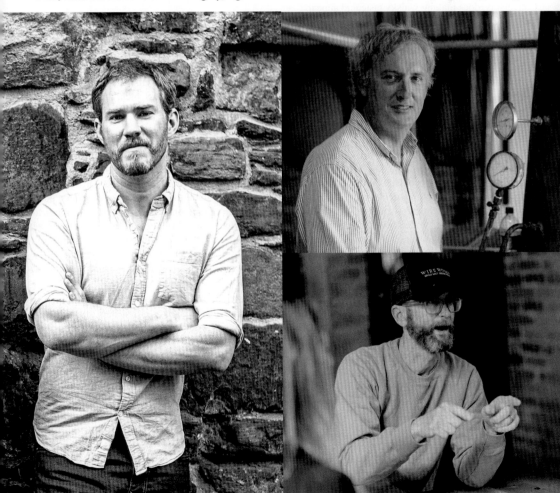

Angus MacRaild (left), Richard Seale (top right) and Max Vaughan (bottom right)

derstanding and appreciation of these elements by consumers. In tequila, terroir plays a fundamental role, too. The origin and quality of the agave has a strong impact on the final liquid. Just like people recognise the importance of the raw ingredient used to make a single malt whisky, people start to understand that, in tequila, the choice of the agave matters."

The dangers of crossover

So there are clearly convergences between these once distinct dark spirits categories. Elements of origin and storied craft, prestige ingredients and maturation are all desirable attributes to a dark spirit, and are no doubt seen as huge selling points for consumers.

But is there really a need for more crossover between them? In many respects, bringing them closer together certainly creates a shared audience, but is that the right thing to do commercially in the future? Conversely, does making whisky taste and appear more like its challengers just diminish what is fundamentally at its heart?

Richard Seale is particularly salient on this point. "For me, maturing Scotch in an ex-tequila cask makes no sense. It is not a primary cask, it's [usually] an ex-whisky (bourbon) cask that had tequila in it. Yes, Scotch does use refill casks; that is its heritage, but it is refilling high quality casks from primary sources with historical links."

"I think the vast majority of these 'cask tinkering' projects do not produce good quality whiskies, offers Angus MacRaild. "I believe that what most casual consumers want is something delicious, at a fair price, with an age statement – which is something visually immediate and understandable. I think people are increasingly wising up to, and are repelled by gimmickry, which is what almost all these cask finishing things are: gimmicks."

So does wilder innovation actually just play further into the hands of the competitor spirits? Is it there to pick up new whisky consumers from those spirits categories, or does it actually convince whisky drinkers to appreciate new, but more disparate flavours – consequently just pulling them further away from the whisky category?

"I think there is always a balance, reasons Iain Weir, Brand Director for Ian Macleod Distillers - home of Tamdhu, Glengoyne and now Rosebank distilleries.

"I am in favour of innovation, but we must never forget that first and foremost we are promoting high quality Scotch whisky at its heart! I think there are consumer segments that are attracted by innovation,

and it creates new headlines and awareness to help continue recruiting new consumers and further growing the market. But I also think that originality and affordability will always be a strong undercurrent of the Scotch whisky market and will help us hold onto many existing and loyal consumers."

White Peak's Max Vaughan takes a slightly different approach here.

"In a sense, the world needs wild innovators to spend time at the boundaries of possibility and creativity. For a long time, single malt in general has not really come across as a creative category, poised with open arms to welcome new and diverse consumers, but this is changing with both the new perspectives of world whisky distilleries (flavour, whisky-making, brand positioning, etc) and also with established whisky brands re-imagining themselves. I see the general theme of innovation as a good thing for broadening the category and bringing in consumers."

What can whisky learn?

So what can whisky learn from its challengers? Are there any transferrable elements that can, in essence, be adopted by the spirit to enhance the experience – in particular single malt Scotch, that won't diminish its core pillars too much, or confuse the future, would-be whisky drinker?

"One thing that might be stronger in tequila than in single malt these days is the 'cool factor'", suggests Charles Dos Santos. 'Tequila is the new aspirational drink that all celebrities have in their parties. But, talking more about the product itself, I believe that single malt is sometimes perceived as too complicated and potentially daunting and that you need to be a 'connoisseur' to really understand and appreciate it. So providing guidance to consumers in their journey of exploration and discovery of single malts is important", he continues.

"In that sense, some consumers might need long drinks or even cocktails as a first step, although many experts would argue that it is not 'the right way' to drink single malt."

Tomáš Mačuga over at Nestville is sympathetic to the cause of whisky, but positive about what the wider spirits consumer base takes from its competitors: a certain versatility.

"For years, whisky was seen as a strong drink that was to be enjoyed neat, especially when talking about single malt style whisky, which often doesn't come cheap. In the recent years with the rise of the RTD category and cocktail culture, companies are looking into options how can whisky be drank with

One way of being relevant for younger consumers is offering single malts in whisky cocktails

a mixer: served with tonic, mixed with vermouth or grapefruit soda as a spritz. That way it becomes easy drinking and more approachable."

So in the future, can whisky maintain the mantle as King Of The Spirits? Can it keep a firm hand on its direction, whilst understanding that the consumer needs more versatility alongside the things which make it prestigious and desirable. More poignantly, can it resist the challenges of its heirs-to-the-throne?

"Look, our reputation is 500 years in the making," laughs Whyte & Mackay's Kieran Healey-Ryder. "That said, we are never complacent. It is important to remember behind every cracking whisky are people dedicated to advance the future of art and science in whisky making. That has been a constant in the success story of Scotch. Investment is important – both to be a modern industry today – and for tomorrow to establish the choices we make now, ensure there will be responsibly produced, high-quality, distinctive, flavourful whisky laid down for generations to come."

I leave the final word to Angus MacRaild.

"Scotch needs to look honestly – and with an open mind – at what other, quality-focused spirits producers are doing around the world and try to understand their successes, or failures, and learn from them. Make the quality of the more humble, sub-£100 bottles better. If more drinkers, can afford better quality drams, that's a big part of Scotch whisky's ongoing success. Rather than obsessing about absolute volume, think about products that are marginally more expensive to allow for a genuinely more interesting and distinctive production process, that creates a better product that is worth the extra £5-10 per bottle."

Succession might have ended *spoiler alert* with Logan dead and buried. However, his children, Kendall, Shiv and Roman, the pretenders to his throne, tried – and failed – to unite, to create a more successful future legacy of their own, mostly because their vision was unfocused, too reactionary and short term. Something tells me that whisky is smarter than them all and has a few wily tricks up its sleeve to continue leading the charge, so long as it stays true to itself: one step ahead of its challengers for many years yet.

Just as Logan Roy barked to his squabbling offspring in a moment of clarity:

"When it's all said and done, there's only one thing you have to know: How to hold the reins."

Neil writes about whisky and other fine spirits for a number of publications globally, including Decanter and The Daily and Sunday Telegraph. He is a Keeper Of The Quaich and a Liveryman in the Worshipful Company Of Distillers. Neil regularly presents a drinks feature on the popular TV food and drink show, Channel Four Sunday Brunch. His first book, (written with Gavin D. Smith) 'Let Me Tell You About Whisky' was published in 2013 and since then, he has co-authored six further books including 'Distilled', with Joel Harrison, the World Atlas Of Gin and the World Of Whisky. His latest book, 60 Second Cocktails was released in October 2022.

Oxidation
- a fascinating enigma

by Ian Wisniewski

When newmake spirit has been filled into a cask,
a number of processes start to transform it into mature whisky.
One of them is oxidation – perhaps the least understood of them all. Under the
influence of oxygen, sulphur compounds are deconstructed and new flavours
are created. Ian Wisniewski explains why a breathing cask
is fundamental to create a good whisky.

The rhythm changes but the process continues: inhaling, exhaling, whether we are asleep or awake. Being autonomic, no effort or even awareness is required. When casks breathe the frequency and mechanics differ but the process is the same: air gives life to the ageing process.

Air is dominated by nitrogen at around 78% of the total, but this has no influence within a cask. Oxygen accounts for a mere 21% but facilitates oxidation, which refines malt whisky and increases complexity. It takes at least 5-7 years to discern the effects of oxidation, though the process begins when a cask is filled. Casks must be emptied of any previous occupant, such as sherry, before filling. But empty casks are, nevertheless, full of air. Filling from the bottom, by lowering a filling lance (pipe) into position, expels air from the cask, some air caught within the spirit bubbles up to the surface, while some air is also 'trapped' in the cask by the spirit.

"Filling pushes air into a cask's cracks and crevices, with the char layer of a bourbon barrel offering plenty of both, and this is the first instance of oxygen integrating with the new make spirit," says Ian Palmer, Managing Director, Inchdairnie.

The level to which casks are filled varies, and has a consequence for oxidation. Some distilleries fill to 95% capacity, ensuring a headspace (ie. 'empty area' between the surface of the spirit and top of the cask) where air accumulates.

But even casks filled 100% develop a headspace within 24-48 hours due to 'indrink,' when staves 'drink in' (absorb) spirit, which lowers the level in the cask. This is typically 3% of the total amount filled, but varies among cask types.

"Fresh casks have staves that are still saturated with the previous occupant, such as sherry, so the level of indrink is minimal. Dechar/rechar and STR (Shave, Toast, Rechar) casks have so much alcohol burned out when rejuvenated that they end up with much drier staves, and the level of indrink is much higher. The same applies to virgin casks," says Stuart Harvey, Master Blender, International Beverage (previously known as Inver House Distillers).

Air channels

Air has two routes into the headspace, one is short haul, through gaps between staves and around the bung; the other is long haul, going through the staves.

A bourbon barrel stave is 25 mms thick, with a char layer of 2-4 mms, while sherry cask staves are 28-30 mms, with a toasted layer of 1-2 mms. However, the journey is far longer than the number of mms suggest, as there aren't direct paths leading straight through a stave.

Air enters the exterior surface of a stave and navigates its way through pores, essentially empty spaces leading onto each other. But pores also lead to a junction with xylem, conduits running the length of the stave (which originally conducted water and nutrients throughout the tree). The only option is to turn left or right, and continue along a conduit, until reaching a junction with pores which provides an exit. Pores lead to another junction with the next conduit, and so it repeats.

Air also reaches the interior of a cask instantaneously, by passing through gaps between staves and joints, as well as around the bung. Natural variations in the size and shape of bung holes (even among the same cask types) can prevent the bung from doing its job.

"Bung application is most important, and over the past 20 years we have advocated 8 different sizes of bung for all our casks to cover variations in bung hole size. We also moved away from oak bungs to poplar which provide a tighter fit," says Sandy Hyslop, Ballantine's Master Blender.

Direct routes for air become more accessible as staves around the bung dehydrate (having lost contact with spirit) and shrink. This expands cracks between staves facilitating air flow, but is also subject to seasonality.

"In summer conditions in the ageing warehouses are hotter and drier, making staves contract and the spaces between them open up. This means a greater ingress of air during the summer. In winter humidity levels increase, causing wood to expand, which seals spaces between staves and reduces opportunities for air to enter the cask," says Alexandre Sakon, Founder, ASC Barrels.

Another aspect of seasonality is that higher and lower temperatures prompt different outcomes.

"Oxidation depends on the ambient temperature in the ageing warehouse. Below 10-12 degrees centigrade, oxygen is not solubilised and there are no oxidation reactions," says Dr Nicolas Vivas, Director of Research, Demptos Research Centre.

The temperature in Scotland peaks in July-August and air pressure builds. This causes the spirit to physically expand filling the head space, which also expels air and vapours from the cask.

"Air chooses the path of least resistance, it is estimated that more than 60% of air being pushed out of the headspace exits through the cracks between the staves and around the bung," says Kim Møller-Elshøj, Distiller and Blender, Whiskymaker & Co.

Spirit filling up the headspace can rehydrate bung staves which sounds advantageous, but also exacts a price.

"Cracks can appear, typically in the bung hole stave, due to the pressure of the spirit expanding, with ethanol expanding considerably more than water. I've seen the pressure of expanding spirit force bungs out of the bung hole and drench the exterior of the cask with alcohol," says Kim Møller-Elshøj.

As the temperature cools the spirit contracts, which draws fresh air from the exterior into the newly 'li-

Kim Møller-Elshøj, distiller and blender at Whiskymaker & Co. (photo: Robert Wengler)

berated' headspace, enabling oxygen to interact with the surface of the spirit.

So, with the headspace receiving air between gaps and also through staves, how do they compare ?

"A study on the transfer of oxygen through dry wood revealed that the majority of oxygen, 70-80%, passed through the stave, with 20-30% passing through the bung and joints. Above the headspace the wood is typically much drier than below the surface of the spirit, where the staves are saturated," says Dr Nicolas Vivas.

Going below the surface

Saturation poses a double dilemma for air passing through staves below the surface of the spirit: at the point of entry on the exterior of the cask, and again within the 'internal zone' of a stave, which is saturated to a depth of around 4-12 mms.

"If the exterior surface of the cask is humid it's harder for air to enter the stave in the first place. If the humidity level increases by 15-20% there is a 10% reduction in the capacity for air to pass through," says Dr Nicolas Vivas.

Air passing through gaps and cracks avoids the saturation challenge, and is in immediate contact with spirit. Interactions occur by the edge of a stave, and potentially within the bulk of the spirit.

Comparing oxidation levels below the surface of

the spirit to the headspace, the surface area of spirit in the headspace is smaller, and intensity of reactions may be lower.

"Air interacting with spirit adjacent to, or within the charred or toasted walls of the cask, is where the action is, rather than interaction between air and the surface of the liquid in the headspace," says Sandy Hyslop.

Oxidation remains one of the least understood aspects of the ageing process, which is frustrating, but also means there's a lot to explore, and that's exciting.

"The first stage of oxidation is for oxygen to become soluble, it happens rapidly when oxygen is in contact with liquid; water and ethanol can solubilise oxygen, turning it into hydrogen peroxide. This increases the oxidation potential of the maturing spirit, and is also a self-perpetuating process. The more oxygen is solubilised the greater the capacity for the liquid to absorb more oxygen and at a faster rate," says Dr Nicolas Vivas.

The mechanics of oxidation vary, oxygen molecules can interact or simply rendezvous with other compounds.

"Oxidation is not always a case of molecules integrating, sometimes two molecules integrate into one molecule, though two molecules can also combine and then divide up into new ones," says Kim Møller-Elshøj.

According to Bill Lumsden the minty notes of some Glenmorangie expressions come from oxidation

Oxygen molecules are capable of varied interactions, but limited by not being particularly reactive. However, catalysts within the spirit enable oxygen molecules to become more interactive. Research is still confirming the catalysts, and how they operate, but one certainty is copper (present in new make spirit due to distilling in copper pot stills).

"A trace of copper is enough to have a catalytic effect, though higher levels of copper don't increase the catalytic effect. Oxygen is not attracted by copper, it's copper that moves towards oxygen to instigate a rendezvous," says Dr Nicolas Vivas.

Which reactions oxygen participates in before, and after being catalysed is not currently known, the scale of oxidation reactions makes this challenging.

"Oxidation is really a chain reaction which entails a sequence of events. Reactions are taking place among compounds measured in parts per million or trillion, and thousands of compounds line-up to make this happen," says Brian Kinsman, Master Blender, William Grant & Sons.

Candidates for oxidation are alcohol and flavour compounds. Filling with new make spirit at 63.5% abv means alcohol accounts for 63.5% of the total, almost 36.5% is water, with flavour compounds less than 1%.

Interaction between oxygen and water is limited to very low levels of oxygen being absorbed (water contains less than 1% oxygen), and is of no consequence to flavour development.

"Oxygen in water is so highly bonded it doesn't have the freedom to interact with ethanol or flavour compounds, whereas oxygen within air is free to interact," says Brian Kinsman.

Oxygen and alcohol molecules experience more of a rendezvous than integration (and more than once).

"When alcohol oxidises it can turn into acid aldehyde, and when this oxidises it can become acetic acid, and when this reacts with alcohol again it can turn into the ester ethyl acetate, which has a fruity note that most people find pleasant, but this sort of reaction is not linear and could turn into a different compound," says Kim Møller-Elshøj.

A transformative process

The first congeners on the agenda are sulphur compounds, being very sensitive to oxygen. Such sensitivity is surprising considering sulphur compounds are domineering, imparting sweaty, vegetal, rubbery, earthy notes, which overwhelm refined characteristics such as fruit and sweetness.

And yet oxidation deconstructs sulphur compounds, rendering them mellower (admittedly evaporation and absorption by a cask's char/toasted layer also lower levels of sulphur compounds). This in turn enables fruit notes and sweetness to show more clearly, changing the profile profoundly.

Ameliorating big, bold compounds is actually a superpower oxidation possesses.

"Flavour compounds such as polyphenols are greatly influenced by oxidation. This decreases their levels of dryness and bitterness which means they make a much mellower contribution to the maturing spirit," says Dr Magali Picard, R&D Spirit Project Manager, Demptos Research Centre.

Spirit continually enters and exits the staves, which provides a liquid highway for flavour compounds to reach the bulk of the spirit. These extractives include acids, which interact with ethanol to create fruityness and floral notes. But acids also inhibit oxidation.

"After distillation the new make spirit has a ph level of 6.5, and this higher ph level is more sensitive to oxygen, leading to more intense oxidation. But even within a few weeks of maturation, acids released by the oak decrease the ph level to around 4.5. This level remains stable as the ageing process continues, and means a lower rate of oxidation compared to a ph of 6.5," says Dr Magali Picard.

The results of oxidation are maximised by using second and third fill casks, as each time a cask is filled its influence becomes milder, allowing the distillery character and oxidation greater prominence.

Filling strengths and fill levels provide additional opportunities.

"There are fruit flavours that chime more often with casks filled to a lower capacity, and a lower filling strength. This allows more oxygen in the cask, and oxygen seems to have a greater influence when the alcoholic strength is lower. Comparing Tormore casks from the early 1990s with different filling strengths, melon is really apparent in casks with lower filling strengths but not present in casks with higher filling strengths," says Oliver Chilton, Head Blender & Business Manager, Elixir Distillers.

Oxidation also makes specific contributions to other malts, exactly how depends on each distillery's house style.

"Glenmorangie has very nice, minty, mentholic top notes, a lot of that is down to oxidation. Mint is also a very small component of the new make spirit, but oxidation-derived mint notes are more delicate and fragrant, adding nuance," says Dr Bill Lumsden, Director of Distilling, Whisky Creation & Whisky Stocks, Glenmorangie.

And this highlights a principal role of oxidation: enhancing flavours in the new make spirit.

"Littlemill's fruit notes such as gooseberry are intensified, grapefruit becomes sharper, and lime is sweeter, which adds freshness and vibrancy," says Michael Henry, Master Blender, Loch Lomond Group. John Campbell, Production Director, Lochlea, adds, "Oxidation enhances the crisp, green apple flavour in Lochlea's new make spirit, and at around 4 years oxidation moves this on to riper, red apple notes."

Oxidation can also provide additional flavours that complement the distillery character.

"Tomatin new make spirit is fruity, sweet and soft, to which oxidation adds some cinnamon, Fisherman's Friend, strawberry liqueur and pineapple, and it's this balance of sweet, spicy, fruity notes that gives complexity," says Graham Eunson, Distillery Operations Director, Tomatin.

Vanilla is one of the most universal flavours in malt whisky, enjoyable in its own right, while also making fruit notes seem riper and more indulgent. But oxidation has the same effect on vanilla.

"Cask influences such as vanilla notes are also enhanced by oxidation. In younger spirit this resembles vanilla essence, but after 4 years oxidation takes it to vanilla pods," says John Campbell.

When the influence of oxidation peaks depends on the role each master blender wishes it to play.

"In Glenmorangie Original and 18 year old mint is a signature aroma, with mint, orange peel and sweet wood extractives a perfect combination adding balance and complexity to the flavour profile. I think 18 years is the sweet spot for oxidation-derived mint to show," says Dr Bill Lumsden.

Longer ageing allows oxidation greater influence, but not greater visibility in the resulting malt whisky, as the level of flavour compounds from the cask continually increases. When oxidation has an optimum presence depends on each distillery.

"After 20 years the flavour of Littlemill gains real clarity. At 27 years the palate has green apple, grapefruit and pineapple, while continued oxidation means a 45 year old shows more intense elderflower, kiwi and pineapple, with a longer, mouthwatering finish of juicy, tart fruit, kiwi, lime and citrus," says Michael Henry.

Oxidation I love you! You give so much, and yet remain a fascinating enigma. I would like to know you better, but I think you prefer to be appreciated rather than understood. I would like to do both.

Ian Wisniewski is a freelance drinks writer focusing on spirits, particularly Scotch whisky. He contributes to various publications including Whisky Magazine France, and is the author of twelve books, the latest being 'A Passion For Whisky: How the tiny Scottish island of Islay creates malts that captivate the world,' published October, 2023. He regularly visits distilleries in Scotland to learn more and is a Master of the Quaich.

Picture of Ian Wisniewski by Alastair Duncan

Back to the Future
The Revival of Tradition

by Kristiane Sherry

Malt makers are turning to the past
to revive old philosophies and lost practices – and we're all lapping it up.
Kristiane Sherry explores why we've got a collective taste for whisky nostalgia,
and whether the wider world is ready.

Tucked away against the banks of the River Derwent lies an old wireworks. Surrounded by woods and accessed via a humdrum industrial estate, the brick building is unassuming. But look closer and it is, in fact, a distillery. It's also, like many others, a portal where heritage collides with modernity in fascinating form.

It's a juxtaposition that's familiar and increasingly desirable. The distillery in question is Derbyshire's White Peak. The English maker is at the forefront of a new category in a nation with a vibrant but fledgling industry. Like an increasing band of new distilleries, its philosophies are entrenched in the past as much as the present. "We are using a process for making whisky which has been around for hundreds of years," co-founder Max Vaughan tells me inside the converted factory. He's a new-generation distiller with an old soul.

Up and down the UK and indeed around the world, makers have embarked on a quest. It's like something from a fairytale – chemists looking to recreate the past. But instead of sorcerers we have distillers. In the place of eternal youth, it's about recreating taste, texture and aroma. The result is not just a plethora of new distilleries, but within that a cohort of producers committed to bringing heritage to life.

What's driven the fascination? And how even to define what 'historical' whisky is? For Angus MacRaild, co-founder at the under-construction Kythe Distillery, it was the next step in a long-running fascination with old and rare whisky bottlings.

"I was always struck by the differences in style and flavour," he says. "After quite extensive tasting experience, I really started to see the broad changes in Scotch whisky's character over the decades. Not just in single malts – in blends, too."

"For us that is defined as a much more textural, fatter and fuller distillate, with flavours of exotic fruits

Crafty Maltsters in Fife, supplying many of the new distilleries, are an important part of the heritage movement and waxes," he continues. "You could also define it as a drier and more balanced style where the distillate has a more equal voice alongside the wood."

With business partner Jonny McMillan, he realised this profile was "virtually extinct" in Scotland. "We felt there was an obvious gap in the market to create a single malt like this again." Their distillery is set to start production in late 2024.

According to MacRaild, heritage distilling is intentionality, setting out to craft precise flavour characteristics. For Simon Thompson, who, alongside his brother Phil, is pursuing old-style whisky production at the renowned Dornoch Distillery, it's more of a hands-off approach.

"You're leaving room for nature," he states. Production includes a range of fermentation times, direct-fired stills and ultimately low yields. It's about replicating low-tech methods as much as chasing a specific profile. "It's like you're herding cattle," he says. "There's control, and you're pointing things in the right direction, but you're not managing every single step."

Dornoch produces circa 12,000 litres of pure alcohol a year, he says. It's a tiny figure, and one that puts them at the "kind of yield that would be respectable for early-to-mid 20th century."

For others, producing a historical whisky means staying true to the long-held flavour characteristics of a region. Alasdair Day, co-founder of R&B Distillers, which owns island producer Raasay, is looking to Campbeltown for his next venture: Machrihanish Distillery.

"I think it's got to be nutty, oily, maybe a bit salty," he says of the planned distillate. A small portion will be peated, too. The vision is to be very in-keeping with the region's long-held character.

Regionality was also a consideration for White Peak's Vaughan. "We've got legitimacy around that conversation," he states. The yeast used in his fermentation comes live from a neighbouring brewery – a time-honoured practice of old.

"Brewing beer is a big part of this region's history. If we were making whisky on some remote island where there's never been any beer, would I have gone out of my way to use live beer [yeast] for heritage purposes? No. It's about that local provenance story."

Anti-homogenisation

Regardless of the reasons for it, heritage production is resonating with consumers. From social media discussions to online forums, at whisky festivals, clubs

and beyond, we're all fascinated by – infatuated with – the romance of whisky history. Where is this trend coming from? And will it last?

"People want quality and they want interesting whisky made by interesting people," MacRaild states. "They're bored of mediocrity and the homogenisation of mainstream Scotch," he says. "It has put a lot of focus on older style whiskies and old bottles."

It's an interesting conversation. Although there's fervour around older styles, it seemingly goes hand-in-hand with the understanding that age in terms of maturation doesn't necessarily mean 'better'.

"Consumers are more educated, more interested in these kinds of details and more ready to embrace newer, smaller producers making products designed specifically for them," he continues.

It seems social media has a positive role in all this. Matt McKay, director of whisky creation and outreach at Dunphail, cites internet culture as a reason for meaningful engagement with the concept. John Campbell, the ex-Laphroaig distillery manager now at Lochlea, reckons the brand, with its grain-to-glass approach, is resonating with a younger audience. Day attributes YouTube and other channels as useful. People are learning from each other, and they're cutting out spin.

"There's not an ambassador or a sales rep standing in front of you," Day says. "It's only the truth."

Vaughan offers some realism. "There probably are some consumers that don't really care," he says, adding that brand perceptions might offer enough of a point of difference. But he also draws parallels with the organic movement across food and drink.

"It's raised people's awareness and consciousness about where their food or drinks products may be coming from," he states. Once you know a little bit, there's a thirst to pursue more.

Capturing the essence of history

We have an idea of what heritage distilling is. But what does this look like when it comes to making whisky? How are distillers capturing the tastes, textures and aromas of the past?

It starts with barley. Alison Milne, from the family that owns specialist Crafty Maltsters (which supplies Dornoch, among others), says that the heritage movement was born from an industry stuck in its ways.

"I was really struck by how fixed people's mindsets were," she recalls the time when the family farm moved into rare barley varietals. Although it had been growing malting barley for generations, this was new. In brewing, hops had become central.

Floor malted barley and a direct fired still are two of the traditional features at the new Dunphail Distillery near Forres

"You open your eyes a little bit wider and think 'what can the barley do?'."

"We looked at a variety of ways we could add value," she explains. A gap in the market was identified: small-scale distillers looking for provenance in a highly commoditised, industrialised sector that just couldn't meet their needs. She looked to America and the boom not only in distillers, but small maltsters, too. The next stop was the James Hutton Institute for crop research.

"They very kindly helped us set up seven trial plots on the farm," she continues. The following year they narrowed it to three. Before long they were specialists in Bere barley, Scotch Common and Scotch Annat. Last widely used during the 1800s, Milne's work really is the Jurassic Park of arable farming.

"We had a lot of interest from brewers and distillers of all shapes and sizes, including really big distilling companies," she continues. But in terms of philosophy, vision and ways of working, she committed to only working with small producers.

It's not just the varietal alone that offers flavour. "You could have north-facing fields, south-facing fields," states Lochlea's Campbell, evoking the language of viticulture.

The next step in production, and a hot topic in heritage whisky-making circles, is floor maltings. A rare sight in Scotland, just seven distilleries out of close to 150 are understood to have retained their own facilities that allow malt to germinate. Surely heritage makers would embrace them?

"It's something we're wrestling with right now," Campbell admits. "I think the emotional answer is yes, 100%." Aside from space concerns, Lochlea is already producing and there's a real risk it could change the flavour profile.

Dunphail is shouting from the rooftops about its floor malting plans. Even at 200,000 LPA production, the distillery will malt 100% of its own barley. That's quite the achievement – and one that sets it apart in Scotland.

For Simon Thompson, it's "fermentation above all else" that harks back to heritage. While the standard length up at Dornoch is a little over or under a week, he's also experimented with much longer.

"We've got some historical records which exalt the benefits of longer fermentation times in the early 20th century," he details. "But then some of the best whiskies ever were made with much shorter." The solution? "We mix it up." The longest fermentation spell at Dornoch has stretched to over three weeks.

"For the latter stages, we run open-top fermentation vessels. They're open to the elements of whatever microbes are floating around," he continues. He also avoids deep chemical cleans to maintain bacteria. "It all adds to the biological complexity, and the more biological complexity you can squeeze out on the front end, the greater the possibility, the greater the amount of complex flavours that can develop in maturation."

Then you've got distillation, which brings up a host of complexities. To direct fire or not? "It achieves the Maillard reaction for texture and bodyweight of the spirit," Dunphail's McKay says, referring to the 'sticking' patches which can create 'cooked'-type flavours.

"We're looking for those heat spots, where the temperature is higher, thus achieving the value-added effect of burning in heavier compounds leftover from the fermentation," he explains.

Up at Kythe, the spirit still will be direct-fired, this time by wood. The team will also make use of worm-tub condensers, the most traditional option.

"There will be many choices to be made once we

For Phil (left) and Simon Thompson at Dornoch Distillery, long fermentations are essential   Photo: Marcel van Gi

start distilling around where to intervene, when to step back and allow something to take place more naturally or slowly," MacRaild, details. Much will have to be tested once the set-up is commissioned, with the "critical" phase two-to-three years in once variations have been isolated.

Casks take up little airtime, mostly because the discussion is centred around the distillate. There's certainly a move to ex-bourbon and traditional sherries. Few STR casks can be seen here.

The sticky sustainability question

With all the talk of direct-fired stills and time-honoured methods, it becomes clear that there's an elephant in the room. The climate crisis is real, and it is urgent. Should distillers be actively pursuing less sustainable production methods at all? What are the environmental ethics of heritage distilling? There's a definite tension between the new and old worlds.

"One of the trade-offs that people wouldn't think about is that your reduction in yield has a carbon cost," says Thompson. "You're being less efficient with your production because you're exchanging efficiency for flavour." In other words, he concedes there is an environmental argument for yielding more whisky.

MacRaild is also realistic that whisky-making in general is not a sustainable process. "However it is very important to us that we do everything we can

to be as sustainable and environmentally sensitive as possible," he states.

He wants to run a sustainable business, he continues, and he recognises that consumers are increasingly aware of the carbon cost of their purchases.

At Dunphail, McKay says it's about looking at all the energy requirements "in the round". "It's then trying to do the best job we can to be friendly with it." He adds that the distillery isn't making claims to be carbon-neutral. "We have made as many reductions as feasibly possible."

The area that has perhaps made the biggest sustainability gains is the barley itself. "We have been very purposeful," Crafty Maltsters' Milne states. While she's not going to make any bold claims, "everything we've done behind the scenes is 'soil up'."

"With the heritage grains, you definitely need less input," she continues. "Less fertiliser, less chemicals. Because they're indigenous, they're where they're supposed to be."

Ultimately the consumer will decide how much they are willing to sacrifice in terms of sustainability for a heritage whisky. There is a collective sense though that more could be done. But the technology – and maybe the will? – isn't there yet.

It is remarkable that small whisky producers hold much clout at all. Especially in Scotch, a highly consolidated industry where big players dominate. And yet. The craft movement which spilled into spirits from beer still has momentum behind it. Could the taste for the past have a wider impact on malt whisky?

"You see occasional bottlings being brought out where they start to talk more about yeast or fermentation as the key differential behind that whisky," says MacRaild, citing Ardbeg, Laphroaig and some Diageo malts as recent examples."I don't think you'd have seen such bottlings at all ten years ago." But he's not convinced the mainstream will ever meaningfully stray into his lane.

"You can never compete with the likes of Diageo or Pernod in terms of cost efficiency and volume – why would you want to? But you can absolutely approach things with a different business model that achieves value through quality."

McKay is a little more optimistic. "It's a sounding bell to the wider industry," he says. They need to do more to offer more diverse whiskies. "Not necessarily craft ones or heritage in the same way, but people are looking for uniqueness, for differences, for exploration. I think you can absolutely see that."

Day is adamant that there's a halo effect. "If I was a multinational company with 30-plus distilleries, I'd be really interested in what people don't buy," he says. "They see when people compete." 'Time will tell' is a tired adage. But when many of these producers are new, and their stock will take time to mature, there will inevitably be a lag time before we see any large producers following suit.

Ultimately though, what the rise of heritage production has done is place provenance front and centre in the conversation once more. "The one universal about the drink itself, whatever country your whisky is from, the one key question you as a whisky lover can ask is 'how did they make this?'" MacRaild concludes.

And the provenance movement is being taken seriously. "I wouldn't say it's a duty, but I'd say that it is an honour to be part of preserving and showcasing some of those traditions which have underpinned the industry since its formation," McKay muses thoughtfully.

There's a fascinating argument behind all of this. That the distilleries best equipped to mimic, to revive, to resurrect whiskies from the past are conversely the most modern, the most high-spec, the most cutting-edge.

Could it be the best way to preserve the past is through production technology we've not even invented yet? Let's regroup over a dram in ten years' time and see.

Kristiane Sherry is a freelance drinks writer, editor, educator, presenter and spirits judge, and consults on brand strategy and creative marketing. Her career has seen her head up the content team at multi-award-winning ecommerce site Master of Malt, edit The Spirits Business magazine, and serve as Head of Brand at luxury wine platform FINE+RARE. Kristiane has chaired and judged at numerous tasting competitions, including the IWSC, the American Distilling Institute's Judging of Craft Spirits, and the Global Spirits Masters.

Alasdair Day, founder of Raasay Distillery and planning to build a distillery in Campbeltown   Photo: Peter Sandground

Is heritage still relevant?

by Joel Harrison

With a tradition that goes back 600 hundred years,
how do producers of Scotch whisky blend modernism with history?
How do you stay relevant in the world of today
without ignoring the richness of your past?

Walk in to any bar in the world, and ask one of the patrons to close their eyes and think of a Scotch single malt whisky distillery. If they were to describe it, you would likely find that the image they describe is of a white-washed walled building, set in a verdant valley with a river snaking past the door. Ask them to linger on the image a little longer, and they might see a stag hidden in the mist, and the sound of a piper's tune floating through the air. This scene, to some degree, is 'Brand Scotland'; an idealistic view of Alba, immortalised on shortbread tins and tourism posters worldwide.

However idealist and dreamlike this image may seem, it is also one rooted in reality. Anyone who has made the pilgrimage to Scotland to visit their favourite whisky producer, this image is often fulfilled.

Just think of many of the storied names within Scottish single malt, from small distilleries such as Glen Garioch, to the major players of The Glenlivet and Glenfiddich. Even the 'urban' distillery of Auchentoshan, nestled just off the Great Western Road on the outskirts of Glasgow, fits most of these tick-boxes.

It was, until recently, rare to find a modernist distillery in Scotland. Even those built in the middle of the last century seem to blend in with their rural idil surrounds. I challenge anyone to find a location in Speyside as pretty as the site of Allt-a-Bhainne distillery. The buildings themselves stand apart from what the traditional ideal of a Scotch distillery should look like, with an interesting mid-century modernity to it, but it still somehow manages to sit comfortably within the shadows of the looming Ben Rinnes mountain.

Yet it is this whimsical ideal of Scotland's countryside - the tartan, heather, weather and bagpipes - on which a billion-dollar business has been built. It is the very foundation of the business. You only need to see old Glenfiddich tins featuring stags and Clansmen or antique bottles of The Glenlivet embossed with gold thistles. Then there is the 'world's most expensive bottle of Scotch', the legendary The Macallan 1926.

This most rare of whiskies comes in two artist-led editions: one with a very forward-thinking label from Italian master of modern art, Valerio Adami. The other, hand painted by Irish artist Michael Dillon, shows an illustration of the Scottish Highlands, complete with a stag standing proud in the distillery estate; a real life example of the value of 'Scottishness' on a bottle.

What is more important, and far more interesting, is the juxtaposition between the two; one showing futurism, the other a retro past. Even more interestingly, is the way that these two bottles reflect what is now on the Macallan estate: a modern distillery sitting next to the old, original facility, now mothballed. The physical manifestation of the move to modernise the image of single malt Scotch.

Modernity in motion

Macallan is not the only distillery to have been busy with modern designers. Glenmorangie, often the vanguard of innovation in single malt Scotch whisky, has built an extension to their original distillery. Walk down the sloping path towards the Dornoch Firth that runs alongside buildings constructed in the early 1800s, and you'll find a brand new, tall glass structure nicknamed 'The Lighthouse'. This facility has been built to house the experimental side of production, lead by Dr. Bill Lumsden.

Lumsden has always looked to push Scotch forward, and take it out of its comfort zone of trad-marketing. "I've come to the conclusion that Sales and Marketing is kind of important, and if you can work in conjunction with them [as a whisky-maker], then that's a good thing", he says.

"A great example of the marketing and the whisky-making coming together, is A Tale of Cake, which tickled my fancy in every way to the extent that I happily posed for a photograph where a cream cake was splatted in my face", and image that could not be further away from the traditional stags in the mist", Lumsden says with a smile.

Yet history is not to be disregarded, notes the Doctor. "Obviously the history [of Scotland] is tremendously important because it shaped the industry as we know it today, and it has determined the style of product that we produce. It is important that we don't completely lose that. It is equally important that we don't allow ourselves to be shackled by that, either. That's the big challenge".

"It is about trying to find a balance of offering your consumer and consumers something new, but also something unashamedly Scotch whisky. There is no question that centuries of tradition have shaped where we are just now. If we end up in a position where we are hamstrung [by tradition] we are going to lose out to other categories of drinks throughout the world."

For a brand that doesn't rely too heavily on heritage, Glenmorangie has always sought ways to engage the consumer with interesting and innovative communication, their giant giraffe mascot being one. "We aren't doing anything bonkers-mad!", exclaims Lumsden."We are just offering people a slightly different way of looking at things. I think the very traditional images of bagpipes and heather has had its day", he concludes. "I can't imagine we are going to entice too many new people into the category by showing them the latest tartan plaid."

"I remember vividly when we relaunched the Glenmorangie brand under new ownership of Moet Hennessy, with Lasanta, Quinta Ruban, and The Nectar D'Or", Lumsden recalls. "I won't say we were widely ridiculed, but there were questions ask. Now everyone and their dog is doing [this type of naming and communication]. It is about trying to differentiate, and if it is done properly, then you can tell a story and give a bit of a clue as to the taste profile of the product, too."

Tradition travels

How well is this approach taken outside of Scotland, where tradition, history and heritage are often lauded as the cornerstones of quality? Stephen Notman, Keeper of the Quaich and Founder of the Whisky L! tasting events held widely across Asia, believes there is huge value in the traditional values of Scotch whisky when it comes to overseas markets.

Bill Lumsden, Head of Distilling and Whisky Creation at Glenmorangie, salutes the balance between heritage and innovation

"History plays varying roles within a consumer's relationship with Scotch whisky," he notes.

"It provides the initial integrity and quality credentials when entering into new markets, and new consumer appeal. This is underscored when consumers can overtly taste traditional methods in their glass, whether it be the use of local peat in the malting, or the use of sherry casks within maturation."

The big question however, is if history and heritage actually adds value to the product for the consumer. Notman thinks so.

"From a collector's perspective history is extremely important as there's perceived value in old production style methods or closed distilleries".

Single malt is made in the Scottish style from Tasmania to Taiwan. To some degree this frees these 'new world' producers of the shackles of history, and we see progressive distillers such as Starward in Melbourne, Australia, or Denmark's Stauning creating innovative liquid with packaging and communication to match. However, the historic ideals behind Scotch are still important, and it is what new producers are using as a jumping off point.

"The successful historic Scotch whisky framework has inspired new world distilleries to be built with many using the 1915 immature spirits act as a benchmark for minimum maturation, or commissioning the knowhow from the likes of coppersmiths Forsyth's of Rothes to install pot stills in new established distilleries in China or South Korea", Notman explains. Scotch is not just an export of a tangible product, but of skills, technique and knowledge, too.

"These new distilleries will be in a position to take advantage of being able to implement localised thumb-prints on their whiskies, and a freedom to talk about their products without the weight of history on their shoulders. This will continue to shake Scotch into innovation, for which there is a genuine thirst. The success of market exclusives such as Singleton 13 year old finished in Sauternes or the Glenlivet 13 and 15 year old Oloroso sherry cask, cask strength editions for the Taiwan markets are recent examples of how innovation and positive communication can inject interest and new life into established brands", Notman concludes.

Selling history

The consumer is king when it comes to the marketing and communication of single malts. Take the

Ian Palmer of Inchdairnie Distillery says "we are a modern distillery producing a traditional product".

rise and rise of Springbank, for example who apply a diffident approach to their marketing, mostly leaving word-of-mouth to do the heavy lifting of a whisky that is built around old-school production, and traditional values.

"Their process is historically valid; they're not making it up, and Springbank deserve their success", says Arthur Motley, Managing Director of retailer Royal Mile Whiskies.

"This [love for Springbank] is an interesting response from the market which shows a desire for whisky not to change, and there are significant numbers of people who do not want whisky to change".

Is the success of Springbank simply down to their unique flavour profile? Motley thinks not.

"It is not just about flavour, it is about soul, it is about creating something beautifully, and in a way that customers want and expect."

Motley is also a revered whisky historian, and one half of the YouTube channel Liquid Antiquarian with writer Dave Broom. From his experience exploring the history of single malt, Motley muses that "the past is a lot more interesting than many people realise".

He adds, "How we look at history, how we use history as a tool probably needs to change a little bit. Looking back at the tremendous success of single malt from the 1990s to today, we can see how history has been used to promote whisky through things such as 'distillery origin stories' and other elements which we now know are a bit sketchy. There are holes in some it. Once a distillery puts an inaccurate foundation date on a bottle, or they weave a florid tale about their founder, it is quite hard to unpick it, and some distillers are finding themselves in an awkward position. More and more highly informed consumers are saying, 'this isn't right' and sometimes I think this holds the industry back a bit."

So what is the answer if doubling-down on the past isn't an option.

"The most important customer in the industry has changed. It used to be a tight group of blenders trading casks. Now single malts can be sold, at value, in their own right, so there is a lot of choice in single malt these days. The key thing for me is new people coming along and doing things in an interesting way, with a lot of soul. And even better if existing distillers change in positive ways, and do a good job. A job that appeals to consumers who care; customers who want to connect with the place, the people and the process," says Motley.

When it comes to a more modern view of single malt, Motley calls out InchDairnie as one to watch.

Located in Fife, InchDairnie was founded in 2015 and has taken a radical direction on their packaging and marketing.

"There is a growing group of people who understand whisky is a traditional product, but who are willing to take a look at products that take a slightly different view on the world, and that's us," says Ian Palmer, Managing Director of InchDairnie.

"Of course, we are very respectful of the industry's traditions. Without them, we wouldn't be here. We have to acknowledge that the traditions are there, and they play a part. But our position is that we use those traditions as a way of going forward; they point us in a direction. We have no heritage here; we are building our own traditions and our own heritage", Palmer continues.

Was Palmer tempted to build something more traditional, more in keeping with the idillic ideal of a white-washed walled single malt distillery?

"People often ask us why we built our distillery in Fife, and not in Speyside," he replied. "Part of the answer is that Speyside distilleries come with huge expectations of what people perceive as a Speyside whisky distillery. Here in Fife, we almost had a blank sheet of paper".

"When we were developing the InchDairnie brand, I said to our agency 'If you ever present me with heather, haggis or tartan, you've lost the job!' We are a modern distillery with a different outlook on life. We can't have an industry that is preserved in aspic. We will then fail to evolve and fail to meet the needs of the modern consumer. At InchDairnie, we are a modern distillery producing a traditional product", Palmer says passionately.

And here in lies the key. History is the warp and heritage the weft of whisky; individually they are loose threads, but woven together they give a secure blanket of quality and authenticity. Modernism is simply a cut of the cloth, creating a style that will define and reflect the current age.

Joel Harrison is an award winning author, communicator and industry consultant, whose work has been published in over 20 countries, across 16 different languages. His writing work can be seen in publications such as The Wall Street Journal India and The Daily Telegraph in the UK. Harrison also appears regularly on British television across a number of shows as a whisky specialist. He sits as a judge for the International Wine and Spirits Competition (IWSC) where today he holds the role of a Trophy Judge and Chairman across Scotch whisky and other spirits. In 2013 Harrison was made a Keeper of the Quaich.

The Cairn Distillery, (photo John Paul)

Malt distilleries

Including the subsections:
Scottish distilleries | New distilleries
Distilleries around the globe

A brief explanation

There are five protected whisky regions or localities in Scotland today; Highlands, Lowlands, Speyside, Islay and Campbeltown. Where useful we mention a location within a region e.g. Orkney, Northern Highlands etc.

The year in which the distillery was founded is usually considered as when construction began and capacity is expressed in litres of pure alcohol (LPA). The historical chronology focuses on the official history of the distillery and (vc) under status means the distillery is open to visitors.

For all the Scottish distilleries we present tasting notes of what, in most cases, can be called the core expression (mainly their best selling 10 or 12 year old). The whiskies have been tasted either by Gavin D Smith (GS), a well-known whisky authority and author of 20 books on the subject or by Ingvar Ronde (IR). All notes have been prepared especially for Malt Whisky Yearbook 2024.

Distilleries that have not started production yet or are in a planning stage are all presented in the chapter The Year That Was, pages 263-266.

Closed distilleries

In previous editions of the Malt Whisky Yearbook there has been a chapter dedicated to closed distilleries. With closed distilleries we mean distilleries that stopped production after 1970. The reason for that cut-off point is that bottlings from all of them were able to buy when the first Yearbook was published in 2005.

Today, stock from most of them have been depleted and only rarely will you be able to find them. At the same time a huge number of new distilleries have been founded. In order for the Yearbook not to grow out of proportion, we decided this year to simply list the closed ones here.

For a deeper knowledge about them, we happily refer to the excellent book "Scotch Missed", written by Brian Townsend and published by Neil Wilson. Here is the list;

Banff • Ben Wyvis • Caperdonich • Coleburn • Convalmore
Dallas Dhu • Glen Albyn • Glenesk • Glen Flagler
Glenlochy • Glen Mhor • Glenugie • Glenury Royal • Imperial
Inverleven • Killyloch • Kinclaith • Ladyburn • Littlemill
Lochside • Millburn • North Port • Pittyvaich • St Magdalene

Aberfeldy

[ah•bur•fell•dee]

Owner:
John Dewar & Sons
(Bacardi)

Region/district:
Southern Highlands

Founded: 1896

Status: Active (vc)

Capacity: 3 400 000 litres

Address: Aberfeldy, Perthshire PH15 2EB

Website: aberfeldy.com

Tel: 01887 822010 (vc)

Aberfeldy distillery was built by the Dewar's brothers on the estate belonging to the Earls of Breadalbane and the Campbell Clan.

Just 10 kilometers west of Aberfeldy lies what used to be the family castle, Taymouth Castle, one of the most impressive in Scotland. The castle was gambled away in the casinos of Monte Carlo in the 1920s, by the 7th Earl of Breadalbane and has since had a checkered history – luxury hotel, hospital for Polish troops during the Second World War and a boarding school for American children. Today it is owned by an American development company which embarked on a £300m renovation in autumn 2022. The plans include residential properties, a 148-bedroom hotel, a golf course and a restaurant.

Aberfeldy malt has been the backbone of the Dewar's blend for more than a century. The Dewar's brand sold 42 million bottles in 2022 (an impressive increase of 25%) and is the best selling Scotch on the American market. The Aberfeldy single malt led a hidden existence for a long time but following a relaunch in 2014, sales have increased substantially to 1.4 million bottles annually.

The equipment at Aberfeldy consists of a 7.5 ton stainless steel, full lauter mash tun, eight washbacks made of larch and three made of stainless steel with an average fermentation time of 72 hours, and four stills. During 2023 the plan is to mash 24 times per week which equates to 3.4 million liters of alcohol. The distillery also has one of the best visitor centers in the industry – Dewar's World of Whisky.

The core range consists of **12, 16** and **21 years old**. Recent limited expressions in 2023 include an **18 year old** finished in red wine casks from Napa Valley and a **15 year old** Cadillac white wine finish. For the duty free market there are two widely available expressions; a **16 year old** and a **21 year old** both of them finished for up to 12 months in Madeira casks (ex-Bual and ex-Malvasia Malmsey respectively). Included are also two **25 year olds** finished in white wine- and red winecasks respectively.

History:
1896 John and Tommy Dewar embark on the construction of the distillery, a stone's throw from the old Pitilie distillery which was active from 1825 to 1867. Their objective is to produce a single malt for their blended whisky - White Label.
1898 Production starts in November.
1917 The distillery closes.
1919 The distillery re-opens.
1925 Distillers Company Limited (DCL) takes over.
1972 Reconstruction takes place, the floor maltings is closed and the two stills are increased to four.
1991 The first official bottling is a 15 year old in the Flora & Fauna series.
1998 Bacardi buys John Dewar & Sons from Diageo at a price of £1,150 million.
2000 A visitor centre opens and a 25 year old is released.
2005 A 21 year old is launched in October, replacing the 25 year old.
2009 Two 18 year old single casks are released.
2010 A 19 year old single cask, exclusive to France, is released.
2011 A 14 year old single cask is released.
2014 The whole range is revamped and an 18 year old for duty free is released.
2015 A 16 year old is released.
2018 A 16 year old and a 21 year old madeira finish are released for duty free.
2020 A limited 15 year old finished in Pomerol casks is released.
2021 A limited 18 year old finished in Côte Rôtie casks is released.
2022 Limited 15 year and 18 old finished in red wine casks are released.
2023 A limited 18 year finished in red wine Napa Valley casks and a 15 year old Cadillac white wine cask finish are released.

12 years old

Tasting notes Aberfeldy 12 years old:
GS – Sweet, with honeycombs, breakfast cereal and stewed fruits on the nose. Inviting and warming. Mouth-coating and full-bodied on the palate. Sweet, malty, balanced and elegant. The finish is long and complex, becoming progressively more spicy and drying.

Aberlour

[ah•bur•lower]

Owner: Chivas Brothers Ltd (Pernod Ricard)

Region/district: Speyside

Founded: 1879

Status: Active (vc)

Capacity: 3 800 000 litres

Address: Aberlour, Banffshire AB38 9PJ

Website: aberlour.com

Tel: 01340 881249

A ravaging fire in 1896 resulted in a major refurbishment of Aberlour but the expansion that is happening at the moment is no doubt the biggest make-over of Aberlour since it began distilling in 1879.

The plans for it were submitted to the local council in summer 2017 and were later withdrawn, but revised plans sent in later were approved in autumn 2020. In summary they will lead to Aberlour doubling its capacity with a new still house, tun room and mash house including an additional four stills and another 16 washbacks. There are also plans to upgrade the visitor center. There is a good reason for this expansion. Aberlour is the 8th best selling single malt in the world (around 4 million bottles annually) and also an important contributor to the blends from Chivas Brothers. For the future, a middle-sized distillery with a capacity of close to 4 million liters of pure alcohol would not be enough. Aberlour was the first Scotch malt distillery acquired by Pernod Ricard, almost 50 years ago.

Currently, the distillery is equipped with a 12 ton semi-lauter mash tun, six stainless steel washbacks and two pairs of large and wide stills in a spacious still room. To achieve the desired character of the new make – fruity – the operators run a very slow distillation. With a 7.5 hour spirit cycle, the middle cut (73-63%) takes two hours to complete.

The core range includes **12, 14, 16** and **18 year olds** – all matured in a combination of ex-bourbon and ex-sherry casks. Another core expression is **Casg Annamh** which is bourbon/oloroso matured. There is also **Aberlour a'bunadh**, bottled at cask strength and matured in ex-oloroso casks and, available in the American market, **a'bunadh Alba** matured in American oak. For select markets **12 year old** non chill-filtered and **Millesime White Oak** are available and for France the **10 year old Forest Reserve** and for China a **20 year old**. Two limited **15 year olds** were recently released and there are three single casks (**10,12** and **14 years old**) which can be found at the Chivas visitor centres in the Distillery Reserve Collection.

History:

1879 The local banker James Fleming founds the distillery.

1892 The distillery is sold to Robert Thorne & Sons Ltd who expands it.

1896 A fire rages and almost totally destroys the distillery. The architect Charles Doig is called in to design the new facilities.

1921 Robert Thorne & Sons Ltd sells Aberlour to a brewery, W. H. Holt & Sons.

1945 S. Campbell & Sons Ltd buys the distillery.

1962 Aberlour terminates floor malting.

1973 Number of stills are increased from two to four.

1974 Pernod Ricard buys Campbell Distilleries.

2000 Aberlour a'bunadh is launched.

2001 Pernod Ricard buys Chivas Brothers and merges Chivas Brothers and Campbell Distilleries under the brand Chivas Brothers.

2002 A new, modernized visitor centre is inaugurated in August.

2008 The 18 year old is also introduced outside France.

2013 Aberlour 2001 White Oak is released.

2014 White Oak Millenium 2004 is released.

2018 Casg Annamh is released.

2019 A'bunadh Alba is released.

2021 A 14 year old is released.

12 years old

Tasting notes Aberlour 12 year old:

GS – The nose offers brown sugar, honey and sherry, with a hint of grapefruit citrus. The palate is sweet, with buttery caramel, maple syrup and eating apples. Liquorice, peppery oak and mild smoke in the finish.

Allt-a-Bhainne

[alt a•vain]

Owner: **Region/district:**
Chivas Brothers Ltd   Speyside
(Pernod Ricard)

Founded: **Status:**   **Capacity:**
1975   Active   4 200 000 litres

Address: Glenrinnes, Dufftown, Banffshire AB55 4DB

Website: **Tel:**
allt-a-bhainne.com   01542 783200

Few places in Scotland are as beautiful as the area in the Cromdale Hills between Tomintoul and Dufftown. A part thereof consists of the Glen of the Livet named after the river which converges into the Avon as it meanders its way towards the coast.

The star distillery in this part of Scotland is Glenlivet but there are a few considerably less famous distilleries in the area, of which Allt-a-Bhainne is one. Built in the mid 1970s it has always been a producer of malt whisky for blends and, in particular, 100 Pipers, a brand which was introduced in 1966 by the legendary Sam Bronfman of Seagram's and first launched in the US. Over the years it became popular in the UK and in some other European countries but following introductions to Korea and Thailand in the early 1990s, the main market for the brand today has shifted to Asia and not least India. The brand reached its peak in 2005 when 42 million bottles were sold and it was the 8th best selling Scotch in the world. Since then sales have fallen by 40% and the brand now occupies spot number 16 on the global sales chart.

The equipment consists of a nine ton lauter mash tun, eight stainless steel washbacks with a fermentation time of 48-50 hours and two pairs of stills. In recent years, the distillery has been working seven days a week with 25 mashes resulting in 4 million litres of alcohol. For a number of years Allt-a-Bhainne has periodically been producing peated whisky. Usually it constitutes 30-50% of the total production and has a phenol specification in the barley between 10 and 20ppm. Chivas Brothers have embarked upon a programme making all their distilleries carbon neutral. First out was Glentauchers and with the work being finished there, Allt-a-Bhainne is now next in line.

Allt-a-Bhainne single malt is used for blends, not least 100 Pipers, and official bottlings are few. A lightly peated **Allt-a-Bhainne NAS** was launched in 2018 and there is also a **15 year old cask strength** in the Distillery Reserve Collection, available at all Chivas' visitor centres.

History:

1975   The distillery is founded by Chivas Brothers, a subsidiary of Seagrams, in order to secure malt whisky for its blended whiskies. The total cost amounts to £2.7 million.

1989   Production has doubled.

2001   Pernod Ricard takes over Chivas Brothers from Seagrams.

2002   Mothballed in October.

2005   Production restarts in May.

2018   An official, lightly peated bottling is released.

Allt-a-Bhainne NAS

Tasting notes Allt-a-Bhainne NAS:

IR – Subtle smokiness is mixed with butterscotch, honey, apples and a touch of pepper. Sweet peat on the palate, oranges, ginger, melon, more pepper and vanilla.

Ardbeg

[ard•beg]

Owner:
The Glenmorangie Co
(Moët Hennessy)

Region/district:
Islay

Founded: 1815
Status: Active (vc)
Capacity: 2 400 000 litres

Address: Port Ellen, Islay, Argyll PA42 7EA

Website: ardbeg.com
Tel: 01496 302244 (vc)

Saturday the 20th of March 2021 was a very special day for Ardbeg and marked the beginning of a new time of increased production – essential to cope with the ever increasing demand for the single malt.

The day before the old stillhouse was decommisoned with the two old stills still in place. The next day the new still house with two pairs of stills was used for the first time. It is in a beautiful building with high ceilings and an extraordinary view towards the sea. A large glass wall which can be opened to let the breeze in adds to the overall feeling of a coastal distillery.

Sales figures for Ardbeg have been increasing consistently in the last decade and the distillery has struggled to keep up with demand. In the last few years it became apparent for the owners that they had to increase capacity. In 2019 the new still house was built but due to the covid pandemic it took almost another two years before two additional stills were commissioned. The latest available sales figures (2021) indicate that Ardbeg is now in third place amongst the Islay malts (well ahead of Lagavulin) with almost 2.4 million bottles sold.

Today the equipment consists of a five ton stainless steel semi lauter mash tun and 12 Oregon pine washbacks holding 23,000 litres. The last four were installed in January 2022 and the fermentation time is now 66-72 hours. Furthermore, there are two pairs of stills with the spirit stills being fitted with purifiers to help create the special fruity character of the spirit. The phenol specification of the malt is 50-55ppm and the cut points for the heart go from 72.5% down to 62.5% which means the heavier compounds are avoided at the end of the distillation. The plan for 2023 is to make 26 mashes per week which would mean around 2.5 million litres of alcohol. There are two dunnage and three racked warehouses on site holding a total of 18,000 casks.

The core range consists of the **10 year old, Uigeadail,** a marriage of bourbon and sherry casks, **Corryvreckan,** a combination of bourbon casks and new French oak, **An Oa,** a vatting of whiskies that have been married together for a minimum of three months in three huge vats and the **5 year old Wee Beastie,** matured in a combination of bourbon and oloroso casks. A sixth member appeared in January 2021 when a **25 year old** was launched.

Recent limited bottlings include the 13 year old **Fermutation** with the longest fermentation in Ardbeg history, the 4th batch of **Traigh Bhan** and **8 years old For Discussion.** The Ardbeg Day expression for 2023 was **Heavy Vapours** where the purifier on the spirit still had been disconnected in order to create a heavier. In spring 2023 **Bizzarebq** (bottled at 50,9%) was released which had been matured in a combination of double charred casks, toasted PX sherry casks and heavily charred Barsero casks. August 2023 saw the debut release in a new, expeimental series called Ardbeg Anthology. The first installment was the **13 year old Harpy´s Tale** matured in a combination of bourbon and sauternes casks. The travel retail exclusive is **Smoketrails.**

History:

1794 First record of a distillery at Ardbeg. It was founded by Alexander Stewart.

1798 The MacDougalls, later to become licensees of Ardbeg, are active on the site through Duncan MacDougall.

1815 The current distillery is founded by John MacDougall, son of Duncan MacDougall.

1853 Alexander MacDougall, John's son, dies and sisters Margaret and Flora MacDougall, assisted by Colin Hay, continue the running of the distillery. Colin Hay takes over the licence when the sisters die.

1888 Colin Elliot Hay and Alexander Wilson Gray Buchanan renew their license.

1900 Colin Hay's son takes over the license.

1959 Ardbeg Distillery Ltd is founded.

1973 Hiram Walker and Distillers Company Ltd jointly purchase the distillery for £300,000 through Ardbeg Distillery Trust.

1977 Hiram Walker assumes single control of the distillery. Ardbeg closes its maltings.

1979 Kildalton, a less peated malt, is produced over a number of years.

1981 The distillery closes in March.

1987 Allied Lyons takes over Hiram Walker and thereby Ardbeg.

1989 Production is restored. All malt is taken from Port Ellen.

1996 The distillery closes in July.

1997 Glenmorangie plc buys the distillery for £7 million. Ardbeg 17 years old and Provenance are launched

History continued:

1998 A new visitor centre opens.

2000 Ardbeg 10 years is introduced and the Ardbeg Committee is launched.

2001 Lord of the Isles 25 years and Ardbeg 1977 are launched.

2002 Ardbeg Committee Reserve and Ardbeg 1974 are launched.

2003 Uigeadail is launched.

2004 Very Young Ardbeg (6 years) and a limited edition of Ardbeg Kildalton are launched.

2005 Serendipity is launched.

2006 Ardbeg 1965 and Still Young are launched. Almost There (9 years old) and Airigh Nam Beist are released.

2007 Ardbeg Mor, a 10 year old in 4.5 litre bottles is released.

2008 The new 10 year old, Corryvreckan, Rennaissance, Blasda and Mor II are released.

2009 Supernova is released.

2010 Rollercoaster and Supernova 2010 are released.

2011 Ardbeg Alligator is released.

2012 Ardbeg Day and Galileo are released.

2013 Ardbog is released.

2014 Auriverdes and Kildalton are released.

2015 Perpetuum and Supernova 2015 are released.

2016 Dark Cove and a Twenty Something 21 year old are relased.

2017 An Oa, Kelpie and Twenty Something 23 year old are released.

2018 Grooves and Twenty Something 22 year old are released.

2019 Drum and Traigh Bhan are released.

2020 Blaaack, Wee Beastie and Traigh Bhan batch 2 are released.

2021 An 8 year old, a 25 year old, Arrrrrrrdbeg, Scorch and Traigh Bhan batch 3 are released.

2022 Fermutation, Ardcore, Smoketrails and Traigh Bhan batch 4 are launched.

2023 Bizzarebq, Heavy Vapours and the 13 year old Harpy´s Tale are launched.

Tasting notes Ardbeg 10 year old:

GS – Quite sweet on the nose, with soft peat, carbolic soap and Arbroath smokies. Burning peats and dried fruit, followed by sweeter notes of malt and a touch of liquorice in the mouth. Extremely long and smoky in the finish, with a fine balance of cereal sweetness and dry peat notes.

Anthology Harpy´s Tale   Heavy Vapours   Bizzarebq

An Oa   Wee Beastie   Smoketrails

10 years old   Uigeadail   Corryvreckan

Ardmore

[ard•moor]

Owner: **Region/district:**
Beam Suntory   Highland

Founded: **Status:**   **Capacity:**
1898   Active   4 900 000 litres

Address: Kennethmont, Aberdeenshire AB54 4NH

Website: **Tel:**
ardmorewhisky.com   01464 831213

Few distilleries have had such a long and solid relationship with the same blended Scotch as Ardmore has had with Teachers. Founded by the Teacher family in 1898, Ardmore and its single malt has always been the backbone of the famous brand.

The most important market by far for Teachers is India where it is one of the top Scotch. Recently however, the brand has experienced a decline in other markets. Ten years ago it was one of the Top 10 blends in the world while it is found in spot 20 today. Ardmore single malt, on the other hand, has increased with 260% to 700,000 bottles in the same period.

Ardmore is the only Highland distillery that consistently has been producing peated whisky from the very start. For around 50% of the production, the phenol specification of the malted barley is 12-14ppm and to a large extent local peat is used. In 2021 a $4m project to restore 1,300 hectares of peatland near the distillery was initiated to safeguard the local supply.

The distillery is equipped with a cast iron semi lauter mash tun with a copper lid. The mash charge is 12.5 tonnes. There are 16 Douglas fir washbacks – six of them with a capacity of 90,000 litres and ten with 45,000 litres. Two of the former were added recently, in April 2022. The distillery produces two styles of single malt – the medium peated Ardmore, and the unpeated Ardlair which is used for blending purposes only. The reason for the additional two washbacks was to allow for the same fermentation time (70 hours) for both styles. Finally there are four pairs of stills in a large still house. In 2023 the distillery will be working a 7-day week with 23 mashes, focusing on Ardmore from June to December while the rest of the year will be devoted to Ardlair. The goal is to reach 4.9 million litres of alcohol.

The core expression is **Legacy**, a mix of 80% peated and 20% unpeated malt. Also, the **12 year old Port Finish** which was discontinued for a while is now back in the range. **Tradition** and **Triple Wood** are exclusive to travel retail.

History:

1898 Adam Teacher, son of William Teacher, starts the construction of Ardmore Distillery which eventually becomes William Teacher & Sons´ first distillery. Adam Teacher passes away before it is completed.

1955 Stills are increased from two to four.

1974 Another four stills are added, increasing the total to eight.

1976 Allied Breweries takes over William Teacher & Sons and thereby also Ardmore. The own maltings (Saladin box) is terminated.

1999 A 12 year old is released to commemorate the distillery's 100th anniversary. A 21 year old is launched in a limited edition.

2002 Ardmore is one of the last distilleries to abandon direct heating (by coal) of the stills in favour of indirect heating through steam.

2005 Jim Beam Brands becomes new owner when it takes over some 20 spirits and wine brands from Allied Domecq for five billion dollars.

2007 Ardmore Traditional Cask is launched.

2008 A 25 and a 30 year old are launched.

2014 Beam and Suntory merge. Legacy is released.

2015 Traditional is re-launched as Tradition and a Triple Wood and a 12 year old port finish are released.

2017 A 20 year old, double matured is released.

2018 A 30 year old is released.

Legacy

Tasting notes Ardmore Legacy:

GS – Vanilla, caramel and sweet peat smoke on the nose, while on the palate vanilla and honey contrast with quite dry peat notes, plus ginger and dark berries. The finish is medium to long, spicy, with persistently drying smoke.

An inside comment on...

The State of Whisky

Paul John
Whisky Hall of Fame inductee No. 77
Owner and Chairman of John Distilleries

What was your objective for entering the whisky business?

I ventured into the alcobev business primarily because my father ran a chain of liquor stores. India is one of the largest whisky markets in the world so it was the obvious choice to enter in the whisky segment if one was in the alcobev industry. I have been in the Indian domestic market for over 25 years now and I have been selling mass brands which are still a large part of my portfolio of offerings. Today the top 10 largest selling whisky brands in the world by volume are from India and we rank 8th for my brand called Original Choice. Over the years as I travelled widely I grew to enjoy single malts and eventually decided to see if we could produce single malts of our own in India. I set up the malt plant in Goa in 2008 and we launched our malts in the UK in 2012.

What would you say are the best ways to attract new, young whisky consumers?

Typically it's a progression for most consumers from beers, gins etc to whiskies and then culminating with malts. To catch them new would be to offer the novelty of learning to experience the exotic flavours of a single malt. Basically we need to offer a quality product with modern packaging at a great value proposition delivered through a premium drinking experience.

Can one whisky, objectively, be better than the other? Isn't it all down to your personal taste and preferences?

Whiskies are heterogenous and good whisky more so. It has many variables starting from raw material, process of making, ageing and blending. What appeals to personal taste and preference is built over time on what has been available but palate expansion across geographies and generations is ever evolving.

Do you feel there is enough innovation in the whisky business and is there still a place for preserving and honouring traditional methods?

Innovation is necessarily not only disruptive at whim but can help build thoughtfully on legacy. Newer products across categories, newer modes of packaging, newer experiences towards reaching the consumer, the advent of social media are all drivers of innovation. There is substantial innovation already happening in the whisky business and as we move ahead we expect to see a lot more. Preserving and honouring traditional methods has been tested and proven, however scope for improvement is always there.

What ever line of business you're in, sustainability is on every company's agenda. Do you feel the whisky industry is at the forefront or could things happen faster?

There will never be enough work done in sustainability, this is continuous and work-in-progress towards leaving a better planet for our future generations than what we have inherited. I can only surmise that the work has started in the right direction.

Investing in whisky has become more and more popular. Is that a good or a bad thing?

Investing in Whisky was always there, it began for distilleries to remain afloat when stocks were maturing but today the purpose of investing in whisky has different motivation and aspiration and that is always a good thing. Simply said good quality whisky will always be a great investment.

I'm sometimes reminded that the readers of the Malt Whisky Yearbook – usually well informed but eager to learn more – represent a miniscule part of the whisky consumers around the world. How important would you say that small consumer segment is for the producers?

This small segment sits on top of the consumption pyramid and influences the larger audience who are in different stages of their whisky discovery. In fact, I won't say this is a minuscule part of whisky consumers anymore, but a growing tribe that are the truest Brand Ambassadors of Whisky and in fact the backbone of the future for malt producers like us.

With young people sometimes questioning the use of alcohol and others exchanging it for cannabis or other drugs – do you feel whisky is still relevant for Generation Z (born 1997-2012)?

I personally believe whisky is here to stay and will continue to be a choice. Yes, Gen Z seem to have an inkling for recreational drugs however these would be very early days to comment on these new trends.

As opposed to thirty years ago, whisky today is produced in a huge number of countries around the world. How would you say that has affected the category/industry as a whole?

It has unequivocally grown the industry and will continue to grow as more countries and regions join in. It's surely a welcome sign and countries that one did not think could produce good quality whiskies have discovered their ability to do so while improving quality as well. This development in my view, will even redefine what we call whisky in a conventional sense of palate, definition, innovation etc.

Please describe your perfect time and place for a dram.

Preferably quiet evenings with close friends and family.

Auchentoshan

[ock•en•tosh•an]

Owner:
Beam Suntory

Region/district:
Lowlands

Founded: **Status:** **Capacity:**
1823 Active (vc) 2 500 000 litres

Address: Dalmuir, Clydebank, Glasgow G81 4SJ

Website: **Tel:**
auchentoshan.com 01389 878561

A 20 minute drive to the west of Glasgow, in Clyde-bank, a town famous since the late 1800s for its shipyards, lies Auchentoshan. Together with Glen-kinchie it was the sole surviving Lowland distillery after Rosebank closed in 1995.

Nearly 30 years later the picture has changed completely and there are now twenty working whisky distilleries in that same part of Scotland. There has been a significant change for Auchen-toshan as well, not least in terms of sales. In the early years of the new millenium, the Japanese owners were struggling to sell 300,000 bottles per year. Then a visitor centre was built, a new range was introduced and bottlings for travel retail were launched. In 2013, Auchentoshan sold over one million bottles for the first time and in 2021 the two million mark was passed. Celebrating its 200th anniversary in 2023, the distillery seems to be moving steadily in the right direction.

The equipment consists of a semi-lauter mash tun with a 7.05 ton charge. There are four Oregon Pine washbacks and five made of stainless steel – all 38,000 litres and with a fermentation time of 70 hours (previously 52 hours). There are three stills; a wash still (17,500 litres), an intermediate still (8,200 litres) and a spirit still (11,500 litres). The distillery is on a 7-day production which means that it will be completing 19 mashes per week during 2023 which translates to around 2.2 million litres of alcohol in the year. Auchentoshan is the sole distillery in Scotland practi-cing triple distillation for the entire production.

The core range consists of **American Oak**, without age statement, **12 years, Three Woods, 18 years** and **21 years**. The duty free range is made up of **Blood Oak**, matured in a combination of bourbon and red wine casks, **American Oak Reserve** matured in first fill bourbon and **Dark Oak** which is a vatting of whiskies matured in ex-bourbon, PX and oloroso casks. A limited **Sauvignon Blanc Finish** introduced in 2019 can still be found in some key markets. Finally, in connection with the distillery´s 200th anniversary, a few very limited expressions will be released in autumn 2023.

History:
1817 First mention of the distillery Duntocher, which may be identical to Auchentoshan.
1823 The distillery is founded by John Bulloch.
1823 The distillery is sold to Alexander Filshie.
1878 C.H. Curtis & Co. takes over.
1903 The distillery is purchased by John Maclachlan.
1941 The distillery is severely damaged by a German bomb raid.
1960 Maclachlans Ltd is purchased by the brewery J. & R. Tennent Brewers.
1969 Auchentoshan is bought by Eadie Cairns Ltd who starts major modernizations.
1984 Stanley P. Morrison, eventually becoming Morrison Bowmore, becomes new owner.
1994 Suntory buys Morrison Bowmore.
2002 Auchentoshan Three Wood is launched.
2004 More than a £1 million is spent on a new, refurbished visitor centre. The oldest Auchentoshan ever, 42 years, is released.
2006 Auchentoshan 18 year old is released.
2007 A 50 year old, the oldest ever Auchentoshan to be bottled, was released.
2008 New packaging as well as new expressions - Classic, 18 year old and 1988.
2010 Two vintages, 1977 and 1998, are released.
2011 Two vintages, 1975 and 1999, and Valinch are released.
2012 Six new expressions are launched for the Duty Free market.
2013 Virgin Oak is released.
2014 American Oak replaces Classic.
2015 Blood Oak and Noble Oak are released for duty free.
2017 Bartender´s Malt is launched.
2018 Bartender´s Malt 2 and 1988 PX Cask are released.
2019 American Oak Reserve and Dark Oak are released for the travel retail market.

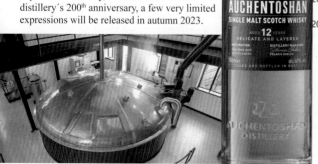

12 years old

Tasting notes Auchentoshan 12 year old:
IR – Green and herbal on the nose with notes of pine needles, citrus and fresh oak. Quite dry on the palate with spicy notes coming through (nutmeg, clove and bay leaf) as well as vanilla and roasted nuts and sunflower seeds.

Auchroisk

[ar•thrusk]

Owner:
Diageo

Region/district:
Speyside

Founded: 1974 **Status:** Active **Capacity:** 5 900 000 litres

Address: Mulben, Banffshire AB55 6XS

Website: malts.com

Tel: 01542 885000

Within the Diageo group there are now, with the soon to be re-opened Port Ellen, 30 malt whisky distilleries operating. And to the company´s credit – there are official bottlings from all of them. Even Roseisle turned up in this year's Special Releases.

Some of these distilleries are represented by one expression each – in the Flora & Fauna range. The name of the range was actually conceived by the immortalized Michael Jackson and saw the light of day in 1991. In total, 22 distilleries have appeared as Flora & Fauna bottlings but half of them are now either a brand of their own or have been sold off. One of the remaining expressions is the 10 year old Auchroisk. In order to choose from a wider selection, one would have to rely on independent bottlers and not least the Scotch Malt Whisky Society (SMWS). To this date they have released more than 80 single casks of Auchroisk.

Starting in 1974 and situated on the B9103 between Keith and Craigellachie, Auchroisk produces a whisky which was sold under the name Singleton for more than twenty years until 2001. Volumes of single malt for the consumer market were small, however, and the real purpose was always to produce malt for blends. The style of the Auchroisk new make has changed over the years depending on the requirements for the blends in the company. Today it can be characterized as nutty/malty and this flavour is achieved through a quick mash, cloudy wort and short fermentations.

The equipment consists of a 12 ton stainless steel semi-lauter mash tun, eight stainless steel washbacks with a fermentation time of 53 hours and four pairs of stills. The washbacks are large (holding 50,000 litres each) and one washback can serve all four wash stills which hold 12,700 litres each. The spacious still house served as the role model for the still house of Diageo's Roseisle distillery. Auchroisk is working 24/7 with 24 mashes per week, producing 5.8 million litres of alcohol per year.

The only official bottling is the **10 year old Flora & Fauna**. The most recent limited bottling was a **47 year old** in the **Prima & Ultima** range in September 2021.

History:

1972 Building of the distillery commences by Justerini & Brooks (which, together with W. A. Gilbey, make up the group IDV) in order to produce blending whisky. In February the same year IDV is purchased by the brewery Watney Mann which, in July, merges into Grand Metropolitan.

1974 The distillery is completed and production begins.

1978 The first bottling appears.

1986 From this year the malt is sold under the name Singleton.

1997 Grand Metropolitan and Guinness merge into the conglomerate Diageo. Simultaneously, the subsidiaries United Distillers (to Guinness) and International Distillers & Vintners (to Grand Metropolitan) form the new company United Distillers & Vintners (UDV).

2001 The name Singleton is abandoned and the whisky is now marketed under the name of Auchroisk in the Flora & Fauna series.

2003 A 28 year old from 1974, the distillery's first year, is launched in the Rare Malt series.

2010 A Manager´s Choice single cask and a limited 20 year old are released.

2012 A 30 year old from 1982 is released.

2016 A 25 year old from 1990 is released.

2021 A 47 year old Prima & Ultima from 1974 is launched.

10 year old
Flora & Fauna

Tasting notes Auchroisk 10 year old:

GS – Malt and spice on the light nose, with developing nuts and floral notes. Quite voluptuous on the palate, with fresh fruit and milk chocolate. Raisins in the finish.

Aultmore

[ault•moor]

Owner:
John Dewar & Sons
(Bacardi)

Region/district:
Speyside

Founded: **Status:** **Capacity:**
1896   Active   3 200 000 litres

Address: Keith, Banffshire AB55 6QY

Website:
aultmore.com

Tel:
01542 881800

The distillery faces an exciting future by way of a huge expansion scheduled to be completed some time in 2024.

In April 2022, the owners sent in a planning application to Moray council which was approved in October. The intention is to double the capacity to over 6 million litres of pure alcohol which will make it the largest in the Dewar's group of distilleries. The two wash stills in the current still house will be removed and a third spirit still will be installed. The still house will then be expanded to the west to house three new wash stills. A new tun room north of the new still house will hold nine washbacks and a new boiler house and new cooling towers are also included in the plans.

The £15m expansion is not made to secure more spirit for the Aultmore single malt brand which wasn't promoted until 2014 and currently sells around 125,00 bottles per year. The whisky however is an important part of two of the biggest blended brands in the world – William Lawson's Finest and Dewar's.

The last time Aultmore was rebuilt was in the beginning of the 1970s and the distillery is equipped with a 10.25 ton Steinecker full lauter mash tun. There are six wooden washbacks (five made of larch and one of Douglas fir) with a minimum fermentation time of 56 hours. Finally, there are two pairs of stills. With slightly descending lyne arms, not allowing for very much reflux, and a generous middle cut between 73% and 61%, the new make carries a body and character which can make a lot of difference in a blend. Since 2008 production has been running seven-days a week, which for 2023 means 16 mashes per week and just over 3.2 million litres of alcohol.

The core range includes a **12 year old**, an **18 year old** and a **21 year old** as well as a **25 year old** exclusive to Asia. There are also limited releases for the travel retail market in the **Exceptional Cask Series** – most recently a **21 year old Colheita port finish**.

History:

1896 Alexander Edward, owner of Benrinnes and co-founder of Craigellachie Distillery, builds Aultmore.

1897 Production starts.

1898 Production is doubled; the company Oban & Aultmore Glenlivet Distilleries Ltd manages Aultmore.

1923 Alexander Edward sells Aultmore for £20,000 to John Dewar & Sons.

1925 Dewar's becomes part of Distillers Company Limited (DCL).

1930 The administration is transferred to Scottish Malt Distillers (SMD).

1971 The stills are increased from two to four.

1991 United Distillers launches a 12-year old Aultmore in the Flora & Fauna series.

1996 A 21 year old cask strength is marketed as a Rare Malt.

1998 Diageo sells Dewar's and Bombay Gin to Bacardi for £1,150 million.

2004 A new official 12 year old bottling is launched

2014 Three new expressions are released – 12, 25 and 21 year old for duty free.

2015 An 18 year old is released.

2019 Three 22 year old single casks with different second maturations are released for duty free.

2021 A 21 year old is added to the core range.

12 years old

Tasting notes Aultmore 12 years old:

GS – A nose of peaches and lemonade, freshly-mown grass, linseed and milky coffee. Very fruity on the palate, mildly herbal, with toffee and light spices. The finish is medium in length, with lingering spices, fudge, and finally more milky coffee.

Balblair

[bal•blair]

Owner:
Inver House Distillers
(International Beverage Holdings)

Region/district:
Northern Highlands

Founded: 1790
Status: Active (vc)
Capacity: 1 800 000 litres

Address: Edderton, Tain, Ross-shire IV19 1LB

Website: balblair.com
Tel: 01862 821273

To most consumers, Balblair is a surprisingly unknown single malt. With global sales of just 150,000 bottles it is not even among the top 60 Scotch single malts in the world.

One would have thought that Balblair, founded already in 1790 and thus with the benefit of being the fourth oldest distillery in Scotland, would have a more prominent place in the whisky ranking. It is owned by Inver House Distillers where Old Pulteney and Speyburn are the malts that have received the most attention in the last decades. On top of that, the company has a popular blend, Hankey Bannister, and its focus is currently on these three brands. Inver House is part of International Beverage Holdings which was formed in 2006 as the international business of Thai-Bev, the largest producer of beer and alcohol in Thailand. That company was founded in 2003 by Charoen Sirivadhanabhakdi and is still run by him and his family. In spring 2023 there was a rumour that the company was looking to sell its spirit division but the comment to that was "there are no concrete plans".

Sustainable production has been a key objective for the Scotch whisky industry in recent years. The process is energy-intensive and in order to loose as little energy as possible in the still house, Balblair installed a TVR (thermal vapour recompression) system in summer 2023.

The distillery is equipped with a stainless steel, 4.5 tonnes semi lauter mash tun, six Oregon pine washbacks and one pair of stills. A couple of years ago the distillery went from a five-day week to a seven-day week and in 2023, 19 mashes per week are planned, which means a target of 1.5 million litres for the full year. It also entails that fermentation time is now 60 hours instead of mixing short (60 hours) and long (90 hours) fermentations.

The core range consists of **12, 15, 18 and 25 year old**. All except the 18 year old are also available in travel retail with the addition of a **17 year old** finished in first fill sherry butts. There have been few limited releases lately but one with a substantial age has been announced for autumn 2023.

History:

1790 The distillery is founded by James McKeddy.

1790 John Ross takes over

1836 John Ross dies and his son Andrew Ross takes over with the help of his sons.

1872 The distillery is moved to the present location.

1873 Andrew Ross dies and his son James takes over.

1894 Alexander Cowan takes over and rebuilds the distillery

1911 Cowan is forced to cease payments and the distillery closes.

1941 The distillery is put up for sale.

1948 Robert Cumming buys Balblair for £48,000.

1949 Production restarts.

1970 Cumming sells Balblair to Hiram Walker.

1988 Allied Distillers becomes the new owner through the merger between Hiram Walker and Allied Vintners.

1996 The distillery is sold to Inver House Distillers.

2000 Balblair Elements and the first version of Balblair 33 years are launched.

2001 Thai company Pacific Spirits (part of the Great Oriole Group) takes over Inver House.

2004 Balblair 38 years is launched.

2005 12 year old Peaty Cask, 1979 (26 years) and 1970 (35 years) are launched.

2006 International Beverage Holdings acquires Pacific Spirits UK.

2007 Three new vintages replace the former range.

2008 Vintage 1975 and 1965 are released.

2009 Vintage 1991 and 1990 are released.

2011 Vintage 1995 and 1993 are released.

2012 Vintage 1975, 2001 and 2002 are released. A visitor centre is opened.

2013 Vintage 1983, 1990 and 2003 are released.

2014 Vintage 1999 and 2004 are released for duty free.

2016 Vintage 2005 is released.

2019 A new range with age statements is launched.

Tasting notes Balblair 12 year old:

IR – Sugary and malty on the nose with herbal and earthy notes coming through. Rich, creamy and sweet on the palate, grilled corn cobs, caramel, honey and some bitter, oaky notes.

12 years old

Balmenach

[bal•men•ack]

Owner:
Inver House Distillers
(International Beverage Holdings)

Region/district:
Speyside

Founded: 1824   **Status:** Active   **Capacity:** 2 900 000 litres

Address: Cromdale, Moray PH26 3PF

Website: inverhouse.com   **Tel:** 01479 872569

In the last couple of years, a lot of focus has been on producing sustainably at Balmenach and to reduce its carbon footprint.

A £3m investment has resulted in an anaerobic digestion plant which uses microorganisms to break down waste products from the production, creating biogas which is then used to generate electricity for the entire site. The new plant runs alongside a wood-pellet biomass boiler generating steam for the distillery.

Entering into Speyside on the A95, coming from Grantown on Spey, Balmenach is the first distillery one encounters. While open for tours of the gin side (Caorunn) of the production, visitors are, unfortunately, not admitted to the whisky distillery itself. There are no official bottlings of the single malt. Hopefully both the distillery and the whisky will get some well-deserved attention in the near future.

Balmenach is equipped with an eight ton stainless steel semi-lauter mash tun with a copper dome and a seven hour mash cycle and there are six washbacks made of Douglas fir – two of them replaced in 2023. There are also plans to add another two washbacks but nothing has yet been confirmed. For quite some time the distillery has been working a 5-day week with seven short fermentations (54 hours) and seven long (90-100 hours). After the summer break in 2023, the production increased to seven days per week with an even 54 hour fermentation. Finally, there are three wash stills and three spirit stills, all equipped with boil balls, descending lyne arms and connected to worm tubs. The distillation is fairly quick with little reflux and that, together with the unusually wide spirit cut (72-58%), results in a meaty and heavy newmake. The production plan is for 14 mashes per week in 2023 for the first six months and then increase to 20 which translates to 2.4 million litres of alcohol.

There used to be a 12 year old from the previous owners but the last time an official bottling of Balmenach turned up was in 2002 when a 25 year old was launched to celebrate the Queen's Golden Jubilee. Aberko though, has been working with the distillery for a long time and has released Balmenach under the name Deerstalker.

History:

1824 The distillery is licensed to James MacGregor who operated a small farm distillery by the name of Balminoch.

1897 Balmenach Glenlivet Distillery Company is founded.

1922 The MacGregor family sells to a consortium consisting of MacDonald Green, Peter Dawson and James Watson.

1925 The consortium becomes part of Distillers Company Limited (DCL).

1930 Production is transferred to Scottish Malt Distillers (SMD).

1962 The number of stills is increased to six.

1964 Floor maltings replaced with Saladin box.

1992 The first official bottling is a 12 year old.

1993 The distillery is mothballed in May.

1997 Inver House Distillers buys Balmenach from United Distillers.

1998 Production recommences.

2001 Thai company Pacific Spirits takes over Inver House at the price of £56 million. The new owner launches a 27 and a 28 year old.

2002 To commemorate the Queen's Golden Jubilee a 25-year old Balmenach is launched.

2006 International Beverage Holdings acquires Pacific Spirits UK.

2009 Gin production commences.

Tasting notes Deerstalker 12 years old:

IR – The nose is sweet and fruity, with green garden notes and sweet liquorice coming through. Sweet, fruity barley on the palate with notes of honey, custard, apricots, peaches and slightly bitter notes from the oak.

Deerstalker 12 years old

Balvenie

[bal•ven•ee]

Owner:
William Grant & Sons

Region/district:
Speyside

Founded: 1892

Status: Active (vc)

Capacity: 7 000 000 litres

Address: Dufftown, Keith, Banffshire AB55 4DH

Website:
thebalvenie.com

Tel:
01340 820373

Not only is Balvenie one of the most sold single malts in the world with well over 4 million bottles last year. It is also one of a few distilleries in where you can follow every step of the production.

Balvenie has its own floor maltings producing 10-15% of the needs and there is also a coppersmith and a cooperage on site. Unlike its sister distillery on the same grounds, Glenfiddich, which predominantly focuses on maturation in ex-bourbon barrels, Balvenie has built its fame on double maturation – ex-bourbon and ex-sherry. The first Doublewood release appeared 30 years ago and this method is still the backbone of the flavour profile. The man behind the success of Balvenie is David Stewart who joined the company in 1962 and became Master Blender at the age of 29. Lately he has been joined by Kelsey McKechnie as his eventual successor.

The distillery is equipped with an 11.8 ton full lauter mash tun where one ton of their own floor-malted barley is part of every batch. There are nine wooden and five stainless steel washbacks with a fermentation time of 64-68 hours. In the original still house there are six spirit stills. In an extension to the building, the five wash stills are more or less packed together. For 2023, the production plan is 30 mashes per week and 7 million litres of alcohol. The main part is unpeated but each year one week of production comes from peated barley (20-40 ppm) which is used for both Balvenie and Glenfiddich.

The core range consists of **Doublewood 12, Caribbean Cask 14, French Oak 16** and **Portwood 21**. There is also the **Rare Marriage** series (**25, 30** and **40 years old**). Recent limited releases include a **60 year old** celebrating David Stewart's six decades with Balvenie. In The Balvenie Stories series **A Rare Discovery From Distant Shores 27 years rum finish** was launched in July 2022 followed by **A Revelation of Cask and Character 19 years** in August 2023. The latter highlights the work of the people at the Balvenie cooperage. Exclusive to duty free are **The Creation of a Classic**, a **15 year old Madeira Cask**, an **18 year old PX Cask** and **The Week of Peat 19 years**.

History:

1892 William Grant rebuilds Balvenie New House to Balvenie Distillery.

1893 The first distillation takes place in May.

1957 The two stills are increased by another two.

1965 Two new stills are installed.

1971 Another two stills are installed.

1973 The first official bottling appears.

1982 Founder's Reserve is launched.

1996 Two vintage bottlings and a Port wood finish are launched.

2001 The Balvenie Islay Cask is released.

2002 A 50 year old is released.

2006 New Wood 17 years old, Roasted Malt 14 years old and Portwood 1993 are released.

2007 Vintage Cask 1974 and Sherry Oak 17 years old are released.

2008 Signature, Vintage 1976, Balvenie Rose and Rum Cask 17 year old are released.

2009 Vintage 1978, 17 year old Madeira finish, 14 year old rum finish and Golden Cask 14 years old are released.

2010 A 40 year old, Peated Cask and Carribean Cask are released.

2011 Second batch of Tun 1401 is released.

2012 A 50 year old and Doublewood 17 years old are released.

2013 Triple Cask 12, 16 and 25 years are launched.

2014 Single Barrel 15 and 25 years, Tun 1509 and two new 50 year olds are launched.

2015 The Balvenie DCS Compendium is launched.

2016 A 21 year old madeira finish is released.

2017 The Balvenie Peat Week 2002 and Peated Triple Cask are released.

2018 A limited 25 year old is relased.

2019 The Balvenie Stories is launched.

2020 A 21 year old is released together with a fourth instalment in the Balvenie Stories series.

2021 The Second Red Rose, The Tale of the Dog and a 25 year old are released.

2022 French Oak 16 years and A Rare Discovery From Distant Shores are released.

2023 A Revelation of Cask and Character 19 years are released.

Tasting notes Balvenie Doublewood 12 years:

GS – Nuts and spicy malt on the nose, full-bodied, with soft fruit, vanilla, sherry and a hint of peat. Dry and spicy in a luxurious, lengthy finish.

Doublewood 12 years old

Ben Nevis

[ben nev•iss]

Owner:	**Region/district:**
Ben Nevis Distillery Ltd	Western Highlands
(Nikka, Asahi Breweries)	

Founded:	**Status:**	**Capacity:**
1825	Active (vc)	2 000 000 litres

Address: Lochy Bridge, Fort William PH33 6TJ

Website:	**Tel:**
bennevisdistillery.com	01397 702476

While many times overshadowed by distilleries that recently have been re-invented in either branding, expansion or refurbishing, there are still distilleries that keep on producing as they have always done and delighting a small, yet loyal, fanbase.

Ben Nevis is one such distillery. The Japanese influence (Nikka has owned the distillery since 1989) has secured the distillery's existence but there has always been a sense of the "absentee landlord" when it comes to the ownership. No doubt some investments have been made and Ben Nevis newmake has for a long time been an important part of Japanese blend such as Black Nikka. In two years from now the distillery will celebrate its 200th anniversary and the location in Fort William, a popular tourist resort, has prompted the owners to make recent investments in the distillery visitor centre.

During three decades towards the end of the 1800s there were three working distilleries in Fort William. Two of them, Ben Nevis and its sister distillery Nevis, were of such a magnitude that their joint production far exceeded distilleries such as Macallan and Glenlivet a the time. The reason for this can be ascribed to the success of the blend Dew of Ben Nevis, which was introduced by the legendary distillery owner "Long" John MacDonald.

Ben Nevis is equipped with a nine ton full lauter mash tun made of stainless steel, six stainless steel washbacks and two made of Oregon pine with a 48 hour fermentation as well as two pairs of stills. In 2023 the plan is to mash 13 times per week and a total of 2 million litres of alcohol. Around 50,000 litres of this will be heavily peated (40ppm in the barley).

The **10 year old** was relaunched with a new design in August 2021. There is also the peated **MacDonald's Traditional Ben Nevis** as well as the recently launched **Coire Leis** without age statement. Very old versions of Ben Nevis have turned up and three vintages from **1966**, **1967** and **1968** were released in Taiwan in 2019.

History:

1825 The distillery is founded by 'Long' John McDonald.

1856 Long John dies and his son Donald P. McDonald takes over.

1878 Demand is so great that another distillery, Nevis Distillery, is built nearby.

1908 Both distilleries merge into one.

1941 D. P. McDonald & Sons sells the distillery to Ben Nevis Distillery Ltd headed by the Canadian millionaire Joseph W. Hobbs.

1955 Hobbs installs a Coffey still which makes it possible to produce both grain and malt whisky.

1964 Joseph Hobbs dies.

1978 Production is stopped.

1981 Joseph Hobbs Jr sells the distillery back to Long John Distillers and Whitbread.

1984 After restoration and reconstruction totalling £2 million, Ben Nevis opens up again.

1986 The distillery closes again.

1989 Whitbread sells the distillery to Nikka Whisky Distilling Company Ltd.

1990 The distillery opens up again.

1991 A visitor centre is inaugurated.

1996 Ben Nevis 10 years old is launched.

2006 A 13 year old port finish is released.

2010 A 25 year old is released.

2011 McDonald's Traditional Ben Nevis is released.

2014 Forgotten Bottlings are introduced.

2015 A 40 year old "Blended at Birth" single blend is released.

2018 Ben Nevis 10 years old Batch No. 1 is released.

2021 The design of the 10 year bottle is revamped and Coire Leis is released.

10 years old

Tasting notes Ben Nevis 10 years old:

GS – The nose is initially quite green, with developing nutty, orange notes. Coffee, brittle toffee and peat are present on the slightly oily palate, along with chewy oak, which persists to the finish, together with more coffee and a hint of dark chocolate.

Benriach

[ben•ree•ack]

Owner:	**Region/district:**
BenRiach Distillery Company	Speyside
(Brown Forman)	

Founded:	**Status:**	**Capacity:**
1897	Active (vc)	2 800 000 litres

Address: Longmorn, Elgin, Morayshire IV30 8SJ

Website:	**Tel:**
benriachdistillery.com	01343 862888

After the foundation in 1897, Benriach only distilled for three years before it was mothballed. The only operation on the site that continued was the floor maltings which provided nearby sister distillery Longmorn with malted barley.

This continued for 65 years until BenRiach was reopened and in 1998 the maltings were decommissioned. Fifteen years later the floors opened up again for a few weeks of malting every year. That was a bold decision as the inefficiency of traditional floor malting are well-known. On the other hand, advantages are that other flavours can be achieved and, not least, visitors will have the opportunity to experience a method of malting that was pre-valent in Scotland for centuries. The operations, however, lasted just ten years and in 2023 the maltings stopped and the owners are now working on various other solutions.

Under the reigns of Billy Walker, BenRiach was known for a multitude of new releases every year. While appreciated by many enthusiasts, a sense of moderation was implemented when Brown Forman took over in 2016 and four years later master blender Rachel Barrie introduced a tighter and very well-composed range.

BenRiach is equipped with a 5.8 ton traditional cast iron mash tun with a stainless steel shell, eight washbacks made of stainless steel with short (55 hours) and long fermentations (+100 hours) and two pairs of stills. In 2023 the plan is to produce 1.8 million litres of pure alcohol which includes peated spirit at 35ppm as well as 40,000 litres of triple-distilled spirit.

The core range consists of **The Original Ten, The Smoky Ten, The Twelve, The Smoky Twelve, The Twenty One, The Twenty Five** and **The Thirty**. In November 2022 **The Sixteen** (matured in a combination of bourbon, sherry and virgin oak) and **The Forty** (bourbon and port casks) werealso added to the range. Exclusive to travel retail is **The Forty Octave Cask Matured** which was released in 2023.

History:
1897 John Duff & Co founds the distillery.
1900 The distillery is closed.
1965 The distillery is reopened by the new owner, The Glenlivet Distillers Ltd.
1972 Production of peated Benriach starts.
1978 Seagram Distillers takes over.
1985 The number of stills is increased to four.
1998 The maltings is decommissioned.
2002 The distillery is mothballed in October.
2004 Intra Trading, buys Benriach together with the former Director at Burn Stewart, Billy Walker.
2004 Standard, Curiositas and 12, 16 and 20 year olds are released.
2005 Four different vintages are released.
2006 Sixteen new releases, i.a. a 25 year old, a 30 year old and 8 different vintages.
2007 A 40 year old and three new heavily peated expressions are released.
2008 Peated Madeira finish, a 15 year old Sauternes finish and nine single casks are released.
2009 Two wood finishes (Moscatel and Gaja Barolo) and nine single casks are released.
2010 Triple distilled Horizons and heavily peated Solstice are released.
2011 A 45 year old and 12 vintages are released.
2012 Septendecim 17 years is released.
2013 Vestige 46 years is released. The maltings are working again.
2015 Dunder, Albariza, Latada and a 10 year old are released.
2016 Brown Forman buys the company for £285m. BenRiach cask strength and Peated Quarter Cask are launched.
2017 10 year old Triple Distilled and Peated Cask Strength are released.
2018 A 12 and a 21 year old, Temporis 21 years and Authenticus 30 years are released.
2019 Batch 16 of the Cask Bottlings is released.
2020 The entire core range is relaunched with seven new expressions.
2021 Malting Season First Edition is launched.
2022 The Sixteen is released.

Tasting notes BenRiach The Twelve:

IR – Fresh on the nose with notes of furniture polish, eucalyptus, tropical fruits, honey and brown sugar. A dry start on the palate is followed by raisins soaked in port, baked apples with vanilla, chocolate, cinnamon and almonds.

The Twelve

Benrinnes

[ben rin•ess]

Owner:
Diageo

Region/district:
Speyside

Founded: **Status:** **Capacity:**
1826 Active 3 500 000 litres

Address: Aberlour, Banffshire AB38 9NN

Website: **Tel:**
malts.com 01340 872600

For those travelling the southern parts of Speyside, the mountain of Benrinnes is a well-known feature in the landscape. From its peak, at 840 metres above sea level, one can see eight different Scottish counties.

With its location, right at the foot of the mountain, it is also appropriate that Benrinnes distillery has taken the same name. It draws its process water from wells on the mountain in the same way as four other distilleries located a little bit further away – namely Aberlour, Allt-a-Bhainne, Dailuaine and Glenfarclas. There are no visible remains of the first Benrinnes distillery dating back to 1826. In fact it was situated a few kilometres from where the current one is. Nor can the second distillery be found, instead what you will see is dating from the 1950s.

When Benrinnes closed down the floor maltings in 1964 they didn´t turn to commercial maltsters for their needs like most other distilleries. Instead they installed a so-called Saladin box, named after Charles Saladin who invented it in the 1890s. This is a long concrete box with revolving rakes. The barley is steeped and turned by the rakes and air circulates through perforated floors to keep the temperature under control. To dry, the green malt goes into a kiln which is simply a large, self-filling and self-emptying box with air blowing through it. Benrinnes closed their maltings finally in 1984.

The equipment consists of an 8.5 ton semi-lauter mash tun, eight washbacks made of Oregon pine with a fermentation time ranging from 65 to 100 hours. There are also two wash stills and four spirit stills connected to worm tubs. These were replaced during 2023 and after the temporary closure, the distillery moved to full capacity which means 21 mashes per week and 3.5 million litres. The fact that the spirit vapours are cooled using worm tubs contribute to the character of Benrinnes newmake, which is light sulphury. The unusually wide spirit cut (73%-58%) also plays its part in creating a robust and meaty spirit.

There is only one official single malt from benrinnes, the **Flora & Fauna 15 year old**. In 2014 a 21 year old Special Release appeared.

History:

1826 Lyne of Ruthrie distillery is built at Whitehouse Farm by Peter McKenzie.

1829 A flood destroys the distillery and a new distillery is constructed by John Innes a few kilometres from the first one.

1834 John Innes files for bankruptcy and William Smith & Co takes over.

1864 William Smith & Co goes bankrupt and David Edward becomes the new owner.

1896 Benrinnes is ravaged by fire which prompts major refurbishment. Alexander Edward takes over.

1922 John Dewar & Sons takes over ownership.

1925 John Dewar & Sons becomes part of Distillers Company Limited (DCL).

1956 The distillery is completely rebuilt.

1964 Floor maltings is replaced by a Saladin box.

1966 The number of stills doubles to six.

1984 The Saladin box is taken out of service and the malt is purchased centrally.

1991 The first official bottling from Benrinnes is a 15 year old in the Flora & Fauna series.

1996 United Distillers releases a 21 year old cask strength in their Rare Malts series.

2009 A 23 year old is launched as a part of this year´s Special Releases.

2010 A Manager´s Choice 1996 is released.

2014 A limited 21 year old is released.

15 years old

Tasting notes Benrinnes 15 years old:

GS – A brief flash of caramel shortcake on the initial nose, soon becoming more peppery and leathery, with some sherry. Ultimately savoury and burnt rubber notes. Big-bodied, viscous, with gravy, dark chocolate and more pepper. A medium-length finish features mild smoke and lively spices.

Benromach

[ben•<u>ro</u>•mack]

Owner:
Gordon & MacPhail

Region/district:
Speyside

Founded: | **Status:** | **Capacity:**
1898 | Active (vc) | 700 000 litres

Address: Invererne Road, Forres,
Morayshire IV36 3EB

Website:
benromach.com

Tel:
01309 675968

There are only two distilleries on the Scottish mainland that use peated malt for virtually all their production; the newly re-opened Brora and Benromach in Forres.

A third distillery, Ardmore south of Huntly, uses peated malt for everything that is bottled as single malt but they also produce an unpeated version intended for blends. In the case of Benromach, the standard phenol specification of the malt is 10-12ppm but for two weeks per year, heavily peated is produced. When Gordon & MacPhail re-opened Benromach in 1998 it was with the intention of recreating an old-school Speyside single malt and back in the days it would have shown a smokier character than today.

Gordon & MacPhail is one of the oldest, and possibly the best known, independent bottlers and their shop in South Street in Elgin is legendary. At the moment it is temporarily closed, undergoing a transformation into a visitor experience which will open 2024. A pop-up shop in High Street opened in April 2023.

Benromach is equipped with a 1.5 ton semi-lauter mash tun with a copper dome and 13 washbacks – nine made of European larch and four from Scottish larch and with a fermentation time between 67 and 115 hours. There is also one pair of stills with straight lyne arms and with exterior condensers. The 2023 plan entails 18 mashes per five-day week for 44 weeks and 500,000 litres of pure alcohol. There are six dunnage and one racked warehouse on site with space for 35,000 casks and one more warehouse may be added during 2023.

The core range consists of **10, 15** and **21 year old** as well as **Cask Strength Vintage**. In August 2021 the first of annual releases of a **40 year old** appeared and the third arrived in summer 2023. There are also special editions in the Contrasts range; **Organic 2014, Peat Smoke 2014** and, released in summer 2023, **Air Dried Oak** and **Kiln Dried Oak**. The last two, both distilled in 2012, were released to show the subtle differences in flavour that come from the different techniques used to dry the staves for the casks. Finally a **Vintage 2011**, finished in Bordeaux casks, was released in autumn 2023.

History:

1898 Benromach Distillery Company starts the distillery.

1911 Harvey McNair & Co buys the distillery.

1919 John Joseph Calder buys Benromach and sells it to Benromach Distillery Ltd.

1931 The distillery is mothballed.

1937 The distillery reopens.

1938 Joseph Hobbs buys Benromach and sells it on to National Distillers of America (NDA).

1953 NDA sells Benromach to Distillers Company Ltd.

1968 Floor maltings is abolished.

1983 Benromach is mothballed.

1993 Gordon & McPhail buys Benromach.

1998 The distillery is once again in operation.

2004 The first bottle distilled by the new owner is 'Benromach Traditional'.

2005 A Port Wood finish, a Vintage 1968 and Classic 55 years ar released.

2006 Benromach Organic is released.

2007 Peat Smoke, the first heavily peated whisky from the distillery, is released.

2008 Benromach Origins Golden Promise is released.

2009 Benromach 10 years old is released.

2011 New edition of Peatsmoke, a 2001 Hermitage finish and a 30 year old are released.

2015 A 15 year old and two wood finishes (Hermitage and Sassicaia) are released.

2016 A 35 year old and 1974 single cask are released.

2017 A 1976 single cask and a 2009 Triple Distilled are released.

2018 A 20th Anniversary bottling and a Sassicaia 2010 are released.

2019 Peat Smoke Sherry Cask Matured and a 50 year old are released.

2020 A new core range is released.

2021 A 40 year old is released together with Peat Smoke Sherry Cask Matured 2012.

2022 Cara Gold and Triple Distilled are released.

2023 Air Dried Oak and Kiln Dried Oak are released.

Tasting notes Benromach 10 year old:

GS – A nose that is initially quite smoky, with wet grass, butter, ginger and brittle toffee. Mouth-coating, spicy, malty and nutty on the palate, with developing citrus fruits, raisins and soft wood smoke. The finish is warming, with lingering barbecue notes.

10 years old

Bladnoch

[blad•nock]

Owner:
David Prior

Region/district:
Lowlands

Founded: 1817

Status: Active (vc)

Capacity: 1 500 000 litres

Address: Bladnoch, Wigtown, Wigtonshire DG8 9AB

Website: bladnoch.com

Tel: 01988 402605

Taking over a closed distillery can many times be a challenge. One costly issue can be exchanging dilapidated equipment but at least that can be solved if you have enough funds. The worst challenge is probably the possible lack of maturing whisky.

If there is not enough stock of whisky to build a brand, only time will save you. Bladnoch is an example of that conundrum. There was no production between 1993 and 2000, small production between 2000 and 2009 and virtually no whisky was produced between 2009 and 2017. That was what David Prior had to face when he took over the distillery in 2015. It seems like an impossible equation but the solution is to hire experienced people who know how to handle the existing stock and at the same time produce whisky for the future.

Prior approached two top profiles in the Scotch whisky industry; Ian MacMillan who at the time was master distiller and master blender at Burn Stewart and (a couple of years later) Nick Savage who was the master distiller at Macallan for three years. Today, due to their expertise, there is a wide range of bottlings and a visitor centre has also opened.

Bladnoch is equipped with a five ton stainless steel semi-lauter mash tun and six Douglas fir washbacks. Fermentations used to be a combination of short and long ones but due to increased production it is now at 60 hours. There is also two pairs of stills. In 2023, 16 mashes per week are planned which will amount to 1.5 million litres of pure alcohol. That includes a small part (480 tonnes) of heavily peated production (60-80ppm).

The core range consists of four expressions with no age statement; the entry level **Vinaya**, **Samsara**, the peated **Alinta** and **Liora**. There are also three expressions with age statements; **11, 14** and **19 years old.** In May 2023 the **Dragon Series** was launched with five no age statement expressions – **The Field, The Spirit, The Casks, The Ageing** and **The Decision**. Two months later **The Samhla Collection** with three ultra rare vintages from **1966, 1990** and **2008** was released.

History:

1817 Founded by Thomas and John McClelland.

1878 John McClelland's son Charlie reconstructs and refurbishes the distillery.

1905 Production stops.

1911 Dunville & Co. buys T. & A. McClelland Ltd. Production is intermittent until 1936.

1937 Dunville & Co. is liquidated and Bladnoch is wound up. Ross & Coulter from Glasgow buys the distillery after the war. The equipment is dismantled and shipped to Sweden.

1956 A. B. Grant (Bladnoch Distillery Ltd.) takes over and restarts production with four new stills.

1964 McGown and Cameron becomes new owners.

1973 Inver House Distillers buys Bladnoch.

1983 Arthur Bell and Sons take over.

1985 Guiness Group buys Arthur Bell & Sons which, from 1989, are included in United Distillers.

1988 A visitor centre is built.

1993 United Distillers mothballs Bladnoch in June.

1994 Raymond Armstrong buys Bladnoch in October.

2000 Production commences in December.

2003 The first bottles from Armstrong are launched, a 15 year old cask strength from UD casks.

2008 First release of whisky produced after the take-over in 2000 - three 6 year olds.

2009 An 8 year old of own production and a 19 year old are released.

2014 The distillery is liquidated.

2015 The distillery is bought by David Prior.

2016 Samsara, Adela and Talia are released.

2017 Production starts again and a Vintage 1988 is released.

2018 A 10 year old is released.

2019 A visitor centre is opened.

2020 An 11 year old and the Waterfall collection is launched.

2022 Alinta and Liora are released together with 5 single casks.

2023 The Dragon Series and the Samhla Collection are launched.

Tasting notes Bladnoch 10 year old:

IR – Fresh and grassy on the nose with sweet notes of honey and lilac, citrus, vanilla and a hint of cardamom. Rich and herbal on the palate with eucalyptus, ginger, pineapple, liquorice and milk chocolate coming through. Lovely mouthfeel.

11 years old

Blair Athol

[blair ath•ull]

Owner: **Region/district:**
Diageo   Southern Highlands

Founded: **Status:**   **Capacity:**
1798   Active (vc)   2 800 000 litres

Address: Perth Road, Pitlochry, Perthshire PH16 5LY

Website: **Tel:**
malts.com   01796 482003

Most distilleries, especially the ones owned by larger companies, tend to distill for either five days or seven days per week. This is, however, not decided on a weekly – or even monthly – basis but rather from year to year.

It all depends on how much stock of certain ages they currently have in the warehouses and the estimate of how much of it will be needed for the next 3-5 years. Quite a few of the Diageo distilleries, especially those producing malt for blends (including Blair Athol), have increased to seven-day production during 2022/2023. The main impact (apart from producing larger volumes) is that in a seven-day production you don't have a combination of short and long fermentations with washbacks resting through the weekend.

The amount of Blair Athol single malt released by the owners is a mere trickle amounting to a few thousand bottles. The importance lies in the effect on blends and in particular on Bell´s and this is the sixth best selling Diageo blend. Due to a substantial loss in sales in 2022 (-22%), it has now fallen to place sixteen on the global list with 22 million bottles sold in 2022. It is still number two in the UK however after Famous Grouse. Blair Athol is the spiritual home of Bell's blended whisky with a magnificent visitor centre attracting between 80-90,000 people every year. One reason for this high number is the exquisite location close to the A9 leading up to the Highlands. A small detour on the A924 takes you to Pitlochry where the distillery is situated.

The distillery is equipped with an 8.2 ton semi-lauter mash tun, six washbacks made of stainless steel with a fermentation time of 46 hours and two pairs of stills. A cloudy wort, together with the short fermentation time, gives Blair Athol newmake a nutty and malty character. The plan for 2023 is to mash 16 times per week and produce 2.8 million litres of alcohol.

The only official bottling is the **12 year old Flora & Fauna**. In autumn 2017, however, a **23 year old**, matured in ex-bodega European oak butts was released as part of the Special Releases.

History:

1798   John Stewart and Robert Robertson found Aldour Distillery, the predecessor to Blair Athol. The name is taken from the adjacent river Allt Dour.

1825   The distillery is expanded by John Robertson and takes the name Blair Athol Distillery.

1826   The Duke of Atholl leases the distillery to Alexander Connacher & Co.

1860   Elizabeth Connacher runs the distillery.

1882   Peter Mackenzie & Company Distillers Ltd of Edinburgh (future founder of Dufftown Distillery) buys Blair Athol and expands it.

1932   The distillery is mothballed.

1933   Arthur Bell & Sons takes over by acquiring Peter Mackenzie & Company.

1949   Production restarts.

1973   Stills are expanded from two to four.

1985   Guinness Group buys Arthur Bell & Sons.

1987   A visitor centre is built.

2003   A 27 year old cask strength from 1975 is launched in Diageo's Rare Malts series.

2010   A distillery exclusive with no age statement and a single cask from 1995 are released.

2016   A distillery exclusive without age statement is released.

2017   A 23 year old is released as part of the Special Releases.

12 years old

Tasting notes Blair Athol 12 years old:

GS – The nose is mellow and sherried, with brittle toffee. Sweet and fragrant. Relatively rich on the palate, with malt, raisins, sultanas and sherry. The finish is lengthy, elegant and slowly drying.

Bowmore

[bow•moor]

Owner:
Beam Suntory

Region/district:
Islay

Founded: 1779
Status: Active (vc)
Capacity: 2 150 000 litres

Address: School Street, Bowmore, Islay, Argyll PA43 7GS

Website:
bowmore.com

Tel:
01496 810441

Dating back to at least 1779, Bowmore is by far the oldest distillery on Islay and the second oldest working distillery in Scotland. It also prides itself of Warehouse No. 1, right next to the sea, which is the oldest whisky warehouse still in use in Scotland.

However, there is evidence that David Simpson may have built Bowmore around the same time as Daniel Campell 'The younger' began planning the village with the same name – circa 1768. On the other hand, the owners of Glenturret recently discovered documents to prove that their distillery was working already in 1763 so it looks like Bowmore has to settle for being at least 'la grande dame' of Islay distilleries.

Bowmore is one of three distilleries on the island with its own floor maltings (Laphroaig and Kilchoman are the other two). One malting on three floors produces 42 tonnes of green malt which is kilned in three batches starting with 10 hours on peat and then 34 hours on dry air. Around 25% of the malt requirement is produced in-house. The remaining part is bought from Simpson's. Both parts have a phenol specification of 25-30 ppm and are always mixed in a ratio of 2 tons in-house malt and 6 tons of malt from Simpsons.

Bowmore is equipped with an eight ton stainless steel semi-lauter mash tun. The original six washbacks made of Oregon pine were complemented by a seventh in April 2023 in order to increase the fermentation time from 62 hours to 72 hours. Finally there are two wash stills (30,940 litres) and two spirit stills (14,750 litres) with a foreshot of 35 minutes in the spirit run and a cut between 74% and 61%. In 2023, the plan is to do 16 mashes per week which amounts to 2.15 million litres of alcohol. Around 20% of the newmake starts in sherry casks while the rest is filled into either first- or second-fill bourbon. In terms of sales, Laphroaig has been the number one Islay malt for many years now but there is fierce competition for the second and third place between Bowmore and Ardbeg. Figures from 2021 put Bowmore in second place, with almost 2.5 million bottles sold.

The core range includes **12, 15, 18** and **25 years**. There are also recurrent but limited release of a **30 and 40 year old**. Recent limited bottlings include the Timeless Collection from spring 2021 with a **27 year old** and a **31 year old**. They were followed by a **29 year old** in September 2023. In 2022 there was also the **25 year old Distiller´s Anthology**. The Feis Ile bottling for 2023 was an **18 year old** matured in oloroso and PX sherry casks. Finally the distillery has entered into a collaboration with car maker **Aston Martin** where the third release appeared in September 2023.

The duty free range consists of **10 year old**, **15 year old** and **18 year old**. Limited releases also include several vintage single casks including one from **1965** and expressions from the No Corners To Hide collection (**22, 23, 33** and **36 year old**) made in collaboration with the artist Frank Quitely. Finally there are a **21 year old** and a **22 year old** from PX sherry casks.

History:
1779 Bowmore Distillery is founded by David Simpson and becomes the oldest Islay distillery.

1837 The distillery is sold to James and William Mutter of Glasgow.

1892 After additional construction, the distillery is sold to Bowmore Distillery Company Ltd, a consortium of English businessmen.

1925 J. B. Sheriff and Company takes over.

1929 Distillers Company Limited (DCL) takes over.

1950 William Grigor & Son takes over.

1963 Stanley P. Morrison buys the distillery and forms Morrison Bowmore Distillers Ltd.

1989 Japanese Suntory buys a 35% stake in Morrison Bowmore.

1993 The legendary Black Bowmore is launched.

1994 Suntory now controls all of Morrison Bowmore.

1996 A Bowmore 1957 (38 years) is bottled at 40.1% but is not released until 2000.

1999 Bowmore Darkest with three years finish on Oloroso barrels is launched.

2000 Bowmore Dusk is launched.

2001 Bowmore Dawn with two years finish on Port pipes is launched.

2002 A 37 year old Bowmore from 1964 and matured in fino casks is launched.

2003 Another two expressions complete the wood trilogy which started with 1964 Fino - 1964 Bourbon and 1964 Oloroso.

2005 Bowmore 1989 Bourbon (16 years) and 1971 (34 years) are launched.

2006 Bowmore 1990 Oloroso (16 years) and 1968 (37 years) are launched.

2007 An 18 year old is introduced. 1991 (16yo) Port and Black Bowmore are released.

History continued:

2008 White Bowmore and a 1992 Vintage with Bourdeaux finish are launched.

2009 Gold Bowmore, Maltmen´s Selection, Laimrig and Bowmore Tempest are released.

2010 A 40 year old and Vintage 1981 are released.

2011 Vintage 1982 and new batches of Tempest and Laimrig are released.

2012 100 Degrees Proof, Springtide and Vintage 1983 are released for duty free.

2013 The Devil´s Casks, a 23 year old Port Cask Matured and Vintage 1984 are released.

2014 Black Rock, Gold Reef and White Sands are released for duty free.

2015 New editions of Devil´s Cask, Tempest and the 50 year old are released as well as Mizunara Cask Finish.

2016 A 9 year old, a 10 year old travel retail exclusive and Bowmore Vault Edit1on are released as well as the final batch of Black Bowmore.

2017 No. 1 is released together with three new expressions for travel retail.

2018 Vintner´s Trilogy is launched.

2019 Vault Edit1on Peat Smoke, a 21 year old for duty free and the 36 year old Dragon Edition are released.

2020 Black Bowmore DBS is launched.

2021 Timeless 27 and 31 years old are released.

2022 The second batch of No Corners To Hide Collection is launched.

2023 Timeless 29 years old is released.

Tasting notes Bowmore 12 year old:

GS – An enticing nose of lemon and gentle brine leads into a smoky, citric palate, with notes of cocoa and boiled sweets appearing in the lengthy, complex finish.

No Corners To Hide 23 year old — 18 year old Feis Ile 2023 — No Corners To Hide 36 year old

12 year old — 15 year old — 25 year old

Braeval

[bre•vaal]

Owner:	**Region/district:**
Chivas Brothers (Pernod Ricard)	Speyside
Founded: **Status:**	**Capacity:**
1973　　　　　Active	4 200 000 litres

Address: Chapeltown of Glenlivet, Ballindalloch, Banffshire AB37 9JS

Website:	**Tel:**
secret-speyside.com	01542 783042

For those of you who want to travel to as many distilleries as possible in a short amount of time, Speyside is an absolute haven. There are more than 50 distilleries and many of them are easily visible when moving through the district.

Braeval is certainly an exception. When you drive on the B9008 from the north (the road everyone takes to go to Glenlivet), you continue until you reach the small hamlet Auchnarrow, which is just a mile south of Tamnavulin. From there you follow a narrow road east towards Chapeltown until it ends. Set in an idyllic and pastoral environment, lies the modern yet surprisingly impressive and beautiful distillery. This area was regarded as a haven for illicit distillers from the 1780s to the early 1800s and the whisky was smuggled out of the valley along narrow paths.

Braeval was built in 1973, the last decade before the second golden age of Scotch whisky came to an end, and was mothballed for six years in the early millenium. Its purpose was always to produce malt for blends and it was through independent bottlers that whisky enthusiasts became aware of the distillery.

The equipment at Braeval consists of a nine ton stainless steel, a full lauter mash tun, 13 stainless steel washbacks with a fermentation time of 70 hours and six stills. Two of them are wash stills with aftercoolers and four are spirit stills, and - with the possibility of producing 26 mashes per week - the distillery can now make 4.2 million litres per year. Recently, Braeval became Chivas Brothers' first zero direct carbon distillery by switching to a rapeseed residue based bio-fuel.

The first official bottling appeared in 2017: a 16 year old single cask available only at Chivas' visitor centres. Then, in July 2019, a new range called The Secret Speyside Collection was launched – a total of 15 bottlings from four different distilleries where Braeval was one. The three from Braeval are **25, 27** and **30 year old**, all matured in ex-bourbon barrels and hogsheads. Finally there is an **18 year old** available in the Distillery Reserve Collection available at the visitor centres.

History:

1973　The distillery is founded by Chivas Brothers (Seagram´s) and production starts in October.

1975　Three stills are increased to five.

1978　Five stills are further expanded to six.

1994　The distillery changes name to Braeval.

2001　Pernod Ricard takes over Chivas Brothers.

2002　Braeval is mothballed in October.

2008　The distillery starts producing again in July.

2017　The first official bottling, a 16 year old single cask, is released.

2019　Three new official bottlings in a new range, The Secret Speyside Collection, are released.

25 years old

Tasting notes Braeval 16 year old:

GS – Marzipan, milk chocolate-coated Turkish Delight and orange peel on the nose. The palate is sweet and fruity, with stewed apples, sugared almonds, nutmeg and ginger. Medium to long in the finish, consistently sugary and spicy.

An inside comment on...

The State of Whisky

Alan Winchester
Whisky Hall of Fame inductee No. 80
Director of Cabrach Distillery

What was your objective for entering the whisky business?

On leaving school, I became a Distillery Guide at Glenfarclas ostensibly just for the summer, however my career path of being a sailor did not come to fruition. At the end of the summer I was offered a role in the Distillery, by that time I had found something that really interested myself, in all facets.

What would you say are the best ways to attract new, young whisky consumers?

That's a difficult question, as society is always concerned about how young people are exposed to alcohol. I think good education should always be about moderation and responsibility. On how young people approach whisky should be about how they want to drink whisky, whether it's by cocktails or an education on exploring flavours.

Can one whisky, objectively, be better than the other? Isn't it all down to your personal taste and preferences?

As a distiller, yes there can be whiskies that are definitely better than others due to faults with the production process and cask maturation. On a well matured whisky I agree it can be subjective. Take sulphur, its incurrence in minute quantities can be off putting to certain consumers. Peat flavour has its fans, and its detractors in equal measure, the old saying one person's meat can be another person's poison.

Do you feel there is enough innovation in the whisky business and is there still a place for preserving and honouring traditional methods?

I do think there are lots of very interesting innovations, but also the rediscovery of things that were carried out in the past, provide a rich basis for modern distillers to innovate with. I do agree that the Scotch Whisky Regulations maybe require review on an ongoing basis. Malted rye is classed as grain whisky, and chestnut wood does not meet the whisky definition in Scotland, though these regulations have provided consumers with confidence over the years, which I think is very important.

Whatever line of business you´re in, sustainability is on every company´s agenda. Do you feel the whisky industry is at the forefront or could things happen faster?

As alcohol production has been around for centuries, it will have to adapt to climate change at all levels as it evolves. Not least in response to concerns on effluent discharge and energy usage. Sustainability is seen as important for the reputation of the products we make. I feel the industry is making great strides on meeting these challenges and maintaining quality; the move away from fossil fuels, the use of mechanical vapor recompression in the heating of stills, green electricity, digestion of co products and exploring new technology in the production of green gas.

Investing in whisky has become more and more popular. Is that a good or a bad thing?

I think many of us have felt with the benefit of hindsight, that I should have kept a bottle when I see its current worth. No doubt a new release is often seen as a chance to invest and has stimulated the market in these products. Maybe as some collectors do, buy 3 bottles... one for drinking, one for swapping/trading and one for the collection. I have a collection but many of my bottles are an emotional connection and may be tasted at some point.

However, it's a concern when I see folk offering investment opportunities that promise returns that just seem to be too good to be true. Take professional advice as you would with money. Investments can go down as well up, but at least if the value goes down, we can always enjoy as it as a dram.

I´m sometimes reminded that the readers of the Malt Whisky Yearbook – usually well informed but eager to learn more – represent a miniscule part of the whisky consumers around the world. How important would you say that small consumer segment is for the producers?

That's maybe so but your Malt Whisky Yearbook has been used as a reference by many on what's going on in the distilling front. The knowledge available now can be quite niche but what an amount of information there is available. Also Liquid Antiquarian has challenged and educated on the established history around the industry. Jason with his Glen Mhor website has taken a lost Distillery to life, by finding much forgotten information. The consumer in their quest for different things has certainly resulted in the companies changing what was on offer. I am pleasantly surprised how knowledgeable consumers are now. Though I know many consumers will enjoy a dram, without think too much about it.

With young people sometimes questioning the use of alcohol and others exchanging it for cannabis or other drugs – do you feel whisky is still relevant for Generation Z (born 1997-2012)?

As an old distiller, I am maybe not the best authority on that, so perhaps a question for the marketeers. I hope enough of this generation give whisky a try though and find with experimentation how diverse whisky can be.

As opposed to thirty years ago, whisky today is produced in a huge number of countries around the world. How would you say that has affected the category/industry as a whole?

All great news, none more than the revival of Irish Whisky and the return of distilling in New Zealand and Australia. Also how malt whisky is being made in the United States and its introduction to countries not normally thought of as whisky countries. I feel it stimulates interest in whisky and also the growth of small scale production, which has seen even more innovation.

Please describe your perfect time and place for a dram.

Anytime or place with friends, but particularly when we rediscover an illicit distillers bothy, with a dram and with the water supply of that bothy.

Bruichladdich

[brook•lad•dee]

Owner: Rémy Cointreau

Region/district: Islay

Founded: 1881

Status: Active (vc)

Capacity: 2 000 000 litres

Address: Bruichladdich, Islay, Argyll PA49 7UN

Website: bruichladdich.com

Tel: 01496 850221

In March 2023 Bruichladdich launched their first rye whisky. Given the difficulties of mashing a rye mashbill in a traditional mashtun, whisky enthusiasts have discussed how Bruichladdich managed to do it.

First of all, the milling is crucial because there are no husks on rye. In Bruichladdich´s case 55% of the mashbill is rye. The rye goes into the mashtun first together with a very hot, first water. After 45 minutes the malted barley is added and the enzymes start to kick in. The second water is added from the bottom of the mash tun and effectively lifts up the sticky, porridge-like bed of grains to facilitate the mashing. Rye has never been commercially grown on Islay but it is a well-known fact that crop rotation is beneficial for the land. With this rye (**The Regeneration Project**) Bruichladdich collaborated with nearby Coull Farm.

The distillery is equipped with a 7 ton cast iron, open mash tun with rakes and six 60,000 litre washbacks made of Oregon pine but only filled with 35,000 litres. The fermentation time varies between 70 and 100 hours. Furthermore there are two wash stills (17,300 litres) and two spirit stills (12,300 litres). All whisky produced is based on Scottish barley and 40% has been grown on Islay. Organic barley (one week production of the year) comes from the mainland. In 2023 there will be 12 mashes per week making 1.4 million litres of alcohol. The breakdown of the three whisky varieties is 55% Bruichladdich, 40% Port Charlotte and 5% Octomore. The unusually low volume of Octomore is due to the recent problems of sourcing heavily peated malt. The plans of reinstating the maltings that were closed in 1961, were delayed by the pandemic but are very much a part of the near future.

Bruichladdich has three product lines; unpeated Bruichladdich, heavily peated (40ppm) Port Charlotte and ultra-heavily peated (in the excess of 100ppm) Octomore. The only core expressions are **The Classic Laddie**, **Port Charlotte 10 year old** and **Octomore Ten Aged Years**. In summer 2023 the tin of The Classic Laddie was eliminated and the new glass bottle (made from 60% recycled glass) was made 32% lighter. The following appear every year with new batches/vintages; for Bruichladdich there are **Islay Barley 2014**, **Bere Barley 2013** and **The Organic Barley 2012** and for Port Charlotte, **Islay Barley 2014** and **PMC:01** matured in Pomerol casks. In September 2023, another batch of the heavily peated Octomore, was released; **14.1** made from Scottish barley peated to 128.9ppm and matured in ex-bourbon casks, **14.2** made from the same malt as 14.1 but matured in a combination of oloroso and amarone casks and **14.3** made from locally grown barley peated to 214.2ppm and matured in a combination of bourbon casks and wine casks. Recent bottlings for Feis Ile 2023 were **Rock'ndaal 02.1**, a 16 year old Bruichladdich matured in bourbon and Sauternes casks and **Rock'ndaal 02.2**, a Port Charlotte 2006 Vintage matured in a combination of refill wine casks and sherry butts. In November 2023 **Bruichladdich Black Art 10** was released and for travel retail there is **The Laddie Eight**.

History:

1881 Barnett Harvey builds the distillery with money left by his brother William III to his three sons William IV, Robert and John Gourlay.

1886 Bruichladdich Distillery Company Ltd is founded and reconstruction commences.

1929 Temporary closure.

1936 The distillery reopens.

1938 Joseph Hobbs, Hatim Attari and Alexander Tolmie purchase the distillery through the company Train & McIntyre.

1952 The distillery is sold to Ross & Coulter.

1960 A. B. Grant buys Ross & Coulter.

1961 Own maltings ceases.

1968 Invergordon Distillers take over.

1975 The number of stills increases to four.

1983 Temporary closure.

1993 Whyte & Mackay buys Invergordon Distillers.

1995 The distillery is mothballed in January.

1998 In production again for a few months.

2000 Murray McDavid buys the distillery from JBB Greater Europe for £6.5 million.

2001 The first distillations of Port Charlotte and Bruichladdich starts in July.

2002 Octomore, the world's most heavily peated whisky (80ppm) is distilled.

2004 Second edition of the 20 year old (nick-named Flirtation) and 3D, also called The Peat Proposal, are launched.

2005 Infinity, Rocks, Legacy Series IV, The Yellow Submarine and The Twenty 'Islands' are launched.

2006 The first official bottling of Port Charlotte; PC5.

2007 New releases include Redder Still, Legacy 6, PC6 and an 18 year old.

2008 More than 20 new expressions including the first Octomore, Bruichladdich 2001, PC7, Golder Still and two sherry matured from 1998.

History continued:

2009 New releases include Classic, Organic, Black Art, Infinity 3, PC8, Octomore 2 and X4+3 - the first quadruple distilled single malt.

2010 PC Multi Vintage, Organic MV, Octomore/3_152, Bruichladdich 40 year old are released.

2011 The first 10 year old from own production is released as well as PC9 and Octomore 4_167.

2012 Ten year old versions of Port Charlotte and Octomore are released as well as Laddie 16 and 22, Bere Barley 2006, Black Art 3 and DNA4. Rémy Cointreau buys the distillery.

2013 Scottish Barley, Islay Barley Rockside Farm, Bere Barley 2nd edition, Black Art 4, Port Charlotte Scottish Barley, Octomore 06.1 and 06.2 are released.

2014 PC11 and Octomore Scottish Barley are released.

2015 PC12, Octomore 7.1 and High Noon 134 are released.

2016 The Laddie Eight, Octomore 7.4 and Port Charlotte 2007 CC:01 are released.

2017 Black Art 5 and 25 year old sherry cask are launched. The limited Rare Cask series is launched.

2018 The Port Charlotte range is revamped and a 10 year old and Islay Barley 2011 are released.

2019 Bere Barley 10, Organic 10, Black Art 7 and Octomore 10.1, 10.2, 10.3 and 10.4 are released.

2020 Port Charlotte OLC:01, Port Charlotte 16 year old and four new Octomore are released.

2021 Port Charlotte PAC:01 and Islay Barley 2013 are launched together with Bruichladdich Islay Barley 2012, Bere Barley 2011 and The Organic 2010. Three new Octomore are also released.

2022 The Biodynamic Project, Port Charlotte SC:01, Brucihladdich 1988/30 and Black Art 09.1 are launched.

2023 The Regeneration Project made from rye is released.

Tasting notes The Classic Laddie:

IR – Fresh on the nose with notes of pears, green apples, vanilla, citrus and paint. The palate starts with a sweet maltiness and lively pepper followed by malted barley, vanilla and pears.

Tasting notes Port Charlotte 10 year old:

IR – Smoked herring and clams on the nose together with notes of tobacco, mint, dried grass and a hint of orange. Great mouth feel with a soothing smokiness, apple pie, digestive, liquorice, nutmeg, roasted coco flakes and some honey sweetness.

Bere Barley 2013 The Regeneration Islay Barley 2014
Project

The Classic Laddie

Port Charlotte
PMC:01 2013

Port Charlotte
10 year old

Bunnahabhain

[buh•nah•hav•enn]

Owner:
CVH Spirits

Region/district:
Islay

Founded: | **Status:** | **Capacity:**
1881 | Active (vc) | 3 500 000 litres

Address: Port Askaig, Islay, Argyll PA46 7RP

Website:
bunnahabhain.com

Tel:
01496 840646

For most distilleries the amount of barley put into the mash tun and then mixed with water is more or less set in stone unless changing to a tun of a different size. For Bunnahabhain, this has not been the case in recent years.

For many years it used to be 12.5 tons, was increased to 15 tons for the last couple of years and now the team has settled for 8 tons but more mashes. The new process means that the capacity has increased by another 500,000 litres without any additional equipment. On top of the hill, before you drive down to the distillery, lies a new bio plant (which is not owned by the distillery) providing the site with steam by burning both wood chips and draff from the distillery. Since last year there is also a new and elegant shop/bar with a stunning view over Jura.

The distillery is equipped with a traditional stainless steel mash tun with a copper lid. There are six 70,000 litre washbacks made of Oregon pine of which two (the last couple dating back to 1963/64) were replaced in summer 2022. With a 24/7 production, the fermentation time is now 52-54 hours. Finally, there are two pairs of stills with slightly descending lyne arms. The intention for 2023 is to make 22 to 24 mashes per week and 3.25 million litres of pure alcohol split between 33% peated (35-45ppm and 67% unpeated.

The core range consists of **12, 18, 25, 30** and a **40 year old**. There is also the **12 year old cask strength** which appeared in 2021 with yearly batches. The peated side of Bunnahabhain is represented by **Toiteach a Dha** without age statement and matured in both bourbon and sherry casks, **Stiùireadair**, matured in first and re-fill sherry casks and (exclusive to the Nordic market) **Moine**. Recent limited releases for Feis Ile 2023 are **Canasta Cask Matured, 1998 Manzanilla Cask Finish** and the **17 year old Triple Cask Moine**. There are also three travel retail exclusives – the young and heavily peated **Cruach-Mhòna, Eirigh Na Greine**, a vatting of whisky from bourbon, sherry and red wine casks and the sherry-matured **An Cladach**.

History:

1881 William Robertson founds the distillery together with the brothers William and James Greenless.

1883 Production starts in January.

1887 Islay Distillers Company Ltd merges with William Grant & Co. in order to form Highland Distilleries Company Limited.

1963 The two stills are augmented by two more.

1982 The distillery closes.

1984 The distillery reopens. A 21 year old is released to commemorate the 100th anniversary.

1999 Edrington takes over Highland Distillers and mothballs Bunnahabhain but allows for a few weeks of production a year.

2001 A 35 year old from 1965 is released.

2002 Auld Acquaintance 1968 is launched.

2003 Edrington sells Bunnahabhain and Black Bottle to Burn Stewart Distilleries for £10 million. A 40 year old from 1963 is launched.

2004 The first limited edition of the peated version is a 6 year old called Moine.

2005 Three limited editions are released - 34 years old,18 years old and 25 years old.

2006 14 year old Pedro Ximenez and 35 years old are launched.

2008 Darach Ur is released for travel retail and Toiteach is launched in few selected markets

2010 The peated Cruach-Mhòna and a limited 30 year old are released.

2013 A 40 year old is released.

2014 Eirigh Na Greine and Ceobanach are released.

2017 Moine Oloroso, Stiùireadair and An Cladach are released.

2018 Toiteach a Dha and a 20 year old Palo Cortado are released.

2019 A 2007 brandy finish and a 39 year old are released.

2020 A 2008 manzanilla, a 1997 PX finish and a 2005 burgundy finish are released.

2021 12 year old cask strength is launched.

2023 Three bottlings are released for Feis Ile.

Tasting notes Bunnahabhain 12 years old:

GS – The nose is fresh, with light peat and discreet smoke. More overt peat on the nutty and fruity palate, but still restrained for an Islay. The finish is full-bodied and lingering, with a hint of vanilla and some smoke.

12 years old

Caol Ila

[cull eel•a]

Owner: Diageo	**Region/district:** Islay
Founded: 1846	**Status:** Active (vc)	**Capacity:** 6 500 000 litres

Address: Port Askaig, Islay, Argyll PA46 7RL

Website: malts.com	**Tel:** 01496 302760

Having alternated between 5- and 7-day production during the last decade, Caol Ila seems, since November 2022, firmly set on distilling at full capacity. The decision has had an impact on other Islay distilleries.

Caol Ila, as well as Lagavulin, get all their malted barley from Port Ellen maltings – all three owned by Diageo. In August 2022 it was announced that henceforth the company would only be able to supply malt to their own distilleries. Historically, most of the other seven distilleries on Islay have to some extent purchased their malt from Port Ellen. Bowmore and Bunnahabhain have for a long time relied on maltsters on the mainland but for Ardbeg, Laphroaig and, not least, Kilchoman the decision from Diageo prompted some re-thinking on from where to source their malted barley.

Caol Ila was in for a huge change on the visitor's side in summer 2022 when the tiny shop on the premises was replaced by an impressive visitor centre. This is part of the Four Corners of Scotland project (Glenkinchie, Cardhu and Clynelish being the other three) initiated by Diageo to highlight four distilleries playing an integral part of the Johnnie Walker blend. The exhibition, shop and bar/restaurant provides a stunning view towards the Sound of Islay and Jura.

Caol Ila is equipped with a 12.5 ton full lauter mash tun. There are eight wooden washbacks and two made of stainless steel, all with a volume of 58,000 litres and a fermentation time of 55-60 hours. Finally, there are three wash stills with descending lyne arms and three spirit stills with straight lyne arms. The distillery is by far the largest on Islay with 26 mashes per week and a total production of 6.5 million litres of pure alcohol. Caol Ila is best known for its peated whisky but unpeated new-make is also produced.

The core range consists of **Moch** without age statement, **12, 18** and **25 year old** and **Distiller's Edition** with a moscatel finish. The release for Feis Ile 2023 was a **13 year old**, matured in PX and oloroso butts and bottled at 60,4%. In August 2022 a **14 year old Four Corners of Scotland** distillery exclusive was launched.

History:

1846 Hector Henderson founds Caol Ila.

1852 Henderson, Lamont & Co. is subjected to financial difficulties and Henderson is forced to sell Caol Ila to Norman Buchanan.

1863 Norman Buchanan sells to the blending company Bulloch, Lade & Co. from Glasgow.

1879 The distillery is rebuilt and expanded.

1920 Bulloch, Lade & Co. is liquidated and the distillery is taken over by Caol Ila Distillery.

1927 DCL becomes sole owners.

1972 All the buildings, except for the warehouses, are demolished and rebuilt.

1974 The renovation, which totals £1 million, is complete and six new stills are installed.

1999 Experiments with unpeated malt.

2002 The first official bottlings since Flora & Fauna/Rare Malt appear; 12 years, 18 years and Cask Strength (c. 10 years).

2003 A 25 year old cask strength is released.

2006 Unpeated 8 year old and 1993 Moscatel finish are released.

2007 Second edition of unpeated 8 year old.

2009 The fourth edition of the unpeated version (10 year old) is released.

2010 A 25 year old, a 1999 Feis Isle bottling and a 1997 Manager's Choice are released.

2011 An unpeated 12 year old and the unaged Moch are released.

2012 An unpeated 14 year old is released.

2013 Unpeated Stitchell Reserve is released.

2014 A 15 year old unpeated and a 30 year old are released.

2016 A 15 year old unpeated is released.

2017 An 18 year old unpeated is released.

2018 Two bottlings in the Special Releases - a 15 year old and a 35 year old.

2020 A 35 year old is released as part of the new Prima & Ultima range.

2022 A 24 year old anniversary bottle and a 14 year old Four Corners of Scotland are released.

2023 A 13 year old, sherry-matured Feis Ile is launched.

Tasting notes Caol Ila 12 year old:

GS – Iodine, fresh fish and smoked bacon feature on the nose, along with more delicate, floral notes. Smoke, malt, lemon and peat on the slightly oily palate. Peppery peat in the drying finish.

12 years old

Cardhu

[car•doo]

Owner: Diageo
Region/district: Speyside

Founded: 1824
Status: Active (vc)
Capacity: 3 400 000 litres

Address: Knockando, Aberlour, Moray AB38 7RY

Website: malts.com
Tel: 01479 874635

When four Diageo distilleries a few years ago were selected to have their visitor centres completely re-made and expanded, they were chosen because of their connection with the Johnnie Walker blend – the most sold Scotch in the world.

Caol Ila, Clynelish, Glenkinchie and Cardhu are all important keystones in Johnnie Walker but the case Cardhu is even more special. In 1893 this became the first malt distillery owned by the Walker family and the ties between the distillery and the brand have been solid ever since.

Until last year, Johnnie Walker's best year in terms of volumes was 2012 when 236 million bottles were sold. Ten years later, however, the record was broken when sales reached 272 million. They are still number one by far but during the same decade the number two, Ballantine´s increased by an impressive 54%. But today's whisky market is less about volumes and more about values. With Johnnie Walker Red Label and Black Label being the backbone of the brand, there is a third category of Johnnie Walker consisting of super premium and highly expensive expressions. This de luxe segment has grown by more than 100% in the last ten years.

Cardhu is equipped with an eight ton stainless steel full lauter mash tun with a copper top, ten washbacks (eight of wood and two of stainless steel), all with a fermentation time of 75 hours, and three pairs of stills. For several years now, the distillery has been producing seven days a week with 21 mashes per week and a total of 3.4 million litres of alcohol. Cardhu is the third best selling single malt from Diageo after The Singleton and Talisker with 3.5 million bottles sold in 2021.

The core range from the distillery consists of **12, 15** and **18 year old** and two expressions without age statement – **Amber Rock** and **Gold Reserve**. In April 2021 a limited **16 year old Four Corners of Scotland** bottling, available only at the distillery, was launched. Recent limited releases include a **16 year old Special Releases** in autumn 2022 – finished in Jamaican rum casks and bottled at 58%.

History:

1824 John Cumming applies for and obtains a licence for Cardhu Distillery.

1846 John Cumming dies and his wife Helen and son Lewis takes over.

1872 Lewis dies and his wife Elizabeth takes over.

1884 A new distillery is built to replace the old.

1893 John Walker & Sons purchases Cardhu for £20,500.

1908 The name reverts to Cardow.

1960 Expansion of stills from four to six.

1981 The name changes to Cardhu.

1998 A visitor centre is constructed.

2002 Diageo changes Cardhu single malt to a vatted malt with contributions from other distilleries in it.

2003 The whisky industry protests sharply against Diageo's plans.

2004 Diageo withdraws Cardhu Pure Malt.

2005 The 12 year old Cardhu Single Malt is relaunched and a 22 year old is released.

2009 Cardhu 1997, a single cask in the new Manager´s Choice range is released.

2011 A 15 year old and an 18 year old are released.

2013 A 21 year old is released.

2014 Amber Rock and Gold Reserve are launched.

2016 A distillery exclusive is released.

2019 A 14 year old appears in the Special Releases and Cardhu is also part of the Game of Thrones series.

2020 An 11 year old Rare by Nature bottling is released.

2021 A 14 year old Rare by Nature and a 16 year old Four Corners of Scotland bottling are released.

2022 A 16 year old rum finish is released.

12 year old

Tasting notes Cardhu 12 years old:

GS – The nose is relatively light and floral, quite sweet, with pears, nuts and a whiff of distant peat. Medium-bodied, malty and sweet in the mouth. Medium-length in the finish, with sweet smoke, malt and a hint of peat.

Whisky in Social Media

There are a lot of blogs, websites
and YouTube channels discussing whisky
and other spirits. Some are excellent and others are
not so great. Below are the ones I follow frequently and
while these are all well worth visiting or tuning into,
the ones marked with * are my personal favourites.

Aqvavitae (Youtube) *

bestshotwhiskyreviews.com *

blog.thewhiskyexchange.com *

canadianwhisky.org *

dramface.com *

First Phil Whisky (Youtube)

greatdrams.com

GWhisky (Youtube)

insidethecask.com *

islaywhisky.se

jeffwhisky.com

maltandoak.com

maltermagasin.se *

maltfascination.com

maltimpostor.com

malt-review.com *

masterofmalt.com/blog *

meleklerinpayi.com

nononsensewhisky.com*

ozwhiskyreview.com.au *

Ralfydotcom (Youtube)

scotchmaltwhisky.co.uk *

scotchnoob.com

Scotch Test Dummies (Youtube)

scotchwhisky.com *

scotch-whisky.org.uk

thedramble.com *

The Single Malt Review (YouTube)

thewhiskeyjug.com *

thewhiskeywash.com *

thewhiskyphiles.com *

The Whiskey Tribe (Youtube)

thewhiskyardvark.com

thewhiskyviking.com

thewhiskywire.com *

timeforwhisky.com

tjederswhisky.se *

whiskyandwisdom.com *

whiskyboys.com

whiskycast.com *

whiskycritic.com

whisky-distillery.net *

whiskyfacile.com

whiskyfanblog.de

whiskyforeveryone.blogspot.com *

whiskyfun.com *

whiskyintelligence.com *

whiskyisrael.co.il *

Whisky Jason (Youtube)

whiskymylife.wordpress.com *

whisky-news.com *

whiskynotes.be *

whiskeyreviewer.com

whiskyreviews.net

whiskysaga.com *

whiskysponge.com *

whiskytalk.fireside.fm *

wordsofwhisky.com

Clynelish

[cline•leash]

Owner:		Region/district:
Diageo		Northern Highlands

Founded:	Status:	Capacity:
1967	Active (vc)	4 800 000 litres

Address: Brora, Sutherland KW9 6LR

Website:	Tel:
malts.com	01408 623003 (vc)

The newmake character of a single malt Scotch can be divided into a handfull of flavour camps; nutty, green/grassy, fruity, sulphury and – the rarest of them all – waxy.

The latter is produced by just a few distilleries; Deanston, Aberfeldy, Dailuaine and, in particular, Clynelish. There are different ways to achieve it, including the fermentation, but in the case of Clynelish the waxiness comes from residues being built up over time in the feints and foreshots receiver. The distillery was closed to be refurbished and expanded for an entire year in 2016. During that time Dailuaine (another Diageo distillery) switched to waxy newmake to secure the unique character essential not least for Johnnie Walker Gold Label. With all the new, clean equipment at Clynelish, a special group within Diageo named "the waxy project" was formed to make sure the distillery would be able to create the same spirit character also after the expansion. This is a brilliant example of just how special and handcrafted a whisky from one of the largest Scottish distilleries can be! Since 2021 there is a new visitor centre at Clynelish, The Highland Home of Johnnie Walker, including a terrace bar overlooking the North Sea with an opportunity to enjoy whisky cocktails of all sorts.

Clynelish is equipped with a 12.2 ton full lauter mash tun, eight wooden washbacks and two made of stainless steel with a 58,000 litre capacity and a fermentation time of 85 hours. The still room holds three pairs of stills. During 2023, Clynelish will be operating a 7-day week and with 18 mashes per week it will produce around 4.8 million litres of alcohol. On site there is also a plant which takes care of the copper residues that derive from the spent lees during the distillation process.

The only official core expression is a **14 year old**. The Distiller's Edition, has recently been discontinued. In 2021 a **16 year old** distillery exclusive (Four Corners of Scotland) matured in ex-bourbon hogsheads was launched and this was followed in autumn 2023 by a **10 year old Special Release** matured in first fill bourbon. At the same time a **26 year old** Prima & Ultima matured in PX and oloroso sherry casks appeared.

10 years old
Special Releases 2023

History:

1819 The 1st Duke of Sutherland founds a distillery called Clynelish Distillery.

1827 The first licensed distiller, James Harper, files for bankruptcy and John Matheson takes over.

1846 George Lawson & Sons become new licensees.

1896 James Ainslie & Heilbron takes over.

1912 James Ainslie & Co. narrowly escapes bankruptcy and Distillers Company Limited (DCL) takes over together with James Risk.

1916 John Walker & Sons buys a stake of James Risk's stocks.

1931 The distillery is mothballed.

1939 Production restarts.

1960 The distillery becomes electrified.

1967 A new distillery, also named Clynelish, is built adjacent to the first one.

1968 'Old' Clynelish is mothballed in August.

1969 'Old' Clynelish is reopened as Brora and starts using a very peaty malt.

1983 Brora is closed in March.

2002 A 14 year old is released.

2006 A Distiller's Edition 1991 finished in Oloroso casks is released.

2009 A 12 year old is released for Friends of the Classic Malts.

2010 A 1997 Manager's Choice single cask is released.

2014 Clynelish Select Reserve is released.

2015 Second version of Clynelish Select Reserve is released.

2017 The distillery produces again after a year long closure for refurbishing.

2019 Clynelish House Tyrell is released as part of the Game of Thrones series.

2020 A 26 year old Prima & Ultima is released.

2021 A 16 year old Four Corners of Scotland is launched.

2022 A 12 year old Special Release is launched.

2023 A 10 year old Special Release is launched together with a 26 year old Prima & Ultima matured in PX and oloroso sherry.

Tasting notes Clynelish 14 year old:

GS – A nose that is fragrant, spicy and complex, with candle wax, malt and a whiff of smoke. Notably smooth in the mouth, with honey and contrasting citric notes, plus spicy peat, before a brine and tropical fruit finish.

Cragganmore

[crag•an•moor]

Owner:
Diageo

Region/district:
Speyside

Founded: 1869
Status: Active (vc)
Capacity: 2 200 000 litres

Address: Ballindalloch, Moray AB37 9AB

Website: malts.com
Tel: 01479 874700

The fact that Cragganmore was selected as the Speyside representative of the Classic Malts back in 1988 may seem a bit surprising today, 35 years later. Although the whisky has always had its fans, it was never a big seller.

It was always too complex in style to act as the "generic" fruity Speyside malt. The distilling regime with little reflux in the wash stills, more so in the spirit stills with their long lyne arms and then worm tubs that are run cold with very little copper contact results in a newmake which is heavy and sometimes sulphury. Maturation will of course transform the spirit and there was always more to Cragganmore single malt than what met the eye.

Today it's only the 10th best selling Diageo malt but seasoned whisky drinkers tend to adore it. The beautiful location in a secluded glen off the busy A95 and just a couple of 100 metres from the banks of river Spey add to the overall impression.

Cragganmore is equipped with a 7 ton stainless steel full lauter mash tun clad with wood and with a copper canopy. There are six washbacks made of Oregon pine and since they are working a five-day week there will be six short (50 hours) and six long (100 hours) fermentations. Finally, there are two large wash stills with sharply descending lyne arms and two considerably smaller spirit stills with boil balls and long, slightly descending lyne arms. The two spirit stills are most peculiar with flat tops, which had already been introduced during the times of the founder, John Smith. The stills are attached to worm tubs on the outside for cooling the spirit vapours. In spring 2022, the cast iron tubs were replaced by new ones made from stainless steel. In 2023, the production will amount to around 1.5 million litres of alcohol.

The official core range of Cragganmore is made up of a **12 year old** and a **Distiller's Edition** with a finish in port pipes. A limited release in the Prima & Ultima range appeared in 2022 – a 48 year old matured in refill hogsheads. The spirit was distilled just after the distillery went from coal-fired stills to using steam.

History:

1869 John Smith, who already runs Glenfarclas distillery, founds Cragganmore.

1886 John Smith dies and his brother George takes over operations.

1893 John's son Gordon, at 21, is old enough to assume responsibility for operations.

1901 The distillery is refurbished and modernized with help of the famous architect Charles Doig.

1912 Gordon Smith dies and his widow Mary Jane supervises operations.

1917 The distillery closes.

1918 The distillery reopens and Mary Jane installs electric lighting.

1923 The distillery is sold to the newly formed Cragganmore-Glenlivet Distillery Co. where Mackie & Co. and Sir George Macpherson-Grant of Ballindalloch Estate share ownership.

1927 White Horse Distillers is bought by DCL which thus obtains 50% of Cragganmore.

1964 The number of stills is increased from two to four.

1965 DCL buys the remainder of Cragganmore.

1988 Cragganmore 12 years becomes one of six selected for United Distillers´ Classic Malts.

1998 Cragganmore Distillers Edition Double Matured (port) is launched for the first time.

2002 A visitor centre opens in May.

2006 A 17 year old from 1988 is released.

2010 Manager´s Choice single cask 1997 and a limited 21 year old are released.

2014 A 25 year old is released.

2016 A Special Releases vatting without age statement and a distillery exclusive are released.

2019 A 12 year bottled at cask strength appears in the Special Releases series.

2020 A 48 year old and a 20 year old are released.

2022 A 48 year old Prima & Ultima is released.

Tasting notes Cragganmore 12 years old:

GS – A nose of sherry, brittle toffee, nuts, mild wood smoke, angelica and mixed peel. Elegant on the malty palate, with herbal and fruit notes, notably orange. Medium in length, with a drying, slightly smoky finish.

12 years old

Craigellachie

[craig•ell•ack•ee]

Owner:
John Dewar & Sons
(Bacardi)

Region/district:
Speyside

Founded: 1891 **Status:** Active **Capacity:** 4 100 000 litres

Address: Aberlour, Banffshire AB38 9ST

Website:
craigellachie.com

Tel:
01340 872971

The whisky boom in the late 19th century put pressure on the big, blending companies. Stocks were running low due to the rapidly increased demand and building or buying a distillery, became necessary.

Peter Mackie, admittedly, already owned Lagavulin, but the sales of his White Horse blend increased so quickly that he needed another distillery and, together with Alexander Edward, he built Craigellachie. He established a sales office in London but became annoyed with the competition from the large producers of grain whisky which, according to him, sold "young, cheap, fiery whisky". During his entire life he was an advocate for quality products and his opinion was crystal clear: "What the public wants is age and plenty of it" – an interesting and still debated opinion over a century later. White Horse now belongs to Diageo (who still use Craigellachie single malt in the blend) but a lot of the malt these days land in Dewar's White Label and William Lawson's – two of the top 15 blends in the world.

The heavy character of Craigellachie single malt is partly due to the worm tubs, but short fermentation as well as massive stills with straight lyne arms adding little reflux, also influences it. In order to balance the character with fruitier notes, the wort is clear and the cut point for the middle cut (75-64%) welcome some of the early esters but avoid the more pungent notes towards the end.

The distillery is equipped with a 10 ton full lauter mash tun, eight 47,000 litre washbacks made of larch with a fermentation time of 56-60 hours and two pairs of massive stills attached to worm tubs. The old cast iron tubs were exchanged for stainless steel in 2014 and the existing copper worms were moved to the new tubs. The production plan for 2023 involves 21 mashes per week and 4.1 million litres of alcohol.

The core range consists of **13, 17, 23** and **33 year old**. The limited Cask Collection, was introduced in spring 2022 by way of a **13 year old** with a one year finish in Armagnac casks. Limited releases for the travel retail market include the Exceptional Cask Series – most recently a **27 year old brandy finish**.

History:

1890 The distillery is built by Craigellachie–Glenlivet Distillery Company which has Alexander Edward and Peter Mackie as part-owners.

1891 Production starts.

1916 Mackie & Company Distillers Ltd takes over.

1924 Peter Mackie dies and Mackie & Company changes name to White Horse Distillers.

1927 White Horse Distillers are bought by Distillers Company Limited (DCL).

1930 Administration is transferred to Scottish Malt Distillers (SMD), a subsidiary of DCL.

1964 Refurbishing takes place and two new stills are bought, increasing the number to four.

1998 United Distillers & Vintners (UDV) sells Craigellachie together with Aberfeldy, Brackla and Aultmore and the blending company John Dewar & Sons to Bacardi Martini.

2004 The first bottlings from the new owners are a new 14 year old which replaces UDV's Flora & Fauna and a 21 year old cask strength from 1982 produced for Craigellachie Hotel.

2014 Three new bottlings for domestic markets (13, 17 and 23 years) and one for duty free (19 years) are released.

2015 A 31 year old is released.

2016 A 33 year old and a 1994 Madeira single cask are released.

2018 A 24 year old and and a 17 year old palo cortado finish are released for duty free and the oldest official Craigellachie so far, 51 years old, is launched.

2019 A 19 and a 23 year old are released.

2020 A 39 year old is launched.

2021 A 33 year old is added to the core range.

2022 A 13 year old Armagnac finish is released.

13 years old

Tasting notes Craigellachie 13 years old:

GS – Savoury on the early nose, with spent matches, green apples and mixed nuts. Malt join the nuts and apples on the palate, with sawdust and very faint smoke. Drying, with cranberries, spice and more subtle smoke.

Dailuaine

[dall•yoo•an]

Owner:
Diageo

Region/district:
Speyside

Founded: **Status:** **Capacity:**
1852 Active 5 200 000 litres

Address: Carron, Banffshire AB38 7RE

Website: **Tel:**
malts.com 01340 872500

Distilleries rarely alter the basic style of their spirit, at least not in such a substantial way as Dailuaine did. In 2015, the production team changed the character of their newmake from nutty to waxy. The reason could be found 200 kilometres to the north.

Clynelish was due to close for a major upgrade and refurbishing and since that was the only distillery within Diageo producing a waxy newmake, a character essential not least for some of the Johnnie Walker versions, another distillery (Dailuaine) would have to make up for the temporary loss. At Clynelish the waxiness came from residues built up over time in the feints and foreshots receiver. With all the new, clean equipment going in it took longer than expected to get back to the classic Clynelish character. They even formed a special group named "the waxy project" to deal with the problem. With the problem finally solved, Dailuaine could go back to their original, nutty style of newmake in summer 2022.

On the site of the distillery lies a number of very pretty dunnage warehouses which, however, haven't been used since 1989. Dailuaine has also kept their spectacular malting floors which were last used in 1960 when Saladin maltings were installed. Today the malt comes from one of the large, commercial maltsters.

The distillery is equipped with a stainless steel, 11.25 ton full lauter mash tun. There are also eight washbacks made of Douglas fir plus two stainless steel ones placed outside – all with a charge of 54,000 litres. Finally there are three pairs of stills. When working on waxy newmake, the fermentation times were very long (between 80 and 107 hours) but since 2022 they have gone back to just 46 hours. Dailuaine has also switched from 5-day production to 7 days with around 22 mashes per week.

Dailuaine is focusing on producing malt for blends and the only core bottling is the **16 year old Flora & Fauna**. In 2015, a **34 year old** from 1980 was launched as part of the Special Releases.

History:
1852 The distillery is founded by William Mackenzie.
1865 William Mackenzie dies and his widow leases the distillery to James Fleming, a banker from Aberlour.
1879 William Mackenzie's son forms Mackenzie and Company with Fleming.
1891 Dailuaine-Glenlivet Distillery Ltd is founded.
1898 Dailuaine-Glenlivet Distillery Ltd merges with Talisker Distillery Ltd and forms Dailuaine-Talisker Distilleries Ltd.
1915 Thomas Mackenzie dies without heirs.
1916 Dailuaine-Talisker Company Ltd is bought by the previous customers John Dewar & Sons, John Walker & Sons and James Buchanan & Co.
1917 A fire rages and the pagoda roof collapses.
1920 The distillery reopens.
1925 Distillers Company Limited (DCL) takes over.
1960 Refurbishing. The stills increase from four to six and a Saladin box replaces the floor maltings.
1965 Indirect still heating through steam is installed.
1983 On site maltings is closed down and malt is purchased centrally.
1991 The first official bottling, a 16 year old, is launched in the Flora & Fauna series.
1996 A 22 year old cask strength from 1973 is released as a Rare Malt.
1997 A cask strength version of the 16 year old is launched.
2000 A 17 year old Manager's Dram matured in sherry casks is launched.
2010 A single cask from 1997 is released.
2012 The production capacity is increased by 25%.
2015 A 34 year old is launched as part of the Special Releases.

16 years old

Tasting notes Dailuaine 16 years old:
GS – Barley, sherry and nuts on the substantial nose, developing into maple syrup. Medium-bodied, rich and malty in the mouth, with more sherry and nuts, plus ripe oranges, fruitcake, spice and a little smoke. The finish is lengthy and slightly oily, with almonds, cedar and slightly smoky oak.

Dalmore

[dal•moor]

Owner:
Whyte & Mackay Ltd
(Emperador Inc)

Region/district:
Northern Highlands

Founded: **Status:**
1839   Active (vc)

Capacity:
4 500 000 litres

Address: Alness, Ross-shire IV17 0UT

Website:
thedalmore.com

Tel:
01349 882362

For quite some time now, Dalmore has been closed to visitors as parts of the distillery grounds have been (and still are) a construction site. The visitor centre itself will be refurbished but there are also grander plans for the distillery afoot.

With an investment of £40m, Whyte & Mackay aims to double the capacity of the distillery. A completely new still house is being built where the, now demolished, Saladin maltings used to sit. Apart from another eight stills, the new distillery will have its own mash tun and washbacks. When finished in August 2024 Dalmore will have a total capacity of 9 million litres of alcohol making it one of the ten largest malt distilleries in Scotland. Once the new plant is operational, the old distillery will shut down for three months for upgrading and making it more sustainable.

The expansion has been discussed ever since Emperador took over Whyte & Mackay in 2014 and the timing couldn't be better. Dalmore is one of the fastest growing single malt Scotch and volumes have increased by almost 300% in the last decade to reach almost 3 million bottles in 2022.

Dalmore distillery is equipped with a 10.4 ton stainless steel, semi-lauter mash tun, eight washbacks made of Oregon pine with a fermentation time of 50 hours and four pairs of stills. All the wash stills have peculiar flat tops while the spirit stills are equipped with water jackets, which allow cold water to circulate between the reflux bowl and the neck of the stills, thus increasing the reflux. The owners anticipate mashing 23 times per week during 2023, producing 4.5 million litres of alcohol which is more or less less the capacity for the distillery.

The core range consists of **12, 12 Sherry Cask Select, 15, 18, 21** and **25 year old, King Alexander III, Cigar Malt Reserve** and **Port Wood Reserve**. For travel retail the range is composed of **The Trio, The Quartet** and **The Quintet** as well as a **20 year old** and a new version of **King Alexander III**. Recent limited bottlings include a **30 year old**, **Dalmore Vintages, The Decades of Dalmore** and (new in September 2023) the first installment in the **Cask Curation Series**.

History:

1839   Alexander Matheson founds the distillery.

1867   Three Mackenzie brothers run the distillery.

1891   Sir Kenneth Matheson sells the distillery for £14,500 to the Mackenzie brothers.

1917   The Royal Navy moves in to start manufacturing American mines.

1922   The distillery is in production again.

1956   Floor malting replaced by Saladin box.

1960   Mackenzie Brothers (Dalmore) Ltd merges with Whyte & Mackay.

1966   Number of stills is increased to eight.

1982   The Saladin box is abandoned.

1990   American Brands buys Whyte & Mackay.

1996   Whyte & Mackay changes name to JBB (Greater Europe).

2001   Through management buy-out, JBB (Greater Europe) is bought from Fortune Brands and changes name to Kyndal Spirits.

2002   Kyndal Spirits changes name to Whyte & Mackay.

2007   United Spirits buys Whyte & Mackay. A 15 year old, and a 40 year old are released.

2008   1263 King Alexander III is released.

2009   New releases include an 18 year old, a 58 year old and a Vintage 1951.

2010   The Dalmore Mackenzie 1992 is released.

2011   More expressions in the River Collection and 1995 Castle Leod are released.

2012   The visitor centre is upgraded and Constellaton Collection is launched.

2014   Emperador Inc buys Whyte & Mackay.

2016   Three new travel retail bottlings are released as well as a 35 year old and Quintessence.

2017   Vintage Port Collection is launched.

2018   The Port Wood Reserve is released.

2019   A new travel retail range is launched.

2020   A 51 year old is released.

2021   A 30 year old and The Decades of Dalmore are released.

2022   A 21 year old is released.

2023   Cask Curation Series is launched.

Tasting notes Dalmore 12 years old:

GS – The nose offers sweet malt, orange mar-malade, sherry and a hint of leather. Full-bodied, with a dry sherry taste though sweeter sherry develops in the mouth along with spice and citrus notes. Lengthy finish with more spices, ginger, Seville oranges and vanilla.

12 years old

Dalwhinnie

[dal•whin•nay]

Owner:	**Region/district:**
Diageo	Speyside
Founded: **Status:**	**Capacity:**
1897 Active (vc)	2 200 000 litres

Address: Dalwhinnie, Inverness-shire PH19 1AB

Website:	**Tel:**
malts.com	01540 672219 (vc)

Dalwhinnie was chosen as one of the six original Classic Malts in 1988 representing the Highlands. Today it is Diageo's 5th best selling single malt with 1.3 million bottles in 2022.

It is also a key malt in two major Scotch blends – Buchanans and Black & White. Both brands were established in the 1890s by one of Scotch whisky's most prominent profiles – James Buchanan. Born in Canada by Scottish emigrants he returned to Scotland and started as a whisky blender in 1884. While Black & White soon became the second best selling whisky in the UK, Buchanan's sales were less remarkable. In the second half of the 20th century, Black & White had lost most of its popularity and from the start of the new millenium it was Buchanans that harvested success, not least in Latin America. Buchanan's is still doing well but in the last decade, Black & White has made one of the most extraordinary come-backs in the industry. Sales have gone up by 200% to 43 million bottles and it is now the 6th best selling Scotch in the world!

Dalwhinnie is probably the most easily spotted distillery in Scotland. Nobody travelling by car on the busy A9 between Perth and Inverness will be able to miss it when the road reaches its highest point (462 metres), the Drumochter Summit, in the Cairngorms.

Dalwhinnie is equipped with a 7.3 ton full lauter mash tun and six wooden washbacks (two of them replaced in 2021). There is one pair of stills attached to worm tubs. For the first time since 2015, the distillery will be working 7 days per week in 2023, doing 15 mashes. This means all fermentations will be 60 hours and the total production around 2.2 million litres of alcohol.

The core range is made up of a **15 year old**, **Distiller's Edition** with a finish in oloroso casks and **Dalwhinnie Winter's Gold**. In spring 2019, Dalwhinnie was also part of the series named after the popular TV series Game of Thrones with **Winter's Frost**. Finally, in autumn 2020, a **30 year old** bottled at 51,9% was launched in the Special Releases range.

History:

1897 John Grant, George Sellar and Alexander Mackenzie commence building the facilities. The first name is Strathspey.

1898 The owner encounters financial troubles and John Somerville & Co and A P Blyth & Sons take over and change the name to Dalwhinnie.

1905 Cook & Bernheimer in New York, buys Dalwhinnie for £1,250 at an auction.

1919 Macdonald Greenlees & Willliams Ltd headed by Sir James Calder buys Dalwhinnie.

1926 Macdonald Greenlees & Williams Ltd is bought by Distillers Company Ltd (DCL) which licences Dalwhinnie to James Buchanan & Co.

1930 Operations are transferred to Scottish Malt Distilleries (SMD).

1934 The distillery is closed after a fire in February.

1938 The distillery opens again.

1968 The maltings is decommissioned.

1987 Dalwhinnie 15 years becomes one of the selected six in United Distillers' Classic Malts.

1991 A visitor centre is constructed.

1992 The distillery closes and goes through a major refurbishment costing £3.2 million.

1995 The distillery opens in March.

2002 A 36 year old is released.

2006 A 20 year old is released.

2012 A 25 year old is released.

2014 A triple matured bottling without age statement is released for The Friends of the Classic Malts.

2015 Dalwhinnie Winter's Gold and a 25 year old are released.

2016 A distillery exclusive without age statement is released.

2018 Lizzie's Dram, a distillery exclusive bottling, is released.

2019 Dalwhinnie Winter's Frost, part of the Game of Thrones series, is released as well as a 30 year old in the annual Special Releases.

2020 A 30 year old is released as part of the Rare by Nature series.

Tasting notes Dalwhinnie 15 years old:

GS – The nose is fresh, with pine needles, heather and vanilla. Sweet and balanced on the fruity palate, with honey, malt and a very subtle note of peat. The medium length finish dries elegantly.

15 years old

Deanston

[deen•stun]

Owner: CVH Spirits
Region/district: Southern Highlands

Founded: 1965
Status: Active (vc)
Capacity: 3 000 000 litres

Address: Deanston, Perthshire FK16 6AG

Website: deanstonmalt.com
Tel: 01786 843010

Deanston, together with Bunnahabhain and Tobermory, have been used to ownership changes over the last three to four decades. The latest, first announced in 2021, was when the Dutch brewer Heineken took over the reigns.

Heineken placed a bid on Distell (owner of the three Scottish distilleries) with the aim, as it later turned out, to take control of a large part of the South African and Namibian beer and cider market. The spirit side of the business was never their focus. When the South African competition tribunal finally gave the go-ahead to Heineken in April 2023, the whisky interests were taken over by CVH Spirits (formerly known as Capevin Holdings)

Deanston is equipped with a traditional, open top, stainless steel mash tun with rakes and the charge was recently increased from 10.5 to 12 tonnes. There are eight stainless steel washbacks and since the distillery is now working seven days a week, the fermentation time is an even 85 hours. Finally there are two pairs of stills with ascending lyne arms. A hydro turbine installed in 2020 (replacing an older one) provides the entire site with electricity. During 2023 the distillery will be mashing 12-13 times per week and 2.5 million litres of alcohol. Having started in 2000, organic spirit is produced every year but due to the demand for "traditional" Deanston single malt, the volume has been reduced to around 10,000 litres per year.

The core range is a **12** and an **18 year old**, the **Virgin Oak** matured in ex-bourbon and with a finish in virgin oak casks and (released in limited quantities) the **15 year old Organic**. Recent limited bottlings include a Tequila Cask Finish, a Virgin Oak Distillery Edition and (in September 2023) a Virgin Oak Cask Strength. The only available duty-free exclusive is a **10 year old Bordeaux red wine cask finish**. Finally, there are three fairly recent distillery exclusives – a **2008 PX cask finish**, a **2013 recharred hogshead** and **Warehouse 4: 2013 bourbon barrel** single cask.

History:

1965 A weavery from 1785 is transformed into Deanston Distillery by James Findlay & Co. and Brodie Hepburn Ltd.

1966 Production commences in October.

1971 The first single malt is named Old Bannockburn.

1972 Invergordon Distillers takes over.

1974 The first single malt bearing the name Deanston is produced.

1982 The distillery closes.

1990 Burn Stewart Distillers from Glasgow buys the distillery for £2.1 million.

1991 The distillery resumes production.

1999 C L Financial buys an 18% stake of Burn Stewart.

2002 C L Financial acquires the remaining stake.

2006 Deanston 30 years old is released.

2009 A new version of the 12 year old is released.

2010 Virgin Oak is released.

2012 A visitor centre is opened.

2013 Burn Stewart Distillers is bought by South African Distell Group for £160m

2014 An 18 year old cognac finish is released.

2015 An 18 year old is released.

2016 Organic Deanston is released.

2017 A 40 year old and Vintage 2008 are released.

2018 A 10 year old Bordeaux finish is released for duty free.

2019 1997 Palo Cortado finish, 2006 Cream Sherry finish and a 2012 Beer finish are launched.

2020 A 1991 Muscat finish, a 2002 Organix PX and a 2002 Pinot Noir finish are released.

2021 Kentucky Cask and Dragon´s Milk are released.

12 years old

Tasting notes Deanston 12 years old:

GS – A fresh, fruity nose with malt and honey. The palate displays cloves, ginger, honey and malt, while the finish is long, quite dry and pleasantly herbal.

Dufftown

[duff•town]

Owner:
Diageo

Region/district:
Speyside

Founded: **Status:**
1896   Active

Capacity:
6 000 000 litres

Address: Dufftown, Keith, Banffshire AB55 4BR

Website:
malts.com
thesingleton.com

Tel:
01340 822100

Like most companies in the consumer products business, the larger whisky producers try to position their products towards different customer segments, determinated by the level of experience within them.

As the name indicates `discovery malts` are aimed towards those who wish to find a whisky which will lift them to the next level of satisfaction. `Recruitment malts` on the other hand are there to awaken the interest in malt whisky. A perfect example of the latter was The Singleton brand introduced in 2006/2007. It consisted (and still does) of three sub-brands – Glen Ord, Glendullan and Dufftown, each with their own character and destined for different markets. Dufftown was aimed at the European market.

The strategy was debated, not least amongst bewildered consumers who weren't sure of what distillery was behind the whisky they were drinking (even though it said so on the label). The commercial result 17 years after the launch however speaks for itself. In 2007 Diageo (always known as a blending company) sold 12 million bottles of single malt. In 2021 that figure had risen to 22 million and 8 million of these refer to The Singleton.

Dufftown distillery is equipped with a 14 ton full lauter mash tun, 12 stainless steel washbacks and three pairs of stills. Furthermore, all stills have sub coolers. The style of the newmake is green and grassy which is achieved by a clear wort and long fermentation (75 hours minimum). The fore shots in the spirit still run for 15 minutes and the middle cut is collected between 73 and 58% abv. In a seven-day week, there are 23 mashes per week which translates into six million litres per year.

The core range consists of **Malt Master's Selection** and **The Singleton of Dufftown 12, 15** and **18 year old**. A range for duty-free consists of **Trinité, Liberté** and **Artisan**. In 2020 a **17 year old** was part of the Special Releases and in 2021 – the **54 old Singleton of Dufftown** was released which was the oldest official bottling of a Diageo single malt ever. Finally, in October 2023, a **37 year old** was part of the 4th Prima & Ultima range.

History:

1895   Peter Mackenzie, Richard Stackpole, John Symon and Charles MacPherson build the distillery Dufftown-Glenlivet in an old mill.

1896   Production starts in November.

1897   The distillery is owned by P. Mackenzie & Co., who also owns Blair Athol in Pitlochry.

1933   P. Mackenzie & Co. is bought by Arthur Bell & Sons for £56,000.

1968   The floor maltings is discontinued and malt is bought from outside suppliers. The number of stills is increased from two to four.

1974   The number of stills is increased from four to six.

1979   The stills are increased by a further two to eight.

1985   Guinness buys Arthur Bell & Sons.

1997   Guinness and Grand Metropolitan merge to form Diageo.

2006   The Singleton of Dufftown 12 year old is launched as a special duty free bottling.

2008   The Singleton of Dufftown is made available also in the UK.

2010   A Manager's Choice 1997 is released.

2013   A 28 year old cask strength and two expressions for duty free - Unité and Trinité - are released.

2014   Tailfire, Sunray and Spey Cascade are released.

2016   Two limited releases are made - a 21 year old and a 25 year old.

2018   Malt Master's Selection is released.

2020   A 30 year old Prima & Ultima and a 17 year old Rare by Nature are released.

2021   A 54 year old is released.

2023   A 37 year old bottled at 47,7% is launched as part of the Prima & Ultima range.

Singleton of Dufftown 12 year

Tasting notes Dufftown 12 years old:

GS – The nose is sweet, almost violet-like, with underlying malt. Big and bold on the palate, this is an upfront yet very drinkable whisky. The finish is medium to long, warming, spicy, with slowly fading notes of sherry and fudge.

Edradour

[ed•ra•dow•er]

Owner:
Signatory Vintage
Scotch Whisky Co. Ltd

Region/district:
Southern Highland

Founded: 1825
Status: Active (vc)
Capacity: 260 000 litres

Address: Pitlochry, Perthshire PH16 5JP

Website: edradour.com
Tel: 01796 472095

For many years Edradour was one of the most visited distilleries in Scotland. Its location, just a 5 minute drive off the A9 when you reach Pitlochry heading towards the Highlands, was perfect for a stop.

In 2009 more than 80,000 people came here but numbers started to decline when the owners switched to receiving smaller groups rather than coach parties. It was then one of few distilleries not to re-open to visitors after the pandemic and it now seems that the closure of the visitor centre is permanent.

On the other hand, the distillery itself is thriving. Following an expansion in 2018 the site is now made up of two distilleries. The combined equipment for the two consists of two open, traditional cast iron mash tuns with a mash size of 1.1 tons, two Morton refrigerators to cool the wort and eight washbacks made of Oregon pine, with enough room left to install more in the future. The two stills in each distillery are attached to worm tubs on the outside and new warehouses have also been erected next to the new still house. Lately, Edradour has been making 5 mashes per week at each distillery with three short at 48 hours and two long at 96 hours. This will equate to 200,000 litres of alcohol. The amount of peated production (for the Ballechin brand) has diminished in the last couple of years and, due to lack of peated malt, there will probably be no peated production during 2023.

Apart from the distillery, the owner, Andrew Symington, has been one of the most influential independent bottlers in Scotland since the 1980s through his company Signatory.

The core range consists of a **10 year old** and the **12 year old Caledonia Selection** and there is also the **10 year old peated Ballechin**. Due to low stocks, the usual limited bottlings of Ibisco bourbon and sherry as well the straight-from.the-cask expressions have been temporarily suspended. Some cask strength bottlings will appear however and a **13 year old** and an **18 year old Ballechin** have also been announced.

History:

1825 Probably the year when a distillery called Glenforres is founded by farmers in Perthshire.

1837 The first year Edradour is mentioned.

1841 The farmers form a proprietary company, John MacGlashan & Co.

1886 John McIntosh & Co. acquires Edradour.

1933 William Whiteley & Co. buys the distillery.

1982 Campbell Distilleries (Pernod Ricard) buys Edradour and builds a visitor centre.

1986 The first single malt is released.

2002 Edradour is bought by Andrew Symington from Signatory for £5.4 million. The product range is expanded with a 10 year old and a 13 year old cask strength.

2003 A 30 year old and a 10 year old are released.

2004 A number of wood finishes are launched as cask strength.

2006 The first bottling of peated Ballechin is released.

2007 A Madeira matured Ballechin is released.

2008 A Ballechin matured in Port pipes and a 10 year old Edradour with a Sauternes finish are released.

2009 Fourth edition of Ballechin (Oloroso) is released.

2010 Ballechin #5 Marsala is released.

2011 Ballechin #6 Bourbon and a 26 year old PX sherry finish are relased.

2012 A 1993 Oloroso and a 1993 Sauternes finish as well as the 7th edition of Ballechin (Bordeaux) are released.

2013 Ballechin Sauternes is released.

2014 The first release of a 10 year old Ballechin.

2015 Fairy Flag is released.

2017 New releases include an 8 year old vatting of Edradour and Ballechin.

2018 The new distillery is commissioned.

10 years old

Tasting notes Edradour 10 years old:

GS – Cider apples, malt, almonds, vanilla and honey ar present on the nose, along with a hint of smoke and sherry. The palate is rich, creamy and malty, with a persistent nuttiness and quite a pronounced kick of slightly leathery sherry. Spices and sherry dominate the medium to long finish.

Fettercairn

[fett•er•cairn]

Owner: **Region/district:**
Whyte & Mackay (Emperador)   Eastern Highlands

Founded: **Status:**   **Capacity:**
1824   Active (vc)   2 200 000 litres

Address: Fettercairn, Laurencekirk, Kincardineshire AB30 1YB

Website: **Tel:**
fettercairnwhisky.com   01561 340205

One of the first distilleries to become licensed, Fettercairn is steeped in tradition. It was also, for more than a century, owned by the Gladstones, a family which amongst other things contributed a four time British Prime Minister – William Gladstone.

Although heritage may be important, the distillery has now entered into a new era of innovative and sustainable production. The owners, Whyte & Mackay, together with Bairds Malt have founded the Fettercairn 200 Club which is a partnership together with 200 local farms within a 50 miles radius of the distillery. From now on all the barley required for the production will be locally sourced. There is also the Scottish Oak programme, an exploration both in new flavours and in the sustainability of whisky production, initiated by the blender Gregg Glass and which involves all the other distilleries in the group.

Fettercairn distillery is equipped with a traditional, 5 ton cast iron mash tun and eleven washbacks with a fermentation time of 60 hours. There are also two pairs of stills. The spirit stills are quite unique in Scotland. They both have a cooling ring attached which sprays the head of the stills with water which is then collected at the base for circulation towards the top again. The whole idea is to increase the reflux during distillation. The goal for 2023 is 24 mashes per week and 2.2 million litres.

The core range consists of **12, 16, 22** and **28 year old**. In autumn 2022 an **18 year** old was added to the range – the first from the distillery in the Sottish oak programme. Initially matured in ex-bourbon American oak the finish took place in Scottish oak. Older versions in the range include **40, 46** and **50 year old**. In 2021 the first in a new series named Warehouse 2 was released where Batch No. 1 had been matured in a combination of bourbon, sherry and port casks. **Batch 4** appeared in August 2022. The final addition to the series (although now from **Warehouse 14**) had been finished in three different beer barrels and appeared in March 2023. For the duty free market there is a **12 year old PX sherry finish** and a **23 year old**.

History:

1824 Sir Alexander Ramsay founds the distillery.

1830 Sir John Gladstone buys the distillery.

1887 A fire erupts and the distillery closes for repair.

1890 Thomas Gladstone dies and his son John Robert takes over. The distillery reopens.

1912 John Gladstone buys out the other investors.

1926 The distillery is mothballed.

1939 The distillery is bought by Associated Scottish Distillers Ltd. Production restarts.

1960 The maltings discontinues.

1966 The stills are increased from two to four.

1971 The distillery is bought by Tomintoul-Glenlivet Distillery Co. Ltd.

1973 Tomintoul-Glenlivet Distillery Co. Ltd is bought by Whyte & Mackay Distillers Ltd.

1974 The mega group of companies Lonrho buys Whyte & Mackay.

1988 Lonrho sells to Brent Walker Group plc.

1989 A visitor centre opens.

1990 American Brands Inc. buys Whyte & Mackay for £160 million.

1996 Whyte & Mackay and Jim Beam Brands merge to become JBB Worldwide.

2001 Kyndal Spirits buys Whyte & Mackay from JBB Worldwide.

2002 The whisky changes name to Fettercairn 1824.

2003 Kyndal Spirits changes name to Whyte & Mackay.

2007 United Spirits buys Whyte & Mackay.

2009 24, 30 and 40 year olds are released.

2010 Fettercairn Fior is launched.

2012 Fettercairn Fasque is released.

2015 Emperador Inc buys Whyte & Mackay.

2018 A new range is launched; 12, 28, 40 and 50 year old.

2019 A 12 year old PX finish is released for duty free.

2020 A 16 year old and a 22 year old are added.

2021 Two first batches of Warehouse 2 are released.

2022 An 18 year old and batch 4 of Warehouse 2 is released.

2023 Warehouse 14 is released.

Tasting notes Fettercairn 12 years old:

IR – A delicious combination of pineapple, banana and mango together with coffee beans, cured ham and dried flowers. Still fruity on the palate but also becomes more spicy and malty and with a bit of mint at the end.

12 years old

Glenallachie

[glen•alla•key]

Owner:
The Glenallachie Distillers Co.

Region/district:
Speyside

Founded: **Status:** **Capacity:**
1967 Active (vc) 4 000 000 litres

Address: Aberlour, Banffshire AB38 9LR

Website: **Tel:**
theglenallachie.com 01236 422120

In 1989 Glenallachie became the third Scotch malt distillery (following Aberlour in 1974 and Edradour in 1982) that Pernod Ricard acquired and the ownership lasted for 28 years until the distillery was sold to a consortium lead by Billy Walker.

In the last 18 years Pernod Ricard has sold five of their distilleries with a combined capacity of 19 million litres. On the other hand expansion at some of their remaining sites has added 26 million litres and within a couple of years another 14 million will be created (Aberlour and Miltonduff). The company is determined to, at the very least, remain the second largest player in the Scotch category after Diageo but has no problem relinquishing some of their distilleries. Diageo on the other hand, with a whisky background dating back to at least 1877, hasn't sold one distillery since 1998 and at that time they were forced to by the authorities in order to preserve competition in the industry. During the Pernod Ricard days, Glenallachie mainly produced malt to become part of blends, especially Clan Campbell. With Billy Walker at the helm the focus quickly shifted and Glenallachie is now very much a single malt brand of its own.

GlenAllachie is equipped with a 9.4 ton semi-lauter mash tun and six washbacks made of mild steel but lined with stainless steel. There are also two pairs of unusually wide stills. Fermentations are long, up to 160 hours. In 2023 the production will be 5 mashes per week and around 1 million litres of alcohol of which ten percent will be heavily peated.

The Glenallachie core range consists of an **8 year old**, a **10 year old cask strength**, **12**, **15** and **18 year old**. There are also a **21 year old** cask strength matured in PX casks and a **30 year old** cask strength from PX, oloroso and chinquapin virgin oak. Recent limited expressions include batch 2 of the **Virgin Oak Finish** series, a **2012 Cuvée Cask Finish** and the **50th Anniversary Trilogy**. Wood finishes exclusive to various markets were released in August 2023; **11 year old Marsala** (UK), **12 year old Moscatel** (Europe) and **10 year old Port** (Asia).

History:

1967 The distillery is founded by Mackinlay, McPherson & Co., a subsidiary of Scottish & Newcastle Breweries Ltd. William Delmé Evans is architect.

1985 Scottish & Newcastle Breweries Ltd sells Charles Mackinlay Ltd to Invergordon Distillers which acquires both Glenallachie and Isle of Jura.

1987 The distillery is decommissioned.

1989 Campbell Distillers (Pernod Ricard) buys the distillery, increases the number of stills from two to four and takes up production again.

2005 The first official bottling for many years is a Cask Strength Edition from 1989.

2017 Glenallachie Distillery Edition is released and the distillery is sold to The Glenallachie Consortium.

2018 A series of single casks is released followed by a core range consisting of 12, 18 and 25 year old.

2019 A range of wood finishes is launched as well as a 15 year old core bottling. A visitor centre is opened.

2020 A 21 year old cask strength and three new wood finishes are launched; rye, port and moscatel.

2021 A 30 year old cask strength and the Wine Cask Finish series are launched.

2022 The 50th Anniversary Trilogy is launched together with 2012 Cuvée Cask Finish.

Tasting notes Glenallachie 12 years old:

IR – Baked apples with almonds and custard, lemon zest and pine needles on the nose. Rich and lively on the palate, sweet spices, ginger, bananas, liquorice, raisins and hints of pepper.

12 years old

Glenburgie

[glen•<u>bur</u>•gee]

Owner: **Region/district:**
Chivas Brothers   Speyside
(Pernod Ricard)

Founded: **Status:**   **Capacity:**
1810   Active   4 250 000 litres

Address: Glenburgie, Forres, Morayshire IV36 2QY

Website: **Tel:**
-              01343 850258

Glenburgie has played a prominent part in the blending of Ballantine´s, the world's second most sold blend for many years. On the Top list it is also one of the brands that has grown the most, up by 24% in the past four years.

In 2022 it sold 110 million bottles which means a share of almost 10% of the entire Scotch whisky market. A the moment the six most sold blends dominate the category more than any other time in the past 25 years. Apart from Ballantine´s, the brands are Johnnie Red Label and Black Label, Chivas Regal, Grant's and Famous Grouse. This handful of brands make up 41% of all Scotch whisky sold (blends and malts combined).

In 1927, Glenburgie appointed the first female distillery manager in the Scotch whisky industry when Margaret Nicol took over the reigns. Admittedly, there had been other women in leading roles before, none more so than Elizabeth Cumming of Cardhu, but that was always at distilleries that had been inherited by wives of the owners.

Glenburgie distillery lies well hidden at the end of a side road to the A96 between Forres and Elgin. It was founded in 1810 as Kilnflat distillery, but the buildings that we see today are of a much later date, having been built in 2003 when the old distillery was demolished. Glenburgie is equipped with a 7.5 ton full lauter mash tun with a copper dome and 12 stainless steel washbacks with a fermentation time of 52 hours. There are also three pairs of large stills with straight lyne arms producing a fruity newmake. The majority of the production is filled into bourbon casks and a part thereof is matured on site in four dunnage, two racked and two palletised warehouses.

There are two official bottlings of Glenburgie – **15** and **18 year old** both aged in ex-bourbon casks and bottled at 40%. A **17 year old cask strength** in the range The Distillery Reserve Collection is also available at Chivas's visitor centres.

History:

1810   William Paul founds Kilnflat Distillery. Official production starts in 1829.

1870   Kilnflat distillery closes.

1878   The distillery reopens under the name Glenburgie-Glenlivet, Charles Hay is licensee.

1884   Alexander Fraser & Co. takes over.

1925   Alexander Fraser & Co. files for bankruptcy and the receiver Donald Mustad assumes control of operations.

1927   James & George Stodart Ltd (owned by James Barclay and R A McKinlay since 1922) buys the distillery which by this time is inactive.

1930   Hiram Walker buys 60% of James & George Stodart Ltd.

1936   Hiram Walker buys Glenburgie Distillery in October. Production restarts.

1958   Lomond stills are installed producing a single malt, Glencraig. Floor malting ceases.

1981   The Lomond stills are replaced by conventional stills.

1987   Allied Lyons buys Hiram Walker.

2002   A 15 year old is released.

2004   A £4.3 million refurbishment and reconstruction takes place.

2005   Chivas Brothers (Pernod Ricard) becomes the new owner through the acquisition of Allied Domecq.

2006   The number of stills are increased from four to six in May.

2017   A 15 year old is released.

2019   An 18 year old is released.

15 years old

Tasting notes Glenburgie 15 years old:

IR – Very fruity on the nose with notes of pears, apple pie, honey, marzipan and roasted nuts. The palate reveals tropical fruits, white chocolate, marmalade, vanilla and caramel.

Glencadam

[glen•ka•dam]

Owner: | **Region/district:**
Angus Dundee Distillers | Eastern Highlands

Founded: | **Status:** | **Capacity:**
1825 | Active | 1 300 000 litres

Address: Brechin, Angus DD9 7PA

Website: | **Tel:**
glencadamwhisky.com | 01356 622217

At one time there were eight distilleries on the east coast between Aberdeen and Dundee. These were (and still are) fertile lands and the proximity to high quality barley was the reason for the establishment.

Two of them, Auchinblae and Glencoull, closed already in the 1920s and with the big whisky crisis in the mid 1980s, another four were forced to cease production – Glenesk, Glenury Royal, North Port and Lochside. The only two survivors were Fettercairn and, further to the south in the town of Brechin, Glencadam. The latter was treated by their owners, Allied Domecq, as a supplier of malt for their blends and in 2000 they mothballed the distillery. Three years later it was taken over by Angus Dundee Distillers. Even though they also use the output as a blend- and bulk whisky, they have since 2005 put a lot of effort into establishing Glencadam as a single malt on its own merits.

The construction of a long anticipated visitor centre at Glencadam got the green light from the local council in November 2022 and it will be opened in 2025 when the distillery celebrates its 200th anniversary. The water wheel that was re-installed in 2021 measures 4.3 metres in diameter and its purpose in not just ornamental but to supply the distillery with electricity as well.

The equipment consists of a traditional, 4.9 ton cast iron mash tun, six stainless steel washbacks with a fermentation time of 52 hours and one pair of stills. On site, two dunnage warehouses from 1825, three from the 1950s and one modern racked can be found. The distillery is currently working a seven-day week, which enables 16 mashes per week and 1.3 million litres of alcohol. The owners also produce a large number of blends and there are blended in 16 huge steel tanks next to the distillery.

The core range consists of **Origin 1825, Reserva Andalucia, American Oak, 10, 13, 15, 21** and **25 year old**. A new addition was made in July 2023 – the re-introduction of the **18 year old**. A limited release in May 2023 was the **15 year old Reserva de Jerez 2007** with an oloroso finish.

History:

1825 George Cooper founds the distillery.

1827 David Scott takes over.

1837 The distillery is sold by David Scott.

1852 Alexander Miln Thompson becomes the owner.

1857 Glencadam Distillery Company is formed.

1891 Gilmour, Thompson & Co Ltd takes over.

1954 Hiram Walker takes over.

1959 Refurbishing of the distillery.

1987 Allied Lyons buys Hiram Walker Gooderham & Worts.

1994 Allied Lyons changes name to Allied Domecq.

2000 The distillery is mothballed.

2003 Allied Domecq sells the distillery to Angus Dundee Distillers.

2005 The new owner releases a 15 year old.

2008 A re-designed 15 year old and a new 10 year old are introduced.

2009 A 25 and a 30 year old are released in limited numbers.

2010 A 12 year old port finish, a 14 year old sherry finish, a 21 year old and a 32 year old are released.

2012 A 30 year old is released.

2015 A 25 year old is launched.

2016 Origin 1825, 17 year old port finish, 19 year old oloroso finish, an 18 year old and a 25 year old are released.

2017 A 13 year old is released.

2019 The 15 year old is back in the range and batch two of the 25 year old is released.

2020 Reserva Andalucia is released.

2022 American Oak is released.

2023 The 18 year old re-appears and a limited 15 year old with an oloroso finish in released.

10 years old

Tasting notes Glencadam 10 years old:

GS – A light and delicate, floral nose, with tinned pears and fondant cream. Medium-bodied, smooth, with citrus fruits and gently-spiced oak on the palate. The finish is quite long and fruity, with a hint of barley.

GlenDronach

[glen•dro•nack]

Owner:
Benriach Distillery Co
(Brown Forman)

Region/district:
Highlands

Founded: 1826
Status: Active (vc)
Capacity: 2 000 000 litres

Address: Forgue, Aberdeenshire AB54 6DB

Website:
glendronachdistillery.com

Tel:
01466 730202

The owner of GlenDronach, Brown Forman, is widely known as the producer of the most sold American whiskey in the world – Jack Daniels. Historically though, these mega producers have always been careful not to put all their eggs in one basket.

One of the best examples is the interest that the Canadian companies Seagrams and Hiram Walker took in Scotch in the 1950´s and 60´s. They realised early on that a focus on just Canadian whisky would not suffice. Brown Forman had a small share of Glenmorangie until 2005. The acquisition of GlenDronach, BenRiach and Glenglassaugh in 2016 however was an evidence of how important it is to be relevant in all the major categories of whisky.

With a fan base since many decades, it seems that GlenDronach was the ultimate target while the other two distilleries were brands that needed considerable efforts. With almost a million bottles sold in 2022 Glendronach is still the number one of the three and the fame of the brand rests very much on sherry cask maturation.

The equipment consists of a 3.7 ton cast iron mash tun with rakes, nine washbacks made of larch with a fermentation time of 50 to 65 hours, two wash stills with sharply descending lyne arms while those on the spirit stills have a much less accentuated angle. The production plan for 2023 is 28 mashes per week and a volume shy of 2 million litres. The distillery is currently in for a major upgrade including more stills and washbacks and when completed in 2025 the capacity will have doubled.

The core range consists of **Original 12 years, Revival 15 years, Allardice 18 years** and **Parliament 21 years**. Rumour has it though that the 18 and 21 will be discontinued. Recent limited releases include the 11th edition of the **Grandeur** (28 years old). In autumn 2023, another batch of the **Cask Strength Bottlings** was launched including **12 single casks**. Finally, the range for duty-free consists of the **10 year old Forgue** (PX and oloroso) and the **16 year old Boynsmill** (PX, oloroso and port).

History:

1826 The distillery is founded by a consortium with James Allardes as one of the owners.

1837 Parts of the distillery is destroyed in a fire.

1852 Walter Scott (from Teaninich) takes over.

1887 Walter Scott dies and Glendronach is taken over by a consortium from Leith.

1920 Charles Grant buys Glendronach for £9,000.

1960 William Teacher & Sons buys the distillery.

1966 The number of stills is increased to four.

1976 Allied Breweries takes over William Teacher & Sons.

1996 The distillery is mothballed.

2002 Production is resumed on 14th May.

2005 The distillery closes to rebuild from coal to indirect firing by steam. Reopens in September. Chivas Brothers (Pernod Ricard) becomes new owner through the acquisition of Allied Domecq.

2008 Pernod Ricard sells the distillery to the owners of BenRiach distillery.

2009 Relaunch of the whole range including 12, 15 and 18 year old.

2010 A 31 year old, a 1996 single cask and a total of 11 vintages and four wood finishes are released. A visitor centre is opened.

2011 The 21 year old Parliament and 11 vintages are released.

2012 A number of vintages are released.

2013 Recherché 44 years and a number of new vintages are released.

2014 Nine different single casks are released.

2015 The Hielan, 8 years old, is released.

2016 Brown Forman buys the distillery. Peated GlenDronach and Octaves Classic are released.

2017 A range of new single casks is released.

2018 Two bottlings for duty free are released - 10 year old Forgue and 16 year old Boynsmill.

2019 Port Wood, Traditionally Peated and batch 18 of the Cask Bottlings are released.

2021 Cask Strength batch 9 is released.

2022 A 50 year old is released.

2023 Cask Strength batch 12 is released.

Tasting notes GlenDronach 12 years old:

GS – A sweet nose of Christmas cake fresh from the oven. Smooth on the palate, with sherry, soft oak, fruit, almonds and spices. The finish is comparatively dry and nutty, ending with bitter chocolate.

12 years old Original

Glendullan

[glen•dull•an]

Owner:
Diageo

Region/district:
Speyside

Founded:
1897

Status:
Active

Capacity:
5 000 000 litres

Address: Dufftown, Keith, Banffshire AB55 4DJ

Website:
thesingleton.com

Tel:
01340 822100

When Diageo released the Singleton concept in 2006, more than one whisky consumer raised their eyebrows. The idea was to market three distilleries under one brand but with each distillery name visible on the label.

Customers were confused (and many still are) but in hindsight, seventeen years later, it was probably a brilliant decision. Glen Ord was the only of the three chosen distilleries that was, at least vaguely, known as a brand of its own. Dufftown and Glendullan were completely anonymous. To build a brand is extremely expensive. If Diageo had chosen to do that separately for each of the three distilleries it would probably have cost them far more than going with the Singleton concept. Today The Singleton sells over eight million bottles and is the fifth biggest malt in the world.

Glendullan is situated just a one minute's drive east of Glenfiddich near a river which, despite of the distillery's name isn't Dullan, but the Fiddich. The confluence of the two rivers lies just a mile to the south of Glendullan. Some remains of the original distillery built in 1896 can still be seen today but the current plant was built in 1972. The two distilleries were working parallel to each other for 13 years until 1985, when the old one was closed.

Glendullan is equipped with a 12 ton full lauter stainless steel mash tun, 8 washbacks made of larch and 2 made of stainless steel with a fermentation time of 75 hours as well as three pairs of stills. In 2023 the distillery plans to make 21 mashes per week, producing five million litres of alcohol. The character of the newmake is green/grassy and of the three Singletons, Glendullan is definitely the lightest.

The core range consists of **12, 15** and **18 year old**. The Singleton Reserve Collection with **Classic** (American oak), **Double Matured** (American and European oak and then married together) and **Master's Art** (Muscat finish) is exclusive to duty free. The most recent limited expressions include a **14 year old**, part of the Special Releases 2023 series, and with a finish in Chardonnay de Bourgogne French oak casks.

History:
1896 William Williams & Sons, a blending company with Three Stars and Strathdon among its brands, founds the distillery.
1902 Glendullan is delivered to the Royal Court and becomes the favourite whisky of Edward VII.
1919 Macdonald Greenlees buys a share of the company and Macdonald Greenlees & Williams Distillers is formed.
1926 Distillers Company Limited (DCL) buys Glendullan.
1930 Glendullan is transferred to Scottish Malt Distillers (SMD).
1962 Major refurbishing and reconstruction.
1972 A brand new distillery is constructed next to the old one and both operate simultaneously during a few years.
1985 The oldest of the two distilleries is mothballed.
1995 The first launch of Glendullan in the Rare Malts series is a 22 year old from 1972.
2005 A 26 year old from 1978 is launched in the Rare Malts series.
2007 Singleton of Glendullan is launched in the USA.
2013 Singleton of Glendullan Liberty and Trinity are released for duty free.
2014 A 38 year old is released.
2015 Classic, Double Matured and Master´s Art are released.
2018 The Forgotten Drops 40 years old is released.
2019 House of Tully, part of the Game of Thrones series, as well as a 41 year old are released.
2021 A 19 year old with a cognac finish and a 28 year old with a second maturation in madeira casks are released.
2023 A 14 year old Chardonnay finish is a part of the 2023 Special Releases.

12 years old

Tasting notes Singleton of Glendullan 12 years:
GS – The nose is spicy, with brittle toffee, vanilla, new leather and hazelnuts. Spicy and sweet on the smooth palate, with citrus fruits, more vanilla and fresh oak. Drying and pleasingly peppery in the finish.

Glen Elgin

[glen el•gin]

Owner:	**Region/district:**
Diageo	Speyside
Founded: **Status:**	**Capacity:**
1898 Active	2 700 000 litres

Address: Longmorn, Morayshire IV30 8SL

Website:	**Tel:**
malts.com	01343 862100

Glen Elgin has been closed for quite some time now and production will most likely not be resumed until 2024. This doesn't mean that the site has been dormant – quite the opposite.

A substantial amount of refurbishing is going on; two stills are being replaced as well as two of the washbacks and four of the six wormtubs, new roofs on the warehouses, new operator facilities in the distillery and an upgrade of the office are just some of the things on the agenda.

Glen Elgin, the first Scottish distillery to start production in the 20th century, lies in a small hamlet called Fogwatt which is on the busy A941 between Elgin and Rothes. It takes 30 seconds to drive through Fogwatt and it is not possible to spot the distillery from the road. There are two streets leading from the main road to the distillery but since this is a working plant with a no visitor policy it is recommended you park your car on one of the side roads and walk a couple of minutes to reach the distillery. Take your pictures when you've reached the distillery office but avoid walking onto the premises. As is the case for most distilleries, health and safety regulations are nowadays not taken lightly.

The distillery is equipped with an 8.4 ton Steinecker full lauter mash tun, nine washbacks (39,400 litres) made of larch and six small stills. The stills are connected to six wooden worm tubs in which the spirit vapours are condensed. Although worm tubs might indicate a heavy and perhaps sulphury newmake, the long fermentation (90 hours on a 7-day production) and the slow distillation produces a fruity spirit with depth, perfect for a blended whisky. When the distillery starts to produce again in 2024 it will initially be a 5-day week with 12 mashes and then ramping it up to seven days production with 16 mashes.

Glen Elgin has for a long time been a signature malt in the blend White Horse which is one of the 10 best selling Scotch in the world with a particular stronghold in Brazil and Japan. The only official bottling of the single malt is a **12 year old**, but a limited **18 year old**, matured in ex-bodega European oak butts was one of the Special Releases in 2017.

History:

1898 The former manager of Glenfarclas, William Simpson and banker James Carle found Glen Elgin.

1900 Production starts in May but the distillery closes just five months later.

1901 The distillery is auctioned for £4,000 to the Glen Elgin-Glenlivet Distillery Co. and is mothballed.

1906 The wine producer J. J. Blanche & Co. buys the distillery for £7,000 and production resumes.

1929 J. J. Blanche dies and the distillery is put up for sale again.

1930 Scottish Malt Distillers (SMD) buys it and the license goes to White Horse Distillers.

1964 Expansion from two to six stills plus other refurbishing takes place.

1992 The distillery closes for refurbishing and installation of new stills.

1995 Production resumes in September.

2001 A 12 year old is launched in the Flora & Fauna series.

2002 The Flora & Fauna series malt is replaced by Hidden Malt 12 years.

2003 A 32 year old cask strength from 1971 is released.

2008 A 16 year old is launched as a Special Release.

2009 Glen Elgin 1998, a single cask in the new Manager´s Choice range is released.

2017 An 18 year old is launched as part of the Special Releases.

12 years old

Tasting notes Glen Elgin 12 years old:

GS – A nose of rich, fruity sherry, figs and fragrant spice. Full-bodied, soft, malty and honeyed in the mouth. The finish is lengthy, slightly perfumed, with spicy oak.

Glenfarclas

[glen•fark•lass]

Owner:	**Region/district:**
J. & G. Grant	Speyside

Founded:	**Status:**	**Capacity:**
1836	Active (vc)	3 500 000 litres

Address: Ballindalloch, Banffshire AB37 9BD

Website:	**Tel:**
glenfarclas.com	01807 500257

When Alfred Barnard published his ground-breaking book on distilleries in the UK in 1887, he devoted but one page to Glenfarclas and he did not seem overwhelmed by what he saw.

At that time, the distillery had been owned by George Grant for 20 years and his interest was devoted more to the farm than the distillery. A few years after he died in 1890 his two sons soon decided to enter partnership with the Pattison brothers who, with their fraudulent actions, initiated a disaster for the entire whisky industry. From 1905, however, the entire ownership of the distillery was safely back in the hands of the Grant family and has remained so with the 5th generation currently working the business.

The current chairman of the company is John Grant who joined Glenfarclas in 1974. At that time single malt had not taken off as a category. Glenfiddich globally released their Straight Malt in 1963 but most of the competitors were slow to follow. John Grant however saw the opportunity and reserved more and more of the stock for single malts. Glenfarclas was also the second distillery in Scotland to open a visitor centre which increased the interest in the brand. Today Glenfarclas single malt is a classic with a large fan base. Their whiskies, especially the older releases, are also competitively priced which perhaps comes from the fact that it is family-owned without share holders interested in quick revenues. In the last ten years, Glenfarclas single malt has climbed the single malt sales list, and with 2.4 million bottles sold in 2021 it is ahead of brands such as Ardbeg, Highland Park and Lagavulin.

The distillery is equipped with a 16.5 ton semi-lauter mash tun, the largest in Scotland, and twelve stainless steel washbacks with a minimum fermentation time of 60 hours but with a current average of 106 hours. There are three pairs of directly fired stills (a most unusual feature in the industry today) and the wash stills are equipped with rummagers to prevent solids from sticking to the copper. The goal for 2023 is to make 3.1 million litres with 12 mashes per week. On site are no less than 42 dunnage warehouses!

The Glenfarclas core range consists of **8, 10, 12, 15, 21** and **25 year old**, as well as the lightly sherried **Heritage** which comes without an age statement and the **105 Cask Strength**. The latter was the first commercially available cask strength single malt in the industry. There is also a **17 year old** destined for the USA, Japan and Sweden. The **30** and **40 year olds** are limited but new editions occur regularly. A **35 year old** was released in 2022 and later in the year, a **50 year old** to celebrate John Grant (the fifth generation of the owning family) being involved in the whisky industry for 50 years. There are also plans for an early 2024 release of a 70 year old - a first for Glenfarclas. In collaboration with Pol Roger, their distributor in the UK, a **20 year old Port Pipe Decanter** was released in June 2023. The owners also continue to release bottlings in their **Family Casks** series with vintages ranging from **1954** to **2008**.

History:

1836 Robert Hay founds the distillery on the original site since 1797.

1865 Robert Hay passes away and John Grant and his son George buy the distillery. They lease it to John Smith at The Glenlivet Distillery.

1870 John Smith resigns in order to start Cragganmore and J. & G. Grant Ltd takes over.

1889 John Grant dies and George Grant takes over.

1890 George Grant dies and his widow Elsie takes over the license while sons John and George control operations.

1895 John and George Grant take over and form The Glenfarclas-Glenlivet Distillery Co. Ltd with the infamous Pattison, Elder & Co.

1898 Pattison becomes bankrupt. Glenfarclas encounters financial problems after a major overhaul of the distillery but survives by mortgaging and selling stored whisky to R. I. Cameron, a whisky broker from Elgin.

1914 John Grant leaves due to ill health and George continues alone.

1948 The Grant family celebrates the distillery's 100th anniversary, a century of active licensing. It is 9 years late, as the actual anniversary coincided with WW2.

1949 George Grant senior dies and sons George Scott and John Peter inherit the distillery.

1960 Stills are increased from two to four.

1968 Glenfarclas is first to launch a cask-strength single malt. It is later named Glenfarclas 105.

1972 Floor maltings is abandoned and malt is purchased centrally.

1973 A visitor centre is opened.

1976 Enlargement from four stills to six.

2002 George S Grant dies and is succeeded as company chairman by his son John L S Grant.

History continued:

2005 A 50 year old is released to commemorate the bi-centenary of John Grant´s birth.

2007 Family Casks, a series of single cask bottlings from 43 consecutive years, is released.

2008 New releases in the Family Cask range. Glenfarclas 105 40 years old is released.

2009 A third release in the Family Casks series.

2010 A 40 year old and new vintages from Family Casks are released.

2011 Chairman´s Reserve and 175th Anniversary are released.

2012 A 58 year old and a 43 year old are released.

2013 An 18 year old for duty free is released as well as a 25 year old quarter cask.

2014 A 60 year old and a 1966 single fino sherry cask are released.

2015 A 1956 Sherry Cask and Family Reserve are released.

2016 40 year old, 50 year old, 1981 Port and 1986 cask strength are released.

2018 A 22 year old version of the 105 Cask Strength is released.

2019 Glenfarclas Trilogy is released.

2020 Pagoda Ruby Reserve 62 and 63 years old are released.

2021 A 185th anniversary bottling is launched together with a 35 year old.

2022 A 50 year old is released.

Tasting notes Glenfarclas 10 year old:

GS – Full and richly sherried on the nose, with nuts, fruit cake and a hint of citrus fruit. The palate is big, with ripe fruit, brittle toffee, some peat and oak. Medium length and gingery in the finish.

105 Cask Strength

50 years old

12 years old

18 years old

Family Cask 1959

21 years old

40 years old

Glenfiddich

[glen•fidd•ick]

Owner:
William Grant & Sons

Region/district:
Speyside

Founded: 1886
Status: Active (vc)
Capacity: 21 000 000 litres

Address: Dufftown, Keith, Banffshire AB55 4DH

Website:
glenfiddich.com

Tel:
01340 820373 (vc)

Of all the malt whisky distilleries in the world, Glenfiddich has the largest capacity! To be accurate it shares the top spot with its fiercest competitor Glenlivet but when it comes to the number of stills Glenfiddich reigns supreme.

No less than 43 copper stills produce what used to be the number one selling single malt in the world every year since 1963. Lately Glenlivet has occupied the top spot on a couple of occasions but the importance of Glenfiddich for the growth of the single malt category in the last decades is huge. The launch of their Straight Malt in 1963 was a major milestone in the history of Scotch and paved the way for other brands and the entire category of single malts. The man behind it was Sandy Grant Gordon whose great grandfather William Grant had built Glenfiddich in the late 1800s. When Sandy, together with his brother Charles, took over the leadership of the company in 1953, he put a lot of effort into launching the single malt, which was used for their famous blend, as a brand of its own and his methods were quite progressive. Global marketing campaigns, also on television, made the brand visible in all corners of the world.

Following a huge expansion which was completed in December 2020, Glenfiddich is now equipped with four, stainless steel full lauter mash tuns – all with a ten ton mash. There are 48 washbacks (40,000 litres) made of Douglas fir with a fermentation time of 74 hours. The total number of stills is 43; 16 wash stills (9,500 litres) and 27 spirit stills (5,900 litres) and 15 of them, in the old still house number two, are directly fired using gas. An interesting new project, completed in 2022, was to install separate receivers on one wash still and two spirit stills. This will enable the owners to run experimental trials without interfering with the normal production. The plan for 2023 is to do 105 mashes per week and 21 million litres of pure alcohol.

The Glenfiddich core range consists of **12, 15** and **18 year old.** Included are also a **12 year old amontillado** (exclusive to Taiwan), **14 year old bourbon barrel reserve** (USA, Canada, France and Israel) and **Triple Oak Twelve** (France). A separate range is the Grand Series with **21 year old Gran Reserva, 22 year old Grand Cortes, 23 year old Grand Cru, 26 year old Grand Couronne** and the new **29 year old Grand Yozakura** finished in ex-Awamori casks. In the Time series we find **30, 40** and **50 year olds** and the Experimental Series include **IPA Experiment, Project XX, 21 year old Winter Storm, Fire & Cane** and **The Orchard Experiment.**

Recent limited releases include **Glenfiddich The Original, 38 year old Glenfiddich Ultimate** and vintages in the **Rare Collection.** An entire new range for travel retail, **Perpetual Collection,** was launched in autumn 2022; **Vat 01** and **Vat 02** without age statements, the **15 year old Vat 03** and the **18 year old Vat 04.** Another duty free exclusive is **Rare Oak 25 years.** Finally, a **15 year old Distillery Edition** is available at the distillery.

History:

1886 The distillery is founded by William Grant.

1887 The first distilling takes place on Christmas Day.

1892 William Grant builds Balvenie.

1898 The blending company Pattisons, largest customer of Glenfiddich, files for bankruptcy and Grant decides to blend their own whisky. Standfast becomes one of their major brands.

1903 William Grant & Sons is formed.

1957 The famous, three-cornered bottle is introduced.

1958 The floor maltings is closed.

1963 Glennfiddich becomes the first whisky to be marketed as single malt in the UK and the rest of the world.

1964 A version of Standfast's three-cornered bottle is launched for Glenfiddich in green glass.

1969 Glenfiddich becomes the first distillery in Scotland to open a visitor centre.

1974 16 new stills are installed.

2001 1965 Vintage Reserve is launched in a limited edition of 480 bottles. Glenfiddich 1937 is bottled (61 bottles).

2002 Glenfiddich Gran Reserva 21 years old, Caoran Reserve 12 years and Glenfiddich Rare Collection 1937 (61 bottles) are launched.

2003 1973 Vintage Reserve (440 bottles) is launched.

2004 1991 Vintage Reserve (13 years) and 1972 Vintage Reserve (519 bottles) are launched.

2006 1973 Vintage Reserve, 33 years (861 bottles) and 12 year old Toasted Oak are released.

2007 1976 Vintage Reserve, 31 years is released.

2008 1977 Vintage Reserve is released.

2009 A 50 year old is released.

History continued:

2010 Rich Oak, 1978 Vintage Reserve, the 6th edition of 40 year old and Snow Phoenix are released.

2011 1974 Vintage Reserve and a 19 year old Madeira finish are released.

2012 Cask of Dreams and Millenium Vintage are released.

2013 A 19 year old red wine finish and 1987 Anniversary Vintage are released. Cask Collection is released for duty free.

2014 The 26 year old Glenfiddich Excellence, Rare Oak 25 years and Glenfiddich The Original are released.

2015 A 14 year old for the US market is released.

2016 Finest Solera is released for travel retail. Two expressions in the Experimental Series are launched; Project XX and IPA Experiment.

2017 Winter Storm is released.

2018 Fire & Cane is released.

2019 Grand Cru 23 year old and Rare Collection Cask No. 20050 are released.

2020 Gran Cortes 22 year old, Grande Couronne 26 year old and two 1975 Vintages are released. The distillery capacity is doubled.

2022 The cider finished Orchard Experiment and the Perpetual Collection are released.

2023 The 29 year old Grand Yozakura is launched.

Tasting notes Glenfiddich 12 year old:

GS – Delicate, floral and slightly fruity on the nose. Well mannered in the mouth, malty, elegant and soft. Rich, fruit flavours dominate the palate, with a developing nuttiness and an elusive whiff of peat smoke in the fragrant finish.

Project XX

Orchard Experiment

IPA Experiment

Perpetual Vat 01

Grand Yozakura
29 years

Our Original
Twelve

Our Solera
Fifteen

Our Small Batch
Eighteen

Glen Garioch

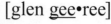
[glen gee•ree]

Owner:
Beam Suntory

Region/district:
Eastern Highlands

Founded: 1797 **Status:** Active (vc) **Capacity:** 1 500 000 litres

Address: Oldmeldrum, Inverurie, Aberdeenshire AB51 0ES

Website:
glengarioch.com

Tel:
01651 873450

Glen Garioch is one of the oldest distilleries in Scotland and also one of the few urban distilleries still operating. Located in the small town of Oldmeldrum, it is one of the first distilleries you encounter coming from Aberdeen towards Speyside.

It is also a distillery heading towards the future by way of looking back at traditional production methods. This was initiated by the owners, Beam Suntory, just two years ago at all five of their Scottish malt distilleries, more prominently so at Glen Garioch. The malting floors, which were last used for a few weeks in 1996, were reinstated with the capacity to supply 25% of the distillery's needs. Around the same time direct gas firing of the wash still was implemented. One of the effects of this method is that a Maillard reaction is obtained from the left-over sugars and amino acids resulting in a more full-bodied spirit. Finally, the distillery is now doing trials with brewer's yeast which a few decades ago lended fruitier notes to most single malts compared to distiller's yeast.

The distillery is equipped with a four ton full lauter mash tun, nine stainless steel washbacks with an average fermentation time of 72 hours, one direct-fired wash still and one spirit still. The two stills have some of the sharpest descending lyne arms in the industry with very little reflux. On the other hand, the condensers are run hot in order to get more copper contact and there is also a sub cooler on the wash still. Together with a very clear wort, the owners attempt to obtain a robust yet fruity newmake. Following a substantial refurbishing, the distillery is now producing at more or less full capacity which during 2023 will mean 19 mashes per week and a total of 1.3 million litres of pure alcohol.

The core range is the **1797 Founder's Reserve** and a **12 year old**. Recent limited expressions include **Virgin Oak, The Renaissance** series, **The American Trilogy** and a number of vintage single casks. The latest, in May 2023, was a **1979 single cask** (44 years old) exclusively available at the distillery.

History:

1797 John Manson founds the distillery.

1798 Thomas Simpson becomes licensee.

1825 Ingram, Lamb & Co. bcome new owners.

1837 The distillery is bought by John Manson & Co.

1884 The distillery is sold to J. G. Thomson & Co.

1908 William Sanderson buys the distillery.

1933 Sanderson & Son merges with the gin maker Booth's Distilleries Ltd.

1937 Booth´s Distilleries Ltd is acquired by Distillers Company Limited (DCL).

1968 Glen Garioch is decommissioned.

1970 It is sold to Stanley P. Morrison Ltd.

1973 Production starts again.

1978 Stills are increased from two to three.

1994 Suntory controls all of Morrison Bowmore Distillers Ltd.

1995 The distillery is mothballed in October.

1997 The distillery reopens in August and from now on, it is using unpeated malt.

2004 Glen Garioch 46 year old is released.

2005 15 year old Bordeaux Cask Finish is launched. A visitor centre opens in October.

2006 An 8 year old is released.

2009 Complete revamp of the range - 1979 Founders Reserve (unaged), 12 year old, Vintage 1978 and 1990 are released.

2010 1991 vintage is released.

2011 Vintage 1986 and 1994 are released.

2012 Vintage 1995 and 1997 are released.

2013 Virgin Oak, Vintage 1999 and 11 single casks are released.

2014 Glen Garioch Renaissance Collection 15 years is released.

2018 The fourth and final installment of the Rennaisance Collection is released.

2021 Floor malting is re-installed.

12 years old

Tasting notes Glen Garioch 12 years old:

GS – Luscious and sweet on the nose, peaches and pineapple, vanilla, malt and a hint of sherry. Full-bodied and nicely textured, with more fresh fruit on the palate, along with spice, brittle toffee and finally dry oak notes.

Glenglassaugh

[glen•gla•ssa]

Owner:
Glenglassaugh Distillery Co
(BenRiach Distillery Co.)

Region/district:
Highlands

Founded: 1875
Status: Active (vc)
Capacity: 1 100 000 litres

Address: Portsoy, Banffshire AB45 2SQ

Website:
glenglassaugh.com

Tel:
01261 842367

Fans of Glenglassaugh have been waiting for a new core range from the distillery and in June 2023 they were finally rewarded for their patience.

Together with GlenDronach and BenRiach, Glenglassaugh near Portsoy was part of the deal when Billy Walker sold his company to Brown Forman (makers of Jack Daniels) in 2016. Many of us thought that Glenglassaugh would be sold off within a year or two. The distillery was smaller than the other two and having been closed for so many years there was neither much stock left, nor was it known as a brand. Young expressions such as Revival, Evolution and Torfa were released. Following the revamp of the BenRiach range in 2020, the company master blender Rachel Barrie had time (and mature stock) to focus on Glenglassaugh and in June three new bottlings replaced the previous ones.

With very little remaining of the old buildings, Glenglassaugh has a stunning location on the A98 between Portsoy and Cullen, almost sitting on the Moray beach. Admittedly, production has been low in the past few years but a planning application approved by the local council in February 2023 shows that six warehouses will be built within the near future. Also,

The distillery equipment consists of a 5.2 ton Porteus cast iron mash tun with rakes, four wooden washbacks and two stainless steel ones, with a fermentation time between 54 and 80 hours. There is one pair of stills with a 20 minute foreshot in the spirit still and a cut-off of the heart at 61%. In a normal year, the production is around 800,000 litres of pure alcohol, and a small percentage has often been peated (30ppm).

The new core range is headed by a **12 year old** matured in a selection of bourbon, sherry and red wine casks. There are also two expressions with no age statement; **Sandend** matured in bourbon and manzanilla sherry casks and **Portsoy** which comes from a combination of sherry, bourbon and port casks. Limited expressions have been released over the past few years including 30,40 and 50 year olds as well as wood finishes.

History:

1873 The distillery is founded by James Moir.

1887 Alexander Morrison embarks on renovation work.

1892 Morrison sells the distillery to Robertson & Baxter. They in turn sell it on to Highland Distilleries Company for £15,000.

1908 The distillery closes.

1931 The distillery reopens.

1936 The distillery closes.

1957 Reconstruction takes place.

1960 The distillery reopens.

1986 Glenglassaugh is mothballed.

2005 A 22 year old is released.

2006 Three limited editions are released - 19 years old, 38 years old and 44 years old.

2008 The distillery is bought by the Scaent Group for £5m. Three bottlings are released - 21, 30 and 40 year old.

2009 New make spirit and 6 months old are released.

2010 A 26 year old replaces the 21 year old.

2011 A 35 year old and the first bottling from the new owners production, a 3 year old, are released.

2012 A visitor centre is inaugurated and Glenglassaugh Revival is released.

2013 BenRiach Distillery Co buys the distillery and Glenglassaugh Evolution and a 30 year old are released.

2014 The peated Torfa is released as well as eight different single casks and Massandra Connection (35 and 41 years old).

2015 The second batch of single casks is released.

2016 Brown Forman buys the distillery. Octaves Classic and Octaves Peated are released.

2017 Three wood finishes are released.

2018 Batch three in the Rare Cask series and the second release of Octaves are released

2020 Ten single casks in the series Coastal Casks are launched.

2021 A 50 year old is released.

2023 A new core range is introduced; 12 year old, Sandend and Portsoy.

Tasting notes Glenglassaugh 12 years old:

IW – Fresh, ripe fruit drizzled with caramel sauce on the nose, becomes more luscious when butterscotch appears. Light texture on the palate from which butterscotch and caramel emerge. Then fudge joins in, poached fruit in syrup and cinnamon hints make it richer and luscious.

12 year old

Glengoyne

[glen•goyn]

Owner:
Ian Macleod Distillers

Region/district:
Southern Highlands

Founded:
1833

Status:
Active (vc)

Capacity:
1 100 000 litres

Address: Dumgoyne by Killearn, Glasgow G63 9LB

Website:
glengoyne.com

Tel:
01360 550254 (vc)

The company which would eventually become the owner of Glengoyne was established in 1933 as Ian Macleod & Company, working as blenders and bottlers.

In 1963 Ian Macleod was taken over by Peter Russell whose father Leonard had started out in the business in 1936 as a whisky broker. Leonard died in 1956 and Peter took over the company. He was probably the first to recognize the potential of selling whisky in supermarkets and started to supply what we today call "own labels". At the same time, he expanded the business of creating own brands and today King Robert II with sales of 4.5 million bottles is the star of the "own labels" segment.

Peter Russell, joined by his son Leonard in 1989, turned Ian Macleod Distillers into one of the most respected whisky companies in the UK. Eventually the family realized that having your own distilleries would be essential for an independent bottler and blender. In 2003 they bought Glengoyne distillery and eight years later Tamdhu. In 2023 the duo became a trio when Rosebank was re-opened. In 2016 Peter Russell was inducted into the Whisky Hall of Fame and in January 2023 he passed away at the age of 95.

Glengoyne is equipped with a 3.84 ton semi lauter mash tun. There are also six Oregon pine washbacks, as well as the rather unusual combination of one wash still and two spirit stills. Both short (56 hours) and long (110 hours) fermentations are practiced. The plan for 2023 is to produce 16 mashes per week and 1.1 million litres of alcohol.

The core range consists of **10, 12, 15** (re-introduced in late 2022), **18** (only available from the distillery), **21, 25** and **30 year old**. There is also batch ten of the **Cask Strength** released in June 2023. Recent limited expressions include batch 9 of the popular **Teapot Dram** which appeared in May 2023. For travel retail there is The Spirit of Time series which consists of the **10 year old First Fill**, predominantly from ex-bourbon, the **15 year old PX Cask Edition** and the **26 year old** oloroso matured. The pinnacle of the range is the **53 year old** (the oldest official release of a Glengoyne) which was first introduced in China in May 2022.

History:

1833 The distillery is licensed under the name Burnfoot Distilleries by the Edmonstone family.

1876 Lang Brothers buys the distillery and changes the name to Glenguin.

1905 The name changes to Glengoyne.

1965 Robertson & Baxter takes over Lang Brothers and the distillery is refurbished. The stills are increased from two to three.

2001 Glengoyne Scottish Oak Finish (16 years old) is launched.

2003 Ian MacLeod Distillers Ltd buys the distillery plus the brand Langs from the Edrington Group for £7.2 million.

2005 A 19 year old, a 32 year old and a 37 year old cask strength are launched.

2006 Nine "choices" from Stillmen, Mashmen and Manager are released.

2007 A new version of the 21 year old, two Warehousemen´s Choice, Vintage 1972 and two single casks are released.

2008 A 16 year old Shiraz cask finish, three single casks and Heritage Gold are released.

2009 A 40 year old, two single casks and a new 12 year old are launched.

2010 Two single casks, 1987 and 1997, released.

2011 A 24 year old single cask is released.

2012 A 15 and an 18 year old are released as well as a Cask Strength with no age statement.

2013 A limited 35 year old is launched.

2014 A 25 year old is released.

2018 A new range for duty free is released – Cuartillo, Balbaine, a 28 year old and Glengoyne PX.

2019 Glengoyne Legacy is launched.

2020 A 50 year old and Glengoyne Legacy Chapter Two are released.

2022 The Spirit of Time series is released for travel retail.

12 years old

Tasting notes Glengoyne 12 years old:

GS – Slightly earthy on the nose, with nutty malt, ripe apples, and a hint of honey. The palate is full and fruity, with milk chocolate, ginger and vanilla. The finish is medium in length, with milky coffee and soft spices.

Glen Grant

[glen grant]

Owner: Campari Group

Region/district: Speyside

Founded: 1840

Status: Active (vc)

Capacity: 6 200 000 litres

Address: Elgin Road, Rothes, Banffshire AB38 7BS

Website: glengrant.com

Tel: 01340 832118

With the possible exceptions of Aberlour in France and The Glenlivet in USA, few Scotch malt brands have dominated a single country in the way Glen Grant did (and to some extent still does) in Italy.

The background to the popularity of Glen Grant in Italy is exciting and unorthodox. An Italian businessman and hotel owner, Armando Giovinetti, was in 1960 determined on introducing malt whisky to the Italian consumers. This was a time when malt whisky was almost unheard of and the Scotch market was dominated by blends. Giovinetti travelled to Speyside in 1961 and met with Douglas Mackessack, owner of Glen Grant and a direct descendant of the founders. Giovinetti left the distillery with an order for 50 cases of their 5 year old single malt. In 1970 he was selling 60,000 cases in Italy. Today, more than 50 years later, Italy is still one of the ten biggest export markets for single malt Scotch.

It may seem odd that Pernod Ricard let go of a large distillery like Glen Grant in 2005, producing the 4th best selling single malt at the time. A short time prior to the sale of Glen Grant, Pernod Ricard had acquired Allied Domecq, the third largest spirits company. This merger got the attention of the European Commission. The company was growing too big and competition was threatened. Pernod Ricard had already agreed to sell on Teacher´s and Laphroaig to Fortune Brands but the authorities were still not satisfied. Another sacrifice was needed. So, the French company decided to put up Glen Grant for sale as well and there was no shortage of potential buyers. The lucky winner was Campari who took over Glen Grant for the sum of 115 million Euros.

Glen Grant distillery is equipped with a 12.3 ton semi-lauter mash tun, ten Oregon pine washbacks with a minimum fermentation time of 48 hours and four pairs of stills. The wash stills are peculiar in that they have vertical sides at the base of the neck and all eight stills are fitted with purifiers. The plan for 2023 is to mash 24 times per week for 33 weeks which will result in 4 million litres of alcohol. An extremely efficient £5m bottling hall was inaugurated in 2013. It has a capacity of 12,000 bottles an hour and Glen Grant is unique among the large distillers in bottling its entire production on site.

The core range for Glen Grant is made up by **The Major's Reserve** without age statement, **Arboralis**, matured in a combination of ex-bourbon and ex-sherry, a **10 year old**, a **12 year old** matured in both bourbon and sherry casks, a **15 year old batch strength,** an **18 year old** bourbon matured and, added in early 2023, a **21 year old** aged in a combination of oloroso sherry and bourbon casks. There is currently one bottling exclusively available at the distillery – a **12 year old Peat Finish**. The oldest official bottling of Glen Grant ever appeared in autumn 2023. As a nod to Queen Elizabeth II and her 70 years on the throne, seven decanters of a **70 year old** bottled at 55,5% were released. The first decanter was auctioned via Sotheby´s and the proceeds were donated to Royal Scottish Forestry Society.

History:

1840 The brothers James and John Grant, managers of Dandelaith Distillery, found the distillery.

1861 The distillery becomes the first to install electric lighting.

1864 John Grant dies.

1872 James Grant passes away and the distillery is inherited by his son, James junior (Major James Grant).

1897 James Grant decides to build another distillery across the road; it is named Glen Grant No. 2.

1902 Glen Grant No. 2 is mothballed.

1931 Major Grant dies and is succeeded by his grandson Major Douglas Mackessack.

1953 J. & J. Grant merges with George & J. G. Smith who runs Glenlivet distillery, forming The Glenlivet & Glen Grant Distillers Ltd.

1961 Armando Giovinetti and Douglas Mackessak found a friendship that leads to Glen Grant becoming the most sold malt whisky in Italy.

1965 Glen Grant No. 2 is back in production, but renamed Caperdonich.

1972 The Glenlivet & Glen Grant Distillers merges with Hill Thompson & Co. and Longmorn-Glenlivet Ltd to form The Glenlivet Distillers.

1973 Stills are increased from four to six.

1977 The Chivas & Glenlivet Group (Seagrams) buys Glen Grant Distillery. Stills are increased from six to ten.

2001 Pernod Ricard and Diageo buy Seagrams Spirits & Wine, with Pernod acquiring Chivas Group.

History continued:

2006 Campari buys Glen Grant for €115m.

2007 The entire range is re-launched.

2008 Two limited cask strengths - a 16 year old and a 27 year old - are released.

2009 Cellar Reserve 1992 is released.

2010 A 170th Anniversary bottling is released.

2011 A 25 year old is released.

2012 A 19 year old Distillery Edition is released.

2013 Five Decades is released and a bottling hall is built.

2014 A 50 year old and the Rothes Edition 10 years old is released.

2015 Glen Grant Fiodh is launched.

2016 A 12 year old and an 18 year old are launched and a 12 year old non chill-filtered is released for travel retail.

2018 A 15 year old is released for the duty free market.

2020 Arboralis with no age statement is released.

2021 A 60 year old Dennis Malcolm Anniversary bottling is released.

2023 A 21 year old is added to the core range and a 70 year old is launched.

Tasting notes Glen Grant 12 year old:

GS – A blast of fresh fruit – oranges, pears and lemons – on the initial nose, before vanilla and fudge notes develop. The fruit carries over on to the palate, with honey, caramel and sweet spices. Medium in length, with cinnamon and soft oak in the finish.

12 years old   15 years old   21 years old

10 years old   The Major´s Reserve

Glengyle

[glen•gajl]

Owner: Mitchell's Glengyle Ltd

Region/district: Campbeltown

Founded: 2004

Status: Active

Capacity: 750 000 litres

Address: Glengyle Road, Campbeltown, Argyll PA28 6LR

Website: kilkerran.scot

Tel: 01586 551710

Originally founded in 1872 and closed in 1925 the distillery was brought back to life in 2004 by the owners of Springbank. It lies just a three minute walk from Springbank in the heart of Campbeltown.

One of the reasons for reviving the old distillery (in the old building dating back to 1872), was that the Scotch Whisky Association in 1998 had decided to stop referring to Campbeltown as a whisky region. Two distilleries (Springbank and Glen Scotia) were simply not enough. The owner of Springbank, Hedley Wright, noted that with only three distilleries, Lowland was still considered a region and so he decided to resurrect Glengyle.

The distillery is equipped with a 4.5 ton semi-lauter mash tun, two washbacks made of boat skin larch and two made of Douglas fir. The fermentation varies between 72 and 110 hours. There is also one wash still (18,000 litres) and one spirit still (15,000 litres). Malt is obtained both from the neighbouring Springbank and from external maltsters but there are also plans to install drum maltings at Glengyle. Operations between Glengyle and Springbank are managed by the same staff. The capacity is 750,000 litres, but considerably smaller amounts have been produced over the years. However, production has increased in later years and the plan for 2023 is to mash five times per week between September and December. This will amount to around 100,000 litres with 85% made up of 'regular' Kilkerran and the rest of heavily peated spirit.

The whiskies from Glengyle are always sold under the name Kilkerran. After many years of 'work in progress' bottlings, the first core **12 year old** was launched in 2016. In 2017, an **8 year old cask strength** appeared for the first time. The two latest versions in 2023 hade been fully matured in bourbon and sherry casks respectively. The first batch of **Kilkerran Heavily Peated** (with a phenol specification of 80ppm in the barley) was released in spring 2019 with batch 8 appearing in 2023. A **16 year old** was first launched in 2020 and a **17 year old** triple distilled (the oldest Kilkerran so far) was launched in connection with the 2023 Campbeltown Festival.

History:

1872 The original Glengyle Distillery is built by William Mitchell.

1919 The distillery is bought by West Highland Malt Distilleries Ltd.

1925 The distillery is closed.

1929 The warehouses (but no stock) are purchased by the Craig Brothers and rebuilt into a petrol station and garage.

1941 The distillery is acquired by the Bloch Brothers.

1957 Campbell Henderson applies for planning permission with the intention of reopening the distillery.

2000 Hedley Wright, owner of Springbank Distillery and related to founder William Mitchell, acquires the distillery.

2004 The first distillation after reconstruction takes place in March.

2007 The first limited release - a 3 year old.

2009 Kilkerran "Work in progress" is released.

2010 "Work in progress 2" is released.

2011 "Work in progress 3" is released.

2012 "Work in progress 4" is released.

2013 "Work in progress 5" is released and this time in two versions - bourbon and sherry.

2014 "Work in progress 6" is released in two versions - bourbon and sherry.

2015 "Work in progress 7" is released in two versions - bourbon and sherry.

2016 Kilkerran 12 years old is released.

2017 Kilkerran 8 year old cask strength is released.

2019 Kilkerran Heavily Peated is released.

2020 A 16 year old is released.

2021 Batch four of Heavily Peated and batch two of the 16 year old are released.

2022 Two new batches of the 8 year old cask strength are launched.

2023 New batches of the 8 year old and Heavily Peated are released.

Tasting notes Kilkerran 12 year old:

GS – Initially, quite reticent on the nose, then peaty fruit notes develop. Oily and full on the palate, with peaches and more overt smoke, plus an earthy quality. Castor oil and liquorice sticks. Slick in the medium-length finish, with slightly drying oak and enduring liquorice.

12 years old

An inside comment on...

The State of Whisky

Sukhinder Singh
Whisky Hall of Fame inductee No. 85
Co-owner, Elixir Distillers

What was your objective for entering the whisky business?

I started collecting miniatures at an early age, I had very little money so had to start buying and selling minis to support my hobby. After University, I could not find a job so decided to work for my parents for a year. I fell in love with the business and especially whisky. Soon after I started collecting full size bottles, working in the business helped my understand of the industry, by talking to suppliers, visiting distilleries and making contacts.

What would you say are the best ways to attract new, young whisky consumers?

The new consumers are very social media conscious. Whisky has become hugely popular, and it is in the media all the time. This certainly has helped the industry. Consumers today are more open to trying flavours from around the world as we have seen in cuisine, similarly they are open to whiskies from around the world. With so many distilleries doing different things to innovate there is something for everyone.

Can one whisky, objectively, be better than the other? Isn´t it all down to your personal taste and preferences?

There are of course good and not so good whiskies. Overall, I would say whisky is more consistent in terms of quality today than 10 years ago. Taste is such a personal thing, and this is why we like different foods, in a similar way we like some whiskies more than others. A simple example is where some consumers prefer sherry matured whiskies over bourbon casks. I also go through phases and currently I am more in tune with malts matured in ex bourbon and refill casks.

Do you feel there is enough innovation in the whisky business and is there still a place for preserving and honouring traditional methods?

In some ways I believe that brands are trying to innovate too much, mainly in terms of different wood finishing, and some have actually forgotten how to make good clean traditional style whisky! There is too much focus on the more sherried style of whiskies and not enough of the good, old fashioned style from ex bourbon and refill casks. Fortunately, Scotland is still heavily regulated, and this certainly helps to maintain the traditional methods. Outside Scotland, where rules are more relaxed, distillers could do a lot more in terms of innovation including England. A lot of the English distillers have played it safe and are pretty much producing whisky similar to that of Scotland.

What ever line of business you´re in, sustainability is on every company´s agenda. Do you feel the whisky industry is at the forefront or could things happen faster?

It is extremely important, and everyone seems to be doing their share, especially the larger distilleries. However, there needs to be a balance between change for the better and maintaining the quality of the product. Some companies seem to be going too far as sustainability has become a key marketing strategy and they seem to be in the news every two minutes for what they are up to, rather than the quality of their whisky. I feel our industry still has a long way to go, there are just too many challenges to make this happen. Just looking at the sources of energy to run a distillery, most distillers are using some sort of gas or oil. Clean fuel like hydrogen is expensive to implement and there is little infrastructure around its supply.

Investing in whisky has become more and more popular. Is that a good or a bad thing?

Around 20 years ago when single malts were becoming popular, most people bought them to drink. The few that did collect also drank whisky and there was a good balance between drinking and collecting. As demand outstripped supply, whisky became investable, but this was mostly led by the bigger names that released a variety of expressions. What changed is that the other distillers saw the potential of single malts over their core blended whisky business and jumped on the wagon to focus more on this newer, growing sector. As whisky became more and more popular, more and more expressions were launched and at some point, collectability and packaging became more important than the liquid itself. Now that we are in the midst of some sort of a recession, people have less income to spend on whisky and prices in the secondary have started dropping but the important thing to note is that only the so called collectors bottles are down in value. The good drinking whiskies are still in short supply and their prices are holding strong.

I´m sometimes reminded that the readers of the Malt Whisky Yearbook – usually well informed but eager to learn more – represent a miniscule part of the whisky consumers around the world. How important would you say that small consumer segment is for the producers?

That small segment is what I am a part of, and I sometimes feel upset when I see some of the larger brands changing direction from making just good tasting whisky, to making products for the new global mass consumer as well as the high-net-worth individuals. Fortunately, there are hundreds of producers to make it still interesting and it keeps us busy on the chase for the next great whisky.

With young people sometimes questioning the use of alcohol and others exchanging it for cannabis or other drugs – do you feel whisky is still relevant for Generation Z (born 1997-2012)?

I believe that whisky drunk in moderation is a part of life that will never disappear. It is superb and in most parts an honest product with a complexity of flavours that no other category can deliver. There are more younger consumers than ever before. In last year's Whisky Show we had 30% new customers and most were under 35.

As opposed to thirty years ago, whisky today is produced in a huge number of countries around the world. How would you say that has affected the category/industry as a whole?

As more countries produce whisky, this becomes a part of marketing for the category. Consumers today are open to food and drink from around the world, seeking new products and flavours. The Scotch industry is probably the one that has most befitted from this but they also need to watch out as many countries today are producing similar products to Scotland and in some cases much better.

Please describe your perfect time and place for a dram.

I love drinking whisky in my office! I am comfortable with the environment and have plenty of great products to hand. The perfect time is when you are in fine company and share a similar passion.

Glen Keith

[glen keeth]

Owner:		Region/district:
Chivas Brothers (Pernod Ricard)		Speyside

Founded:	Status:	Capacity:
1957	Active	6 000 000 litres

Address: Station Road, Keith, Banffshire AB55 3BU

Website:	Tel:
secret-speyside.com	01542 783042

The mixed history of Glen Keith distillery has more to it than meets the eye. It was one of only three malt distilleries to open in the 1950s, Tormore and Lochside being the other two.

With sales of Scotch whisky entering into a golden age in the years following the end of the second world war, it seems surprising that the building boom of new distilleries didn´t happen until the sixties and early seventies. The decision of turning an old mill in Keith into a distillery came from a man who had seen first hand how the demand for Scotch whisky was growing in the USA. It was Sam Bronfman, owner and chairman of Seagrams.

Born in Russia, Bronfman came to America in 1889. Together with his brothers and merging with the established player Seagrams, he built a spirits conglomerate which would have a huge impact for decades on the whisky business worldwide. Eventually he bought Chivas Brothers in Scotland and this is where Glen Keith comes into the picture. He wanted a light whisky for the growing American market and Glen Keith was the distillery that was destined to supply malt for the new blend 100 Pipers.

Glen Keith is equipped with a Briggs 8.4 ton full lauter mash tun. There are three tun rooms with three wooden washbacks in number one, another six wooden in number two and six made of stainless steel in the third together with the mash tun. Finally there are six stills with unusually long, slightly descending lyne arms. The production is usually between 38 and 41 mashes per week with the possibility to produce 6 million litres of pure alcohol.

Whisky enthusiasts have started to take an interest in Glen Keith single malt but until recently they've had to rely on independent bottlers. In 2017 the official **Distillery Edition**, exclusive to the UK market was released. Two years later, Chivas launched The **Secret Speyside Collection** where Glen Keith is represented by **21, 25** and **28 years old**. Finally, there is a 22 year old cask strength bottling in the Distillery Reserve Collection, available at all Chivas visitor centres.

History:

1957 The Distillery is founded by Chivas Brothers (Seagrams).

1958 Production starts.

1970 The first gas-fuelled still in Scotland is installed, the number of stills increases from three to five.

1976 Own maltings (Saladin box) ceases.

1983 A sixth still is installed.

1994 The first official bottling, a 10 year old, is released as part of Seagram's Heritage Selection.

1999 The distillery is mothballed.

2001 Pernod Ricard takes over Chivas Brothers from Seagrams.

2012 The reconstruction and refurbishing of the distillery begins.

2013 Production starts again.

2017 A Distillery Edition is launched.

2019 Three bottlings in The Secret Speyside Collection are launched.

Tasting notes Glen Keith Distillery Edition:

IR – Sweet and fruity on the nose with notes of toffee and apples. Smooth on the palate, vanilla, tropical fruits, marzipan, sponge cake, honey, pears and a hint of dry oak in the finish.

Distillery Edition

Glenkinchie

[glen•kin•chee]

Owner: **Region/district:**
Diageo   Lowlands

Founded: **Status:**   **Capacity:**
1837   Active (vc)   2 500 000 litres

Address: Pencaitland, Tranent,
East Lothian EH34 5ET

Website: **Tel:**
malts.com   01875 342004

In the past, visitors to Edinburgh wishing to visit a whisky distillery nearby, had one choice – Glenkinchie a 30 minute drive from the city. Today there are three distilleries in the city itself.

However, if you wish to visit a distillery with an almost 200 year old history, it's definitely worthwhile taking the trip to Glenkinchie. The visitor centre was completely refurbished and expanded in 2020 and a large part of the focus is on the importance of Glenkinchie malt for the Johnnie Walker blend. The fact that Glenkinchie is situated in Lothian, often referred to as Scotland's garden county, is also emphasized by a large landscaped garden with an orchard and specially selected plants native to East Lothian.

When Glenkinchie was founded in 1815 there were 155 distilleries in the Lowlands! In the beginning of the new millenium, there were only two malt distilleries left – Auchentoshan and Glenkinchie. Things have changed dramatically and today there are 20 distilleries operating in the region. There are two reasons for Glenkinchie having survived as a distillery when so many others were closed. One was the formation of Scottish Malt Distillers with four other distilleries which took it through the hard years after the First World War. The other is the fact that it was selected one of six Classic Malts in 1988.

The distillery is equipped with a 9 ton full lauter mash tun and six wooden washbacks with a combination of short (66 hours) and long fermentations (110 hours). There are two stills where the wash still has the biggest charge in Scotland – 21,000 litres. The spirit vapours are condensed in a cast iron worm tub. The production regime during 2023 will be a five-day week with 10 mashes, producing just under 2 million litres of alcohol.

The core range consists of a **12 year old** and a **Distiller's Edition** with a finish in amontillado sherry casks. A limited **16 year old** available only at the distillery was released in 2020. In autumn 2023 a **27 year old**, matured in a combination of refill American barrels and European oak butts, appeared in the Special Releases range.

History:

1825 A distillery known as Milton is founded by John and George Rate.

1837 The Rate brothers are registered as licensees of a distillery named Glenkinchie.

1853 John Rate sells the distillery to a farmer by the name of Christie who converts it to a sawmill.

1881 The buildings are bought by a consortium from Edinburgh.

1890 Glenkinchie Distillery Company is founded. Reconstruction and refurbishment is on-going for the next few years.

1914 Glenkinchie forms Scottish Malt Distillers (SMD) with four other Lowland distilleries.

1939- 1945 Glenkinchie is one of few distilleries allowed to maintain production during the war.

1968 Floor maltings is decommissioned.

1969 The maltings is converted into a museum.

1988 Glenkinchie 10 years becomes one of selected six in the Classic Malt series.

1998 A Distiller's Edition with Amontillado finish is launched.

2007 A 12 year old and a 20 year old cask strength are released.

2010 A cask strength exclusive for the visitor centre, a 1992 single cask and a 20 year old are released.

2016 A 24 year old and a distillery exclusive without age statement are released.

2019 A limited version is released in connection with The Royal Edinburgh Military Tattoo.

2020 A new visitor experience is opened and a 16 year old distillery exclusive is released.

2023 A 27 year old is released as part of this year´s Special Releases

12 years old

Tasting notes Glenkinchie 12 years old:

GS – The nose is fresh and floral, with spices and citrus fruits, plus a hint of marshmallow. Notably elegant. Water releases cut grass and lemon notes. Medium-bodied, smooth, sweet and fruity, with malt, butter and cheesecake. The finish is comparatively long and drying, initially rather herbal.

Glenlivet

[glen•liv•it]

Owner: Chivas Brothers (Pernod Ricard)

Region/district: Speyside

Founded: 1824

Status: Active (vc)

Capacity: 21 000 000 litres

Address: Ballindalloch, Banffshire AB37 9DB

Website: theglenlivet.com

Tel: 01340 821720 (vc)

The two-step expansion of Glenlivet distillery made it the largest malt distillery in the world together with Glenfiddich. There are two reasons why the owners increased the production capacity.

An obvious one is that sales of Glenlivet single malt has increased radically in the last decade and for at least two years now Glenlivet has been the best selling single malt globally (just over 20 million bottles in 2022). The other reason is that Chivas Brothers is also very much a blended whisky company. Number two and three on the top list (after Johnnie Walker) are Ballantine´s and Chivas Regal. If you add Passport, 100 Pipers and Clan Campbell (recently sold to Stock Spirits), the top five blends from Chivas Brothers have increased their combined volumes in the last decade by 33% to reach 240 million bottles in 2022. Even though Chivas has other large distilleries providing malt for their blends, Glenlivet is still an important contributor.

In 2002 Alan Winchester became the Chivas Brothers distilling manager which meant that he had the production responsibilities for all the company´s distilleries – at that time seventeen. In 2018 he stepped back from the production duties but remained as The Glenlivet Master Distiller. In 2022 he retired from the company but like many other Scotch whisky icons he cannot loosen his grip on the industry. With his long experience he's been an important part of starting up the Cabrach Trust distillery south of Dufftown

Since 2009 the distillery capacity has been expanded in two steps from 5.8 million litres to the current 21 million. The last step, completed in 2018, was a second distillery at the back of the warehouses. The current complete equipment at Glenlivet consists of two Briggs full lauter mash tuns, each with a 14 ton charge. Sixteen wooden washbacks are complemented by 16 made of stainless steel in the new distillery – all filled with 59,000 litres and with a fermentation time of 50-52 hours. Fourteen pairs of stills with tall necks, long lyne arms and narrow waists are divided into three different rooms.

The core range is made up of **Founder's Reserve, Captain's Reserve** with a finish in cognac casks, **Caribbean Reserve** finished in rum casks, **12 year old Double Oak, 15 year old French Oak Reserve**, and an **18 year old.** There is also a **14 year old cognac finish** exclusive to the American market. The classic 21 year old Archive and Glenlivet XXV were in summer 2022 replaced by two new versions which form The Sample Room Collection. The **21 year old** is triple finished in casks that have held oloroso, cognac and vintage port while the **25 year old** has a finish in PX casks and cognac. The travel retail range includes **Triple Cask Distiller's Reserve, Triple Cask White Oak Reserve** and **Triple Cask Rare Cask**. Recent limited expressions include the **12 year old Licensed Dram**, matured in a combination of first fill European oak sherry casks and first fill American bourbon casks. There is also Cask Finished Edition where a **20 year old rum finish** and a **9 year old finished in Innis & Gunn quarter casks** were the latest.

History:
1817 George Smith inherits the farm distillery Upper Drumin.
1840 George Smith buys Delnabo farm near Tomintoul and leases Cairngorm Distillery.
1845 George Smith leases three other farms, one of which is situated on the river Livet and is called Minmore.
1846 William Smith develops tuberculosis and his brother John Gordon moves back home to assist his father.
1858 George Smith buys Minmore farm and obtains permission to build a distillery.
1859 Upper Drummin and Cairngorm close and all equipment is brought to Minmore which is renamed The Glenlivet Distillery.
1871 George Smith dies and his son John Gordon takes over.
1880 John Gordon Smith applies for and is granted sole rights to the name The Glenlivet.
1890 A fire breaks out and some of the buildings are replaced.
1901 John Gordon Smith dies.
1904 John Gordon's nephew George Smith Grant takes over.
1921 Captain Bill Smith Grant, son of George Smith Grant, takes over.
1953 George & J. G. Smith Ltd merges with J. & J. Grant of Glen Grant Distillery and forms the company Glenlivet & Glen Grant Distillers.
1966 Floor maltings closes.
1970 Glenlivet & Glen Grant Distillers Ltd merges with Longmorn-Glenlivet Distilleries Ltd and Hill Thomson & Co. Ltd to form The Glenlivet Distillers Ltd.
1978 Seagrams buys The Glenlivet Distillers Ltd. A visitor centre opens.
2000 French Oak 12 years and American Oak 12 years are launched

History continued:

2001 Pernod Ricard and Diageo buy Seagram Spirits & Wine. Pernod Ricard thereby gains control of the Chivas group.

2004 This year sees a lavish relaunch of Glenlivet. French Oak 15 years replaces the previous 12 year old.

2005 The Glenlivet 12 year old First Fill and Nadurra are launched.

2007 Glenlivet XXV is released.

2009 Four more stills are installed and Nadurra Triumph 1991 is released.

2010 Another two stills are commissioned and Glenlivet Founder´s Reserve is released.

2011 Glenlivet Master Distiller´s Reserve is released for the duty free market.

2012 1980 Cellar Collection is released.

2013 The 18 year old Batch Reserve and Glenlivet Alpha are released.

2014 Nadurra Oloroso, Nadurra First Fill Selection, The Glenlivet Guardian´s Chapter and a 50 year old are released.

2015 Founder´s Reserve is released as well as Solera Vatted and Small Batch.

2016 The Glenlivet Cipher and the second edition of the 50 year old are launched.

2018 Captain´s Reserve and Code are released. A new distillery is commissioned.

2019 Enigma and a 14 year old cognac finish are released.

2020 Spectra, Carribean Reserve and Illicit Still are released.

2021 The Licensed Dram is released.

2022 The Sample Room Collection is launched.

Tasting notes Glenlivet 12 year old:

GS – A lovely, honeyed, floral, fragrant nose. Medium-bodied, smooth and malty on the palate, with vanilla sweetness. Not as sweet as the nose might suggest. The finish is pleasantly lengthy and sophisticated.

Distiller´s Reserve

Illicit Still 12 years old

Carribean Reserve

21 years old   25 years old

Founder´s Reserve

12 years old   18 years old

Glenlossie

[glen•loss•ee]

Owner: **Region/district:**
Diageo   Speyside

Founded: **Status:**   **Capacity:**
1876   Active   3 700 000 litres

Address: Birnie, Elgin, Morayshire IV30 8SS

Website: **Tel:**
malts.com   01343 862000

When a distillery is working 5 days per week it usually means that some of the fermentations will be long, i. e. the wash will continue to ferment over the closed weekend before being distilled.

A continuous seven-day production, however, entails that all fermentation times are the same. During the past decade Glenlossie has been alternating between 5 and 7 days but at the same time the oily/green character is dependent on a mix of short and long fermentations. The problem to be solved was how one could achieve some longer fermentations even during a 7-day production. The solution back in 2019 was to add another two washbacks. The distillery was temporarily closed from January to August 2023. Production was re-started with 12 mashes per week and then ramped up to 18 mashes including both short (65 hours) and long (106 hours) fermentations.

Together with Glenkinchie and Linkwood, Glenlossie is one of the major contributors to the Haig Gold Label blend. In terms of sales the brand is a far cry from the heydays of the 1970s when more than 30 million bottles were sold. Today (with 3 million bottles) it is not even amongst the 30 most sold Scotch. India, where it was first introduced in 2006, is one of its strongest markets.

Glenlossie is equipped with an eight ton stainless steel full lauter mash tun, eight washbacks made of larch and two, placed outdoors, made of stainless steel. There are three wash stills (15,800 litres) and three spirit stills (13,500 litres), all with horizontal lyne arms and equipped with purifiers. During the last couple of years, the distillery has been mashing 12 times per week producing 2 million litres of alcohol.

To come across a wider variety of Glenlossie single malt, one needs to look at independent bottlers, not least The Scotch Malt Whisky Society which has released more 120 single casks. The only official bottling of Glenlossie single malt available today is a **10 year old Flora & Fauna**.

History:

1876 John Duff, former manager at Glendronach Distillery, founds the distillery. Alexander Grigor Allan (to become part-owner of Talisker Distillery), the whisky trader George Thomson and Charles Shirres (both will co-found Longmorn Distillery some 20 years later with John Duff) and H. Mackay are also involved in the company.

1895 The company Glenlossie-Glenlivet Distillery Co. is formed. Alexander Grigor Allan passes away.

1896 John Duff becomes more involved in Longmorn and Mackay takes over management of Glenlossie.

1919 Distillers Company Limited (DCL) takes over the company.

1929 A fire breaks out and causes considerable damage.

1930 DCL transfers operations to Scottish Malt Distillers (SMD).

1962 Stills are increased from four to six.

1971 Another distillery, Mannochmore, is constructed by SMD on the premises. A dark grains plant is installed.

1990 A 10 year old is launched in the Flora & Fauna series.

2010 A Manager´s Choice single cask from 1999 is released.

10 years old

Tasting notes Glenlossie 10 years old:

GS – Cereal, silage and vanilla notes on the relatively light nose, with a voluptuous, sweet palate, offering plums, ginger and barley sugar, plus a hint of oak. The finish is medium in length, with grist and slightly peppery oak.

An inside comment on...

The State of Whisky

Patrick Maguire
Whisky Hall of Fame inductee No. 50
Director at Maguire & Co Distillery,
ex Sullivans Cove Distillery

What was your objective for entering the whisky business?

To start with, I like whisky! At the time, there was no Australian whisky available, there was a gap in the market. I saw it as an opportunity to be a part of creating something that consumers would hopefully, one day, like and appreciate. This was new territory for Tasmania, I had no idea at the time that we could achieve that outcome which made the challenge all the more attractive.

What would you say are the best ways to attract new, young whisky consumers?

It starts with producing a quality whisky. One that is created with quality in mind from the outset. Using local ingredients, brewed and distilled with attention to detail and bottled when its ready, not just because it reached a certain age. From there it's a matter of letting your potential customers know what you are creating and how you are creating it. Younger whisky consumers tend to drink less but better quality. They are an educated group that like to know how the things they consume are made, the ingredients used and where they come from. It's important to them, so include them on the journey from the start. They want to know the whisky they are buying matches their values. Participate in whisky shows and let them taste it. Talking about it is OK but getting them to taste it is more effective.

Can one whisky, objectively, be better than the other? Isn't it all down to your personal taste and preferences?

Personal taste is a powerful thing, if you like it, drink it, your taste buds can't be wrong. For me, to really enjoy a whisky, it's more than just the taste, it has to have the structure to support and carry the flavours. Structure means viscosity, balance, length. Not all whiskies have that. Those that do, in my opinion are better than those that don't.

Do you feel there is enough innovation in the whisky business and is there still a place for preserving and honouring traditional methods?

I hope there will always be a place for preserving and honouring what we know as "traditional methods". After all, it's the traditional whiskies that have attracted us all along. Thinking about it though, there has always been innovation in whisky. From its humble beginnings in Ireland to the giant global industry it has become. Some use peat, others don't. The casks used have varied over the years depending on availability. Different toasting and charring regimes have developed. Some countries use corn, others wheat, rye or other grains depending on availability. In Australia, we are exploring the use of wine casks and some are exploring local timbers. Others are experimenting with alternative materials to create smoke when malting. Distilling has been an evolution over hundreds of years. I imagine that will always continue.

What ever line of business you're in, sustainability is on every company's agenda. Do you feel the whisky industry is at the forefront or could things happen faster?

Things could always happen faster however I believe the distilling industry is right up there with sustainable thinking and implementation. Distilleries globally that are investing in renewable energy and consumption reduction as any business does. Some are creating energy from their waste products. Many are reducing or stopping the use of plastics with their packaging. Sourcing ingredients from local growers and manufacturers to reduce carbon miles is high on the agenda. There is a lot happening in this space, it's exciting and it's gathering pace.

Investing in whisky has become more and more popular. Is that a good or a bad thing?

It can be a good thing if its managed effectively. A good way for startup distilleries to fund capex and growth. It can also be a good way for whisky enthusiasts to get more involved in the making of it. However it's a long term investment which doesn't suit everyone.

I'm sometimes reminded that the readers of the Malt Whisky Yearbook – usually well informed but eager to learn more – represent a miniscule part of the whisky consumers around the world. How important would you say that small consumer segment is for the producers?

For me the small consumer segment is very important. There are whisky enthusiasts everywhere and their enthusiasm is catching. They want to know everything and anything about distilleries, their whiskies and the people behind them. They love tasting new brands and every edition issued. They turn up to whisky events and are happy to talk endlessly about whisky. These are the people that the less enthusiastic whisky consumers talk to to find out what is new and what is good in the whisky world. We can't live without them.

With young people sometimes questioning the use of alcohol and others exchanging it for cannabis or other drugs – do you feel whisky is still relevant for Generation Z (born 1997-2012)?

Humans seem to need something to take the edge off. And I think it's good that people question the consumption of alcohol. However to replace it with other drugs may not be for everyone either. I think there will always be a place for alcohol (including good whisky) and there will always be alternatives.

As opposed to thirty years ago, whisky today is produced in a huge number of countries around the world. How would you say that has affected the category/industry as a whole?

The global expansion of whisky production has shaken up the whisky world. That's a good thing. Whisky is enjoying a massive resurgence of popularity because of it. It's not just whisky. Boutique beers, wines and spirits are in growing demand as consumers have become more interested and discerning about the things they drink and eat. For a lot of people now, it's not the cheapest or the largest volume they are interested in, it's consume less but better quality. Variety is the spice of life and it's exciting to see how different regions express their version of what whisky is.

Please describe your perfect time and place for a dram.

My perfect time and place for a dram is kicking back with friends at the end of the day on the couch at home or on the boat at anchor somewhere. As long there is peace and quiet and I'm not distracted from just enjoying the dram at hand.

Glenmorangie

[glen•mor•run•jee]

Owner:
The Glenmorangie Co
(Moët Hennessy)

Region/district:
Northern Highlands

Founded:
1843

Status:
Active (vc)

Capacity:
7 100 000 litres

Address: Tain, Ross-shire IV19 1PZ

Website:
glenmorangie.com

Tel:
01862 892477 (vc)

Glenmorangie single malt is the third best selling single malt in the UK and number four on the global list. Together with Talisker it is the single malt that has increased the most in terms of volumes in the past five years.

In 2021 that meant 8.3 million bottles in worldwide sales, which means it has a bit of a climb to do before it reaches the volume of current number three – Macallan. Still, it was a record year for the brand and the sister distillery on Islay, Ardbeg, also sold in record numbers under 2021.

In February 2022 an extension to the distillery, named the Lighthouse, was commissioned. This was to fulfill the need of having an experimental plant on site where trials can be conducted without interfering with the general production. It is equipped with a one ton mash tun but there is also a mash conversion vessel that can handle more complex mash bills. Furthermore, there are two 5,000 litre wash backs and one pair of stills. Other features include a water jacket on the spirit still and it is also equipped with both copper and stainless steel condensers.

The Glenmorangie main distillery is equipped with a full lauter mash tun with a charge that used to be 10.3 tons but since 2023 has increased to 11.5 tons. High gravity mashing (1070 OG), with more barley and less water loaded in the mash tun, lies behind that. The fruity character is still maintained with all the esters coming through but less energy is used to heat water. There are also 12 stainless steel washbacks with a fermentation time of 52 hours and six pairs of stills. The production plan for 2023 is 34 mashes per week and to make around 7.1 million litres of pure alcohol. On site are also 18 warehouses (four dunnage, six racked and eight palletised) but within the next eight years there are plans to build another 16 warehouses at the old Fearn airfield south-east of the distillery.

The core range consists of **Original** (10 year old) and **18 year old**. There are three wood finishes: **Quinta Ruban**, a 14 year old which has been finished in a combination of 225 litre ruby barriques and 670 litre ruby pipes. **Lasanta** is 12 years old with a finish in a combination of oloroso casks (75%) and PX sherry casks (25%). Finally, there is **Nectar D'Or** with no age statement that has been finished in Sauternes casks. Added to the core range is **Signet**, an unusual piece of work with 20% of the whisky made using chocolate malt. A new addition to the core range, designed for mixing with for example tonic, soda, cola or ginger ale, appeared in 2021 when **X by Glenmorangie** was released.

Recent limited releases include the third and fourth installment in the Barrel Select range (introduced in 2021); **Palo Cortado** and **Amontillado**, both 12 years old and finished in the respective sherry casks. In autumn 2022 **A Tale of the Forest** (infused with botanicals during the kilning process) was released. For travel retail there are 12 year old **The Accord**, 14 year old **The Elementa**, 16 year old **The Tribute** and a **19 year old**.

History:

1843 William Mathesen applies for a license for a farm distillery called Morangie, which is rebuilt by them. Production took place here in 1738, and possibly since 1703.

1849 Production starts in November.

1887 The distillery is rebuilt and Glenmorangie Distillery Company Ltd is formed.

1918 40% of the distillery is sold to Macdonald & Muir Ltd and 60 % to the whisky dealer Durham. Macdonald & Muir takes over Durham's share by the late thirties.

1931 The distillery closes.

1936 Production restarts in November.

1980 Number of stills increases from two to four and own maltings ceases.

1990 The number of stills is doubled to eight.

1994 A visitor centre opens. Glenmorangie Port Wood Finish is released.

1995 Glenmorangie´s Tain l´Hermitage is launched.

1996 Two different wood finishes are launched, Madeira and Sherry. Glenmorangie plc is formed.

2001 Cask strength port wood finish, Cote de Beaune Wood Finish and Three Cask (ex-Bourbon, charred oak and ex-Rioja) are launched.

2002 A 20 year old Sauternes finish is launched.

2003 Burgundy Wood Finish and cask strength Madeira-matured are released.

2004 Glenmorangie buys the Scotch Malt Whisky Society. The Macdonald family decides to sell Glenmorangie plc (including the distilleries Glenmorangie, Glen Moray and Ardbeg) to Moët Hennessy at £300 million. A new version of Glenmorangie Tain l´Hermitage (28 years) is released as well as Glenmorangie Artisan Cask.

History continued:

2005 A 30 year old is launched.

2007 The entire range gets a complete makeover with 15 and 30 year olds being discontinued and the rest given new names and packaging.

2008 Astar and Signet are launched.

2009 Sonnalta PX is released for duty free.

2010 Glenmorangie Finealta is released.

2011 28 year old Glenmorangie Pride is released.

2012 Glenmorangie Artein is released.

2013 Glenmorangie Ealanta is released.

2014 Companta, Taghta and Dornoch are released.

2015 Túsail and Duthac are released.

2016 Milsean, Tayne and Tarlogan are released.

2017 Bacalta, Astar and Pride 1974 are released.

2018 Spios, Cadboll and Grand Vintage Malt 1989 and 1993 are released.

2019 Allta, Cask 1784 and Grand Vintage Malt 1991 are launched.

2020 A new range of travel retail exclusives is released as well as the 26 year Truffle Oak, Grand Vintage Malt 1996 and A Tale of Cake.

2021 X by Glenmorangie, Grand Vintage Malt 1997, a 13 year old cognac finish, Signet Ristretto and Tale of Winter are launched.

2022 A Tale of Forest and Barrel Select Palo Cortado are released. An experimental distillery is commissioned.

2023 Barrel Select Amontillado is released.

Tasting notes Glenmorangie Original 10 year old:

GS – The nose offers fresh fruits, butterscotch and toffee. Silky smooth in the mouth, mild spice, vanilla, and well-defined toffee. The fruity finish has a final flourish of ginger.

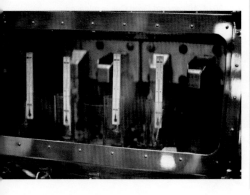

A Tale of Forest   The Elementa   Barrel Select Amontillado

Original 10 years old   La Santa   X by Glenmorangie

Glen Moray

[glen mur•ree]

Owner:
La Martiniquaise (COFEPP)

Region/district:
Speyside

Founded: 1897

Status: Active (vc)

Capacity: 8 500 000 litres

Address: Bruceland Road, Elgin,
Morayshire IV30 1YE

Website:
glenmoray.com

Tel:
01343 542577

When La Martiniquaise took over Glen Moray in 2008, the distillery had a capacity of just 2.2 million litres of alcohol. Within a couple of years another one million litres had been added to that.

A major refurbishing was completed in spring 2016, including installing a new mashtun, which made it possible to produce 5.7 million litres. But already then the company had even grander plans for the Elgin-based distillery. During part of 2023 Glen Moray has resembled a building site when another five washbacks were added. The old mashtun was also refurbished and put to use again and later in the year a fourth wash still was added to the setup. When all the equipment is in place the distillery will have an impressive capacity of 8.5 million litres which makes it one of the 10 largest malt distilleries in Scotland.

The extra capacity is needed. Sales of Glen Moray have grown rapidly and totalled 2.2 million bottles in 2021. On top of that, La Martiniquaise have three major blends in their portfolio demanding more malt whisky. Label 5, Sir Edward´s and Cutty Sark showed combined sales of 58 million bottles in 2022.

The "new" Glen Moray will be equipped with a 10.1 ton full lauter mash tun and a 6 ton semilauter tun. There are 21 stainless steel washbacks placed outside with a fermentation time of 58 hours. Finally there will be ten stills (four wash and six spirit). In 2022, the owners mashed 27 times per week and produced 5 million litres of alcohol. Usually, a small batch of peated newmake (48ppm in the barley) is made every year.

An extensive core range consists of **Classic, Classic Port Finish, Classic Chardonnay Finish, Classic Sherry Finish, Classic Cabernet Sauvignon Finish** and **Classic Peated** as well as **10 year old Fired Oak, 12, 15, 18 year old** and **21 year old portwood finish**. In spring 2023, the cognac-matured **Twisted Vine** was added to the range. The limited Warehouse 1 Collection made its debut in 2021 with three expressions and in 2022 another three bottlings were released; **Amarone Finish, Amontillado Finish** and **Oloroso Full Maturation**.

History:

1897 Elgin West Brewery, dated 1830, is reconstructed as Glen Moray Distillery.

1910 The distillery closes.

1920 Financial troubles force the distillery to be put up for sale. Buyer is Macdonald & Muir.

1923 Production restarts.

1958 A reconstruction takes place and the floor maltings are replaced by a Saladin box.

1978 Own maltings are terminated.

1979 Number of stills is increased to four.

1996 Macdonald & Muir Ltd changes name to Glenmorangie plc.

1999 Three wood finishes are introduced - Chardonnay (no age) and Chenin Blanc (12 and 16 years respectively).

2004 Louis Vuitton Moët Hennessy buys Glenmorangie plc and a 1986 cask strength, a 20 and a 30 year old are released.

2006 Two vintages, 1963 and 1964, and a new Manager's Choice are released.

2007 New edition of Mountain Oak is released.

2008 The distillery is sold to La Martiniquaise.

2009 A 14 year old Port finish and an 8 year old matured in red wines casks are released.

2011 Two cask finishes and a 10 year old Chardonnay maturation are released.

2012 A 2003 Chenin Blanc is released.

2013 A 25 year old port finish is released.

2014 Glen Moray Classic Port Finish is released.

2015 Glen Moray Classic Peated is released.

2016 Classic Chardonnay Finish and Classic Sherry Finish are released as well as a 15 and an 18 year old.

2017 Glen Moray Mastery is launched.

2018 10 year old Fired Oak is released.

2019 Glen Moray Rhum Agricole is released.

2020 A 13 year old Madeira Cask is released.

2021 A 30 year old sherry finish and a 14 year old matured in Sauternes casks are launched.

2022 Batch 2 of the Warehouse 1 Collection is released.

2023 Twisted Vine is launched.

Tasting notes Glen Moray 12 years old:

GS – Mellow on the nose, with vanilla, pear drops and some oak. Smooth in the mouth, with spicy malt, vanilla and summer fruits. The finish is relatively short, with spicy fruit.

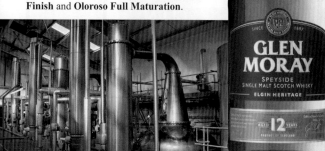

12 years old

Glen Ord

[glen <u>ord</u>]

Owner:	**Region/district:**
Diageo	Northern Highlands
Founded: **Status:**	**Capacity:**
1838 Active (vc)	11 900 000 litres

Address: Muir of Ord, Ross-shire IV6 7UJ

Website:	**Tel:**
malts.com	01463 872004 (vc)

One of the tours at the newly refurbished Glen Ord visitor centre is the Malt to Cask Tour. Apart from a walk around the distillery and a tasting of the Glen Ord range it includes a visit to the adjacent maltings.

In the early 1900s, virtually all the Scottish malt distilleries had their own floor maltings – the traditional way of malting your barley on site. As time progressed, distilleries started to buy their malt from large, commercial maltsters. Today there are only eight distilleries practicing floor malting. Glen Ord however is the only distillery (together with Port Ellen due to reopen in 2023) that has a much larger and more efficient malting operation on site.

The drum maltings were installed in 1968 and today there are 18 drums and four kilns. The total capacity is 45,000 tons per year and, apart for their own need, they produce malt mainly for Talisker. Currently, with most of the distilleries in Scotland running at full capacity, malted barley has become a bottleneck. A fire at Crisp Maltings in Portgordon in spring 2022 added to the problem. Having two larger maltings within the company obviously gives Diageo the edge. When the Singleton brand was introduced in 2006, Glen Ord already had devoted fans. Within the trio of Singleton single malts (Dufftown and Glendullan being the other two), Glen Ord is still the star in terms of sales figures and the brand is targeted towards the Asian market.

Glen Ord is equipped with two stainless steel, full lauter mashtuns, each with a 12.5 ton mash. There are 22 wooden washbacks, allowing for a capacity of 55,000 litres and with a fermentation time of 75 hours. Three wash stills and three spirit stills can be found in still house No. 1 facing the road while the eight latest stills to be installed are all in a new building.

The core range is the **Singleton of Glen Ord 12, 15** and **18 year old**. The duty free range consists of **Signature, Trinité, Liberté** and **Artisan**. Recent limited bottlings include three of substantial age (**38, 39** and **40 year old**). In autumn 2023 a **40 year old** was released – the last in the Epicurean Odyssey Series and with an astonishingly long second maturation (28 years) in Ron Zacapa casks.

History:

1838 Thomas Mackenzie founds the distillery.
1855 Alexander MacLennan and Thomas McGregor buy the distillery.
1870 Alexander MacLennan dies and the distillery is taken over by his widow who marries the banker Alexander Mackenzie.
1877 Alexander Mackenzie leases the distillery.
1878 Alexander Mackenzie builds a new still house and barely manages to start production before a fire destroys it.
1896 Alexander Mackenzie dies and the distillery is sold to James Watson & Co. for £15,800.
1923 John Jabez Watson, James Watson's son, dies and the distillery is sold to John Dewar & Sons. The name changes from Glen Oran to Glen Ord.
1961 A Saladin box is installed.
1966 The two stills are increased to six.
1968 Drum maltings is built.
1983 Malting in the Saladin box ceases.
1988 A visitor centre is opened.
2002 A 12 year old is launched.
2005 A 30 year old is launched.
2006 A 12 year old Singleton of Glen Ord is launched.
2010 A Singleton of Glen Ord 15 year old is released in Taiwan.
2012 Singleton of Glen Ord cask strength is released.
2013 Singleton of Glen Ord Signature, Trinité, Liberté and Artisan are launched.
2015 The Master´s Casks 40 years old is released.
2017 A 41 year old reserved for Asia is released.
2018 A 14 year old triple-matured is launched as part of the Special Releases.
2019 A 43 year old is released as well as an 18 year old in the Special Releases.
2022 A 34 year old Prima & Ultima and a 15 year old Special Release are launched.
2023 A 40 year old with a 28 year secondary maturation in Ron Zacapa rum casks is released.

12 years old

Tasting notes Glen Ord 12 years old:

GS – Honeyed malt and milk chocolate on the nose, with a hint of orange. These characteristics carry over onto the sweet, easy-drinking palate, along with a biscuity note. Subtly drying, with a medium-length, spicy finish.

Glenrothes

[glen•roth•iss]

Owner: **Region/district:**
The Edrington Group   Speyside

Founded: **Status:**   **Capacity:**
1878   Active   5 600 000 litres

Address: Rothes, Morayshire AB38 7AA

Website: **Tel:**
theglenrothes.com   01340 872300

Edrington (the owners of Glenrothes) made it clear a few years ago that their business plan for going forward was to excel in the ultra premium segment of single malts with their three brands – Macallan, Highland Park and Glenrothes.

They sold off the Cutty Sark blend in 2018 and just a few months later Glenturret was sold and the Famous Grouse Experience was closed (the brand however is still part of the company). Macallan is the star, boosted by the astonishing new distillery and visitor centre, and the Orcadian malt Highland Park has a large and devoted group of followers. One question remained – when would Glenrothes get their fair share of attention?

The brand (not the distillery) was sold to Berry Brothers in 2017 but Edrington bought it back five years later. Today the brand sells 600,000 bottles per year (compared to Macallan's 11 million and Highland Park's 2 million). For Edrington the volumes are not that important but rather the values. There are now signs that Glenrothes is due for the next step. The distillery is destined for a long awaited upgrading over the next five years which most likely will include building a brand home. Also, an impressive stock of older Glenrothes will make sure the "ultra premium" status of the brand is secured.

The distillery is equipped with a 5.5 ton stainless steel full lauter mash tun. Twelve washbacks made of Oregon pine are in one room, whilst an adjacent tun room houses eight stainless steel washbacks – all of them with a 58 hour fermentation time. There are also five pairs of stills. For 2023, the aim is 48 mashes per week, producing around 4.2 million litres of alcohol.

The core range of today reflects the owners' commitment to ultra-premium. The ten and twelve year old as well as Whisky Maker's Cut have all been discontinued and today the range consists of **18 year old, 25 year old** and (released in 2023) a **42 year old**. There is also a **40 year old** exclusive to the Chinese market. At the moment there are no bottlings exclusively available for travel retail.

History:

1878 James Stuart & Co. begins planning the new distillery with Robert Dick, William Grant and John Cruickshank as partners.

1879 Production starts in December.

1884 The distillery changes name to Glenrothes-Glenlivet.

1887 William Grant & Co. joins forces with Islay Distillery Co. and forms Highland Distillers Company.

1897 A fire ravages the distillery.

1903 An explosion causes substantial damage.

1963 Expansion from four to six stills.

1980 Expansion from six to eight stills.

1989 Expansion from eight to ten stills.

1999 Edrington and William Grant & Sons buy Highland Distillers.

2002 Four single casks from 1966/1967 are launched.

2005 A 30 year old is launched together with Select Reserve and Vintage 1985.

2008 1978 Vintage and Robur Reserve are launched.

2009 The Glenrothes John Ramsay, Alba Reserve and Three Decades are released.

2010 Berry Brothers takes over the brand.

2011 Editor's Casks are released.

2013 2001 Vintage and the Manse Brae range are released.

2014 Sherry Cask Reserve and 1969 Extraordinary Cask are released.

2015 Glenrothes Vintage Single Malt is released.

2016 Peated Cask Reserve and Ancestor's Reserve are released.

2017 The brand returns to Edrington and The Glenrothes Wine Merchant's Collection is introduced.

2018 The entire range is revamped and four new bottlings with age statements are introduced.

2019 A 40 year old and a 50 year old are released.

2020 A 13 year old Halloween Edition is released.

2023 A 42 year old is launched.

Tasting notes Glenrothes 18 year old:

IR – Ripe pear and sweet vanilla pods, invigorating almond notes and a hint of dried ginger. A rich and deep flavour with sweet ginger, pear and rose water, aromatic fruit and light oak with an undercurrent of creamy vanilla.

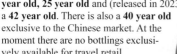

18 years old

An inside comment on...

The State of Whisky

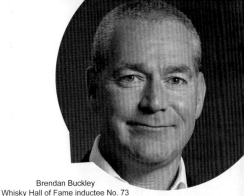

Brendan Buckley
Whisky Hall of Fame inductee No. 73
Global Marketing Director,
Irish Distillers Pernod Ricard

What was your objective for entering the whisky business?

To be fully honest, I more stumbled into the industry rather than setting out with any clear objective in mind. I am a Marketeer by profession and entered the industry that way and before I knew it, my profession also became my passion and I found myself drawn to the amazing history, people and moments which the whiskey business represents.

What would you say are the best ways to attract new, young whisky consumers?

Stop taking itself too seriously. At Jameson, we describe ourselves as the serious whisky that doesn't take itself too seriously and this has arguably been one of the cornerstones of the brand's ability to attract new consumers all over the world. We have never subscribed to the notion that whiskey needed to be appreciated a certain way and drank by certain people. Coming from Ireland where our culture is very egalitarian and where there is a more relaxed outlook, this translates into how we approach our whiskey. From a marketing point of view, we must of course ensure that we are developing communications around our brands which are engaging and relevant and of course, must use media channels which younger consumers consume – most notably, digital and social media. Additionally, we explore ways by which we can build brand engagement in a wider culture.

Can one whisky, objectively, be better than the other? Isn´t it all down to your personal taste and preferences?

Of course. I've never been a huge fan of the rating systems which only perpetuates some of the elitism that surrounds the world of whiskey. I will certainly savour a beautifully made and aged whiskey such as a Redbreast 27 while at the same time derive just as much enjoyment from a Jameson & Ginger Ale with friends.

Do you feel there is enough innovation in the whisky business and is there still a place for preserving and honouring traditional methods?

Yes to both. In fairness to the whiskey business at large, I think that there has been considerable progress in the area of innovation. When I entered the industry over 20 years ago, an innovative whiskey was something with an unusual age statement whereas nowadays one cannot keep up with the variety and number of new innovations – from flavours to finishes and more. That said, there will always be a place for the preservation of traditional practices – it is something which sets this very special industry apart from other beverage industries. Clearly, the relevant regulatory bodies in whiskey producing nations will need to play their role in how they codify innovation. Some countries of origin apply quite strict regulations which can hamper innovation whereas others might facilitate overly flexible regulations which might have the contrary impact of compromising quality perceptions. Happily, I believe that the Irish Whiskey Association has struck the right balance.

What ever line of business you´re in, sustainability is on every company´s agenda. Do you feel the whisky industry is at the forefront or could things happen faster?

Speaking from the perspective of Irish Distillers, we have placed a huge emphasis on sustainability as we believe that in the long run, there will be no whiskey industry unless we protect the planet and nature which provides the raw ingredients. People forget that despite the seeming industrial nature of whiskey distillation, it is an agricultural endeavour behind it all – barley, maize, water, yeast – so we need to protect the environment which provides these ingredients. Furthermore, we need to ensure that we minimize the use of energy and carbon emissions in the making of our whiskeys.

Investing in whisky has become more and more popular. Is that a good or a bad thing?

Each to one's own. Personally, I collect whiskeys to drink and share with others.

I´m sometimes reminded that the readers of the Malt Whisky Yearbook – usually well informed but eager to learn more – represent a miniscule part of the whisky consumers around the world. How important would you say that small consumer segment is for the producers?

Whiskey enthusiasts/nerds/geeks – call them what you will – are incredibly important as I am one myself! As with any area where there is a desire to enhance one's knowledge, those consumers who take the time to learn can become very influential in their own right.

With young people sometimes questioning the use of alcohol and others exchanging it for cannabis or other drugs – do you feel whisky is still relevant for Generation Z (born 1997-2012)?

Yes. Whiskey is a very unique organoleptic and social experience which I don't believe other substances can match. Plus you don't have the same characters and generations of craftsmen and stories and conviviality that whiskey brings to the table.

As opposed to thirty years ago, whisky today is produced in a huge number of countries around the world. How would you say that has affected the category/industry as a whole?

I think that it is great. I recall attending Whisky Live in Paris 15 years ago and I spent my entire time trying whiskeys from India, Taiwan, Australia and it was a thrilling experience. The more variety the better and of course, it can help spread the good word of whiskey to more corners of the globe. Ireland may be considered one of the traditional 'Big Four' whiskey producing nations but let's not forget that for almost 100 years from 1900's to 1990's, Irish whiskey was on a downward spiral and almost became extinct. As much as it may irk some, it took the arrival of a French company (Pernod Ricard) to breathe new life into the Irish whiskey industry vis a vis their acquisition of Irish Distillers and the subsequent transformation of Jameson from being a small regional Irish whiskey brand to its current position as the 4th largest whiskey brand globally. This success paved the way for new entrants into the industry so it is heartening to see so many new producers now playing a role in building a thriving and diverse Irish whiskey category which is rapidly building greater recognition worldwide.

Please describe your perfect time and place for a dram.

I could give you a clicheed answer about 'with close friends' or 'as the sun sets' but my perfect time and place has always been in the magical warehouses of Midleton Distillery with some new people who I am attempting to convert to one of our brands.

Glen Scotia

[glen <u>sko</u>•sha]

Owner:
Loch Lomond Group
(Hillhouse Capital Management)

Region/district:
Campbeltown

Founded: 1832
Status: Active (vc)
Capacity: 800 000 litres

Address: High Street, Campbeltown, Argyll PA28 6DS

Website: glenscotia.com
Tel: 01586 552288

The transition of Glen Scotia, previously known as a worndown and neglected distillery, to becoming a revered brand in just a few years has been nothing less than amazing. And the efforts have certainly paid off.

Master distiller Iain Macallister together with master blender Michael Henry have recreated the classic Campbeltown whisky which in the last few years have earned accolades in various competitions such as "Distillery of the year" and "Worlds best whisky". The attention is reflected in sales figures, and the time has now come to expand production.

For many years the distillery has been one of the smallest in Scotland (800,000 litres yearly) but starting in 2024 the distillery will increase the capacity by 50%. Today Glen Scotia is equipped with a traditional 3 ton cast iron mash tun and nine stainless steel washbacks. From next year another two stills and more wash-backs will be installed increasing the capacity to 1.2 million litres. The existing mash tun will be replaced but keeping the traditional rakes and the fermentation will still include shorts (70 hours) and longs (140 hours). The current wash still (11,800 litres) and spirit still (8,600 litres) will be mirrored by yet another pair.

The standard cut points are 73% to 63% but for peated spirit the lower cut point is 60-61%. To achieve the classic Campbeltown style the worts are cloudy and the stills are short and squat. In 2023 the production will be around 800,000 litres – mostly unpeated but with around 6% peated, either at 23ppm or 55ppm.

The core range consists of **Double Cask, Double Cask Rum Finish, 10, 15, 18** and **25 year old**. There are also **Victoriana** and **Glen Scotia Harbour**, both gently peated. The duty free range consists of **Glen Scotia Campbeltown 1832** finished in PX sherry casks, **Crosshill Cask Strength** (oloroso finish), a **22 year old** (tawny port finish) and a **32 year old**, Recent limited releases include the first install-ment in the Icons of Campbeltown series – **The Mermaid** – and in September 2023 a **48 year old**, the oldest release from the distillery so far.

History:

1832 The families of Stewart and Galbraith start Scotia Distillery.

1895 The distillery is sold to Duncan McCallum.

1919 Sold to West Highland Malt Distillers.

1924 West Highland Malt Distillers goes bankrupt and Duncan MacCallum buys back the distillery.

1930 The distillery closes and Duncan MacCallum commits suicide

1933 Bloch Brothers Ltd take over and production restarts.

1954 Hiram Walker takes over.

1955 A. Gillies & Co. becomes new owner.

1970 A. Gillies & Co. becomes part of Amalgamated Distilled Products.

1979 Reconstruction takes place.

1984 The distillery closes.

1986 Amalgamated Distilled Products is taken over by Gibson International.

1989 Production starts again.

1994 Glen Catrine Bonded Warehouse Ltd takes over and the distillery is mothballed.

1999 The distillery re-starts under Loch Lomond Distillery supervision using staff from Springbank.

2000 Loch Lomond Distillers runs operations with its own staff from May onwards.

2005 A 12 year old is released.

2006 A peated version is released.

2012 A new range is launched.

2014 A 10 year old and one without age statement are released - both heavily peated.

2015 A new range is released; Double Cask, 15 year old and Victoriana.

2017 A 25 year old and an 18 year old as well as two bottlings for duty-free are released.

2019 The distillery is sold to Hillhouse Capital Management. A 2003 Vintage and a 45 year old are released.

2021 A 46 year old is released.

2022 Double Cask Rum Finish is launched.

2023 The Mermaid and a 48 year old are released.

Tasting notes Glen Scotia Double Cask:

GS – The nose is sweet, with bramble and redcurrant aromas, plus caramel and vanilla. Smooth mouth-feel, with ginger, sherry and more vanilla. The finish is quite long, with spicy sherry and a final hint of brine.

Double Cask

Glen Spey

Photo: © Raymond MacDonald

[glen spey]

Owner: Diageo

Region/district: Speyside

Founded: 1878

Status: Active

Capacity: 1 500 000 litres

Address: Rothes, Morayshire AB38 7AU

Website: malts.com

Tel: 01340 831215

Perhaps a bit surprisingly, Glen Spey has for at least three years now been producing gin rather than whisky and it seems likely this will go on for another year or two.

Diego's intention though is to eventually resume whisky distillation. Glen Spey is the fourth smallest of the owners' 30 malt distilleries and the whisky has never been a brand of its own. Therefore it wouldn't have been surprising if such a huge company would decide to sell it and focus on more efficient malt production. For the past 25 years however, that hasn't been the Diageo way. They tend to stick with their distilleries unlike Chivas Brothers who during that period have closed or sold off at least five distilleries. Perhaps the explanation can be found in the fact that the roots of Diageo go back more than a century while Pernod Ricard (owners of Chivas Brothers) made their first foray into Scotch whisky in the late 1980s.

Glen Spey is situated in the middle of the town Rothes, at the foot of the hill where the ruins of Castle Rothes is to be found. This was the home of the Leslie family (Earl of Rothes) for four hundred years until 1662 when it was destroyed in a fire. Only a fragment of the outer walls remain on site, but many of the stones were used for building houses in Rothes.

The distillery is equipped with a 4.4 ton semi-lauter mash tun, eight stainless steel washbacks with both short (46 hours) and long (100 hours) fermentations and two pairs of stills. The two spirit stills are equipped with purifiers which add reflux and also help eliminate the heavier esters. Due to a cloudy wort, the Glen Spey new make is nutty and slightly oily. Even though a new control room was installed in 2017, Glen Spey still operates largely as a manual distillery.

Virtually all of the produce goes into blends and especially that of J&B. The only official single malt is the **12 year old Flora & Fauna** bottling. In 2010, two limited releases were made – a **1996 single cask** from new American oak and a **21 year old** with maturation in ex-sherry American oak.

History:

1878 James Stuart & Co. founds the distillery which becomes known by the name Mill of Rothes.

1886 James Stuart buys Macallan.

1887 W. & A. Gilbey buys the distillery for £11,000 thus becoming the first English company to buy a Scottish malt distillery.

1920 A fire breaks out and the main part of the distillery is re-built.

1962 W. & A. Gilbey combines forces with United Wine Traders and forms International Distillers & Vintners (IDV).

1970 The stills are increased from two to four.

1972 IDV is bought by Watney Mann which is then acquired by Grand Metropolitan.

1997 Guiness and Grand Metropolitan merge to form Diageo.

2001 A 12 year old is launched in the Flora & Fauna series.

2010 A 21 year old is released as part of the Special Releases and a 1996 Manager's Choice single cask is launched.

12 years old

Tasting notes Glen Spey 12 years old:

GS – Tropical fruits and malt on the comparatively delicate nose. Medium-bodied with fresh fruits and vanilla toffee on the palate, becoming steadily nuttier and drier in a gently oaky, mildly smoky finish.

Glentauchers

[glen•tock•ers]

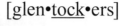

Owner:
Chivas Brothers
(Pernod Ricard)

Region/district:
Speyside

Founded: **Status:**   **Capacity:**
1897   Active   4 200 000 litres

Address: Mulben, Keith, Banffshire AB55 6YL

Website: **Tel:**
-                  01542 860272

Glentauchers has for many years been the most traditional distillery in the Chivas group with much of the process being handled mechanically. In a way the distillery has been used as a trainee plant for employees to learn the basics of whisky production.

Perhaps that was the reason why Glentauchers was chosen to undergo a transformation to become the first carbon-neutral distillery in the company. It was a blank sheet with only the absolutely necessary maintenance performed over the years. The efforts to bring it to sustainable production were successful. Not least the installation of MVR (mechanical vapour recompression) on their stills. The recovery of the energy reduced the site energy demand from 7.7kwh/ltr to 3.6kwh/ltr. The MVR system will now be implemented at all other Chivas distilleries.

From the first days until today, Glentauchers role has been to produce malt whisky for blends. Founded by whisky "baron" James Buchanan, Black & White was obviously the first to rely on Glentauchers for its character. As owners changed hands over the years it became a signature malt for Teacher´s and today it is an integral part of Ballantine´s.

The distillery is equipped with a 12.2 ton stainless steel full lauter mash tun with a copper dome. There are six washbacks made of Oregon pine (two of them replaced in 2022) with a fermentation time of 56 hours and three pairs of stills. The distillery is now doing 18 mashes per week (in a 5-day week it's 12 mashes) and a total of 4 million litres per year.

Official bottlings of Glentauchers have been scarce but in 2017 a **15 year old** was launched as a part of the Ballantine's Single Malt Series. This was later accompanied by a **23 year old**. There are also three cask strength bottlings in the Distillery Reserve Collection, available at all Chivas' visitor centres – two **13 year olds** and one **21 year old**.

History:

1897   James Buchanan and W. P. Lowrie, a whisky merchant from Glasgow, found the distillery.

1898   Production starts.

1906   James Buchanan & Co. takes over the whole distillery and acquires an 80% share in W. P. Lowrie & Co.

1915   James Buchanan & Co. merges with Dewars.

1923   Mashing house and maltings are rebuilt.

1925   Buchanan-Dewars joins Distillers Company Limited (DCL).

1930   Glentauchers is transferred to Scottish Malt Distillers (SMD).

1965   The number of stills is increased from two to six.

1969   Floor maltings is decommissioned.

1985   DCL mothballs the distillery.

1989   United Distillers (formerly DCL) sells the distillery to Caledonian Malt Whisky Distillers, a subsidiary of Allied Distillers.

1992   Production recommences in August.

2000   A 15 year old Glentauchers is released.

2005   Chivas Brothers (Pernod Ricard) become the new owner through the acquisition of Allied Domecq.

2017   A 15 year old is released in the Ballantine´s Single Malt Series.

2021   A 23 year old is launched.

15 years old

Tasting notes Glentauchers 15 years old:

IR – Delicious on the nose, both floral and fruity, vanilla, pastry, heather and honey. Still fruity on the palate with additional notes of roasted nuts, toffee and milk chocolate..

Glenturret

[glen•turr•et]

Owner: Lalique Group/Hansjörg Wyss
Region/district: Southern Highlands

Founded: 1763
Status: Active (vc)
Capacity: 500 000 litres

Address: The Hosh, Crieff, Perthshire PH7 4HA

Website: theglenturret.com
Tel: 01764 656565

When the Swiss Lalique Group took over Glenturret in 2019 from Edrington they obviously had plans. One was to expand the hospitality side of the distillery and early 2022, the restaurant on site was awarded a Michelin star.

The layout of the restaurant and the bar (including the well equipped wine cellar below) has definitely stated an example for all other distilleries. There is also a café for more casual dining or lunch. Another part of the plan was to bring the oldest working distillery in Scotland into the 21st century while still retaining the feeling of a traditional distillery and, not least, the character of the spirit. This took two years under the supervision of long-time head brewer and current distillery manager Ian Renwick. Having been in the shadow of Edrington and Famous Grouse for almost twenty years, Glenturret now seems destined for an existence based on its own merits.

For quite some time consensus has been that Glenturret deserves the title as the oldest workingdistillery in Scotland. It has often been said it was established around the year 1775 as Hosh distillery. Recent findings however indicate the distillery was founded founded even earlier than that. A rental document of Sir Patrick of Ochtertye, who died in 1764, refers to Thurot Distillery.

The distillery is equipped with a new 1.95 ton stainless steel, semilauter mash tun (which replaced the last hand stirred, open mash tun in Scotland in May 2022). There are eight 8,000 litre Douglas fir washbacks with a fermentation time of 100-120 hours and one pair of stills. The production target for 2023 is 7-8 mashes per week and a total of 220,000 litres.

A completely new range was introduced in 2020 and the core range (released in yearly batches with small variations) now consists of seven expressions, all with different abv; **Triple Wood, 7 year old Peat Smoked, 10 year old Peat Smoked, 12, 15, 25** and **30 year old**. A range of very limited bottlings, The Trinity, was also introduced with a **33 year old** as the first expression and in 2023 the third release of the **Manager's Dram** appeared.

History:
- 1763 A distillery by the name of Thurot is operating on the site of todays Glenturret.
- 1818 John Drummond is licensee until 1837.
- 1826 A distillery in the vicinity is named Glenturret, but is decommissioned before 1852.
- 1852 John McCallum is licensee until 1874.
- 1875 Hosh Distillery takes over the name Glenturret Distillery and is managed by Thomas Stewart.
- 1903 Mitchell Bros Ltd takes over.
- 1921 Production ceases and the buildings are used for whisky storage only.
- 1929 Mitchell Bros Ltd is liquidated, the distillery dismantled and the facilities are used as storage for agricultural needs.
- 1957 James Fairlie buys the distillery and re-equips it.
- 1959 Production restarts.
- 1981 Remy-Cointreau buys the distillery and invests in a visitor centre.
- 1990 Highland Distillers takes over.
- 1999 Edrington and William Grant & Sons buy Highland Distillers for £601 million. The purchasing company, 1887 Company, is a joint venture between Edrington (70%) and William Grant (30%).
- 2002 The Famous Grouse Experience, a visitor centre costing £2.5 million, is inaugurated.
- 2003 A 10 year old Glenturret replaces the 12 year old as the distillery's standard release.
- 2007 Three new single casks are released.
- 2013 An 18 year old bottled at cask strength is released as a distillery exclusive.
- 2014 A 1986 single cask is released.
- 2015 Sherry, Triple Wood and Peated are released.
- 2016 Fly's 16 Masters is released.
- 2017 Cameron's Cut, Jamieson's Jigger Edition and Peated Drummond Edition are launched.
- 2019 Lalique Group and Hansjörg Wyss buy the distillery.
- 2020 A completely new core range is launched.
- 2021 Glenturret Jaguar E-Type is released.
- 2023 The third edition of the Manager's Dram is launched.

Tasting notes Glenturret 12 years old:
GS – Initial hints of Christmas cake and old leather, warm spices, dried fruits and old oak. Sweet and rich on the palate with tangy orange notes, cinnamon, dates, walnuts, caramel and lingering ginger.

12 years old

Highland Park

[hi•land park]

Owner:	**Region/district:**
The Edrington Group	Highlands (Orkney)

Founded:	**Status:**	**Capacity:**
1798	Active (vc)	2 500 000 litres

Address: Holm Road, Kirkwall, Orkney KW15 1SU

Website:	**Tel:**
highlandparkwhisky.com	01856 874619

There is evidence to suggest that Highland Park single malt was already exported to Norway, as well as to India in the late 1800s, but it wasn't until 1979 that the owners started promoting the whisky in a more structured manner.

The results were almost immediate and soon the brand had a large number of loyal followers. Unlike some other brands, year on year sales of Highland Park tend not to be a linear progress but rather reaches plateaus where it sits for a while. From 2007 to 2013 sales were around 1.2 million bottles per year. Then they started to rise but have for the past five years levelled out at around 2 million bottles. Last year Highland Park was in 20th place on the sales list. The distillery is one of only nine in Scotland that was founded in the 18th century and celebrates its 225 anniversary in 2023. When you enter through the impressive gates, the layout of the beautiful buildings connected by winding foot paths covered with bricks gives you the feeling of walking through a small 19th century hamlet. Very different from the regular on-site experience of strolling through the premises of a distillery.

Highland Park is equipped with a 12 ton semi-lauter mash tun although with a 6.5 ton mash. The mash tun sits in the same room as 11 washbacks made of Oregon pine and one made of Siberian larch. The distillery is working seven days a week and the fermentation time is an even 60 hours. In a separate building there are two 14,600 litre wash stills and two 9,000 litre spirit stills – all with horizontal lyne arms and condensers outside. The cut points for the spirit run are 74-64%. In the last couple of years there have been 22 mashes per week which means a total of 2.5 million litres of alcohol. Highland Park is malting roughly 25% of its malt on-site and there are five malting floors with a capacity of almost 36 tons of barley. The old kiln is still in place but hasn't been used since 1904 when the new kiln was installed. The malted barley is dried using peat for the first eight hours and coke for the final 19. This gives a phenol specification of 30-40ppm whereas the malt sourced from Simpsons is unpeated.

The core range of Highland Park consists of **12 year old Viking Honour, 15 year old Viking Heart, 18 year old Viking Pride** as well as **21, 25, 30** and **40 year olds**. The 10 year old Viking Scars has recently been discontinued. Included in the core range are also **Cask Strength** which is released in batches and **Dragon Legend**. The duty free range consists of **Spirit of the Bear** (matured mainly in American oak ex-sherry), **Loyalty of the Wolf** (14 years old, matured in a combination of American oak ex-sherry and ex-bourbon), **Wings of the Eagle** (16 years old, predominantly from European oak ex-sherry) and a duty free version of the **18 year old Viking Pride**. Recent limited expressions include the oldest release ever from the distillery – a **54 year old** which was launched in spring 2023. It originally came from four refill butts and six refill hogsheads and was then matured for the last 14 years in first fill sherry butts.

History:

1798 David Robertson founds the distillery. The local smuggler and businessman Magnus Eunson previously operated an illicit whisky production on the site.

1816 John Robertson, an Excise Officer who arrested Magnus Eunson, takes over production.

1826 Highland Park obtains a license and the distillery is taken over by Robert Borwick.

1840 Robert´s son George Borwick takes over but the distillery deteriorates.

1869 The younger brother James Borwick inherits Highland Park and attempts to sell it as he does not consider the distillation of spirits as compatible with his priesthood.

1895 James Grant (of Glenlivet Distillery) buys Highland Park.

1898 The distillery is expanded from two to four stills.

1937 Highland Distilleries buys Highland Park.

1979 Highland Distilleries invests considerably in marketing Highland Park as single malt which increases sales markedly.

1986 A visitor centre, considered one of Scotland's finest, is opened.

1997 Two new Highland Park are launched, an 18 year old and a 25 year old.

1999 Highland Distillers are acquired by Edrington Group and William Grant & Sons.

2005 Highland Park 30 years old is released. A 16 year old for the Duty Free market and Ambassador´s Cask 1984 are released.

2006 The second edition of Ambassador´s Cask, a 10 year old from 1996, is released.

2007 The Rebus 20, a 21 year old duty free exclusive, a 38 year old and a 39 year old are released.

History continued:

2008 A 40 year old and the third and fourth editions of Ambassador´s Cask are released.

2009 Two vintages and Earl Magnus 15 year are released.

2010 A 50 year old, Saint Magnus 12 year old, Orcadian Vintage 1970 and four duty free vintages are released.

2011 Vintage 1978, Leif Eriksson and 18 year old Earl Haakon are released.

2012 Thor and a 21 year old are released.

2013 Loki and a new range for duty free, The Warriors, are released.

2014 Freya and Dark Origins are released.

2015 Odin is released.

2016 Hobbister, Ice Edition, Ingvar and King Christian I are released.

2017 Valkyrie, Dragon Legend, Voyage of the Raven, Shiel, Full Volume, The Dark and The Light are released.

2018 New duty free bottlings include Spirit of the Bear, Loyalty of the Wolf and Wings of the Eagle. The limited Valknut is also released.

2019 Twisted Tattoo, Valfather, Triskelion and a 21 year old are released.

2020 A cask strength is added to the core range.

2021 A 15 year old and a 50 year old are released.

2023 A 54 year old, the oldest expression from Highland Park so far, is launched.

Tasting notes Highland Park 12 year old:

GS – The nose is fragrant and floral, with hints of heather and some spice. Smooth and honeyed on the palate, with citric fruits, malt and distinctive tones of wood smoke in the warm, lengthy, slightly peaty finish.

21 years old   54 year old   Loyalty of the Wolf

Cask Strength

12 years old   15 years old

Inchgower

INCHGOWER DISTILLERY

[inch•gow•er]

Owner:
Diageo

Region/district:
Speyside

Founded: **Status:** **Capacity:**
1871 Active 3 200 000 litres

Address: Buckie, Banffshire AB56 5AB

Website: **Tel:**
malts.com 01542 836700

In 1938 Inchgower distillery was acquired by Arthur Bell & Sons, a highly reputable blending firm dating back to 1865. Arthur Bell himself died in 1900 and at that time Bell´s whisky had acquired a reputation as one of the best blends.

The success of the Bell´s brand from 1900 and onwards was very much due to Arthur's sons Arthur Jr. and Robert. Their father had always been reluctant to put the name Bell on their bottlings and the idea of extensive advertising was unknown territory for him. Ultimately Bell´s became the best selling Scotch in England and today it's number two in the UK after Famous Grouse. Globally the brand sold 22 million bottles in 2022.

Over the years, whisky enthusiasts wishing to enjoy Inchgower have depended on bottlings from the independents. One of the most diligent bottlers of the malt is the Scotch Malt Whisky Society (SMWS). By June 2023 they had released no less than 53 different single casks from the distillery. Celebrating its 40th anniversary in 2023, SMWS was founded by a group of friends with Pip Hills as the driving force. Today the society has close to 50,000 members worldwide and was listed on the London stock exchange in 2021.

The distillery is equipped with an 8.4 ton stainless steel semilauter mash tun, where the cloudy wort adds to the spirit character, and six 50,000 litre washbacks made from Oregon pine divided into two separate rooms. Two wash stills (13,640 litres) and two spirit stills (8,155 litres) are all onion-shaped and with sharply descending lyne arms. A quick distillation and a middle cut which goes down to an unusually low 55% enhance the nutty and robust style of newmake. The production plan for 2023 aims at a seven-day operation with 19 mashes per week and 3.2 million litres. It also entails fermentations of 50-52 hours as opposed to short (42 hours) and long (90 hours) when operating a five-day week.

Besides the official **Flora & Fauna 14 year old**, there have also been a few limited bottlings of Inchgower single malt. The most recent was a **27 year old** in autumn 2018 which was part of the yearly Special Releases.

History:
1871 Alexander Wilson & Co. founds the distillery.
1936 Alexander Wilson & Co. becomes bankrupt and Buckie Town Council buys the distillery and the family's home for £1,600.
1938 The distillery is sold on to Arthur Bell & Sons for £3,000.
1966 Capacity doubles to four stills.
1985 Guinness acquires Arthur Bell & Sons.
1987 United Distillers is formed by a merger between Arthur Bell & Sons and DCL.
1997 Inchgower 1974 (22 years) is released as a Rare Malt.
2004 Inchgower 1976 (27 years) is released as a Rare Malt.
2010 A single cask from 1993 is released.
2018 A 27 year old is launched as part of the Special Releases.

14 years old

Tasting notes Inchgower 14 years old:
GS – Ripe pears and a hint of brine on the light nose. Grassy and gingery in the mouth, with some acidity. The finish is spicy, dry and relatively short.

Jura

[joo•rah]

Owner: **Region/district:**
Whyte & Mackay   Highlands (Jura)
(Emperador Inc)

Founded:	**Status:**	**Capacity:**
1810	Active (vc)	2 500 000 litres

Address: Craighouse, Isle of Jura PA60 7XT

Website: **Tel:**
jurawhisky.com   01496 820240

Recently there has been a change of guards at Jura distillery with Jamie Muir as the new distillery manager and Joe Ricketts as the lead whisky maker.

Jamie started his career at Jura in 2006 and returned to the distillery as manager in late 2022, having worked at Kilchoman and BrewDog in between. Joe has for the past two years been responsible for the Jura range of single malts under the supervision of master blender Greg Glass. The responsibility of taking the reins of the number one selling single malt in the UK is of course huge. The latest available figures show that Jura single malt has a 7.1% market share in the UK, beating Glenfiddich by a whisker.

Jura distillery has a five ton semi-lauter mash tun, six stainless steel washbacks with a fermentation time of 60 hours and two pairs of stills. The foreshots are 20 minutes and the heart of the spirit run starts at 73% and goes down to 60%. The production plan for 2023 is 28 mashes per week and close to 2.4 million litres of alcohol. Usually the distillery has a three-week period of making peated whisky but due to the difficulties of acquiring peated malt all of the production during 2023 will be unpeated. Instead they are planning for six weeks of peated production in 2024. A biomass plant will be installed in 2024 and for the past few years there have been plans of increasing the capacity of the distillery.

The core range consists of **Bourbon Cask** (replacing Journey), **10 year old, 12 year old, 14 year old Rye cask, Seven Wood, 15 year old Sherry Cask, 18 year old** and the **21 year old Tide**. There is also **French Oak** and a series called **Cask Editions** which is part of the signature range but sold seasonally. The latest include **Pale Ale Cask, Red Wine Cask, Winter Edition** and **Rum Cask**. For duty-free there are **The Sound, The Road, The Loch** and the 19 year old **The Paps** – all of them finished in PX casks. There is also the **21 year old Jura Time**, finished in ex-peated malt casks and, exclusive to travel retail in Asia, the **12 year old The Bay**. Recent limited releases include two vintages, **1990** and **1993** and the **Feis Ile 2023** bottling – distilled in 2008 and matured in a first fill bourbon cask.

History:

1810 Archibald Campbell founds a distillery named Small Isles Distillery.

1853 Richard Campbell leases the distillery to Norman Buchanan from Glasgow.

1867 Buchanan files for bankruptcy and J. & K. Orr takes over the distillery.

1876 Licence transferred to James Ferguson & Sons.

1901 Ferguson dismantles the distillery.

1960 Charles Mackinlay & Co. extends the distillery. Newly formed Scottish & Newcastle Breweries acquires Charles Mackinlay & Co.

1963 The first distilling takes place.

1985 Invergordon Distilleries acquires Charles Mackinlay & Co. from Scottish & Newcastle.

1993 Whyte & Mackay (Fortune Brands) buys Invergordon Distillers.

1996 Whyte & Mackay changes name to JBB (Greater Europe).

2001 The management buys out the company and changes the name to Kyndal.

2002 Isle of Jura Superstition is launched.

2003 Kyndal reverts back to its old name, Whyte & Mackay. Isle of Jura 1984 is launched.

2006 The 40 year old Jura is released.

2007 United Spirits buys Whyte & Mackay.

2009 Prophecy and Paps of Jura are released.

2012 The 12 year old Jura Elixir is released.

2013 Camas an Staca, 1977 Juar and Turas-Mara are released.

2014 Whyte & Mackay is sold to Emperador Inc.

2016 The 22 year old "One For The Road" is released.

2017 The limited One and All is released.

2018 A new core range is released; 10, 12 and 18 year old as well as Journey and Seven Wood.

2019 A new range for duty-free is released.

2020 Red Wine Cask and Winter Edition are released.

2021 Cask Editions and two vintages (1990 and 1993) are launched.

2022 The 14 year old Rye Cask is released.

2023 Bourbon Cask replaces Journey.

Tasting notes Jura 10 years old:

GS – Resin, oil and pine notes on the delicate nose. Light-bodied in the mouth, with malt and drying saltiness. The finish is malty, nutty, with more salt, plus just a wisp of smoke.

12 years old

Kilchoman

[kil•ho•man]

Owner:
Kilchoman Distillery Co.

Region/district:
Islay

Founded: 2005
Status: Active (vc)
Capacity: 650 000 litres

Address: Rockside farm, Bruichladdich,
Islay PA49 7UT

Website:
kilchomandistillery.com

Tel:
01496 850011

An important feature for Kilchoman is not only to grow some of their own barley but also to malt it themselves. However, as demand increases it becomes more difficult for the owners to keep up in the fields and on the malting floors.

An extension to the malting floor was therefore completed in 2023 (the previous expansion was as recently as in 2019). Originally the plan was to be able to malt 25% of their needs themselves and buy the rest from Port Ellen. However, the decision in autumn 2022 that Port Ellen would in the future only provide malted barley for the Diageo distilleries forced Kilchoman to re-think. They have now filed a planning application in order to expand their own malting with Saladin boxes. And not only that – they also have plans to build a rum distillery in Barbados!

A second distillery, mirroring the original, was commissioned in 2019 and today the equipment consists of two 1.2 ton stainless steel semi-lauter mash tuns, 16 stainless steel, 6,000 litre washbacks with an average fermentation time of 90 hours and two pairs of stills. But Wills has no intention of stopping there. He already has plans to add another pair of stills and more washbacks in 2023 which would increase the capacity from 650,000 litres of pure alcohol to 975,000. The expansion is financed through a £22.5m funding package secured in early 2022 from Barclays. The production plan for 2023 is 600,000 litres – a 35% increase from the previous year.

The core range consists of **Machir Bay** and **Sanaig**. Limited, but regular releases are **Loch Gorm** matured in oloroso casks and **100% Islay** purely made from barley grown and malted on the island. Recent limited releases include a **10 year old** matured in a combination of oloroso and bourbon for Feis Ile 2023. There has also been a **cognac cask matured**, a **fino cask matured**, a **PX cask matured** and a **16 year old**. For the UK duty free market there is **Coull Point** and for global duty free, **Saligo Bay** is available.

History:

2002 Plans are formed for a new distillery at Rockside Farm on western Islay.

2005 Production starts in June.

2006 A fire breaks out in the kiln causing a few weeks´ production stop but malting has to cease for the rest of the year.

2007 The distillery is expanded with two new washbacks.

2009 The first single malt, a 3 year old, is released on 9th September followed by a second release.

2010 Three new releases and an introduction to the US market. John Maclellan from Bunnahabhain joins the team as General Manager.

2011 Kilchoman 100% Islay is released as well as a 4 year old and a 5 year old.

2012 Machir Bay, the first core expression, is released together with Kilchoman Sherry Cask Release and the second edition of 100% Islay.

2013 Loch Gorm and Vintage 2007 are released.

2014 A 3 year old port cask matured and the first duty free exclusive, Coull Point, are released.

2015 A Madeira cask maturation is released and the distillery celebrates its 10th anniversary.

2016 Sanaig and a Sauternes cask maturation are released.

2017 A Portugese red wine maturation and Vintage 2009 are released.

2018 Original Cask Strength and 2009 Vintage are released.

2019 Capacity is doubled with two more stills. A limited STR Cask Matured is released.

2020 Am Burach and a fino sherry cask are released.

2021 Two bottlings matured in PX sherry cask and madeira cask respectively are launched.

2022 Casado and a Madeira cask matured are released.

2023 Expressions matured in casks that had held cognac, fino sherry and PX sherry are released.

Machir Bay

Tasting notes Kilchoman Machir Bay:

GS – A nose of sweet peat and vanilla, undercut by brine, kelp and black pepper. Filled ashtrays in time. A smooth mouth-feel, with lots of nicely-balanced citrus fruit, peat smoke and Germolene on the palate. The finish is relatively long and sweet, with building spice, chili and a final nuttiness.

Kininvie

[kin•in•vee]

Owner:
William Grant & Sons

Region/district:
Speyside

Founded: 1990   **Status:** Active

Capacity:
4 800 000 litres

Address: Dufftown, Keith, Banffshire AB55 4DH

Website:
kininvie.com

Tel:
01340 820373

You're not actually supposed to come to the Kininvie distillery as it is not open to visitors except for on those rare occasions such as during the Speyside Whisky Festival.

But if you do find yourself standing outside it is actually a rather unobtrusive building holding nine stills. The rest of the equipment is "hidden" within the doors of next-door Balvenie. Kininvie was opened in 1990 to supply the owners with single malt for blends and, later, blended malts. The distilleries that were already owned by W Grants at the time (Glenfiddich and Balvenie) had become far too important as brands of their own and more malt was needed for Grant's blended Scotch. In later years the spirit has also become an integral part of the hugely popular Monkey Shoulder.

As mentioned, Kininvie distillery consists of one separate still house with three wash stills (13, 100 litres) and six spirit stills (8,600 litres). There is a 9.6 ton stainless steel full lauter mash tun which is placed next to Balvenie's in the Balvenie distillery. Ten Douglas fir washbacks with a minimum fermentation time of 70 hours (typically, it is 75 hours long) can be found in two separate rooms, also at Balvenie. The yearly production varies depending on what style is in the making. If it is "floral" (normally 25% of the yearly production) there will be 21 mashes per week with a fermentation time of at least 70 hours. The other style, "cereal", takes 60 hours to ferment and there can be 25 mashes per week. Every year there is also one week of rye whisky production at Kininvie.

The first official bottling appeared in 2013 and since then a few experimental whiskies have been launched; the **KVSM001** is a 5 year old triple distilled single malt while the **KVSG002** is a whisky made of malted rye and malted barley, matured in virgin American oak for three years. Finally, there is **KVSB003** which is a blend of double distilled malt and the aforementioned rye/barley whisky.

History:

1990 Kininvie distillery is inaugurated and the first distillation takes place on 25th June.

1994 Another three stills are installed.

2006 The first expression of a Kininvie single malt is released as a 15 year old under the name Hazelwood.

2008 In February a 17 year old Hazelwood Reserve is launched at Heathrow´s Terminal 5.

2013 A 23 year old Kininvie is launched in Taiwan.

2014 A 17 year old and batch 2 of the 23 year old are released.

2015 Batch 3 of the 23 year old is released and later in the year, the batches are replaced by a 23 year old signature bottling and single casks are launched. Three 25 year old single malts are launched.

2019 Three expressions in the Kininvie Works series are released.

Tasting notes Kininvie 17 years old:

GS – The nose offers tropical fruits, coconut and vanilla custard, with a hint of milk chocolate. Pineapple and mango on the palate, accompanied by linseed oil, ginger, and developing nuttiness. The finish dries slowly, with more linseed, plenty of spice, and soft oak.

Kininvie KVSB003

Knockando

[nock•<u>an</u>•doo]

Owner: Diageo.

Region/district: Speyside

Founded: 1898

Status: Active

Capacity: 1 400 000 litres

Address: Knockando, Morayshire AB38 7RT

Website: malts.com

Tel: 01340 882000

Historically, distilleries in Scotland have sometimes been closed for years only to suddenly rise like phoenixes. When lovers of Knockando single malt finally had given up hope, the distillery started producing again in autumn 2023.

In late 2017, the distillery was closed and there were rumours that the rather small distillery (1.4 million litres) was surplus to Diageo needs. Almost six years later, however, the distillery which is hidden away in a valley close to river Spey, started recruiting staff to re-open. In a way this revives the sentiments of whisky enthusiasts in 2008 when Diageo opened Roseisle distillery and a closing of many small distilleries in favour of the new, huge and versatile distillery was anticipated. Fifteen years later none of the Diageo distilleries has been closed. Instead, two that were closed (Brora and Port Ellen) have been re-opened.

The distillery is equipped with a small (4.4 ton), semi-lauter mash tun, eight Douglas fir washbacks and two pairs of stills. Historically, Knockando has always worked a five-day week with 16 mashes – eight short fermentations (50 hours) and eight long (100 hours). The nutty character of the newmake, a result of the cloudy worts coming from the mash tun, has given it its fame. However, in order to balance the taste, the distillers also wish to create the typical Speyside floral notes by using boiling balls on the spirit stills to increase reflux.

Knockando has always been a vital part of the major blend J&B and for many years there was a fifth warehouse on the site called Ultima after the legendary J&B Ultima blend released in 1994, where whiskies from 128 distilleries (116 malts and 12 grains) were blended together. At the same time it was also one of the first whiskies to be bottled as a single malt and in the early 1990s, it was one of the top ten single malt brands of the world.

The core range which used to consist of four expressions, has recently been diminished to just one – the **12 year old**. The 15 year old Richly Matured, 18 year old Slow Matured and 21 year old Master Reserve have all been discontinued.

History:

1898 John Thompson founds the distillery. The architect is Charles Doig.

1899 Production starts in May.

1900 The distillery closes in March and J. Thompson & Co. takes over administration.

1903 W. & A. Gilbey purchases the distillery for £3,500 and production restarts in October.

1962 W. & A. Gilbey merges with United Wine Traders (including Justerini & Brooks) and forms International Distillers & Vintners (IDV).

1968 Floor maltings is decommissioned.

1969 The number of stills is increased to four.

1972 IDV is acquired by Watney Mann who, in its turn, is taken over by Grand Metropolitan.

1978 Justerini & Brooks launches a 12 year old Knockando.

1997 Grand Metropolitan and Guinness merge and form Diageo; simultaneously IDV and United Distillers merge to United Distillers & Vintners.

2010 A Manager's Choice 1996 is released.

2011 A 25 year old is released.

2017 The distillery closes for refurbishing.

2023 Production is resumed.

12 years old

Tasting notes Knockando 12 years old:

GS – Delicate and fragrant on the nose, with hints of malt, worn leather, and hay. Quite full in the mouth, smooth and honeyed, with gingery malt and a suggestion of white rum. Medium length in the finish, with cereal and more ginger.

Knockdhu

[nock•doo]

Owner: **Region/district:**
Inver House Distillers   Speyside
(International Beverage Holdings)

Founded: **Status:**   **Capacity:**
1893   Active (vc)   2 000 000 litres

Address: Knock, By Huntly, Aberdeenshire AB54 7LJ

Website: **Tel:**
ancnoc.com   01466 771223

Whisky production is energy-intensive and Scottish distilleries have had to adapt to a new reality in the last decades. Knockdhu distillery has always been at the forefront of sustainable whisky production, never shy of adapting new technology.

In 2023 there was an extended summer shut-down to fit a TVR system on the wash still. In order not to loose more energy in the still house than necessary, TVR (thermal vapour recompression) is one way of recovering energy for use in other parts of the distillery. The production costs are expected to be lower as well as, more importantly, carbon emissions. Unlike many other distilleries in the area, Knockdhu doesn't have a large visitor centre. Since a few years, however, it is possible to book a guided tour.

Knockdhu distillery is equipped with a 5 ton stainless steel lauter mash tun with a copper dome and eight washbacks made of Oregon pine (two of them used as intermediate vats). The fermentation time is currently a flat 65 hours. Finally there is one pair of stills with quite tall necks and straight lyne arms connected to worm tubs. Oddly enough there is also a shell and tube condenser fitted on the wash still just before the worm tub. With the right amount of reflux in the stills, condensation using worm tubs (which adds sulphury notes) and a wide spirit cut of 72-62% (catching both esters at the start and heavier notes at the end), the owners are looking for quite a heavy new make which after maturation will transform into sweeter, apple notes. In 2023 the distillery continues to work seven days per week which means 20 mashes and a total of 1.8 million litres of pure alcohol. Typically 200,000 litres of that will be heavily peated (45ppm).

The core range consists of **12, 18** and **24 years old**. In addition to that there is the smoky **Peatheart** where batch 3 was made from 34ppm barley (13ppm in the whisky) and Sherry Cask Finish Peated Edition. Recent limited bottlings include **Vintage 2009** and **Vintage 2006 Sherry Cask** (exclusive to Sweden). For the travel retail market there is **Black Hill Reserve** and the peated (20ppm) **Rùdhan** may still be available.

History:

1893 Distillers Company Limited (DCL) starts construction of the distillery.

1894 Production starts in October.

1930 Scottish Malt Distillers (SMD) takes over production.

1983 The distillery closes in March.

1988 Inver House buys the distillery from United Distillers.

1989 Production restarts on 6th February.

1990 First official bottling of Knockdhu.

1993 First official bottling of anCnoc.

2001 Pacific Spirits purchases Inver House Distillers at a price of $85 million.

2003 Reintroduction of anCnoc 12 years.

2004 A 14 year old from 1990 is launched.

2005 A 30 year old from 1975 and a 14 year old from 1991 are launched.

2006 International Beverage Holdings acquires Pacific Spirits UK.

2007 anCnoc 1993 is released.

2008 anCnoc 16 year old is released.

2011 A Vintage 1996 is released.

2012 A 35 year old is launched.

2013 A 22 year old and Vintage 1999 are released.

2014 A peated range with Rutter, Flaughter, Tushkar and Cutter is introduced.

2015 A 24 year old, Vintage 1975 and Peatlands are released as well as Black Hill Reserve and Barrow for duty free.

2016 Vintage 2001, Blas and Rùdhan are released.

2017 Vintage 2002 and Peatheart are released.

2019 A 16 year old cask strength is released.

2021 Vintage 2009 is released.

2023 Peatheart batch 3 is launched.

12 years old

Tasting notes anCnoc 12 years old:

GS – A pretty, sweet, floral nose, with barley notes. Medium bodied, with a whiff of delicate smoke, spices and boiled sweets on the palate. Drier in the mouth than the nose suggests. The finish is quite short and drying.

Lagavulin

[lah•gah•**voo**•lin]

Owner: Diageo

Region/district: Islay

Founded: 1816

Status: Active (vc)

Capacity: 3 000 000 litres

Address: Port Ellen, Islay, Argyll PA42 7DZ

Website: malts.com

Tel: 01496 302749 (vc)

Peated Islay malts are popular amongst whisky drinkers around the world but most of the distilleries on the island are surprisingly small, including Lagavulin, a few miles north of Port Ellen.

The three million litres of alcohol produced is actually slightly below the average capacity of a malt distillery in Scotland. For quite some time now Lagavulin have been tweeking the production process in order to get more spirit without having to install more equipment. One measure was to increase the mash size two years ago from 4.4 tonnes to 5.4. That means using more malt in the mash tun compared to heated water and this is often called a high gravity mash. Not only can this result in a higher yield but it is often more sustainable as it requires less energy to heat a smaller volume of water. Similar trials have been made at another Diageo distillery, namely Talisker.

Even though Laphroaig became popular in the USA during prohibition in the 1920s, it is probably fair to say that Lagavulin started the whole trend of drinking peated whisky in the 1980s. Until the year 2000 it was the most sold Islay whisky but since then Laphroaig has been the number one. In 2021 Lagavulin came in fourth with both Bowmore and Ardbeg showing larger volumes. Lagavulin sold 1.7 million bottles which is close to the figures from two decades ago.

The location of Lagavulin is steeped in history. On a peninsula next to the distillery stands the ruins of Dunyvaig Castle. In the 14th and 15th centuries this was used by the clan Macdonald (or Lord of the Isles) to protect the island from attacks from sea.

The distillery is equipped with a 5.4 ton stainless steel full lauter mash tun and ten washbacks made of larch with a volume of 21,000 litres and a 55 hour fermentation cycle. Six of the washbacks have been replaced over the past three years. There are two pairs of stills where the spirit stills are actually larger than the wash stills. Three of the stills were replaced in 2021. The newmake is, almost without exception, filled into ex-bourbon hogsheads. There are only 7,000 casks maturing at the distillery and all of the new production is now shipped to the mainland for maturation. The production plan for 2023 is a 7-day week with 29 mashes per week and 3 million litres of alcohol.

The core range of Lagavulin consists of an **8 year old**, a **16 year old** and the **Distiller's Edition**, a PX sherry finish. There is also a **12 year old cask strength** which actually forms part of the yearly Special Releases. In 2023 this version, bottled at 56.4%, was surprisingly finihed in Don Julio añejo tequila casks. In October 2022 the third Offerman Edition, a collaboration with American actor Nick Offerman, appeared in the way of the **11 year old Charred Oak Cask**. The Feis Ile release for 2023, bottled at 58.4%, was a **14 year old** matured in American and European oak and then finished in armagnac casks – a first for Lagavulin. Finally, a **25 year old** distilled in 1997 appeared in the Prima & Ultima range in October 2023.

History:

1816 John Johnston founds the distillery.

1825 John Johnston takes over the adjacent distillery Ardmore.

1836 John Johnston dies and the two distilleries are merged and operated under the name Lagavulin. Alexander Graham, a wine and spirits dealer from Glasgow, buys the distillery.

1861 James Logan Mackie becomes a partner.

1867 The distillery is acquired by James Logan Mackie & Co. and refurbishment starts.

1878 Peter Mackie is employed.

1890 J. L. Mackie & Co. changes name to Mackie & Co. Peter Mackie launches White Horse with Lagavulin included in the blend.

1895 James Logan Mackie retires and Peter Mackie takes over the distillery.

1908 Peter Mackie uses the old distillery buildings to build a new distillery, Malt Mill, on the site.

1924 Peter Mackie passes away and Mackie & Co. changes name to White Horse Distillers.

1927 White Horse Distillers becomes part of Distillers Company Limited (DCL).

1930 The distillery is administered under Scottish Malt Distillers (SMD).

1952 An explosive fire breaks out and causes considerable damage.

1962 Malt Mills distillery closes and today it houses Lagavulin's visitor centre.

1974 Floor maltings are decommisioned and malt is bought from Port Ellen instead.

1988 Lagavulin 16 years becomes one of six Classic Malts.

1998 A Pedro Ximenez sherry finish is launched as a Distillers Edition.

2002 Two cask strengths (12 years and 25 years) are launched.

History continued:

2006 A 30 year old is released.

2010 A new edition of the 12 year old and a Manager's Choice single cask are released.

2011 The 10th edition of the 12 year old cask strength is released.

2012 The 11th edition of the 12 year old cask strength and a 21 year old are released.

2013 A 37 year old and the 12th edition of the 12 year old cask strength are released.

2014 A triple matured for Friends of the Classic Malts and the 13th edition of the 12 year old cask strength are released.

2015 The 14th edition of the 12 year old cask strength is released.

2016 An 8 year old and a 25 year old are launched.

2017 A new edition of the 12 year old cask strength is released.

2018 An 18 year old is released for Feis Ile.

2019 A 19 year old is released for Feis Ile, a 9 year old House Lannister in the Game of Thrones series and a 10 year old for duty free.

2020 The 11 year old Offerman Edition, the 1991 Prima & Ultima and a 20 year old for Feis Ile are released.

2021 A second Offerman Edition, a 13 year old for Feis Ile and a 26 year old are launched.

2022 A third Offerman and a 28 year old Prima & Ultima are released.

2023 A 14 year old Feis Ile bottling and 25 year old 1997 Prima & Ultima are launched.

Tasting notes Lagavulin 16 year old:

GS – Peat, iodine, sherry and vanilla merge on the rich nose. The peat and iodine continue on to the expansive, spicy, sherried palate, with brine, prunes and raisins. Peat embers feature in the lengthy, spicy finish.

Offerman Edition 11 years old

12 year old Special Release 2023

14 years old Feis Ile 2023

16 years old

8 years old

Distiller´s Edition

Laphroaig

[lah•froyg]

Owner: **Region/district:**
Beam Suntory   Islay

Founded: **Status:**   **Capacity:**
1815   Active (vc)   3 300 000 litres

Address: Port Ellen, Islay, Argyll PA42 7DU

Website: **Tel:**
laphroaig.com   01496 302418

For those Islay distilleries that were used to source part of their peated malt from Port Ellen maltings, a message from Diageo in August 2022 caused some disturbance; no malt would in the future be delivered to customers outside the company.

The reason was that Caol Ila went from 5- to 7-day production and that Port Ellen distillery would soon be working again. Diageo needed all the malt for themselves. Laphroaig's way of handling it was to buy more malt from mainland maltsters to complement their own malting floors. They also increased their own malting by 50% to cover just over 20% of their need. Usually 10-12 hours of peat smoke and 15-18 hours of hot air will get them the 50-60ppm needed for the character. Sourced malt has typically been malted to 45 ppm and the two types are almost always blended before mashing. Recently malt from the mainland has sometimes held a lower ppm due to increased demand. In those cases Laphroaig has prolonged the drying over peat to achieve a ppm closer to 75-80ppm before mixing it.

The distillery is equipped with a 5.5 ton stainless steel full lauter mash tun and eight stainless steel washbacks. Two of them (both external) were added in March 2023, not to add to the capacity but to increase fermentation time from 53 hours to 72 hours. This will generate a more complex and fruitier flavour profile. The distillery uses an unusual combination of three wash stills (4,700 litres), one large spirit still (9,400 litres) and three smaller spirit stills half that volume. All stills are fitted with ascending lyne arms and foreshots are unusually long – 45 minutes. The middle cut starts at 72% and goes down to 60%. A new cooling tower was recently installed as well as a new pipe from Kilbride dam to the distillery for the process water. The distillery has been running at full capacity for several years now and with 34 mashes per week, the plan is to produce 3.3 million litres of alcohol during 2023. The idea of increasing the capacity has been discussed for at least eight years and is still very much a part of the plans for the near future. Around 90% of the production is reserved for single malt and a new, huge warehouse currently being built on the left hand side of the road going to Port Ellen, will ensure that at least 75% of the production is matured on Islay.

The core range consists of **Oak Select**, **10 year old**, **10 year old cask strength**, **10 year old Sherry Oak Finish** (with 12 to 18 months in oloroso casks), **Quarter Cask**, **Lore** and a **25 year old cask strength**. The travel retail range consists of **Four Oak,** the **1815 Legacy Edition, Port Wood and PX Cask**. Also a part of the duty free range is the **Bessie Williamson Story 25 years old**. In 2019 a series of five bottlings named **The Ian Hunter Story** was introduced to celebrate the last of the Johnston family to own Laphroaig. **Chapter Five** was released in August 2023 and a month earlier the 17 year old madeira finish, **Francis Mallman edition,** was launched. Finally, this year´s Feis Ile bottling was **Cairdeas White Port & Madeira** bottled at 52.3%.

History:

1815 Brothers Alexander and Donald Johnston found Laphroaig.

1836 Donald buys out Alexander and takes over.

1837 James and Andrew Gairdner found Ardenistiel a stone's throw from Laphroaig.

1847 Donald Johnston is killed in an accident in the distillery. The Manager of neigh-bouring Lagavulin, Walter Graham, takes over.

1857 Operation is back in the hands of the Johnston family when Donald's son Dougald takes over.

1877 Dougald, being without heirs, passes away and his sister Isabella, married to their cousin Alexander takes over.

1907 Alexander Johnston dies and the distillery is inherited by his two sisters Catherine Johnston and Mrs. William Hunter (Isabella Johnston).

1908 Ian Hunter arrives in Islay to assist his mother and aunt with the distillery.

1924 The two stills are increased to four.

1927 Catherine Johnston dies, Ian Hunter takes over.

1928 Isabella Johnston dies and Ian Hunter becomes sole owner.

1950 Ian Hunter forms D. Johnston & Company

1954 Ian Hunter passes away and management of the distillery is taken over by Elisabeth "Bessie" Williamson.

1967 Seager Evans & Company buys the distillery through Long John Distillery, having already acquired part of Laphroaig in 1962. The number of stills is increased from four to five.

1972 Bessie Williamson retires. Another two stills are installed bringing the total to seven.

1975 Whitbread & Co. buys Seager Evans (now renamed Long John International) from Schenley International.

1989 The spirits division of Whitbread is sold to Allied Distillers.

1994 The Friends of Laphroaig is founded.

1995 A 10 year old cask strength is launched.

History continued:

2001 A 40 year old is released.

2004 Quarter Cask is launched.

2005 Fortune Brands becomes new owner.

2007 A vintage 1980 and a 25 year old are released.

2008 Cairdeas and Triple Wood are released.

2009 An 18 year old is released.

2010 Cairdeas Master Edition is launched.

2011 Laphroaig PX and Cairdeas - The Ileach Edition are released.

2012 Brodir and Cairdeas Origin are launched.

2013 QA Cask, An Cuan Mor, 25 year old cask strength and Cairdeas Port Wood Edition are released.

2014 Laphroaig Select is released.

2015 A 21 year old and a 32 year old sherry cask are released and the 15 year old is re-launched.

2016 Lore, Cairdeas 2016 and a 30 year old are released.

2017 Four Oak, The 1815 Edition and a 27 year old are released.

2018 A 28 year old and Cairdeas Fino are released.

2019 A 30 year old is the first release in a new series named The Ian Hunter Story.

2020 The Ian Hunter Story chapter 2, Cairdeas Port & Wine Casks and a 16 year old are released.

2021 A 10 year old sherry oak finish and The Ian Hunter Story chapter 3 are released.

2022 Chapter 4 in the Ian Hunter Story is released.

2023 Chapter 5 (a 34 year old) in the Ian Hunter Story, the Francis Mallman Edition and Cairdeas White Port & Madeira are released.

Tasting notes Laphroaig 10 year old:

GS – Old-fashioned sticking plaster, peat smoke and seaweed leap off the nose, followed by something a little sweeter and fruitier. Massive on the palate, with fish oil, salt and plankton, though the finish is quite tight and increasingly drying.

Oak Select

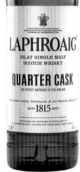
Quarter Cask

Lore

10 years old

Francis Mallman

The 1815 Edition

Ian Hunter Story
Chapter 5

Cairdeas
Feis Ile 2023

Linkwood

[link•wood]

Owner: | | **Region/district:**
Diageo | | Speyside

Founded: | **Status:** | **Capacity:**
1821 | Active | 5 600 000 litres

Address: Elgin, Morayshire IV30 8RD

Website: | **Tel:**
malts.com | 01343 862000

In the whisky world of today it is popular to talk about single estate distilleries and "grain-to-glass" production. It lends an authenticity when everything is produced and manufactured locally.

Sometimes we tend to forget that this was the the majority of Scotch was produced until the early 1900s. Linkwood is one example. Built on the vast Seafield Estates, on the southern outskirts of Elgin, it was run by the estate factor Peter Brown for many years. The barley came from the fields of the estate and the by-products were fed to the cattle. Peter's son William took over in 1872, demolished the distillery and built a new one. By this time, Linkwood single malt had earned a reputation of being one of the best to use for the popular blends of the time. Linkwood managed to keep its independence in 1925 when a huge number of distilleries were acquired by the giant of the time – DCL/SMD. It only lasted eight years until Linkwood finally was absorbed into the company which we today know as Diageo.

The original part of the distillery (equipped with traditional worm tubs) worked in tandem with a new site (built in 1971 and using shell and tube condensers) but stopped producing in 1996. In connection with an upgrade in 2013, the old buildings from the 1800s facing the road were demolished and an extension of the current still house, which houses two of the stills and the tunroom, was conducted. The only original buildings from 1872 left standing are No. 6 warehouse and the redundant, old kiln with the pagoda roof.

Linkwood is equipped with a 12.5 ton full lauter mash tun, 11 wooden washbacks and three pairs of stills. Since July 2022 the distillery is back on a 7-day production with 21 mashes per week which means all fermentations are now 75 hours. In 2024 the existing boiler will be replaced by a wood pellet dust boiler reducing the carbon emissions by 80-90%.

There is only one official core bottling from Diageo - a **12 year old Flora & Fauna**. In 2021, a 39 year old matured in American oak that had been seasoned with both PX and oloroso sherry was launched as part of the Prima & Ultima range.

History:

1821 Peter Brown founds the distillery.

1868 Peter Brown passes away and his son William inherits the distillery.

1872 William demolishes the distillery and builds a new one.

1897 Linkwood Glenlivet Distillery Company Ltd takes over operations.

1902 Innes Cameron, a whisky trader from Elgin, joins the Board and eventually becomes the major shareholder and Director.

1932 Innes Cameron dies and Scottish Malt Distillers takes over in 1933.

1962 Major refurbishment takes place.

1971 The two stills are increased by four. Technically, the four new stills belong to a new distillery referred to as Linkwood B.

1985 Linkwood A (the two original stills) closes.

1990 Linkwood A is in production again for a few months each year until 1996.

2002 A 26 year old from 1975 is launched as a Rare Malt.

2005 A 30 year old from 1974 is launched as a Rare Malt.

2008 Three different wood finishes (all 26 year old) are released.

2009 A Manager´s Choice 1996 is released.

2013 Expansion of the distillery including two more stills.

2016 A 37 year old is released.

2021 A 39 year old in the Prima & Ultima range is released.

12 years old

Tasting notes Linkwood 12 years old:

GS – Floral, grassy and fragrant on the nutty nose, while the slightly oily palate becomes increasingly sweet, ending up at marzipan and almonds. The relatively lengthy finish is quite dry and citric.

Loch Lomond

[lock low•mund]

Owner:	**Region/district:**
Loch Lomond Group	Western Highlands
(Hillhouse Capital et al)	
Founded: **Status:**	**Capacity:**
1965 Active	5 000 000 litres

Address: Lomond Estate, Alexandria G83 0TL

Website:	**Tel:**
lochlomondwhiskies.com	01389 752781

In a short time, Loch Lomond has transitioned from being a brand that few aficionados mentioned to become a whisky with an impressive range of high quality products.

The first step of this metamorphosis happened in 2014 when new owners headed by the current CEO of Loch Lomond Group (including Glen Scotia and Littlemill), Colin Matthews, took over and it was accelerated in 2019 when the Chinese investment firm Hillhouse Capital acquired a controlling part of the company. In February 2023 it was rumoured that Hillhouse is now considering a sale of its stake in the company.

Loch Lomond has an extremely unusual equipment setup. Founded in 1966, one pair of straight neck pot stills were installed. Yet another pair were installed in 1990 and four years later a grain distillery with two continuous stills was opened. One pair of traditional swan neck pot stills were installed in 1998 and in 2007 a single grain coffey still was added. Complemented with a third pair of straight neck stills, the distillery now has 11 stills of four different kinds! Of the 5 million litres on the malt side, 70% is distilled in the Coffey still with Loch Lomond Single Grain being the big seller. The Loch Lomond is distilled in the traditional pot stills but mixed before bottling with whisky from the straight neck stills. The rest of the equipment consists of a 9.5 ton full lauter mash tun, 21 stainless steel washbacks (with a fermentation time of 92 to 160 hours) for the malt side of the production and another 18 for the grain side.

The core range consists of **Loch Lomond Classic, Original, 10, 12** and **18 year old**. Furthermore there is **Loch Lomond Inchmurrin 12 year old** and **Loch Lomond Inchmoan 12 year old**. The duty-free range is made up of **Original, 8 year old Madeira Wood Finish, 12 year old, 14 year old Peated** and **18 year old**. There are also four core grain expressions, **Single Grain, Single Grain Peated, Distiller's Choice** and **Cooper's Choice**. Recent limited releases include **Steam and Fire**, finished in heavily charred casks and in October 2023 a **25 year old** was launched followed by a **50 year old** in December.

History:

1965 The distillery is built by Littlemill Distillery Company Ltd owned by Duncan Thomas and American Barton Brands.

1966 Production commences.

1971 Duncan Thomas is bought out.

1984 The distillery closes.

1985 Glen Catrine Bonded Warehouse Ltd buys Loch Lomond Distillery.

1987 The distillery resumes production.

1993 Grain spirits are also distilled.

1997 A fire destroys 300,000 litres of maturing whisky.

1999 Two more stills are installed.

2005 Inchmoan and Craiglodge as well as Inchmurrin 12 years are launched.

2006 Inchmurrin 4 years, Croftengea 1996 (9 years), Glen Douglas 2001 (4 years) and Inchfad 2002 (5 years) are launched.

2010 A peated Loch Lomond with no age statement is released as well as a Vintage 1966.

2012 New range for Inchmurrin released – 12, 15, 18 and 21 years.

2014 The distillery is sold to Exponent Private Equity. Organic versions of 12 year old single malt and single blend are released.

2015 Loch Lomond Original Single Malt is released together with a single grain and two blends, Reserve and Signature.

2016 A 12 year old and an 18 year old are launched.

2017 This year's releases include Inchmoan 12 year old and Inchmurrin 12 and 18 year old.

2018 A 50 year old Loch Lomond is released.

2019 The distillery is sold to Hillhouse Capital Management and a 50 year old is released.

2020 The core range is revamped and expanded.

2021 The 45 year old oloroso finish Remarkable Stills is released.

2022 A range of four grain expressions is launched.

2023 Steam and Fire and a 50 year old are released.

Tasting notes Loch Lomond 12 years old:

IR – Starts out malty on the nose followed by pears, apple pie with custard and digestive. Herbal at first on the palate with cinnamon and thyme, roasted root vegetables and nuts, caramel, vanilla and a hint of peat.

Loch Lomond 12 year old

Lochranza

[lock•ran•sa]

Owner:	**Region/district:**
Isle of Arran Distillers	Highlands (Arran)

Founded:	**Status:**	**Capacity:**
1993	Active (vc)	1 200 000 litres

Address: Lochranza, Isle of Arran KA27 8HJ

Website:	**Tel:**
arranwhisky.com	01770 830264

By many considered one of the new distilleries in Scotland, the Lochranza distillery has actually been producing since 1995. The new distillery on the island of Arran is instead Lagg, owned by the same company.

When Lagg was opened all the peated production was moved there and Lochranza is now all about unpeated whisky even though peated expressions made at the distillery (such as Machrie Moor) are still very much a part of the range

Lochranza is equipped with a 2.5 ton semi-lauter mash tun with a copper top producing a clear wort to retain the fruity elements essential for the distillery character. There are ten 13,000 litre Oregon pine washbacks with the last four having been installed in June 2023 in an extension of the tun room. Even though working seven days per week, with the additional washbacks the owners intend to have both short (50 hours) and long (100-110) fermentations. Finally there are two wash stills (6,500 litres) and two spirit stills (4,500 litres). The production plan for 2023 is to do 13 mashes per week and 850,000 litres of pure alcohol. Some 5% of this will be made from barley grown on Arran. The distillery is by far the most visited distillery in Scotland with around 100,000 people coming here annually.

The core range consists of a **10** and a **25 year old, Quarter Cask The Bothy, Sherry Cask The Bodega, Barrel Reserve** and **Robert Burns**. The 18 year old that used to be is currently out of stock but will return in 2024 while the 21 year old has been discontinued. The peated side of Arran is represented by **Machrie Moor Cask Strength** without age statement as well as a new **10 year old** version. Limited expressions include **Machrie Moor Fingal's Cut** with two varieties; quarter cask finish and sherry finish. Recent limited expressions of the unpeated Lochranza include three wood finishes – **Amarone, Port** and **Sauternes**. Finally a **17 year old** was released in October 2023 together with **Remnant Renegade**, the first in the Arran Signature Series.

History:

1993 Harold Currie founds the distillery.

1995 Production starts in full on 17th August.

1998 The first release is a 3 year old.

1999 The Arran 4 years old is released.

2002 Single Cask 1995 is launched.

2003 Single Cask 1997, non-chill filtered and Calvados finish is launched.

2004 Cognac finish, Marsala finish, Port finish and Arran First Distillation 1995 are launched.

2005 Arran 1996 and two finishes, Ch. Margaux and Grand Cru Champagne, are launched.

2006 After an unofficial launch in 2005, Arran 10 years old is released as well as a couple of new wood finishes.

2007 Four new wood finishes and Gordon's Dram are released.

2008 The first 12 year old is released as well as four new wood finishes.

2009 Peated single casks, two wood finishes and 1996 Vintage are released.

2010 A 14 year old, Rowan Tree, three cask finishes and Machrie Moor (peated) are released.

2011 The Westie, Sleeping Warrior and a 12 year old cask strength are released.

2012 The Eagle and The Devil's Punch Bowl are released.

2013 A 16 year old is released.

2014 A 17 year old and Machrie Moor cask strength are released.

2015 A 18 year old and The Illicit Stills are released.

2017 The Exciseman is released.

2018 A 21 year old and Brodick Bay are released.

2019 The core range is revamped and the limited Lochranza Castle is released.

2020 A 25 year old and the 21 year old Kildonan & Pladda are released.

2021 Drumadoon Point and two 15 year olds are released.

2022 Ten year old Machrie Moor and Rare Batch are released.

2023 A 17 year old and Remnant Renegade are launched.

Tasting notes Arran 14 year old:

GS – Very fragrant and perfumed on the nose, with peaches, brandy and ginger snaps. Smooth and creamy on the palate, with spicy summer fruits, apricots and nuts. The lingering finish is nutty and slowly drying.

10 years old

Longmorn

[long•morn]

Owner:
Chivas Brothers
(Pernod Ricard)

Region/district:
Speyside

Founded:
1894

Status:
Active

Capacity:
4 500 000 litres

Address: Longmorn, Morayshire IV30 8SJ

Website:
secret-speyside.com

Tel:
01343 554139

It is a well-known fact that most malt whiskies of today tasted differently a century ago. The reasons for that are many; the yeast, the barley and, not least, the production methods.

In the excellent book "The Distilleries of Great Britain & Ireland" published by James Eadie Ltd. a visit to Longmorn in November 1924 is accounted for. The distillery is described as "up to date in every sense of the word" but the interesting part is about their floor malting. To dry the malt two thirds of peat from the nearby Mannoch Hill were used to one third of coke and for the first 20 hours the kiln was fired by peat. Peat was abundant and had been used as fuel for centuries all across Scotland. The Longmorns of latter days however carry no trace of smoke. Its popularity amongst aficionados comes from being a complex single malt aging well in both ex-bourbon and ex-sherry casks.

In 2016 a remake of the official range indicated that the owners, Chivas Brothers, had the intention of building a brand that would be able to compete with some of the other super premium malts. At the moment though there are signs indicating that the current core range could be replaced as well as the bottlings in the Secret Speyside Collection. Nothing has been revealed by the owners though.

Longmorn distillery is equipped with an 8.5 ton Briggs full lauter mash tun and ten stainless steel washbacks. There are eight, large onion-shaped stills with declining lyne arms producing a rich new make combining both depth and fruitiness. In the last few years, production has been running for five days per week with 18 mashes which means roughly three million litres of alcohol.

The current core range consists of **The Distiller's Choice**, a **16 year old** and a **23 year old**. In 2019, another three bottlings (**18, 23** and **25 year old**) appeared in a series named The Secret Speyside Collection. Finally, there are four cask strength bottlings in the Distillery Reserve Collection, available at all Chivas's visitor centres – from **15** to **24 years old**.

History:

1893 John Duff & Company, which founded Glenlossie already in 1876, starts construction. John Duff, George Thomson and Charles Shirres are involved in the company. The total cost amounts to £20,000.

1894 First production in December.

1897 John Duff buys out the other partners.

1898 John Duff builds another distillery next to Longmorn which is called Benriach (at times aka Longmorn no. 2). Duff declares bankruptcy and the shares are sold by the bank to James R. Grant.

1970 The distillery company is merged with The Glenlivet & Glen Grant Distilleries and Hill Thomson & Co. Ltd. Own floor maltings ceases.

1972 The number of stills is increased from four to six. Spirit stills are converted to steam firing.

1974 Another two stills are added.

1978 Seagrams takes over through The Chivas & Glenlivet Group.

1994 Wash stills are converted to steam firing.

2001 Pernod Ricard buys Seagram Spirits & Wine together with Diageo and Pernod Ricard takes over the Chivas group.

2004 A 17 year old cask strength is released.

2007 A 16 year old is released replacing the 15 year old.

2012 Production capacity is expanded.

2015 The Distiller´s Choice is released.

2016 A 16 year old and a 23 year old are released.

2019 Three expressions in the new The Secret Speyside Collection are released.

Distiller´s Choice

Tasting notes Longmorn Distiller´s Choice:

GS – Barley sugar, ginger, toffee and malt on the sweet nose. The palate reveals caramel and milk chocolate, with peppery Jaffa orange. Toffee, barley and a hint of spicy oak in the medium-length finish.

Macallan

[mack•al•un]

Owner:
Edrington Group

Region/district:
Speyside

Founded: **Status:** **Capacity:**
1824 Active (vc) 15 000 000 litres

Address: Easter Elchies, Craigellachie, Morayshire
AB38 9RX

Website: **Tel:**
themacallan.com 01340 871471

A few distilleries have been responsible for the main portion of global single malt sales for many years. In 2021 the top six malts represented more than 43% of the sales – the largest share since 2009.

The only distillery of the Top 6 that hasn't increased its market share in the last five years is Macallan with 7% of the world sales in 2021. In 2017 it was 8.3%. Volumes, however, isn't everything. Macallan is still the best selling malt in terms of value. The last decade of focusing on premium and ultra-premium releases has paid off. The distillery has plenty of old stock in their warehouses and is usually the number one on lists of most investible whiskies.

The ownership of Macallan is more complex than most other Scottish distilleries. Highland Distilleries (which assumed control over Macallan but also e g Highland Park in 1996) was acquired in 1999 by a new company under the name The 1887 Company. The ownership was divided between Edrington (with The Robertson Trust in the background) owning 70% and William Grant & Sons controlling 30%. Ten years previously Japanese Suntory had bought 25% but only of Macallan. On top of that, in January 2020, The Robertson Trust sold part of Edrington to Suntory who now hold 10% of the shares in The Edrington Group aside from their share of Macallan.

Macallan is equipped with a full lauter mash tun with a 17 ton mash and there is also room for another tun, should this be needed in the future. There are 21 washbacks made of stainless steel with a fermentation time of 60 hours and 12 wash stills and 24 spirit stills – quite small and with steeply descending lyne arms. They are not attached to any spirit safe and the spirits go into a buffer tank and from there to the spirits filling store. Since the opening of the new distillery in 2019, the production has continuously been ramped up and in 2023 they are looking to do 41-42 mashes per week resulting in 12.5-13 million litres of pure alcohol. There are 16 dunnage and 35 racked warehouses on site. In spring 2022 the cooperage that used to be located at the sister distillery Glenrothes was moved to Macallan.

The core range of Macallan consists of **Sherry Oak 12, 18, 25** and **30 years old** and **Double Oak 12, 15, 18** and **30 years old** Included is also **Macallan Estate.** Triple Cask (which used to be named Fine Oak) has been discontinued. The number of limited expressions is huge; **The Red Collection** with old and ultra-rare bottlings, the M Collection with **M, M Black** and **M Copper,** the Harmony Collection with **Rich Cacao, Fine Cacao, Intense Arabica** and **Smooth Arabica**, **Edition** with No. 6 as the latest, **Distil Your World** and the **Fine & Rare** with single casks from 1926 to 1993. In 2022, the oldest ever bottled Scotch single malt, the 81 year old **The Reach**, was also released.

The Macallan Quest Collection is reserved for duty-free including **Quest, Lumina, Terra** and **Enigma** as well as **Oscuro** and **Rare Cask Black.** In 2023 a new range of 5 whiskies for travel retail named **The Colour Collection** was announced.

History:

1824 The distillery is licensed to Alexander Reid under the name Elchies Distillery.

1847 Alexander Reid passes away and James Shearer Priest and James Davidson take over.

1868 James Stuart takes over the licence. He founds Glen Spey distillery a decade later.

1886 James Stuart buys the distillery.

1892 Stuart sells the distillery to Roderick Kemp from Elgin. Kemp expands the distillery and names it Macallan-Glenlivet.

1909 Roderick Kemp passes away and the Roderick Kemp Trust is established to secure the family's future ownership.

1965 The number of stills is increased from six to twelve.

1966 The trust is reformed as a private limited company.

1968 The company is introduced on the London Stock Exchange.

1974 The number of stills is increased to 18.

1975 Another three stills are added, now making the total 21.

1984 The first official 18 year old single malt is launched.

1986 Japanese Suntory buys 25% of Macallan-Glenlivet plc stocks.

1996 Highland Distilleries buys the remaining stocks. 1874 Replica is launched.

1999 Edrington and William Grant & Sons buys Highland Distilleries for £601 million through The 1887 Company with 70% held by Edrington and 30% by William Grant & Sons. Suntory still holds 25% in Macallan.

2000 The first single cask from Macallan (1981) is named Exceptional 1.

2002 Elegancia, 1841 Replica, Exceptional II and Exceptional III are launched.

History continued:

2003 1876 Replica and Exceptional IV, single cask from 1990 are released.

2004 Exceptional V, single cask from 1989 is released as well as Exceptional VI, single cask from 1990. The Fine Oak series is launched.

2005 New expressions are Macallan Woodland Estate, Winter Edition and the 50 year old.

2007 1851 Inspiration and Whisky Maker´s Selection are released as a part of the Travel Retail range.

2008 Estate Oak and 55 year old Lalique are released.

2009 The mothballed No. 2 stillhouse is re-opened. The Macallan 1824 Collection and a 57 year old Lalique bottling is released.

2010 Oscuro is released for Duty Free.

2011 Macallan MMXI is released for duty free.

2012 Macallan Gold, the first in the new 1824 series, is launched.

2013 Amber, Sienna and Ruby are released.

2014 1824 Masters Series (with Rare Cask, Reflexion and No. 6) is released.

2015 Rare Cask Black is released.

2016 Edition No. 1 and 12 year old Double Cask are released.

2017 Folio 2 is released. The new distillery is commissioned.

2018 The Quest Collection is released for duty free and Macallan M Black and Genesis are launched. Concept No. 1 and a 72 and a 52 year old are released.

2019 Macallan Estate, Edition No. 5 and Concept No. 2 are released.

2020 Double Cask 15 and 18 year old are released as well as the Red Collection.

2021 The third and final bottling in the Concept range is launched as well as Tales of The Macallan Volume I.

2022 The Harmony Collection, a 30 year old Double Cask and the 81 year old The Reach are released.

2023 The Colour Collection is launched.

Tasting notes Macallan 12 year old Sherry oak:
GS – The nose is luscious, with buttery sherry and Christmas cake characteristics. Rich and firm on the palate, with sherry, elegant oak and Jaffa oranges. The finish is long and malty, with slightly smoky spice.

Double Cask 30 years   Estate   Sherry Oak 12 years

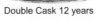
Double Cask 12 years

Harmony Fine Cacao   78 years old   A Night On Earth

M Copper   Rare Cask Black   Rare Cask Batch 3

Macduff

[mack•duff]

Owner:	**Region/district:**
John Dewar & Sons Ltd	Highlands
(Bacardi)	

Founded:	**Status:**	**Capacity:**
1960	Active	3 400 000 litres

Address: Banff, Aberdeenshire AB45 3JT

Website:	**Tel:**
lastgreatmalts.com	01261 812612

Although the French and Italien markets showed great interest in Glen Deveron single malt (as it was called in the early millenium), The Deveron was largely unknown to other markets until the rebranding in 2015. Today it sells 350,000 bottles per year.

These are impressive numbers for a "new" malt, yet one third of the spirit produced is used for William Lawson's blended Scotch while the remaining volume is equally split between own single malts and reciprocal use. William Lawson's was registered in 1889 by an Irish blending company called E. & J. Burke. The whisky is named after William Lawson who became export manager of the company one year before the blend was launched.

While sales increased year by year, it wasn't until Martini & Rossi took over in 1963 that volumes began to skyrocket. In 2015 it was the 6th best selling Scotch blend in the world with a volume of 40 million bottles. Since then a couple of competitors have caught up and in 2022 sales were at 42 million bottles (number 8 on the top list). At the moment the brand's heavy exposure on the Russian and Ukrainian markets is problematic.

In August 2022 a new Steinecker full lauter mash tun with a 7.6 ton mash was installed at Macduff. Included in the rest of the equipment are nine stainless steel washbacks (33,000 litres each) and with a fermentation time of 55 hours. Finally there are two wash stills with vertical condensers and three spirit stills with horizontal condensers and sub coolers. Foreshots run for 20 minutes and the cut points for the spirit run are between 74% and 64%. During 2023 the production will be based on 26 mashes per week for 48 weeks resulting in 3.3 million litres of alcohol. There is space for another six washbacks and two more stills should the owners decide to increase the capacity in the future.

The core range from the distillery is known under the name The Deveron and consists of a **10 year old** and a **12 year old**. For duty free there is a range, first launched in 2013, named Glen Deveron The Royal Burgh encompassing a **16**, a **20** and a new **28 year old**.

History:

1960 The distillery is founded by Marty Dyke, George Crawford, James Stirrat and Brodie Hepburn (who is also involved in Tullibardine and Deanston). Macduff Distillers Ltd is the name of the company.

1964 The number of stills is increased from two to three.

1967 Stills now total four.

1968 The first bottling from the distillery is launched - the 5 year old Macduff Pure Highland Malt Scotch Whisky.

1972 William Lawson Distillers, part of General Beverage Corporation which is owned by Martini & Rossi, buys the distillery from Glendeveron Distilleries.

1990 A fifth still is installed.

1993 Bacardi buys Martini Rossi (including William Lawson) and eventually transfered Macduff to the subsidiary John Dewar & Sons.

2013 The Royal Burgh Collection (16, 20 and 30 years old) is launched for duty free.

2015 A new range is launched - 10, 12 and 18 years old.

10 years old

Tasting notes The Deveron 12 years old:

GS – Soft, sweet and fruity on the nose, with vanilla, ginger, and apple blossom. Medium-bodied, gently spicy, with butterscotch and Brazil nuts. Caramel contrasts with quite dry spicy oak in the finish.

Mannochmore

[man•och•moor]

Owner: Diageo **Region/district:** Speyside

Founded: 1971 **Status:** Active **Capacity:** 6 000 000 litres

Address: Elgin, Morayshire IV30 8SS

Website: malts.com **Tel:** 01343 862000

Speyside is full of distilleries – actually more than fifty – and most of them are easy to find. A few can even be seen from miles around. Mannochmore does, however, not belong to that category.

If you travel along the A941 towards Rothes and stop to take pictures of Longmorn on your left side, you can see on your right hand side in the distance the rooftops of warehouses and a huge, white building with smoke coming out of the chimney. Mannochmore you think but you're not quite correct. The building is a dark grains plant sitting on the same site as the distillery.

Even if you drive right up to the distillery, you'll have difficulties spotting it. What you see is Glenlossie's old kiln house with the pagoda roof. To be able to detect Mannochmore, you have to enter the site (which you shouldn't as visitors are not allowed) where you will find a still house with large windows and another building for the mash tun and eight of the washbacks.

Mannochmore and Glenlossie are sister distilleries but built almost a century apart. During the first decade of the new millenium, the two distilleries shared the same crew working at Glenlossie for six months and then moving on to Mannochore for the rest of the year. For quite some time, both distilleries have been working more or less at full capacity.

Mannochmore is equipped with an 11.1 ton Briggs full lauter mash tun, eight wooden washbacks, another eight external washbacks made of stainless steel and four pairs of stills. Clear wort and long fermentations (up to 100 hours) create a new-make spirit with a fruity character and the distillery is currently running a seven-day production with 5,8 million litres planned for 2023.

Mannochmore is the signature malt for Haig, a brand first introduced in the late 1880s and which today sells a little more than 3 million bottles per year. The only current official bottling is a **12 year old Flora & Fauna**. A limited release in the Prima & Ultima range was announced in June 2022 – a **31 year old** bottled at 45.1% having spent almost thirty years in virgin European oak.

History:

1971 Distillers Company Limited (DCL) founds the distillery on the site of their sister distillery Glenlossie. It is managed by John Haig & Co. Ltd.

1985 The distillery is mothballed.

1989 In production again.

1992 A Flora & Fauna series 12 years old becomes the first official bottling.

2009 An 18 year old is released.

2010 A Manager's Choice 1998 is released.

2013 The number of stills is increased to eight.

2016 A 25 year old cask strength is released.

2022 A 31 year old Prima & Ultima is released.

31 year old
Prima & Ultima

Tasting notes Mannochmore 12 years old:

GS – Perfumed and fresh on the light, citric nose, with a sweet, floral, fragrant palate, featuring vanilla, ginger and even a hint of mint. Medium length in the finish, with a note of lingering almonds.

Miltonduff

[mill•ton•duff]

Owner: | **Region/district:**
Chivas Brothers | Speyside
(Pernod Ricard) |

Founded: | **Status:** | **Capacity:**
1824 | Active | 5 800 000 litres

Address: Miltonduff, Elgin, Morayshire IV30 8TQ

Website: | **Tel:**
- | 01343 547433

The next two years will be extremely busy at Miltonduff. The distillery is facing a major expansion which will make it the third largest malt whisky distillery in Scotland.

The project was announced by Chivas Brothers already in spring 2022 but a planning application wasn't submitted to the local council until January 2023 and 31 May it was approved. A number of warehouses northwest of the existing distillery will be demolished to make space for a new distillery with nine or ten pairs of stills. The new capacity will be an impressive 16 million litres of alcohol and the total investment is £88m. That also includes a major expansion of Aberlour. The plans for Miltonduff are also to make the distillery carbon-neutral which is an overall goal within the next few years for all distilleries owned by Chivas Bros.

The reason for this expansion is the continued success for Ballantine´s blended Scotch where Miltonduff malt is a vital component. In the last four years, volumes of the second best selling Scotch in the world has increased by 37% to 112 million bottles. The corresponding figures for Johnnie Walker Red Label (number one on the list with 132 million bottles) is up 10% and Ballantine's is closing the gap. However, if one adds the volumes of Johnnie Walker Black Label (another 70 million bottles) it is visible just how dominant the Johnie Walker brand is.

Miltonduff is currently equipped with an eight ton full lauter mash tun with a copper dome, 16 stainless steel washbacks with a fermentation time of 56 hours and six large stills.

Official bottlings of Miltonduff single malt were rare until 2017 when it, together with Glenburgie and Glentauchers, was released in a new range called Ballantine's Single Malt Series. The official bottling is a **15 year old** and it was accompanied in 2020 by a **19 year old**, exclusive to Asia. There is also a **12 year old cask strength** in the Distillery Reserve Collection, available at all Chivas' visitor centres.

History:

1824 Andrew Peary and Robert Bain obtain a licence for Miltonduff Distillery. It has previously operated as an illicit farm distillery called Milton Distillery but changes name when the Duff family buys the site it is operating on.

1866 William Stuart buys the distillery.

1895 Thomas Yool & Co. becomes new part-owner.

1936 Thomas Yool & Co. sells the distillery to Hiram Walker Gooderham & Worts. The latter transfers administration to the newly acquired subsidiary George Ballantine & Son.

1964 A pair of Lomond stills is installed to produce the rare Mosstowie.

1974 Major reconstruction of the distillery.

1981 The Lomond stills are decommissioned and replaced by two ordinary pot stills, the number of stills now totalling six.

1986 Allied Lyons buys 51% of Hiram Walker.

1987 Allied Lyons acquires the rest of Hiram Walker.

1991 Allied Distillers follow United Distillers´ example of Classic Malts and introduce Caledonian Malts in which Tormore, Glendro-nach and Laphroaig are included in addition to Miltonduff. Tormore is later replaced by Scapa.

2005 Chivas Brothers (Pernod Ricard) becomes the new owner through the acquisition of Allied Domecq.

2017 A 15 year old is released.

2020 A 19 year old exclusive to Asia is released.

15 years old

Tasting notes Miltonduff 15 years old:

IR – Fresh citrus and honey on the nose together with heather, ginger and peaches. More spicy on the palate with cinnamon and clove, vanilla, honey, red berries and liquorice.

Mortlach

[mort•lack]

Owner: Diageo	**Region/district:** Speyside

Founded: 1823	**Status:** Active	**Capacity:** 3 800 000 litres

Address: Dufftown, Keith, Banffshire AB55 4AQ

Website: mortlach.com, malts.com	**Tel:** 01340 822100

Mortlach was the first distillery to be founded in Dufftown. Despite this the distillery failed to make an impact on whisky history during its initial 30 years.

Many owners replaced each other, including the brothers James and John Grant who later founded Glen Grant, and at times there was no production at all. Not until George Cowie joined the company as part owner in 1853, did the situation start to change. Cowie was an engineer and a railway surveyor who had worked with the expansion of the railway in Banffshire. He streamlined production and made sure that Mortlach single malt was to be sold beyond Scotland's borders. His son, Alexander, joined the company in 1896, expanded the distillery and introduced the 2.81 distillation that is still in use today.

Mortlach is equipped with a 12 ton full lauter mash tun and six washbacks made of Douglas fir. For many years there have been both short and long fermentations but since June 2022, the distillery is working at full capacity seven days a week with 16 mashes which means all fermentations are 55 hours. There are three wash stills and three spirit stills – all of them attached to worm tubs for cooling the spirit vapours. The No. 3 pair acts as a traditional double distillation. The low wines from wash stills No. 1 and 2 are directed to the remaining two spirit stills according to a certain distribution. In one of the spirit stills, called Wee Witchie, the charge is redistilled twice and, with all the various distillations taken into account, it could be said that Mortlach is distilled 2.81 times.

The core range consists of **12 year old Wee Witchie**, **16 year old Distiller's Dram**, **20 year old Cowie's Blue Seal** and, for duty-free, the **14 year old Alexander's Way**. In 2022 the **30 year old Midnight Malt** and in autumn 2023 an unusual **Special Release** bottling appeared which had been matured in a combination of ex-Kanosuke Japanese whisky casks and ex-pinot noir casks. In 2021 Diageo (through Distil Ventures) made an investment in Kanosuke distillery.

History:

1823 The distillery is founded by James Findlater.

1824 Donald Macintosh and Alexander Gordon become part-owners.

1831 The distillery is sold to John Robertson for £270.

1832 A. & T. Gregory buys Mortlach.

1837 James and John Grant of Aberlour become part-owners. No production takes place.

1842 The distillery is now owned by John Alexander Gordon and the Grant brothers.

1851 Mortlach is producing again after having been used as a church and a brewery for some years.

1853 George Cowie joins and becomes part-owner.

1867 John Alexander Gordon dies and Cowie becomes sole owner.

1896 Alexander Cowie joins the company.

1897 The number of stills is increased to six.

1923 Alexander Cowie sells the distillery to John Walker & Sons.

1925 John Walker becomes part of Distillers Company Limited (DCL).

1964 Major refurbishment.

1968 Floor maltings ceases.

1996 Mortlach 1972 is released as a Rare Malt.

1998 Mortlach 1978 is released as a Rare Malt.

2004 Mortlach 1971, a 32 year old cask strength is released.

2014 Rare Old, Special Strength, 18 year old and 25 year old are released.

2018 A new range is presented; 12 year old Wee Witchie, 16 year old Distiller´s Dram and 20 year old Cowie´s Blue Seal.

2019 The oldest official Mortlach bottling ever, 47 years, is released and a 26 year old appears in the Special Releases.

2020 A 25 year old Prima & Ultima is released followed by a 21 year old Rare by Nature.

2021 A 13 year old, partly matured in virgin oak, is released as well as a 25 year old Prima & Ultima.

2022 The 30 year old Midnight Malt is launched.

2023 A NAS Special release bottling appears, partly matured in ex-Japanese casks.

Tasting notes Mortlach 12 years old:

IR – Fresh and intense on the nose with notes of sherry, apple cider, dark plums, tobacco and toffee. The palate is robust with orange marmalade, dark chocolate, espresso and chili pepper.

Special Release 2023

Oban

[oa•bun]

Owner:		Region/district:
Diageo		Western Highlands

Founded:	Status:	Capacity:
1794	Active (vc)	870 000 litres

Address: Stafford Street, Oban, Argyll PA34 5NH

Website:	Tel:
malts.com	01631 572004 (vc)

In the old days, it was common that a son followed in his father's footsteps and started working at the same distillery. Today the younger generations tend to find other careers.

At Oban, however, three generations have been in charge of the whisky production and this has, so far, been commemorated by two special releases. In 2019 Old Teddy was released in honour of Teddy Maclean who started at the distillery in 1953 and eventually became the master distiller. His skills were inherited by his son Teddy who joined the company in 1985 and the limited Young Teddy was launched in spring 2023. Now we are only waiting for the third installment to celebrate Derek Maclean, the third generation, who took up the position as senior operator at Oban in 2017.

Oban is one of few urban distilleries remaining and in this case the town of Oban (officially founded in 1820) was actually built around the distillery which opened in 1793. Today, completely surrounded by shops and restaurants in the busiest part of Oban, the distillery stands no chance of expanding even if it wanted to.

The equipment consists of a 7 ton stainless steel mash tun with rakes. The four wooden washbacks are made from Oregon pine and there is one wash still (16,880 litres) and one spirit still (8,296 litres) attached to a stainless steel worm tub. One washback and the spirit still were replaced in spring 2023. The fruity character of Oban single malt is partly due to long fermentations, hence only six mashes per week with five long (110 hours) and one short (65 hours) can be managed. The production plan is to distill around 840,000 litres in 2023.

The core range consists of **Little Bay**, a **14 year old**, an **18 year old** exclusive to the US market and a **Distiller's Edition** with a montilla fino sherry finish. Recent limited editions include the **Night's Watch – Oban Bay Reserve, Old Teddy, Young Teddy** and an **11 year old** Carribean rum cask finish, which was released in autumn 2023 in the Special Releases series. At the same time a **26 year old** matured in refill European oak was released as part of the Prima & Ultima range.

History:

1793 John and Hugh Stevenson found the distillery.

1820 Hugh Stevenson dies.

1821 Hugh Stevenson's son Thomas takes over.

1829 Bad investments force Thomas Stevenson into bankruptcy. His eldest son John takes over.

1830 John buys the distillery from his father's creditors for £1,500.

1866 Peter Cumstie buys the distillery.

1883 Cumstie sells Oban to James Walter Higgins who refurbishes and modernizes it.

1898 The Oban & Aultmore-Glenlivet Co. takes over with Alexander Edwards at the helm.

1923 The Oban Distillery Co. owned by Buchanan-Dewar takes over.

1925 Buchanan-Dewar becomes part of Distillers Company Limited (DCL).

1931 Production ceases.

1937 In production again.

1968 Floor maltings ceases and the distillery closes for reconstruction.

1972 Reopening of the distillery.

1979 Oban 12 years is on sale.

1988 United Distillers launches Classic Malts and Oban 14 year old is included.

1998 A Distillers' Edition is launched.

2002 The oldest Oban (32 years) so far is launched.

2010 A no age distillery exclusive is released.

2013 A limited 21 year old is released.

2015 Oban Little Bay is released.

2016 A distillery exclusive without age statement is released.

2018 A 21 year old is launched as a part of the Special Releases.

2019 Night's Watch - Oban Bay Reserve and Old Teddy are released.

2021 A 12 year old Rare by Nature is released.

2022 A 10 year old Special Release with an amontillado finish is launched.

2023 Young Teddy and an 11 year old Special Release rum finish are launched.

Tasting notes Oban 14 years old:

GS – Lightly smoky on the honeyed, floral nose. Toffee, cereal and a hint of peat. The palate offers initial cooked fruits, becoming spicier. Complex, bittersweet, oak and more gentle smoke. The finish is quite lengthy, with spicy oak, toffee and new leather.

11 years old
Special Releases 2023

Pulteney

[poolt•ni]

Owner: **Region/district:**
Inver House Distillers   Northern Highlands
(International Beverage Holdings)

Founded: **Status:**   **Capacity:**
1826   Active (vc)   1 700 000 litres

Address: Huddart St, Wick, Caithness KW1 5BA

Website: **Tel:**
oldpulteney.com   01955 602371

With its location in Wick, the largest port for herring fisheries in Europe in the mid 1800s, the coastal connection has always been important for Pulteney distillery and Old Pulteney single malt.

The start of a new range of whiskies, the Coastal Series, in autumn 2022 highlights the maritime bond even further. The bottlings, with the first of four matured in Pineau des Charentes casks from Charente-Maritime, will all be inspired by coastal locations around the world.

Pulteney (together with Balblair, Balmenach, Knockdhu and Speyburn) is owned by Inver House Distillers. They make up part of a group named International Beverage Holdings. InBev is the spirits arm of one of Asia´s top drinks producers, ThaiBev, controlled by the Thai billionaire Charoen Sirivadhanabhakdi and his family. With 700,000 bottles sold in 2021, Old Pulteney is Inver House´s best selling single malt.

The distillery is equipped with a stainless steel semi-lauter mash tun clad with wood and with a copper canopy and seven stainless steel washbacks. Fermentation time is a mix of short (50 hours) and long cycles (110 hours). The wash still, equipped with a huge boil ball and a very thick lye pipe, is quaintly chopped off at the top. Both stills use stainless steel worm tubs for condensing the spirit. For the past few years, the distillery has been working a 5-day week producing around 1.3 million litres of alcohol.

The core range is made up of **12 years old**, the smoky **Huddart** and **15, 18** and **25 years old**, all three matured in a combination of bourbon and sherry casks. For the travel retail market there is a **10 year old** matured in bourbon barrels, a new **13 year old** finished in Spanish oak casks and a **16 year old** with a finish in oloroso casks. Recent limited releases include the aforementioned **Coastal Series Pineau des Charentes** and a **38 year old** oloroso sherry finish single cask for the Chinese market. The **Flotilla** series, finally, continued with a new vintage – 2012.

History:

1826   James Henderson founds the distillery.

1920   The distillery is bought by James Watson.

1923   Buchanan-Dewar takes over.

1930   Production ceases.

1951   In production again after being acquired by the solicitor Robert Cumming.

1955   Cumming sells to James & George Stodart, a subsidiary to Hiram Walker & Sons.

1958   The distillery is rebuilt.

1959   The floor maltings close.

1961   Allied Breweries buys James & George Stodart.

1981   Allied Breweries changes name to Allied Lyons.

1995   Allied Domecq sells Pulteney to Inver House Distillers.

1997   Old Pulteney 12 years is launched.

2001   Pacific Spirits (Great Oriole Group) buys Inver House at a price of $85 million.

2004   A 17 year old is launched.

2005   A 21 year old is launched.

2006   International Beverage Holdings acquires Pacific Spirits UK.

2010   WK499 Isabella Fortuna is released.

2012   A 40 year old and WK217 Spectrum are released.

2013   Old Pulteney Navigator, The Lighthouse range (3 expressions) and Vintage 1990 are released.

2014   A 35 year old is released.

2015   Dunnet Head and Vintage 1989 are released.

2017   Three vintages (1983, 1990 and 2006) are released together with a 25 year old.

2018   A completely new core range is launched.

2020   A limited 34 year old is released.

2022   A limited 38 year old is released.

2023   The Coastal Series is introduced and a 13 year old is launched for duty free.

12 years old

Tasting notes Old Pulteney 12 years old:

GS – The nose presents pleasingly fresh malt and floral notes, with a touch of pine. The palate is comparatively sweet, with malt, spices, fresh fruit and a suggestion of salt. The finish is medium in length, drying and decidedly nutty.

Royal Brackla

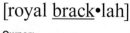
[royal brack•lah]

Owner:
John Dewar & Sons
(Bacardi)

Region/district:
Highlands

Founded: **Status:** **Capacity:**
1812 Active 4 300 000 litres

Address: Cawdor, Nairn, Nairnshire IV12 5QY

Website: **Tel:**
lastgreatmalts.com 01667 402002

Royal Brackla was the first distillery ever to carry a Royal Warrant. King William IV recognized the distillery in 1835 and the warrant was renewed by Queen Victoria three years later when she had accessed the throne.

Particular to Royal Warrants, however, is that they need to be renewed by the new monarch and in spite of the name, Royal Brackla today does not hold a warrant. However, the distillery did experience a regal connection in 1986 when a 60 year old (distilled in 1924), bottled in crystal decanters by Buchanans's, was released for the Japanese market to celebrate the 60th anniversary of emperor Hirohito.

Royal Brackla is connected to an important character of the Scotch whisky industry – Andrew Usher, who is credited for creating one of the first commercial blends of Scotch whiskies. He set up his own business in 1813 and later became an agent for Royal Brackla where he launched his first blended whisky (a vatting of malt whiskies) called Old Vatted Glenlivet. After his death in 1853 his son, Andrew II, continued the experiments but now used grain whisky and malt whisky as components. Andrew II later became one of the directors of Royal Brackla.

Royal Brackla is equipped with a 12.9 ton full lauter mash tun with a six hour mash cycle. There are six wooden washbacks and another two made of stainless steel – all with a fermentation time of 68 hours. Finally, there are also two pairs of large stills with tall necks and slightly ascending lyne arms. In 2023, the production plan is to alternate between 17 and 18 mashes per week, translating into 4.3 million litres of alcohol which equates to the full capacity of the distillery.

The core range consists of a **12 year old oloroso finish**, an **18 year old palo cortado finish** and a **20 year old** finished in a combination of PX, oloroso and palo cortado. There are also limited releases for the travel retail market in the Exceptional Cask Series – most recently a **25 year old oloroso finish**.

History:

1812 The distillery is founded by Captain William Fraser.

1833 Brackla becomes the first of three distilleries allowed to use 'Royal' in the name.

1852 Robert Fraser & Co. takes over the distillery.

1897 The distillery is rebuilt and Royal Brackla Distillery Company Limited is founded.

1919 John Mitchell and James Leict from Aberdeen purchase Royal Brackla.

1926 John Bisset & Company Ltd takes over.

1943 Scottish Malt Distillers (SMD) buys John Bisset & Company Ltd and thereby acquires Royal Brackla.

1964 The distillery closes for a big refurbishment
-1966 and the number of stills is increased to four. The maltings closes.

1970 Two stills are increased to four.

1985 The distillery is mothballed.

1991 Production resumes.

1993 A 10 year old Royal Brackla is launched in United Distillers´ Flora & Fauna series.

1997 UDV spends more than £2 million on improvements and refurbishing.

1998 Bacardi–Martini buys Dewar´s from Diageo.

2004 A new 10 year old is launched.

2014 A 35 year old is released for Changi airport in Singapore.

2015 A new range is released; 12, 16 and 21 year old.

2019 A new range for travel retail, including 12, 18 and 20 year olds, is launched.

2021 The 18 year old palo cortado finish and the 20 year old sherry finish (three different types of sherry) become part of the core range.

12 years old

Tasting notes Royal Brackla 12 years old:

GS – Warm spices, malt and peaches in cream on the nose. The palate is robust, with spice and mildly smoky soft fruit. Quite lengthy in the finish, with citrus fruit, mild spice and cocoa powder.

Royal Lochnagar

[royal loch•nah•gar]

Owner: Diageo

Region/district: Eastern Highlands

Founded: 1845

Status: Active (vc)

Capacity: 500 000 litres

Address: Crathie, Ballater, Aberdeenshire AB35 5TB

Website: malts.com

Tel: 01339 742700

Diageo is the world's largest producer of spirits with megabrands such as Johnnie Walker, Smirnoff, Guinness and Baileys. It is also the number one supplier of Scotch to the world.

Their dominance has accelerated in the new millenium and in 2021 Diageo's market share of Scotch was 41% – the highest since 1996. The following years (1997/1998) the share dropped considerably due to the fact that all Dewar´s distilleries (owned by UDV, the precursor of Diageo) were sold off to Bacardi. That deal was enforced by the regulators to preserve competition in the liquor industry following the merger between Guinness and Grand Metropolitan (forming Diageo).

It is interesting though that in this huge conglomerate there is still room for a tiny distillery such as Royal Lochnagar, producing just half a million litres per year. The provenience of the distillery is also special. Following a visit by Queen Victoria and Prince Albert in 1848, Lochnagar was granted a royal warrant and this was renewed as recently as December 2021. The royal connection was further emphasized in May 2023 when a special bottling celebrating the coronation of King Charles III was released. The only other Scotch distillery currently holding a royal warrant is Laphroaig, granted by Prince Charles in 1994.

The distillery is equipped with a 5.4 ton open, traditional stainless steel mash tun. There are two wooden washbacks with short fermentations of 70 hours and long ones of 110 hours. The two stills are small with a charge in the wash still of 6,100 litres and 4,000 litres in the spirit still and the spirit vapours are condensed in cast iron worm tubs. The whole production is filled on site with 1,000 casks being stored in its only warehouse, while the rest is sent away. Four mashes per week during 2023 will result in 450,000 litres of pure alcohol.

The official core range of single malts consists of the **12 year old** and **Selected Reserve**. The latter is a vatting of casks, usually around 18-20 years of age. A limited release in the Prima & Ultima range appeared in June 2022 – a **40 year old** matured in refill hogsheads, bottled at 52.5%.

History:

1823 James Robertson founds a distillery in Glen Feardan on the north bank of River Dee.

1826 The distillery is burnt down by competitors but Robertson decides to establish a new distillery near the mountain Lochnagar.

1841 This distillery is also burnt down.

1845 A new distillery is built by John Begg, this time on the south bank of River Dee. It is named New Lochnagar.

1848 Lochnagar obtains a Royal Warrant.

1882 John Begg passes away and his son Henry Farquharson Begg inherits the distillery.

1896 Henry Farquharson Begg dies.

1906 The children of Henry Begg rebuild the distillery.

1916 The distillery is sold to John Dewar & Sons.

1925 John Dewar & Sons becomes part of Distillers Company Limited (DCL).

1963 A major reconstruction takes place.

2004 A 30 year old cask strength from 1974 is launched in the Rare Malts series (6,000 bottles).

2008 A Distiller´s Edition with a Moscatel finish is released.

2010 A Manager´s Choice 1994 is released.

2013 A triple matured expression for Friends of the Classic Malts is released.

2016 A distillery exclusive without age statement is released.

2019 House Baratheon is released as part of the Game of Thrones series.

2021 A 16 year old Rare by Nature is released.

2022 A 40 year old Prima & Ultima is released.

12 years old

Tasting notes Royal Lochnagar 12 years old:

GS – Light toffee on the nose, along with some green notes of freshly-sawn timber. The palate offers a pleasing and quite complex blend of caramel, dry sherry and spice, followed by a hint of liquorice before the slightly scented finish develops.

Scapa

[ska•pa]

Owner:		Region/district:
Chivas Brothers		Highlands (Orkney)
(Pernod Ricard)		

Founded:	Status:	Capacity:
1885	Active	1 300 000 litres

Address: Scapa, St Ola, Kirkwall, Orkney KW15 1SE

Website:	Tel:
scapawhisky.com	01856 876585

Seasoned whisky drinkers will remember a time in the 1970s when "those-in-the-know" were looking for Scapa single malt as well as Glen Scotia. The whiskies were good and both distilleries were located in remote and exciting places.

The Orcadian Scapa and Glen Scotia way down south in (almost) forgotten Campbeltown experienced closures and intermittent production in the 1990s and early new millenium. Workers from nearby Highland Park and Springbank respectively assisted with the production from time to time. Interestingly enough, both distilleries were also owned by the Bloch brothers until Hiram Walker took over in 1954.

In the last decade Glen Scotia has made a remarkable come-back and Scapa, having to compete for attention with another eleven distilleries in the Chivas group, might be on the same track. A visitor centre was opened in 2015 and in 2022 a stunning tasting room with a view to Scapa Bay was built. An extended range of whiskies would make the transformation complete.

The equipment at Scapa consists of a 2.9 ton semi-lauter mash tun with a copper dome. In 2019 another four washbacks were installed to achieve the very long (160 hours) fermentation time that was usually applied at Scapa. There are now 12 washbacks made of stainless steel. Finally there are two stills. The wash still, sourced from Glenburgie distillery in 1959, is only one of two surviving Lomond stills in the industry. However, the adjustable plates were removed from it in 1979.

For quite a while the core range has consisted of **Skiren** with no age statement and matured in first fill bourbon as well as **Glansa**, matured in American oak and then finished in casks that previously held peated whisky. Although not confirmed there are signs that this may change in the near future. Recent limited releases include four different cask strength bottlings (**8 to 19 years**) in the **Distillery Reserve Collection**, available at all Chivas' visitor centres as well as a **14 year old** available only at the distillery.

History:

1885 Macfarlane & Townsend founds the distillery with John Townsend at the helm.

1919 Scapa Distillery Company Ltd takes over.

1934 Scapa Distillery Company goes into voluntary liquidation and production ceases.

1936 Production resumes.

1936 Bloch Brothers Ltd (John and Sir Maurice) takes over.

1954 Hiram Walker & Sons takes over.

1959 A Lomond still is installed.

1978 The distillery is modernized.

1994 The distillery is mothballed.

1997 Production takes place a few months each year using staff from Highland Park.

2004 Extensive refurbishing takes place at a cost of £2.1 million. Scapa 14 years is launched.

2005 Production ceases in April and phase two of the refurbishment programme starts. Chivas Brothers becomes the new owner.

2006 Scapa 1992 (14 years) is launched.

2008 Scapa 16 years is launched.

2015 The distillery opens for visitors and Scapa Skiren is launched.

2016 The peated Glansa is released.

2020 Three vintages are released - 1977, 1979 and 1990.

Scapa Skiren

Tasting notes Scapa Skiren:

GS – Lime is apparent on the early nose, followed by musty peaches, almonds, cinnamon, and salt. More peaches on the palate, with tinned pear and honey. Tingling spices in the drying finish, which soon becomes slightly astringent.

Speyburn

[spey•burn]

Owner:
Inver House Distillers
(International Beverage Holdings)

Region/district:
Speyside

Founded: **Status:** **Capacity:**
1897 Active (vc) 4 500 000 litres

Address: Rothes, Aberlour, Morayshire AB38 7AG

Website: **Tel:**
speyburn.com 01340 831213

The small village of Rothes in Speyside is home to four whisky distilleries but only one, Glen Grant, is open to visitors. This is about to change however. It has been revealed that there are plans for Speyburn to open its doors to the public as well.

During the 2023 Speyside Festival a small number of visitors were taken round on guided tours for the first time and the distillery is now permanently open to visitors. The distillery has a couple of rare features that makes for an exciting tour. A worm tube is used to condense the spirit and, not least, a rare drum malting (last used in the late 1960s) is still there to see.

When Speyburn opened up in 1897 an interesting decision was made when they turned their back on traditional floor malting and instead installed a brand new device called the Galland-Henning pneumatic drum. Patented in the late 1800s by Nicholas Galland and Julius Henning most of the equipment was later made by a company in Milwaukee. Drum malting, however, never took off at single malt distilleries. Instead floor malting was eventually abandoned and replaced by a few large commercial maltsters.

Speyburn is equipped with a 6.25 ton stainless steel, semilauter mash tun. There are four wooden washbacks and 15 rather new made of stainless steel. Fermentation time in a 7-day week is 72 hours and working 5 days there are both short (72 hours) and long (120 hours) fermentations. Finally there is one wash still connected to a shell and tube condenser and two spirit still attached to a worm tub. The production during 2023 will be 40 mashes per week and 4.5 million litres.

The core range consists of **10, 15** and an **18 year old** and **Bradan Orach** without age statement. Limited bottlings include **Companion Cask**, a series of single casks matured in first fill ex Buffalo Trace bourbon casks and, limited to USA, **Arranta Casks**. Three bottlings are available in travel retail; a **10 year old** (ex-bourbon and ex-sherry), the **Hopkins Reserve**, matured in casks that previously held a peated whisky and a **16 year old** aged in ex-bourbon barrels.

History:

1897 Brothers John and Edward Hopkins and their cousin Edward Broughton found the distillery through John Hopkins & Co. They already own Tobermory. The architect is Charles Doig. Building the distillery costs £17,000 and the distillery is transferred to Speyburn-Glenlivet Distillery Company.

1916 Distillers Company Limited (DCL) acquires John Hopkins & Co. and the distillery.

1930 Production stops.

1934 Productions restarts.

1962 Speyburn is transferred to Scottish Malt Distillers (SMD).

1968 Drum maltings closes.

1991 Inver House Distillers buys Speyburn.

1992 A 10 year old is launched as a replacement for the 12 year old in the Flora & Fauna series.

2001 Pacific Spirits (Great Oriole Group) buys Inver House for $85 million.

2005 A 25 year old Solera is released.

2006 Inver House changes owner when International Beverage Holdings acquires Pacific Spirits UK.

2009 The un-aged Bradan Orach is introduced for the American market.

2012 Clan Speyburn is formed.

2014 The distillery is expanded.

2015 Arranta Casks is released.

2017 A 15 year old and Companion Casks are launched.

2018 Two expressions for duty free are released - a 10 year old and Hopkins Reserve. A core 18 year old is launched.

2023 The distillery opens to the public.

10 years old

Tasting notes Speyburn 10 years old:

GS – Soft and elegant on the spicy, nutty nose. Smooth in the mouth, with vanilla, spice and more nuts. The finish is medium, spicy and drying.

Speyside

[spey•side]

Owner:
Speyside Distillers Co.

Region/district:
Speyside

Founded: 1990

Status: Active

Capacity: 850 000 litres

Address: Glen Tromie, Kingussie, Inverness-shire PH21 1NS

Website:
speysidedistillery.co.uk

Tel:
01540 661060

The days are numbered for one of the prettiest and most romantic distilleries in Scotland. At least in the hands of the current owners.

Together with partners, George Christie started North of Scotland distillery in 1957. It was first and foremost a grain distillery but two pot stills also produced malt whisky for a while. Around the same time he bought a piece of land at Drumguish near Kingussie. The plan was to build a malt distillery and he commissioned a drystone diker to build it. It would take 28 years before the distillery started production and by that time George Christie had already sold the company. Eleven years ago the current owners stepped in and successfully grew the brand.

In 2021 the blender and bulk whisky supplier Glasgow Whisky bought the Tromie Mills Distillery Ltd, the company that owns the land and the buildings that comprise Speyside Distillery. Since 2012, when Harvey's of Edinburgh (with John McDonough at the helm and aided by Taiwanese investors) took over the Spey brand and the running of Speyside distillery, they have been leasing the site and the building. The lease expires in 2025 and now they are looking to build a new distillery. In April 2023 a planning application for a distillery near Strathmashie (around 15 km west of the current site) was submitted to the local council.

Speyside distillery is equipped with a 4.2 ton semi-lauter mash tun, six stainless steel washbacks with a 70-120 hour fermentation time and one pair of stills. For the last few years they have been working a six-day week with a total production of 600,000 litres of alcohol but the additional washbacks have increased the production to 850,000 litres. Peated spirit is produced annually for about two weeks.

The core range of Spey single malt is made up of **Tenné** (with a 6 months port finish), **Trutina** which is a 100% bourbon maturation, **Fumare**, similar to Trutina but distilled from peated barley, **Chairman's Choice** and **Royal Choice**. The latter two are multi-vintage marriages from both American and European oak. Also part of the core range is **Beinn Dubh** which replaced the black whisky Cu Dubh.

History:

1956 George Christie buys a piece of land at Drumguish near Kingussie.

1957 He starts a grain distillery near Alloa.

1962 Christie commissions the drystone dyker Alex Fairlie to build a distillery in Drumguish.

1986 Scowis assumes ownership.

1987 The distillery is completed.

1990 The distillery is on stream in December.

1993 The first single malt, Drumguish, is launched.

1999 Speyside 8 years is launched.

2000 Speyside Distilleries is sold to a group of private investors including Ricky Christie, Ian Jerman and Sir James Ackroyd.

2001 Speyside 10 years is launched.

2012 Speyside Distillers is sold to Harvey's of Edinburgh.

2014 A new range, Spey from Speyside Distillery, is launched (NAS, 12 and 18 year old).

2015 The range is revamped again. New expressions include Tenné, 12 years old and 18 years old.

2016 "Byron's Choice - The Marriage" and Spey Cask 27 are released.

2017 Trutina and Fumare are released.

2019 Cask strength versions of Tenné, Trutina and Fumare are released.

2020 A 10 year old bourbon/port, a peated 12 year old and a 12 year old port cask are released.

Tasting notes Spey Trutina:

IR – A floral nose, with lemon, granola, shortbread and dried grass. A sweet start on the palate, honey, white chocolate, sweet red apples and then ends with a dry, oaky note.

Trutina

An inside comment on...

The State of Whisky

Jota Tanaka
Whisky Hall of Fame inductee No. 79
Master Blender, Fuji Gotemba Distillery

What was your objective for entering the whisky business?

I never expected to be involved in the whisky business at all. When I was a university student, I had a vague idea that I wanted to work abroad, especially in the USA. It was also unexpected, but I had the opportunity to work at a winery in Napa Valley and gradually got involved in the whisky world. I feel very fortunate to have been involved in the whisky business. At the same time, I am very grateful that I did not enter the whisky business from the beginning but instead gained experience in the wine and other alcoholic beverage industries, which has given me a variety of perspectives and made me who I am today.

What would you say are the best ways to attract new, young whisky consumers?

It's about making people realize that whisky is not boring but a lovely and exciting drink. Whisky is a traditional drink, but innovation is taking place, and it is an exciting situation, with new whisky distilleries springing up all over the world, not just in traditional countries. Whisky is not just a high-alcohol beverage but a drink with a lot of history, culture, stories and drama, with many fascinating elements. It is necessary to convey to young people that having whisky around them will help to make their lives more enjoyable and richer.

Can one whisky, objectively, be better than the other? Isn't it all down to your personal taste and preferences?

It depends on what you expect from whisky. It's not a question of good or bad; it depends on personal taste and preference. However, an important criterion to follow as a whisky maker is to make whisky with integrity and to be able to confidently explain what the whisky is about, not to try to deceive the customer. It is essential to make whisky with sincerity, transparency and fairness.

Do you feel there is enough innovation in the whisky business and is there still a place for preserving and honouring traditional methods?

Undoubtedly, I believe that there is still room for innovation in the whisky business. On the other hand, the unique characteristics of whisky should still be preserved, so the production method should be maintained to strict rules, and there should be a clear line between whisky and other category items. I am satisfied that the Japanese Whisky we have recently defined has a clear line of demarcation as Japanese Whisky while still leaving room for innovation.

Whatever line of business you're in, sustainability is on every company's agenda. Do you feel the whisky industry is at the forefront or could things happen faster?

Sustainability is an issue that the whisky industry needs to tackle, but whether it is at the forefront depends on the individual manufacturer's perception of the case, with varying degrees of progress. We believe that we should take the initiative in tackling this issue and are working on the following points:

1. Initiatives to conserve water sources (Water Source Forest activities); managing the water source forests; the program includes tree planting, pruning and thinning, holding lectures on forest regeneration, etc.

2. Wastewater treatment; use of renewable energy through methane gas recovery in anaerobic treatment.

3. Environmental conservation activities around the plant; activities centred on clean-up in the surrounding area (Mt. Fuji)

Investing in whisky has become more and more popular. Is that a good or a bad thing?

Whisky is meant to be tasted and enjoyed as a drink in the first place, but unfortunately, it has become an investment target for certain people. It is inevitable that whisky, which also has aspects of art and craft, becomes an object of investment. However, this is largely due to the marketing activities of the whisky producers, who have been responsible for the iconic luxury items launched in recent years in the name of premiumisation, with a lot of money spent on packaging.

I'm sometimes reminded that the readers of the Malt Whisky Yearbook – usually well informed but eager to learn more – represent a miniscule part of the whisky consumers around the world. How important would you say that small consumer segment is for the producers?

The people keen to gather information, such as the readers of the Malt Whisky Yearbook, may indeed be a minority. Still, we are being trained and nurtured by striving to disseminate information that meets the expectations of these readers. They are vital people because, thanks to them, we can invite new customers by recognizing our current values and creating new ones.

With young people sometimes questioning the use of alcohol and others exchanging it for cannabis or other drugs – do you feel whisky is still relevant for Generation Z (born 1997-2012)?

While young people may be right about cannabis and other drugs if they measure the effects only in terms of psychological changes, the benefits gained through whisky and other alcoholic beverages enrich all aspects of their lives, so it is very relevant for Generation Z people. We should tell them about the many benefits that drugs don't have.

As opposed to thirty years ago, whisky today is produced in a huge number of countries around the world. How would you say that has affected the category/industry as a whole?

It's definitely a good thing for us because the mushrooming of many whisky distilleries worldwide will revitalize the industry and the market and create innovation and a new whisky culture. However, as the history of whisky has shown repeatedly, there will be cases of trouble, and the current global whisky boom will sooner or later come to an end. After that, it will be interesting to see what the whisky map around the world will look like, and I believe that the whole industry will evolve to a new stage again, although it may take some time.

Please describe your perfect time and place for a dram.

It is always a perfect time for me to meet a whisky that inspires me, and when I encounter a moment when people smile when they drink the whisky we make.

Springbank

[spring•bank]

Owner:
Springbank Distillers
(J & A Mitchell)

Region/district:
Campbeltown

Founded: 1828
Status: Active (vc)
Capacity: 500 000 litres

Address: Well Close, Campbeltown, Argyll PA28 6ET

Website: springbank.scot
Tel: 01586 551710

The owner and chairman of J & A Mitchell, Hedley G. Wright, passed away in August 2023 at the age of 92. He had been a part of the Scotch whisky industry for more than six decades and absolutely instrumental in the success of Springbank and later Glengyle.

He was the fifth generation of the Mitchell family to own and operate Springbank and several years ago he secured the company's continuation when he put the majority of the company's shares in a trust to secure its independence. Springbank has always trodden its own path. For the owners, the distillery is not there just to produce whisky, but also to create future jobs and security for the families living in Campbeltown. The hands-on production and a near obsession of adhering to "old-school" production techniques (including floor malting their entire need of barley), has an appeal to many whisky drinkers.

In 2028 Springbank distillery turns 200 years but already in 2023 they released the first installment of five – a 27 year old – in the Countdown Collection. Every year a new expression will be offered to enthusiasts around the world by way of a ballot. Springbank has been sought after for a few decades now but the current hype defies everything. The whisky is on allocation in every market and in secondary markets prices are soaring.

The distillery is equipped with a 3.5 ton open cast iron mash tun and six wooden washbacks with one short fermentation of 72 hours per week while the rest are on 100 hours. There is also one wash still and two spirit stills. The wash still is unique in Scotland, as it is fired by both an open oil-fire and internal steam coils. Ordinary condensers are used to cool the spirit vapours, except in the first of the two spirit stills, where a worm tub is used.

Springbank produces three distinctive single malts with different phenol contents in the malted barley: Springbank is distilled two and a half times (12-15ppm), Longrow is distilled twice (50-55 ppm) and the unpeated Hazelburn is distilled three times. When Springbank is produced, the malted barley is dried using 6 hours of peat smoke and 30 hours of hot air, while Longrow requires 48 hours of peat smoke. The production plan for 2023 is to do 5 mashes per week which means 210,000 litres of Springbank and 25,000 litres each of Longrow and Hazelburn.

The core range is **Springbank 10, 15** and **18 year old** and a **12 year old cask strength**. There are also limited but recurrent releases of a **21 year old**, a **25 year old** and a **30 year old**. Recent limited releases include **Springbank Local Barley 11 years old**, a **10 year old** with a 3 year finish in PX casks and the aforementioned **27 year old Countdown Collection**. The core **Longrow** is without age statement. A limited, annual release is **Longrow Red** with an 11 year tawny port finish launched in autumn 2022. In 2022 a **21 year old**, partly matured in chardonnay casks, was released. For Hazelburn, the core expression is a **10 year old** complemented by limited annual releases. Two of the most recent are **Sherrywood 12 year old** and a **21 year old**.

History:

1828 The Reid family, in-laws of the Mitchells (see below), founds the distillery.

1837 The Reid family encounters financial difficulties and John and William Mitchell buy the distillery.

1897 J. & A. Mitchell Co Ltd is founded.

1926 The depression forces the distillery to close.

1933 The distillery is back in production.

1960 Own maltings ceases.

1979 The distillery closes.

1985 A 10 year old Longrow is launched.

1987 Limited production restarts.

1989 Production restarts.

1992 Springbank takes up its maltings again.

1997 First distillation of Hazelburn.

1998 Springbank 12 years is launched.

1999 Dha Mhile (7 years), the world's first organic single malt, is launched.

2000 A 10 year old is launched.

2001 Springbank 1965 'Local barley' is launched.

2002 Number one in the series Wood Expressions is a 12 year old with five years in rum casks.

2004 Springbank 10 years 100 proof is launched as well as Longrow 14 years old, Springbank 32 years old and Springbank 14 years Port Wood.

2005 Springbank 21 years, the first version of Hazelburn (8 years) and Longrow Tokaji Wood Expression are launched.

2006 Longrow 10 years 100 proof, Springbank 25 years and Hazelburn 8 year old are released.

2007 Springbank Vintage 1997 and a 16 year old rum wood are released.

2008 The distillery closes temporarily. Three new releases of Longrow - CV, 18 year old and 7 year old Gaja Barolo.

2009 Springbank Madeira 11 year old, Springbank 18 year old and Hazelburn 12 year old are launched.

History continued:

2010 Springbank 12 year old cask strength is released.

2011 Longrow 18 year old and Hazelburn 8 year old Sauternes wood expression are released.

2012 Springbank Rundlets & Kilderkins, Springbank 21 year old and Longrow Red are released.

2013 Longrow Rundlets & Kilderkins, a new edition of Longrow Red and Springbank 9 year old Gaja Barolo finish are released.

2014 Hazelburn 10 year old and Springbank 25 years old are launched.

2015 New releases include Springbank Green 12 years old and a new edition of the Longrow Red.

2016 Springbank Local Barley and a 9 year old Hazelburn barolo finish are released.

2017 Springbank 14 year old bourbon cask and Hazelburn 13 year old sherrywood are released.

2018 Local Barley 10 year old, 14 year old Longrow Sherry Wood and a new Longrow Red are released.

2019 Springbank 25, Hazelburn 14 and a 21 year old Longrow are released.

2020 Springbank Local Barley 10 years old, a 17 year old madeira finish and Longrow Red Cabernet Sauvignon are released.

2021 Longrow Red 10 year old malbec is released.

2022 Longrow Red 15 year old pinot noir, a 21 year old Hazelburn and a 30 year old Springbank are released.

2023 Longrow Red 11 year old tawny, Local Barley 11 and 27 year old Countdown Collection are released. Hedley G. Wright dies.

Tasting notes Springbank 10 years old:

GS – Fresh and briny on the nose, with citrus fruit, oak and barley, plus a note of damp earth. Sweet on the palate, with developing brine, nuttiness and vanilla toffee. Coconut oil and drying peat in the finish.

Tasting notes Longrow NAS:

GS – Initially slightly gummy on the nose, but then brine and fat peat notes develop. Vanilla and malt also emerge. The smoky palate offers lively brine and is quite dry and spicy, with some vanilla and lots of ginger. The finish is peaty with persistent, oaky ginger.

Tasting notes Hazelburn 10 years old:

GS – Pear drops, soft toffee and malt on the mildly floral nose. Oiliness develops in time, along with a green, herbal note and ultimately brine. Full-bodied and supple on the smoky palate, with barley and ripe, peppery orchard fruits. Developing cocoa and ginger in the lengthy finish.

Longrow 18 years Springbank 18 years Hazelburn 10 years

Longrow NAS Longrow Red

Springbank 10 years old

Springbank 30 years old Springbank Local Barley

Strathisla

Strathisla is the oldest working distillery in Speyside and third oldest in Scotland after Glenturret and Bowmore. With the double pagodas and the water wheel in the foreground it epitomizes the classic Scottish whisky distillery.

Despite its seniority as a distillery, the whisky has never in earnest been promoted as a single malt in its own right but rather as an important part of blended whisky and in particular Chivas Regal. Its connection with the third best selling Scotch in the world is comparatively new. Strathisla (or Milton distillery as it was known at the time) was bought in 1950 by Chivas Brothers, a highly reputable whisky company established already in 1857. A year before, Chivas Bros itself had been bought by the Canadian spirits giant Seagrams. Headed by the famous spirits tycoon Sam Bronfman, Seagrams transformed Chivas Regal into one of the best known Scotch of all time and eventually Strathisla became the brand home for the blend.

During the past decade Chivas Regal has been competing with Grant's regarding third place on the global list of best selling Scotch and with 62 million bottles sold in 2022 Chivas Regal is in the lead. One of the latest additions to the range is the Extra 13 year old which has been fully matured in ex-oloroso casks.

The distillery is equipped with a 5.12 ton traditional mash tun with a raised copper canopy, seven washbacks made of Oregon pine and three of larch – all with a 54 hour fermentation cycle. There are two pairs of stills. The wash stills are of lantern type with descending lyne arms and the spirit stills have boiling balls with the lyne arms slightly ascending.

As already mentioned, Strathisla is a key malt in Chivas Regal, the third biggest blend in the world. The only core expression is the **12 year old** but a limited **18 year old** sherry matured bottled at 47.7% has also recently been released. In the **Distillery Reserve Collection**, available at all Chivas' visitor centres, there are five recent single casks aged from **10** to **20 years** with the **16 year old** unusually finished in a cognac cask.

[strath•eye•la]

Owner:
Chivas Bros (Pernod Ricard)

Region/district:
Speyside

Founded: **Status:**
1786 Active (vc)

Capacity:
2 450 000 litres

Address: Seafield Avenue, Keith, Banffshire AB55 5BS

Website:
chivas.com

Tel:
01542 783044

History:

1786 Alexander Milne and George Taylor found the distillery under the name Milltown, but soon change it to Milton.

1823 MacDonald Ingram & Co. purchases the distillery.

1830 William Longmore acquires the distillery.

1870 The distillery name changes to Strathisla.

1880 William Longmore retires and hands operations to his son-in-law John Geddes-Brown. William Longmore & Co. is formed.

1890 The distillery changes name to Milton.

1942 Jay Pomeroy acquires a majority of the shares in William Longmore & Co. Pomeroy is jailed as a result of dubious business transactions and the distillery goes bankrupt in 1949.

1950 Chivas Brothers buys the run-down distillery at a compulsory auction for £71,000 and starts restoration.

1951 The name reverts to Strathisla.

1965 The number of stills is increased from two to four.

1970 A heavily peated whisky, Craigduff, is produced but production stops later.

2001 The Chivas Group is acquired by Pernod Ricard.

2019 Chivas Distillery Collection Strathisla 12 year old is released.

Tasting notes Strathisla 12 years old:

GS – Rich on the nose, with sherry, stewed fruits, spices and lots of malt. Full-bodied and almost syrupy on the palate. Toffee, honey, nuts, a whiff of peat and a suggestion of oak. The finish is medium in length, slightly smoky and with a final flash of ginger.

12 years old

Strathmill

[strath•mill]

Owner:
Diageo

Region/district:
Speyside

Founded: 1891   **Status:** Active   **Capacity:** 2 600 000 litres

Address: Keith, Banffshire AB55 5DQ

Website: malts.com   **Tel:** 01542 883000

Strathmill, beautifully embedded in the greenery along the River Isla at the perimeter of Keith, is certainly not of the more well-known Scottish distilleries. Despite that, many drinkers have probably tasted it as it since long has been an essential ingredient in J&B blended Scotch.

Scotch whisky history has its share of mergers and acquisitions but few have been of such a magnitude as when Grand Metropolitan Plc and Arthur Guinness, Son & Co merged in 1997 to form Diageo. The value of the deal was a staggering £24 billion. Of the 30 Scottish malt distilleries owned and operated by Diageo today, only four came from Grand Met in that deal, namely Strathmill, Auchroisk, Knockando and Glen Spey. The rest (with the obvious exception of newly built Roseisle) came from Guinness who in their turn hade acquired them when they bought Distillers Company Limited (DCLI) a decade earlier.

While still a major brand with 35 million bottles sold globally, J&B has lost some of its former glory when it was number three in the world. Today it comes in as number seven and the need for Strathmill single malt has declined to such an extent that the distillery has been producing gin for the last couple of years. The grapevine suggests, however, that single malt whisky will be on the agenda any time soon.

The equipment consists of a 9.1 ton stainless steel semi-lauter mash tun and six stainless steel washbacks. There are two pairs of stills and Strathmill is one of few distilleries still using purifiers on the spirit stills. This device is mounted between the lyne arm and the condenser and acts as a mini-condenser, allowing the lighter alcohols to travel towards the condenser and forcing the heavier alcohols to go back into the still for another distillation. The result is a lighter spirit.

Over the years, Strathmill has been an important part of the J&B blend and the only official bottling is the **12 year old Flora & Fauna**, but a limited **25 year old** was launched in 2014 as part of the Special Releases.

History:
1891 The distillery is founded in an old mill from 1823 and is named Glenisla-Glenlivet Distillery.

1892 The inauguration takes place in June.

1895 The gin company W. & A. Gilbey buys the distillery for £9,500 and names it Strathmill.

1962 W. & A. Gilbey merges with United Wine Traders (including Justerini & Brooks) and forms International Distillers & Vintners (IDV).

1968 The number of stills is increased from two to four and purifiers are added.

1972 IDV is bought by Watney Mann which later the same year is acquired by Grand Metropolitan.

1993 Strathmill becomes available as a single malt for the first time since 1909 as a result of a bottling (1980) from Oddbins.

1997 Guinness and Grand Metropolitan merge and form Diageo.

2001 The first official bottling is a 12 year old in the Flora & Fauna series.

2010 A Manager´s Choice single cask from 1996 is released.

2014 A 25 year old is released.

12 years old

Tasting notes Strathmill 12 years old:
GS – Quite reticent on the nose, with nuts, grass and a hint of ginger. Spicy vanilla and nuts dominate the palate. The finish is drying, with peppery oak.

Talisker

[tal•iss•kur]

Owner:	**Region/district:**
Diageo	Highlands (Skye)

Founded:	**Status:**	**Capacity:**
1830	Active (vc)	3 500 000 litres

Address: Carbost, Isle of Skye,
Inverness-shire IV47 8SR

Website:	**Tel:**
malts.com	01478 614308 (vc)

For a long-established distillery such as Talisker, a change in the way one produces whisky doesn't come along that often. Usually it's changing from dry to liquid yeast or something similar.

Most essential is keeping the character of the spirit and the ethos "if it's not broken, don't mend it" is the key. However, the current focus on sustainability have lead quite a few distilleries to turn to high gravity mash. That means they are using more malt in the mash tun compared to heated water which results in less energy being used. The idea is generally not to change the character nor yield but depending on your fermentation process more fruity esters may be added. Talisker has just embarked on a trial of high gravity mash which means the usual charge of 8 tonnes of malt into the mash tun has changed to 8.75 and they are no strangers to increasing to 9 tons and beyond. Two decades ago Diageo decided to turn Talisker into one of the major single malt brands in the world. At that time it sold 500,000 bottles yearly and was in 15th place on the list. Today Talisker sells 4.3 million bottles and is the seventh best selling Scotch single malt. The distillery visitor centre was recently refurbished in a major way and attracts 65,000 people every year.

The distillery is equipped with a stainless steel lauter mash tun with a capacity of 8.75 tonnes and eight washbacks made of Oregon pine. Before mashing, the malted barley is mixed to a ratio of 25% unpeated and 75% peated which has a phenol specification of 20-25ppm. There are five stills – two wash stills and three spirit stills. The wash stills are equipped with a special type of "purifiers" or, more specifically, return pipes, which use the colder outside air, and there is also a u-bend in the lyne arms. The return pipes and the peculiar bend of the lyne arms allow for more copper contact and increases the reflux during distillation. All of the stills are connected to wormtubs. The fermentation time is around 60 hours and the middle cut from the spirit still is collected between 76% and 65% which, together with the phenol specification, gives a medium peated spirit. In 2023, 20 mashes per week are planned which, with the high-gravity mash, could result in 3.5 million litres of alcohol.

Talisker's core range consists of **Skye** and **Storm**, both without age statement, **10, 18, 25** and **30 year old, Distiller's Edition** with an Amoroso sherry finish and **Port Ruighe**, finished in ruby port casks. There is also **Dark Storm** which is exclusive to duty free together with **Surge**. In May 2022 the 44 year old **Forests of the Deep** was released where the finishing casks had been charred using sea kelp. It was part of the ambition to preserve sea forests around the planet and in spring 2023 it was followed up by **Wilder Seas**, released in collaboration with Parley for the Seas, an organisation dedicated to rewilding the ocean forests. This was also the first Talisker finished in ex-cognac casks. A limited **37 year old** in the Prima & Ultima range was released in June 2022 and in autumn 2023, a **Special Release** finished in three different types of port casks was launched.

History:

1830 Hugh and Kenneth MacAskill found the distillery.

1848 The brothers transfer the lease to North of Scotland Bank and Jack Westland from the bank runs the operations.

1854 Kenneth MacAskill dies.

1857 North of Scotland Bank sells the distillery to Donald MacLennan for £500.

1863 MacLennan experiences difficulties in making operations viable and puts the distillery up for sale.

1865 MacLennan, still working at the distillery, nominates John Anderson as agent in Glasgow.

1867 Anderson & Co. from Glasgow takes over.

1879 John Anderson is imprisoned after having sold non-existing casks of whisky.

1880 New owners are now Alexander Grigor Allan and Roderick Kemp.

1892 Kemp sells his share and buys Macallan Distillery instead.

1894 The Talisker Distillery Ltd is founded.

1895 Allan dies and Thomas Mackenzie, who has been his partner, takes over.

1898 Talisker Distillery merges with Dailuaine-Glenlivet Distillers and Imperial Distillers to form Dailuaine-Talisker Distillers Company.

1916 Thomas Mackenzie dies and the distillery is taken over by a consortium consisting of, among others, John Walker, John Dewar, W. P. Lowrie and Distillers Company Limited (DCL).

1928 The distillery abandons triple distillation.

1960 On 22nd November the distillery catches fire and substantial damage occurs.

1962 The distillery reopens after the fire.

1972 Own malting ceases.

1988 Classic Malts are introduced, Talisker 10 years included. A visitor centre is opened.

History continued:

1998 A Distillers Edition with an amoroso sherry finish is released.

2004 Two new bottlings appear, an 18 year old and a 25 year old.

2005 Talisker 175th Anniversary is released.

2006 A 30 year old and the fourth edition of the 25 year old are released.

2008 Talisker 57° North is launched.

2009 New editions of 25 and 30 year old are released.

2010 A 1994 Manager´s Choice single cask and a new edition of the 30 year old are released.

2013 Four new expressions are released – Storm, Dark Storm, Port Ruighe and a 27 year old.

2014 A bottling for the Friends of the Classic Malts is released.

2015 Skye and Neist Point are released.

2018 A 40 year old, the first in the new Bodega Series, and an 8 year old Special Release are launched.

2019 A 41 year old Bodega Series and House Greyjoy in the Game of Thrones series are released.

2020 A 31 year old Prima & Ultima and an 8 year old rum finish Rare by Nature are released.

2021 A 43 year old and an 8 year old Special Releases are released.

2022 The 27 year old Talisker Elements, the 44 year old Forests of the Deep and Talisker Surge are launched.

2023 Wilder Seas and a port finished Special Release are launched.

Tasting notes Talisker 10 years old:

GS – Quite dense and smoky on the nose, with smoked fish, bladderwrack, sweet fruit and peat. Full-bodied and peaty in the mouthy; complex, with ginger, ozone, dark chocolate, black pepper and a kick of chilli in the long, smoky tail.

Port Ruighe

Storm

Forests of the Deep

18 years old

Surge

10 years old

Wilder Seas

Special Release 2023

Tamdhu

[tam•doo]

Owner:	**Region/district:**
Ian Macleod Distillers	Speyside
Founded: **Status:**	**Capacity:**
1897 Active	4 000 000 litres

Address: Knockando, Aberlour, Morayshire AB38 7RP

Website:	**Tel:**
tamdhu.com	01340 872200

Taking over "unwanted" or closed distilleries has become the signature of independent bottler Ian Macleod. The first was Glengoyne in 2003, followed by Tamdhu in 2011 and, most recently, the resurrection of Rosebank in 2023.

But buying a distillery entails more than investing millions of pounds into it and creating a range of whiskies. It is about the people who run it and the passion they put into the daily work. A comforting thought when some of today's distilleries can be operated by two people and a computer. At Tamdhu there are now 20 people working – all guided by distillery manager Sandy McIntyre. After an eight year spell with Diageo, Sandy headed Tamdhu distillery in 2014 and his dedication, which gave him a Distillery Manager of the Year award in 2019, has meant a lot to the distillery and the brand.

Tamdhu is equipped with an 11.85 ton semilauter mash tun and nine Oregon pine washbacks with a fermentation time of 59 hours. There are three 22,500 litre wash stills with sustainable TVR (thermal vapour recompression) installed in autumn 2023 and three 18,300 litre spirit stills. An on-site cooperage for repairing and testing casks became operational in 2019. The production plan for 2023 is set on 20 mashes per week and 3.8 million litres of pure alcohol. On site there are also no less than 28 warehouses (dunnage, racked and palletised) storing not only Tamdhu but also Glengoyne and future casks of Rosebank.

The core range consists of a **10 year old** exclusive to UK, a **12 year old**, a **15 year old** and the **18 year old** which was launched in 2022. The non-chill filtered **Batch Strength** (with the 8th edition launched in August 2023) is released yearly but not as part of the core range. Recent limited releases include the third release of **Cigar Malt** in September 2023 and **Tamdhu Distinction III** one month later. Finally, there are two expressions reserved for the travel retail market; **Ámbar Vintage 2009** and the **Gran Reserva**.

History:

1896 The distillery is founded by Tamdhu Distillery Company, a consortium of whisky blenders with William Grant as the main promoter. Charles Doig is the architect.

1897 The first casks are filled in July.

1898 Highland Distillers Company, which has several of the 1896 consortium members in managerial positions, buys Tamdhu Distillery Company.

1911 The distillery closes.

1913 The distillery reopens.

1928 The distillery is mothballed.

1948 The distillery is in full production again in July.

1950 The floor maltings is replaced by Saladin boxes when the distillery is rebuilt.

1972 The number of stills is increased from two to four.

1975 Two stills augment the previous four.

1976 Tamdhu 8 years is launched as single malt.

2005 An 18 year old and a 25 year old are released.

2009 The distillery is mothballed.

2011 The Edrington Group sells the distillery to Ian Macleod Distillers.

2012 Production is resumed.

2013 The first official release from the new owners – a 10 year old.

2015 Tamdhu Batch Strength is released.

2017 A 50 year old is released.

2018 A 12 year old, a 15 year old and the Dalbeallie Dram are released.

2019 Two expressions for duty-free - Ámbar and Gran Reserva First Edition.

2020 Iain Whitecross Single Cask and Cigar Malt are launched.

2021 Quercus Alba Distinction is released.

2022 Tamdhu Club Single Cask, Tamdhu Distinction II and an 18 year old are launched.

2023 Tamdhu Distinction III is launched.

Tasting notes Tamdhu 12 years old:

IR – Distinct sherry notes on the nose with raisins and prunes as well as menthol and green leaves. The taste is wellbalanced with dried fruit, crème brûlée, roasted nuts, bananas and cinnamon.

12 years old

Tamnavulin

[tam•na•voo•lin]

Owner:	Region/district:
Whyte & Mackay (Emperador)	Speyside

Founded:	Status:	Capacity:
1966	Active	4 200 000 litres

Address: Tomnavoulin, Ballindalloch, Banffshire AB3 9JA

Website:	Tel:
tamnavulinwhisky.com	01807 590285

The combination of a good spirit and a very decent price has made Tamnavulin one of the fastest growing Scotch single malts in recent years and in Sweden it is actually the top seller.

In 2021 Tamnavulin sold just over 2 million bottles worldwide and there are now plans to follow up on the brand's popularity by adding a brand home to welcome visitors. It probably won't be until 2025/26 but the intention is to use the same building from the 1830s which used to house a visitor centre between 1985 and 1995. New distillery manager since 2022 is Leon Webb who was the master distiller for Shelter Point Distillery on Vancouver Island in Canada for six years before he returned to Scotland.

With the exception for a few weeks of distillation in 2002, the distillery was closed between 1996 and 2007. Two modifications took place shortly after the restart which improved the quality of the spirit considerably. First of all the maturing stock was re-racked into better wood. Secondly, new spirit stills with shorter necks and purifiers were installed giving the newmake spirit more complexity and body.

Tamnavulin distillery is equipped with a full lauter mash tun with an 11 ton charge, nine washbacks made of stainless steel with a fermentation time of 57-60 hours and three pairs of stills. The wash stills, with horizontal lyne arms, are all equipped with sub-coolers while the spirit stills with their descending lyne arms have purifiers. The foreshots are running for 25 minutes and the heart is collected from 75% down to 60% resulting in a slightly grassy new make. A new cooling tower was built in August 2022. In 2023 the distillery will be working 24/7 with 22 mashes per week, aiming for 4.3 million litres of alcohol.

The core expression is **Double Cask** with a sherry finish. In 2019 a **Sherry Cask Edition** with a finish in three types of oloroso casks was launched and in 2020 three wine cask finishes were added – **Cabernet Sauvignon, Grenache** and **Pinot Noir**. These were recently followed by a **Sauvignon Blanc** finish. There is also a **Tempranillo finish** for duty free and four limited **vintages** (from 1970 to 2000) only available in Asia.

History:

1966 Tamnavulin-Glenlivet Distillery Company, a subsidiary of Invergordon Distillers Ltd, founds Tamnavulin.

1993 Whyte & Mackay buys Invergordon Distillers.

1995 The distillery closes in May.

1996 Whyte & Mackay changes name to JBB (Greater Europe).

2000 Distillation takes place for six weeks.

2001 Company management buy out operations for £208 million and rename the company Kyndal.

2003 Kyndal changes name to Whyte & Mackay.

2007 United Spirits buys Whyte & Mackay. Tamnavulin is opened again in July after having been mothballed for 12 years.

2014 Whyte & Mackay is sold to Emperador Inc.

2016 Tamnavulin Double Cask is released.

2019 Sherry Cask Edition and Tempranillo Finish are released.

2020 Three wine cask finishes are released; cabernet sauvignon, grenache and pinot noir.

2022 A sauvignon blanc finish is released.

Double Cask

Tasting notes Tamnavulin Double Cask:

GS – The nose offers malt, soft toffee, almonds and tangerines. Finally, background earthiness. Smooth on the palate, with ginger nut biscuits, vanilla and orchard fruits, plus walnuts. The finish is medium in length, with lingering fruity spice.

Teaninich

[tee•ni•nick]

Owner: Diageo	**Region/district:** Northern Highlands

Founded: 1817	**Status:** Active	**Capacity:** 10 200 000 litres

Address: Alness, Ross-shire IV17 0XB

Website: malts.com	**Tel:** 01349 885001

Teaninich is the third largest distillery within Diageo. Only Roseisle and Glen Ord produce more. Yet it is virtually unknown amongst whisky consumers.

It is the second oldest of the distilleries north of Inverness that survived into the new millenium (Balblair was founded 27 years earlier) and at one time, back in the 1970s, it was one of the largest distilleries in Scotland with a capacity of 6 million litres. Situated in what is today an industrial area of Alness, one would have thought that a distillery with such a heritage would have had spells of glory over the years but it very much continued making whisky for blends. Not even during the three decade-long ownership of Robert Innes Cameron, a respected whisky broker from Elgin and chairman of the Malt Distillers Association did the distillery make any impression in the history of whisky.

Instead, the distillery received attention in 2000 when a hammer mill and a mash filter were installed as opposed to using a traditional mill and a mash tun. This was the first time in Scotch whisky history and the only distilleries to follow (in recent days) are Inchdairnie and (to a certain extent) the Lighthouse experimental distillery at Glenmorangie. The process entails grinding the grain into a fine flour without husks. The grist is then mixed with water in a conversion vessel. Once the conversion from starch to sugar is performed, the mash passes through a mash filter which consists of a number of mesh bags. The filter compresses the bags and the wort is collected for the next step – fermentation. The yield is higher and the versatility of the process gives the opportunity to process a wider range of cereals.

The equipment consists of a Meura hammer mill, a Meura mash filter (two times 7 ton mash) with 76 plates, 18 wooden and two stainless steel washbacks with a fermentation time of 78 hours and six pairs of stills. Since the re-opening in summer 2022 the distillery has been producing att full capacity also making rye when requested by the blending team.

The only official core bottling is a **10 year old** in the Flora & Fauna series but a limited **17 year old** matured in refill American oak was launched in autumn 2017 as part of the Special Releases.

10 years old

History:

1817 Captain Hugh Munro, owner of the estate Teaninich, founds the distillery.

1831 Captain Munro sells the estate to his younger brother John.

1850 John Munro, who spends most of his time in India, leases Teaninich to the infamous Robert Pattison from Leith.

1869 John McGilchrist Ross takes over the licence.

1895 Munro & Cameron takes over the licence.

1898 Munro & Cameron buys the distillery.

1904 Robert Innes Cameron becomes sole owner of Teaninich.

1932 Robert Innes Cameron dies.

1933 The estate of Robert Innes Cameron sells the distillery to Distillers Company Limited.

1970 A new distillation unit with six stills is commissioned and becomes known as the A side.

1975 A dark grains plant is built.

1984 The B side of the distillery is mothballed.

1985 The A side is also mothballed.

1991 The A side is in production again.

1992 United Distillers launches a 10 year old Teaninich in the Flora & Fauna series.

1999 The B side is decommissioned.

2000 A mash filter is installed.

2009 Teaninich 1996, a single cask in the new Manager's Choice range is released.

2015 The distillery is expanded with six new stills and the capacity is doubled.

2017 A 17 year old is launched as part of the Special Releases.

Tasting notes Teaninich 10 years old:

GS – The nose is initially fresh and grassy, quite light, with vanilla and hints of tinned pineapple. Mediumbodied, smooth, slightly oily, with cereal and spice in the mouth. Nutty and slowly drying in the finish, with pepper and a suggestion of cocoa powder notes.

Tobermory

[tow•bur•mo•ray]

Owner:		Region/district:
CVH Spirits		Highland (Mull)

Founded:	Status:	Capacity:
1798	Active (vc)	1 200 000 litres

Address: Tobermory, Isle of Mull, Argyllsh. PA75 6NR

Website:	Tel:
tobermorydistillery.com	01688 302647

For more than 130 years, until it closed in 1930, the distillery was known as Tobermory. When it was opened again in 1972 the name was changed to Ledaig and then back again to Tobermory when Burn Stewart took over in 1993.

The name Ledaig, however, certainly thrives as the brand name for the peated version of the whisky. In fact, it has become so popular that since some time back it stands for 70-80% of the distillery's output. Made from malted barley with a phenol specification of 35-40ppm it tends to mature quicker than the unpeated Tobermory and it also lends itself well to second maturations in a variety of wine casks. Even if the Isle of Mull has been inhabited since 5,000 BC, the main town, Tobermory, wasn't founded until 1788. It was actually created by the British Fisheries Society in an attempt to attract the people working on the land to become fishermen. It never came out that way, but during a few years kelp was harvested to be used when manufacturing soap and glass. For many years now, tourism (not least ecotourism due to the islands amazing wildlife) has been the main source of income for the island's 2,800 inhabitants

The equipment consists of a 7.5 ton, stainless steel semi lauter mash tun, installed in 2022, and four washbacks made of Oregon pine with a fermentation time of 52 to 110 hours. Finally there are four stills, two of which were replaced in 2014 and the other two in summer 2019. The production plan for 2023 is to do 9-10 mashes per week.

The core range consists of the **12 year old Tobermory** and the **10** and **18 year old Ledaig** as well as the NAS **Ledaig Sinclair rioja finish**. In 2021 a new limited, series named The Hebridean was introduced. The first out of five expressions was a **23 year old** which had received an 8 year finish in oloroso casks. This was followed in 2022 by a **24 year old** and in February 2023 by a **25 year old** which was aged in a combination of oloroso and González Byass casks. Recent limited expressions include a **9 year old Ledaig 2012** fully matured in red wine Bordeaux casks.

History:

1798 John Sinclair founds the distillery.

1837 The distillery closes.

1878 The distillery reopens.

1890 John Hopkins & Company buys the distillery.

1916 Distillers Company Limited (DCL) takes over.

1930 The distillery closes.

1972 A shipping company in Liverpool and the sherrymaker Domecq buy the buildings and embark on refurbishment. When work is completed it is named Ledaig Distillery Ltd.

1975 Ledaig Distillery Ltd files for bankruptcy and the distillery closes again.

1979 The estate agent Kirkleavington Property buys the distillery, forms a new company, Tobermory Distillers Ltd and starts production.

1982 No production. Some of the buildings are converted into flats and some are rented to a dairy company for cheese storage.

1989 Production resumes.

1993 Burn Stewart Distillers buys Tobermory.

2002 CL Financial buys Burn Stewart Distillers.

2005 A 32 year old from 1972 is launched.

2007 A Ledaig 10 year old is released.

2008 A Tobermory 15 year old is released.

2013 Burn Stewart Distillers is sold to Distell Group Ltd. A 40 year old Ledaig is released.

2015 Ledaig 18 years and 42 years are released together with Tobermory 42 years.

2018 Two 19 year old Ledaig are released.

2019 A 12 year old Tobermory is released.

2020 A 23 year old Tobermory oloroso finish and Ledaig Sinclair rioja finish are released.

2021 A new series, The Hebridean, is launched.

2023 A 25 year old Tobermory is released.

Tasting notes Tobermory 12 years old:

IR – Butterscotch and heather honey on the nose with peaches and a hint of orange peel. Mouthcoating, rich and malty with notes of fudge, Danish pastry, citrus, pineapple and a hint of pepper. The finish is slightly salty.

Tasting notes Ledaig 10 years old:

GS – The nose is profoundly peaty, sweet and full, with notes of butter and smoked fish. Bold, yet sweet on the palate, with iodine, soft peat and heather. Developing spices. The finish is medium to long, with pepper, ginger, liquorice and peat.

Ledaig 10 years old

Tomatin

[to•mat•in]

Owner: **Region/district:**
Tomatin Distillery Co   Highland
(Takara Shuzo Co., Kokubu & Co., Marubeni Corp.)

Founded: **Status:**   **Capacity:**
1897   Active (vc)   5 000 000 litres

Address: Tomatin, Inverness-shire IV13 7YT

Website: **Tel:**
tomatin.com   01463 248144 (vc)

Tomatin is probably one of the best examples of a distillery that has changed from the production of bulk whisky into one building a brand.

This becomes very apparent when one looks at the production figures which have gone from 12 million litres annually in the late 1970s to 2.3 million litres for 2023. For Tomatin there is obviously more money to be made from a range of aged quality single malts than selling tanks of young whisky to third parties. This transition slowly started fifteen years ago when the hard-to-find 10 year old was traded for a range of different varieties. Since then, the range has been expanded and a sub-range of peated expressions, Cù Bòcan, has also been introduced.

The distillery is equipped with a 9.5 ton stainless steel, full lauter mash tun, 12 stainless steel washbacks with a long fermentation time (+140 hours) and six pairs of stills (with only four of the spirit stills being used). Lately they have been looking into using one of the redundant spirit stills to occasionally balancing the distillation due to the higher gravity mash. With the normal 12 mashes per week and 21 mashes for 12 weeks, the goal for 2023 is to increase the production to 2.3 million litres. The aim is also to increase production by 10% year on year going forward. Around 200 tones of peated malt (40ppm)is used yearly.

The core range consists of **Legacy, 12, 18, 30** and **36 year old** as well as **Cask Strength** and **14 year old port finish**. Recent limited releases (September 2023) include three expressions in the **Italian Collection** where 10 year old whisky was matured for another two years in casks that had held marsala, amarone and barolo wines respectively. The distillery's duty free range consists of **8, 12, 16, 21** and **45 year old**. The smoky side of Tomatin is represented by **Cù Bòcan** with **Signature** and a **12 year old** rum maturation. There is also **Creation #3** (matured in Moroccan cabernet sauvignon and rye casks), **Creation #4** (tawny port and cognac casks) and, released in March 2023, **Creation #5** (matured in Andean oak casks). Finally, in October 2023 there was also a **Cù Bòcan 15 year old**, matured in oloroso sherry casks.

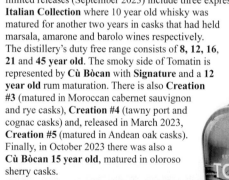

History:

1897 The distillery is founded by Tomatin Spey Distillery Company.

1906 Production ceases.

1909 Production resumes through Tomatin Distillers.

1956 Stills are increased from two to four.

1958 Another two stills are added.

1961 The six stills are increased to ten.

1974 The stills now total 23 and the maltings closes.

1985 The distillery company goes into liquidation.

1986 Takara Shuzo Co. and Okara & Co., buy Tomatin through Tomatin Distillery Co.

1998 Okara & Co is liquidated and Marubeni buys out part of their shareholding.

2004 Tomatin 12 years is launched.

2005 A 25 year old and a 1973 Vintage are released.

2006 An 18 year old and a 1962 Vintage are launched.

2008 A 30 and a 40 year old are released.

2009 A 15 year old, a 21 year old and four single casks are released.

2010 The first peated release - a 4 year old exclusive for Japan.

2011 A 30 year old and Tomatin Decades are released.

2013 Cù Bòcan, the first peated Tomatin, is released.

2014 14 year old port finish, 36 year old, Tomatin Cuatro and Cù Bòcan Sherry Cask are released.

2015 Cask Strength and Cù Bòcan Virgin Oak are released.

2016 A 44 year old Tomatin and two Cù Bòcan vintages (1988 and 2005) are released.

2017 New releases include Wood, Fire and Earth as well as a 2006 Cù Bòcan.

2018 A 30 and a 50 year old are released.

2019 The entire range of Cù Bòcan is relaunched with three new expressions.

2020 A Vintage 1975 is released.

2021 The French Collection is released.

2022 Cù Bócan Creation #3 and #4 are released together with the Portuguese Collection.

2023 Cù Bócan 15 year old and Creation #5 are released together with Tomatin Italian Collection.

Tasting notes Tomatin 12 years old:

GS – Barley, spice, buttery oak and a floral note on the nose. Sweet and medium-bodied, with toffee apples, spice and herbs in the mouth. Medium-length in the finish, with sweet fruitiness.

12 years old

Tomintoul

[tom•in•towel]

Owner:
Angus Dundee Distillers

Region/district:
Speyside

Founded: 1965
Status: Active
Capacity: 3 300 000 litres

Address: Ballindalloch, Banffshire AB37 9AQ

Website: tomintouldistillery.co.uk
Tel: 01807 590274

The owner of Tomintoul and Glencadam, Angus Dundee Distillers, may not be that well-known to the consumer but the company is one of the most prominent players in the Scotch whisky industry.

The company was formed as a broker and blender in 1950 and was acquired by Terry Hillman in 1988. Born in 1933 he is still one of the directors but the daily business has been run by his children Tanya and Aaron for many years. The success of the company is very much built on selling its own blends and, not least, providing bulk whisky or blended whisky for supermarkets or third party customers. In 2012 they established a company in India which gave access to one of the most promising whisky markets. Tomintoul is a typical 1960s distillery built with efficient production in mind rather than to be a pretty sight for visiting tourists. The surrounding scenery is, however, among the most beautiful in Speyside, with Tomintoul town, the highest situated village in the Highlands, just to the south of the distillery.

Tomintoul is equipped with a 12 ton semi lauter mash tun, six stainless steel washbacks with a fermentation time of 54-60 hours and two pairs of stills. There are currently 15 mashes per week, which means that capacity is used to its maximum, and the 13 warehouses have a storage capacity of 120,000 casks. The malt used for mashing is unpeated, but every year since 2001, heavily peated (55ppm) spirit has also been produced. In 2023 that part will be 440,000 litres split between June and December to coincide with the following silent seasons.

The core range consists of **Tlàth** and **Seiridh**, both without age statement, **10, 14, 16, 18, 21, 25 year old** and **Cigar Malt.** The peaty side of Tomintoul is represented by **Peated** without age statement and **Peaty Tang 15 year old**. As a stand-alone range, there is also the heavily peated **Old Ballantruan** without age statement as well as a **10** and **15 year old**. Recent limited releases include **seven different cask finishes** without an age statement as well as a **12 year old oloroso finish** (August 2023). Finally, a new range of expression for travel retail was launched in spring 2023; **Tor, Tundra** and **Tarn.**

History:

1965 The distillery is founded by Tomintoul Distillery Ltd, which is owned by Hay & MacLeod & Co. and W. & S. Strong & Co.

1973 Scottish & Universal Investment Trust, owned by the Fraser family, buys both the distillery and Whyte & Mackay.

1974 The two stills are increased to four and Tomintoul 12 years is launched.

1978 Lonhro buys Scottish & Universal Investment Trust.

1989 Lonhro sells Whyte & Mackay to Brent Walker.

1990 American Brands buys Whyte & Mackay.

1996 Whyte & Mackay changes name to JBB (Greater Europe).

2000 Angus Dundee plc buys Tomintoul.

2002 Tomintoul 10 year is launched.

2003 Tomintoul 16 years is launched.

2004 Tomintoul 27 years is launched.

2005 The peated Old Ballantruan is launched.

2008 1976 Vintage and Peaty Tang are released.

2009 A 14 year old and a 33 year old are released.

2010 A 12 year old Port wood finish is released.

2011 A 21 year old, a 10 year old Ballantruan and Vintage 1966 are released.

2012 Old Ballantruan 10 years old is released.

2013 A 31 year old single cask is released.

2015 Five Decades and a 40 year old are released.

2016 A 40 year old and Tlàth without age statement are launched.

2017 15 year old Peaty Tang and 15 year old Old Ballantruan are launched.

2018 Tomintoul 1965 The Ultimate Cask is released.

2020 Seiridh and a number of bottlings celebrating Robert Fleming´s 30th anniversary are released.

2021 A 16 year old Sauternes finish is released.

2023 Tor, Tundra and Tarn are released for travel retail.

Tasting notes Tomintoul 10 years old:

GS – A light, fresh and fruity nose, with ripe peaches and pineapple cheesecake, delicate spice and background malt. Medium-bodied, fruity and fudgy on the palate. The finish offers wine gums, mild, gently spiced oak, malt and a suggestion of smoke.

10 years old

Tormore

[tor•more]

Owner:
Elixir Distillers

Region/district:
Speyside

Founded: 1958
Status: Active
Capacity: 4 800 000 litres

Address: Tormore, Advie, Grantown-on-Spey, Morayshire PH26 3LR

Website: -
Tel: 01807 510244

For more than a year now, the distillery has been under the ownership of whisky specialist Elixir Distillers, owned by brothers Sukhinder and Rajbir Singh.

They bought it, including stock of maturing whisky, from Pernod Ricard in June 2022 and around the same time the brothers' retail company, The Whisky Exchange, was taken over by Pernod Ricard. The first distillation under Elixir ownership was 9th January 2023 and the company will continue to produce single malt for Chivas' blends as well as for their own needs.

A large re-racking programme on mature stocks has been initiated and from autumn 2023 they hope to have reinstated the filling store so that they can fill their own casks. In the pipeline is also a rationalisation of the site and planning for a visitor centre in the future.

The distillery is equipped with a 10.4 ton stainless steel full lauter mash tun and eleven stainless steel washbacks with a fermentation time of around 60 hours. In a very spacious still house, there are four 18,500 litre wash stills (filled at 12,300 litres) and four 13,900 litre spirit stills (6-7,000 litres fill), all equipped with purifiers which together with a clear wort and slow distillation gives a light and fruity character to the newmake. Currently the distillery is working a 5-day week with 18 mashes and 3,2 million litres of alcohol.

Before a 2014 re-launch, there had been two attempts to establish Tormore single malt as a brand. In 1991 it became part of Caledonian Malts, a range introduced by Allied Distillers. The second time was in 2004 when a 12 year old was launched under the name "The Pearl of Speyside". Currently the brand sells around 40,000 bottles per year.

The only official bottlings are a **14 year old** bottled at 43% and a **16 year old**, non chill-filtered, bottled at 48%. There are also two cask strength bottlings (**12 and 20 years old**) in the Distillery Reserve Collection, which used to be available at all Chivas' visitor centres.

History:

1958 Schenley International, owners of Long John, founds the distillery.

1960 The distillery is ready for production.

1972 The number of stills is increased from four to eight.

1975 Schenley sells Long John and its distilleries (including Tormore) to Whitbread.

1989 Allied Lyons (to become Allied Domecq) buys the spirits division of Whitbread.

1991 Allied Distillers introduce Caledonian Malts where Miltonduff, Glendronach and Laphroaig are represented besides Tormore. Tormore is later replaced by Scapa.

2004 Tormore 12 year old is launched as an official bottling.

2005 Chivas Brothers (Pernod Ricard) becomes new owners through the acquisition of Allied Domecq.

2012 Production capacity is increased by 20%.

2014 The 12 year old is replaced by two new expressions - 14 and 16 year old.

2022 The distillery is sold to Elixir Distillers.

14 years old

Tasting notes Tormore 14 years old:

GS – Vanilla, butterscotch, summer berries and light spice on the nose. Milk chocolate and tropical fruit on the smooth palate, with soft toffee. Lengthy in the finish, with a sprinkling of black pepper.

Tullibardine

[tully•bar•din]

Owner:
Terroirs Distillers
(Picard Vins & Spiritueux)

Region/district:
Highlands

Founded: 1949
Status: Active (vc)
Capacity: 3 000 000 litres

Address: Blackford, Perthshire PH4 1QG

Website:
tullibardine.com

Tel:
01764 682252

Tullibardine is the wonderful story of a distillery that was deemed surplus in the aftermath of the huge decline for Scotch in the mid 1980s. Mothballed in 1994, it was revived ten years later by new owners.

A consortium of private investors took over Tullibardine with plans to include a retail village adjacent to the distillery. The property crash in 2009 radically changed the prospects. A new owner stepped in – the French spirits company Picard. They had been involved with blending and bottling Scotch for a few years and in 2008, when Glenmorangie decided to stop making blends, they took over the highly reputed Highland Queen brand as well as Muirhead's. What they lacked was a distillery making malt whisky and buying Tullibardine in 2011 was the perfect solution.

They new owners invested heavily in the distillery which resulted in a new visitor centre, a bottling line, a vatting hall, more warehouses and even a small cooperage used for repairing casks. The location in Blackford, on the busy A9 from Stirling to Perth, is perfect for attracting visitors on their way to the Highlands. While the investment in Tullibardine may have been prompted by the need for single malts to become a part of their blends, the owners have put a lot of effort into promoting Tullibardine as a brand of its own. The lack of older stock due to the distillery not producing between 1994 and 2003 does not help however.

The distillery equipment consists of a 6.2 ton stainless steel semi-lauter mash tun, nine stainless steel washbacks with a fermentation of 55-60 hours, two 21,000 litre wash stills and two 16,000 litre spirit stills. During 2023, they will be working 27 mashes per week which will result in 3 million litres of alcohol.

The core range consists of **Sovereign** without age statement, **225 Sauternes finish, 228 Burgundy finish, 500 Sherry finish** and a **15 year old**. The 25 year old has been discontinued and an **18 year old** was added in late 2023. The changes are due to stock issues caused by the stop in production between 1994 and 2003. Twelve expressions have so far been released in the Marquess Collection with the latest being **2008 The Triple Port**. This had been finished in a combination of port casks; white, tawny and ruby port.

History:

1949 The architect William Delmé-Evans founds the distillery.

1953 The distillery is sold to Brodie Hepburn.

1971 Invergordon Distillers buys Brodie Hepburn Ltd.

1973 The number of stills increases to four.

1993 Whyte & Mackay buys Invergordon Distillers.

1994 Tullibardine is mothballed.

1996 Whyte & Mackay changes name to JBB (Greater Europe).

2001 JBB (Greater Europe) is bought out from Fortune Brands by management and changes name to Kyndal (Whyte & Mackay from 2003).

2003 A consortium buys Tullibardine for £1.1 million. The distillery is in production again.

2005 Three wood finishes from 1993, Port, Moscatel and Marsala, are launched together with a 1986 John Black selection.

2006 Vintage 1966, Sherry Wood 1993 and a new John Black selection are launched.

2007 Five different wood finishes and a couple of single cask vintages are released.

2008 A Vintage 1968 40 year old is released.

2009 Aged Oak is released.

2011 Three vintages and a wood finish are released. Picard buys the distillery.

2013 A completely new range is launched – Sovereign, 225 Sauternes, 228 Burgundy, 500 Sherry, 20 year old and 25 year old.

2015 A 60 year old Custodian Collection is released.

2016 A Vintage 1970 and The Murray from 2004 are released.

2017 Vintage 1962 and The Murray Chateauneuf-du-Pape are released.

2018 The Murray Marsala Finish is released.

2019 A Vintage 1964 is released.

2020 A 15 year old is released.

2021 The Murray Double Wood Finish is released.

2023 An 18 year old and The Murray Triple Port are released.

Tasting notes Tullibardine Sovereign:

GS – Floral on the nose, with new-mown hay, vanilla and fudge. Fruity on the palate, with milk chocolate, brazil nuts, marzipan, malt, and a hint of cinnamon. Cocoa, vanilla, a squeeze of lemon and more spice in the finish.

Sovereign

Final work at Port of Leith Distillery in April 2023

New
distilleries

Until Kilchoman was founded in 2005,
only two malt distilleries had been opened in Scotland during
the preceeding 15 years. Since 2005, no less than 44 new distilleries
have been built! Even though many of them have released whisky, and
some of them of a considerable age, we still call them New Distilleries in
this section. Many more are yet to come – read more about them in the
chapter The Year That Was, pages 263-266

8 Doors

[eyt doars]

Owner:
Kerry and Derek Campbell

Region/district:
Highlands

Founded: 2022
Status: Active (vc)
Capacity: 150 000 litres

Address: John O´Groats, Wick KW1 4YR

Website:
8doorsdistillery.com

Tel:
01955 482000

For many years, Pulteney was Scotland's most northerly situated mainland whisky distillery. Then Wolfburn in Thurso came in 2013 but their claim to the title only lasted nine years.

In September 2022 the 8 Doors Distillery started production in John O´Groats which is about as far north you can get on the mainland. The founders, Kerry and Derek Campbell, managed to hire John Ramsay as their whisky creator. With a 40 year long career as master blender for the Edrington Group (Macallan, Highland Park, Glenrothes etc.), Ramsay is a legend in the whisky industry.

While there is no mill on site, the grist is bought from an external supplier. The equipment at 8 Doors is interesting as the owners have decided on both a mash conversion vessel and a 0.4 ton semi lauter mash tun to process the grains. The MCV can be used to process grains other than malted

barley but for now it's used as the first step of of the barley mash conversion. They are also looking for a clear wort with a slightly higher gravity. With five stainless steel wash backs (2,000 litres each) the distillery is currently working a 5-day week with two short (70 hours) and three long (120 hours) fermentations.There is also one 1,700 litre wash still and one 1,300 litre spirit still, both from Speyside Copperworks and with slightly descending lyne arms. The foreshots last 10 minutes and they they cut the spirit between 74% and 64% aiming for a fruity new make spirit.

In waiting of their own spirits to mature the owners have launched a range of sourced Scotch blends and single malts under the name The Seven Sons. There is also the 874 Club, named after the distance by road between Land's End and John O´Groats (the whole length of Great Britain), where fans initially could buy there own cask from the distillery.

Aberargie

[aber•ar•jee]

Owner:
Morrison Scotch Whisky
Distillers Ltd.

Region/district:
Lowlands

Founded: 2017
Status: Active
Capacity: 750 000 litres

Address: Aberargie, Perthshire PH2 9LX

Website:
morrisondistillers.com

Tel:
01738 787044

The distillery was built on the same grounds in Fife as Morrison & Mackay, independent bottler and producer of Scottish liqueurs, and a company which can trace it´s roots back to 1982.

Founded as John Murray & Co., the company was taken over in 2005 by Kenny Mackay and Brian Morrison, once the chairman of Morrison Bowmore, and his son Jamie. The production of liqueurs, continued while bottling of Scotch single malts (The Carn Mor) was added to the business. Later on, they also took over the Old Perth brand from Whyte & Mackay and relaunched it as a blended malt. The company name was changed to Morrison & Mackay in 2014. In 2019, when Brian and Jamie Morrison became the sole owners, the name was changed to Morrison Scotch Whisky Distillers Ltd.

The company has a blending and bottling facility in Fife and just a stone´s throw from that, construction on a whisky distillery started in summer 2016 and the first spirit was distilled in November 2017.

The distillery is equipped with a 2 ton semilauter mash tun, six stainless steel washbacks with a fermentation time of 72 hours, one 15,000 litre wash still and one 10,000 litre spirit still. The stills, both with steeply descending lyne arms, were made by Forsyths and are heated with panels instead of coils or pans. With a maturation in a mixture of first fill sherry butts, first fill bourbon barrels and second fill sherry/bourbon casks, the owners are aiming for a fruity character which will be enhanced by occasional peated spirit runs. Different barley varieties are being used, including Golden Promise, and they are all grown in 300 acres of field owned by the Morrison family and that surround the distillery.

Abhainn Dearg

[aveen jar•rek]

Owner:	**Region/district:**
Mark Tayburn	Highlands (Isle of Lewis)
Founded: **Status:**	**Capacity:**
2008 Active (vc)	c 20 000 litres

Address: Carnish, Isle of Lewis,
Na h-Eileanan an Iar HS2 9EX

Website:	**Tel:**
abhainndeargdistillery.co.uk	01851 672429

In September 2008, spirit flowed from a newly constructed distillery in Uig on the island of Lewis in the Outer Hebrides.

This was the first distillery on the island since 1840 when Stornoway distillery was closed. The conditions for new distilleries being built at that time were not improved when James Matheson, a Scottish tradesman, bought the entire island in 1844. Even though he had made his fortune in the opium trade, he was an abstainer and a prohibitionist and did not look kindly on the production or use of alcohol.

The Gaelic name of the new distillery is Abhainn Dearg which means Red River, and the founder and owner is Mark "Marko" Tayburn who was born and raised on the island. There are two 500 kg mash tuns made of stainless steel and two 7,500 litre washbacks made of Douglas fir with a fermentation time of 4 days. The wash still has a capacity of 2,112 litres and the spirit still 2,057 litres. Both

have very long necks and steeply descending lye pipes leading out into two wooden worm tubs. Both bourbon and sherry casks are used for maturation. The plan is to use 100% barley grown on Lewis and in 2013 the first 6 tonnes of Golden Promise (15% of the total requirement) were harvested. Over the years, production has been limited to around 10,000 litres of pure alcohol yearly even though the distillery has the capacity to do more.

The first release from the distillery was The Spirit of Lewis in 2010 and the first single malt was a limited release of a 3 year old in October 2011, followed up by a cask strength version (58%) in 2012. The distillery's first 10 year old appeared in late 2018 when 10,000 bottles were released, bottled at 46%. At the same time 100 bottles of a limited 10 year old single cask, also bottled at 46% were launched. Since then a number of single casks with different maturations (including madeira and sauternes) have been released for various markets.

Ailsa Bay

[ail•sah bey]

Owner:	**Region/district:**
William Grant & Sons	Lowlands
Founded: **Status:**	**Capacity:**
2007 Active	12 000 000 litres

Address: Girvan, Ayrshire KA26 9PT

Website:	**Tel:**
ailsabay.com	01465 713091

Commissioned in September 2007, it only took nine months to build this distillery on the same site as Girvan Distillery near Ayr on Scotland's west coast.

Initially, it was equipped with a 12,1 tonne full lauter mash tun, 12 washbacks made of stainless steel and eight stills. In 2013 however, it was time for a major expansion when yet another mash tun, 12 more washbacks and eight more stills were commissioned, doubling the capacity to 12 million litres of alcohol. Each washback will hold 50,000 litres and fermentation time is 60 hours for the heavier styles and 72 hours for the lighter "Balveniestyle". The stills are made according to the same standards as Balvenie's and one of the wash stills and one of the spirit stills have stainless steel condensers instead of copper. That way, they have the possibility of making batches of a more sulphury spirit if desired. To increase efficiency and to get more alcohol,

high gravity distillation is used. Maturation for the part that is bottled as single malt starts in small (25-100 litres) ex-bourbon barrels from Tuthilltown distillery and after 6-9 months the spirit is tranferred to regular sized barrels as well as into new oak. The production plan is normally to do around 50 mashes per week, producing 10 million litres of alcohol.

Five different types of spirit are produced. The most common is a light and rather sweet spirit. Then there is a heavy, sulphury style and three peated with the peatiest having a malt specification of 50ppm. The production is mainly used for Grant's blended Scotch but in 2016, a peated single malt Ailsa Bay was released. This was followed up in 2018 by Ailsa Bay Sweet Smoke and the same year Aerstone Land Cask was launched which is a 10 year old Ailsa Bay single malt matured inland. Shortly after, Aerstone Sea Cask was launched which had been matured in warehouses on the coastal site of Girvan.

Annandale

[ann•an•dail]

Owner:		Region/district:
Annandale Distillery Co.		Lowlands

Founded:	Status:	Capacity:
2014	Active (vc)	500 000 litres

Address: Northfield, Annan, Dumfriesshire DG12 5LL

Website:	Tel:
annandaledistillery.com	01461 207817

In 2010 Professor David Thomson and his wife, Teresa Church, obtained consent from the local council for the building of the new Annandale Distillery in Dumfries and Galloway in the south-west of Scotland.

The old one had been producing since 1836 and was owned by Johnnie Walker from 1895 until it closed down in 1918. From 1924 to 2007, the site was owned by the Robinson family, who were famous for their Provost brand of porridge oats. David Thomson began the restoration of the site in June 2011 with the two, old sandstone warehouses being restored to function as two-level dunnage warehouses. The distillery was in a poor condition and the mash house and the tun room was largely reconstructed while the other buildings were refurbished substantially.

The distillery is equipped with a 2.5 ton semi-lauter mash tun with a copper dome. There are three wooden washbacks (a fermentation time of 72-96 hours), one wash still (12,000 litres) and two spirit stills (4,000 litres). In June 2023 a £3.6m project was announced which will use a new thermal energy storage technology enabling Annandale to produce a carbon-neutral whisky.

The first cask was filled in November 2014 and both unpeated and peated (45ppm) whisky is distilled. In June 2018, the first two single malts were released, both matured in ex-Buffalo Trace barrels. The Man O´Words is unpeated while the Man O´Swords is heavily peated. All expressions are bottled at cask strength, un chill-filtered and without colouring. The Founder´s Selection range are all single casks and there are also two other ranges, Vintage and Rare Vintage, that are vattings of several casks. Recent limited releases include Storyman in collaboration with actor James Cosmo.

Arbikie

[ar•bi•ki]

Owner:		Region/district:
The Stirling family		Eastern Highlands

Founded:	Status:	Capacity:
2015	Active	200 000 litres

Address: Inverkeilor, Arbroath, Angus DD11 4UZ

Website:	Tel:
arbikie.com	01241 830770

The Stirling family has been farming since the 17th century and the 2000-acre Arbikie Highland Estate in Angus has now been in their possession for four generations.

The three brothers (John, Iain and David) started their careers within other fields but have now returned to the family lands to open up a single-estate distillery. The definition of a single-estate distillery is that, not only does the whole chain of production take place on site, but all the ingredients are also grown on the farm.

The first vodka from potatoes was distilled in October 2014 which was followed by gin in May 2015. Trials with malt whisky, started in March 2015, went over to full production in October 2015. Responsible for the production side at the distillery is master distiller Kirsty Black. The barley is grown in fields of their own and then sent to Boorts malt in Montrose. The distillery is equipped with a stainless steel, semi-lauter mash tun with a 0.75 ton charge and four washbacks (two 4,400 litre and two 9,000 litre) with a fermentation time of 96-120 hours. There is also one 4,000 litre wash still and one 2,400 litre spirit still. For the final stage of vodka and gin production, there is a 40 plate rectification column. The Stirlings don´t intend to launch their first single malt whisky until 2029/2030.

In 2015 Arbikie started trials with rye whisky made from 52% unmalted rye, 33% unmalted wheat and 15% malted barley grown on their own farm. Matured for three years in American oak and finished in ex-PX casks, it was released in December 2018 as the first rye whisky made in Scotland for more than 100 years. The third edition of the 1794 Highland Rye Scotch appeared in autumn 2022 and had been finished in a Jamaican rum barrel. In 2021, Arbikie was awarded craft producer of the year in Whisky Icons of Scotland.

Ardnahoe

[ard•na•<u>hoe</u>]

Owner:
Hunter Laing & Company

Region/district:
Islay

Founded: 2017
Status: Active (vc)
Capacity: 1 000 000 litres

Address: Isle of Islay, Port Askaig PA46 7RU

Website:
ardnahoedistillery.com

Tel:
01496 840711

All but one distillery on Islay (Kilchoman) are beautifully located close to the sea and especially the ones on the northern tip of the island offer a breathtaking view.

While both Bunnahabhain and Caol Ila may be situated right by the water it is probably the one in the middle, Ardnahoe, that takes first prize for the most scenic site. Even though it's around 200 metres to the sea, the elevation of the surrounding landscape gives an extraordinary view of the Sound of Islay with Jura on the other side and Mull in the distance. The distillery visitor centre is surprisingly huge (given the size of the distillery) with a large shop and a café/whisky bar

Ardnahoe is the newest distillery on Islay, at least until Port Ellen and Portintruan are commissioned, and is owned by independent bottler Hunter Laing. It is equipped with

a 2.75 ton semi lauter mash tun with a copper lid. The lauter gear is used as little as possible to get a clear wort. There are four 25,000 litre washbacks made from Oregon pine with an average fermentation time of 72 hours, one wash still (12,500 litres) and one spirit still (8,000 litres) with a slow distillation, both with the longest lyne arms in Scotland (7.5 metres). The spirit is collected between 74% and 63% and the character of the newmake is fruity. The distillery is also equipped with wooden worm tubs – the only ones on Islay.

Around 90% of the production is peated (using malt typically peated to 40ppm) while the rest is unpeated. Eighty percent of the newmake goes into first fill bourbon. There are currently three warehouses on site with plans to build another four. Even though the first whisky in the warehouse is now five years old, there is no set plan when the inaugural single malt will be released.

Ardnamurchan

[ard•ne•<u>mur</u>•ken]

Owner:
Adelphi Selection

Region/district:
Western Highlands

Founded: 2014
Status: Active (vc)
Capacity: 500 000 litres

Address: Glenbeg, Ardnamurchan, Argyll PH36 4JG

Website:
adelphidistillery.com

Tel:
01972 500 285

It takes a good 90 minutes to drive from Fort William to the distillery, on the Ardnamurchan peninsula north of Mull, but it's well worth the pilgrimage.

The distillery is owned by independent bottler Adelphi Selection. Early on, they realised that the supply of whisky could become scarce in years to come for those companies not having a distillery of their own.

Ardnamurchan is equipped with a two tonne semi-lauter stainless steel mash tun with a copper canopy, seven washbacks; four wooden (three made from Oregon pine and one from oak) and three made of stainless steel. The fermentation time is 72-96 hours. There is one wash still (10,000 litres) and one spirit still (6,000 litres) and quite recently, sub-coolers made from stainless steel were also fitted. Two different styles of whisky are produced; peated (30-35ppm)

and unpeated. The goal for 2023 is to do 10-12 mashes per week and 370,000 litres of alcohol. Around 60% of that will be peated. There are also plans to malt some of their barley themselves in the future.

Due to the remote location of the distillery, the importance of a functional circular economy is the essence of their operation. All power and heat requirements for the distillery come from local renewables. The river that provides the cooling water has a hydro-electricity generator and the biomass boiler is fuelled by woodchip from local forestry.

In October 2020 the inaugural single malt was released – the AD/09.20:01. In 2022, the distillery launched their AD Limited Edition Cask Strength. Recent releases include a sherry cask released in July 2023 and a 6 year old unpeated, finished in champagne barriques from Paul Lanois. There is also The Glover 6 – a fusion between Ardnamurchan and the japanese distillery Chichibu.

Ardross

[ard•ross]

Owner: Greenwood Distillers

Region/district: N Highland

Founded: 2019 **Status:** Active

Capacity: 1 000 000 litres

Address: Ardross Mains, Ardross, Alness

Website: theardross.com **Tel:** -

Of all the new distilleries opening up in Scotland, the vast number have their eyes set on a visitor centre as well, including tours, restaurant and a shop. Ardross is an exception.

Commissioned in August 2019, this distillery north of Inverness is owned by Greenwood Distillers, a company with a mezcal producer in Mexico, a producer of armagnac in France, a cooperage in Japan and a new bourbon distillery in Kentucky under their umbrella. This is not the typical Scotch whisky company and their ambitions at Ardross also stand out. Apart from the existing distillery, a new experimentation plant on the site called Theodore House was opened in September 2023. The idea is to have the opportunity of experimenting without interfering with the daily production at Ardross.

Theodore House is equipped with a 0.65 ton mash tun,

three wooden washbacks and three stills made up of one wash still, one cooker for grains and one small distillation column. The aim is to have the possibility of producing different types of spirits.

The main Ardross distillery is equipped with a 3.5 ton semi-lauter mash tun, ten wooden washbacks, 20,000 litres each and with a fermentation time of 100-130 hours, one 15,000 litre wash still and one 12,000 litre spirit still both fitted with purifiers although these are currently not used. The capacity is an impressive one million litres of pure alcohol and in 2023 the plan is to mash 10 times per week and 700,000 litres. The signature style will be unpeated but peated newmake (55ppm in the malted barley) will amount to 300,000 litres. There is also a designated gin still.

The first release of a single malt is probably not due until it has reached the age of 8-10 years. The first product from the distillery however was Theodore gin which appeared in August 2019.

Ballindalloch

[bal•lin•da•lock]

Owner: The Macpherson-Grant family

Region/district: Speyside

Founded: 2014 **Status:** Active (vc)

Capacity: 100 000 litres

Address: Ballindalloch, Banffshire AB37 9AA

Website: ballindallochdistillery.com **Tel:** 01807 500 331

The location for Ballindalloch distillery couldn't be better chosen: right by the busy A95 where it can't be missed yet in tranquil and pastoral surroundings.

To the west are distilleries such as Craggamore and Tormore. If you go south you will soon end up at Glenlivet and, heading north, you enter into the very heartland of Speyside with all its distilleries. The land and the distillery is owned by the Macpherson-Grants who live in the nearby Ballindalloch Castle which has been home of the family since 1546. The concept of turning an old steading from 1848 into a distillery was conceived in 2011. From the very start the idea was to build an "estate distillery" where the barley was grown in the surrounding fields and the draff from the production was fed back to the herd of Black Angus owned by the family.

The distillery is equipped with a 1 ton semi lauter, copper clad mash tun with a copper dome. There are four washbacks made of Oregon pine with four long fermentations (140 hours) and one short (92 hours). Finally there is a 5,000 litre lantern-shaped wash still and a 3,600 litre spirit still with a reflux ball. Both stills are connected to two wooden worm tubs for cooling the spirit vapours. The worms are run sligthly hotter than conventional worms in an attempt to increase the conversion between the spirit vapour and the copper. The water from the tubs is also passed over a cooling tower and returned to the tub. These features result in a very light, delicate and fruity spirit. The distillery is working 5 days a week, making 100,000 litres of alcohol. The first two expressions (matured in ex-bourbon and ex-oloroso respectively) were released at the distillery in August 2023 while the first widely available single malt is expected in 2024. The distillery is open for visitors by appointment.

Bonnington

[bon•ing•tun]

Owner:		Region/district:
Halewood Artisinal Spririts		Lowlands

Founded:	Status:	Capacity:
2020	Active	720 000 litres

Address: 21 Graham Street, Edinburgh EH6 5QN

Website:	Tel:
crabbiewhisky.com	0151 480 8800

The second malt whisky distillery to open up in Edinburgh in recent times is owned by a company that was started in 1978 by John Halewood.

Run as a family company for many years it was in 2015, with new investors, transformed into one of the largest spritits distillers and distributors in the UK. In 2020 they changed the name of the company to Halewood Artisinal Spirits and they have interests in such diverse countries as the UK, USA, Australia, South Africa and China. Their portfolio of brands include Crabbie´s Scotch whisky. The Pogues Irish whiskey, J.J. Whitley gin, Dead Man´s Finers rum and Aber Falls Welsh whisky. In 2021 Kirstie McCallum, with a background at Burn Stewart and Glen Moray, was hired as the company´s Director of Distilleries.

Construction of the Bonnington distillery in Leith started in January 2019 and was finished in December that year. But, already in 2018 a small pilot distillery (Chain Pier) was opened in Granton not far away from the current distillery. Here the owners could trial different malts, yeasts, fermentation lengths, cut points and distillation methods before starting at Bonnington.

The first distillation took place in March 2020 and the distillery is equipped with a 2 ton semi lauter mash tun, 15 stainless steel washbacks with a fermentation time of 48-70 hours, a 10,500 litre wash still and an 8,000 litre spirit still. Nine of the washbacks were installed in spring 2023 as part of a major expansion which eventually could give the distillery a capacity of one million litres. From May 2023 the production was increased moving from 12 mashes per week to 28. Around 5% of that will be made using peated malt (50ppm). The newmake is filled into a variety of casks (bourbon, sherry, virgin oak, port, marsala and sweet wine).

The Borders

[boar•ders]

Owner:		Region/district:
Borders Distillery Co. Ltd.		Lowlands (Sc. Borders)

Founded:	Status:	Capacity:
2017	Active (vc)	1 600 000 litres

Address: Commercial Road, Hawick TD9 7AQ

Website:	Tel:
thebordersdistillery.com	01450 374330

On the 6th of March 2018, the first whisky distillery in the Borders in 180 years started production and the distillery opened to the public a few weeks later.

Behind the Borders Distillery in Hawick is a company called Borders Distillery Company Limited which was founded in 2013 by four men who had all previously worked for William Grant & Sons – George Tait, Tony Roberts, John Fordyce and Tim Carton. In 2016, the company started to renovate the beautiful buildings dating from the late 1880s and which used to be an electric company and turned it into a distillery. The river Teviot is running just behind the distillery and the distillery uses it for cooling the spirit vapours.

The distillery is equipped with a 5 ton mash tun, eight stainless steel washbacks with a fermentation time of 80 hours, two wash stills (12,500 litres) and two spirit stills (7,500 litres) with all equipment provided by Forsyths. The whisky produced is un-peated and floral. Other spirits are also produced, for instance vodka and gin. In spring 2022, the distillery established a partnership (Borders Growers & Distillers) together with Simpsons Malt and 12 farms, all located within a 30 mile radius of the distillery. The aim is to support sustainable farming and improve the traceability of the supply chain.

The first bottling of spirit was released in 2018 when William Kerr´s Borders Gin was launched and this was later followed by Puffing Billy Steam Vodka. The company then released a blended Scotch from sourced whisky called Clan Fraser and a new series of Scotch whiskies named Workshop Series appeared in autumn 2022 with Borders Malt & Rye, the first blended Scotch to leave the Scottish Borders in 185 years, as the first installment. This was later followed by Long and Short of It.

Brew Dog

[bru•dog]

Owner: Brewdog plc.	**Region/district:** Highlands
Founded: 2016	**Status:** Active	**Capacity:** 450 000 litres

Address: Balmacassie Commercial Park, Ellon, Aberdeenshire AB41 8BX

Website: brewdog.com	**Tel:** 01358 724924

In spring 2019, the distillery changed the name from Lone Wolf to Brew Dog in order to tap into the name and fame of the well-known brewery

Founded in 2007 Brew Dog grew to become the biggest independent brewery in the UK and in 2014 a decision was taken to open up also a distillery. It is situated next to the brewery in Ellon outside of Aberdeen and as director distilling operations, Steven Kersley who had a background at several Diageo distilleries, was called in. In autumn 2018, David Gates who previously ran Diageo Futures and worked as brand director for Johnnie Walker, joined the company as managing director.

From the very start, gin and vodka was an important part of the production and as time passed and the demand increased for their white spirits, the owners realised they had to improve the capacity in order to fulfill their ambitions on the whisky side. A new distillery was recently built on site and all the existing equipment was moved there including two 3,000 litre copper pot stills. A new 10,000 litre still was added as well as a 19 metre tall rectification column and this will increase whisky production from eight casks per week to 30-35 casks and there will also be more space to produce rum.

Gin and vodka were launched in spring 2017 and rum has since been released but no whisky. In 2017, Lone Wolf became one of the first Scottish distilleries in modern times to distill a rye whisky. In spring 2019, the company entered into a collaboration with three other whisky makers (Millstone, Compass Box and Duncan Taylor) who all designed one whisky each to be paired with Brew Dog beers. In late 2022, 50 casks of whisky were offered to consumers in partnership with whisky auction house Whisky Hammer.

Brora

[bro•rah]

Owner: Diageo	**Region/district:** Northern Highlands
Founded: 2021 (1819)	**Status:** Active (vc)	**Capacity:** 800 000 litres

Address: Clynelish Rd, Brora, Sutherland KW9 6LR

Website: malts.com	**Tel:** -

Brora distillery was closed in 1983 and as the years passed, the prospects of a resurrection more or less vanished. Not even the biggest enthusiasts believed it would produce again.

That's why it came as a huge surprise in October 2017 when Diageo announced that not only Brora but also Port Ellen were to be restored and rebuilt as a part of a £35m investment. Brora was founded as Clynelish in 1819 by the 1st Duke of Sutherland and operated under that name until 1969 when it was changed to Brora. At that time a modern distillery had also been built on the same site and was named Clynelish. Both distilleries worked in tandem for 16 years with Brora focusing on peated spirit. The final distillation at the old distillery was in 1983.

Starting 2019 the distillery has been meticulously restored to its former glory. The original stills (wash still 14,400 litres and spirit still 13,200) with slightly descending lyne arms, were sent to Abercrombie in Alloa for refurbishing while a new traditional 6 ton mash tun with rake and plough and 6 new washbacks (28,800 litres each and a fermentation time of 120 hours) made of Oregon pine were manufactured in accordance with the old drawings and specifications. The stills are attached to wooden worm tubs with a magnificent view towards the North Sea and currently the distillery is working 7 days per week. The character of the newmake is fruity/waxy and lightly peated. The first cask was filled in May 2021 and the first distillery manager for the new Brora, Stewart Bowman, was succeeded by Jackie Robertson (ex-Talisker) in autumn 2021.

Recent limited bottlings include a set of three 50cl bottles named Brora Triptych, made up of three vintages; 1972 (48 years), 1977 (43 years) and 1982 (38 years). In October 2023 a 45 year old bottling distilled in 1977 appeared as part of the 4th Prima & Ultima range.

Burnobennie

[burn•o•benni]

Owner:	**Region/district:**
Ardent Spirits	Eastern Highlands

Founded:	**Status:**	**Capacity:**
2020	Active	680 000 litres

Address: Burn Ó Bennie Road, Banchory,
Aberdeenshire AB31 5NN

Website:	**Tel:**
burnobennie.com	01330 202172

In 2017, Mike Bain opened up a small experimental craft distillery in Banchory and named it Deeside Distillery. It only worked for 18 months though before it closed.

It was a part of Deeside Brewery in Lochton of Leys, also owned by Bain, but it was more or less intended from the beginning that this would serve as a pilot distillery where the team could put some of their ideas into practice. Only 100 casks were filled at Deeside of which 88 were sold to help finance the new distillery. The remaining 12 will be matured for at least ten years before being bottled.

In 2019 Mike Bain teamed up with Liam Pennycook and moved the operation to larger premises in a business park in near-by Hill of Banchory. The new distillery, which started production in 2020, has recently been expanded and is now equipped with a 1,6 ton mash tun which is designed specifically to accomodate wash for whisky distillation as well as beer and rye wash. Furthermore, there are 13 (used to be five) stainless steel wash-backs with a fermentation time of 168 hours, one 5,000 litre wash still and one 3,600 litre spirit still. Fore-shots are one hour and a slow distillation is practiced.

The distillery is definitely at the forefront when it comes to searching for new flavours. Recently they hired Sam Shrimpton as a consultant and he will continue with the distillery´s experimentations on yeast, fermentation, fractional distillation and sour beer washes.

The distillery produces both peated and unpeated single malt as well as small batches of rye and corn whisky. One feature which stands out is the owners' interest in various speciality malts that are typically used in the brewing business but not so much by distilleries. These include for instance crystal and chocolate malt but also the use of the heritage bere barley.

The Cairn

[cairn]

Owner:	**Region/district:**
Gordon & MacPhail	Speyside

Founded:	**Status:**	**Capacity:**
2022	Active (vc)	1 000 000 litres

Address: Craggan, Grantown-on-Spey PH26 3NT

Website:	**Tel:**
thecairndistillery.com	01479 816543

The planning application for The Cairn was approved by the local council in October 2019, just a few months before the covid pandemic hit the world.

The fact that the owners, Gordon & MacPhail, managed to distill the first spirit only two and a half years later and open the to the public in October 2022 was impressive. Quite a few distillery projects around Scotland have been delayed for years due to the pandemic. Located on the outskirts of Grantown-on-Spey, at the foothills of the beautiful Cairngorms, it is the first distillery you see when you enter the Speyside area coming from the west on the A95.

This is the second distillery owned by the most influential of the independent bottler Gordon & Macphail. The first was the then dormant Benromach which was bought in 1993 and brought back to life five years later.

The Cairn distillery is equipped with a 5.8 ton full lauter mash tun. There are six 27,000 litre stainless steel washbacks with cooling jackets and both short (67 hours) and long (110 hours) fermentations. Finally, there are two traditional wash stills and four spirit stills. The production plan for 2023 is to do 9 mashes per week which will result in one million litres of pure alcohol – the actual, current capacity. With an additional six washbacks in the future, the capacity would rise to 2 million litres.

The intention is to produce an unpeated single malt, definitely lighter in style compared to the owners´ other distillery Benromach, and the newmake is fruity with sweet, malty notes. As distillery manager, the owners managed to hire Mhairi Winters with more than 20 years´ experience in the industry, most recently at Balvenie and Kininvie. The first whisky from the distillery is not expected to be released until the mid 2030s.

The Clydeside

[klajdsajd]

Owner:
Morrison Glasgow Distillers

Region/district:
Lowlands

Founded: **Status:** **Capacity:**
2017 Active (vc) 620 000 litres

Address: 100 Stobcross Road, Glasgow G3 8QQ

Website: **Tel:**
theclydeside.com 0141 2121401

Clydeside was the second whisky distillery to be opened in Glasgow in modern times and if the first (Glasgow Distillery) was built as a production facility with no regards being open to the public - Clydeside did the opposite

The distillery is beautifully situated on the river Clyde with well-known attractions such as the Riverside Museum, Glasgow Science Centre and the SEC Centre as its closest neighbours. The area (the Queen's Dock) is filled with whisky history from the past century with ships coming in with barley and coal and going out with barrels of whisky, Originally known as Stobcross Dock it was opened by Queen Victoria in 1877 and evenually closed in 1969 due to a decline in river traffic.

The founder of the distillery, Tim Morrison, represents the fourth generation of one of Scotland's best known whisky families. Today, Tim's son Andrew is the managing director of Clydeside Distillery.

The equipment consists of a 1.5 ton semi lauter mash tun made of stainless steel, 8 stainless steel washbacks with a fermentation time of 72 hours, a 7,500 litre wash still and a 5,000 litre spirit still. The foreshots are 15 minutes with a slow distillation and the cutpoints for the spirit run are 76-71%. The production plan for 2023 is to do 19 mashes per week and a total of 490,000 litres of pure alcohol. In late 2020, the first spirit reached the age of three but it would last until autumn 2021 before the inaugural release of a Clydeside single malt was released. It was named Stobcross after a cross that once marked the route to Dumbarton Rock which was later demolished to make way for the Queen's Dock. The latest bottling is 5 years old and a cask strength version has also been recently released.

Daftmill

[daf•mil]

Owner:
Francis Cuthbert

Region/district:
Lowlands

Founded: **Status:** **Capacity:**
2005 Active c 65 000 litres

Address: By Cupar, Fife KY15 5RF

Website: **Tel:**
daftmill.com 01337 830303

Since the first whisky from one of the smallest distilleries in Scotland was released, it has often been done by way of a ballot. That is how small the volumes are.

Ever since December 2008, when the spirit legally became whisky, questions to the owners Francis and Ian Cuthbert about when the first whisky would be launched have always been answered by "when it's ready". In 2017, they signed a distribution agreement with Berry Brothers and in May 2018, a ballot was opened for buying one of the first 629 bottles of a 12 year old matured in ex-bourbon casks. The first release was followed by a Summer Relase in June where seven casks rendered 1665 bottles. More bottlings have followed, including single casks exclusive to certain markets or retailers and in 2022, the first 15 year old appeared. One of the latest releases was the Daftmill 2010 Winter Batch Release in 2023, a batch of 25 first-fill ex-bourbon casks.

Daftmill's first distillation was in 2005 and it is run as a typical farmhouse distillery. The barley is grown on the farm and they also supply other distilleries. The equipment consists of a one tonne semi-lauter mash tun with a copper dome, two stainless steel washbacks with a fermentation between 72 and 100 hours and one pair of stills. The stills are designed to give a lot of copper contact and a lot of reflux. The wash still has a capacity of 3,000 litres and the spirit still 2,000 litres. The Cuthbert's aim is to do a light, Lowland style whisky. In order to achieve this they have very short foreshots (five minutes) and the spirit run starts at 78% to capture all of the fruity esters and already comes off at 73%. Taking care of the farm obviously prohibits Francis from producing whisky full time. Whisky production is therefore reserved for two months in the summertime and two in the winter.

Dalmunach

[dal•moo•nack]

Owner:
Chivas Brothers

Region/district:
Speyside

Founded: **Status:** **Capacity:**
2015 Active 10 000 000 litres

Address: Carron, Banffshire AB38 7QP

Website: **Tel:**
\- \-

One of the largest new distilleries in Scotland, and one of the most beautiful, has been built on the site of the former Imperial distillery.

Imperial distillery was founded in 1897, the year of Queen Victoria´s Diamond Jubilee and on the top of the roof there was even a large cast iron crown to mark the occasion. The founder was Thomas Mackenzie who at the time already owned Dailuaine and Talisker. The timing was not the best though. One year after the opening, the Pattison crash brought the whisky industry to its knees and the distillery was forced to close. Eventually it came into the hands of DCL who owned it from 1916 until 2005, when Chivas Brothers took over. It was out of production for 60% of the time until 1998 when it was mothballed. The owners probably never planned to use it for distillation again as it was put up for sale in 2005 to become available as residential flats. Soon after, it was withdrawn from the market and, in

2012, a decision was taken to tear down the old distillery and build a new. Demolition of the old distillery began in 2013 and by the end of that year, nothing was left, except for the old warehouses.

Construction on the new Dalmunach distillery started in 2013 and it was commissioned in October 2014. The exceptional and stunning distillery is equipped with an efficient (4 hour mash) 13 ton Briggs full lauter mash tun and 16 stainless steel washbacks charged with 56,000 litres and with a fermentation time of 56-62 hours. There are four pairs of stills of a considerable size – wash stills 28,000 litres and spirits stills 18,000. They are all positioned in a circle with a hexagonal spirit safe in the middle. The distillery, which cost £25m to build, is the company´s most ennergy efficient distillery and uses 38% less energy and 15% less water than the industry average. In autumn 2019, the first official release of Dalmunach single malt appeared – a 4 year old bottled at cask strength (59%).

Dornoch

[dor•nock]

Owner:
Thompson Bros Distillers

Region/district:
Northern Highlands

Founded: **Status:** **Capacity:**
2016 Active 12 000 litres

Address: Castle Street, Dornoch, Sutherland, IV25 3 SD

Website: **Tel:**
thompsonbrosdistillers.com 01862 810 216

It is probably fair to say that the recent trend of using time honoured production techniques amongst newly established Scottish distilleries, started with the Thompson brothers.

The Dornoch Castle Hotel, owned by the Thompson family, are famous for their well-stocked whisky bar and the second generation, Phil and Simon, are passionate about old-style whisky. So passionate that they decided in 2016 to open a distillery in an old fire station at the back of the hotel. The idea was to try and recreate whisky as it was made decades ago, not worrying about yield. The distillery building is only 47 square metres and all the barley is floor malted, often using old heritage varieties and different strains of brewer´s yeast. They are also working as independent bottlers having released more than 100 expressions.

Currently, the distillery is equipped with a 300 kg stainless steel, semi-lauter mash tun, six washbacks made of oak with a minimum fermentation time of seven days, a 1,000 litre wash still and a 600 litre spirit still. The stills are directly fired using gas but they are also equipped with steam coils. There is also a 2,000 litre still with a column for the production of gin and other spirits. The first single malt release appeared in November 2020 and more releases have since followed. The brothers have had plans for a much larger distillery and in December 2022 a planning application (pending approval) was submitted to the Highland council. The proposed site is a derelict building a couple of 100 metres south of the exisiting distillery and overlooking the Dornoch firth. The distillery will be equipped with no less than 12 washbacks and one pair of stills and the capacity is 175,000-200,000 litres of pure alcohol. A visitor centre is also in the plans.

Dunphail

[done•fail]

Owner:
Dunphail Distillery Ltd.

Region/district:
Highlands

Founded: 2023
Status: Active (vc)
Capacity: 200 000 litres

Address: Wester Greens, Dunphail, Forres IV36 2QR

Website:
dunphaildistillery.com

Tel:
01309 611309

When Dariusz and Ewelina Plazewski opened up Bimber distillery in west London in 2015, their focus was on whisky production with a flavour of heritage as well as innovation.

Floor malted barley and long fermentation times were essential parts of the the process. While the success was instant, the owners already had their minds set on yet another distillery where they could malt all of their barley themselves and this time they decided on building a distillery in Scotland. The location of Dunphail, near Forres was chosen because of the proximity to the supply of Sassy grain from the Altyre Estate and mineral-rich water from a borehole on site. The first distillation took place in September 2023.

The distillery is equipped with a one ton semi-lauter mash tun and 12 open-top washbacks made from Douglas fir, each holding 5,000 litres. Fermentations are long, usually around six days. There are two 2,250 litre wash stills and one 2,250 litre spirit still – all of them direct fired. On top of that they have a 5 ton floor malting which makes it the second distillery in Scotland (after Springbank) malting all their barley on site. One unique feature (at least for Scottish distilleries) is that they don't redistill the foreshots. These are considered by-products used for car screen wash and similar.

The owners produce both unpeated and peated whisky (in a ratio of 60/40) and for both styles they are looking for a fruity newmake. The cask policy will favour refill wood over first fill. Initially Dunphail will produce 100,000 litres of pure alcohol while the maximum capacity is 200,000. All in all, Dunphail is one of the best representatives of new distilleries featuring time-honoured processes to achieve and preserve as much as possible of the character from the production (malting, fermentation and distillation) rather than relying on the influence of the casks.

Eden Mill

[eden mill]

Owner:
Inverleith LLP

Region/district:
Lowlands

Founded: 2012
Status: Active (vc)
Capacity: 100 000 litres

Address: 96 Market St, St Andrews, Fife, KY16 0UU

Website:
edenmill.com

Tel:
01334 834038

In 2012, Eden Mill was founded in Guardbridge just west of St. Andrews. It was Scotland's first single-site brewery and distillery.

Ten years later, the original founders, Tony Kelly and Paul Miller, sold a majority stake in the company to investment company Inverleith. What started as a brewery in 2012 was extended in 2014 with a distillery and the first whisky (as well as gin) was distilled that same year. The distillery was situated in an old paper mill and only 50 metres away, there was a distillery called Seggie which was operative between 1810 and 1860 and owned by the Haig family.

Eden Mill distillery, with a 100,000 litre capacity, is equipped with two wash stills and one spirit still of the alembic type. Made by Hoga in Portugal, all three stills are of the same size – 1,000 litres. The first release of a single malt appeared in 2018, matured in a combination of French virgin oak, American virgin oak, and Pedro Ximenez casks.

Since then a series of different 20cl bottlings called the Hip Flask Series has been launched. All of them have been made from different mashbills and matured in different types of casks. Every year an Eden Mill Single Malt is released in celebration of St. Andrews Day. There are two versions, bottled at 46,5% and at cask strength.

In 2018, the owners announced that they had plans to move the entire operation to a new distillery at the mouth of the River Eden. In 2019, whisky production stopped (although distillation of gin continued) and the owners started working on the plans for the new distillery. In March 2022 they received planning permission for a distillery which will be powered by University of St Andrews solar plant. The equipment will consist of six 15,000 litre washbacks, one 15,000 litre wash still and one 11,500 litre spirit still. If everything goes according to plan, the new distillery will be producing in 2024 and at the same time a visitor centre will also open.

Falkirk

[fall•kirk]

Owner:
Stewart family

Region/district:
Lowlands

Founded: **Status:**
2020   Active (vc)

Capacity:
1 200 000 litres

Address: Grandsable Rd, Polmont, Falkirk FK2 0WA

Website:
falkirkdistillery.com

Tel:
01324 281086

The road from idea to distillery is not always as straightforward as planned. Falkirk is a good example of navigating a long and winding road.

As early as in 2008 the plans for this distillery on the outskirts of Falkirk were on the table. Planning approval was granted in 2010 but Historic Scotland raised objections that the distillery would be built too close to the remnants of the Roman Antonine Wall built in the 2nd century. That prompted a lot of compulsory surveys, including archaeological digs, before the green light was given. The founders, local businessman George Stewart and his daughter Fiona, didn't lose hope though. They adjusted their plans and carried on and in July 2020 the distillery became fully operational and in September the first drops of spirit were distilled.

The distillery is equipped with a 4,6 ton ex-Caperdonich traditional mash tun with rakes made of stainless steel and with a copper top, six 20,000 litre stainless steel washbacks

with a fermentation time of 100 plus hours, one 10,000 litre wash still and a 7,100 litre spirit still – both also from Caperdonich. The plan is to produce a light, traditional Lowland malt which will mature mainly in ex-oloroso and first fill bourbon casks. At the moment the production is two mashes per week but the plan is to scale that up by end of 2023 or start of 2024. Newmake has already been released and the plan is to launch the inaugural single malt in late 2023 or early 2024.

As distillery manager, the family hired Graham Brown, formerly of Distell where he had worked at both Tobermory and Deanston. In September 2022 he was succeeded by Stuart Hughes from Ardnahoe Distillery who has over 30 years of experience in the industry. A visitor centre is due to be opened by end of 2023 and benefitting from Falkirk's three existing visitor attractions (Callendar House, The Falkirk Wheel and The Kelpies) the owners hope to attract over 80,000 visitors every year.

Glasgow

[glas•go]

Owner:
Liam Hughes, Ian McDougall

Region/district:
Lowlands

Founded: **Status:**
2015   Active

Capacity:
365 000 litres

Address: Deanside Rd, Hillington, Glasgow G52 4XB

Website:
glasgowdistillery.com

Tel:
0141 4047191

When Glasgow Distillery was opened in Hillington Business Park, it became the first new whisky distillery in Glasgow in modern times.

There were stills within the Strathclyde grain distillery producing the malt whisky Kinclaith from 1958-1975 but Liam Hughes, Mike Hayward and Ian McDougall built the first proper malt distillery in Glasgow in more than a hundred years. The distillery started production in February 2015 and the first distillation of whisky was unpeated. Since then peated spirit (50ppm) has become part of the production and since January 2017, triple distillation is also practised one month per year. The distillery is equipped with a one ton mash tun, 8 stainless steel washbacks with a minimum fermentation of 72 hours, two 2,500 litre wash still, two 1,400 litre spirit still and one 450 litre gin still – all from Firma Carl in Germany. Two of the stills were installed in November 2019.

The first product to be bottled was the Makar gin which now exists in several versions. In the beginning, the owners also bottled old, sourced single malts under the name Prometheus. The first single malt from their own production appeared in June 2018. Aged in ex-bourbon barrels and finished in virgin oak, the whisky was called 1770 Glasgow Single Malt, named after Glasgow's first distillery which was founded at Dundashill in 1770. Since then a signature range of three whiskies has evolved; The Original, Peated and Triple Distilled. They are released in batches with the type of wood changing slightly for every batch. In June 2020 the owners launched Malt Riot Blended Malt with their own malt as the main part and in 2021, the first distillery exclusive, The Cooper's Cask Release, appeared. A new range, Small Batch Series, was introduced in 2022 with a peated malt finished in cognac casks and an unpeated finished in a tequila cask. The latest, in 2023, had been finished in a combination of port and Bordeaux red wine..

GlenWyvis

[glen•wivis]

Owner:
GlenWyvis Distillery Ltd.

Region/district:
Highlands

Founded: 2017   **Status:** Active (vc)

Capacity: 140 000 litres

Address: Upper Docharty, Dingwall IV15 9UF

Website: glenwyvis.com

Tel: 01349 862005

In 2015, the local farmer John McKenzie, came up with the idea to establish a distillery that was owned by the local people – the first ever 100% community-owned distillery.

A planning application was submitted to the local council in March 2016 and by summer more than £2.5 million had been raised via a community share offer with more than 3,000 people investing. Construction started in January 2017 and later that year, the owners managed to hire one of the most experienced distillers in Scotland as the manager, Duncan Tait, who was succeeded by Matthew Farmer in August 2020. The first distillation was on the 30th of January 2018 and the production goal for 2021 is to average 6 mashes per week and produce 55,000 litres of pure alcohol. The distillery is equipped with a 0.5 ton semi lauter mash tun, six washbacks (4,400 litres each) made of stainless steel with a fermentation time of 96-144 hours, one 2,500 litre wash still and one 1,700 litre spirit still. In October 2019 there was a fire in the distillery´s woodchip store and even though the fire was contained to a small area, it took until March 2020 before they were producing again. They have one dunnage warehouse on site and are currently working on the restoration of an old farm steading into a second one.

The style of the newmake is a combination o fruity and green/grassy and the unpeated spirit, which is mainly filled into American oak, was released for sale in 2019. A first, limited whisky release for shareholders appeared in 2020 while the inaugural public release was in December 2021. The whisky had been matured in a combination of bourbon and moscatel casks. This was followed in June 2022 where the maturation had been in casks that had held bourbon and oloroso with an added proportion of refilled hogsheads.

Harris

[har•ris]

Owner:
Isle of Harris Distillers Ltd.

Region/district:
Highlands (Isle of Harris)

Founded: 2015   **Status:** Active (vc)

Capacity: 399 000 litres

Address: Tarbert, Isle of Harris, Na h-Eileanan an Iar HS3 3DJ

Website: harrisdistillery.com

Tel: 01859 502212

Finally the time has come for the Isle of Harris distillery to release their inaugural bottling. On 23rd September 2023 The Hearach single malt was officially launched.

More than ten years ago, Anderson Bakewell conjured up an idea to build a distillery on the Isle of Harris. Joining Bakewell, who had been connected to the island for more than 40 years, was Simon Erlanger, a former marketing director for Glenmorangie and now the MD of the distillery. Construction started in 2014 and the distillery came into production in September 2015. The total cost for the whole project was £11.4m. The distillery, located in Tarbert, was the second distillery after Abhainn Dearg on Lewis to be founded in the Outer Hebrides.

The first spirit to be distilled in September 2015 was gin and this was followed by whisky in December. The gin was released early on and apart from traditional botanicals, local ingredients are also used such as sugar kelp.

The equipment consists of a 1.2 tonne semi lauter mash tun made of stainless steel but clad with American oak and 8 washbacks made of Oregon pine with a fermentation time of 72-96 hours. There are also one 7,000 litre wash still and a 5,000 litre spirit still - both with descending lyne arms and made in Italy. For 2023 the goal is to do 10 mashes and 200,000 litres of pure alcohol or more. Two new warehouses were built in 2022, adjacent to the original warehouse at Ardhasaig. The style of the whisky is medium peated with a phenol specification in the barley of 12-14ppm although they have also distilled a few batches of heavily peated malt (30ppm) made with local peat. Before the pandemic, the distillery received no less than 100,000 visitors in a year. Obviously the numbers have fallen since but in 2022 the figures had recovered to an impressive 69,000 people.

Holyrood

[holly•rude]

Owner:
The Holyrood Distillery Ltd.

Region/district:
Lowlands

Founded: 2019

Status: Active (vc)

Capacity: 250 000 litres

Address: 19 St Leonard's Lane, Edinburgh EH8 9SH

Website:
holyrooddistillery.co.uk

Tel:
0131 2858977

The first whisky distillery in almost 100 years to open up in Edinburgh, Holyrood has become known as one of the most innovative Scottish distilleries practising what could best be described as a holistic view on whisky production.

The distillery uses a variety of different types of yeast as well as different mash bills based on traditionally malted barley, including heritage strains such as Chevalier and Golden Promise, but also including speciality varieties such as crystal and chocolate malt. In 2022, the distillery used 23 different yeasts within 99 different mash recipes. There is a private cask programme which in 2023 focused on cloudy wort vs. clear wort. In short, Holyrood's pioneering approach is not aiming for a 'Holyrood-style', but at creating interesting whiskies across a spectrum of flavours.

Holyrood, which made its first distillation in September

2019, is equipped with a one ton semi-lauter mash tun and six 5,000 litre washbacks made of stainless steel. The fermentation time is typically between 48 and 120 hours but experiments with more than 300 hours of fermentation have also been conducted. There is one 5,000 litre wash still and one 3,750 litre spirit still – both very tall and fitted with descending lyne arms and boil balls. Attached to the spirit still is a water-cooled purifier. The newmake is filled into a variety of casks, including ex-bourbon, sherry, rum and virgin oak.

The first single malt is due to arrive in autumn 2023 but the distillery already sells different types of new make, available also to enjoy in the distillery bar, neat as well as in a cocktail.

Located in the centre of Edinburgh, the distillery also houses a visitor centre which now hosts the annual Mash-Up Festival – a celebration of craft beer and new wave whiskies and their unique relationship.

InchDairnie

[inch•dairnie]

Owner:
InchDairnie Distillery Ltd

Region/district:
Lowlands

Founded: 2015

Status: Active

Capacity: 4 000 000 litres

Address: Whitecraigs Rd, Glenrothes, Fife KY6 2RX

Website:
inchdairniedistillery.com

Tel:
01595 510010

When Inchdairnie was established in 2015 it was unusually large compared to other new distilleries founded at the same time.

This was, however, just the beginning. A large owner, the Danish spirits company MacDuff International, together with Ian Palmer as the distillery manager (and co-owner) indicated that something major was in the works. And true enough – in 2023 it was announced that the distillery was about to be expanded with more washbacks and stills to reach a capacity of 4 million litres by the end of the year.

The distillery is equipped with a hammer mill and a Meura mash filter, instead of a traditional mash tun. There are four washbacks with a fermentation time of 72 hours and one pair of traditional pot stills with double condensers and after-coolers increasing the copper to spirit ratio. The two stills are complemented by a Lomond still with six plates to provide the opportunity for triple and experimen-

tal distillation. A unique yeast recipe is used and the team is working with both the standard spring barley as well as winter barley to give the possibility for a broader palette of flavours.

Five different types of whisky are produced; first of all Inchdairnie Single Malt which will form the core range together with RyeLaw made from malted rye and malted barley and KinGlassie which is a peated expression, distilled once a year for only two weeks. Furthermore there is Strathenry which constitutes 80% of the distillery's production and will be used for blended whisky. The final expression is The PrinLaws Collection which will be a range of spirits from different yeasts, cereals and oaks. The first core expression appeared in May 2023 when RyeLaw (made from 53% malted rye and 47 % malted barley) was released. In summer 2023 InchDairnie also started trials with a pot still style of whisky including 35% unmalted barley.

Isle of Raasay

[ajl ov rassay]

Owner:	**Region/district:**
R&B Distillers	Highlands (Raasay)
Founded: **Status:**	**Capacity:**
2017 Active (vc)	220 000 litres

Address: Borodale House, Raasay, By Kyle IV40 8PB

Website:	**Tel:**
raasaydistillery.com	01478 470177

Raasay distillery is a stunning example of a a whisky distillery established in a remote area (in this case an island east of Skye), creating job opportunities for the locals.

An old Victorian house was turned into both a distillery and a six bedroom hotel and recently the visitor centre was upgraded with a new tasting room and a new bar. With a magnificent view towards the Cuillin Mountains on the Isle of Skye, this is an excellent way of spending a night on Raasay.

The distillery is equipped with a 1.1 ton mash tun and six stainless steel (5,000 litre) washbacks with cooling jackets currently with four short fermentations (67 hours) and six long (118 hours) adding up to 210,000 litres of alcohol in 2023. The 5,000 litre wash still has a cooling jacket around the lyne arm and there's also a 3,600 litre spirit still with

a copper column attached should they want to use it for special runs. The production is a 50/50 combination of peated (48-52 ppm) and unpeated spirit. Some of the barley is grown on Raasay while the production in 2023 also will include Siena barley from Orkney, Laureate from Campbeltown and Bere barley from a maltster in Berwickshire. All Raasay single malt is distilled, matured and bottled on the island.

The first release of their signature malt (R01), matured in a combination of virgin chinkapin oak, Bordeaux red wine barriques and first fill rye casks, appeared in June 2021. New releases in 2023 include R01.2 and R02.2 as well as a distillery only bottling named "Tourism Destination of the Year" matured in ex manzanilla pasada american oak, Dun Cana matured in ex rye casks finished in a mix of oloroso and PX quarter casks and a Distillery of the Year bottling matured in ex bourbon and ex rye and finished in Andean/Colombian oak (*Quercus humboldtii*).

Jackton

[jack•ton]

Owner:	**Region/district:**
Raer Scotch Whisky Ltd.	Lowlands
Founded: **Status:**	**Capacity:**
2020 Active	300 000 litres

Address: Hayhill Road, Jackton G74 5AN

Website:	**Tel:**
raer.co.uk	01355 202 590

Usually the opening up of a new whisky distillery in Scotland is known to a wide group of whisky interested people long before the first distillation.

News are spread through company press releases, fundraising and on social media even before a planning application has been submitted. On rare occasions though, projects fall under the radar like the Lochlea Distillery in South Ayrshire. It wasn't until 2021 that most people knew about it even though it started distillation in 2018.

There are certainly similarities between Lochlea and Jackton Distillery in that sense. A planning application to convert the O'Cathain Farm near East Kilbride in South Lanarkshire south of Glasgow to a distillery was approved in June 2019. Only eight months later, the first spirit was distilled! Gin was soon on the market as well as sourced

whisky under the name Raer but few people were actually aware that they were also distilling their own malt whisky.

Behind the project is the Kean family, hailing from nearby East Kilbride. The distillery is equipped with a one ton stainless steel, semi-lauter mash tun and six 7,000 litre stainless steel washbacks (with room for another six in the future) with a fermentation time of 90 hours. There are two stills from Kothe – a 5,000 litre wash still and a 2,000 litre spirit still. At the moment the owners are commissioning a malting plant on site which will consist of two 5 drum systems in which they can manufacture 4 tons in a drum every 8 days. There are both dunnage and racked warehouses on site and the owners use a variety of casks for the maturation; bourbon, sherry, rum, port and different wine casks. The distillery is currently not open to visitors but on site is the Wee Distillery Shop where you can sample and purchase the products.

Kingsbarns

[kings•barns]

Owner:		Region/district:
Wemyss family		Lowlands

Founded:	Status:	Capacity:
2014	Active (vc)	600 000 litres

Address: East Newhall Farm, Kingsbarns,
St Andrews KY16 8QE

Website:	Tel:
kingsbarnsdistillery.com	01333 451300

Located on the East Neuk of Fife, near St Andrews, the distillery was opened by the Wemyss Family in November 2014.

The idea was to restore a derelict farm-steading from the late 18th century and turn it into a modern distillery. Planning permission was received in March 2011 and in 2012 the Wemyss family invested £3m into the project and became the new owners. Wemyss Family Spirits are also known for their independent whisky bottling brand, Wemyss Malts and their Scottish gin, Darnley's Gin, which is distilled at Kingsbarns Distillery.

The distillery is equipped with a 1.5 ton stainless steel mash tun, four 7,500 litre stainless steel washbacks with a fermentation time of 72-120 hours, one 7,500 litre wash still and one 4,500 litre spirit still. A slow distillation and an early cut are important to achieve the fruity character. In the near future they are looking to install more washbacks to increase the capacity yet maintain the long fermentations. More warehouses are also being built offsite but still in Fife. Mainly first fill bourbon barrels are used for maturation together with STR casks (wine barriques that have been shaved, toasted and re-charred), however the distillery continue to experiment with cask types. The first casks were filled in March 2015 and the current yearly production is 200,000 litres of alcohol.

The inaugural whisky was in 2018 but the first widely available release, Dream to Dram, a vatting of ex-bourbon casks and STR red wine casks, appeared in 2019. In 2023 this was succeeded by Doocot, twice the age of the predecessor. Before that they added an ex-oloroso matured single malt, Balcomie, to the range. The latest limited release, in August 2023, was Bell Rock – matured in a combination of bourbon and oloroso casks and bottled at 61.1%.

Lagg

[laag]

Owner:	Region/district:
Isle of Arran Distillers Ltd.	Lowlands (s. Arran)

Founded:	Status:	Capacity:
2019	Active (vc)	750 000 litres

Address: Kilmory, Isle of Arran KA27 8PG

Website:	Tel:
laggwhisky.com	01770 870565

Lagg means hollow or deep end and the distillery has been beautifully integrated in the extraordinary landscape in the most southern parts of Arran.

Starting in 2019 it became the second distillery on the island owned by Arran Distillers. The idea was to move all the peated production from the Lochranza site to Lagg and while different phenol specifications in the barley are used, 50ppm is the core. At the moment 6% of the barley has been grown on Arran while the rest is sourced from Aberdeenshire.

It is a bit of a drive from Brodick (where the ferry lands) to Lagg but the location and the excellent and contemporary visitor centre has already drawn large numbers of visitors from the mainland. The view from the stills towards the sea is stunning! On the other side of the road, 3,000 apple trees have been planted with a view to make apple brandy in the future.

The distillery, with all the equipment conveniently gathered on one level, has a four ton semilauter mash tun with a copper top, four Oregon pine washbacks holding 25,000 litres and with a fermentation time of either 54 or 72 hours, one wash still (10,000 litres) and one spirit still (6,500 litres). However, there is space for an additional four washbacks and one more pair of stills in the future. The cloudy wort, slightly descending lyne arms and a quick distillation gives a green/grassy newmake and the plan for 2023 is to do 8 mashes per week and 500,000 litres of alcohol.

In August 2022 the first limited single malts from the distillery appeared; matured in bourbon, oloroso and red wine casks. These were followed in summer 2023 by the first core bottlings – Kilmory (46%, bourbon matured) and Corriecravie (55%, bourbon matured and with a sherry finish).

Lindores Abbey

[linn•doors aebi]

Owner:
The Lindores Distilling Co.

Region/district:
Lowlands

Founded: 2017
Status: Active (vc)
Capacity: 225 000 litres

Address: Lindores Abbey House, Abbey Road, Newburgh, Fife KY14 6HH

Website:
lindoresabbeydistillery.com

Tel:
01337 842547

Building a distillery at the old monastery of Lindores was a stroke of genius from the owners, Drew and Helen McKenzie.

In a letter from King James IV to Friar John Cor in 1494 he instructed the monk to make "aqua vitae from VIII bolls of malt". The archaeological and historical evidence for Lindores being the birthplace of Scotch whisky are by no way inconclusive but further excavations of the site may reveal some evidence.

Be that as it may, the location is stunning and with all the production equipment on one level you have a spectacular view of the surroundings. If you look down from the second floor you see the remnants of the old monastery and if you look further away you see Dundee.

The equipment consists of a 2 ton semi lauter mash tun with a copper lid, four Douglas fir washbacks with two

short (68 hours) and three long (114 hours) fermentations, one 10,000 litre wash still and two 3,500 litre spirit stills. The foreshots are 15-20 minutes and the spirit cut starts at 75% and goes down to 67% with the obvious aim of catching the fruity esters in the beginning and avoiding the pungent congeners at the end. The plan for 2023 is to do 5 mashes per week, producing 188,000 litres of pure alcohol. All the barley used in the distillery has been grown in the surrounding fields

In spring 2021, the first 1494 bottles of their inaugural release, available only to members of The 1494 Preservation Society, appeared and this was followed in July by the first widely available expression - the Lindores MCDXCIV bottled at 46%. Recently (in spring 2023), the limited Friar John Cor Chapter 1 was released which was a marriage of different casks and bottled at cask strength and Chapter 2, a marriage of different casks, followed shortly after.

Lochlea

[lock•lee]

Owner:
Lochlea Distilling Co.

Region/district:
Lowlands

Founded: 2018
Status: Active
Capacity: 200 000 litres

Address: Lochlea Farm, South Ayrshire KA1 5NN

Website:
lochleadistillery.com

Tel:
07585 661 605

While commissioning the distillery more or less under the radar, Lochlea released their first single malt in early 2022.

A few months before that they managed to hire John Campbell, with 27 years at the Laphroaig distillery (the last 16 as distillery manager), as the production director and master blender. Loch Lea is situated on a farm from the 1700s in Ayrshire just south of Kilmarnock. What makes it so special is that Robert Burns, the famous bard, actually lived and worked here during his formative years (1777-1784) and it was at that time he wrote some of his most famous poems and also founded the Bachelor's Club. The founder and owner of Lochlea is Neil McGeoch with interests in a variety of businesses including property and renewable energy.

The distillery is equipped with a 2 ton semi-lauter mash

tun, six Douglas fir washbacks with both short (66 hours) and long (116) fermentations and two, tall stills (10,000 and 6,250 litres respectively). The production plan for 2023 is five mashes per week and as close to 200,000 litres of pure alcohol as they can get. All the barley used for the whisky is grown on the farm.

In April 2023, Lochlea was named the global winner of Single Estate Distillery of the Year at the Icons of Whisky Awards.

The style of the spirit is more full-bodied than a traditional Lowland and peated production is also in the pipeline. The inaugural, limited whisky appeared in early 2022. Until the first whisky with an age statement appears (in 2026) the range of Our Barley, built on a combination of bourbon, sherry and STR casks, will continue with new releases. There is also the Sowing Edition, a limited edition released every spring.

Moffat

[moff•at]

Owner:
Dark Sky Spirits

Region/district:
Lowlands

Founded: 2023

Status: Active (vc)

Capacity: 12 000 litres

Address: Moffat DG10 9FE

Website:
moffatdistillery.com

Tel:
07761 930167

While the vast majority of new Scottish distilleries are quite small in terms of capacity, Moffat is definitely on the far side of the spectrum – probably the smallest distillery to date.

The founder, Nick Bullard, is aiming for around 12,000 litres per year. Prior to entering the whisky business Bullard was a corporate coach, based in the US and working with pharmaceutical companies all over the world. In 2017 he founded Dark Sky Spirits, a whisky blending company, in Moffat in Dumfries & Galloway and in 2018 the blended malt The Moffat was released. The name of the company comes from the fact that Moffat was the first town in Europe to be named a "dark sky town" due to the installation of eco-friendly street lighting that keeps light pollution to a minimum.

Shortly after Nick, aided by his wife Erin, had started the

company, he decided to expand it with a small distillery honouring traditional production technique. The distillery was granted planning permission in January 2020 and at the same time they received a fund of £320,000 from the South of Scotland Economic Partnership. Delayed by the pandemic, the distillery finally came on stream in summer 2023.

The distillery is equipped with an 0.1 ton semi lauter mash tun and two 400 litre stainless steel washbacks. There is one 350 litre wash still, directly fired using locally sourced wood logs, and one electrically-heated 200 litre spirit still. The aim is to use both short fermentations to get the malty character and long where they obtain the fruity, estery notes. Ninety percent of the barley is grown, malted and milled on a single estate. There is also a visitor centre focusing on both the distillery and the artisanal products from Dark Sky Spirits.

Nc´nean

[nook•knee•anne]

Owner:
Nc´nean Distillery Ltd.

Region/district:
Western Highlands

Founded: 2017

Status: Active (vc)

Capacity: 100 000 litres

Address: Drimnin, By Lochaline PA80 5XZ

Website:
ncnean.com

Tel:
01967 421698

Sustainability has been at the heart of the founder Annabel Thomas and her team from the moment the first plans for Nc´nean distillery were drawn up.

In 2021 Nc´nean became a certified net zero emissions whisky distillery – the first in the UK to achieve this and 20 years ahead of the Scotch industry target. In 2022 the distillery was one of two distilleries in Scotland to become a certified B Corporation for its social and environmetal standards. The distillery is powered with 100% renewable energy from a biomass boiler fired by woodchips from a nearby forest and all the trees are replanted.

The distillery is equipped with a one ton semi lauter mash tun and four stainless steel washbacks with a fermentation time between 65 and 115 hours. Furthermore there is a 5,000 litre wash still and a 3,500 litre spirit still, both with

slightly descending lyne arms and sub coolers although the latter are currently not being used. The owner is working on two basic recipes of fruity whisky – "new style" to be enjoyed young and "old style", with lower cut points and destined for a longer maturation.

A botanical spirit (still part of the range) was launched in autumn 2018. The first single malt, Ainnir, matured in red wine casks and American bourbon barrels, was released in 2020 and this was followed by a core expression which is now bottled in batches. Quiet Rebels, introduced in 2021 and bottled every autumn, is a series of whiskies chosen by each individual working at Nc´Nean. A new spring series, Huntress, focusing on the distillery´s experiments with yeast, was introduced in April 2022 with Woodland Candy as the second release in 2023. Finally, there have been a number of single cask bottlings under the name Aon. The distillery is situated on the Drimnin estate on the Morvern peninsula with an astounding view towards Mull.

Port Ellen

[port ell•en]

Owner: Diageo

Region/district: Islay

Founded: 1825

Status: Active

Capacity: 750 000 litres

Address: Port Ellen, Isle of Islay, Argyll PA42 7AJ

Website: -

Tel: -

Adding Port Ellen to active distilleries in the Yearbook may have been a bit premature. There were signs that an opening was to happen in 2023 but it now looks like it will be 2024.

The fact that it will become operational again is in itself amazing. It closed, seemingly for good in 1983, together with another twenty distilleries at a time when the Scotch whisky industry encountered decreasing demand for its products. Thirtyfore years later, with Scotch in a boom, Diageo announced they would reopen both Port Ellen and Brora.

Unlike Brora, there were just a few of the existing buildings at Port Ellen that could be used and all the equipment was gone. Instead Diageo used the old drawings to recreate the equipment. And not only that – there will also be a second, smaller pair of stills with the intention of creating experimental whiskies. The distillery, with an 800,000 litre capacity, should be up and running sometime in 2024.

The history of Port Ellen tells us that it had actually been closed for almost 40 years when it was re-opened with a doubled capacity in 1967. Six years later, a huge drum malting was opened on the site (which is still there) and in 1980 Queen Elizabeth came to visit. On its height, Port Ellen was capable of producing 1,7 million litres of alcohol per year.

Even though the distillery closed there was still stocks of whisky available. From 2001 bottlings of the rare spirit were released by the owners and the whisky was all of a sudden revered by the enthusiasts and prices soared. Some of the latest bottlings (in October 2023) included a 43 year old in the Prima & Ultima range, matured in the last four American oak hogsheads from 1978 in the warehouse and bottled at 53,4%.

Port of Leith

[port of leeth]

Owner: Muckle Brig

Region/district: Lowlands

Founded: 2023

Status: Active (vc)

Capacity: 400 000 litres

Address: 11 Whisky Quay, Edinburgh EH6 6FH

Website: leithdistillery.com

Tel: 0131 6000 144

When it comes to the architecture and the design, the Port of Leith distillery in Edinburgh is definitely one of the most unusual in Scotland, perhaps even in the world.

To start with, it's 42 metres high (the Swedish Mackmyra comes in at 37 metres) with no less than 10 floors and solar panels on the roof. The top five floors hold the hospitality area with bars, private dining areas, visitor centre and shop. The lower floors contain the production parts with a CTS mill and hopper on the top floor, followed by a 1,5 semi lauter mash tun and seven insulated, 7,500 litre washbacks with a 72 hour fermentation. Further down are one wash still and one spirit still, made in Elgin and both with slightly descending lyne arms. The water for the production comes from a 132 metre deep bore hole on the site.

The two founders, Paddy Fletcher and Ian Stirling, chose the location with great care. The distillery can be found in the port in Leith, just 50 metres from the Royal Yacht Britannia which receives 400,000 visitors per year. The historical aspect of Leith being an important area for shipping and warehousing whisky until the late 1990s, also played an important part.

The view from all floors towards the North Sea is also stunning. The distillery opened in summer 2023 and the spirit will be unpeated with various strains of yeast and barley varieties being an important part. The newmake will be filled into first and refill bourbon and oloroso along with a smaller part of various wine casks.

Already four years ago the owners started trials of whisky making in a small pilot distillery and in May 2022 they opened The Lind & Lime Distillery in Coburg Street. The name pays hommage to Dr. J Lind who discovered the effect of citrus fruits on those suffering from scurvy.

Rosebank

[rows•bank]

Owner:
Ian Macleod Distillers

Region/district:
Lowlands

Founded: 2022 **Status:** Active **Capacity:** 1 000 000 litres

Address: Camelon Road, Falkirk FK1 5JR

Website: rosebank.com **Tel:** -

In October 2017, just 24 hours after Diageo had announced that they were to re-open Brora and Port Ellen, news broke that another legendary distillery would be brought back from the dead.

With a history of distillation on the site going back to 1798, the distillery which would later become famous was founded in 1840 on the site of the Camelon maltings. In 1919, the distillery became a part of Distillers Company (DCL), the embryo of today's Diageo. Over the years, Rosebank earned a reputation of being the finest Lowland malt. The need for substantial and costly refurbishing however prompted Diageo to close it for good in 1993.

Rumours of a ressurection floated about until Ian Macleod Distillers, owners of Glengoyne and Tamdhu, finally acquired the buildings from Scottish Canals and the trademark and stock from Diageo in 2017. Since then the buildings

have been refurbished and expanded. Most of the equipment was stolen already in 2008 and the only remaining piece from the old distillery that is used today is the Boby mill. With the help of the old drawings from Abercrombie & Smith, the three stills were replicated at Forsyths.

The distillery is equipped with 3,2 ton semi lauter mash tun with a copper dome. There are eight 15,000 litre Douglas fir washbacks with a fermentation time of 56-72 hours. Rosebank is triple distilled in a 15,000 litre wash still, a 7.7 metre high 10,000 litre intermediate still and an 8,000 litre spirit still. The swan neck on the wash still is chopped off and capped and the lyne arm stuck on the side of the neck. The spirit is cooled in individual worm tubs on the outside.

The first cask was filled in July 2023. It will of course take a while before the first whisky from the new production will appear but Ian Macleod have already released several limited bottlings from the old stock.

Roseisle

[rose•eyel]

Owner:
Diageo

Region/district:
Speyside

Founded: 2009 **Status:** Active **Capacity:** 12 500 000 litres

Address: Roseisle, Morayshire IV30 5YP

Website: - **Tel:** 01343 832100

Roseisle distillery is located on the same site as the already existing Roseisle maltings just west of Elgin. The distillery has won several awards for its ambition towards sustainable production.

The distillery is equipped with two stainless steel, full lauter mash tuns with a 12.5 tonne charge each. There are 14 huge (112,000 litres) stainless steel washbacks and 14 stills with the wash stills being heated by external heat exchangers while the spirit stills are heated using steam coils. The spirit vapours are cooled through copper condensers but on three spirit stills and three wash stills there are also stainless steel condensers attached, that you can switch to for a more sulphury spirit. The fermentation time for a Speyside style of whisky is 90-100 hours and for a heavier style it is 50-60 hours. The plan for 2020 is to do 23 mashes per week and a total of 12 million litres of alcohol.

The total cost for the distillery was £40m and how to use the hot water in an efficient way was very much a focal point from the beginning. For example, Roseisle is connected by means of two long pipes with Burghead maltings, 3 km north of the distillery. Hot water is pumped from Roseisle and then used in the seven kilns at Burghead and cold water is then pumped back to Roseisle. The pot ale from the distillation is piped into anaerobic fermenters and transformed into biogas and the dried solids act as a biomass fuel source. The biomass burner on the site, producing steam for the distillery, covers 72% of the total requirement and green technology has reduced the emission of carbon dioxide to only 15% of an ordinary distillery.

In 2017, Roseisle single malt was part of the blended malt Collectivum XXVIII and in the 2023 Special Releases it was for the first time released as a single malt – a 12 year old matured in first fill bourbon and refill casks.

Strathearn

[strath•earn]

Owner: Douglas Laing

Region/district: Southern Highlands

Founded: 2013

Status: Active

Capacity: 140 000 litres

Address: Bachilton Farm Steading, Methven PH1 3QX

Website: strathearndistillery.com

Tel: -

When Strathearn distillery was founded in 2013, just ten kilometres west of Perth, it was one of Scotland's first craft distilleries.

Craft in the sense that it was extremely small but also due to the fact that it approached whisky production in a very innovative and challenging way. The founder, Tony Reeman-Clark, was keen to challenge the rules stipulated by the Scotch Whisky Association. One example was their experimentation with different types on non-oak wood for maturation – chestnut, mulberry and cherry wood. They also used old barley varieties, including Maris Otter, where the yield was less important than the flavour.

The distillery was taken over in 2019 by the independent bottler Douglas Laing (who currently have plans to build a new distillery in Glasgow named Clutha) and while they've stopped using alternative wood for the maturation, they continue the exploration of heirloom and speciality malts.

The equipment consists of a new copper-clad, 0.4 ton stainless steel mash tun, eight stainless steel washbacks, two 1,000 litre wash stills and one 1,000 litre spirit still. The fermentations are long, averaging 144 hours and the plan for 2023 is to make around 57,000 litres of pure alcohol. The previous owner used to make also peated whisky but now it's all about un-peated. Following a four year career in beer brewing, Angela Brown has for the past two years been the lead distiller at Strathearn.

The first single malt Scotch from the distillery was released in December 2016. The first from the new owners however, appeared in December 2019. Distilled in 2013 and 2014 the whisky had matured in a combination of virgin European oak and first fill oloroso. In July 2022, 1,800 bottles of a new single malt spirit named "The Heart", bottled at 63,5%, was launched. Finally, the first single malt release from Strathearn made by Douglas Laing is due for release end of 2023.

Torabhaig

[tor•a•vaig]

Owner: Mossburn Distillers

Region/district: Highlands (Skye)

Founded: 2016

Status: Active (vc)

Capacity: 500 000 litres

Address: Teangue, Sleat, Isle of Skye IV44 8RE

Website: torabhaig.com

Tel: 01471 833447

The plans for a second whisky distillery on Skye (with Talisker being the first) were conceived by Sir Iain Noble – a Skye landowner who was known for his interest in and dedication to the Gaelic language.

Sir Ian founded Sabhal Mór Ostaig, a Gaelic college on the Sleat peninsula just a mile south of Torabhaig. When Sir Iain died in 2010 Mossburn Distillers took over and finalised the plans for a distillery. It is located in a farmstead from the 1820s and some of the buildings have been meticulously restored while others have been added. Mossburn distillers (with a Swedish owner) has become known as an independent bottler but they also recently opened the small Reivers distillery in the Scottish Borders with plans to build a much larger one in a few years.

The entire set of production equipment at Torabhaig is situated on one level with a 1.5 ton stainless steel semi lauter mash tun with a copper top. There are eight washbacks made of Douglas fir (10,000 litres) with a fermentation time between 80 and 120 hours, one 8,000 litre wash still and one 5,000 litre spirit still. The production plan for 2023 is to do 18 mashes per week in the winter and 12 in the summer aiming for 500,000 litres of pure alcohol. The whisky produced is heavily peated with a phenol specification of up to 75ppm in the malted barley.

The first single malt from the distillery, "2017. The Legacy Series", was released in February 2021. Made from heavily peated barley (55-60ppm) it had matured in first fill bourbon barrels. It was followed in autumn 2021 by Allt Gleann matured in a combination of first fill bourbon barrels and re-fill casks. The second edition of Allt Gleann appeared in 2022 and was followed by a cask strength version in late 2023. In 2024 this will be followed by Cnoc na Moine.

Uile-bheist

[ewl•uh•<u>vehst</u>]

Owner:
Jon and Victoria Erasmus

Region/district:
Northern Highlands

Founded: 2023

Status:
Active (vc)

Capacity:
20 000 litres

Address: Ness Bank, Inverness IV2 4SG

Website:
uilebheist.com

Tel:
01463 234308

Until the mid 1980s Inverness had three malt distilleries operating; Glen Albyn, Glen Mhor and Millburn. The first two closed in 1983 followed by Millburn two years later.

One of them, Glen Mhor, was considered to be a malt of superior quality and with a bit of luck (and quite a lot of money) it is still possible to find. Since 2023 however, there is a new distillery in town. Unlike many other new distilleries, Uile-bheist began production in 2023 very much under the radar. It was founded by Jon and Victoria Erasmus – a couple that started the Glen Mhor Hotel at Ness bank in 2006. They have grown their business since then to also include self-catered apartments.

Since at least 2014, the couple have contemplated adding a brewery to the existing hotel and eventually a whisky distillery was added to the plans. This is the first distillery to open in Inverness in 130 years. It is built on sustainability and is powered both by water from river Ness through a system using shallow water wells as well as rooftop solar installations.

The distillery is equipped with a 1.5 ton mash tun and 4 stainless steel washbacks with a fermentation between 72 and 96 hours using brewer's yeast. Furthermore there is one 1,000 litre wash still and one 500 litre spirit still. The equipment comes from the German manufacturer Kaspar Schultz and the stills are designed to create a high reflux which together with the brewer's yeast will make for a light and fruity new make. The first distillation was in April 2023 and recently Andrew Shearer, who previously worked at Glen Turner and the Kinrara distillery in the Cairngorms, was hired as the Head Distiller. The combined brewery and distillery cost £7m to build and there is also a visitor centre and a restaurant. In July 2023, 500 bottles of their newmake were released.

Wolfburn

[wolf•burn]

Owner:
Aurora Brewing Ltd.

Region/district:
Northern Highlands

Founded: 2013

Status:
Active (vc)

Capacity:
135 000 litres

Address: Henderson Park, Thurso, Caithness KW14 7XW

Website:
wolfburn.com

Tel:
01847 891051

While age isn't everything when it comes to whisky, far from it, it is a definitive milestone when a distillery releases its first ten year old.

This happened to Wolfburn in spring 2023 when a new permanent member of the core range, matured in 2nd fill oloroso sherry casks, was launched. Once known as the most northerly distillery on the Scottish mainland, Wolfburn lost its geographic uniqueness in 2022 to 8 Doors distillery in John O'Groats, a couple of miles further to the north from Thurso. This probably didn't bother the owners of Wolfburn that much. The distillery and the brand has come a long way in ten years and devoted fans care more about the spirit than the location.

Construction of Wolfburn commenced in August 2012 and the first newmake came off the stills at the end of January 2013. The distillery is equipped with a 1.1 ton semi-lauter stainless steel mash tun with a copper canopy, four stainless steel washbacks with a fermentation time of 70-92 hours, holding 5,500 litres each, one wash still (5,500 litres) and one spirit still (3,600 litres). The main part of the malt is unpeated but a lightly peated spirit is also produced.

The inaugural bottling from 2016 had a smoky profile from being partly matured in quarter casks from Islay. This was followed by a more widely available bourbon matured whisky, Northland. Still part of the core range, it has since been complemented by Aurora, partly matured in oloroso sherry casks, the peated Morven, Langskip, matured in ex-bourbon barrels and the 10 year old.

A range of limited bottlings started in 2017 and the most recent, in September 2022, was Batch 458 matured in a combination of first fill bourbon and first fill PX sherry. Another limited range is Kylver where batch 11 (Isa) was released in spring 2023. Other limited releases include a cask strength as well as Coronation to celebrate King Charles III ascending the throne.

Active distilleries per owner

Diageo
Auchroisk
Benrinnes
Blair Athol
Brora
Caol Ila
Cardhu
Clynelish
Cragganmore
Dailuaine
Dalwhinnie
Dufftown
Glendullan
Glen Elgin
Glenkinchie
Glenlossie
Glen Ord
Glen Spey
Inchgower
Knockando
Lagavulin
Linkwood
Mannochmore
Mortlach
Oban
Port Ellen
Roseisle
Royal Lochnagar
Strathmill
Talisker
Teaninich

Chivas Brothers (Pernod Ricard)
Aberlour
Allt-a-Bhainne
Braeval
Dalmunach
Glenburgie
Glen Keith
Glenlivet
Glentauchers
Longmorn
Miltonduff
Scapa
Strathisla

Edrington Group
Glenrothes
Highland Park
Macallan

**Inver House
(International Beverage Holdings)**
Balblair
Balmenach
Knockdhu
Pulteney
Speyburn

John Dewar & Sons (Bacardi)
Aberfeldy
Aultmore
Craigellachie
Macduff
Royal Brackla

William Grant & Sons
Ailsa Bay
Balvenie
Glenfiddich
Kininvie

Whyte & Mackay (Emperador)
Dalmore
Fettercairn
Jura
Tamnavulin

Beam Suntory
Ardmore
Auchentoshan
Bowmore

Glen Garioch
Laphroaig

CVH Spirits
Bunnahabhain
Deanston
Tobermory

Benriach Dist. Co. (Brown Forman)
Benriach
Glendronach
Glenglassaugh

Loch Lomond Group
Glen Scotia
Loch Lomond

J & A Mitchell
Glengyle
Springbank

Glenmorangie Co. (LVMH)
Ardbeg
Glenmorangie

Angus Dundee Distillers
Glencadam
Tomintoul

Ian Macleod Distillers
Glengoyne
Rosebank
Tamdhu

Campari Group
Glen Grant

Isle of Arran Distillers
Lagg
Lochranza

Signatory
Edradour

Tomatin Distillery Co.
Tomatin

J & G Grant
Glenfarclas

Rémy Cointreau
Bruichladdich

David Prior
Bladnoch

Gordon & MacPhail
Benromach
The Cairn

La Martiniquaise
Glen Moray

Ben Nevis Distillery Ltd (Nikka)
Ben Nevis

Picard Vins & Spiritueux
Tullibardine

Harvey's of Edinburgh
Speyside

Kilchoman Distillery Co.
Kilchoman

Cuthbert family
Daftmill

Mark Tayburn
Abhainn Dearg

Aurora Brewing Ltd
Wolfburn

Douglas Laing
Strathearn

Annandale Distillery Co.
Annandale

Adelphi Distillery Co.
Ardnamurchan

Wemyss
Kingsbarns

Mcpherson-Grant family
Ballindalloch

Inverleith LLP
Eden Mill

Isle of Harris Distillers
Harris

The Glasgow Distillery Company
Glasgow Distillery

John Fegus & Co. Ltd
Inchdairnie

Stirling family
Arbikie

Brewdog plc
Brew Dog Distillery

Thompson family
Dornoch

Mossburn Distillers
Torabhaig

R & B Distillers
Isle of Raasay

The Lindores Distilling Company
Lindores Abbey

Morrison Glasgow Distillers
Clydeside

Nc'nean Distillery Ltd.
Nc'nean

Borders Distillery Company Ltd.
The Borders

The Glenallachie Distillers Co.
Glenallachie

Morrison Scotch Whisky Distillers
Aberargie

GlenWyvis Distillery Ltd.
GlenWyvis

Hunter Laing
Ardnahoe

The Holyrood Distillery Ltd.
Holyrood

Greenwood Distillers
Ardross

Lalique Group/Hansjörg Wyss
Glenturret

John Crabbie & Co.
Bonnington

Lochlea Distilling Co.
Lochlea

Stewart family
Falkirk

Ardent Spirits
Burnobennie

Raer Scotch Whisky Ltd.
Jackton

Elixir Distillers
Tormore

Kerry and Derek Campbell
8 Doors Distillery

Dunphail Distillery Ltd.
Dunphail

Dark Sky Spirits
Moffat

Muckle Brig
Port of Leith

Jon and Victoria Erasmus
Uile-bheist

Distilleries
around the globe

Including the subsections:
Europe
North America | Australia & New Zealand
Asia | Africa | South America

It´s no longer a surprise to anyone that whisky is now produced in every corner of the world. This development has been evident since the first edition of the Malt Whisky Yearbook was published in autumn 2005. And why indeed should we be surprised? Whisky is made from grain, water and yeast – ingredients that are accessible in any country. And the consumer interest in whisky – a prerequisite for a producer aiming at the home market – is growing.

But with every booming market comes a number of producers wanting to make as much money as possible in the shortest period of time and, often, breaking the written or unwritten rules. What can I as a consumer expect from a whisky labelled as Japanese, Bourbon or Irish whiskey? Protecting intellectual property has become increasingly important. The global forum for these matters is World Intellectual Property Organization (WIPO) and Geographical Indication (GI) is one of the tools for the producer to protect the uniqueness of their products.

GI applies to anything from Swiss watches to parmesan cheese and can at best be defined as the geographic origin giving it a specific quality, reputation or other characteristic. Scotch whisky was certified as a GI product in the EU in 2011 and the ratification in countries ouside the EU has followed since. Irish whiskey received the status in 2016 and bourbon is recognised in 44 countries in the world.

Smaller whisky regions are eager to distinguish themselves and in 2015 whisky made in Brittany, France (Whisky Breton) achieved GI status followed by Welsh whisky in 2023. One region that could follow in a few years is the Nordics. An inaugural meeting with Nordic whisky producers in June 2023 indicated a will to work towards a GI status for their local produce.

To achieve GI status means having established some kind of a technical file regulating how whisky from a particular region should be produced. That can also be the downside for some distilleries arguing that a more or less strict definition of a whisky could hamper innovation. This argument has been put forward not least by some producers of English whisky.

In China, one of the latest countries to produce whisky, China Alcoholic Drinks Association (CADA) has recently been formed. The aim is to protect the reputation of Chinese whisky from the very start instead of dealing with the issue further on.

The historical parallell of all these current activities around the world trying to define whisky from a consumer point of view, date back to the "What Is Whisky" inquiry in England in 1905 which is interesting to say the least. It´s obvious that there´s nothing new under the sun.

Opposite page: Jane and Casey Overeem from Overeem Distillery in Australia

Europe

Austria

Destillerie Haider
Roggenreith, founded in 1995

waldviertlerwhisky.at

The owners released the first Austrian whisky in 1998. In 2005, they opened up a Whisky Experience World with tours and tastings. The distillery is equipped with two Christian Carl copper stills. The main part of the production is made from either 100% malted rye or a combination of rye and malted barley while the rest is from malted barley. Five expressions make up the core range and apart from them there are peated versions as well and limited releases are launched regularly - some of them up to 15 years old.

Broger Privatbrennerei
Klaus, founded in 1976 (whisky since 2008)

broger.info

The production of whisky is supplementing the distillation and production of eau de vie from apples and pears. The distillery is equipped with a 150 litre Christian Carl still. The current range of whiskies consists of Triple Cask, Medium Smoked, Burn Out and the limited Distiller´s Edition. A separate range of five whiskies is Hoamat with the different grains coming from neighbouring farms.

Other distilleries in Austria

Arno Pauli, Brennerei
Absam, founded in 1930 (whisky since 2005)

arnopauli.at

Whisky is produced in this combination of a guesthouse, brewery and distillery. Besides a single malt from barley, they have also released whiskies made from maize, dinkel and wheat.

Dachstein Destillerie
Radstadt, founded in 2007

mandlberggut.com

Apart from production of various spirits from berries, malt whisky is also produced. Their core expression is the five year old Rock-Whisky and in December 2022 a limited 12 year old was released.

Farthofer, Destillerie
Öhling, founded in 1867 (whisky since 2014)

destillerie-farthofer.at

A classic Austrian distillery that has been producing schnapps and various liqueurs for more than a century. Whisky production started in recent years and apart from the blend AWA, the owners have released both single rye and single malt whiskies. The production is organic and they also have their own maltings.

Franz Kostenzer, Edelbrennerei
Maurach/Achensee, founded in 1998, whisky since 2006

schnaps-achensee.at

A huge range of different spirits as well as whisky is produced. Several expressions under the name Whisky Alpin have been released including a 13 year old single malt sherry cask finish, an 11 year old amarone finish and a 6 year old heavily peated.

Hermann Pfanner, Destillerie
Lauterach, founded in 1854 (whisky since 2005)

pfanner-weine.com

Two core expressions are produced, Pfanner Single Malt Classic and Single Malt Red Wood with a maturation in red wine casks. There are also several limited releases including a PX single barrel and the 9 year old White Wood - both released in 2022.

Keckeis Destillerie
Rankweil, founded in 2003 (whisky since 2008)

destillerie-keckeis.at

The core expression is Keckeis Single Malt but in early 2021 the limited Stillman´s Finest was launched. Part of the barley has been smoked with beech and maturation is in small ex-sherry casks.

Kuenz Naturbrennerei
Dölsach, founded in1643 (whisky since 2014)

kuenz-schnaps.at

The distillery recently added whisky to their range. The first single malt, named Rauchkofel, was released in 2017 and since then several different batches have appeared including a smoked one.

Old Raven
Neustift, founded in 2004

oldraven.at

A brewery supplies the wash for the whisky. The core expression is the triple distilled Old Raven and special versions include the 5 year old Smoky Devil, the 10 year old Lockdown and Black Edition.

Puchas, Destillerie (former Lagler, Spezialitätenbrennerei)
Kukmirn, founded in 2009

destillerie-puchas.at

One of few distilleries that are using vacuum distillation. Two single malts are available under the name Kukmirn.

Reisetbauer & Son
Kirchberg-Thening, founded in 1994 (whisky since 1995)

reisetbauer.at

Specialising in brandies and fruit schnapps, a range of malt whiskies is also produced. The current range of whiskies have all been matured in casks that have previously contained Chardonnay and Trockenbeerenauslese and include 7, 12, 15 and 21 year old.

Rogner, Destillerie
Rappottenstein, founded in 1997

destillerie-rogner.at

The whisky range consists of Rogner Waldviertel Whisky 3/3, Rye Whisky No. 13 and a single malt, Whisky No. 2. The 20 year old Red Road and the sherry finished Phönix were released in 2022 and in August 2023 the 18 year old rye Old John appeared.

See-Destillerie
St. Wolfgang im Salzkammergut, founded in 2018

see-destillerie.at

Originally a liqueur distillery the first expression of Wolfgangsee Whisky 1528 was launched in 2021 and there are now four different varieties including two peated.

Weutz, Destillerie
St. Nikolai im Sausal, founded in 2002

weutz.at

The distillery added whisky to the range in 2004. Some of the whiskies are produced in the traditional Scottish style while others are more unorthodox, for example based on elderflower.

Wieser Destillerie
Wösendorf in der Wachau, founded in 1996

wieserwachau.com

Traditionally producing schnaps and liqueur, they have also launched the quadruple distilled Uuahouua whisky; American oak, French oak, Pinot Noir and Smoke on the Water.

Belgium

Belgian Owl Distillery

Grâce Hollogne, founded in1997

belgianwhisky.com

The first Belgian whisky distillery has certainly come a long way since they released their first expression in 2008. They are now exporting to Eastern Europe, Asia and the USA and the range of special expressions is growing. The last two, both 5 years old, had been finished in casks that had held chocolate spirit and coffee spirit respectively. The core expressions are usually 3 years old and bottled at 46% or cask strength but there is a rumour about an imminent 15 year old as well. The distillery is equipped with two stills that were retrieved from the closed Caperdonich distillery.

De Molenberg Distillery

Blaasveld, founded in 1471 (whisky since 2003)

stokerijdemolenberg.be

In 2010, the brewer Charles Leclef started a distillery at the family estate Molenberg. The wash still has a capacity of 3,000 litres and the spirit still 2,000 litres. The first bottles under the name Gouden Carolus Single Malt 3 years old appeared in 2008 and this, including a special sherry oak version and the smoky Blaasveld Broek, is still the core expression. In 2022 a 9th anniversary edition with a 3 year cognac finish was launched.

Other distilleries in Belgium

Braeckman Distillery

Oudenaarde, founded in 1918 (whisky since 2007)

braeckman.eu

A genever distillery with whisky also on the map. Their first release was a 9 year old single grain and currently there are four single grains available, the oldest a 13 year old. They are also distilling the San Graal 5 and 7 year old single malt for the De Graal brewery.

Filliers

Bachte-Maria-Leerne, founded in 1880 (malt whisky since 2008)

filliersdistillery.com

In 2007 a whisky was launched under the name Goldlys. Today the sherrymatured single malt is sold under the name Filliers and currently a 10 year old is available. In 2018 two pot stills from Forsyths were installed.

Pirlot, Brouwerij

Zandhoven, founded in 1998 (whisky since 2011)

brouwerijpirlot.be

Originally a brewery, the distillery is equipped with a continuous still and the spirit is matured in a combination of ex-bourbon and quarter casks from Laphroaig. The first of Kempisch Vuur single malt was released in 2016 and several releases have followed.

Radermacher, Distillerie

Raeren, founded in 1836

distillerie.biz

In a wide range of products from this classic distillery, there is also whisky to be found. The brand name is Lambertus and the range consists of both single grain and single malt, aged up to 10 years.

Sas Distillery

Stekene, founded in 2014

sasdistilleries.com

In a 200 litre column still, Sas is producing gin, rum, absinthe and whisky according to old recipes. In 2019 the Ignis Templi single malt was released with batch 2 appearing in 2022.

Wilderen, Brouwerij & Distilleederij

Wilderen-St. Truiden, founded in 2011

brouwerijwilderen.be

A combination of a beer brewery with a history going back to 1642 and a distillery. The current core bottling of a single malt is Wild Weasel bottled at either 46% or 60% as well as a limited sherry cask finish.

Etienne Bouillon - founder and owner of Belgian Owl Distillery

Czech Republic

Svachovka Distillery
České Budějovice, founded in 2016
svachovkadomu.cz

Owned by Vaclav Cvach, this is a combination of a brewery, distillery, hotel, restaurant and spa. Equipped with stainless steel washbacks and copper stills the distillery produces fruit brandy as well as 5-10,000 litres of Svach´s Old Well single malt whisky yearly. The first 3 year old single malt was launched in autumn 2019 and a wide variety of expressions have been released since.

Gold Cock Distillery
Vizovice, founded in 1877
rjelinek.cz

The main product is slivovitz but whisky is produced in three versions – a 3 year old blended whisky, a 12 year old single malt and different versions of Small Batch single malt. Production was stopped for a while but after the brand and distillery were acquired by R. Jelinek a.s. the whisky began life anew.

Denmark

Stauning Whisky
Stauning, founded in 2006
stauningwhisky.dk

The first Danish purpose-built malt whisky distillery entered a more adolescent phase in 2009, after having experimented with two small pilot stills bought from Spain. More stills were installed in 2012. The preconditions, however, were completely changed in 2015 when Diageo´s incubator fund project, Distil Ventures, invested £10m to increase the capacity. In 2018, it became evident what the investment had meant to the company. A new distillery with no less than 24 copper stills, all directly fired, was opened. The floor malting were increased to 1,000 m² on four floors and the total production capacity is now 900,000 litres of pure alcohol. The core range consists of Rye, Kaos Triple Malt (both rye and barley) and Smoke Single Malt. Recent limited expressions include a Kaos rum finish, a single cask rye maple cask finish and, in summer 2023,

Douro Dreams – a rye that had matured in a combination of heavy charred American white oak and port casks. In the 2023 World Whiskies Awards Stauning won Sustainable Distillery of the Year.

Braunstein
Köge, founded in 2005 (whisky since 2007)
braunstein.dk

Denmark's first micro-distillery in Køge, just south of Copenhagen. The wash comes from the own brewery and a Holstein type of still is used for distillation. A substantial part of the required barley is ecologically grown in Denmark. The first release from the distillery and the first release of a malt whisky produced in Denmark was in 2010. Recent releases include Library Collection 23:1, matured in oloroso sherry casks and finished in casks that held Chateau d´Yquem and Edition No: 14, peated and oloroso sherry matured. There is also Danica reserved for the duty-free market.

Other distilleries in Denmark

Als, Destilleriet
Sydals, founded in 2018
destillerietals.dk

Built as a combined gin- and whisky distillerie with aid from Henric Molin of Spirit of Hven fame, the whisky is distilled in a 350 litre column still. Their second release, a 4 year old PX maturation, appeared in spring 2023.

Copenhagen Distillery
Copenhagen, founded in 2014
copenhagendistillery.com

Although founded in 2014 the distillery moved a few years ago to the southern parts of Copenhagen. A wide range of gin, vodka and liqueurs have been produced as an initial "bread and butter" but this is first and foremost a whisky distillery with some unusual features. The grain is milled using a Skiold plate mill and then mashed in a 0.6 ton mash tun. Following a 7-10 day fermentation on the grain, the liquid is distilled one time in a 1,050 litre copper hybrid still by Müller which has a 2-plate column attached as well as dephlegmator to increase the options while distilling. The spirit is mainly matured in toasted 100-litre casks made of Hungarian oak but more unusual casks are used as well. There are three different ranges; Refine which is a more traditional whisky, Raw where the

Jakob Stjernholm and Andreas Poulsen from Thy Distillery

all the flavours are "dialled up" and the experimental Rare bottlings where sometimes alternative grains are used. The First Edition was released in February 2020 and has been followed by a number of limited bottlings.

Enghaven, Braenderiet

Mellerup, founded in 2014

braenderiet-enghaven.dk

Producing also rum and gin, the first whisky, in autumn 2017, was a rye matured in both bourbon casks and port casks and in 2018, the first single malt from a rum cask was released. The latest were a wine-finished single malt as well as a rye in late 2020.

Falster Destilleri & Bryghus

Væggerløse, founded in 2019

falsterdestilleri.dk

A combined brewery and distillery producing several different types of spirits in two Portuguese pot stills, including malt whisky. The first whisky, matured in a combination of bourbon, oloroso and PX sherry was released in February 2023 and was then followed by a peated version in June.

Fary Lochan Destilleri

Give, founded in 2009

farylochan.dk

The main part of the malted barley is imported from the UK but they also malt some themselves. The first whisky was released in 2013 and a number of bottlings have been released since then. One of the latest, in spring 2023, was the 7 year old Sweet & Spicy Sauternes with a double maturation in bourbon and sauternes barriques. The distillery has also been represented in Nordic Casks from Berry Brothers.

Limfjorden, Braenderiet

Roslev, founded in 2013

braenderiet.dk

The distillery moved to a new location in 2018 and a brewery was added. Apart from peated and unpeated single malt and rye, the distillery also produces gin and rum. The first single malt was released in 2016 while the latest, in spring 2022, was the 9 year old, peated Solvognen matured in an ex-oloroso cask.

Mosgaard Whisky

Oure, founded in 2015

mosgaardwhisky.dk

Three alambic stills were designed by the owners and made in Portugal. There is also a 150 kilo mash tun and four stainless steel washbacks with a 7 day fermentation. The whisky is produced from organically grown barley and the maturation takes place primarily in small 50 litre casks. The first single malts appeared in spring 2019. Since then a number of expressions, some times matured or finished in an unusual combination of casks and both peated and unpeated, have appeared. The latest, in June 2023, was a 5 year old matured in a combination of amontillado and madeira casks.

Nyborg Destilleri

Nyborg, founded in 1997 (whisky since 2009)

fioniawhisky.com

Opened as an extension to an existing brewery, the distillery moved in 2017 to new premises. The distillery is equipped with two copper pot stills with attached columns. The first release of Isle of Fionia single malt was in 2012. The core range includes Little Isle, Danish Oak, Peated and Peated Black. Another range of limited releases is Adventurous Spirit which currently includes La Plume and Skipper´s Mist, which had been matured in a combination of virgin French oak and ex-bourbon.

Radius Distillery

Præstø, founded in 2019

radiusdistillery.com

A farmhouse distillery focused on gin and apple brandy but also producing malt whisky from their own barley. Unusually, the whisky is distilled on the grain with an anticipated release in 2024.

Sall Whisky Distillery

Sall, founded in 2018

sallwhisky.com

Gin but above all, malt whisky made from ecologically grown barley from the land of the owners is produced. New make was launched in 2019 and the inaugural single malt appeared in February 2023. This was later followed by a peated version and an ex-oloroso maturation.

Søgaards Bryghus

Aalborg, founded in 2010 (whisky since 2018)

soegaardsbryghus.dk

Originally a brewery, the owners embarked on an exciting distillery adventure in 2018. Farmers on four different islands in northern Jutland were sent Odyssey sowing barley in spring 2018. The barley was harvested and malted in autumn that same year and used at the brewery/distillery in Aalborg to distill new make in spring 2019. This was filled into Jack Daniels casks and then sent back to each of the islands for maturation. The four whiskies were released in June 2023 under the name Vindblæst (Windswept).

Thornaes Destilleri

Helsing, founded in 2018

thornaes.com

A distillery in North Zealand specialising in whisky but also producing gin. No mature single malt is available but their new make, both peated and unpeated, is sold under the name Year Zero.

Thy Whisky

Fjerritslev, founded in 2009 (whisky since 2011)

thy-whisky.dk

A family-owned farm distillery where the ecological barley used for the production is grown in fields surrounding the distillery. The owners also use innovative smoking material for their whiskies. The first Thy single malt was released in 2014 and at least 22 editions have occured since. The most recent, in May 2023, was a beechsmoked single malt matured in first fill PX casks. The distillery has also been represented in Nordic Casks from Berry Brothers.

Trolden Distillery

Kolding, founded in 2011

trolden.com

The distillery is a part of a brewery and the first single malt release was Nimbus in 2014 and in May 2020, the distillery moved to new premises. In November 2022 the Nimbus Stratus Peated was released and this was followed by more, limited releases including one matured in merlot casks.

Ærø Whisky

Ærøskøbing, founded in 2013

ærøwhisky.dk

Situated on the island of Ærø the distillation started in stills from Portugal. In 2016, larger stills were installed and the production increased. The first bottling was in 2017 and today the core expression is matured in a combination of American oak, virgin oak and sherry casks. Limited editions are released on a regular basis.

England

English Distillery, The

Roudham, Norfolk, founded in 2006

englishwhisky.co.uk

Originally known as St. George´s Distillery, it was started by father and son, James and Andrew Nelstrop near Thetford in Norfolk. It became the first English malt whisky distillery for over a hundred years. In 2009, it was time for the release of the first whisky called Chapter 5. This was then followed by several more chapters (up to 17) but the sometimes uncomprehensible range was then exhanged for a range with two core expressions; The English Original and The English Smokey. In 2020 The English 11 years old was released for the first time and it is now a limited yet recurrent expression There are also regular, limited releases in the Small Batch series with Vintage 2010, Founder´s Private Cellar 15 years old, Triple Distilled and Heavily Smoked Sherry Butt as some of the latest. Other ranges are the Single Cask Series and The Norfolk, the latter including innovative expressions made from different grains. The distillery is equipped with a semi-lauter mash tun, stainless steel washbacks with a fermentation time of 85 hours and one pair of stills. There is also an excellent visitor centre including a shop with more than 300 different whiskies.

Cotswolds Distillery

Stourton, founded in 2014

cotswoldsdistillery.com

The distillery is the brainchild of Dan Szor and production of both whisky and gin started in September 2014. Originally equipped with four stills; one wash still (2,400 litres), one spirit still (1,600 litres) and two Holstein stills, the distillery was substantially expanded in autumn 2022. A completely new distillery was built to house both some of the old equipment as well as a new 2 ton mash tun and two much larger stills (10,000 and 6,000 litres respectively. This meant a quadrupling of the capacity to 500,000 litres. All the barley is grown locally and is floor malted at Warminster Maltings.

The first product for sale was gin in 2014 while the first single malt, the 3 year old Odyssey, was launched in 2017. In early 2018, the distillery started experimenting with rye whisky and in August

that same year the owners made their first trials producing rum. The two core expressions in the Classics Collection are Signature and Reserve, both matured in a combination of ex-bourbon and STR casks. The Cask Expressions Collection, all bottled at cask strength, include Founder´s Choice (STR matured), Peated Cask (matured in ex peated quarter casks), Sherry Cask and Bourbon Cask. Finally there is the limited Hearts & Craft Collection with Banyuls Cask (full maturation) as the fourth and latest installment. In May 2023 there was also a limited Coronation Cask release.

Lakes Distillery

Bassenthwaite Lake, founded in 2014

lakesdistillery.com

Headed by Paul Currie a consortium of private investors founded the distillery. The distillery is equipped with two stills for the whisky production, each with both copper and stainless steel condensers, and a third still for the distillation of gin. A £4.25m investment from Comhar Capital made it possible to install another eight washbacks in 2020 thereby increasing the production capacity to more than 1 million bottles per year. The inaugural bottling, The Lakes Malt Genesis, was released in 2018. A widely available core expression has yet to emerge. Instead the single malts are divided into different series. In September 2019, the distillery launched its first limited edition in the sherry-led Whiskymaker´s Reserve series with the sixth expression being released in 2023. There is also the Whiskymaker´s Editions, with Iris, Infinity, Revelation and Odyssey as the latest additions. Finally there is the limited collection Elements from March 2023 with seven whiskies matured in different sherry casks. In 2023, the whisky maker Dhavall Gandhi was succeeded by Sarah Burgess who had been working as a blender at Macallan for a number of years.

Spirit of Yorkshire Distillery

Hunmanby, founded in 2016

spiritofyorkshire.com

The distillery, founded by Tom Mellor and David Thompson, is actually situated in two separate locations with a mash tun and washbacks standing at Tom´s farm which also houses Wold Top Brewery while the wash still and the spirit still are 2,5 miles down the road in Hunmanby. A four plate column is designed to run in tandem with the spirit still and part of the production is distilled

Lakes Distillery in the heart of Lake District

using the column to achieve a lighter character of the new make. All the barley comes from the farm and the distillery also produces small volumes made from rye. There are plans to increase capacity and the distillery also has a visitor centre with daily tours. Their core bottling, first released in 2019, is the bourbonmatured Filey Bay Flagship. Limited expressions in 2023 include Double Oak #2 finished in American new oak, Filey Bay Peated Finish batch #3 and Yorkshire Day, a distillery exclusive matured in bourbon and madeira casks.

Bimber Distillery

London, founded in 2015

bimberdistillery.co.uk

An innovative distillery equipped with open top wooden washbacks, direct-fired alembic stills and using floor malted barley. Distillation began in May 2016 and the first release from the distillery was a vodka. Today, however, only whisky is produced. In September 2019, it was time for the distillery´s inaugural single malt bottling and a number of releases have followed since including their first peated in 2022. In July 2023 a collaboration with Compass Box resulted in the blended malt Duality and later in the year a 7 year old from one their first casks was released. In September 2023 the owners opened up a second distillery (Dunphail) near Forres in Scotland.

Other distilleries in England

Abingdon Distillery

Abingdon, founded in 2022

abingdondistillery.com

Starting with rum and gin, malt whisky is now also produced in a 650 litre hybrid still from a wash that has fermented for seven days.

Ad Gefrin Distillery

Wooler, founded in 2022

adgefrin.co.uk

Founded by the Ferguson family, this distillery in Northumberland even includes an Anglo-Saxon museum. Equipped with two pot stills, the first casks were filled in December 2022.

Adnams Copper House Distillery

Southwold, founded in 2010

adnams.co.uk

Adnams Brewery in Suffolk added distillation of spirits to their production in 2010 and, apart from whisky – gin, vodka and absinthe are produced. The first whisky was released in 2013 and the range now consists of Single Malt, Rye Malt and Triple Malt. Limited releases matured in oloroso sherry, port and bourbon casks respectively can be found in the Distiller´s Choice range.

Bankhall Distillery

Blackpool, founded in 2019

facebook.com/bankhallwhiskey/

Owned by Halewood Artisinal Spirits, the distillery has a broad perspective on whisky. Sweet mash whisky and expressions made from rye are produced but the first release, in 2023, was a single malt bottled at cask strength.

Canterbury Brewers and Distillers

Canterbury, founded in 2018

thefoundrycanterbury.co.uk

A fascinating combination of craft brewery, distillery, restaurant and bar located in the heart of Canterbury. Equipped with a 500 litre still, gin and rum has been for sale for quite a while. The first whisky was distilled in August 2019 and in March 2023 the bourbon matured Foundry Streetlight single malt was launched.

Circumstance Distillery

Bristol, founded in 2018

circumstancedistillery.com

The idea is to make whisky and rum in a flexible distillery equipped with a pot still with attached columns. The first bottling in 2019 was Circumstantial Barley 1:1:1:1:6, a spirit made from 100% malted barley. The five digit number in this and following releases is a code identifying batch, fermentation (including mash bill), distillation, maturation and age in months. A number of different expression from a variety of mashbills have occured since and in September 2023 the first 100% rye was released.

Cooper King Distillery

Sutton-on-the-Forest, founded in 2018

cooperkingdistillery.co.uk

Inspired by a trip to Australia, Abbie Neilson and Chris Jaume decided to equip their distillery with a Tasmanian copper pot still. The barley is floor malted at Warminster Maltings, the mash is stirred by hand and fermentation times are 6-7 days. The owners released their first gin in 2018, whisky production started in June 2019 and the first malt whisky is expected in autumn/winter 2023. The distillery practises a combination of vacuum distillation and traditional distillation.

Copper Rivet Distillery

Chatham, founded in 2016

copperrivetdistillery.com

The distillery is equipped with a copper pot still with a column attached as well as a special gin still. Dockyard Gin and Vela Vodka were released early on and in April 2017, Son of a Gun, an 8 week old grain spirit (rye, wheat and barley) was released. The first Masthouse Single Malt was released in 2020 and it was followed by Masthouse Grain Whisky, Masthouse Column Malt and a single malt bottled at cask strength.

Dartmoor Distillery

Bovey Tracey, founded in 2016

dartmoorwhiskydistillery.co.uk

Greg Millar and Simon Crow acquired a 50 year old alembic still in Cognac. The brought it to England, refurbished it and attached a copper "wash warmer" to pre warm the wash. The first single malt was launched in February 2020 and the current core range of three includes ex-bourbon, ex-oloroso and ex-Bordeaux wine casks.

Durham Whisky

Durham, founded in 2014 (whisky since 2018)

durhamwhisky.co.uk

The distillery started producing gin and vodka and in 2018 whisky was added to the range. In 2021, the distillery (as well as bar and visitor centre) moved to larger premises. Using local malt, the distillery is equipped with a 1,200 litre wash still and a 1,000 litre spirit still. So far, no single malt has been released.

East London Liquor Company

London, founded 2014

eastlondonliquorcompany.com

Located in an old glue factory in Bow Wharf near Victoria Park, this combined distillery, bar and restaurant was the first distiller to open up in more than 100 years in East London. A variety of spirits are produced where their gin has become the most popular. On the whisky side there is both rye and single malt made from barley.

Ellers Farm Distillery

Stamford Bridge, whisky since 2022

ellersfarmdistillery.com

Having produced various spirits for some years, this Yorkshire distillery commenced distilling malt whisky in summer 2022 with an aim to present its first release in 2025. Complete with a bar and a visitor centre, the distillery is focused on sustainable production and the owners are looking to become a certified B Corp company

Forest Distillery, The

Macclesfield, founded in 2014

theforestdistillery.com

Established in a 17th century stone barn in the Peak District National Park, the 500 litre pot still was later moved to the legendary Cat & Fiddle Inn and thus becoming Britain's highest altitude whisky distillery. Gin has been released as well as at least 28 blends of their own single malt and sourced whiskies. The first single malt, matured in a cognac cask, appeared in October 2022.

Henstone Distillery

Oswestry, Shropshire, founded in 2017

henstonedistillery.com

Commissioned in December 2017, the distillery first released gin, vodka, apple brandy and (in early 2020) a corn "whisky". The first malt whisky distilled in a Kothe copper hybrid still, was launched in January 2021 and the range is now made up of single malts matured in bourbon, oloroso, PX and peated casks respectively.

Isle of Wight Distillery

Newport, founded in 2015

isleofwightdistillery.com

The distillery is currently focused on vodka and their Mermaid Gin. For the whisky, the fermented wash is bought from a local brewery and distilled in hybrid copper stills. The first whisky was distilled in December 2015 but has not yet been released.

Ludlow Distillery

Craven Arms, founded in 2014

ludlowdistillery.co.uk

Equipped with a 200 litre still, this tiny distillery just south of Shrewsbury released its first single malt, Young Prince, in November 2018. The latest release was a 5 year old Distiller's Cut in November 2022.

Penrock Distillery

Merrymeet, founded in 2021

penrockdistillery.co.uk

Sim Daley was born in Cornwall but moved to the USA to pursue his career as a bluegrass musician. Returning to the the UK after two decades he started the Penrock distillery. Rum has already been released and Sim is also working on sour mash American whisky as well as single malt.

Pocketful of Stones

Penzance, founded in 2019

pocketfulofstones.com

This combination of a distillery, bar and restaurant produces a wide range of different spirits and in August 2022 Hell's Stone Whisky with a rioja finish was released.

Retribution Distilling Co.

Frome founded in 2021

retributiondistillingco.uk

With gin and rum already on the shelves, the owners produce small volumes of Somerset's first malt whisky. The first release is due in 2024 and a version made from local peat is in the plans.

Spirit of Birmingham Distillery

Birmingham, founded in 2021

spiritofbirmingham.co.uk

Makers of both beer and vodka, the owners have also laid down whisky in barrels made from a five grain mash bill including both malted rye and malted barley.

Spirit of Manchester Distillery, The

Manchester, founded in 2016 (whisky since 2022)

spiritofmanchester.co.uk

Situated underneath the former railway arches on Watson Street in Manchester, the distillery started producing gin but since 2022 a malt whisky is also distilled, due to be released in 2025 under the name One Point Six..

Weetwood Brewery & Distillery

Kelsall, founded in 1992 (whisky since 2019)

weetwoodales.co.uk

Established as a brewery thirty years ago, the owners added a distillery to the set-up in 2019. Gin, vodka, run and brandy have were first released and the inaugural Cheshire single malt appeared in September 2022 followed by a second release in April 2023.

West Midlands Distillery, The

Rowley Regis, founded in 2017 (whisky since 2021)

westmidlandsdistillery.co.uk

Gin, vodka and rum have been on the market for quite a while and in 2021 the owners started distilling malt whisky with a possible first release in 2024. Heritage grain from Warminster Maltings and different strains of yeast are a vital part of the production.

Wharf Distillery

Towcester, founded in 2015

wharfdistillery.co.uk

What probably used to be the smallest whisky distillery in England was expanded with yet another still in March 2022. The first malt whisky release appeared in January 2019 followed by Solstice and Equinox. There is also a range of grain whiskies named Fyr Drenc.

White Peak Distillery

Ambergate, Derbyshire, founded in 2017

whitepeakdistillery.co.uk

The distillery started distillation in April 2018. Gin, rum, and a 30 months old malt spirit were released first followed by the inaugural, Wire Works Single Malt in February 2022. Recent expressions include Caduro and Alter Ego.

Whittaker's Distillery

Harrogate, founded in 2015 (whisky since 2019)

whittakersgin.com

The owners have already had success with Whittaker Gin but whisky was in their thoughts from the beginning. In summer 2019, two new, larger stills were installed and whisky production started in the autumn. The release of their single malt is planned for 2025.

Yarm Distillery

Eaglescliffe, founded in 2018

yarmdistillery.com

During the first two years, focus was on gin (both sloe and London dry) and in 2020 the first single malt whisky, made from wash from a local brewery, was distilled in their two alembic copper stills. The inaugural release appeared in August 2023.

Faroe Islands

Einar´s Distillery

Klaksvik, founded in 2016

einarsdistillery.com

The first legal distillery in the Faroe Islands was built adjacent to the Föroya Bjór brewery and the wash obviously comes from the brewery´s 2 ton mash tun and is then fermented in three stainless steel washbacks and distilled in a pot still from Arnold Holstein. The first single malt, matured in a combination of ex-bourbon and ex-oloroso, was released in November 2020. The most recent releases include Músabróður where the spirit had matured in both oloroso and marsala casks while Ternan (in May 2023) was a combination of bourbon and oloroso sherry.

Faer Isles Distillery

Vestmanna, founded in 2023

faer.io

In February 2023 the second distillery in the Faroe Islands started production. With a capacity of 600,000 litres of alcohol, the owners are aiming at 80,000 per annum in the first years. Most of the equipment has been manufactured in Scotland. Vodka, akvavit and gin have already been released. The whisky is matured in ”open” warehouses (*opnahjallur*) similar to the ones that have been used for centuries to dry lamb and fish. The owners expect a substantial impact from the humid, windy and salty weather.

Finland

Teerenpeli

Lahti, founded in 2002

teerenpeli.com

The original distillery, located in a restaurant in Lahti, is equipped with one pair of stills. A completely new distillery, with one 3,000 litre wash still and two 900 litre spirit stills, was opened in 2015 in the same house as the brewery and today the old distillery serves as a ”laboratory” for new spirits. The core range consists of a 10 year old, Kaski which is a 100% sherry maturation, Portti which is finished in port casks, the peated Savu and the 7 year old Kulo,

matured in PX and oloroso casks. Recent limited bottlings include the 10 year old Vetehinen with an amarone finish, a 14 year old (the oldest from the distillery so far) and, in May 2023, an 8 year old single cask madeira.

Other distilleries in Finland

Helsinki Distilling Company

Helsinki, founded in 2014

hdco.fi

Equipped with one mash tun, three washbacks and two stills. A gin was released in 2014 and on the whisky side, the focus is on malted rye but also single malt made from barley and whisky made from corn. The latest single malt from barley was a 4 year old PX finish in 2020. In spring 2021 they distilled their first organic whisky.

Nagu Distillery

Lillandet, founded in 2018

nagudistillery.com

Located in an old boat factory in the southwestern Finnish archipelago the owners have released a number of gins and vodkas. Malt whisky is still maturing in the warehouses.

Ägräs Distillery

Fiskars, founded in 2017

agrasdistillery.com

Located in the south of Finland in a small factory village dating back to the 17th scentury. Today it is renowned for its artisan community with a variety of activities within art, craft and design, Ägräs Distillery produces various spirit such as aqvavit, gin and also malt whisky. No whisky has yet been released.

France

Distillerie Warenghem

Lannion, Bretagne, founded in1900 (whisky since 1993)

distillerie-warenghem.com

Leon Warenghem founded the distillery and in 1967, his grandson Paul-Henri Warenghem, together with his associate, Yves Leizour,

Teerenpeli Distillery in Finland

took over the reins. They moved the distillery to its current location on the outskirts of Lannion in Brittany. Gilles Leizour, Yves' son, took over at the end of the 1970's and it was he who added whisky to the Warenghem range. WB, a blend from malted barley and wheat, saw the light in 1987 and Armorik – the first ever French single malt – was released in 1998. The distillery is equipped with a 6,000 litre semi-lauter mashtun, six stainless steel washbacks and two, traditional copper pot stills (a 6,000 litre wash still and a 3,500 litre spirit still). Around 180,000 litres of pure alcohol (including 20% grain whisky) are produced yearly. The single malt core range consists of Armorik Édition Originale and Armorik Sherry Finish. Both are 4 years old, matured in ex-bourbon casks and with a finish in sherry butts. Armorik Classic, a mix of 4 to 8 year old whiskies and the 7 year old Armorik Double Maturation which has spent time in both new oak and sherry wood are earmarked for export as well as the Armorik Sherry Cask and a 10 year old. Warenghem has also distilled rye whisky with the 10 year old Roof Rye being released in 2021. In 2018 the first peated expression, Triagoz, and in September 2022 a 15 year old was added to the core range. Since July 2023 a special bottlings is released to commemorate the creation of the compnay (1st July 1900). The first Deiz was a 10 year old single PX cask. The owners have also recently added a cooperage and they have plans to also open a micro distillery for experimental spirit trials.

Distillerie Rozelieures

Rozelieures, Grand Est, founded in 1860 (whisky since 2003)

whiskyrozelieures.com

Hubert Grallet (who died in March 2022) and his son-in-law, Christophe Dupic launched the Glen Rozelieures brand in 2007. With a production of 200,000 litres, Rozelieures is one of the largest distilleries in France. Five versions are currently available: Original Collection aged in ex-fino casks, the lightly peated Rare Collection matured in ex-sauternes, Fumé Collection (20ppm) matured in ex-fino, Tourbé Collection and the un-peated Subtil Collection. In 2018 they opened a malting plant and in 2021 they released the first batch of whiskies made from their own barley and malted on site.

Distillerie des Menhirs

Plomelin, Bretagne, founded in 1986 (whisky since 1998)

distillerie.bzh

Originally a portable column still distillery, Guy Le Lay and his

wife Anne-Marie settled down in 1986 and the first lambig with the name Distillerie des Menhirs was released in 1989. Shortly after, Guy Le Lay came up with the idea of producing a 100% buckwheat whisky. Eddu Silver was launched in 2002, followed by Eddu Gold, Eddu Silver Brocéliande and Eddu Diamant. Ed Gwenn, aged for 4 years in ex-cognac barrels, was released in 2016 and in 2019, Les Menhirs released a vintage 2004 which was the first whisky distilled from malted buckwheat. To celebrate the 20th anniversary of the first Eddu, the 21 year old Graal was released in 2022.

Domaine des Hautes-Glaces

Saint Jean d´Hérans, Auvergne-Rhône Alpes, founded in 2009 (whisky since 2014)

hautesglaces.com

Located at an altitude of 900 metres, the distillery grows and malt their own organic barley. Principium, the first whisky made at the distillery has been available since 2014. The distillery was bought by Rémy Cointreau in 2015 and a second distillery started operating in 2020. The core range includes Les Moissons Malt and Les Moissons Rye. In 2021, XOᴼ, the first 10 year old was released together with two single casks – Confluens and Ampelos. In October 2023 the entire range was revamped and is now sold in 50 cl bottles.

Miclo

Lapoutroie, Grand Est, founded in 1970 (whisky since 2012)

distillerie-miclo.com

Originally a producer of fruit spirits, the owners have since 2012 used wort from a local brewery to make whisky in four Holstein waterbath pot stills. In September 2021 the range was revamped and now consists of Welche Classique ex-Sauternes, Welche Fumé, Welche Tourbé and Welche Classique ex-Bourgogne.

Bercloux

Bercloux, Nouvelle Aquitaine, founded in 2000 (whisky since 2014)

distillerie-bercloux.fr

Opened as a brewery, a Stupfler pot still was installed in 2014 to produce whisky. This has later been complemented by a cognac still and a column still. The first bottlings of Bercloux Single Malt Whisky were released in 2018. In 2019, the distillery was bought by

Warenghem Distillery with Armorik single malt is the category leader in France

the company Les Bienheureux. Their intention was to secure stock and production for their own brand – Bellevoye triple malt whisky which now has a range of seven expressions. The original Bercloux brand changed name to Lefort to be sold mainly in supermarkets.

Glann ar Mor

Pleubian, Bretagne, founded in 1999

glannarmor.com

The founder, Jean Donnay, started his first trials in 1999 while regular production commenced in 2005. Two small stills are directly fired and worm tubs are used for condensing the spirit. The fermentation in wooden washbacks is long and the distillation is very slow. There are two versions of the whisky – the unpeated Glann ar Mor and the peated Kornog. Core expressions are usually bottled at 46% but every year a number of limited releases are made. In 2019, Glann Ar Mor released its oldest bottling, a Kornog 12 year old, the triple distilled single malt Teir Gwech and Ar Seizh Greun, distilled from a mash of seven malted cereals. In 2020 Jean Donnay sold the distillery to Maison Villevert.

Hepp, Distillerie

Uberach, Grand Est, founded in 1972 (whisky since 2005)

distillerie-hepp.com

The family-owned Hepp produces two core expressions without age statement; Tharcis Hepp (bourbon and sherry) and Johnny Hepp (bourbon and white wine). In 2018 three new bottlings were released; Ouisky, Tharcis Hepp Tourbé and French Flanker. Hepp is also behind the brand Roborel de Climens, launched in 2019 by Aymeric Roborel. The idea is to present whiskies finished in single grape wine cask. Merlot, Sauvignon, Semillon, Rolle, Grenache and Ugni Blanc have already been released.

Castan, Distillerie

Villeneuve Sur Vère, Occitanie, founded in 1946 (whisky since 2010)

distillerie-castan.com

In 2010 Sébastien Castan moved his portable still into a proper distillery and the same year he distilled his first whisky. In 2016, a brewery was built to supply the beer. The range consists of five bottlings: Villanova Berbie (ex-white wine casks), Gost (new cask), Terrocita (peated), Roja (ex-red wine casks) and Segala (rye). The construction of a new distillery has recently been completed and in 2022 the peated Villanova Argile was launched.

Rouget de Lisle

Bletterans, Bourgogne-Franche Comté, founded in 1994 (whisky since 2006)

brasserie-rouget-lisle.com

The brewery Rouget de Lisle commissioned the Brûlerie du Revermont in 2006 to distil whisky for them. The first Rouget De Lisle single malt whisky was released in 2009 and in 2012 the owners bought their own still. The core range consists of two NAS aged in ex-vin de paille and ex-Macvin casks. In 2022 a number of single casks (8 to 15 years old) were released together with expressions aged in beer and tequila barrels.

Hautefeuille, Distillerie

Beaucourt En Santerre, Hauts de France, founded in 2015

distilleriedhautefeuille.com

The distillery is fitted with an 800 litre Stupfler still. A new warehouse and a filling/bottling room was built in 2020.The first whisky, Loup Hardi distilled at another distillery, was launched in 2018. The first release from their own production appeared in 2020 and end of 2022, Parcelle Hangard was launched.

Ninkasi

Tarare, Auvergne-Rhône Alpes, founded in 2015

ninkasi.fr

The whisky was at first distilled in a 2,500-litre Prulho Chalvignac still and aged in different types of wine barrels. A second still was installed in 2019 and in June 2023 a completely new distillery with two stills operating under vacuum was commissioned. The first whiskies were released in 2018 with the first core expression, Ninkasi Chardonnay, appearing in 2021.

Saint-Palais

Saint-Palais de Negrignac, Nouvelle Aquitaine, founded in 2016

alfredgiraud.com

A distillery equipped with ten stills was built in 1963 with the capacity doubled in 1990. In 1995, Philippe Giraud joined the company to form the Alfred Giraud French Malt Whisky. In 2021 the distillery´s first own single malt, Pointe Blanche, was launched. In 2023 a single malt matured in 14 different types of casks was released under the name Alfred Giraud.

Tessendier

Cognac, Nouvelle Aquitaine, founded in 1880 (whisky since 2019)

cognac-tessendier.com

The famous producer of cognac and other spirits has a distillery fitted with seven stills. The first results of whisky production appeared in September 2022; Arlette matured in a combination of new American oak and ex-bourdon barrels, Mizunara with a finish in Japanese mizunara casks and the peated Tourbé.

Twelve, Distillerie

Laguiole, Occitanie, founded in 2017

whiskytwelve.fr

The distillery was built in the former presbytery of Laguiole. The first whisky, Basalte, was released in 2020 and was later followed by Almandin (ex-rum), Aventurine (ex-cognac) and the peated Azurite. The limited but anual Sobroniel is also available.

Other distilleries in France

Bertrand, Distillerie

Uberach, Grand Est, founded in 1874 (whisky since 2002)

distillerie-bertrand.com

The malt is bought from a local brewer and distilled in Holstein stills. Ageing and finishing whisky in French wine casks has been important from the start. The brand was revamped in 2022 and is now made up of two core expressions – Le Principal matured in French oak and Le Souffle from ex-alsacian wine casks.

Boinaud, Maison

Angeac Champagne, Nouvelle Aquitaine, founded in 1971 (whisky since 2018)

boinaud.com

Equipped with 41 pot stills, Maison Boinaud has become one of the most important cognac distilleries in recent years. Since 2018 they are also producing malt whisky two months per year. The first single malt, Hériose Le Classique, was launched in June 2022.

BOWS

Laure Minervois, Occitanie, founded in 2017

bowsdistillerie.com

Bows, which stands for Brave Occitan Wild Spirits, is a project started by Benoit Garcia, a former engineer. He designed and built the distillery himself and the first whiskies, Benleioc Original and Benleioc Tourbe Intense, both made from a stout beer, appeared in 2021. In 2022 the distillery moved to a new location and new equipment was installed to expand the production.

Brana, Domaine

Ossès, Nouvelle Aquitaine, founded in 1974 (whisky since 2018)

brana.fr

With a history of four generations working in the wine industry, the family started distilling spirits from pears in 1974. A new distillery equipped with three copper pot stills was opened in 2018 and in 2022 Laminak, matured in Irouléguy red wine casks, was launched. A second expression appeared in September 2023.

Breuil, Château du

Le Breuil en Auge, Normandie, founded in 1952 (whisky since 2015)

chateau-breuil.biz

The company is a well-known maker of Calvados and, fitted with two Charentais stills, the distillery also produces malt whisky. The first expressions, including a smoky version after maturation in Laphroaig casks, appeared in 2021 under the name Le Breuil. At the moment the company is up for sale.

Brûlerie du Revermont

Nevy sur Seille, Bourgogne-Franche Comté, founded in 1991 (whisky since 2003)

marielouisetissot-levin.com

Relying upon a unique distillation set-up, a Blavier still with three pots, the Tissot family have been producing single malt whisky since 2003. In 2011 they launched their brand Prohibition with whiskies aged in "feuillettes" which is 114 litre half-casks.

Brunet, Distillerie

Cognac, Nouvelle Aquitaine, founded in 1920 (whisky since 2006)

drinkbrenne.com

The first whisky from the distillery was launched in the USA in 2009 by Allison Parc under the brand Brenne. Since then the brand has gained reputation and it has been taken over by Samson & Surrey which in turn was bought by Heaven Hill in 2022.

Bughes, Distillerie des

Solignac, Auvergne, founded in 2017

homedistillers.fr

The founder, Béranger Mayoux, started with three stills, directly heated using gas and in 2021 a fourth and larger still was installed. Montagnac, aged in sherry casks, was released in 2020 followed by Mandrant matured in ex-red wine casks.

Busnel

Cormeilles, Normandie, founded in 1820 (whisky since 2019)

distillerie-busnel.fr

A classic and well-known producer of calvados entered into whisky four years ago. The first two bottlings appeared in 2023 - Cormeil and Busnel - and Cormeil Peated is expected end of 2023.

Camut, Domaine

La Lande Saint-Léger, Normandie, founded in 1981 (whisky since 2018)

A 6th generation producer of calvados making their whisky debut in 2018. Two bottlings, matured in barrels that held "balsamic" apple vinegar, have been released in 2022/2023.

Castor, Distillerie du

Troisfontaines, Grand Est, founded in 1985 (whisky since 2011)

distillerie-du-castor.com

Equipped with two small stills the distillery produces whisky as well as fruit and pomace brandies. The distillate is aged in ex-white wine (sauvignon blanc) casks and then finished in ex-sherry casks. The whisky is sold under the name St Patrick.

Charlier & Fils

Warcq, Grand Est, founded in 2015

facebook.com/laquinarde

The ambition from start was to create their whisky from indigeneous yeast and practising long fermentations. The first Charlier whisky was released in 2020. The production will increase in the coming years as the owner recently bought another still.

Claeyssens de Wambrechies, Distillerie

Wambrechies, Hauts de France, founded in 1817 (whisky since 2000)

wambrechies.com

The distillery´s first 3 year old whisky was released in 2003 followed by an 8 year old in 2009. In 2019, the distillery was bought by Saint-Germain brewery/distillery and it is currently mothballed. The range consists of Wambrechies 5 year old, Sherry and the peated Tourbé.

Didier Barbe Entreprise

Lusigny Sur Barse, Grand Est, founded in 2012

didierbarbeentreprise.com

Focusing on brandies and gin, the first whisky was produced in 2017 from the wash from local breweries. The first whisky, R, aged in ratafia barrels, was launched in 2020.

Dreumont

Neuville-en-Avesnois, Hauts de France, founded in 2005
ladreum.com

In 2011 Jérôme Dreumont built his own 300 litre still and has since then been filling only one cask per year. His first whisky, was launched in 2015 and has been followed by more releases.

Ergaster, Distillerie

Passel, Hauts de Frances, founded in 2015

distillerie-ergaster.com

Peated and unpeated spirit is aging in Cognac, Pineau des Charentes, Vin Jaune and Banyuls casks. The organic Ergaster Nature was launched in 2018 and the latest was Fût D´Exception in 2022.

Fabrique à Alcools, La

Pecqueuse, Ile de France, founded in 2016

lafabriqueaalcools.com

Founded as Parisis Brewery in 2003, whisky production started in 2017. In 2021 a single cask named Le Premier de la Fabrique was launched followed by Alliage, Chevreuse and Fromenteau.

Fontagard

Neuillac, Nouvelle Aquitaine, founded in 1990 (whisky since 2018)

Equipped with no less than 12 stills, the owners have been producing whisky for the last six years. The first three expressions appeared in late 2021 and the whisky production is now being increased.

Hagmeyer

Balbronn, Alsace, founded in 2016

distillerie-hagmeyer.com

Fruit producers for several generations, the owners started whisky production based on beer from Perle brewery. WAH! was launched in 2019. From time to time, WAH! single cask (riesling) and WAH! cask strength (59%) whiskies have been released since 2022.

Kentan

Tonquedec, Britanny, founded in 2017

kentan.fr

Equipped with a Charentais-style still, the distillery started production in 2018. The first releases, Season One and Season Two, have both been matured in ex-cognac casks.

Lachanenche

Méolans Revel, Provence-Alpes-Côte d´Azur, founded in 2008 (whisky since 2018)

lachanenche.com

Supplied with wash from a local brewery, the owners went from distilling spirits from raspberries to also making whisky. Laverq, matured in white wine and white port casks, appeared in late 2022.

Laurens, Domaine

Clairvaux d'Aveyron, Occitanie, founded in 1983 (whisky since 2014)

domaine-laurens.com

This wine estate started production with the help of a brewery. The first versions. Red Léon, aged in white dry aveyron wine ex-casks, and Blue Léon, red ratafia ex-casks, were launched in 2017.

Lehmann, Distillerie

Obernai, Grand Est, founded in 1850 (whisky since 2001)

distillerielehmann.com

The first bottlings from this family-owned distillery appeared in 2008. The range includes Elsass Origine and Elsass Gold matured in white wine casks, and Elsass Premium matured in Sauternes casks. In 2020 a new range of three bottlings, Birdy, was launched.

Leisen

Malling, Grand Est, founded in 1898 (whisky since 2012)

distillerie-leisen-petite-hettange.fr

Since 1898, the Leisen family has distilled fruit spirits but also spirits made from rye and barley. The distillery is equipped with two Carl stills. In 2018 the first bottles appeared under the JML brand.

Mabillot, Domaine

Sainte-Lizaigne, Centre-Val de Loire, founded in 1992 (whisky since 2021)

domaine-mabillot.fr

The wine-making family recently started producing whisky in a 250 litre Holstein still. In 2021 Mabillot Artry and Les Dordans were released followed in 2023 by the peated Mabillot Bellevue.

Mavela, Domaine

Corsica, founded in 1991 (whisky since 2001)

domaine-mavela.com

Distilled in a Holstein still and aged in ex-Corsican muscat casks, the P&M single malt was sold for the first time in 2004. End of 2017, the distillery released its first 12 year old and in 2018 the owners unveiled a completely new range: P&M Signature, P&M Red Oak (aged in ex-red-wine casks) and P&M Tourbé (peated). In 2021, Armelle and Dominique Sialelli took over and merged with LN Mattei, famous for their fortified wine Mattei Cap Corse.

Merlet & Fils

Saint-Sauvant, Nouvelle Aquitaine, founded in 1850 (whisky since 2015)

distillerie-merlet.com

Renowned for their liqueurs and cognacs, the Merlet family are also into whisky. The first, in 2020, was released under the name Coperies and it was followed by Coperies Les Ocres in 2023.

Meyer, Distillerie

Hohwarth, Grand Est, founded in 1958 (whisky since 2004)

distilleriemeyer.fr

The first bottlings from the distillery were launched in 2007 and currently there are two malt whiskies for sale, Meyer's Pur Malt and Meyer Pur Malt Le Fumé.

Michard, Brasserie

Limoges, Nouvelle Aquitaine, founded in 1987 (whisky since 2008)

bieres-michard.com

The first whisky from this craft brewery was released in 2011 followed by a second batch in 2013. End of 2021 a 15 year old was launched.

Mine d´Or, La

Ploërmel, Bretagne, founded in 2017

laminedor.bzh

Originally fitted with an 800 litre still, a new distillery, with an additional 2,500 litre Charentais still, was opened in 2022. The whisky is sold under the name Galaad.

Moon Harbour

Bordeaux, Nouvelle Aquitaine, founded in 2017

moonharbour.fr

The distillery is equipped with two 1,000 litre Stupfler stills. The first whisky was released in 2020 under the name Dock. In 2021 Dock 2, made from malted corn, and Dock 3 where malted barley smoked with seaweed was used, appeared.

Moutard

Buxeuil, Grand Est, founded in 1892 (whisky since 2017)

famillemoutard.com

Fitted with five pot stills, the distillery buys the wash from 5 local breweries in order to make whisky. Matured in Champagne ratafia barrels, the first whisky was released in 2020. A number of bottlings, all with a reference to the breweries have since been released.

Naguelann, Distillerie

Languenan, Bretagne, founded in 2014

naguelann.bzh

Lenaïck Lemaitre launched Naguelann Company as an independent bottler. While working as a bottler, Lenaïck started to build his own distillery fitted with two small stills. Dieil Tantad released in 2020 is his first bottling from own production. In 2021, a brewery and two more stills were installed.

Nalin, Distillerie

La Chana, Auvergne-Rhône Alpes, founded in 1919 (whisky since 2015)

distillerie-nalin.fr

For generations the Nalin family has distilled pear eaux-de-vie for other companies. In 2015, they started whisky production and the first bottling has been sold under the name of NP since 2018.

Northmaen, Distillerie de

La Chapelle Saint-Ouen, Normandie, founded in 1997 (whisky since 2002)

northmaen.com

Originally a craft brewery but later equipped with a portable still. Over the years Thor Boyo, Sleipnir, the peated Fafnir and Kenning have been released and in 2022 Cuvée 1110 Batch 1 appeared. The still is not portable anymore but now works in a real distillery.

Ouche Nanon

Ourouer Les Bourdelins, Centre-Val de Loire, founded in 2015

ouche-nanon.fr

Equipped with a wood-fired still, they launched La Petite Bertha from Sauternes casks in 2018 followed by the peated Frog´s Peat and single casks or small batch (The Lost Barrel and Cardonaccum).

Paris, Distillerie de

Paris, Île de France, founded in 2016

distilleriedeparis.com

Equipped with a small Holstein still the distillery launched the first Parisian whisky in 2019 and it was followed in 2021 by whiskies made from corn and rice and a cask strength finished in chestnut wood.

Piautre, La

Ménitré Sur Loire, Pays de Loire, founded in 2004 (whisky since 2014)

lapiautre.fr

Originally a brewery, La Piautre is now equipped with two direct-fired stills and malting their own barley. They released their first whiskies in 2018; Malt, Tourbé and Seigle. End of 2022, Ile De Baure, aged in sweet white wine and cognac casks, appeared.

Quintessence, La

Herrberg, Grand Est, founded in 2008 (whisky since 2013)

distillerie-quintessence.com

Nicolas Schott produces fruit spirits and also liqueurs. End of 2016, he surprised everyone with the release of his first single malt whisky, Schott's, bottled at 42%.

Roche Aux Fées, La

Sainte-Colombe, Bretagne, founded in 1996 (whisky since 2010)

distillerie-larocheauxfees.com

A micro-brewery from 1996 was in 2010 turned into a portable automatic batch still. The still is wood-heated and equipped with a worm tub. The first Roc'Elf bottling, distilled from three malted cereals (barley, wheat, oat), was released in 2016 followed by a second in 2017. In 2020, the brewery moved to a new and larger site.

T. O. S. Distillery

Aix-Noulette, Hauts de France, founded in 2017

tosdistillery.fr

Saint-Germain has been one of the greatest successes in the revival of French beer production and in 2017 the owners also took up whisky. Artesia single malt was released in 2020 followed by Artesia Rye and Artesia Sherry in 2021 and Artesia Char#3 in 2023.

Vercors, Distillerie

Saint-Jean En Vercors, Auvergne-Rhône Alpes, founded in 2015 (whisky since 2019)

distillerie-vercors.com

The distillery is equipped with a Charentais copper still and a steel boiler which works under vacuum. Sequoia Première Impression

Copper pot stills from Forsyths at the St Kilian Distillery (photo Ernst Scheiner)

and Sequoïa Tourbé, two malt spirits, were launched in 2018 and in 2020 the first "proper" whisky was launched followed by a peated version in 2021.

Vinet Delpech

Brie Sous Archiac, Nouvelle Aquitaine, founded in 1972 (whisky since 2019)

vinet-delpech.com

With a history of producing cognac and brandy, mainly for the Asian market, the distillery equipped with ten pot stills started whisky production in July 2019. The first whisky, matured in Limousin French oak, was released in September 2022.

Germany

Whisky-Destillerie Blaue Maus

Eggolsheim-Neuses, 1980

fleischmann-whisky.de

The oldest malt whisky distillery in Germany distilling their first whisky in 1983. It took, however, 15 years before the first whisky, Glen Mouse 1986, appeared. A completely new distillery became operational in 2013. All whisky from Blaue Maus are single cask and there are around ten single malts in the range. Some of them are released at cask strength while others are reduced to 40%.

Slyrs Destillerie

Schliersee, founded in 1928 (whisky since 1999)

slyrs.de

The malt, smoked with beech, comes from locally grown grain and the spirit is distilled in 1,500 litre stills. The non chill-filtered whisky is called Slyrs after the original name of the surrounding area, Schliers. The core expressions are a the Classic, the 51 which has matured in casks that previously held sherry, port or sauternes and a 12 year old. There are also a peated version as well as a rye. Limited editions include a number of wood finishes and the Mountain Edition, with a new batch released yearly around 1st of May. In summer 2023 the 8 year old Lakeside Edition was released.

Hercynian Distilling Co (formerly known as Hammerschmiede)

Zorge, founded in 1984 (whisky since 2002)

hercynian-distilling.de

The distillery´s main products used to be spirits from fruit, berries and herbs but whisky distilling was embarked on in 2002. The first bottles were released in 2006. The core range goes under the name Elsburn and one subrange is called Alrik, represented by experimental and smoky whiskies while the Willowburn range consists of whiskies finished in different types of casks and Emperor´s Way is all about peated whisky. Several new releases appear every year in small batches and often sell out quickly.

Bayerwald-Bärwurzerei und Spezialitäten-Brennerei Liebl

Kötzting, founded in 1970 (whisky since 2006)

coillmor.com

In 2009 the first bottles bearing the name Coillmór were released. There is a wide range aged between 4 and 12 years currently available. Recent limited editions include the 12 year old Bayerische Weihnacht 2022 matured in rum casks.

St Kilian Distillers

Rüdenau, founded in 2015

stkiliandistillers.com

St Kilian is one of few German distilleries designed to make

only whisky. Equipped with copper pot stills from Forsyths and wooden washbacks from Joseph Brown in Dufftown, the capacity is now 600,000 litres of pure alcohol. Recently they moved all the maturing casks to new warehouses up in the mountains. The first single malt, Signature Edition One, was released in 2019 and in 2023 two core expressions emerged; Classic and Peated – both matured in a combination of bourbon and sherry casks.

Finch Whiskydestillerie

Heroldstatt, founded in 2001

finch-whisky.de

One of Germany´s biggest distilleries with a yearly production of 250,000 litres. A new distillery was commissioned in 2023. The range of whiskies is large and they are made from a variety of different grains. The age is between 5 and 12 years and include peated expressions as well as rye.

Eifel Whisky

Koblenz, founded in 2009

eifelwhisky.de

This is not a distillery per se. Instead the owner of the company, Stephan Mohr, decides on the mash bills and the malted barley and other grains are then sent to Feinbrennerei Sasse to be processed and distilled to Mohr´s specification. The newmake is then sent back to Eifel Whisky´s warehouses in Koblenz for maturation and blending. There are currently three ranges; Signatur, around 4 years old, Reserve, 6-8 years old and 746.9 Series, 10-12 years old.

Other distilleries in Germany

Altstadthof, Hausbrauerei

Nürnberg, founded in 1984

hausbrauerei-altstadthof.de

The current range of Ayrer´s organic single malts consists of Red, PX, Bourbon and Ayla (peated). Limited expressions include the 5 year old Mastercut, the 5 year old Alligator and three wood finishes.

Am Hartmannsberg, Schaubrennerei

Freital, founded in 2011

hartmannsberger.de

Working on a range of various spirits, the owner also produces small volumes of whisky. The first whisky was released in 2015 and the latest was a 7 year old single malt, matured in ex-sherry casks.

Avadis Distillery

Wincheringen, founded in 1824 (whisky since 2006)

avbrennerei.de

Matured in French oak casks that have previously matured white Mosel wine. Threeland Whisky is between 3 and 6 years old and the range also consists of finishes in oloroso and port casks.

Bellerhof Brennerei

Owen, founded in 1925 (whisky since 1990)

dannes.de

The production of whisky made from barley, wheat and rye started in 1990 and today there is a range of various whiskies under the name Danne´s.

Bergwelt Brennerei

Pfaffenhausen-Salgen, founded in 2017

bergwelt-brennerei.de

Apart from a variety of spirits made from herbs, the distillery also produces gin and a single malt whisky under the brand name White

Mountain. The mash bill is made up of five different malt varities.

Birgitta Rust Piekfeine Brände

Bremen, founded in 2011

br-piekfeinebraende.de

A producer of gin and other spirits but also single malt whisky. One of the latest releases is the Van Loon 6 year old single malt with a Tokajer finish.

Birkenhof-Brennerei

Nistertal, founded in 1848 (whisky since 2002)

birkenhof-brennerei.de

The first release from the distillery in 2008 was the 5 year old rye Fading Hill followed by a single malt. The current range consist of single malt, both peated and unpeated, and a rye.

Bosch Edelbrand

Lenningen, founded in 1948 (whisky since 1997)

bosch-edelbrand.de

A family company run by the third generation, the distillery produces gin, edelbrände and single malt whisky. The range consists of whiskies (both grain and malt) up to ten years of age.

Brauhaus am Lohberg

Wismar, whisky since 2010

brauhaus-wismar.de, hinricusnoyte.de

The first release of Baltach single malt, a 3 year old sherry finish, was in 2013. Today there is also a peated version, finished in PX sherry casks.

Burger Hofbrennerei

Burg, founded in 2007 (whisky since 2012)

sagengeister.de

Apart from distillates from fruits and berries, the distillery also produces whisky made from malted barley. The first release of Der Kolonist single malt was in spring 2015.

Dolleruper Destille

Dollerup, founded in 1990 (whisky since 2014)

dolleruper-destille.de

A huge variety of spirits from fruits, berries and nuts are produced but also single malt whisky. A variety of different bottlings, including peated, have been released.

Drexler, Destillerie

Arrach, whisky since 2007

drexlers-baerwurz.de

Malt whisky has been produced since 2009. The first release of Bayerwald Single Malt was in 2011 and the latest, in November 2022, was a 5 year old single cask matured in a cognac cask.

Druffel, Brennerei

Oelde-Stromberg, founded in 1792 (whisky since 2010)

brennerei-druffel.de

A variety of spirits are produced including malt whisky. One of the latest releases of Prum single malt (autumn 2020) was a 5 year old matured in a combination of PX, bourbon and plum wood.

Dürr Edelbranntweine

Neubulach, founded in 2002

blackforest-whiskey.com

The first release from the distillery, the 4 year old Doinich Daal,

reached the market in 2012. Two of the latest expressions were Baurahaib and Vogelsang - both finished in apple aperitif casks.

Edelbrände Senft

Salem-Rickenbach, founded in 1988 (whisky since 2009)

senft-destillerie.de

The first Senft Bodensee Whisky was released in 2012 and then followed by a cask strength version. One of the latest releases, Edition Herbert, was a 6 year old amarone finish.

Evermann-Whisky (Bimmerle KG)

Sasbach, founded in 1966 (whisky since 2015)

evermann-whisky.de

This family owned company, although of a signicant size, is focused on fruit brandies but recently malt whisky has become a part of the range. Currently the range consists of Wilhelm single malt and Theo blended whisky.

Faber, Brennerei

Ferschweiler, founded in 1949

faber-eifelbrand.de

A producer of eau-de vie from fruits and berries, whisky has also been included in the production. The only whisky so far is a single malt that has matured for 6 years in American white oak.

Feller, Brennerei

Dietenheim-Regglisweiler, founded in 1820 (whisky since 2008)

brennerei-feller.de

In 2012 the 3 year old single malt Valerie matured in bourbon casks, was released. It has since been followed by the smoky Torf and 6 to 10 year old grain whiskies under the name Augustus.

Fitzke, Kleinbrennerei

Herbolzheim-Broggingen, founded in 1874 (whisky since 2004)

kleinbrennerei-fitzke.de

The first release of Derrina single malt was in 2007 and new batches have been launched ever since. The different varieties are made from malted grains (barley, rye, wheat, oats) or unmalted (barley, oats, buckwheat, rice, triticale, sorghum or maize).

Glina Whiskydestillerie

Werder a.d. Havel, founded in 2004

glina-whisky.de

The first Glina Single Malt was released in 2008. Most of the whiskies are between 3 and 8 years old. The oldest whisky so far is a 12 year old single rye, fully matured in port casks.

Grumsiner Distillery

Angermünde, founded in 2015

grumsiner.de

The first whiskies were released in 2019 and the latest release of Mammoth single malt was the 8 year old Edition 2023 finished for 3 years in PX casks. Single rye and single grain are also available.

Gutsbrennerei Joh. B. Geuting

Bocholt Spork, founded in 1837 (whisky since 2010)

muensterland-whisky.de

The first releases, two single malts and two single grain, appeared in 2013. More releases of the J.B.G. Münsterländer Single Malt have followed, the latest a 6 year old matured in ex-bourbon casks.

Henrich, Brennerei

Kriftel, founded in 1983 (whisky since 2008)

brennerei-henrich.de, www.gilors.de

The first release was the 3 year old single malt Gilors in 2012. In 2023 the Gilors No. 1 was released to celebrate the company's 50th anniversary. Different casks from 2008-2010 had been married together for two years in bourbon casks and bottled at 55,1%.

Höhler, Brennerei

Aarbergen, founded in 1895 (whisky since 2001)

brennerei-hoehler.de

The first whisky was released in 2004 as a 3 year old. One of the more recent releases of their Whesskey is a 6 year old matured in chestnut casks.

Kammer-Kirsch, Destillerie

Karlsruhe, founded in1961 (whisky since 2006)

kammer-kirsch.de

Working with a brewery the distillery is making their own Black Forest Rothaus whisky as well as thesingle malt Bird of Prey range for the spirits company Bauernkirsch.

Kinzigbrennerei

Biberach, founded in 1937 (whisky since 2004)

biberacher-whisky.de

The first single malt release was the 4 year old Biberacher in 2010. Later releases include Schwarzwälder Rye, Kinzigtäler and Geroldsecker. The oldest whisky so far is the 15 year old Annorum XV bottled at both 40% and cask strength (54%).

Kymsee Whisky

Grabenstätt, founded in 1994 (whisky since 2012)

kymsee-whisky.de

In 2015 the first triple-distilled Kymsee single malt was released. Later editions include Triple Oak and two finishes - quarter cask and sherry cask.

Landgasthof Gemmer

Rettert, founded in 1908 (whisky since 2008)

landgasthof-gemmer.de

The only single malt released is the 3 year old Georg IV which has matured for two years in toasted Spessart oak casks and finished for one year in casks that have contained Banyuls wine.

Lübbehusen Malt Distillery

Emstek, founded in 2014

theluebbehusen.com

With one of the largest pot stills in the country, the distillery currently has three single malts in the range; Unpeated small batch 4 years old, Peated small batch 5 years old and a Vintage 2014.

Marder Edelbrände

Albbruck-Unteralpfen, founded in 1953 (whisky since 2009)

marder-edelbraende.de

The first release was the 3 year old Marder Single Malt. The oldest expression so far is a 10 year old matured in ex-Islay casks.

Märkische Spezialitäten Brennerei

Hagen, whisky since 2010

msb-hagen.de

The spirit is distilled four times and matured in a cave. The first DeCavo whisky was released in 2013 and the latest, in June 2023, was a 6 year old made from Chevalier heritage barley.

Mösslein, Destillerie

Zeilitzheim, founded in 1984 (whisky since 1996)

weingeister.de

Originally a winery, the first whisky was released in 2003 and the current range consists of single malt and a grain whisky including the 5 year old Bergwerk-Whisky.

Nordik Edelbrennerei

Horneburg, founded in 2012

nordik-edelbrennerei.de

A variety of spirits including whisky are produced. Their latest single malts, released in 2020, include two 5 year olds matured in red wine casks. The distillery moved to a new location in 2022.

Nordpfälzer Edelobst & Whiskydestille Höning

Winnweiler, founded in 2008

nordpfalz-brennerei.de

The first release was in 2011, a 3 year old single malt by the name Taranis with a full maturation in a Sauternes cask. Every year in September, a new version is released.

Number Nine Spirituosen-Manufaktur

Leinefelde-Worbis, founded in 1999 (whisky since 2013)

number-nine.eu

Production was expanded in 2013 to include rum, gin and whisky. The first single malt under the label The Nine Springs was launched in 2016. The latest release was the peated Festival Whisky 2023.

Old Sandhill Whisky

Bad Belzig, founded in 2012

sandhill-whisky.com

The first whisky was released in 2015. The current range of six expressions include Oloroso, Bordeaux, German oak, American oak, Port and the 5 year old Bio Whisky.

Preussische Whiskydestillerie

Mark Landin, founded in 2009

preussischerwhisky.de

The spirit is distilled five to six times in a 550 litre copper still with a rectification column. Since 2013 only organic barley is used. The first whisky was launched as a 3 year old in 2012. Since 2015, all the whiskies have been at least 5 years old.

Ralf Hauer, Destillerie

Bad Dürkheim, founded in 1989 (whisky since 2012)

sailltmor.de

The first release, in 2015 was the 3 year old Saillt Mor single malt. The current range are all 5-6 years old; PX Sherry, Double Wood, Port Cask, Woodford Reserve and Pfälzer Eiche.

Rieger & Hofmeister

Fellbach, founded in 1994 (whisky since 2006)

rieger-hofmeister.de

First release was in 2009 and there are now five expressions – a single malt matured in pinot noir casks, a malt & grain from chardonnay casks, a malted rye, a single grain and a smoky, 8 year old triple wood.

Sauerländer Edelbrennerei

Kallenhardt, founded in 2000 (whisky since 2004)

sauerlaender-edelbrennerei.de

The first release of the 3 year old Thousand Mountains McRaven appeared in 2007. One of the latest bottlings was the highly limited

Golt with a finish in red wine, bourbon and sherry casks.

Scheibel Mühle

Kappelrodeck, founded in 2015

scheibel-muehle.de

Originally distillers of Kirschwasser, the owners are now also producing whisky. The Emill range of single malts consists of Feinwerk, Stockwerk, Kraftwerk and the 7 year old Fasswerk.

Schlitzer Destillerie

Schlitz, founded in 2006

schlitzer-destillerie.de

Apart from a range of different spirits, whisky is also produced. There are currently three Schlitzer single malt - Classic, Peaty and and Woody, the last one matured in virgin oak.

Schloss Neuenburg, Edelbrennerei

Freyburg, founded in 2012

schlossbrennerei.eu

The first whisky appeared in August 2016 and one of the most recent expression is is Schlosswhisky No. 8 matured in a tokaji cask.

Schwarzwaldbrennerei Walter Seeger

Calw-Holzbronn, founded in 1952 (whisky since 1990)

krabba-nescht.de

The first single malt was launched in 2009. Currently there are two expressions in the range; the 4 year old Black-Wood single malt matured in amontillado casks and an 8 year old wheat whisky.

Seitz, Gasthof

Gräfenberg, founded in 2007 (whisky since 2013)

gasthof-seitz.de, elch-whisky.de

A combination of a brewery and a distillery. The latest releases include the 7 year old Elch matured in cognac casks and the smoky Torf vom Dorf.

Simon´s Feinbrennerei

Alzenau-Michelbach, founded in 1879 (whisky since 1998)

simon-brennt.de

A single pot still whisky has been produced since 2013 and the range also includes a blend, a rye and a whisky made from emmer.

Singold Whisky

Wehringen, founded in 2017

singold-whisky.de

Although founded in 2017, the brand was produced at another distillery already in 2012. The core range consists of Singold Malt Whisky including a cask strength version and Singold Sherry Cask.

Steinhauser Destillerie

Kressbronn, founded in 1828 (whisky since 2008)

weinkellerei-steinhauser.de

The main products are spirits derived from fruits, but whisky also has its niche. The first release was the single malt Brigantia which appeared in 2011 and an 8 year old has followed since.

Steinwälder Hausbrennerei

Erbendorf, founded in 1818 (whisky since 1920)

brennerei-schraml.de, stonewood-whisky.de

A kind of whisky was made here already in the early 1900s but was sold as "Kornbrand". When the current owner took over, the

spirit was relaunched as a 10 year old single grain by the name Stonewood 1818. Latest releases include an 8 year old, amarone matured single malt and Drà Doublewood One.

Stork Club Whiskey-Destillerie

Schlepzig, founded in 2004

stork-club-whisky.com

The distillery had a history of producing a wide range of spirits but new owners decided to focus mainly on rye whisky. The range is called Stork Club and also includes a single malt made from barley

Störtebeker Brennerei

Mönchgut/Rügen, founded in 2009

stoertebeker-whisky.com

The first whisky was released in 2014 and the current core expression is Klassik. Recent limited editions include two finishes - rum casks and cognac casks. The distillery was expanded in 2023 with a new still.

Tecker Whisky-Destillerie

Owen, founded in 1979 (whisky since 1989)

tecker.eu

Apart from a variety of other spirits, whisky is also produced. The core expression is the 10 year old Tecker Single Malt matured for five years in ex-bourbon barrels, followed by five years in oloroso casks. Recently an 18 year old port cask matured has been released.

Thomas Sippel, Destillerie

Weisenheim am Berg, founded in 1992 (whisky since 2011)

destillerie-sippel.de

Wines as well as distillates of all kinds are on the menu with whisky being introduced in 2011. The first release of the Palatinatus Single Malt came in 2014 and several expressions matured in different casks have since been released.

Vielanker Distillery

Vielank, whisky since 2008

vielanker.de

A combination of a restaurant, hotel, beer brewery and, most recently, a distillery. The brand name of their single malt is Aur Ox and the two oldest expressions so far are a 10 and a 12 year old.

Volker Theurer, Brennerei

Tübingen, founded in 1991

schwaebischer-whisky.de

The first whisky was released in 2003 as a 7 year old. Since then they have released the 8 year old Sankt Johann and the 10 year old Tammer (both single malts) as well as the blend Original Ammertal.

Wild Brennerei

Gengenbach, founded in 1855 (whisky since 2002)

wild-brennerei.de

Three 5 year old whiskies have been released so far – Wild Whisky Single Malt matured for 3 years in American white oak and another 2 in either sherry or port casks, Blackforest Wild Whisky Sherry Cask and Blackforest Wild Whisky Peated.

Zeitzer Whisky Manufaktur

Zeitz, founded in 2014

whisky-zeitz.de

The distillery is equipped with a Lomond still as well as a still built in Germany in 1935. Latest releases include a number of whiskies matured or finished in casks such as tequila, moscatel, gin, madeira and marsala.

Ziegler, Brennerei

Freudenberg, founded in 1865

brennerei-ziegler.de

Maturation takes place not only in oak casks, but also made from chestnut! Their single malt brand, Aureum 1865, was recently complimented by Freud Whisky matured in bourbon and chestnut casks and finished in their Obstbrand barrels.

Hungary

Gemenc Distillery

Pörböly, founded in 2014

gemencdistillery.hu

Unlike so many other distilleries in Hungary producing pálinka, Gemenc is completely focused on whisky. The owner´s, Lajos Szöke, interest lies mainly in various grain whiskies which are matured in casks made from Hungarian oak or acacia. Since 2017, Szöke has also filled casks with both peated and unpeated single malt made from barley.

Agárdi Distillery

Gárdony, founded in 2002

agardi.hu

A classic pálinka producer located by Lake Velence who also distills small amounts of Agárdi single malt and rye whisky.

Iceland

Eimverk Distillery

Garðabær, founded in 2012

flokiwhisky.is

The country´s first whisky distillery where only organic barley grown in Iceland is used for the production and everything is malted on site. Both peat and sometimes sheep dung is used to dry the malted barley. The distillery has a capacity of 100,000 litres where 50% is reserved for gin and aquavite and the rest for whisky. The first, limited release of a 3 year old whisky was in late 2017 and more bottlings have followed since then including one finished in beer casks and one with a partial maturation in birch casks.

Republic of Ireland

Midleton Distillery

Midleton, Co. Cork, founded in 1975

irishdistillers.ie

Midleton is by far the biggest distillery in Ireland and the home of Jameson´s Irish Whiskey. The production at Midleton comprises of two sections – grain whiskey and single pot still whiskey. The grain whiskey is needed for the blends, where Jameson´s is the biggest seller. Single pot still whiskey, on the other hand, is unique to Ireland. This part of the production is also used for the blends but is being bottled more and more on its own.

Instead of mash tuns, Midleton is equipped with three mash filters and following several major upgrades of the distillery in the last decade, the distillery is now equipped with 48 washbacks, 6 column stills and 10 pot stills. The total capacity of the distillery is 70 million litres of pure alcohol. In 2015 a micro distillery

The size of the Midleton Distillery complex is impressive

adjacent to the existing distillery was opened to be used mainly for experiments and innovation. The owners announced in June 2022 that they would invest €50 million over the next four years to make the distillery carbon neutral by the end of 2026. A couple of months later, in September, Irish Distillers declared that they were going to build another distillery across the Dungourney river, just across the existing distillery. The investment is €250 million and the distillery should be operational by 2025 . Another €13 million investment will redevelop the visitor centre at Midleton to include a multi-sensory whiskey experience, interactive whiskey tours and tastings. It will also be completed by 2025 to coincide with the 200th anniversary of the first Midleton distillery.

Of all the brands produced at Midleton, Jameson´s blended Irish whiskey is by far the biggest. In 2022 the brand sold 125 million bottles! Apart from the core expression with no age statement, there are Crested, Black Barrel, Black Barrel Proof, Triple Triple and Jameson Bow Street 18 years. There is also the Caskmates series with two finishes – Stout and IPA. Finally a single pot still, Five Oak Cask Release, was recently launched in the core range.

Other blended whiskey brands include Powers, including a 100% rye version launched in 2023, and the exclusive, yearly releases of Midleton Very Rare. The latter is also the name of a newly released series of exceptionally old whiskies – Midleton Very Rare Silent Distillery. They have all been distilled at the old Midleton Distillery which closed in 1975. The fourth installment, in May 2023, was a 48 year old blend of grain and pot still and the oldest Irish whiskey ever to be released.

In recent years, Midleton has invested increasingly in their second category of whiskey – single pot still. The main brand is Redbreast with a core range of 12, 12 cask strength, 15, 21, Lustau Edition, PX Edition and a 27 year old. Recent limited releases include the Redbreast Dream Cask 30 year old Double Cask and a 19 year old fully matured in oloroso casks. Other single pot stills whiskies can be found in the Spot range; Green Spot without age statement, the 12 year old Leoville Barton bordeaux finish, the Chateau Montelena finish and Quails´ Gate, Yellow Spot 12 year old, Red Spot 15 year old, Blue Spot 7 year old and, released in June 2022, the 9 year old Gold Spot. Powers John´s Lane and Three Swallow and Barry Crocket Legacy are other examples of their single pot still whiskies and so is the Dair Ghaelach range of single casks, finished in virgin Irish oak and aged between 13 and 26 years.

The innovative side of production at Midleton was displayed in 2017 when a first range of experimental whiskeys was introduced under the name Method and Madness. Recent releases include the single pot still Garryana Oak Edition and one that had been made from 60% oats and 40% malted barley.

Tullamore Dew Distillery

Clonminch, Co. Offaly, founded in 2014

tullamoredew.com

Until 1954, Tullamore D.E.W. was distilled at Daly´s Distillery in Tullamore. When it closed, production was temporarily moved to Power´s Distillery in Dublin, and was later moved to Midleton Distillery and Bushmill´s Distillery. William Grant & Sons acquired Tullamore D.E.W. in 2010 and in May 2013, they started to build a new distillery at Clonminch, situated on the outskirts of Tullamore. The four stills produce both malt whiskey and single pot still whiskey and the capacity is 3.6 million litres of pure alcohol. In autumn 2017, a bottling hall and a grain distillery with a capacity of doing 8 million litres of grain spirit was opened on the same site. All whiskies at Tullamore are triple distilled. Tullamore D.E.W. is the second biggest selling Irish whiskey in the world after Jameson with 17 million bottles sold in 2022. The core range consists of Original (without age statement), 12 year old Special Reserve and 14 and 18 year old Single Malts. Exclusive to duty free and select markets there are also the Cider Cask Finish and Carribean Rum Cask Finish and in 2021 the 13 year old Rouge (finished in ex-Pomerol casks) was launched at Dublin Airport. Warehouse Release can only be found at the distillery visitor centre.

Cooley Distillery

Cooley, Co. Louth, founded in 1987

thetyrconnellwhiskey.com, connemarawhiskey.com

John Teeling has played a huge part in the resurrection of Irish whiskey – a category which during the second half of the 20th century continuosly lost ground amongst the consumers. By the late 1980s there were only two distilleries left in the country. In 1987 he bought the disused Ceimici Teo distillery (an industrial alcohol plant) and renamed it Cooley distillery. Two years later he installed two pot stills and in 1992 he released the first single malt from the distillery, called Locke´s Single Malt. A number of brands were launched over the years. In 2011 Beam Inc. acquired the distillery and today Cooley is owned by Beam Suntory. The range of whiskies is made up of several brands. Connemara single malts, which are all more or less peated, consist of a no age Original, a 12 year old and a cask strength. Another brand is Tyrconnell with a core expression bottled without age statement. Other Tyrconnell varieties include three 10 year old wood finishes and Tyrconnell 16 year old with a finish in both oloroso and moscatel casks.

Teeling Distillery

Dublin, founded in 2015

teelingwhiskey.com

After the Teeling family had sold Cooley and Kilbeggan distilleries to Beam in 2011, the family started a new company, Teeling Whiskey. John Teeling´s two sons, Jack and Stephen, then opened a new distillery in Newmarket, Dublin in June 2015. This was the first new distillery in the city in 125 years. In 2017, Bacardi acquired a minority stake (40%) in Teeling Whiskey and in autumn 2022 there were rumours that they were looking to make another bid to take over the majority of the company. The distillery also has an impressive visitor centre. Teeling is equipped with two wooden washbacks, four made of stainless steel and three stills made in Italy; wash still (15,000 litres), intermediate still (10,000 litres) and spirit still (9,000 litres) and the capacity is 500,000 litres of alcohol. Both pot still and malt whisky is produced.

The core range from the distillery consists of the blend Small Batch, the biggest seller, which has been finished in rum casks, Single Grain which has been fully matured in Californian red wine barrels, Single Malt - a vatting of five different whiskies that have been finished in five different types of wine casks and Single Pot Still (50% malted and 50% unmalted barley). In 2020 an extension to the range appeared when Blackpitts Peated Single Malt, triple distilled and matured in ex-bourbon and ex-Sauternes, was released. Recent limited bottlings include Wonders of Wood where two expressions had been finished in virgin Portuguese oak and Chinkapin oak respectively. There is also the new Explorers Series where a 15 year old had been matured for the final 4 years in Japanese shochu casks.

Dingle Whiskey Distillery, The

Milltown, Dingle, Co. Kerry, founded in 2012

dingledistillery.ie

The distillery is equipped with a very unusual wooden mash tun and wooden washbacks with a minimum fermentation time of 72 hours. There are also three pot stills and a combined gin/vodka still. The first production of whiskey was in December 2012 and the first general release of a single malt whiskey was in autumn 2016. Since then a range of six different ”small batches” of single malt and five of single pot still have been released. A limited series named Wheel of the Year (reflecting the Celtic solar calendar) was recently launched with the fourth edition (out of eight), Lúnasa, released in August 2023.

Roayl Oak Distillery (fomerly known as Walsh Whiskey Distillery)

Carlow, Co. Carlow, founded in 2016

royaloakdistillery.com, thebusker.com

With succesful brands such as The Irishman and Writer´s Tears, Bernard Walsh opened his own distillery at Royal Oak, Carlow.

With a back-up from the major Italian drinks company, Illva Saronno, the distillery was commissioned in 2016. The capacity is 2.5 million litres of alcohol and all types of whiskey is produced including grain- malt- and pot still whiskey. In 2019 Illva Saronno took full control of the distillery while Bernard Walsh continued with the brands Writer´s Tears and The Irishman. Walsh Whiskey was later acquired by Latvian based Amber Beverage Group. The new owners of Roayl Oak introduced their own brand, Busker, in November 2020 and the range now consists of Single Grain, Single Malt, Single Pot Still and Triple Cask.

Great Northern Distillery
Dundalk, Co. Louth, founded in 2015
gndireland.com

In 2013, the Irish Whiskey Company (IWC), with John Teeling as the majority owner, took over the Great Northern Brewery in Dundalk and turned it into a distillery. When it became operational in August 2015, it was the second biggest distillery in Ireland (and still is), with the capacity to produce 3.6 million litres of pot still whiskey and 8 million litres of grain spirit. A recent expansion, including another six pot stills and an additional eight washbacks has brought the capacity to 16 million litres. The idea behind the distillery is to sell new make or whiskey to other companies. Around 60% of the volume sold is new make but the share of mature whiskey (including blends) is growing. The master distiller and general manager, Brian Watts, died suddenly in October 2022 at the age of 60. Before moving to Ireland Watts had a long career at The North British Distillery in Scotland.

Waterford Distillery
Waterford, Co. Waterford, founded in 2015
waterforddistillery.ie

Founded by the former co-owner of Bruichladdich distillery, Mark Reynier. In 2014 he bought Waterford Brewery and in December 2015, the first spirit was distilled. The distillery is equipped with two pot stills (which replaced the old Inverleven stills in August 2021) and one column still and, even though grain spirit will be produced, malt whiskey is the number one priority. The distillery also has a mash filter instead of a mash tun. There is a focus on local barley sourced from more than 70 farms on 19 different soil types. After having distilled Ireland´s first organic whiskey in 2016, Reynier decided to also produce the first biodynamic whiskey in 2018. Pilgrimage, the first general whiskey release from the distillery, appeared in April 2020 and, what could be considered as the core expression going forward, Cuvée Concept, was released in 2021. It was followed by Cuvée Argot in March 2023. There is also the Arcadian Farm Origin series where one of the latest releases was Heritage Hunter, made from a barley variety that hasn´t been used since the 1970s. The Single Farm Origin series is made up of whisky distilled at the individual farms and the Organical Single Farm Origin range was recently introduced with Killone as the first installment.

Roe & Co. Distillery
Dublin, founded in 2019
roeandcowhiskey.com

The opening of Roe & Co Distillery marked Diageo´s return to the Irish whiskey scene which they left in 2014 when they sold Bushmills. A blend named Roe & Co made from sourced whiskies was launched already in 2017 and at the same time plans to build a distillery in Dublin were revealed. The distillery is situated in The Liberties district in the former Guinness Power Station. Three stills and wooden washbacks make up part of the equipment and the production capacity of double- and tripledistilled whiskey is 500,000 litres. In November 2020 the first whiskies, sourced from another distillery, appeared. The latest were a 13 year old single malt, a 13 year old single grain and, in October 2022, Cask & Keg - a whiskey finished in coffee stout casks.

West Cork Distillers
Skibbereen, Co. Cork, founded in 2004
westcorkdistillers.com

The distillery, equipped with eight pot stills, two column stills and with a yearly capacity of no less than 4,5 million litres of pure alcohol, produces both malt whiskey and grain whiskey and some of the malting is done on site. The whiskey range is quite substantial and include single malts, single pot stills, cask finished whiskies with a second maturation in cask that have held for example port, stout, IPA and sherry and finally, the Glengarriff series with peated expressions. The two most recent releases (in December 2022) were a 5 year old single pot still and a 7 year old single malt. In autumn 2019 the founders bought out the majority stake in the business held by Halewood Group and in 2020 the company moved to a new and expanded distillery in Marsh Road in Skibbereen.

Blackwater Distillery
Ballyduff Upper, Co. Waterford, founded in 2014
blackwaterdistillery.ie

Originally located in Cappoquin, Co. Waterford, the distillery moved in 2018 to Ballyduff. At that time the company was already famous for their gin. In their new distillery, equipped with two former grappa stills from Frilli in Italy, whiskey is now also produced. Director and co-founder Peter Mulryan, with a background as TV-producer and whisky writer, is passionate about single pot still. The current legislation says it must be produced from malted and unmalted barley and that only 5% of other grains can be a part of the mash bill. According to legislators this is the traditional way. Going through hundreds of recipes from the 19th and 20th century Irish distilleries, Mulryan has shown that a substantially higher percentage of other grains were involved. A revised version of the technical file for production of single pot still was anticipated to be implemented by the end of 2022 but so far nothing has happened. Apart from distilling single malt, Mulryan is making single pot still from a huge variety of these ancient recipes. The first releases, named Dirtgrain Irish Whisky, were released in November 2022. Four different mashbills (inlcuding wheat, oats and rye) matured in four different types of casks were presented.

Other distilleries in Ireland

Achill Island Distillery
Achill Island, Co. Mayo, founded in 2019
irishamericanwhiskeys.com

Situated on the most westerly tip of Europe, this is Irelands first island-based whiskey distillery, owned by the IrishAmerican Trading Company, a family owned company with offices both in Dublin and Boston. The distillery is equipped with two copper pot stills. The first products for sale were sourced whiskies aged 6 to 19 years but their inaugural release from own production, matured in bourbon and Bordeaux casks, appeared in December 2022.

Ballykeefe Distillery
Ballykeefe, Co. Kilkenny, founded in 2017
ballykeefedistillery.ie

A classic farm distillery growing their own barley. The distillery is equipped with three copper pot stills and the first triple distillation was in spring 2018. Gin, vodka and poitin were released early on while the first Ballykeefe single pot still appeared in March 2021 followed by a single malt in November.

Baoilleach Distillery
Carrickart, Co. Donegal, founded in 2018
baoilleachdistillery.ie

Michael O´Boyle started off distilling gin, rum and poitín and later ventured into whiskey made from malted and unmalted barley. A new, direct-fired still was installed in March 2022. The Mountain Dew series of malt spirits (not old enough to be called whiskey) as well as new make have been launched.

Blacks Brewery & Distillery

Kinsale, Co. Cork, founded in 2013 (whiskey since 2020)

blacksbrewery.com

Starting off as a brewery, the owners later went on with distillation of gin and rum. In 2020, they purchased two copper pot stills from Frilli in Italy and the first whiskey distillation was made later that year. Both single malt whiskey and single pot still are produced and souced whiskey is currently for sale.

Boann Distillery

Drogheda, Co. Meath, founded in 2016

boanndistillery.ie

The distillery, founded by Pat Cooney, is equipped with three Italian-made copper pot stills and a gin still. Releases of sourced whiskey under the name The Whistler appeared early on. The first single pot still whiskey distillation was in December 2019 and in December 2022 the first whiskey from their own production, the PX-matured The Solstice, was released. The owners have also started trials with different mash bills in order to revive the old Irish way of using a range of different grains.

Burren Distillery

Ballyvaughan, Co. Clare, founded in 2019

burrendistillers.com

The owners are using locally grown barley which is floor malted at the distillery, distillation takes place in traditional copper pot stills and for some of the maturation, casks made of Irish oak are used. Both single pot still and single malt whiskey is produced.

Church of Oak Distillery

Ballykelly Mills, Monasterevin, Co. Kildare, founded in 2021

churchofoak.com

Under the supervision of Ian MacMillan, who worked for Burn Stewart Distillers for many years, a large distillery owned by

Jewelfield Ltd with Bono as a shareholder was recently opened. The stills were delivered from Forsyths in August 2021 and the first spirit was distilled in May 2022. The whiskey is either double or triple distilled (and occasionally 2,5 times).

Clonakilty Distillery

Clonakilty, Co. Cork, founded in 2016

clonakiltydistillery.ie

For nine successive generations, the Scully family have farmed the coastal lands near the resort town Clonakilty in West Cork. Production started in spring 2019 with Paul Corbett (former Teeling Whiskey Company) as the head distiller. The main product will be a triple distilled pot still whiskey and the first release is planned for spring 2024 with sourced whiskey already in the range.

Connacht Whiskey Company

Ballina, Co. Mayo, founded in 2016

connachtwhiskey.com

Equipped with three pot stills the distillery has the capacity to produce 300,000 litres of pure alcohol per year. The first distillation of whiskey (double-distilled) was made in 2016 and in 2017, triple distillation started as well. Apart from malt whiskey and single pot still, the owners also produce vodka, gin and poitín. In June 2021 a limited release from the first cask as well as a general release of Single Malt Batch 1 occured. Sourced whiskies are also sold.

Crolly Distillery

Crolly, Co. Donegal, founded in 2020

thecrollydistillery.com

The former Crolly Doll factory from 1902 has been converted into a distillery with two beautiful cognac stills and the ability to produce 50,000 litres of pure alcohol yearly. The first distillation was in November 2020 and sourced whiskey is currently sold.

Dublin Liberties Distillery, The

Dublin founded in 2018

thedld.com

After eight years of preparations, the distillery finally started the

Connacht Whiskey Company

production in early 2019. It is owned by Quintessential Brands (75%) and East European drinks company Stock Spirits (25%). The three coper pot stills produce both double and triple distilled whiskey as well as peated expressions and the total capacity is 700,000 litres of pure alcohol per year. The whiskeys currently available have all been produced at either Bushmills or Cooleys.

Kilbeggan Distillery

Kilbeggan, Co. Westmeath, founded in 1757

kilbegganwhiskey.com

Brought back to life in 2007, Kilbeggan is the oldest producing whiskey distillery in the world, equipped with a wooden mash tun, four Oregon pine washbacks and two stills. The first single malt from the new production came in 2010 and the current range consists of a blended whiskey, a single pot still, a small batch rye and triple cask (whish used to be called single grain). Limited releases include the peated Kilbeggan Black and an 11 year old single malt for travel retail.

Killarney Distillery

Scart, Co. Kerry, founded in 2020

torcbrewing.ie

Aidan Forde and John Keane, owners of Torc Brewing Company, opened a distillery equipped with two 2,000 litre stills manufactured in house and the first spirit was distilled in spring 2020 with a possible inaugural release in 2023.Currently the owners are working on the idea of opening another distillery 12 kilometres to the south in Aghadoe, on the outskirts of Killarney.

Lough Gill Distillery

Hazelwood House, Co. Sligo, founded in 2019

loughgilldistillery.com, athru.com

A group of investors led by David Raethorne came up with the idea in 2014 to build a distillery adjacent to the 18th century Hazelwood House. Planning permission was secured in 2017 and in late 2019 the distillery was commissioned. Equipped with three pot stills from Frilli, the distillery has a capacity of 1 million litres. Sourced whiskey can be found under the brand name Athrú. In summer 2022 The Sazerac Company (Buffalo Trace and Southern Comfort) acquired the distillery and at the same time Bushmill´s former master blender Helen Mulholland joined the team.

Lough Ree Distillery

Lanesborough, Co. Longford, founded in 2018

lrd.ie

A family owned distillery west of Dublin, famous for its Slingshot Gin. Production of whiskey didn´t start until 2022 but sourced whiskey from Great Northern Distillery is sold under the name Bart´s.

Micil Distillery

Salthill, Co. Galway, founded in 2016

micildistillery.com

The first steps into distillation six years ago were producing gin and poitin. In 2021, the operation was expanded into whiskey making, not least using local peat from Inverin to dry the barley. According to the owners the Micil family represents Irelands longest unbroken family distilling tradition. Apart from their own gin and poitin, sourced whiskey is currently for sale.

Pearse Lyons Distillery

Dublin, founded in 2017

pearselyonsdistillery.com

Dr Pearse Lyons, who passed away in 2018, was a native of Ireland and used to work for Irish Distillers in the 1970s. In 1980 he changed direction and founded a company specializing in animal nutrition and feed supplements. In 2008, he opened a whiskey distillery in Lexington, Kentucky. Four years later he started a distillery in Carlow, Ireland. After a few years, the stills were moved to Dublin where Dr Lyons restored the old St James´ church and converted it to a distillery. The distillery is equipped with a traditional wash still with a descending lyne arm while the spirit still has four rectification plates to further refine the spirit. The first distillation was in September 2017 but the owners already have a range of aged malt whiskies made from whisky produced at Carlow and other distilleries. In July 2019 they also started distilling pot still whiskey and in 2020 they began using oats in some of their mashbills. The range consists of two blended whiskies (5 and 7 years) and two single malts (5 and 12 years).

Powerscourt Distillery

Enniskerry, Co. Wicklow, founded in 2017

powerscourtdistillery.com

The distillery is situated at the Powerscourt Estate, owned by the Slazenger family, south of Dublin. Equipped with hree pot stills, distillation started in autumn 2018 and a visitor centre was opened in summer 2019. For the first five years Noel Sweeney from Cooley Distillery was in charge of the distillery which has a capacity of producing 1 million bottles per year. A range of sourced whiskies have already been released under the name Fercullen.

Shed Distillery, The

Drumshanbo, Co. Leitrim, founded in 2014

thesheddistillery.com

Founded by entrepreneur and drinks veteran P J Rigney, the distillery is equipped with five pot stills, three column stills and six washbacks. The focus for the owners is triple distilled single pot still whiskey but Drumshanbo gin has been on the market for years. The first whiskey distillation was in late 2014 and in 2019 the 5 year old Drumshanbo Single Pot Still was released.

Slane Distillery

Slane, Co. Meath, founded in 2017

slaneirishwhiskey.com

The Conyngham family established a whiskey brand a few years ago which became popular not least in the USA. The whiskey was produced at Cooleys but the family decided to start a distillery of their own. After an unsuccesful partnership with Camus Wine & Spirits, Brown-Forman stepped in and took over the entire project in 2015. Equipped with three copper pot stills, six column stills and washbacks made of wood, the distillery started production in summer 2018 and three types of whiskey are produced; single malt, single pot still and grain whiskey. Currently in the range are Triple Casked Blend, Batch Strength, Special Edition and, the latest, Extra Sherry Wood - the first release in the Wood Series.

Sliabh Liag Distillers (Ardrara Distillery)

Ardara, Co. Donegal, founded in 2021

sliabhliagdistillers.com

Starting with gin production, James and Moira Doherty always had their eyes set on a whiskey distillery. Planning was granted in August 2019 and in early 2022 the first whiskey was produced from the three stills made by Forsyths. In 2020, Japanese drinks giant Asahi Group invested €3m in the distillery. The current capacity is 440,000 litres but a crowd funding campaign launched in June 2022 is expected to take the production up to 600,000 litres in the future. Meanwhile, the Dohertys have with great success been selling a blended whiskey named Silkie and their first single malt, the smoky The Kilcar Release, appeared in September 2023.

Tipperary Boutique Distillery

Clonmel, Co. Tipperary, founded in 2020

tipperarydistillery.ie

Jennifer Nickerson and her husband Liam Ahearn chose the

Ahearn family farm, Ballindoney, between Clonmel and Tipperary as the spot for Tipperary Boutique Distillery. Sourced whiskey was released from early on and in November 2020, the first whiskey made from their own barley and distilled at another Irish distillery was released. Simultaneously, the owners made their first distillation at their own distillery which is equipped with four stills from Hoga in Portugal.

Italy

Puni Destillerie

Glurns, South Tyrol, founded in 2012

puni.com

The design of the distillery – a 13-metre tall cube made of red brick – is unusual as is the combination of three malted cereals in the recipe – barley, rye and wheat. The distillery is equipped with five washbacks with a fermentation time of 96 hours. There is also one pair of stills. The first single malt was released in 2015 and the core range consists of Sole (two years in ex-bourbon and two years in PX casks), Gold (5 years in ex-bourbon) and Vina (5 years in marsala casks). Recent limited releases include the third version of Arte made from 100% malted barley and matured in ex-sherry casks, the third edition of Aura, an 8 year old matured in virgin French oak and, in July 2023, Cubo - the first distillery exclusive.

Psenner Destillerie

Tramin, founded in 1947 (whisky since 2013)

psenner.com

A producer of fruit spirits and grappa, tried their hands at whisky for the first time 7 years ago. Their inaugural release of the 3 year old single malt eRètico appeared in 2016 and had been matured in a combination of ex-grappa and ex-oloroso casks.

The Netherlands

Zuidam Distillers

Baarle Nassau, founded in 1974 (whisky since 1996)

zuidam.eu

Zuidam Distillers was started in 1974 as a traditional, family distillery producing liqueurs, genever, gin and vodka and is today managed by Patrick van Zuidam. The first release of the Millstone single malt was bottled in 2007 as a 5 year old. The current range is a 5 year old which comes in both peated and unpeated versions, American oak 10 years, French oak 10 years, Sherry oak 12 years and PX Cask 1999. Apart from single malts there is also the Millstone 100 Rye which is bottled at 50% and its younger sibling 92 Rye. Limited expressions include the 8 year old Double Sherry Cask (oloroso and PX), American Oak Peated Moscatel, the 7 year old Peated PX and (in 2023) a 6 year old fully matured in Amarone casks. The oldest release so far is a 23 year old oloroso single cask. Two more stills from Forsyths were commissioned in 2020 and the distillery has also started to grow their own barley and rye at a nearby farm.

Other distilleries in The Netherlands

Bus Whisky

Loosbroek, founded in 2015

buswhisky.com

An estate distillery using barley from their own fields. The whisky starts the maturation in ex-bourbon and may then receive a finish in other types of casks. The first expression was released in 2019 and the latest batch (23) appeared in 2023. The whisky is only sold at the distillery or in their own webshop.

Cley Distillery

Rotterdam, founded in 2015

cleywhisky.com

The triple distilled Cley whisky is matured in ex-bourbon and finished in virgin American oak. Both single malts and combinations of malt and rye are bottled. One of the latest was a 4 year old finished in Islay casks.

Den Hool Distillery

Holsloot, founded in 2015

denhoolwhisky.nl

Originally a farm, the owners started brewing beer in the late 1990s. In 2009 some of the wash was sent to Zuidam Distillers for distillation into whisky. The first release of Veenhar single malt was in 2016 and the latest, in spring 2023, a 7 year old year old matured in a combination of new American oak, bourbon and PX sherry. Since 2015, distillation is carried out on the farm and they are also taking care of their own malting.

Drumlin Distillery

Havelte, founded in 2018

drumlindistillery.com

The first release from this new distillery was a gin but both malt whisky and rye are also produced. In January 2023, the first bottling of Cromlech single malt (a 3 year old distilled in 2019) appeared.

Eaglesburn Distillery

Ede, founded in 2015

eaglesburn.com

The owner, Bart Joosten, is a firm believer in long fermentation - at least 10-12 days. The first release was in October 2018 and in early 2023 the third installment in the Double Wood series appeared, matured in a combination of bourbon and rum casks.

Hemel Brewery and Distillery, De

Nijmegen, founded in 1983

brouwerijdehemel.nl

Situated in a 12th century monastery, a brewery has now been complemented by a distillery. The two releases of Anima whisky are technically "Bierbrands", i. e. distilled from a hopped beer.

Horstman Distillery

Losser, founded in 2000

distilleerderijhorstman.nl

Producers of genever and whisky, the distillery released their first bottling in 2016 (a 5 year old matured in port casks). The current range includes both grain and single malt, matured in various casks.

Ijsvogel Distillery, De

Arcen, founded in 2012

ijsvogel.com

A huge variety of different spirits are distilled including malt whisky. The first whisky was bottled in 2015 and the latest, released in September 2023, was a 50 months old matured in a combination of ex-Laphroaig and Vino de Naranja casks.

Kalkwijck Distillers

Vroomshoop, founded in 2009

kalkwijckdistillers.nl

The distillery is equipped with a 300 litre pot still with a column attached. In spring 2015, the first Eastmoor single malt was released as a 3 year old and in 2023 batch 9 appeared. Recently a new range named Higgledy Piggledy was introduced made up of grain, rye and corn whiskies.

Lepelaar Distillery

Texel, founded in 2009 (whisky since 2014)

landgoeddebontebelevenis.nl/Texelse-Whisky

This distillery, producing single malt (both peated and unpeated) as well as grain whisky and genever, is a part of a larger crafts centre. A first, limited release of Texelse Whisky was made for the crowd funders in 2018 and was later followed by a general release.

Stokerij Sculte

Ootmarsum, founded in 2004 (whisky since 2011)

stokerijsculte.nl

The distillery is equipped with a 500 litre stainless steel mashtun, 4 stainless steel washbacks and two stills. The first Sculte Twentse Whisky was released in 2014 and has been followed by a number of different releases. One of them, the fourth batch of the peated, appeared in autumn 2023.

Us Heit Distillery

Bolsward, founded in 2002

usheit.com

Frysk Hynder was the first Dutch whisky and made its debut in 2005 at 3 years of age. The barley is grown in the surrounding area and malted at the distillery. The whisky (3 to 5 years old) is matured in a variety of casks and there is also a cask strength version.

Northern Ireland

Bushmill's Distillery

Bushmills, Co. Antrim, founded in 1784

bushmills.com

This, the second biggest of the Irish distilleries after Midleton, was sold by Pernod Ricard to Diageo in 2005 who, in turn.sold it to Proximo (producer of the José Cuervo tequila) in 2014. The new owners applied for a planning permission to expand the capacity and also to build another 29 warehouses over the next two decades on adjacent farmland. The local council gave the green light in 2019 and in spring 2023 a second distillery on the site, named Causeway Distillery, was opened. Equipped with one mash tun, eight washbacks and ten stills, it means that Bushmills has doubled their capacity to 9 million litres. Bushmills is the third most sold Irish whiskey after Jameson and Tullamore D.E.W. and in 2022 it broke the 1 million cases barrier.

At Bushmill's, triple distilled single malt whiskey is produced. For their range of blended whiskies, the grain part is brought in from Midleton Distillery. The blended range consists of Bushmill's Original, Black Bush and Red Bush. In April 2021 two Bushmills Original Cask Finish were released. The single malt part of the two whiskies had been finished in American oak and rum respectively.

The core range of Bushmill's single malts consists of a 10 year old, a 16 year old Triple Wood with a finish in Port pipes and a 21 year old finished in Madeira casks for two years. In 2022 a 12 year old with a finish in Marsala casks is added to the range. Two limited small batch expressions appeared in April 2023; a 25 year old with 21 years in ruby port pipes and a 30 year old with a 16 year long secondd maturation in PX sherry butts. December 2020 saw the launch of the first expression in the limited The Causeway Collection where, over the years, a total of ten single malts, aged up to 33 years that had been finished in different casks were bottled at cask strength.

Other distilleries in Northern Ireland

Copeland Distillery

Donaghadee, Co. Down, founded in 2016

copelanddistillery.com

In early 2019, the founder Gareth Irvine moved his distillery in Saintfield 20 kilometres south of Belfast to Donaghadee by the coast. Already established as a gin producer, the owners filled their first cask of malt whiskey in November 2019 and the first release is planned for 2025. Currently a sourced blended whiskey is sold.

Echlinville Distillery

Kircubbin, Co. Down, founded in 2013

echlinville.com

Founded by Shane Braniff and located near Kircubbin on the Ards Peninsula, the distillery started production in August 2013. The

Bushmills Distillery has recently doubled its capacity to 9 million litres

distillery, having its own floor maltings, has been expanded over the years and a visitor centre has also been opened. Apart from single pot still and single malt whiskey, vodka and gin is also produced. Using sourced whiskey Braniff has revived the old Dunville´s brand of blended whiskey and included also single malt. The Matt D´Arcy brand was also recently added to their range. The first whiskey from their own distillation is expected in 2023.

Hinch Distillery

Ballynahinch, Co. Down, founded in 2020

hinchdistillery.com

The owner of Chateau de La Ligne in Bordeaux, Terry Cross, is the founder of this distillery within the grounds of Killaney Lodge just south of Belfast. A wide range of sourced whiskies were launched early on. The covid pandemic delayed the opening of the distillery but in November 2020, the first distillation was made. The distillery, practising triple distillation, is equipped with three pot stills (10,000 l, 5,500 l and 2,500 l).

Killowen Distillery

Newry, Co. Down, founded in 2017

killowendistillery.com

Founded by Brendan Carty, the distillery started producing gin in 2017 and in 2019 the first batch of pot still whiskey was distilled. The spirit is double distilled and peated and the mash bill contains not only malted and unmalted barley but also other grains (like oats). Fermentation takes place in open top wash backs for a week or longer, the two Portuguese stills are direct heated and worm tub condensers are being used. In 2019 the first in a range of sourced whiskeys called Bonded Experimental and they have also released a number of different poitin. Collaborations have been carried out with both Blackwater in Ireland and Belgrove in Tasmania and in October 2022 it was time for their first whiskey release from their own distillation. Under the name Barántúil , two single cask single pot still whiskeys were launched.

Mourne Dew Distillery

Warrenpoint, Co. Down, founded in 2018

mournedew.com

The distillery is unusually equipped with two vacuum stills as well as a conventional 500 litre hybrid still. The first products to be launched were poitin, gin and vodka but recently their triple distilled whiskey has been launched both in way of a blend as well as a single malt. For maturation ex-bourbon casks are used together with virgin oak and casks that have held rye whisky and IPA.

Rademon Estate Distillery

Downpatrick, Co. Down, founded in 2012

shortcrosswhiskey.com

Shortcross gin became a success for Rademon very quickly and in summer 2015 the production was expanded into whiskey, both single malt and single pot still. Through a £2.5m investment, the capacity of the distillery was further increased in 2018 with a new gin still as well as a new still for the whiskey production. The first release of a Shortcross single malt was a 5 year old in December 2021 which had been matured in Bordeaux red wines casks and finished in chinquapin oak. It was followed by Shortcross Rye & Malt in April 2022 and in 2023 a peated single malt as well as a malt and potstill distillery exclusive.

Titanic Distillers

Belfast, Co. Antrim, founded in 2022

titanicdistillers.com

In 1911 The Titanic was moved from the ship builder Harland & Wolff to the newly constructed Thompson Dry Dock for the final fitting. More than hundred years later a distillery has been constructed in the old pump-house. Equipped with three copper pot stills from Forsyth, the distillery was founded by Peter Lavery, Richard Irwin and Stephen Symington with the venture capital firm Norlin Ventures as the principal owner. The project has cost close to £8m and in March 2023 the distillery was opened to visitors and started distilling in early August. Whisky and vodka under the brand Titanic has been on the market for some time, distilled at the Great Northern Distillery in Dundalk.

The first distillation at Titanic Distillery in Belfast was in August 2023

Norway

Det Norske Brenneri
Grimstad, founded in 1952 (whisky since 2009)

eiktyrnewhisky.com

Founded in 1952 the company mainly produced wine from apples and other fruits. Whisky production started in 2009 and two Holstein stills are used for the distillation. In 2012, Audny, the first single malt produced in Norway was launched. Recent bottlings include Eiktyrne Fransk Eik Countdown 3 which appeared in November 2021.

Myken Distillery
Myken, founded in 2014

mykendestilleri.no

Situated on Myken, a group of islands in the Atlantic ocean, 32 kilometres from mainland Norway. Both peated and unpeated whisky is produced. The first launch of their single malt was in 2018. Recent expressions in 2023 include the 5 year old Sabotör #2 and two 4 year old expressions named Two Islands. One of them (Echoes of Smoke) was made from unpeated Myken malt that had matured in ex-islay casks and the other (Chorus of Smoke) from peated Myken malt maturing in the same type of casks.

Other distilleries in Norway

Anora (former Arcus)
Gjelleråsen, founded in 1996 (whisky since 2009)

arcus.no

Anora is the biggest supplier and producer of wine and spirits in Norway. The first whisky produced by the distillery was launched in 2013. Under the name Gjoleid, two whiskies made from malted barley and malted wheat were released. More and older expressions have followed and in 2021 the 10 year old Mesterens Utvalgte made from 85% malted barley and 15% malted wheat was released.

Aurora Spirit
Tromsö, founded in 2016

bivrost.com

At 69.39°N, Aurora is the northernmost distillery in the world. In the beginning the mash was bought from a brewery but since 2021 they do the mashing inhouse. Apart from single malt whisky, the owners also produce gin, vodka and aquavit. All their products are sold under the name Bivrost and until the first core bottling is released (around 2025) a number of limited expressions will occur. The most recent are the smoky Helheim and Vanaheim with a teak cask finish. In 2019 the owners embarked on an exciting project involving barley grown in the distillery´s Arctic surroundings.

Berentsen Distillery
Egersund, founded in 1895 (whisky since 2018)

berentsens.no

A producer of mineral water for more than 100 years, the company has started producing beer and spirits in recent years. By way of a £5m investment and using stills from Arnold Holstein in Germany the owners hope to become one of the biggest whisky producers in Norway. In March 2023 the inaugural 3 year old Vardberg Born single malt was released.

Feddie Ocean Distillery
Island of Fedje, founded in 2019

feddiedistillery.no

On Fedje, the most westerly, populated island in Norway, an already existing brewery was complemented by a distillery in 2019 and production of organic whisky started. Founded by Anne

Koppang, the distillery is owned by more than 100 investors. The bigger goal for the company is to contribute to the island by way of investments and inspiration. The 1000th cask was recently filled and the owners have plans to install a mash filter within the next couple of years. The first release of their whisky is expected in November 2024.

Klostergården Distillery
Tautra, founded in 2017

klostergardentautra.no

Equipped with two copper stills from Hoga in Portugal (1,000 and 600 litres repectively), this distillery is situated on the island of Tautra in the Trondheim fiord. There is also a brewery, hotel, restaurant and shop. No official bottling has yet been released.

Oss Craft Distillery
Flesland, founded in 2016

osscraft.no

Specialising in gin and other spirits made from herbs and botanicals, the distillery has already launched a range of spirits under the name Bareksten. In 2017, production of malt whisky began as well and in 2019 the distillery was expanded.

Poland

Piasecki Distillery
Stawiguda, founded in 1964 (whisky since 2014)

mazurskiemiody.pl/destylarnia/

A wide range of spirits are produced and recently also malt whisky. The 3 year old Langlander was released in 2017 and there is also Bee Keeper blended whisky.

Karczma Wrzos
Ustrón, whisky since 2019

karczma-wrzos.pl

A combination of a restaurant, brewery and distillery producing a variety of spirits including whisky. The 3 year old Glen Vistula, matured in virgin oak, was released in December 2022.

Millside Distillery
Debrzno, founded in 2023

millside.pl

What started in 2013 as a whisky shop (and later an independent bottler) has recently been complemented with a distillery. It is equipped with a 1,000 litre wash still, a 500 litre spirit still and a column still for making vodka. Golden Promise barley is used for the whisky and the distillery started production in late 2023.

Portugal

Venakki Distillery
Alpiarça, founded in 2012

portuguesewhisky.com

Founded by Jay Venakki the distillery produces a wide range of spirits including malt whisky. They are using Spanish grain for the whisky and every step of the production is carried out on site. In 2022 a larger still replaced the original 350 litre still. Their Woodwork single malts whiskies start their maturation in ex-bourbon barrels and are then finished in a variety of different Portuguese wine casks.

Slovakia

Nestville Distillery

Hniezdne, founded in 2008

nestville.sk

The distillery is owned by BGV and focuses mainly on production of ethanol and grain alcohol for industrial use. Whisky production started in 2008 and in 2012 the first Nestville whisky, a blend, was released as a three year old. Currently there are six different blends, all based on 90% grain made with a mash bill of malted barley, triticale and corn and 10% malt whisky. The first single malt was released in 2018 followed by a 6 year old in 2019.

Slovenia

Broken Bones Distillery

Ljubljana, founded in 2016

brokenbones.si

A family owned craft distillery producing gin and whisky. Two expressions of their single malt are available, un-peated and peated, and they are bottled without chill filtration and artificial colouring.

Spain

Distilerio Molino del Arco

Segovia, founded in 1959

dyc.es

Equipped with six copper pot stills, the distillery has the capacity for producing eight million litres of grain whisky and two million litres of malt whisky per year. The big seller when it comes to whiskies is a blend simply called DYC which is around 4 years old. It is supplemented by an 8 year old blend and also by DYC Pure Malt, a blend of malt from the distillery and from Scottish distilleries. A new range called Colección Maestros Destiladores was launched in 2018 with a 12 year old blend as the first release. This was followed by a 20 year old single barrel in 2022.

Other distilleries in Spain

Destilerias Liber

Padul, Granada, founded in 2001

destileriasliber.com

Apart from whisky, the distillery produces rum, marc, gin and vodka. Maturation takes place in PX sherry casks that have been previously used in a solera system for 20-30 years. Whiskies on the market include the 5 year old single malt called Embrujo de Granada and the 13 year old Liber. Starting 2020, a number of single casks aged 12-16 years have been released in small numbers.

Sweden

High Coast Distillery (former BOX Distillery)

Bjärtrå, founded in 2010

highcoastwhisky.se

Set in buildings from the 19th century, the distillery started production in November 2010 and in 2018 it was expanded. The equipment now consists of a semilauter mash tun with a capacity of 1,5 tonnes, ten stainless steel washbacks, two wash stills (3,800 litres) and two spirit stills (2,500 litres). This increased the capacity from 100,000 litres to 300,000. In 2014 an excellent visitor centre was opened which today attracts more than 10,000 visitors yearly. The distillery makes two types of whisky – fruity/unpeated and peated. With a slow distillation, the flavour of the spirit is also impacted by the effective condensation using 2-6ºC water from a nearby river. A fermentation time of 72-96 hours also affects the character. The first whisky was released in 2014 and three years later the first core expression, Dàlvve, was launched. This was replaced in 2019 by a new core range; Timmer, Hav, Älv and Berg. Limited releases in 2023 include Chevaleresk Estate, the third installment in the Harbours Collection (Lunde), Cinco II, matured in five types of sherry casks, Moncolica, matured in Asian oak and Doubles - matured in rum casks.

Mackmyra Svensk Whisky

Valbo, founded in 1999

mackmyra.com

Mackmyra´s first distillery was built in 1999 and in 2012 a new distillery was built a few miles from the first one. The construction is quite extraordinary and with its 37 metre structure, it is one of the tallest distilleries in the world. Since 2017 the old distillery serves as a "lab" where new spirits, for example gin, are created. Mackmyra whisky is based on two basic recipes, one which produces a fruity and elegant whisky, while the other is smokier. The first release was in 2006 and the distillery now has four core expressions; Svensk Ek, Brukswhisky, the peated Svensk Rök and MACK by Mackmyra. A range of limited editions called Moment was introduced in 2010 by the Master Blender, Angela D´Orazio who left the company in 2021. In spring 2023 a new range of limited releases named Small Batch was introduced. The first expression, Muddus, had been partially matured in casks that had previously contained wine from raspberries and cloudberries. Later in the year, Sweden´s oldest malt whisky (a 20 year old) was released. In June 2023 the distillery hosted the first Nordic Whisky Forum with participants from all five Nordic countries

Spirit of Hven

Hven, founded in 2007

hven.com

The distillery, situated on the island of Hven right between Sweden and Denmark, was founded by Henric Molin, a trained chemist. It is equipped with a 0,5 ton mash tun, six washbacks made of stainless steel, one wash still, one spirit still and a designated gin still. Apart from that, a unique wooden Coffey still has been installed to be used mainly for distillation of rye and corn. Part of the barley is malted on site using Swedish peat, sometimes mixed with seaweed and sea-grass, for drying. Apart from whisky, other products include rum made from sugar beet, vodka, gin and aquavit.

Their first whisky was the lightly peated Urania, released in 2012. Several limited releases have followed and the first core expression, Tycho´s Star, was released in 2015. New and innovative bottlings include Sweden´s first rye whisky, Hvenus Rye, and Mercurious, the first whisky in Sweden made predominantly (88%) from corn. The first Swedish blended whisky appeared in spring 2022.

Smögen Whisky

Hunnebostrand, founded in 2010

smogenwhisky.se

Founded by Pär Caldenby, the distillery is equipped with three washbacks, a 900 litre wash still and a 600 litre spirit still. An interesting addition to the equipment setup was made in 2018 when worm tubs were installed. Heavily peated malt is imported from Scotland and the aim is to produce an Islay-type of whisky. The first release from the distillery was the 3 year old Primör in 2014. This has over the years been followed by many limited releases, mostly single casks. In 2020 a wider release of a 6 year old "100 proof" from sherry seasoned quarter casks appeared. Recent expressions include the fourth edition of the 8 year old matured in PX casks, batch 3 of a bourbonmatured 9 year old and a 10 year old first fill oloroso single cask.

Agitator Whiskymakare
Arboga, founded in 2017

agitatorwhisky.se

The owners of this new distillery have chosen some rather unusual techniques in the production. Water is added during the milling and the fermented wash is split in half and distributed to the two pairs of stills. The stills operate under vacuum which is extremely rare in pot still whisky making. The distillery is experimenting with different kinds of grain apart from barley. The capacity is 500,000 litres of pure alcohol and the first distillation was made in 2018. The first two bottlings (in November 2021) were made from the unpeated recipe. The current core range consists of two single malts (peated and unpeated), one blend and the Blind Seal rye. Recent limited editions include a single malt that had matured in a combination of new American oak and barrels that had contained maple syrup, one matured in chestnut casks and, finally, a whisky that had been matured in a combination of PX and ex-Islay casks.

Other distilleries in Sweden

Bergslagens Destilleri
Örebro, founded in 2014 (whisky since 2019)

bergslagensdestilleri.se

A family-owned distillery equipped with one Holstein still and four washbacks producing a number of different spirits including malt whisky. In 2016 the company bought the whisky stock from the closed Grythyttans distillery and have since then released a vast number of expressions. The first bottling from their own production has not yet appeared.

Gammelstilla Whisky
Torsåker, founded in 2005

gammelstillawhisky.se

Built by the owners, the wash still has a capacity of 600 litres and the spirit still 300 litres and the annual capacity is 20,000 litres per year. The first, limited release for shareholders was in May 2017 with a general release in January 2018 of the 4 year old Jern. The most recent releases are "2023", Smedjan and the second batch of Jern.

Gotland Whisky
Romakloster, founded in 2011

gotlandwhisky.se, isleoflime.com

The distillery is equipped with a 1,600 litre wash still and a 900 litre spirit still. Local barley is ecologically grown and part of it is malted on site. Unpeated and peated whisky is produced and the capacity is 60,000 litres per year. The first release of Isle of Lime was in 2017 and the 13th edition (in November 2022) was the 7 year old Shareholder´s Edition, matured in a combination of bourbon and virgin American oak followed in June 2023 by the 6 year old, rum cask matured Salvorev.

Nordmarkens Destilleri
Årjäng, founded in 2014 (whisky since 2018)

nordmarkensdestilleri.se

In 2015 the owners produced newmake spirit at another Swedish distillery and following maturation at Nordmarken, Traukiol was released in March 2021. The first whisky distillation on their own premises, where gin and aqvavit are also produced, was in summer 2018 and both peated and unpeated malt spirit is distilled.

Norrtelje Brenneri
Norrtälje, founded in 2002 (whisky since 2009)

norrteljebrenneri.se

The production consists mainly of spirits from fruits and berries. Since 2009, a single malt whisky from ecologically grown barley is also produced. The first bottling was released in summer 2015 and the latest was a PX sherry matured in September 2022.

Tevsjö Destilleri
Järvsö, founded in 2012 (whisky since 2014)

tevsjodestilleri.se

The owners are primarily focused on distillation of aquavit and other white spirits but whisky production is also included. In December 2019 the first malt whisky and "bourbon" were released. At the moment they are in the midst of an expansion which will increase the capacity by ten.

High Coast Distillery with a stunning location in Northern Sweden

Switzerland

Luchs & Hase (formerly known as Käsers Schloss)

Elfingen, Aargau, founded in 2001

luchsundhase.ch

The first whisky from this distillery, founded by Ruedi Käser, reached the market in 2004. It was a single malt under the name Castle Hill. Since then, under the range of Ruedi´s sons Michael and Raphael, the range of malt whiskies has been expanded. In July 2023 the distillery changed its name to Luchs & Hase and the year before the entire range was revamped. Today there are ´180 Grad´, an 8 year old with a 2 year madeira finish, the smoky ´Rauchzeichen´, ´Fassgeschichten´ with a maturation in multiple casks and ´Best of Vintage´ where the latest was a 12 year old from new, toasted French oak.

Brauerei Locher

Appenzell, founded in 1886 (whisky since 1999)

saentismalt.com

Brauerei Locher is unique in using old beer casks for the maturation, sometimes with a finish in other types of casks. The core range consists of three expressions; Himmelberg, Dreifaltigkeit which is slightly peated having matured in toasted casks and Sigel which has matured in very small casks. There is also a range of limited bottlings with the fourth batch of Edition Genesis in 2023 being one of the latest.

Langatun Distillery
Langenthal, Bern, founded in 2007

langatun.ch

The distillery was built under the same roof as a brewery. A variety of casks are used for maturation and the single malts include Old Deer, Old Bear and the smoky Old Crow and Old Wolf. Other bottlings are Old Eagle rye, Old Mustang ”bourbon” and the organic Old Woodpecker. Recent limited releases include a 6 year old Langatun fully matured in a rioja cask.

Other distilleries in Switzerland

Etter Distillerie

Zug, founded in 1870 (whisky since 2007)

etter-distillerie.ch

The main produce from this distillery is eau de vie from various fruits and berries but whisky production commenced in 2007. The first release of Johnett Single Malt was made in 2010 and in June 2022 a smoky 10 year old appeared.

Hollen, Whisky Brennerei

Lauwil, Baselland, founded in 1999

single-malt.ch

The first Swiss whisky! In the beginning most bottlings were 4-5 years old but in 2009 the first 10 year old was released and there has also been a 12 year old from the distillery.

Humbel Brennerei

Stetten, Aargau, founded in 2004

humbel.ch

With a history going back to 1918, the distillery uses a wash from the brewery Unser Bier in Basel to produce their ValeReuss Whisky.

Lüthy, Bauernhofbrennerei

Muhen, Aargau, founded in 1997 (whisky since 2005)

brennerei-luethy.ch

The distillery is equipped with its own malting floor and the first single malt was Insel-Whisky, matured in Chardonnay casks and released in 2008. Several releases have since followed. Starting in 2010, the yearly bottling was given the name Herr Lüthy and the 13th release, matured in a combination of oloroso casks and first fill bourbon barrels, was followed by a 14th release in 2023. Whisky from rye, corn, rice and dinkel are also produced.

Macardo Distillery

Amlikon-Bissegg, Thurgau, founded in 2007

macardo.ch

Built on a former cheese factory, the distillery moved to new premises in 2020. The core single malt, without age statement, is bottled at 42%. One of the latest releases, in summer 2023, was The Life Cycle of a Cask, a cask strength expression maured in port wine casks.

Rugen Distillery

Interlaken, Bern, founded in 2010

rugenbraeu.ch

An old brewery which was later expanded with a distillery. The whisky brand name is Swiss Mountain and the core range consists of Classic, Double Barrel and the 7 year old Rock Label. A limited yet yearly expression is Ice Label where the latest edition (10 years old and released in 2023) received a second maturation of 6 years in the ice of Jungfraujoch at an altitude of 3,454 m.

Sempione Distillery

Brig-Glis, Valais, founded in 1976 (whisky since 2011)

sempione-distillery.ch

A family-owned distillery of fruits and berries but now focusing on whisky. Current single malts made from barley are Wallisky, Swiss Stone Eagle and the limited Reine des Reines while Sempione and 1815 – 3 Sterne also include dinkel and rye.

Stadelmann, Brennerei

Altbüron, Luzern, founded in 1932 (whisky since 2003)

schnapsbrennen.ch

The distillery is equipped with three Holstein-type stills and the first generally available bottling (a 3 year old) appeared in 2010. Small volumes of Luzerner Hinterländer Single Malt, up to 10 years old, have since been released.

Z´Graggen Distillerie

Lauerz, Schwyz, founded in 1948

zgraggen.ch

Focusing on spirits distilled from fruits and berries, the owners also produce gin, vodka and whisky. The distillery is quite large, with a combined production of 400,000 litres per year. There are three single malts in the range – the 3 year old Heimat, the 10 year old Bergsturz and Z´Graggen without age statement.

Zürcher, Spezialitätenbrennerei

Port, Bern, founded in 1954 (whisky from 2000)

lakeland-whisky.ch

The main focus of the distillery is specialising in various distillates of fruit, absinth and liqueur but a Lakeland single malt is also in the range. The lastest expression was a 9 year old with a full mauration in a port cask.

Wales

Penderyn Distillery

Penderyn, founded in 2000

penderyn.wales

When Penderyn began producing in 2000, it was the first Welsh distillery in more than a hundred years. A new type of still, developed by David Faraday for Penderyn, differs from the Scottish and Irish procedures in that the whole process from wash to new make takes place in one single still producing a spirit at 92% abv. In 2013, a second still (almost a replica of the first still) was commissioned and in 2014, two traditional pot stills, as well as their own mashing equipment was installed. In May 2021, the owners opened yet another distillery in Llandudno in north Wales. This is also equipped with the trademark Faraday still but production at the new distillery will be focused on production of peated single malt. The distillery has a visitor centre which the owners hope will attract 60,000 people yearly. In summer 2023, Copperworks Distillery, the third in the Penderyn group, opened in Swansea. This is the largest of the three bringing the combined capacity to 900,000 litres of alcohol. It is equipped with two Faraday stills and one pair of traditional pot stills. Penderyn has been influential advocating for a GI status (geographical indication) for Welsh whisky and this became fruitious in summer 2023. The first single malt was launched in 2004. The core range today is divided into two groups. Dragon consists of the Madeira finished Legend, Myth which is fully bourbon matured and Celt with a peated finish. The other range is Gold with Madeira, Peated, Portwood, Sherrywood and Rich Oak. The smoky notes from the distillery´s peated expressions comes from maturation in ex-Islay casks. A limited range is Icons of Wales where the 9th edition, Headliner, was released in 2022 and the distillery also releases single casks regularly. An exclusive to travel retail is Penderyn Faraday.

Other distilleries in Wales

Aber Falls Distillery

Abergwyngregyn, founded in 2017

aberfallsdistillery.com

In common with other distilleries, Aber Falls started producing and selling gin. Malt whisky, however, is also produced and in spring 2019, they distilled rye for the first time. Their inaugural, limited single malt was released in May 2021 followed by a core expression in August and a couple of limited Distiller´s Cut.

Dà Mhìle Distillery

Llandyssul, founded in 2013

damhile.co.uk

Focusing on gin and grain whisky, malt whisky is also produced in a wood fired still. Aged, organic single malts, distilled by Springbank back in the 1990s, have been offered for a while and in December 2019, their first organic single malt from own production was released - The Tarian Edition from a single first fill oloroso cask. It was followed in 2021 by Glynhynod and more releases have then appeared.

In The Welsh Wind

Tan-y-groes, founded in 2021

inthewelshwind.co.uk

Located on the west coast north of Cardigan, the distillery has already launched several bottlings of gin. Whisky made from local barley is maturing in the warehouses with a probable first release due in 2024.

A view from the visitor centre at Copperworks Distillery in Swansea - the third and newest in the Penderyn group of distilleries

North America

USA

Westland Distillery

Seattle, Washington, founded in 2011

westlanddistillery.com

Until 2012, Westland was a medium sized craft distillery where they brought in the wash from a nearby brewery and had the capacity of doing 60,000 litres of whiskey per year. During the summer of 2013 the owners moved to another location equipped with a 6,000 litre brewhouse, five 10,000 litre fermenters and two Vendome stills (wash still 5,670 litres and spirit still 4,540 litres). The distillery capacity is now 260,000 litres per year. In 2017, global spirits giant Remy Cointreau bought Westland Distillery. Sine the start the distillery has been focusing on local barley varieties and also local peat.

The flagship single malt (first released in 2013) is Westland American Single Malt Whiskey is based on a 6-malt grain bill and has matured for a minimum of 40 months in a combination of five different types of casks. There is also the Heritage Collection with American Oak, Sherry Oak and Peated. A limited range called Outpost has been introduced in order to highlight the owners´ interest in exploring new frontiers of whiskey making. Currently there are three expressions; Garryana where the native garry oak has been used for the maturation, Colere which has been made using the local six-row winter barley Alba and Solum (released in March 2023) which gets its character from local peat. A number of limited expressions, some available only at the distillery, are also released on a regular basis.

Balcones Distillery

Waco, Texas, founded in 2008

balconesdistilling.com

Originally founded by Chip Tate who left the company in 2014. The same year, another four, small stills were installed. The big step though, was a completely new distillery which was built 5 blocks from the old site. Distillation started in February 2016 and the official opening was in April. The new distillery is equipped with two pairs of stills and five fermenters with a capacity of 350,000 litres per year. In November 2022 it was announced that Diageo had bought the company for an undisclosed sum. All of Balcones´ whisky is mashed, fermented and distilled on site and they were the first to use Hopi blue corn for distillation. The core range currently consists of seven expressions; Texas Single Malt, Lineage Single Malt, Baby Blue and True Blue (both made from blue corn, Texas Rye 100 Proof, Pot Still Bourbon and the smoky Brimstone. Limited but yearly expressions include Rumble Cask Reserve, Single Malt rum finish, True Blue Cask Strength, Blue Corn Bourbon, Mirador Single Malt, Peated Single Malt and Wheated Bourbon. Special releases during 2022 include the second batch of Tres Hombres made from blue corn, barley and rye and the High Plains single malt.

Stranahans Whiskey Distillery

Denver, Colorado, founded in 2003

stranahans.com

Founded by Jess Graber and George Stranahan, the distillery was bought by New York based Proximo Spirits in 2010. Rob Dietrich took over as head distiller in 2011 but left the company in 2019. His succesor Owen Martin began revamping part of the range. The Classic expression was in spring 2021 replaced by Original made up of older whiskies. Before that, in 2020, the four year old Blue Peak, matured using a solera system, was launched together with the oldest expression so far from the distillery - the 10 year old Mountain Angel fully matured in new American oak. In spring 2021 a new, limited range called Experimental Series was launched. From the old range there is still Diamond Peak, a vatting of casks that are around 4 years old, a Single Barrel and Sherry cask. In May

2022 the Añejo Cask was released where the whiskey had received a second maturation in tequila casks.

Hood River Distillers

Hood River, Oregon, 1934

hrdspirits.com

Since the foundation, the company acts as importer, distiller, producer and bottler of all kinds of spirits. Some of the products are distilled in-house while others are sourced. The role in the single malt segment came through buying Clear Creek Distillery in 2014. Founded by Steve McCarthy in 1985, Clear Creek Distillery was the first to produce single malt whiskey in the USA. The only single malt whiskey produced by the company is the peated McCarthy´s Oregon Single Malt available both as a 3 year old and as a 6 year old. There is also a 6 year old finished in PX casks. In December 2017, Clear Creek closed their distillery in Portland and moved to Hood River. Steve McCarthy, suffering from Parkinson´s Disease, died in January 2023 at the age of 79.

Hudson Whiskey (Tuthilltown Distillery)

Gardiner, New York, founded in 2003

hudsonwhiskey.com

The distillery was founded by Ralph Erenzo and Brian Lee. In 2010, William Grant & Sons aquired the Hudson Whiskey brand while the founders still owned the distillery. In spring 2017, William Grant followed up the deal by buying the entire company. Launched in 2006, the brand has undergone a complete revamp in late 2020 and it looks as though their single malt has been discontinued, at least for the time being. In an attempt to highlight the fact that the four whiskies in the new core range are made in New York, they are now called Bright Lights Big Bourbon (a straight bourbon), Do The Rye Thing (a straight rye), Short Stack (rye finished in maple syrup casks) and Back Room Deal (a rye finished in barrels that had previously contained peated Scotch). There is also the Four Part Harmony made from a mash bill of 60% corn, 15% rye, 15% wheat and 10% malted barley.

Copper Fox Distillery

Sperryville, Virginia, founded in 2000

copperfoxdistillery.com

Founded in 2000 by Rick Wasmund, the distillery moved to another site in 2006 and in November 2016, he opened up a second distillery in Williamsburg. He is currently planning for a third distillery. Wasmund does his own floor malting of barley and it is dried using smoke from selected fruitwood (apple and cherry). After mashing, fermentation and distillation, the spirit is filled into oak barrels, together with hand chipped and toasted chips of apple wood and oak wood. In 2019 the entire range was rebranded and the core single malt expressions are the signature Original Single Malt, Peachwood Single Malt, Apple Brandy Barrel Finish and Port Style Barrel Finish. There also various bourbon and rye expressions as well as a blend (corn, barley, oats) that has been matured using chestnut chips.

St. George Distillery

Alameda, California, founded in 1982

stgeorgespirits.com

The distillery is situated in a hangar at Alameda Point, the old naval air station at San Fransisco Bay. It was founded by Jörg Rupf, who became one of the forerunners when it comes to craft distilling in America. In 1996, Lance Winters joined him and today he is Distiller, as well as co-owner. In 2022 Lance was introduced in the Whisky Hall of Fame. In 2005, the two were joined by Dave Smith who now has the sole responsibility for the whisky production. The main produce is based on eau-de-vie and a vodka named Hangar One. Whiskey production was picked up in 1996 and the first single malt appeared on the market in 1999. St. George Single Malt, based on a highly complex mashbill, used to be sold as a three year old but nowadays comes to the market as a blend of whiskeys aged from 5 to 22 years! The latest release is Lot 23 in autumn 2023. In October 2022 a special 40th anniversary bottle was released. Introduced a few years ago there is also the single malt Baller which has been matured in a combination of ex-bourbon barrels and French oak wine casks.

Westward Whiskey (House Spirits Distillery)

Portland, Oregon, founded in 2004

westwardwhiskey.com

In 2015, Christian Krogstad and Matt Mount moved their distillery a few blocks to bigger premises. That was also the year when fermentation of the wash was brought in-house, having relied on local breweries before.In the early days, the main products for House Spirits used to be Aviation Gin and Krogstad Aquavit but with their new equipment they drastically increased whiskey capacity. In 2018, Diageo´s "spirits accelerator" Distill Ventures acquired a minority stake in the brand which helped expand the capacity even further. The first three whiskies were released in 2009 and in 2012 it was time for the first, widely available single malt under the name of Westward American Single Malt. In autumn 2020 the brand was revamped and the core range now consists of American Single Malt, a cask strength version of the same, American Single Malt Stout Cask and American Single Malt Pinot Noir Cask. Limited expressions are released regularly with the Grand Cru Sauternes Cask in February 2023 being one of the latest.

Corsair Distillery

Nashville, Tennessee, founded in 2008

corsairdistillery.com

The two founders of Corsair, Darek Bell and Andrew Webber, first opened up a distillery in Bowling Green, Kentucky and two years later, another one in Nashville, Tennessee (followed by a second one in Nashville a few years later). The Bowling Green operation was closed in 2019 but a much larger distillery is currently being built in Ashland City which will have a production capacity of 24,000 barrels per year. Corsair Distillery has always had a wide range of whiskies often made from experimental grains. This changed in 2020 when the owners settled for both a new design of the bottles and a more comprehensive range. This now consists of Triple Smoke, a single malt smoked using cherry wood, beech wood and peat, Dark Rye made from malted rye and chocolate rye and two gins - barreled and unbarreled. Once in a while however, limited releases appear.

Kings County Distillery

Brooklyn, New York, founded in 2010

kingscountydistillery.com

Founded by Colin Spoelman and David Haskell, this is the oldest distillery in Brooklyn. The wash is fermented in open-top, wooden fermenters and they practise double distillation in copper pot stills. The distillery is primarily focused on bourbon and rye but a single malt (60% unpeated and 40% peated) was released already in 2016 and it is still in the range as a limited yet yearly release. In Spring 2022 a 2 year old Irish style, triple distilled whiskey was released.

Virginia Distillery

Lovingston, Virginia, 2008 (production started 2015)

vadistillery.com

The whole idea for this distillery was conceived in 2007. The copper pot stills arrived from Turkey in 2008 but following several changes in ownership and struggling with the financing, the first distillation didn´t take place until November 2015. The distillery is equipped with a 3.75 ton mash tun, 8 washbacks, a 10,000 litre wash still and a 7,000 litre spirit still. Their first single malt from own production was a very limited release of Prelude: Courage & Conviction in 2019 followed by a general launch in 2020. This is now the flagship expression made up of 50% matured in bourbon casks and 25% each matured in ex-sherry and ex.wine (cuvée) casks respectively. In March 2021, another three versions representing

Steve McCarthy, creator of the first single malt whiskey from USA released in 1999, passed away in January 2023

each of the individual maturation styles were launched. Limited releases include a single malt that has been finished in barrels that held small-batch coffee.

Long Island Spirits

Baiting Hollow, New York, founded in 2007

lispirits.com

Long Island Spirits, founded by Rich Stabile, is the first distillery on the island since the 1800s. The starting point for The Pine Barrens Whisky, the first single malt from the distillery, is a finished ale with hops and all. The whisky was first released in 2012 and was followed in 2018 by a bottle-in-bond version (at least four years old) and later by an expression that is cherrywood smoked. The whiskey range also includes Rough Rider and Field & Sound bourbon and rye.

Great Wagon Road Distilling Co.

Charlotte, North Carolina, founded in 2014

gwrdistilling.com

The distillery, founded by Ollie Mulligan, started with a 15 litre still but moved to a new location in 2020 and is now equipped with a 3,000 litres Kothe still and in 2021 a second still was installed. The mash comes from a neighbouring brewery and the fermentation is made in-house. The first batch of the Rua Single Malt was launched in 2015 and was later complemented by Rua Gold. A limited 4 year old edition named The Caledonia Edition was released in February 2023.

Hamilton Distillers

Tucson, Arizona, founded in 2011

whiskeydelbac.com

Stephen Paul came up with the idea of drying barley over mesquite, instead of peat. He started his distillery using a 40 gallon still but since 2014, a 500 gallon still is in place. In 2015, new malting equipment was installed which made it possible to malt the barley in 5,000 lbs batches, instead of the previous 70 lbs! The first bottlings of Del Bac single malt appeared in 2013 and they now have four expressions – aged Mesquite smoked (Dorado), aged unsmoked (Classic), unaged Mesquite smoked (Old Pueblo) and aged unsmoked, bottled at cask strength (Distiller´s Cut) which appears in different batches throughout the year. Three limited but annual expressions are Frontera (PX finish), Normandie (calvados finished) and Ode to Islay (heavily mesquited).

Deerhammer Distilling Company

Buena Vista, Colorado, founded in 2010

deerhammer.com

The location of the distillery at an altitude of 2,500 metres with drastic temperature fluctuations and virtually no humidity, have a huge impact on the maturation of the spirit. Owners Lenny and Amy Eckstein released their first single malt, aged for only 9 months, in 2012. More and older batches (2 to 3 years) of their Deerhammer Single Malt have followed including several different finishes. In autumn 2019, the first edition of a new series, Progeny, was released. The second release was the 5 year old single malt Cask Savant made from a hopped beer from the local brewery Crooked Stave and the third, in June 2022, was the 4 year old Honeycomber finished in ex-mead casks from Redstone Meadery.

Hillrock Estate Distillery

Ancram, New York, founded in 2011

hillrockdistillery.com

Originally equipped with a 250 gallon Vendome pot still and five fermentation tanks, the distillery was substantially expanded in 2019 with a new pot still, a lauter mash tun and more fermentation tanks which tripled the capacity. The owners also floor malt their own barley. The first release from the distillery was in 2012, the Solera Aged Bourbon. Today, the range has been expanded with

a Single Malt and a Double Cask Rye. Over the years, limited bottlings have appeared such as the peated Single Malt, a Napa cabernet cask finished bourbon and an 8 year old single malt rye.

Santa Fe Spirits

Santa Fe, New Mexico, founded in 2010

santafespirits.com

Colin Keegan uses copper stills from Christian Carl in Germany for his distillation and the whiskey gets a hint of smokiness from mesquite. The first product, Silver Coyote released in 2011, was an unaged malt whiskey. The first release of an aged single malt whiskey, Colkegan, was in 2013. Since then, the range has been expanded to include also a version finished in apple brandy casks, a four year old finished for one year in PX sherry casks, a cask strength and, added in October 2022, Colkegan Unsmoked.

Copperworks Distilling Company

Seattle, Washington, founded in 2013

copperworksdistilling.com

The distillery is currently equipped with two, large copper pot stills for the whiskey production, one smaller pot still for the gin and one column still. However, they are planning for a major expansion/relocation in the near future which entails increasing production substantially and adding mutiple new locations. The first distillation was in 2014 and the first batch of the single malt was launched in 2016. One of the latest releases, in November 2022, was a 4 year old pale malt whiskey that had matured in American oak and then finished in Jamaican rum casks.

Rogue Ales & Spirits

Newport, Oregon, founded in 2009

rogue.com

The company consists of one brewery, two combined brewery/pubs and two distillery pubs scattered over Oregon, Washington and California. The main business is producing Rogue Ales but apart from whiskey - rum and gin are also distilled. The first malt whiskey, Dead Guy Whiskey, was launched in 2009 and is still in the core range. Later additions are three expressions that have been finished in stout casks, wine casks and cherry casks respectively. Another, limited, release is the very ligthly smoked Morimoto single malt.

Golden Moon Distillery

Golden, Colorado, founded in 2008

goldenmoondistillery.com

Distillery veteran Stephen Gould has built a distillery equipped with six custom designed pot stills as well as four antique stills. Working also as an independent bottler the products from the company are a combination of sourced whiskey (mainly bourbon) and whiskies produced in-house. At least 15 different kinds of spirits are distilled and three single malts whiskies have so far been released, the latest being Principium and Triple - the latter being a triple distilled, Irish-style whiskey.

High West Distillery

Park City, Utah, founded in 2007

highwest.com

The founder, David Perkins, made a name for himself mainly as a blender of sourced rye whiskies. None of these were distilled at High West distillery. In 2015, they opened another distillery at Blue Sky Ranch in Wanship, Utah and in 2016 Constellation Brands bought High West Distillery for a sum of $160 million. Even though they consider themselves blenders first and foremost, the 2018 versions of Rendezvous Rye and Double Rye, were the first expressions which included whiskey from their own production. The distillery is highly focused on rye and bourbon but in December 2019, the first single malt made entirely by themselves and named High Country, was released.

FEW Spirits

Evanston, Illinois, founded in 2010

fewspirits.com

Former attorney Paul Hletko started this distillery in Evanston, a suburb to Chicago in 2010. It is equipped with three stills; a Vendome column still and two Kothe hybrid stills. The first single malt (preceeded by both bourbon and rye) was released in 2015. Apart from a Single Malt smoked with cherry wood, the core range consists of a variety of bourbon and rye.

Sons of Liberty Spirits Co.

South Kingstown, Rhode Island, founded in 2010

solspirits.com

The distillery is equipped with a stainless steel mash tun, stainless steel, open top fermenters and a combined pot and column still from Vendome and is first and foremost a whiskey distillery. The two core expressions are Uprising American Whiskey made from a stout beer and Battle Cry made from a Belgian style ale. Both versions are also released as 5 to 6 year old single barrels and at a higher abv.

Talnua Distillery

Arvada, Colorado, founded in 2017

talnua.com

With a career in the oil- and gas business, Patrick and Meagan Miller started the distillery with the aim to produce single pot still whiskey in the traditional Irish style. That means, in their case, using a mashbill of 50% unmalted and 50% malted barley as well as practising triple distillation. Their single pot still range, aged 3 years or more, is currently made up of Peated Cask, Continuum, Bourbon Cask & Stave and Virgin White Oak. There is also Heritage which is a blend of single pot still and grain. Limited releases include a Bottled-in-Bond in July 2022 and, in March 2023, this year's limited release of Olde Saint's Keep, a single pot still finished in former madeira and cognac barrels, was released.

Oak & Grist Distilling Co.

Black Mountain, North Carolina, founded in 2015

oakandgrist.com

The owners are focusing on whiskey made from locally grown and malted barley. The first couple of years they relied on single barrel releases aged up to 3 years. Since 2021, the expressions are blended from several barrels with release #3 launched in October 2022. Experiments with smoked whiskies (hickory and peach wood) started a couple of years ago and are still maturing. Two of the founders are father and son Ed and Russell Dodson. Ed, with a 40 year plus track record in the Scotch whisky industry, was the distillery manager of Glen Moray until 2005. Another co-founder is William Goldberg who is also the head distiller.

Other distilleries in USA

2nd Street Distilling Co

Walla Walla, Washington, founded in 2011

2ndstreetdistillingco.com

Formerly known as River Sands Distillery. Gin and vodka are produced, as well as a single malt – R J Callaghan. In 2016 a 100% malted rye, Reser's Rye, was also released.

10th Street Distillery

San José, California, founded in 2017

10thstreetdistillery.com

Inspired by a trip to Islay, Virag Saksena and Vishal Gauri went on to build their own distillery. So far they have released Peated Single Malt, STR Single Malt, Distiller's Cut and a Port Malt and in spring 2022 they moved to a new location in San José.

Acre Distilling

Fort Worth, Texas, founded in 2015

acredistilling.com

The distillery produces gin, vodka, bourbon, rye and different versions of single malt. The core expression, Texas Single Malt, is complemented by Smoked Single Malt and Matthew McD's Straight Malt Whiskey - a blend of malted and unmalted barley.

Alley 6 Craft Distillery

Healdsburg, California, founded in 2014

alley6.com

A small craft distillery in Sonoma county with rye whiskey as the main product. The first bottles were released in summer 2015 followed by a single malt in May 2016. The owners are experimenting with a range of different barley varieties.

Amalga Distillery

Juneau, Alaska, founded in 2017

amalgadistillery.com

The distillery uses a 250 gallon pot still from Vendome and they are also floor malting their own barley, some of it grown in Alaska. The first core single malt was released in August 2020 with their Flagship Batch 11 released in February 2023.

Andalusia Whiskey

Blanco, Texas, founded in 2016

andalusiawhiskey.com

Focusing on whiskey production, the spirit is double-distilled in a 250 gallon pot still and the first single malts were released in 2016. Core expressions are the mesquite-smoked Stryker, the lightly peated Revenant Oak and Triple-Distilled.

Arizona Distilling Company

Tempe Arizona, founded in 2012

azdistilling.com

The first release from the distillery was Copper City bourbon followed by Desert Durum made from wheat, Humphrey's, a single malt first released in 2014 and Copper City Straight Rye. The distillery is one of few using open top fermenters.

ASW Distillery

Atlanta, Georgia, founded in 2016

aswdistillery.com

Equipped with two traditional Scottish copper pot stills the distillery also has three tasting rooms in Atlanta. Among the latest malt releases are Duality, made from 50% malted barley and 50% malted rye, the heavily peated Tire Fire, the triple distilled Druid Hill, Maris Otter and Burns Night Single Malt.

Atelier Vie Distillery

New Orleans, Louisiana, founded in 2012

ateliervie.com

The first product, released in 2013, was Riz - a whiskey made from Louisiana rice. Owner Jedd Haas then went on to distil also malt whiskey from barley. Louisiana Single Malt was first released in 2019 with a 5 year old cask strength appearing in January 2023.

Axe and the Oak Distillery

Colorado Springs, Colorado, founded in 2013

axeandtheoak.com

A combination of a distillery, bar and restaurant, Axe and the Oak have so far released both bourbon and rye whiskey but there is also single malt maturing.

Bellemara Distillery

Hillsborough, New Jersey, 2021

bellemaradistillery.com

Founded by Camden Winkelstein, who spent a year at Heriot-Watt University in Edinburgh earning his masters in brewing and distilling, and his wife Christina Lee. The distillery is very much focused on single malt whisky, which has yet to be released, but gin and single malt aquavit has already been launched.

Bendt Distilling Co. (former Witherspoon Distillery)

Lewisville, Texas, founded in 2011

bendtdistillingco.com

Originally named Wiherspoon, the distillery recently inroduced a new core range with Staright Malt, Straight Bourbon and Straight Wheat. There is also the blended whiskey Bendt No. 5.

Bogue Sound Distillery

Bogue, North Carolina, founded in 2018

boguesounddistillery.com

The distillery is equipped with a 500-gallon still and produces gin, vodka, rye and bourbon. A single malt, to be released under the John A.P. Conoley brand, is currently maturing.

Breckenridge Distillery

Breckenridge, Colorado, founded in 2008

breckenridgedistillery.com

Situated at a an altitude of 2,900 metres and claiming to be the world´s highest distillery, Breckenridge produces mainly bourbon and not least many cask finished versions. There is also the limited Dark Arts single malt, aged up to 10 years.

Breuckelen Distilling

Brooklyn, New York, founded in 2010

brkdistilling.com

The company focused first on gin and whiskies made from rye, corn and wheat. When locally malted barley became available the range was expanded and the first single malt, the 6 year old Brownstone Malt Whiskey, was released in 2020.

Brickway Brewery & Distillery (former Borgata)

Omaha, Nebraska, founded in 2013

drinkbrickway.com

The owners are focused on single malt whiskey but they also produce smaller amounts of bourbon and rye as well as gin and rum. Their first whisky appeared in 2014 and one of the most recent releases was a 5 year old bottled-in-bond single malt in 2022 with the next release scheduled for November 2023.

Brother Justus

Minneapolis, Minnesota, founded in 2014

brotherjustus.com

Phil Steger and his team spent the first years quitely working away in an underground distillery to find a perfect recipe for a single malt using local peat from Minnesota. The unusual approach is that they let the whisky rest in barrels with peat instead of burning it to dry the barley. The first whiskies, including Cold-Peated Whiskey, appeared in late 2020. The distillery has now moved onto street level and is combined with a bar and restaurang.

Bull Run Distillery

Portland, Oregon, founded in 2011

bullrundistillery.com

The distillery is focused on 100% Oregon single malt whiskey although aged bourbons as well as brandy and gin are also in the range. The first release of a single malt was a 4 year old in 2016. The current expression is 7 years old and there is also a recent, limited 9 year old available.

Caiseal Beer & Spirits Company

Hampton, Virginia, founded in 2017

caiseal.com

A combined brewery and distillery where the brewery produces the mash for various distilled products. The first spirits included vodka, gin and bourbon and was followed in 2019 by a single malt. Since then a peated version has also been added to the range.

Cedar Ridge Distillery

Swisher, Iowa, founded in 2003

cedarridgewhiskey.com

The first single malt was launched in 2013 and the core expression is The Quintessential. A special version named Murphy Quint has been finished in a first fill sherry cask. Other spirits in the range include both bourbon, malted rye and malted wheat.

Charbay Winery & Distillery

St. Helena, California, founded in 1983

charbay.com

With a wide range of products such as wine, vodka, grappa, pastis, rum and port, the owners decided in 1999 to also enter in to whiskey making. They were pioneers distilling whiskey from hopped beer and over the years several releases have been made including Double-Barrel Release, Doubled & Twisted, Pilsner Whiskey and Charbay R5.

Chattanooga Whiskey

Chattanooga, Tennessee, founded in 2015

chattanoogawhiskey.com

The distillery, which moved to larger premises in 2017, is mainly focused on bourbon but a few whiskies made from malted barley have appeared. One of the latest, made from roasted, toasted and caramel malt, had been finished in cabernet casks.

Coppersea Distilling

New Paltz, New York, founded in 2011

coppersea.com

A distillery with malting on site, open-top wooden washbacks and direct-fired alembic stills. One thing that makes Coppersea stand out is that they don´t dry the malted barley but instead produce a mash from green, unkilned barley. Big Angus is made from 100% green barley and in the range there is also bourbon and rye.

Cotherman Distilling

Dunedin, Florida, founded in 2015

cothermandistilling.com

All the whiskies are made from 100% malted barley. First launched in July 2016 and several batches have followed since. Apart from whiskey – gin, rum and vodka are also produced.

Current Spirits

Elmsford, New York, founded in 2019

currentspirits.com

Scott Vaccaro opened up a distillery next door to his brewery focusing on gin, vodka, rye and many versions of bourbon. In 2020 the first cask strength version of their single malt was released and in 2023, Perpetual single malt was released - matured in a combination of bourbon, rye and sherry casks.

Cut Spike Distillery (formerly Solas Distillery)

La Vista, Nebraska, founded in 2009

cutspike.com

In 2010 single malt whiskey was distilled and the first bottles were launched in 2013. New batches of the whiskey have then appeared regularly and various special editions include single malt aged in cabernet barrels as well as finished in maple syrup barrels, oatmeal stout barrels and PX sherry casks. Peated production commenced in January 2020.

Dampfwerk Distillery, The

St. Louis Park, Minnesota, founded in 2016

thedampfwerk.com

The distillery offers fruit brandies and herbal liqueurs as well as gin and whiskey. The first single malt (4 years old), made from pale ale and chocolate malt and finished in red wine barrels, was launched in January 2021 and more batches have followed.

Dark Island Spirits

Alexandria Bay, New York, founded in 2015

darkislandspirits.com

By way of a device inside the casks, the owners are maturing their spirits with the help of soundwaves created by different genres of music. A variety of different spirits have been released including single malt under the name Eleanor Glen. The latest versions are Phantom Piper, Highlander and the peated 1000 Islays.

Dirty Water Distillery

Plymouth, Massachusetts, founded in 2013

dirtywaterdistillery.com

Starting with vodka, gin and rum, the distillery expanded into malt whiskey in 2015. The first release of Bachelor Single Malt, came in 2016 and the most recent release in November 2022 was Night Shift Santilli IPA made from a beer wash. The distillery moved to larger premises in autumn 2022.

Distillery 291

Colorado Springs, Colorado, founded in 2011

distillery291.com

The core range consists of several ryes, bourbons and American whiskies. In an experimental range there have also been two single malts made from 100% barley. In February 2021, the distillery moved to a new facility and doubled their capacity.

Dogfish Head Distillery

Milton, Delaware, founded in 2002

dogfish.com

Opened up as a brewery, the company later expanded into being a distillery as well. Two copper stills and a copper column are used to make rum, gin and vodka. On the malt whiskey side there are Straight Whiskey, Let´s Get Lost and a number of different finishes.

Door County Distillery

Sturgeon Bay, Wisconsin, founded in 2011

doorcountydistillery.com

Originally a winery which was later complemented by a distillery. Gin, vodka and brandy are the main products but they also make single malt whiskey. The first Door County Single Malt was released in 2013 and there are also bourbon and rye in the range.

Dorwood Distillery

Buellton, California, founded in 2014

dorwood-distillery.com

The distillery dries the barley using mesquite smoke and the triple distillation takes place in two reflux stills. The unaged White Hawk Malt Whiskey has so far been released.

DownSlope Distilling

Centennial, Colorado, founded in 2008

downslopedistilling.com

Made from 65% malted barley and 35% rye, Double-Diamond Whiskey was released in 2010 and it is still the core expression. It was followed by a number of varieties of bourbon, rye and a 4 year old single malt matured in a combination of four different casks.

Dry Diggings Distillery

El Dorado Hills, California, founded in 2012

drydiggings.com

In 2015, Dry Diggings bought Amador Distillery and has since then produced spirits under both brand names. Together with gin, vodka, rye and bourbon there is also one single malt - Bodie 5 Dog.

Dry Fly Distilling

Spokane, Washington, founded in 2007

dryflydistilling.com

Several types of whisky have been released including the single pot still O´Danaghers made from malted and unmalted barley. The distillery moved to a new location in 2021.

Eastern Kille Distillery (former Gray Skies Distillery)

Grand Rapids, Michigan, founded in 2014

easternkille.com

Bourbon and rye are produced and the first bottle of Michigan Single Malt appeared in 2016 while the latest batch (six years old) appeared in 2022. The distillery will be moving to a new location in Rockford in autumn 2023, just north of Grand Rapids.

Edgefield Distillery

Troutdale, Oregon, founded in1998

mcmenamins.com

Part of the McMenamin chain of pubs and hotels in Oregon and Washington. Some of the pubs have adjoining microbreweries and the chain's first distillery opened in 1998 in Troutdale with Hogshead Whiskey being bottled in 2002. Limited releases occur every year on St Patrick´s Day under the name The Devil´s Bit with the 2023 edition being a 5 year old single malt distilled from Oregon barley and matured in Oregon oak. A second distillery was opened in 2011 at Cornelius Pass Roadhouse in Hillsboro.

Eleven Wells Distillery

St. Paul, Minnesota, founded in 2013

11wells.com

Equipped with open-top fermenters and two stills, whiskey is the main product and the first two releases, aged bourbon and rye, were released in 2014 followed by a wheat whiskey in 2015 and finally a subtly smoky single malt made from malted barley.

Elgin Distillery (Arizona Craft Beverage)

Elgin, Arizona, founded in 2015

azwhiskies.com

What started out as a winery founded in 1982 by Bill Letarte, was later expanded to also a brewery and a distillery. Gin, rum, bourbon, rye and a 5 year old malt whiskey from 100% barley are produced.

Elk Fence Distillery

Santa Rosa, California founded in 2020

elkfencedistillery.com

The first craft distillery in Santa Rosa, founded by Scott Woodson and Gail Coppinger. Equipped with two copper Trident stills from maine, the distillery produces vodka, gin, rum and a single malt whisky named The Briny Deep.

Fainting Goat Spirits

Greensboro, North Carolina, founded in 2015

faintinggoatspirits.com

First spirits on the shelves were gin and vodka. In 2017 Fisher's single malt whiskey was launched as a 2 year old and today there is also a Distiller's Reserve with the latest being a madeira finish.

Glacier Distilling

Coram, Montana, founded in 2010

glacierdistilling.com

The distillery produces a wide range of all kinds of spirits. On the malt whiskey side there is Bearproof flavoured with huckleberry juice, Wheatfish which is a malted wheat whiskey and Two Med made from an ale from Great Northern Brewing Company.

Grand Teton Distillery

Driggs, Idaho, founded in 2012

tetondistillery.com

The first and foremost product from the distillery is vodka made from potatoes. Various whiskies are also produced, including a 4 year old single malt matured in ex-bourbon barrels and finished in Jackson Hole Winery red wine barrels.

Great Lakes Distillery

Milwaukee, Wisconsin, founded in 2004

greatlakesdistillery.com

Included in the extensive range of various spirits are bourbon, rye and malt whiskey. The Kinnickinnic blend has been around for a few years and in 2019 the limited 10 year old Menomonee single malt was launched.

Herman Marshall Whiskey

Wylie, Texas, founded in 2008

hmwhiskey.com

The first products in the Herman Marshall range were launched in 2013 and were at that time produced at Dallas Distilleries in Garland. Late 2021 the brand was sold to Dry County Distilleries who moved the production in 2022 to Wylie. Bourbon, rye and single malt are in the range. Limited releases include the 7 months old Temptress and the 22 months old Divine.

Hewn Spirits

Pipersville, Pennsylvania, founded in 2013

hewnspirits.com

Apart from rum, gin and vodka the distillery produces bourbon, rye and the Reclamation American Single Malt Whiskey. After maturing the malt whiskey in barrels for 1-4 months, it receives a second maturation in stainless steel vats where staves of reclaimed chestnut, hickory and oak wood add to the profile.

High Peaks Distilling

Lake George, New York, founded in 2016

highpeakdistilling.com

High Peaks obtains all of their fermented wash from the Adirondack Brewery which is then distilled and matured on site. The first release in spring 2018 was the peated Cloudsplitter Single Malt which was later followed by bourbon and rye.

Highside Distilling

Bainbridge Island, Washington, founded in 2018

highsidedistilling.com

Several expressions of gin and amaro had been released when production of single malt whiskey started in 2019. The first version, 3 years old, appeared in January 2023.

Hinterhaus Distilling

Arnold, California, founded in 2020

hinterhausdistilling.com

This family distillery in the Sierra Nevada has released gin, vodka and sourced bourbon and rye. Rye and single malt from their own production are currently maturing in the warehouse.

Hogback Distillery

Boulder, Colorado, founded in 2017

hogbackdistillery.com

The distillery founder and owner is the Scotsman Graeme Wallace who moved to Colorado. The focus is to do a Scottish style single malt made from malt from Gleneagles Maltings, some of it peated. The first single malt (peated) was released in September 2020 and this was followed by limited releases in the Wallace Collection.

Hollerhorn Distilling

Naples, New York, founded in 2018

hollerhorn.com

Hollerhorn started off focusing on spirits made from maple syrup but eventually expanded into whiskey made from malted barley. Singe malt whiskey as well as whiskey infused with habanero has been released and in March 2022 a Malt in Motion Heavily Peated Single Malt was launched. The distillery burned to the ground in May 2022 but was rebuilt and opened again in summer 2023.

Idlewild Spirits

Winter Park, Colorado, founded in 2015

idlewildspirits.com

Production of the first batch of malt whiskey was in June 2016. Fermentation and distillation being on the grain add to the over-all character. Their Colorado Single Malt was first released in 2018.

Immortal Spirits

Medford, Oregon, founded in 2008

immortalspirits.com

A wide range of spirits are produced including gin, rum, vodka and limoncello. The only whiskey made from barley (unmalted) is the 5 year old Single Grain. The Single Barrel range of selected casks has sometimes been represented by a single malt.

Ironton Distillery

Denver, Colorado, founded in 2018

irontondistillery.com

The distillery produces vodka, gin, genever, whiskey and rum. The first whiskies (bourbon, rye and malt) were all released in 2019. The malt is made from malted barley smoked with beech and a straight version was released in March 2022.

Jersey Spirits Distilling Co

Fairfield, New Jersey, founded in 2015

jerseyspirits.com

Apart from gin and vodka, the owners have two bourbon varieties. The first single malt distillation was in 2018 and in 2020, Apple Wood Smoked and Cherry Wood Smoked were released. The latest addition (November 2022) was the 5 year old Celtic Riviera.

John Emerald Distilling Company

Opelika, Alabama, founded in 2014

johnemeralddistilling.com

With the wash being fermented on the grain, the main product is John´s Alabama Single Malt which gets its character from barley smoked with a blend of southern pecan and peach wood. The first release was made in 2015 and is currently aged for three years.

Journeyman Distillery

Three Oaks, Michigan, founded in 2010

journeymandistillery.com

The range of whiskies distilled at Journeyman include bourbon, rye, wheat and single malt. The first release of Three Oaks Single Malt Whiskey was in 2013 and it has been aged in a combination of casks that have previously contained bourbon, rye and rum.

Judson & Moore

Chicago, Illinois, founded in 2020

judsonandmoore.com

Located in a former leather tannery in Chicago, the distillery focuses on whiskey; bourbon, rye and a single malt made from 65% smoked malted barley and 35% unsmoked. First releases were in spring 2022.

Krobar Craft Distillery

San Luis Obispo, California, founded in 2012

krobardistillery.com

Two wine businesses inherited by Stephen Kroner and Joe Barton turned into a distillery and today they are producing gin, vodka and whiskey. The current single malt expression has been matured for at least two years and finished in port barrels.

Laws Whiskey House

Denver, Colorado, founded in 2011

lawswhiskeyhouse.com

Most of their bourbon and rye whiskies are released in batches

with the latest including whiskey aged up to 10 years. The flagship in the range is Four Grain Straight Bourbon but they also have a 4 year old single malt called Henry Road on the menu. In 2020 the distillery was substantially upgraded.

Liberty Call Spirits

Spring Valley, California, founded in 2014

libertycall.com

The distillery uses a range of barley varieties including caramel malts and the rare Maris Otter. Apart from bourbon, gin and rum there is also a single malt named Old Ironsides. In spring 2020, they opened up a second restaurant/distillery in Barrio Logan, south central San Diego.

Liquid Brands Distillery

Spokane, Washington, founded in 2018

warriorliquor.com

Rich and Mary Clemson produce gin, vodka, bourbon, rye whiskey and the Warrior single malt made from malted barley.

Liquid Riot Bottling Co.

Portland, Maine, founded in 2013

liquidriot.com

At the waterfront in the Old Port, Liquid Riot, Maine´s first brewery/distillery/resto-bar, produces an extensive range of beers and spirits which include bourbon, rye, oat, rum, vodka, agave spirit and the three years old Old Port Single Malt.

Los Angeles Distillery

Culver City, California, founded in 2013

ladistillery.com

While gin and rum may be a part of the product range, the distillery is very much focusing on whiskey. Different versions of bourbon and rye are produced as well as a number of varieties of malt whiskey from barley. The latest addition to the range is The Trio which encompasses Tokaji Cask (aged solely in Tokaji casks), Double (aged in a combination of Tokaji casks and virgin oak) and

Los Angeles Distillery

Triple Cask (a blend of Tokaji, Bordeaux and virgin oak). All three are 8 years old.

Mad River Distillers

Warren, Vermont, founded in 2011

madriverdistillers.com

The distillery was built on a 150 year old farm in the Green Mountains. Focus is on rum, brandy and whiskey. The only single malt so far is Hopscotch which was first released in late 2016 with the latest beimng distilled from an IPA and aged for three years.

Maine Craft Distilling

Portland, Maine, founded in 2013

mainecraftdistilling.com

The distillery offers vodka, gin, rum as well as the Fifty Stone single malt in limited batches. The barley is floor malted on site and both peat moss and seaweed is used to dry the barley.

Maplewood Brewery and Distillery

Chicago, Illinois, founded in 2014

maplewoodbrew.com

This brewery/distillery has released four malts; Fat Pug made from pale malt, dark crystal, dark munich, chocolate malt and roasted malt, Oaty Otter with Maris Otter barley and oats, Fest inspired by festbier and Sour Mash Pils - a blend of pilsner and Vienna malt.

Montgomery Distillery

Missoula, Montana, founded in 2012

montgomerydistillery.com

The owners use a hammer mill and the wash is then fermented on the grain. The first whiskey was a rye in 2015, followed up by the 3 year old Montgomery Single Malt in 2016. The latest release, in November 2022, was a 5 year old.

Motor City Gas

Royal Oak, Michigan, founded in 2014

motorcitygas.com

The owners have an experimental approach using rare grains, different yeasts and unusual woods. The range includes rye, bourbon and single malt. Two of the latest single malts are the 5 year old Vienna and the 4 year old, peated Lockness. In 2021 the company bought a farm in Ann Arbour where they will grow their own organic heirloom grain.

New Holland Brewing Co.

Holland, Michigan, founded in 1996 (whiskey since 2005)

newhollandbrew.com

The first cases of New Holland Artisan Spirits were released in 2008 and among them were Zeppelin Bend, a 3 year old straight malt whiskey which is now their flagship brand. Included in the range is also the 4 year old Zeppelin Bend Reserve which has been finished in sherry casks.

New Liberty Distillery

Philadelphia, Pennsylvania, founded in 2014

newlibertydistillery.com

A distillery working with whiskey on two tracks - the New Liberty produced at the distillery (including a Smoked Malt and Dutch Malt Whiskey) and Kinsey which is sourced from other distilleries.

Noco Distillery

Fort Collins, Colorado, founded in 2016

nocodistillery.com

With a fermentation of up to three weeks, slow distillation and up to nine different types of woods for maturation, the distillery produces gin, rum, vodka, bourbon, rye whiskey as well as single malt. The latter was first released in March 2019. New hybrid stills were installed in early 2022.

Old Home Distillers

Lebanon, New York, founded in 2014

oldhomedistillers.com

The distillery produces bourbon, corn whiskey and New York Single Malt Whiskey. The mash is fermented on the grain for 4-5 days and the distillation takes place in a hybrid column still.

Old Line Spirits

Baltimore, Maryland, founded in 2014

oldlinespirits.com

Distilling started in 2016 and a peated version was launched in 2017 with a sherry cask finish appearing in 2018 and a cask strength a year later. From April 2023 there is a new core range with Flagship 95 and Navy Strength 114.

Old Trestle Distillery

Truckee, California, founded in 2012

oldtrestle.com

Using their own underground aquifer as the water source, the distillery is focused on whiskey production but the first spirit releases were vodka and gin. In summer 2020, their 3 year old Sierra Bourbon was launched and their first single malt was released in spring 2023.

Orange County Distillery

Goshen, New York, founded in 2013

orangecountydistillery.com

The distillery malts their own barley and use their own peat when needed. Since 2014, they have launched a wide range of whiskies, including corn, bourbon, rye and peated single malt. The first aged single malt was launched in 2015 and more releases have followed.

Orcas Island Distillery

Orcas, Washington, founded in 2014

orcasislanddistillery.com

Apple brandy is the main produce but the 3 year old West Island Single Malt Whiskey, first released in 2018, is also in the range.

Painted Stave Distilling

Smyrna, Delaware, founded in 2013

paintedstave.com

Most of the production is centered on bourbon and rye but there is also Diamond State Pot Still Whiskey made from malted barley and rye and Double TroubleD made from a hopped beer.

Peach Street Distillers

Palisade, Colorado, founded in 2005

peachstreetdistillers.com

An extensive range of various spirits is complemented by a bourbon (first released in 2008), a smoky rye, a hop flavoured whiskey, a peated single malt and, released in December 2021, an 8 year old single barrel version of the peated single malt.

Perlick Distillery

Sarona, Wisconsin, founded in 2014

perlickdistillery.com

A family distillery with American Yeoman Vodka made from wheat and barley as the core product. Small amounts of single malt whiskey made from barley grown on the farm is also produced. The first release (a 5 year old) is planned for summer 2023.

Pilot House Distilling

Astoria, Oregon, founded in 2013

pilothousedistilling.com

Starting off with vodka and gin, the owners eventually broadened the range to include also whisky. The main product is the A-O American Whiskey made from corn and malted barley but small amounts of single malt are also produced and the first 2 year old was released in August 2021. The distillery moved to a new location in Astoria in spring 2022.

Pioneer Whisky (formerly known as III Spirits)

Talent, Oregon, founded in 2014

pioneerwhisky.com

Focusing mainly on single malts, there are currently two single malts in the range; Oregon Highlander made from a grain bill of brewer´s malt, Munich malt and crystal malt and Islay Style Peated Whisky produced from 100% heavily peated malt from Scotland.

PostModern Distilling

Knowville, Tennessee, founded in 2017

postmodernspirits.com

While focusing on gin, vodka and liqueur, the owners released their first single barrel single malt whiskey in 2018. The current core expression is the Straight Malt Whiskey.

Prichard´s Distillery

Kelso and Nashville, Tennessee, founded in 1999

prichardsdistillery.com

The main track of the production is rum. The first single malt was launched in 2010 and later releases usually have been vattings from barrels of different age (some up to 10 years old).

Quincy Street Distillery

Riverside, Illinois, founded in 2011

quincystreetdistillery.com

The distillery produces a range of spirits including gin, vodka, absinth, bourbon, corn whiskey and rye. The only single malt released so far is the 2 year old Golden Prairie which was launched in 2015 for the first time only to return in October 2022.

Ranger Creek Brewing & Distilling

San Antonio, Texas, founded in 2010

drinkrangercreek.com

Focusing on beer brewing and whiskey production, the first whiskey release was Ranger Creek .36 Texas Bourbon in 2011. Their core single malt, Rimfire, was launched in 2013. In 2019, Heavy Smoke Rimfire made from mesquite smoked barley, was released. The latest version, in March 2023, was Rimfire "304" finished in barrels that originally held peach brandy.

Rennaisance Artisan Distillers

Akron, Ohio, founded in 2013

renartisan.com

Apart from whiskey, the distillery produces gin, brandy, grappa and limoncello. The first whiskey release, The King´s Cut single malt, was made from a grain bill including toasted and caramel malts. In March 2021 Kilted Peat Malt Whiskey was released.

Rock Town Distillery

Little Rock, Arkansas, founded in 2010

rocktowndistillery.com

A grain-to-glass distillery where the backbone of the production is made up of several bourbons, rye, wheat whiskey and vodka but there is also a 4 year old single malt finished in ex-cognac casks.

Rock Valley Spirits

Long Eddy, New York, founded in 2018

rockvalleyspirits.com

A small, family-owned farm distillery located in the Catskill Mountains. First spririts that were launched were gin and vodka and they were followed in December 2021 by a single malt whisky.

Routt Distillery

Steamboat Springs, Colorado, founded in 2022

routtdistillery.com

Founded by Brad Christensen, the distillery/tasting room started by releasing gin and vodka and now has American single malt maturing in the warehouse. For the maturation, the owner uses rye and bourbon barrels from another distillery.

Sand Creek Distillery

Hugo, Colorado, founded in 2013

sandcreekdistillery.com

Founded by Lucas Hohl, this micro distillery is entirely focused on American malt whiskey. The first Sand Creek single malt was released in 2017 and it was followed by American Redux in 2020.

San Diego Distillery

Spring Valley, California, founded in 2015

sddistillery.com

A distillery focused almost entirely on whiskey. In 2016 the first six whiskies were released including an Islay peated single malt. Since then several single malts have been appeared.

SanTan Spirits

Chandler and Phoenix, Arizona, founded in 2007 (2015)

santanbrewing.com

With two locations in Arizona, this brewery/restaurant added distilling to its concept in 2015. Sacred Stave Single Malt occurs in two, core versions both finished in red wine barrels with one being bottled at cask strength.The limited 4 year old Crimson Oath was released in March 2022.

Seattle Distilling

Vashon, Washington, founded in 2013

seattledistilling.com

The distillery produces gin, vodka, coffee liqueur and malt whiskey. The latter, named Idle Hour, is made from both malted and unmalted barley with an addition of honey and matured in barrels that used to hold local cabernet sauvignon wine.

Seven Caves Spirits

San Diego, California, founded in 2016

the7caves.com

Apart from gin and rum, Geoff Longenecker also makes whiskey from malted barley. One of the latest (in August 2022) was a peated 4 year old matured in a rum barrel.

Shadow Ridge Spirits

Oceanside, California, founded in 2017

srdistilled.com

While rum and gin may be a part of the range, the distillery is focused on whiskey; bourbon, rye and single malt. The latter has been made from a combination of different malts and also comes in a special, smoked version where peat and cherry wood were used.

Shelter Distilling

Mammoth Lakes, California, founded in 2018

shelterdistilling.com

Apart from gin, vodka, rum and liqueurs the distillery produces bourbon, rye and single malt. The latest releases include Embers Peated Whiskey, Dark Sky and High Sierra which had been matured in a combination of Hungarian and American oak.

Sinister Distlling

Albany, Oregon, founded in 2015

sinisterdeluxe.com

Part of a brewstillery with DeLuxe Brewing as the other half. A variety of spirits are produced in a pot still from Portugal including the 4 year old single barrel Howard Jacob single malt.

Snitching Lady Distillery

Fairplay, Colorado, founded in 2018

snitchingladydistillery.net

The distillery, which moved to new premises in August 2019, has so far released peach brandy, bourbon, rye and blue corn spirit. Single malt made from barley was distilled for the first time in March 2019 and released in September 2022.

Solar Spirits

Richland, Washington, founded in 2018

solarspirits.com

A "farm-to-bottle" distillery using 100% renewable energy thanks to onsite solar panels. The range currently consists of gin, vodka, brandy and a single malt whiskey.

South Mountain Distilling

Connelly Springs, North Carolina, founded in 2015

southmountaindistillery.com

Focus is very much on moonshine but there are also matured whiskies in the range including Dignified Single Malt and a corn whiskey named Sinister.

Spirit Hound Distillers

Lyons, Colorado, founded in 2012

spirithounds.com

The signature spirits are gin and malt whiskey. The barley for the whiskey is grown, malted and peat-smoked in Alamosa by Colorado Malting. The first bottles hit the shelves in 2015 and there is now also a cask strength version available as well as rye and bourbon.

Spirit Lab Distilling

Charlottesville, Virginia, founded in 2016

spiritlabdistilling.com

Founded by the Norway immigrant Ivar Aass, the distillery is making gin, brandy and American malt whiskley. Using a solera system, batches of the cask strength Aass Single Malt are released regularly. In September 2022 their first single barrel was launched.

Spirits of St Louis Distillery (formerly known as Square One)

St. Louis, Missouri, founded in 2006

spiritsofstlouisdistillery.com

A combined brewery and restaurant. Apart from rum, gin, vodka and absinthe, the owners also produce J.J. Neukomm Whiskey, a malt whiskey made from 25% cherry wood smoked malt.

Stark Spirits

Pasadena, California, founded in 2013

starkspirits.com

The first single malt whiskey was distilled in 2015 and the first official distillery release of single malt (both peated and un-peated) came in February 2017. They have two stills with one reserved for all the peated production.

Storm King Distilling Co.

Montrose, Colorado, founded in 2017

stormkingdistilling.com

Inspired by a passion for whiskey, the owners have released wheat whiskey, bourbon and rye while single malt is still maturing. Currently for sale are also gin, vodka, rum and different spirits made from agave.

Stoutridge Distillery

Marlboro, New York, founded in 2017

stoutridge.com

Originally a winery it was expanded with a distillery with direct fired stills and their own floor maltings in 2017. The range consists of vodka, gin, brandy and whiskey. Their Southern Ulster Single Malt is made from in-house malted barley and matured in ex-Laphroaig casks.

Sugar House Distillery

Salt Lake City, Utah, founded in 2014

sugarhousedistillery.net

The first release from the distillery in 2014 was a vodka, followed by a single malt whisky. More releases of the single malt have followed (as well as bourbon, rye and rum) and a limited single malt finished in Malbec casks was launched in February 2021.

Sweetgrass Distillery

Portland, Maine, founded in 2007

sweetgrasswinery.com

Focusing from the start on wine and the distillation of gin, brandy, rum and liqueur, the distillery went on to producing malt whiskey. The latest batch of their Sunk Haze malt whiskey in November 2022 had been matured for eight years.

Thumb Butte Distillery

Prescott, Arizona, founded in 2013

thumbbuttedistillery.com

A variety of gin, dark rum and vodka, as well as whiskey are produced by the owners. Crown King Single Malt as well as rye and bourbon has been released. The latest version of the single malt has been made from barley smoked by using Arizona pecan wood.

Timber Creek Distillery

Crestview, Florida, founded in 2014

timbercreekdistillery.com

Fermentation and distillation is off the grain and they use a traditional worm tub to cool the spirits. Releases include a rye, a wheated bourbon, a four grain whiskey and Florida Single Malt.

Town Branch Distillery

Lexington, Kentucky, founded in 1999

lexingtonbrewingco.com

In 1980 Dr Pearse Lyons founded Alltech Inc, a biotechnology company specializing in animal nutrition and feed supplements. Alltech purchased Lexington Brewing Company in 1999 and in 2008, two traditional copper pot stills were installed. The first single malt whiskey was released in 2010 under the name Pearse Lyons Reserve and has since been replaced by the 7 year old Town Branch Malt. Alltech opened yet another distillery in Pikeville - Dueling Barrels Brewery and Distillery.

Triple Eight Distillery

Nantucket, Massachusetts, founded in 2000

ciscobrewers.com

Apart from whiskey, Triple Eight also produces vodka, rum and gin. The first 888 bottles of single malt whiskey were released on 8th August 2008 as an 8 year old. More releases of Notch have followed and currently there is a 12 year old and a 15 year old.

Two James Spirits

Detroit, Michigan, founded in 2013

twojames.com

Equipped with a 500 gallon pot still with a rectification column attached, the distillery has released vodka, gin, bourbon (even a peated version) and rye while a single malt is still maturing in the warehouse. Aged in ex-sherry casks the whiskey has been made from peated Scottish barley.

Up North Distillery

Post Falls, Idaho, founded in 2015

upnorthdistillery.com

Randy and Hilary Mann had their eyes set on malt whiskey when they started production but the first releases were honey spirits and apple brandy. The first release of North Idaho Single Malt Whiskey in autumn 2020 has been followed by more batches.

Van Brunt Stillhouse

Brooklyn, New York, founded in 2012

vanbruntstillhouse.com

The distillery made their first release of Van Brunts American Whiskey in 2012. This has been followed by bourbon, rye and corn whiskey. The Van Brunt Single Malt is bottled regularly, produced from a mash bill of nine different brewer´s malts and fermented on the grain. The latest batch appeared in early 2023.

Vapor Distillery (formerly known as Roundhouse Spirits)

Boulder, Colorado, founded in 2007

vapordistillery.com, boulderspirits.com

Since 2014 and using a 3,800 litre copper pot still, the owners focus on American malt whiskey but also make bourbon with an unusually high proportion of malted barley in the mash bill. Currently the distillery has four single malt whiskies in the range – Boulder American Single Malt Whiskey, a peated version of the same, one bottled in bond and one port finish. There is also the limited 4 year old Trailhead PX finish available only at the distillery.

Venus Spirits

Santa Cruz, California, founded in 2014

venusspirits.com

Production is focused on whiskey, but gin and spirits from blue agave have also been released. The first single malt was Wayward Whiskey, matured in port and sherry casks and released in 2015. This was followed up by a rye and later a bourbon.

Vikre Distillery

Duluth, Minnesota, founded in 2012

vikredistillery.com

Together with whisky - gin, vodka and aquavit are produced at the distillery. Whiskies include Iron Range American Single Malt, Northern Courage Smokey Rye, Sugarbush Whiskey and the blended Honor Brand Hay & Sunshine.

Warfield Distillery

Ketchum, Idaho, founded in 2015

drinkwarfield.com

Warfield Organic American Whiskey was launched in 2019 with a fourth release in August 2022. Gin, vodka, brandy and beer is also produced. In summer 2020 the distillery was expanded with two copper pot stills (3,800 litres each) made by Forsyths in Scotland.

Woodstone Creek Distillery

Cincinnati, Ohio, founded in 1999

woodstonecreek.com

Opened as a farm winery in 1999, a distillery was added to the business in 2003. The first bourbon, was released in 2008 followed by a 10 year old single malt. Whiskey production is very small and just a handfull of releases have appeared since.

Town Branch Distillery in Kentucky

Wood´s High Mountain Distillery

Salida, Colorado, founded in 2011

woodsdistillery.com

The first expression (and current big seller), Tenderfoot Whiskey, is a triple malt and so is the release that followed, Sawatch, a 4-5 year old made from malted barley (a mix of chocolate malt and cherrywood smoked malt), malted rye and malted wheat. The latest version (with a second release in November 2021) is the 5 year old Dawn Patrol made from 45% cherry-wood smoked barley.

Wright & Brown Distilling Co.

Oakland, California, founded in 2015

wbdistilling.com

The distillery is focused on barrel aged spirits. The first release, a rye whiskey, appeared in 2016 and was followed by a bourbon in 2017. Early 2020 it was time for the first single malt, a bottled in bond expression aged for 4,5 years with batch 2 launched in 2021. The latest, 6.5 years, was released in December 2022.

Canada

Shelter Point Distillery

Vancouver Island, British Columbia, founded in 2009

shelterpoint.ca

Founded by dairy farmer Patrick Evans who in 2005 switched to growing crops and four years later added a distillery. Distillation started in 2011 and the barley used is grown on the farm. Apart from whisky, gin and vodka is also produced. In 2016, the Artisanal 5 year old single malt was released and this is still the core expression. Other releases in a substantial range include Ripple Rock (matured in ex-bourbon and virgin oak), the triple distilled Montfort made from unmalted barley, Double Barrel (finished in wine casks), The Forbidden (made from malted wheat), Cask Strength and a 10 year old. There is also Smoke Point where the fumes from smoked wood and local peat is piped into the wood of ·the maturing casks. A recent release, and part of the Evans Family Reserve series, is a Carribean Rum Cask Finish.

Macaloney´s Island Distillery

Victoria, British Columbia, founded in 2016

macaloneydistillers.com

Founded by the Scotsman Graeme Macaloney the distillery is equipped with a one ton semilauter mash tun, 7 stainless steel washbacks, a 5,500 litre wash still and a 3,600 litre spirit still. Some of the barley is malted on site and there is also a craft beer brewery. Glenloy, the inaugural single malt and signature release, appeared in December 2020 together with two single casks (bourbon and STR cask) named Invermallie. The first 3 year old single malt was released in December 2020. More releases in the Invermallie range have appeared together with the Invernahaven matured in PX and oloroso casks. The latest additions include the lightly peated An Aba matured in a combination of six different types of casks, An Loy matured in a combination of bourbon, sherry and STR casks and the sherried Cath-Nah-Aven.

Glenora Distillery

Glenville, Nova Scotia, founded in 1990

glenoradistillery.com

Situated in Nova Scotia, Glenora was the first malt whisky distillery in Canada. The first launch of in-house produce came in 2000, an 8 year old named Glen Breton Rare and a 10 year old is now the core expression. Many other expressions have appeared over the years - 14, 19, 21 and 25 year olds including also peated versions. Glen Breton Ice, aged in an ice wine barrel, was launched in 2006 and the latest edition was a 19 year old. A recent limited release is

the Glen Breton Alexander Keith´s 18 year old which was distilled from an IPA made at a local brewery.

Still Waters Distillery

Concord, Ontario, founded in 2009

stillwatersdistillery.com

The distillery is equipped with a 3,000 litre mash tun, two 3,000 litre washbacks and a Christian Carl 450 litre pot still. The still also has rectification columns. The focus is on whisky but they also produce vodka, brandy and gin. Their first single malt, named Stalk & Barrel Single Malt, was released in 2013 and it was followed in 2014 by the first rye whisky. The range now consists of Rye and Single Malt, both bottled at 46% and at cask strength.

Other distilleries in Canada

Arbutus Distillery

Nanaimo, British Columbia, founded in 2014

arbutusdistillery.com

The distillery is focusing on vodka, gin and other spirits but rye and single malt whisky is also on the agenda. The first 3 year old single malt appeared in December 2018.

Bridgeland Distillery

Calgary, Alberta, founded in 2018

bridgelanddistillery.com

Equipped with an unusual copper pot still where the lyne arm is extended with a large copper spiral leading to a condenser. A single malt spirit was released in August 2019 and in July 2022 the first single malt named Glenbow appeared.

Central City Brewers & Distillers

Surrey, British Columbia, founded in 2013

centralcitybrewing.com

One of Canada´s largest craft breweries added a distillery in 2013. The whisky is sold under the Lohin McKinnon Single Malt brand including special bottlings such as peated, tequila finish and one aged with cocoa from a local chocolatier.

De Vine Wine & Spirits

Victoria, British Columbia, founded in 2007

devinevineyards.ca

Starting as winemakers, the owners added a distillery in 2014. The first whisky was the 3 year old single malt Glen Saanich which was first released in 2017 and batch 8 released in autumn 2023. Made from floor malted barley it was complmented by a Wine Cask Finish in spring 2022. Ancient Grains made from a combination of barley, spelt, emmer, einkorn and kamut is also in the range.

Dubh Glas Distillery, The

Oliver, British Columbia, founded in 2015

thedubhglasdistillery.com

The whisky is double distilled in an Arnold Holstein still and gin is also produced. Initial products were Noteworthy Gin and Virgin Spirits Barley (a newmake). The first release of a single malt was the peated Against All Odds in June 2019. The owner, Grant Stevely, releases a huge number of whiskies every year where the latest include Happy Days, Stout of Water, New Adventures and Smoke & Oak.

Eau Claire Distillery

Turner Valley, Alberta, founded in 2014

eauclairedistillery.ca

The distillery´s first limited single malt whisky appeared in 2017 with Batch 6 (a combination of new Hungarian oak, ex-bourbon and ex-sherry) being the latest. The range also includes the Stampede Rye and the blend Rupert´s Whisky.

Ironworks Distillery

Lunenburg, Nova Scotia, founded in 2010

ironworksdistillery.com

Focusing on rum, brandy and vodka, Lynne MacKay and Pierre Guevremont started to produce also whisky. Heart Iron single malt was released in 2020 with a fourth edition in January 2023.

Last Mountain Distillery

Lumsden, Saskatchewan, founded in 2010

lastmountaindistillery.com

Equipped with two copper stills with columns the distillery produces vodka, gin, rum, limoncello and whisky including rye, wheat and single malt from barley. Currently there is a 6 year old single malt and in March 2022 the Smoky Single Malt was released.

Last Straw Distillery

Vaughan, Ontario, founded in 2016

madebyhand.laststrawdistillery.com

A wide range of spirits are produced including whisky made from various grains. The latest release (in March 2023) was the 5 year old Rice & Rye.

Liberty Distillery, The

Vancouver, British Columbia, founded in 2010

thelibertydistillery.com

The distillery produces gin, vodka and a wide range of whiskies made from organic grain. Sold under the brand name Trust Whiskey, there are three single malts matured in madeira, port and burgundy casks and a sherry version is coming soon.

Lucky Bastard Distillers

Saskatoon, Saskatchewan, founded in 2012

luckybastard.ca

Founded by Michael Goldney, Cary Bowman and Lacey Crocker. The first releases were vodka, gin and a variety of liqueurs. In 2016 the first single malt appeared and this is now released intermittently in small batches.

Maison Sivo

Hinchinbrooke, Quebec, founded in 2014

maisonsivo.ca

Inspired by production of fruit brandies in Hungary where he grew up, Janos Sivo produces different kinds of spirit including whisky. Le Single Malt finished in Sauternes casks and Le Rye were both released in 2018. There is also the limited Le Sélection Single Malt.

Moon Distillery

Victoria, British Columbia, founded in 2012

moondistillery.ca

Clay Potter is producing both beer and a variety of spirits including single malt whisky. Two of the latest single malts, Antifogmatic Bliss and 3 Sheets, were followed by a series of three whiskies infused with cacao nibs, coffee beans and dark cherries.

North of 7 Distillery

Ottawa, Ontario, founded in 2013

northof7distillery.ca

First releases, waiting for their whiskies to mature, were gin and other spirits. These were followed by whiskies made from various mash bills and in June 2022 a 5 year old single malt appeared.

Casks maturing at Macaloney´s Island Distillery

Odd Society Spirits

Vancouver, British Columbia, founded in 2013

oddsocietyspirits.com

The first two whiskies appeared in late 2018; the Commodore single malt and the Prospector rye. This was followed in late 2019 by Maple - a single malt that had been smoked with maple wood and matured in casks that had previously contained maple syrup.In January 2023 a 5 year old, lightly peated single barrel appeared.

Okanagan Spirits

Vernon and Kelowna, British Columbia, founded in 2004

okanaganspirits.com

The first Okanagan distillery was started in 1970 but closed in 1995. In 2004 Okanagan Spirits was established and a distillery was opened in Vernon (and later, one in Kelowna). A variety of spirits including gin, vodka and whisky are being produced. In 2013 the Laird of Fintry single malt was released where a number of different expression have been releasecd since. Two new single malts were added to the range in 2023, the 1 Malt and Chadwick Double Wood Mezcal Finish.

Phillips Fermentorium

Victoria, British Columbia, founded in 2014

fermentorium.ca

Started as a brewery, distillation of spirits was added 13 years later. The first limited whisky release was the 5 year old Small Talk in late 2019.

Rig Hand Distillery

Nisku, Alberta, founded in 2014

righanddistillery.com

The distillery produces whisky. vodka, rum and gin with the first whisky appearing in 2017. Bar M was a blended whisky made from wheat, barley and rye. This was followed by the Diamond S single malt, the Rocking R rye and, in autumn 2019, the Lazy B corn whisky.

Sheringham Distillery

Langford, British Columbia, founded in 2015

sheringhamdistillery.com

Gin, akvavit and vodka were the first to be bottled while the inaugural release of their Red Fife and Woodhaven whiskies came in 2019. In 2023 the distillery moved to a new location.

Stillhead Distillery

Duncan, British Columbia, founded in 2017

stillhead.ca

All kinds of whisky including rye, wheat and "bourbon" style are produced, including malt whisky. Recent releases include a 5 year old with a 3 year second maturation in Hungarian oak, the port cask finish Potent Port-ables and one matured in madeira casks.

Yukon Spirits

Whitehorse, Yukon, founded in 2009

twobrewerswhisky.com

All of the whisky produced is made from malted grains but not only barley but also wheat and rye. The first bottles of the 7 year old Two Brewer´s Yukon Single Malt Whisky were released in 2016 and the current portfolio is based on four styles; Classic, Peated, Special Finishes and Innovative.

The Dyck family - owners of Okanagan Spirits

Australia & New Zealand

Australia

Lark Distillery

Cambridge, Tasmania, founded 1992

Pontville, Tasmania, founded in 2015

larkdistillery.com

In 1992, Bill Lark was the first person for 153 years to take out a distillation licence in Tasmania. The success of the distillery forced Bill Lark to bring in investors in the company to generate future growth and since April 2018, Australian Whisky Holdings (AWH) holds a majority of the shares. Bill Lark is still working with the company as the Global Ambassador. In 2020, AWH changed name to Lark Distilling Co and in autumn 2021 they bought the Shene Estate, 30 minutes north of Hobart, in a deal worth £21.5m. Behind the Shene Estate distillery was Damian Mackey who started distilling whisky already in 2007. In 2016, with the aid of investor John Ibrahim and Anne and David Kernke, the opportunity came for him to move the production to the Shene Estate at Pontville. When Lark Distilling bought Shene, an already existing distillery with a 350,000 litre capacity and stock of maturing whisky was included in the deal. This gave the two distilleries (the original distillery in Cambridge and the one at Shene Estate) a combined capacity of almost 600,000 litres. The Pontville distillery (Shene) was opened in March 2022 in connection with Lark´s 30th anniversary and there are now plans to increase the production to one million litres per year.

The core products in the Lark whisky range are the Classic Cask, Classic Cask Cask Strength, Rebellion and the new Tasmanian Peated. Limited bottlings include Dark Lark, Origins, Chinotto Cask II, Muscat Cask II, Para 100 and the 20 year old Legacy. One of the latest (in November 2022) was the Tokay 100 Rare Cask.

Bakery Hill Distillery

North Balwyn, Victoria, founded 1998

bakeryhill.com

The first spirit at Bakery Hill Distillery, founded by David Baker, was produced in 2000 and the first single malt was launched in autumn 2003. In 2016, David was joined by his son Andrew and father and son started planning for a move to larger premises and adding a second still. The plan is to move to a new location in Kensington and to help with the financing, a crowd funding campaign was launched in 2022. Five different core expressions are available – Classic and Peated (both matured in ex-bourbon casks) and Double Wood (ex-bourbon and a finish in French Oak). Classic and Peated are also available at cask strength. Two of the most recent limited releases were the 5 year old Peated Double Wood and the second edition of Blunderbluss which is a collaboration with Hop Nation Brewery where the whisky has been finished in casks that held stout beer.

Sullivans Cove Distillery

Cambridge, Tasmania, founded 1994

sullivanscove.com

Founded Robert Hosken in 1994, Patrick Maguire joined the company five years later as head distiller and co-owner. In 2016, Maguire and the other owners sold the distillery to a company led by Adam Sable who was general manager of Bladnoch distillery for two years. The core range from the distillery comprises of American Oak, French Oak (where the barrels have contained tawny) and Double Cask. There is also the Special Cask range where one of the latest releases (in August 2022) was a 12 year old finished in an ex-Apera cask, Old & Rare with whiskies that are 16 years or older and Cask Variations. In March 2023, 200 bottles of a 21 year old were released. While the distillery launched a 21 year old anniversary bottling a couple of years ago, this is the oldest single cask yet released. In 2021 the owners revealed plans to move the entire operation back to Hion Quays on the Hobart waterfront to a site close to where the original distillery was founded. Later that year they received a federal government grant of $3.3m to help fund the project, in May 2022 they received a planning permission and the owners hope to have completed the move by the end of 2023.

Starward Distillery

Melbourne, Victoria, founded 2008

starward.com.au

The distillery, founded by David Vitale, was moved in 2016 to a bigger site in Port Melbourne and the year before Diageo invested in the distillery. The original stills (an 1,800 litre wash still and a 600 litre spirit still) were complemented in 2020 with a new 7,000 litre wash still while at the same time the old wash still became the new spirit still. The first Starward single malt was released in 2013 and the current range consists of Nova (matured in Australian red wine barrels), Solera (matured in casks that had held apera, the Australian version of sherry), Fortis (fully matured in American oak) and Peated Finish (finished in ex-peated casks from Islay for 18 months). There is also the blended whisky Two-Fold (made from malted barley and wheat). Recent limited expressions include Vitalis in October 2022 to celebrate the distillery´s 15 anniversary and in March 2023, the Small Batch Chardonnay Cask which was fully matured in white wine casks.

Hellyers Road Distillery

Burnie, Tasmania, founded 1999

hellyersroaddistillery.com.au

Hellyer´s Road Distillery is one of the larger single malt whisky distilleries in Australia with a capacity of doing 120,000 litres of pure alcohol per year. The distillery is equipped with a 6.5 ton mash tun, a 60,000 litre wash still and a 20,000 litre spirit still. The pots on both stills are made of stainless steel while heads, necks and lyne arms are made of copper. The large stills and a slow distillation call for an unusually long middle-cut, 24 hours. The first whisky was released in 2006 and there are now more than ten different expression in the range, including 10 and 12 year olds, peated as well as unpeated and various finishes. A range of limited releases include whiskies up to 19 years old.

Great Southern Distilling Company

Albany, Western Australia, founded 2004

distillery.com.au

The distillery is located at Princess Royal Harbour in Albany. In 2015, the owners opened a second distillery in Margaret River which will is focused on gin production and in autumn 2018 a third distillery, Tiger Snake in Porongurup, started production. The combined production is 400,000 litres of pure alcohol per year and the company also have their own maltings. The first expression of the whisky, called Limeburners, was released in 2008 and the core range now consists of American Oak, Port Cask, Sherry Cask and Peated. Limited yet yearly editions include the heavily peated Darkest Winter and two Director´s Cut – one finished in a topaque barrel and one in a PX barrel.

Archie Rose Distilling Company

Rosebery and Botany, New South Wales, founded 2014

archierose.com.au

What started as a fairly ordinary distillery, both in terms of size and production technique, was completely changed in November 2020 when their new distillery in Botany in south east Sydney was opened. This is now the largest whisky distillery in Australia but what stands out is how the whisky is produced. The mashing is done with a mash filter (the same is used at Teaninich and Inchdairnie in Scotland). The really unique thing though is how they handle their different malts in the process. The whisky from Archie Rose was from the start based on a six-malt mash bill. In the new distillery, each malt variety is handled separately all the way from milling, through brewing, fermentation, distillation and maturation. Only after that is the whisky blended together. This way each malt variety can be handled with regards to its own specific attributes. This technique, which requires lots of fermenters as well as other equipment, has also been patented by the company.

Apart from producing rye whisky and peated and unpeated single malt, the distillery also makes gin, rum and vodka. The first whisky, Chocolate Rye Malt, was released in June 2019 and today there are two core expressions Single Malt and Rye Malt. Limited releases occur regularly including the Stringybark Smoked Single Malt and the Smoked Heritage Rye Malt Whisky. The distillery also has a service where you can taylor your own, personalised whisky.

Overeem Distillery (former Sawford Distillery)

Kingston, Tasmania, founded in 2017

overeemwhisky.com

While Sawford may be a fairley new distillery there is a background that goes back to 2007. In that year Casey Overeem founded the Old Hobart Distillery and eventually he had made a name for himself with his Overeem single malt and was also joined by his daugther Jane. In 2014, Old Hobart distillery was acquired by Lark Distillery and later by Australian Whisky Holdings. In summer 2020, the Overeem trademark and part of the whisky inventory was sold back to Jane (who was married Sawford) and her husband Mark. The equipment was not included and henceforth Overeem whisky is produced at the new Sawford (recently renamed Overeem) distillery which is equipped with two stills from Knapp Lewer (1,800 and 800 litres respectively). The core range of Overeem single malts (aged for at least 5 years) consists of Port Cask, Sherry Cask and Bourbon Cask bottled at both 43 and 60%. In March 2023, the 12 year old Bourbon Cask single malt was launched - the very last that was crafted by Casey Overeem himself. Recent new releases (November 2022) include Man of Promise Reserve which is a cask marriage of port, sherry and bourbon casks.

Chief´s Son Distillery

Somerville, Victoria, founded in 2017

chiefsson.com.au

The distillery is equipped with a 4,000 litre copper pot still and the owners focus on malt whisky with the first release appeareing in March 2019. They currently have a core range made up of three varieties matured in French oak, bottled either at 43-46% or at 60% – the lightly peated 900 Standard, the 900 Sweet Peat and 900 Pure malt – and also the 900 American Oak. There is also The Tanist, a "double-wood" expression positioned as an entry-level malt. Recent limited expressions include the third edition of Distiller´s Select, distilled from dark beer malts and matured in French oak ex-sherry casks which was released in late 2022.

Other distilleries in Australia

5 Nines Distilling

Uraidla, South Australia, founded in 2017

5ninesdistilling.com.au

The whisky is made primarily with local barley and the first releases appeared in August 2020. Later versions have included one that was finished in a cask that had been seasoned with cola and one that had matured in a cask that had held altar (sacrificial) wine.

7K Distillery

Brighton, Tasmania, founded in 2017

7kdistillery.com.au

A wide range of gins were intially released followed by their first single malt in August 2020. This was followed by more bottlings, for instance an Apera Cask Single Malt in early 2023.

Nosing the whisky at Overeem Distillery

23rd Street Distillery

Renmark, South Australia, founded in 2016

23rdstreetdistillery.com.au

With three used stills, 7,500 litres each, this distillery initially focused on a variety of gin, vodka and rum to start with. In 2019 the first single malt whisky was released. This was followed in May 2021 by a single malt that had entirely (including mashing) been produced at the distillery. More releases have followed.

36 Short Distillery

Virginia, South Australia, founded 2014

36short.com.au

A versatile distillery producing gin, vodka, rakia and also single malt whisky using a 1200 litre copper pot still. The whisky has been matured in a combination of new American oak, ex-bourbon and ex-shiraz casks.

78 Degrees (a k a Adelaide Hills Distillery)

Hay Valley, South Australia, founded in 2016

78degrees.com.au

With his distillery, Sacha La Forgia is leading the way when it comes to producing whisky from Australian native grains. His trials have been numerous and the first bottling in 2019 couldn´t even be called whisky since wattleseed (which was part of the mash bill) isn´t a cereal grain. The whisky is now sold under the name 78 Degrees and in 2021, the distillery (with a capacity of 400,000 litres) was bought by the Australian drinks accelerator Mighty Craft with La Forgia remaining in the company.

2020 Distillery

Cooroy, Queensland, founded 2020

2020distillery.com.au

While gin has already been launched, the owners are also working on single malt (both unpeated and peated), triple distilled single malt and a 100% rye - all of which have yet to be released.

Adams Distillery

Perth, Tasmania, founded in 2016

adamsdistillery.com.au

After less than two years of production, all the equipment was sold to make way for a huge new distillery which started production in March 2019. Around the same time, the first 2 year old single malt was also released. In February 2021, the distillery burned to the ground but soon after the ressurection began and a new distillery was operational in summer 2023. March 2023 saw the release of Signature Series 2 bottled at either 42% or 59%.

Aisling Distillery, The

Griffith, New South Wales, founded in 2015

theaislingdistillery.com.au

With a focus on malt whisky - gin, vodka and rum is also produced. The first two single malts were released in November 2020 and they were followed by more expressions. Tale of the Oak appeared in October 2021 and was followed a year later by Cnoc Neamh.

Amber Lane Distillery

Wyong, New South wales, founded 2017

amberlanedistillery.com

Founded by Rod Berry and Phil Townsend and equipped with a 3,600 litre copper pot still, the distillery focuses entirely on whisky. The first core expression, Destiny, has been followed my a number of limited releases with Equinox as one of the latest.

Backwoods Distilling

Yackandandah, Victoria, founded in 2017

backwoodsdistilling.com.au

Equipped with a 1200 litre copper pot still with an attached column, the first distillation was in 2018 with an inaugural release in August 2020. One of the most recent appeared in November 2022 with the lightly smoked Swagman´s Ghost Expression, matured in a combination of casks that had held apera and corn whisky.

Barossa Distilling Company

Nuriootpa, South Australia, founded in 2016

barossadistilling.com

Located in the historical Old Penfolds Distillery established in 1913, the distillery has focused on gin the first years and have launched a dozen different styles so far. Malt whisky is also produced but is still maturing.

Battery Point Distillery

Battery Point (Hobart), Tasmania, founded 2018

batterypointdistillery.com

Lloyd and Jan Clark founded the distillery and brought on Jack Lark, son of whisky icon Bill Lark as their head distiller. Jack has later moved on but the first releases from the distillery appeared in April 2021. Focus in on single malts finished in a variety of casks; sherry, tawny and bourbon.

Bellarine Distillery

Drysdale, Victoria, founded in 2017

bellarinedistillery.com.au

Located at the unlikely address Scotchman´s Road, the distillery is equipped with four stills, producing both gin and malt whisky. The first whisky, released in spring 2021, had been matured in charred pinot noir barrels and then married in ex-bourbon casks. Latest release was Grey Fantail in December 2022.

Black Gate Distillery

Mendooran, New South Wales, founded in 2012

blackgatedistillery.com

Apart from malt whisky, the distillery produces vodka and rum. The first single malt was in 2015 when a sherrymatured expression was released. More bottlings have followed, including a 5 year old peated version matured in a tawny cask released in December 2022.

Boatrocker Brewers & Distillers

Braeside, Victoria, founded in 2012

boatrocker.com.au

What started out as a brewery was later complemented by a distillery. Apart from beer, gin, vodka and rye, small amounts of single malt whisky is also produced. The first release was the 7 year old Seven Year Itch in summer 2021.

Bogan Road Distillery

Quambay Brook, Tasmania, founded 2018

boganroaddistillery.com

Starting out as bottlers (Tasmanian Whisky Selectors) in 2016, Karin Ketelaar and Shane Spencer decided to build a distillery in 2018 to produce their own spirit. Gin and various liqueurs have already been launched while single malt whisky is still maturing in the warehouse.

Callington Mill Distillery

Oatlands, Tasmania, founded in 2021

callingtonmilldistillery.com.au

In 2017, investor John Ibrahim bought a property 80 kilometres north of Hobart with the intention of turning it into a major distillery. With an investment of $20m construction started in February 2020 and the distillery started producing in 2021. Equipped with two copper pot stills and eight washbacks, the distillery has a capacity of producing 400,000 litres of pure alcohol. In 2022, the Leap of Faith series of eight bottlings distilled at Shene and Old Kempton distilleries was released.

Canberra Distillery, The

Canberra, ACT, founded in 2016

thecanberradistillery.com.au

The main part of the production is gin, vodka and various liqueurs. The first single malt whisky, Old George Reserve, distilled in 2018 and matured in a PX sherry cask was first released in late 2021.

Cape Byron Distillery

McLeods Shoot, New South Wales, founded 2016

capebyrondistillery.com

A family owned distillery situated on a macadamia farm. Some 40% of the 96-acre estate is made up of rainforest which was re-generated by the family. When Eddie Brook was working as the brand manager for Bruichladdich and Botanist gin in Australia he met the legendary Jim McEwan and together they decided to build a distillery. The original intention was to do only gin but in 2019 they also started producing malt whisky. In late 2022 The Original and Chardonnay Cask were launched and recently the distillery was expanded with a second, 4,500 litre, pot still.

Castle Glen Distillery

The Summit, Queensland, founded in 2009

castleglenaustralia.com.au

Established as a vineyard in 1990, Castle Glen moved on to open up also a brewery and a distillery in 2009. Apart from wine and beer, a wide range of spirits are produced. The first whisky, Castle Glen Limited Edition, was released as a 2 year old in 2012 while the latest was a 9 year old single malt.

Coburns Distillery

Burrawang, New South Wales, founded in 2017

coburnsdistillery.com.au

Mark Coburn started production in spring 2017 and has so far released several versions of his gin. The single malt turned two years old in July 2019 but has yet to be released. Coburns is one of very few Australian distilleries with its own peat bog for smoking the barley. Plans for the future include having a set of no less than five 5,000 litre pot stills.

Corowa Distilling Co.

Corowa, New South Wales, founded in 2010

corowawhisky.com.au

Situated in a restored flour mill the distillery is focused entirely on single malt whisky using barley from their own estate. Corowa started distilling in 2016 and the inaugural release from their own production was First Drop (aged in port barrels) in 2018 followed by Bosque Verde (also port) and Quicks Courage (PX sherry). November 2022 saw the release of a hopped whisky and in January 2023 the Rabbit (third in the Lunar New Year series) was launched.

Corra Linn Distillery

Relbia, Tasmania, founded in 2015

corralinndistillery.com.au

John Wielstra made the first distillation in his hybrid column still in autumn 2016. He is using his own yeast and smokes his barley using dried kelp instead of peat. The first release of single malt was in December 2018 and they are sold as single barrels and bottled at cask strength. A limited edition is called Rueben.

Cradle Mountain Whisky

Cradle Mountain, Tasmania, founded in 2019

cradlemountainwhisky.com

The story behind Cradle Mountain Whisky goes back to 1989, thirty years before the current distillery started production. In that year Brian Poke distilled the first Cradle Mountain single malt at his Darwin Distillery. He actually preceeded Bill Lark by a couple of years. Production, although sometimes intermittent, continued under different named (Franklin Distillery and Small Concerns Distillery) until 2015 when Cradle Mountain Whisky (including stock) was bought by the Lahra family. In 2019 they opened up a new distillery with the help of Brian Poke under the name Cradle Mountain. Equipped with a 2,000 litre wash still and a 600 litre spirit still, the owners now produce single malts such as A Walk in the Woods and The Forest Trail. Meanwhile they have also released bottlings from the old stock sometimes aged 23 years and more.

Craft Works Distillery

Capertee, New South Wales, founded 2018

craftworksdistillery.com.au

The first releases from the owner, Crafty Field, were collaborations with other distillers. The first whisky from his own production was I Am..., released in early 2021 and matured in a combination of casks that had held shiraz, cabernet sauvignon and vintage port. It was later followed by I Am Too.

Darby-Norris Distillery

Scottsdale, Tasmania, founded in 2018

darbynorrisdistillery.com.au

The distillery recently moved from Kelso to larger premises in Scottsdale. Gin, vodka and rum have been released but the first single malt isn´t expected at least until 2023.

Derwent Distillery

Dromedary, Tasmania, founded in 2019

derwentdistillery.com.au

The owners, Robbie and Emma Gilligan, had been working in the Tasmanian whisky industry for several years when they decided to set up their own distillery. It was opened in spring 2022 but before that a number of bottlings had been released under the Derwent brand. These whiskies had all been distilled by Robbie at some of the distilleries where he had been working, predominantly Redland and Old Kempton.

Dusty Barrel Distillery

Macclesfield, Victoria, founded 2020

dustybarreldistillery.com.au

An unusual craft distillery, founded by Nick Hope, producing whisky from a variety of different barley malts but also from rice. The 3,800 litre still is directly fired using gas and the neck is a gatlin type which means the vapours rise through a number of smaller pipes before they reach the condenser.

Edge of the World Distillery

Burnine, Tasmania, founded 2019

edgeoftheworlddistillery.com.au

A family owned distillery with the first spirits distilled in late 2019. Focus is on malt whisky with the first bottlings expected in 2022/2023 but other products, including gin, are also in the plans.

Fannys Bay Distillery

Lulworth, Tasmania, founded in 2014

fannysbaydistillery.com.au

The distillery is equipped with a 400 litre copper pot still and they use a long (7-8 days) fermentation. The first whisky was released in

May 2017 and it is now available in four main versions - bourbon, sherry, pinot and port. Most of the releases are single barrels and recently they have started to bottle lightly peated versions as well.

Fleurieu Distillery

Goolwa, South Australia, founded in 2016

fleurieudistillery.com.au

A beer brewery was turned into a distillery in 2016 but whisky had been distilled already since 2014. The first single malt appeared in 2016 and has been followed by several more with names like Never A Dull Moment and Lost Paraguayos. They also do collaborations with other distilleries, for example the blended malt Jumping the Rattler together with Backwoods and Timboon Railway Shed.

Furneaux Distillery

Flinders Island, Tasmania, founded in 2018

furneauxdistillery.com.au

Located on Flinders Island in the Bass Strait north east of Tasmania. The fermented wash is brought in from Launceston Distillery and then distilled at Furneaux. The first single malts, were released in 2020 and in March 2022 a new range was launched with the unpeated Sawyers Bay Double Oak and the peated Flinders Island.

Headlands Distilling Co.

North Wollongong, New South Wales, founded 2018

headlands.com.au

A range of gins and vodka were the first releases from this distillery but in December 2020, the first two single malts were launched, finished in apera and muscat casks respectively.

Hillwood Whisky (Tamar Valley Distillery)

Hillwood, Tasmania, founded in 2018

hillwoodwhisky.com.au

The spirit is distilled in a 600 litre copper pot still and maturation takes place in small casks that have previously held either wine or sherry, bourbon and port. The first releases appeared in summer 2020 and the biggest seller currently is Peated Sherry.

Hobart Whisky (formerly known as Devil´s Distillery)

Moonah, Tasmania, founded in 2015

hobartwhisky.com.au

In the beginning the distillery bought the wash for distillation but since 2017 they have their own brewing and fermentation system. The first core expression was the bourbonmatured Signature in 2020 which was followed by Pedro Ximenez Solera in 2022. There have also been a number of limited wood finishes (pinot noir, rosé, botrytis, stout).

Hunnington Distillery

Kettering, Tasmania, founded 2016

hunningtondistillery.com.au

Focusing on gin and vodka, the owners also produce small volumes of triple distilled single malt whisky. The whisky is bottled barrel by barrel and the first release appeared in August 2020 and was followed by more bottlings.

Iron House Brewery & Distillery

White Sands Resort, Tasmania, founded in 2007

ironhouse.com.au

Established as a brewery but moved into distilling whisky as well in 2010. The first Tasman Whisky (as the brand is called) was released in summer 2019 and the core range currently consists of Port-, Sherry- and Bourbon Cask - all aged for more than 4 years. A limited peated version appeared in autumn 2022.

Joadja Distillery

Joadja, New South Wales, founded in 2014

joadjadistillery.com.au

Initially equipped with just the one small still, the distillery was expanded in 2015 with a 2,400 litre wash still and later also a 6,000 litre still. The main part of the barley is from their own fields. The first whisky was launched in 2017 with a two year old oloroso maturation (release 17) in July 2022 as one of their latest bottlings.

Jones & Smith Distillery

Spring Hill, New South Wales, founded 2017

jonesandsmithdistillery.com.au

A family owned craft distillery which started producing single malt whisky in August 2018. Their Epoch gin was first launched in late 2019 and single malt whisky followed in July 2022.

Kangaroo Island Spirits

Cygnet River, South Australia, founded in 2006

kispirits.com.au

Focusing on gin for the first decade, Jon (brother of Bill Lark) and Sarah Lark started distilling also malt whisky in 2018. In autumn 2021 the distillery was substantially upgraded with larger stills. No whisky has yet been released.

Kilderkin Distillery

Ballarat, Victoria, founded in 2016

kilderkindistillery.com.au

The distillery is equipped with one pair of copper pot stills and have so far released a range of different gins. The whisky is still maturing.

Killara Distillery

Richmond, Tasmania, founded in 2016

killaradistillery.com

Daughter of Bill Lark, Kristy Booth, opened her own distillery in summer 2016 after having worked with her father for 17 years. In autumn 2020 the distillery moved from Hobart to a new site in Richmond. The succesful Apothecary gin has been on the market for a while and in November 2018 it was time for the first single malt release - a cask strength matured for two years in an ex-tawny port cask. More releases have followed with a 5 year old ex-tawny in January 2023 as one of the more recent.

Kinglake Distillery

Kinglake, Victoria, founded in 2018

kinglakedistillery.com.au

Located close to the Yarra Valley, the distillery is focused on malt whisky. Unusual features are a mash tun stirred by hand and open fermenters. The first whisky was released in 2021 and this has been followed by more including one matured in French oak, ex-tawny barrels in November 2022.

Launceston Distillery

Western Junction (near Launceston), Tasmania, founded in 2013

launcestondistillery.com.au

The equipment consists of a 1,100 litre stainless steel mash tun, stainless steel washbacks, a 1,600 litre wash still and a 700 litre spirit still. The newmake is filled into barrels which have previously held bourbon, apera and tawny (Australian port). The first release, matured in Apera casks, appeared in July 2018 and whisky matured in different types of casks, bottled on a batch basis have been launched more or less monthly since then.

Lawrenny Distilling

Ouse, Tasmania, founded in 2017

lawrenny.com

The distillery started off releasing vodka and gin. The first single malt whisky, Ascension, was launched in November 2020 and it was followed up by Descension (matured in a combination of casks including port, bourbon and madeira) in June 2022. Meanwhile there is an ongoing range named Cellar Collection with whiskies matured in different types of casks; sherry, bourbon, port etc.

Lisandras Distillery

Bayswater, Western Australia, founded 2019

lisandrasdistillery.com.au

A family owned distillery which was recently expanded. First two expressions of single malt (matured in Hungarian oak and American oak respectively) were released in 2021. Gin is also produced.

Loch Distillery

Loch, Victoria, founded in 2014

lochbrewery.com.au

A combined brewery and distillery using the wash from their brewery for the whisky production. The first single malt was launched in 2018 and by spring 2023, around 30 different releases had been made including a Rye&Corn.

Lower Marsh Distillery

Apsley, Tasmania, founded 2019

lowermarshdistillery.com

Steve Knight and Corey Hazelwood produce malt whisky from barley grown on their own farm including malting it themselves. The spirit is matured in a variety of casks (apera, port, Jack Daniels) and the first three bottlings appeared in November 2021.

The McLaren Vale Distillery

Blewitt Springs, South Australia, founded in 2014

themclarenvaledistillery.com.au

The wash is bought from a brewery and fermented and distilled at the distillery. In autumn 2021 the distillery was expanded with more stills. In 2017, twenty different malt spirits were launched to showcase different types of maturation and in 2020, the first two malt whiskies were released. More expressions have followed, often matured in casks from local wineries.

McRobert Distillery

Armadale, Western Australia, founded in 2019

mcrobertdistillery.com.au

Using a 1,000 litre hybrid still, the owner produces gin and whisky. Apart from rye, corn and bourbon style whisky there are two single malts in the range - bottled at 40% and 61% respectively.

Manly Spirits Co. Distillery

Brookvale, Sydney, New South Wales, founded in 2017

manlyspirits.com.au

Equipped with two copper pot stills (1,500 l and 1,000 l), the distillery first launched gin, vodka and a white dog malt spirit. The first single malt appeared in October 2021 and the range now consists of a core expression (Nor´easter) and the Element Series (five different small batch single malts).

Morris Whisky

Rutherglen, Victoria, founded 2016

morriswhisky.com

Since 1859 the Morris family have made fortified wines and in 2016 they added a distillery equipped with two hybrid copper pot stills from the 1930s. Their signature release appeared in 2021 and has been followed by other expressions (muscat, sherry, tokay), all of which have been finished in the company´s own wine barrels.

Mountain Distilling

New Gisborne, Victoria, founded 2017

mountaindistilling.com

Focusing mainly on gin, vodka and (not least) agave spirits the distillery has so far also released the peated Red Gum Single Malt.

Mt Uncle Distillery

Walkamin, North Queensland, founded in 2001

mtuncle.com

The owners started out by producing gin, rum and vodka - all of which soon became established brands on the market. Their first single malt, The Big Black Cock, was released in April 2014 matured for five years and was then followed by Watkins Whisky.

Nant Distillery

Bothwell, Tasmania, founded in 2007

larkdistillery.com

The distillery was founded by Keith Batt but was later taken over by Australian Whisky Holdings which has since been renamed Lark Distilling Co. The first bottlings were released in 2010.

Nonesuch Distillery

Dodges Ferry, Tasmania, founded in 2018

nonesuchdistillery.com.au

Established as a gin distillery it soon expanded into making single malt whisky as well. A red wine matured version and a triple grain (corn, rye and barley) are in the range together with the limited Roaming Cask.

Noosa Heads Distillery

Noosaville, Queensland, founded in 2018

noosaheadsdistillery.com

Equipped with a 2,000 litre copper pot reflux still, the distillery launched its first products in 2019 – gin, vodka and a white malt (new make spirit). The first single malt whisky was released in spring 2023.

Old Kempton Distillery

Kempton, Tasmania, founded in 2012

oldkemptondistillery.com.au

Established as Redlands Estate Distillery, the distillery re-located in 2016 to Dysart House in Kempton and later changed the name to Old Kempton Distillery. The distillery is equipped with four stills and the first single malt whisky was launched in 2015. Currently in the range are Classic in two versions, pinot and port, Old Stables and Solera Cask. December 2022 saw the release of a 10th Anniversary limited bottling.

Otter Craft Distilling

St Peters, New South Wales, founded 2017

ocdistilling.com

This small distillery has launched a wide range of vodkas and in summer 2019 the first single malt whisky was released. Several more have followed, always bottled as a single barrel.

Riverbourne Distillery

Jingera, New South Wales, founded in 2016

riverbournedistillery.com

Located close to Canberra, the distillery produces whisky, rum and vodka. The first two single malts, released in June 2018, were The Riverbourne Identity and The Riverbourne Supremacy followed later by Ultimatum, Enigma, Initiative and Objective.

St Agnes Distillery

Renmark, South Australia, founded 1925 (whisky since 2016)

stagnesdistillery.com.au

Starting as wine makers in the late 1800s, the Angove family later became Australia´s leading brandy producer. In 2016 the fifth generation ventured into small scale whisky production as well and in late 2022 the first releases of Camborne single malt appeared. They were all single casks and finished in brandy, sherry, tawny and shiraz casks repectively.

Sandy Gray Distillery

Spreyton, Tasmania, founded 2016

sandygraywhisky.com.au

A micro distillery producing gin and small volumes of single malt that is matured in 25 litre casks. The first whisky was released in September 2019.

Settlers Artisan Spirits

McLaren Vale, South Australia, founded in 2015

settlersspirits.com.au

Initially concentrating on gin, a new pot still in 2018 tripled the whisky production. The only single malt release so far is the port matured Settlers Single Malt.

Souwester Spirits

Margaret River, Western Australia, founded in 2016

souwesterspirits.com

Danielle Costley decided early on that her spirits (gin and malt whisky) would be matured in ex-wine casks. A single malt, matured in an ice chardonnay barrique, was first released in 2020.

Spring Bay Distillery

Spring Beach, Tasmania, founded in 2015

springbaydistillery.com.au

The first release was a gin followed in 2017 by a single malt. More whiskies, matured in port, sherry and bourbon casks, have appeared since. A special version is The Rheban bottled at 58%.

Stillmaker and Sons Distillery

Montville, Queensland, founded 2019

stillmakerdistillery.com.au

A family-owned distillery entirely focused on single malt whisky. A private cask was bottled in early 2023 but the first official release is yet to come.

Sunny Hill Distillery

Arthurton, South Australia, founded in 2018

sunnyhilldistillery.com.au

A family farm since 1872, the distillery produces gin, vodka and liqueurs. The first single malt made from their own barley was released in November 2021 and one of the latest (in February 2023) was the single cask Walandan.

Tara Distillery

Nowra Hill, New South Wales, founded 2019

taradistillery.com

The first spirit from the distillery that was launched was a gin in autumn 2020. The owners also produce an Irish-style single pot still as well as single malt whisky, both of them still maturing altough the Exile poitín has been released.

Taylor & Smith Distilling Co.

Moonah, Tasmania, founded in 2017

taylorandsmith.com.au

Using a self-built, direct-fired 400 litre pot still, the owners produce small volumes of gin and malt whisky. The first single malt was released in October 2020 and several more expressions have followed matured in bourbon, sherry, port or rum casks.

Maturing barrels at Old Kempton Distillery, Tasmania

Timboon Railway Shed Distillery

Timboon, Victoria, founded in 2007

timboondistillery.com.au

Wash from a local brewery is distilled twice in a 600 litre pot still. The first whisky release (Port Expression) was made in 2010 and is still the signature whisky. Other bottlings include Tom´s Surrender, Christie´s Cut and, bottled in early 2023, Governor´s Reserve which had been finished in a Yalumba Port cask.

Tin Shed Distilling Co.

Welland (Adelaide), South Australia, founded in 2013

tinsheddistillingco.com.au

The owners opened their first distillery, Southern Coast Distillers, in 2004. Eventually it was closed and the current distillery started in 2013. The first single malt, under the name Iniquity, was launched as a 2 year old in 2015 and in April 2023 batch 23, a 3 year old matured in a combination of port, sherry and bourbon, was released. Other ranges include the Anomaly Series and Gold Series.

Tiny Bear Distillery

Knoxfield, Victoria, founded in 2017

tinybear.com.au

Currently the main product is various expressions of gin. The first single malt appeared in 2021 followed by a port matured in January 2022 and Barrel 10 in November 2022.

Tria Prima Distillery

Mount Barker, South Australia, founded 2017

triaprima.com.au

Equipped with a 2,200 litre pot still and located in the Adelaide Hills, the distillery is focused on malt whisky. The first single malts, the 3 year old Enchantress and Bruxa, were released in August 2021 and was followed by Shaman - all three available either at 46% or at cask strength.

Turner Stillhouse

Grindelwald, Tasmania, founded in 2018

turnerstillhouse.com

Founded by ex-Californian Justin Turner, the distillery has so far been focusing on gin. A designated whisky still was installed in summer 2019 and the first single malt is expected in 2023.

Waubs Harbour Distillery

Bicheno, Tasmania, founded in 2018

waubsharbourwhisky.com

Inspired by coastal Scottish distilleries like Talisker and the ones on Islay but also staying true to Tasmanian whisky making methods, the distillery was founded by Tim Polmear, his wife Bec and Tim´s brother Rob. The latter had a long career in whisky making working for both Casey Overeem and Bill Lark before becoming the head distiller for Waubs. The first whiskies - Waubs Original, Port Storm and Founder´s Reserve - appeared in April 2023.

White Label Distillery

Huntingfield, Tasmania, founded in 2018

whitelabeldistillery.com.au

This is an unusual distillery in the sense that it is working as a contract brewing and distilling company, producing for other clients. Their customers can either obtain wash for their own distillation or new make spirit distilled to their own specification. The equipment consists of no less than 16 stainless steel washbacks (4,000 litres each) and two pairs of copper pot stills.

Wild River Mountain Distillery

Wondecla, Queensland, founded in 2017

wildrivermountaindistillery.com.au

One of the highest elevated distilleries in Australia, Wild River Mountain released their first single malt, Elevation, in August 2019. The fourth batch was released in August 2022 and in April 2023 a tawny barrel single malt was launched.

William McHenry and Sons Distillery

Port Arthur, Tasmania, founded in 2011

mchenrydistillery.com.au

Originally equipped with a 500 litre copper pot still, a 3,400 litre still was installed in late 2022. The first whisky was released in 2016 and the latest edition (number 32), in October 2022, was named Discovery and had been aged in French oak port barrels.

Winding Road Distilling

Tintenbar, New South Wales, founded 2017

windingroaddistilling.com.au

Apart from single malt whisky, both gin and rum is produced. The first whisky was distilled in spring 2019 in a 1,250 litre copper pot still and the first release of the Hinterland Single Malt appeared in spring 2022 with a second release in late 2022.

Yack Creek Distillery

Yackandandah, Victoria, founded in 2015

yackcreekdistillery.com.au

Equipped with two stills with columns attached, the distillery produces malt whisky, rum, gin and vodka. The first whisky was released in December 2019 and has been followed by more batches, including lightly peated malt. Batch 17 ex-apera in spring 2022 was followed by Batch 19, a wheat malt.

New Zealand

Thomson Whisky Distillery

Auckland, North Island, founded in 2014

thomsonwhisky.com

The company started out as an independent bottler but in 2014, the owners opened up a small distillery based at Hallertau Brewery in North West Auckland. First release was in 2018 and the current core range is made up by Rye & Barley, Manuka Smoke and South Island Peat. Recent limited expression include Full Noise - a cask strength manuka smoked whisky and Cask Martin, made from New Zealand grown barley and matured in local pinot noir casks.

Cardrona Distillery

Cardrona (near Wanaka), South Island, founded in 2015

cardronadistillery.com

The distillery is equipped with 1.4 ton mash tun, six metal washbacks, one 2,000 litre wash still and a 1,300 litre spirit still - both made by Forsyth's in Scotland. Apart from whisky, barrel-aged gin and single malt vodka is also produced. The first 3 year old whisky was released in December 2018 followed by Just Hatched (bourbon and sherry matured). Next came three expressions under the name Growing Wings and in spring 2023 it was time for Full Flight – two 7 year olds, matured in bourbon and PX sherry respectively and bottled at cask strength. September 2023, finally, saw the release of Falcon bottled at 52%.

Pokeno Whisky Company

Pokeno, North Island, founded in 2018

pokenowhisky.com

Equipped with two copper pot stills the owners are working with long fermentation times (+72 hours) and a slow distillation. In August 2022 the first three single malts were released; Origin fully matured in ex-bourbon, Discovery matured in a combination of bourbon, oloroso and PX casks and Revelation which combines bouron and red wine casks. In 2023 they were followed by Triple Distilled, Winter Malt and the world´s first whisky matured in totara wood (*Podocarpus totara*), a species endemic to New Zealand.

Other distilleries in New Zealand

1919 Distilling

Auckland, North Island, founded in 2016

1919distilling.com

The owners have a substantial range of gin and in summer 2020 the first single malt was released. The oldest release so far, in May 2022, is the 5 year old Kirikiriroa. Peated whisky is also produced. A core expression is due in 2024.

Auld Farm Distillery

Scotts Gap, South Island, founded in 2017

aulddistillery.co.nz

For three generations, the Auld family have been growing grain on their farm and in 2017 Rob and Toni also added distilling. The barley comes from their own land and is malted on site. Only new make and a flavoured usquebaugh have so far been released.

Herrick Creek Distillery

Christchurch, South Island, founded in 2020

herrickcreek.co.nz

This micro distillery has already launched gin and three types of whisky are produced - single malt from barley, corn and bourbon style. The current Explorer series is made from sourced whisky.

Kiwi Spirit Company

Golden Bay, South Island, founded in 2002

kiwispiritdistillery.co.nz

For two decades the distillery has produced a wide variety of different spirits including the unique Waitui Single Malt Manuka Honey (currently an 8 year old) where the whisky has matured in casks that had previously held manuka honey.

Lammermoor Distillery

Ranfurly, South Island, founded in 2018

lammermoordistillery.com

Lammermoor is a true "paddock-to-bottle" distillery where the Elliots control every step from organically growing and malting the barley through to distilling and maturation. The manuka smoked First Edition single malt appeared in 2020 and was followed by The Anzac Edition, The Jock Scott and, in August 2023, Double Cask.

Reefton Distilling Co.

Reefton, South Island, founded in 2018

reeftondistillingco.com

Starting off by distilling gin, vodka and liqueur, the owners moved to new premises in 2021, added a second still and started producing Moonlight Creek Whisky which will be available from 2025.

Spirits Workshop Distillery, The

Christchurch, South Island, founded in 2012

thespiritsworkshop.co.nz

For some time now Doug and Anthony Lawry have been making spirits for others in their two copper pot stills including malt whisky for New Zealand Whisky. Recently, however, they have themselves released a single malt under the name Divergence. All are matured in different types of barrels; virgin oak, port, PX sherry and there is also one expression that has been finished in sloe gin barrels.

Waiheke Whisky

Waiheke Island, North Island, founded in 2010

waihekewhisky.com

The distillery was founded by Mark Izzard and Richard Evatt on the Waiheke Island outside Auckland They started by designing a highly unique, geodesic spirit still made up by a number of flat copper panels that were fitted together. The goal was to increase the spirit volume to copper surface area to get more copper contact and a higher reflux. In 2022 the distillery moved into larger premises with more washbacks and a new set of stills. New Zealand peat is used for a lot of the production and the first expressions include Moss, Seris 1, Bog Monster and Dyad I and II.

The extraordinary view from the Cardrona Distillery still room

Asia

China

Daiking Distillery

Zhangzhou, Fujian, founded in 2014

Without any international attention, this malt whisky distillery of a substantial size (a capacity of 8,4 million litres of pure alcohol) was opened already in 2014 and in 2019 their first whisky was launched in the domestic market. The distillery is equipped with no less than five mash tuns (three semi-lauter and two converted starch cookers for brewing). There are 48 stainless steel wash backs with a fermentation time from 60 to 96 hours. A total of ten 10,000 litre wash stills (two made by Forsyths and eight made in China) and eight spirit stills, 6,000 to 10,000 litres (two made by Forsyths and six made in China) are housed in three still houses.

Laizhou Distillery

Qionglai, Sichuan, founded in 2021

bacchusrio.waimaotong.com

In the city of Qionglai, with a long history of producing baijiu, one of China's first malt whisky distilleries in modern times started production in October 2021. Laizhou distillery is owned by Shanghai Baccus, the biggest company in China in the ready-to-drink (RTD) segment and a subsidiary of Bairun. The distillery is equipped with eight copper pot stills made by McMillan in Scotland and equipped with condensers made of copper as well as stainless steel. In addition there are also 7 column stills. The distillery has the capacity to make 5 million litres of malt and 20 million litres of grain yearly. There is also a cooperage on site with nine coopers as well as a custom-made STR-system where wine casks are shaved, toasted and re-charred. The first products to be released will be vodka and gin with whisky coming later.

Chuan Distillery

Emeishan, Sichuan, founded in 2021

pernod-ricard.com

Speculations on when the world's two biggest spirits companies would build their own malt whisky distilleries in China cicrculated for years. Diageo broke ground to their Eryuan Distillery in

Yunnan in November 2021 but by that time Pernod Ricard's Chuan Distillery had been distilling for almost six months. With an investment of $150m the distillery has been equipped with ten stainless steel washbacks with a minimum fermentation time of 78 hours and one pair of pot stills made by Forsyths. The distillery is spectacularly designed and in 2023 a visitor experience with an arte centre will also be opened.

Mengtai Distillery

Ordos, Inner Mongolia, founded in 2023

In 2021 the equipment for an entire whisky distillery was shipped from Forsyths in Scotland to Ordos in Inner Mongolia. It is the first whisky distillery in the region and behind the project is Mengtai Group, one of Inner Mongolia's largest private companies and mainly active in coal production and generation of electricity. Included in the equipment is a two ton mash tun and ten washbacks. One of two production lines, making "bourbon", was commissioned in May 2023 and production of malt whisky commenced in August

Dongwei Distillery

Dong-Ting Lake, Hunan, founded in 2020

thedongwei.com

A craft distillery owned by Weidong Wei who began distilling already in 2014 in a small pilot still. The distillery is equipped with two traditional Scottish-style copper pot stills, designed and built by himself. The wash still is 3,000 litres and spirit still 2,000 litres and the distillery has a capacity of producing 93,000 litres. Chinese barley (two-, four- and six-row) is used and the first 6 year old single malt was released in 2022.

India

Amrut Distilleries Ltd.

Bangalore, Karnataka, founded in 1948

amrutdistilleries.com

The family-owned distillery, based in Kumbalgodu outside Bangalore in southern India, started to distil malt whisky in

Mengtai Distillery in Inner Mongolia - one of the latest (spring 2023) to open up in China

the mid-eighties. The equivalent of 60 million bottles of spirits (including rum, gin and vodka) is manufactured a year, of which 1,5 million bottles is whisky. Most of the whisky goes to blended brands but Amrut single malt was introduced in 2004 and can now be found in more than 50 countries. The distillery was expanded with four more stills in 2018 and with a total of two mash tuns and 12 washbacks it now has the capacity of producing one million litres of pure alcohol. The fermentation time for the single malt is 140 hours and the barley is sourced from the north of India, malted in Jaipur and Delhi and finally distilled in Bangalore before the whisky is bottled without chill-filtering or colouring.

The Amrut core range consists of Indian (unpeated) and Peated Indian, both bottled at 46% as well as at cask strength as well as Fusion which is based on 25% peated malt from Scotland and 75% unpeated Indian malt. Special releases over the years, often released in new batches, include Two Continents, where maturing casks have been brought from India to Scotland for their final period of maturation, Intermediate Sherry Matured where the new spirit has matured in ex-bourbon or virgin oak, then re-racked to sherry butts and with a third maturation in ex-bourbon casks, Kadhambam which is a peated Amrut matured in ex oloroso butts, ex Bangalore Blue Brandy casks and ex rum casks, Portonova with a maturation in bourbon casks and port pipes, Amalgam comprising of Amrut as well as single malts from Scotland and Asia (with a peated version introduced in late 2018), Spectrum where the fourth edition had been matured in casks made of four varieties of oak, Double Cask, a 5 year old combination of ex-bourbon and port pipes and the 100% malted Amrut Rye Single Malt. A big surprise in 2013 was the release of the 8 year old Amrut Greedy Angels. That was an astonishing achievement in a country where the hot climate causes major evaporation. A few years later a 12 year old version was launched with the latest edition released in 2021.

In 2020 the first triple distilled Indian whisky was released - Amrut Triparva - and in 2021 the sherry-finished Bagheera was launched. Late that year the first Master Distiller´s Reserve, a peated version matured in both bourbon and PX sherry casks. A special range called Single Malts of India was launched in 2021 with the peated Neidhal being the first bottling. Distilled at another distillery it had been further matured and bottled by Amrut. A second installment, Kurinji, appeared in 2023.

John Distilleries Jdl
Goa, Konkan and Bangalore, Karnataka, founded in 1992
pauljohnwhisky.com

Paul P John, who today is the chairman of the company, started in 1992 by making a variety of spirits including Indian whisky made from molasses. Their biggest seller today is Original Choice, a blend of extra neutral alcohol distilled from molasses and malt whisky from their own facilities. The brand, which was introduced in 1995 is one of the top selling brands in India. Another brand is Bangalore Malt, a simpler version of Original Choice. John Distilleries owns three distilleries and produces its brands from 18 locations with its head office in Bangalore and a huge distillery and visitor centre in Goa. The basis for their blended whiskies is distilled in column stills with a capacity of 500 million litres of extra neutral alcohol per year. In 2007 they set up their single malt distillery which was equipped with one pair of traditional copper pot stills and in 2017, another pair of stills were added, doubling the capacity to 1.5 million litres. Paul P John recently announced an expansion of the company, both in terms of capacity and in terms of the range. Whisky production will be doubled, gin was recently added to the protfolio and vodka is next in line. The large American spirit producer Sazerac owns 43% of the company while the rest is controlled by Paul P John.

The company released their first single malt in autumn 2012 and this was followed by several single casks. Since 2015 the core range consists of three expressions aged 6 years or more; Brilliance - unpeated and bourbon-matured, Edited - bourbon-matured and lightly peated and Bold - heavily peated. In 2019 an entry level bottling named Nirvana, aged for 3 years and bottled at 40%, was also launched. In 2014, two cask strength bottlings were released; Select Cask Classic and Select Cask Peated and since then, more Select expressions have been released, Oloroso and Pedro Ximenez. Part of a special range called Zodiac are Kanya and Mithuna. Every year a special Christmas Edition is launched. The latest had matured in a combination of ex-bourbon, brandy and peated oloroso casks.

Rampur Distillery
Rampur, Uttar Pradesh, founded in 1943
rampursinglemalt.com

This huge distillery was purchased in 1972 by G. N. Khaitan and

Rampur Distillery in Uttar Pradesh

is today owned by Radico Khaitan, one of the biggest Indian liquor companies. The capacity is 75 million litres of whisky based on molasses and 30 million litres of grain whisky. They also have a distillery producing whisky from malted barley. An expansion in autumn 2019 increased the capacity of that distillery to 3 million litres per year. A larger mash tun was installed as well as a new wash still (25,000 litres) and a new spirit still (16,000 litres). They also own another distillery in Maharashtra with a capacity of 52 million litres. The first whisky brand from Radico (in 1997) was 8PM, which sells around 115 million bottles yearly. The first single malt release, the ex-bourbon matured Select, appeared in 2016 and since then Double Cask matured in bourbon and sherry casks and PX sherry have been released in the core range. Asava, in 2020, was finished cabernet sauvignon casks. This was followed in 2022 by Trigun which had matured in a combination of ex-bourbon as well as champagne and sauternes casks, Jugalbandi #1 with a moscatel finish and Jugalbandi #2 with a calvados finish.

Other distilleries in India

Imperial Distillers & Vintners

Kundaim Industrial Estate, Ponda, Goa, founded in 2009

thecheersgroup.com

The company, which is part of the Cheers Group founded by Mohan Krishna, is the producer of a variety of different spirits and recently they launched the Three Monkeys Single Malt. Equipped with copper pot stills, the distillery has a capacity of 1 million litres of alcohol per year.

Khoday

Bangalore, Karnataka, founded in 1906

khodayindia.com

Khoday is a company working in many areas, including brewing and distillation. The IMFL whisky Peter Scot was launched by the company already in 1968 and in spring 2019, the Peter Scot Black Single Malt was launched.

McDowell´s Distillery

Ponda, Goa, founded in 1988 (malt whisky)

diageoindia.com

Established in the late 1800s, the distillery produces the best selling whisky in the world, McDowell´s No. 1, with 361 million bottles sold in 2021. Owned by Diageo since 2014, the distillery also produces a very small amount of single malt whisky. In early 2022 Diageo India launched a single malt named Godawan named after the threatened Great Indian Bustard. Whether or not this whisky was produced at McDowell´s is uncertain though.

Mohan Meakin

Solan, Himachal Pradesh, founded in 1855

mohanmeakin.com

Founded as a brewery in 1820, possibly by Edward Dyer and incorporated as a company in 1855. It was taken over by H G Meakin in 1887 and finally, Narendra Nath Mohan acquired the business in 1949. Today, the company is making beer, whisky and rum. Their most famous brands are Old Monk rum and Solan No. 1 whisky. Their first general launch of a single malt whisky under the name Solan Gold Single Malt appeared in 2019.

Piccadily Distillery

Indri, Haryana, founded in 1967, whisky since 1994

piccadily.com

Piccadily Agro Industries was founded in 1952 while Piccadily Distillery was registered in 1967 and in 1994 they resumed distilling. The distillery is equipped with two mash tuns (4.5 and 6.5 tons respectively), eight washbacks (60,000 litres each), three 25,000 litre wash stills and three 15,000 litre spiri stills - all pot stills stills and made from copper. The total malt capacity is 4 million litres of pure alcohol but grain spirit is also produced and on a much larger scale. This makes Piccadily the largest independent malt producing distillery in India. In 2020, in a joint venture with Peak Spirits, they launched their first single malt whisky named Kamet. This was followed in spring 2022 with Indri which had been matured in a combination of ex-bourbon, ex-wine and PX sherry casks and in 2023, Indri: Dru, a cask strength version was launched. The master blender behind the whisky is Surrinder Kumar who was the Amrut master blender for many years.

Israel

The Milk & Honey Distillery

Tel-Aviv, founded in 2013

mh-distillery.com

Israel´s first whisky distillery, equipped with a stainless steel mash tun, six stainless steel washbacks and two copper stills. The capacity is 800,000 litres of pure alcohol but there are plans for an expansion in 2024. The first distillation was in March 2015 and the first, limited 3 year old single malt, made before the final equipment was installed, was released in August 2017. A Founder´s Edition appeared in autumn 2019 and in January 2020 their first commonly available and current core expression, Classic, was launched. A series named Elements is based on maturation in ex-bourbon and STR casks with an addition of other cask types for each expression. Currently there are Sherry, Peated and Red Wine, with an annual limited edition of pomegranate wine casks expression for every Jewish new year. Another, limited, range is Apex where the head distiller, Tomer Goren, is experimenting with malts having been fully matured or finished in unusual casks or in extreme conditions. Some recent examples are Mouton, Tequila, Cognac and, one that has attracted a lot of attention, the Dead Sea where the casks had been matured in the lowest place on earth. A third range named Art & Craft focuses on different cask types and while the first edition in 2022 focused on ex-beer casks, the second batch in 2023 was all about dessert wine casks. Finally, in September 2023, the first Israeli whisky made entirely from Israeli barley was launched under the name Local Barley.

Other distilleries in Israel

Golani Distillery

Katzrin, founded in 2014

golanispirit.com

Founded by David Zibell, the distillery is equipped with two artisanal copper stills and some of the whisky is matured in wine casks from the nearby Golan Heights Winery. In spring 2020, a new, one ton mash tun as well as two more washbacks were installed and in autumn 2021 another mash tun, two more washbacks and two new 1,000 litre stills were added. The distillery is focusing on single malt from barley and on grain whisky (51% malted barley and 49% wheat). The first 3 year old whisky appeared in late 2017. A large number of different expressions, mainly single casks, have since been launched. There is also a range of single cask single malts named Unicask where the whiskies have matured mainly in casks that have previously held wine or brandy.

N.G.K. Distillery

Gan Hashomron, founded in 2021

ngk-distillery.com

Founded by Tomer Goren, Milk & Honey's Head Distiller and Amos Nir, in a collaboration with Milk & Honey distillery, it started distillation in May 2022. Equipped with 1 mash tun, 3 stainless steel washbacks and 2 stills, the distillery is producing a lightly peated whisky. There is already plans for an expansion in 2024

Shevet Brewing & Distilling

Pardess Hanna, founded in 2017

shevet.co.il

An impressive brewery founded by Neil Wasserman and Lior Balmas with a distillery attached that is equipped with two traditional copper pot stills. The wash from the brewery is distilled into whisky. A malt whisky by the name Ruach is in the pipeline but has not yet been released.

Yerushalmi Distillery

Jerusalem, founded in 2017

yerushalmidistillery.com

This is David Zibell´s (owner of Golani) second distillery and equipped with a 3,000 litre wash still and a 2,000 litre spirit still it has a capacity of 150,000 litres per year. David´s idea is to concentrate his production of peated whisky to this distillery. The first whisky distillation was in 2019 and recently they have released the peated single malt (35ppm) Mount Moriah and also four peated single casks in a new range named Solum; Sessile Oak (new French charred oak), Pirate Oak (rum cask), Birra Oak (craft beer cask) and Dessert Oak (white dessert wine cask). In March 2023 the peated Burnt Offering was released.

Japan

Yamazaki

Mishima, Osaka, founded in 1923

suntory.com/factory/yamazaki/

1923 marked the 100th anniversary of Japanese whisky and everything started here, in 1923, when Shinjiro Torii built the first malt whisky distillery in Japan. Torii was a pragmatic man, so he decided to build his distillery close to center of commerce at the time, Osaka. The construction of Yamazaki distillery began in late 1922 and was completed the following year. The distillery started out with two pot stills but has been reconfigured and expanded many times over the years, most recently in 2013 when four pot stills were added bringing the count to 16. There's plenty of variety in terms of heating method, shape, size, lyne-arm orientation and condenser type. Eight of the washbacks are wooden and the other nine made from stainless steel. With different peating levels for the barley, different yeast strains and a plethora of cask types, the variety of whisky types created at Yamazaki distillery is quite staggering.

Due to various renovations, the distillery was closed most part of 2023. Suntory also announced it would be investing approximately 10 billion yen into its Yamazaki and Hakushu Distilleries by 2024. The visitor facilities will undergo renovation and at both distilleries, floor-malting facilities will come into use. At Yamazaki, changes were also made to the so-called pilot distillery. This is a small-scale distilling facility which has been used for research and development since 1968.

Yoichi

Yoichi, Hokkaido, founded in 1934

nikka.com/eng/distilleries/yoichi/

Masataka Taketsuru set up Yoichi distillery after leaving Kotobukiya (now Suntory) in 1934. He settled on the town of Yoichi in Hokkaido, because the locale and climate conditions reminded him of Scotland, where he had studied whisky making. The first spirit ran off the stills in 1936, with the first product launched in 1940. Initially equipped with a single still that doubled as spirit and wash still, the distillery now houses 6 stills. Coal-heated and featuring straight heads and downward lyne arms, these produce a robust spirit. Although the 'house style' is peaty and heavy, people tend to forget that – like the other big distilleries in Japan – Yoichi is set up to create a wide range of distillates. Between various peating levels, yeast strains, fermentation times, distillation methods and maturation types, it is said that Yoichi is capable of producing 3,000 different types of malt whisky. Yoichi distillery is steeped in history. On November 19, 2021, ten buildings were added to the list of Important Cultural Properties by the

Milk & Honey Distillery in Israel has achieved an international reputation in just ten years

Japanese Ministry of Education, Culture, Sports and Technology. As far as enjoying the whisky produced at Yoichi goes, the options are somewhat limited. In September 2015, the entire Yoichi range (which included a no-age statement expression as well as a 10, 12, 15 and 20yo) was axed and replaced with a single option without age statement.

Fuji Gotemba

Gotemba, Shizuoka, founded in 1973

fujiwhisky.com

Fuji Gotemba distillery is nestled at the foot of Mt. Fuji, less than 12km from the peak. The 'mother water' is taken from the aquifer running 100 metres underground. Analysis has shown that the water used today fell on Mt Fuji as snow 50 years ago. The distillery was founded by Kirin Brewery, Seagram & Sons and Chivas Brothers as a comprehensive whisky distillery where all production processes – from malt and grain whisky distilling to blending and bottling – take place on site. Unlike most Japanese distilleries, which followed Scottish whisky-making practice, Fuji Gotemba distillery adopted production techniques and methodologies from all over the world. After Seagram started selling off its beverage assets worldwide, Kirin became the sole owner of the distillery.

The distillery is well known for its uniquely different styles of grain whiskey making, using column stills, a kettle and a doubler in a modular way. There are also ongoing projects to further diversify the flavor profile of their malt whisky. In June 2021, two different sets of new pot stills and four wooden washbacks came into use. The year 2023 marked the 50th anniversary of the distillery, and having switched to "Mt. Fuji Distillery" for the past few years, the decision was made to revert back to the original name, "Fuji Gotemba Distillery". This year, also, the two large-size pot stills, which had been in use since the foundation of the distillery, were replaced with brand new ones. The big news in 2023 was the launch of FUJI Single Malt Japanese Whisky in June. According to Master Blender Jota Tanaka, "it results from our efforts to diversify the malt whisky style, which we have been working on for more than ten years. The fruity key malt results from improvements made at every stage of the whisky-making process."

Hakushu

Hokuto, Yamanashi, founded in 1973

suntory.com/factory/hakushu/

Hakushu was built 50 years after the first Suntory malt whisky distillery and is nestled in a vast forest area at the foot of Mt Kaikomagatake in the Southern Alps. It is often referred to as 'the forest distillery': more than 80% of the site owned by Suntory is undeveloped. The original distillery was equipped with 6 pairs of stills. In 1977, capacity was doubled and another 6 pairs of stills added in a building next to 'Hakushu 1'. With its 4 mashtuns, 44 washbacks and 24 stills, Hakushu (1+2) was the biggest distillery in the world at the time. In 1981, Suntory built a new distillery, 'Hakushu 3' or 'Hakushu East' on the site, and decided to phase out production at #1 and #2 in favour of #3. Distilleries 1 and 2 had big stills, but all of the same shape and size, whereas #3 had a variety of stills with different shapes, sizes, lyne-arm orientations, heating methods and condenser types. What they were after was diversity and quality rather than quantity.

The distillery as it is operative now is Hakushu 3, albeit with the addition of two pairs of pot stills in 2014, bringing the total to 8 pairs, just like at Yamazaki distillery. It's also worth noting that there is a small grain whisky facility at Hakushu since December 2010. In February 2023, Suntory announced it would be investing approximately 10 billion yen into its Hakushu and Yamazaki distilleries by 2024. The visitor facilities at both sites will undergo renovation and reopen in autumn 2023 and floor-malting facilities will come into use. The Hakushu distillery will also introduce a process to cultivate yeast.

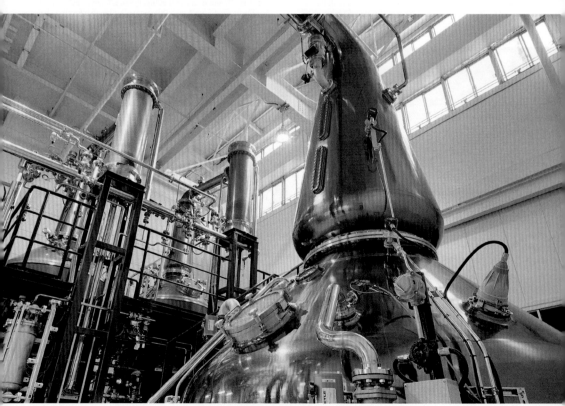

The new wash still at Fuji Gotemba Distillery

Miyagikyo

Sendai, Miyagi, founded in 1969

nikka.com/eng/distilleries/miyagikyo/

Miyagikyo is Nikka's second distillery andegend has it that it took Masataka Taketsuru three years to find the perfect site for it. He settled on the valley that brings the Hirosegawa and Nikkagawa rivers together because of the quality of the water, the suitable humidity and the crisp air. Construction started in 1968 and was completed in May of the following year. Originally known as 'Sendai', the distillery was renamed 'Miyagikyo' when Asahi took control of Nikka in 2001. At present, Miyagikyo is equipped with 22 steel washbacks and 8 huge pot stills of the 'boil ball' type with upward lyne arms, encouraging reflux which – given the slow distillation method (steam-heated) – results in a lighter, cleaner spirit. The site also houses two enormous Coffey stills imported by Taketsuru from Scotland. Moved from Nishinomiya in 1999, these are used to produce grain whisky (Coffey Grain) but, occasionally, are used to distill malted barley (Coffey Malt). Since 2017, they're also churning out Coffey Gin and Coffey Vodka. In September 2015, Nikka discontinued the entire Miyagikyo range due to stock shortages. It was replaced with a new NAS expression, which is the only permanently available Miyagikyo single malt.

Chichibu #1

Chichibu, Saitama, founded in 2007

facebook.com/ChichibuDistillery/

Chichibu distillery started producing in 2008 and the set up is small and compact: a 2,400 litre mashtun (manually stirred with a wooden paddle), eight mizunara washbacks of 3,000 litres each and a pair of 2,000 litre pot stills. Chichibu #1 uses mainly local barley and there is an area for floor malting on site. Between Chichibu #1 and Chichibu #2 distillery, there are 7 warehouses: six dunnage and one racked. The owner, Ichiro Akuto, also has a fully operational cooperage a few minutes down the road from Chichibu #1 distillery. Since 2010, the Chichibu team is buying mizunara wood from Hokkaido and a very small number of casks are made out of local Chichibu mizunara oak. Supply and demand is Ichiro's biggest headache. There simply isn't enough to go around. The latest 'big' single malt release was 'Red Wine Cask 2023' (11,800 bottles) which hit the shelves in the latter half of 2023.

Chichibu #2

Chichibu, Saitama, founded in 2019

facebook.com/ChichibuDistillery/

Around 2014, Ichiro Akuto started thinking about setting up a second distillery. His new distillery is just a two-minute drive away from the 'old' one and construction began in April 2018 and the first spirit came off the stills in July 2019. There are many features of the new distillery that are the same as at Chichibu #1, but the new distillery is five times bigger than the first one. At Chichibu #2, two tonnes of malted barley are processed per batch. Whereas Chichibu #1 uses mostly local barley, Chichibu #2 uses malted barley imported from England and Germany for the most part. Mashing takes place in a semi-lauter tun. For the fermentation process, Ichiro is sticking with wooden vessels, but unlike at Chichibu #1 where the washbacks are made of mizunara, the washbacks at the new distillery are made of French oak. There are 5 washbacks at the moment but there's room for more in the future. The stills are the same shape as at Chichibu #1 but they are much bigger and both stills are direct-fired, whereas those at Chichibu #2 are heated indirectly.

Other distilleries in Japan

Akkeshi

Akkeshi, Hokkaido, founded in 2015

akkeshi-distillery.com/en/

Inspired by Islay and with equipment and methods imported from Scotland, the goal of Akkeshi distillery is to create a whisky that is uniquely shaped by the environment. The production relies heavily on peated malt (50ppm), although non-peated malt is used as well. The distillery has two warehouses on site as well as two near the sea, to explore differences in maturation. Since August 2021, the distillery has also been maturing some of its spirit in central Hokkaido. The 10th release in the distillery's ongoing 24 Solar Terms series ('Keichitsu') was released in February 2023.

Asaka

Koriyama, Fukushima, founded in 2015

sasanokawa.co.jp/asaka-distillery-en/

Sasanokawa Shuzo was founded in 1765. Whisky 'making' started in 1946 but exactly how is lost in the mists of time. Sake production forms the backbone of the company and that allowed them to ride out some of the tougher periods for whisky in Japan. To mark the 250th anniversary of the company in 2015, a proper malt whisky distillery was set up in a disused warehouse on site. By the end of the year, two small pot stills had been installed. The first single malt expression (Asaka The First) was released in 2019 and Asaka The First Peated was released the year after. Because of a fire at the Portgordon Maltings in Scotland in 2022, the distillery couldn't get their usual supply of peated malt. Instead, they used malted barley smoked with New Zealand peat to about 60ppm.

Eigashima

Akashi, Hyogo, founded in 1919 (whisky since 1984)

ei-sake.jp/en/

On paper, this is the oldest whisky producer in Japan, having acquired a whisky production license in 1919, four years before Yamazaki. It took them four decades to get their act together, and another four decades to release their first single malt in 2007. The old spirit and wash still were retired in 2019 and replaced with new ones. In April 2023, a wooden washback was added to the distillery to extend the fermentation time and encourage the lactic acid fermentation. All production is matured on site in old single-story rickety warehouses in a bewildering variety of cask types. In 2022 the company released Eigashima Sextet, a single malt expression created by vatting whisky matured in six different cask types.

Fuji Hokuroku

Fujikawaguchi, Yamanashi, founded in 2020

Fuji Hokuroku Disitllery is a sideproject of Ide Jozoten, a well-known sake producer. The current president of the company, Yogoemon Ide, decided to expand into the field of whisky production and a tiny distillery was set up next to the historical sake brewery. The first milling took place in 2020 and the equipment includes two repurposed enamel-coated steel sake tanks and a single stainless steel still with copper plates in the neck.

Hanyu

Hanyu, Saitama, founded in 2021

toashuzo.com/lineup/whisky/en/

The original Hanyu Distillery was mothballed in 2000 and demolished in 2004. Its whiskies have since become the stuff of legend, changing hands for many thousands of dollars a bottle. In 2002, Toa Shuzo became a subsidiary of Hinode Holdings Co., Ltd and recently the top dogs decided the time was right to revive whisky-making at the company. A brand new distillery equipped with a one ton mash tun, 5 stainless steel washbacks and a pair of steam-heated lantern-shaped pot stills based on the blueprints of the original Hanyu stills started production in February 2021.

Hikari

Konosu, Saitama, founded in 2020

Hikari Distillery is the brainchild of Eric Chhoa and is, for the time being, the closest whisky distillery from Tokyo. They are doing their best to stay out of the spotlight for the first few years and focus on creating quality malt whisky. The Flemish-style design of the buildings is quite striking. Inside the distillery, all equipment is on skids allowing for easy reconfiguration in the future, should the need arise. The equipment consists of a one ton mash tun, six stainless steel washbacks and one pair of stills. From the start the distillery has been making whisky using non-peated malted barley imported from the UK. Occasionally, medium- and heavily-peated malt is used. The first spirit produced is now 3 years old but there are no plans to release anything as of yet.

Iiyama Mountain Farm

Iiyama, Nagano, founded in 2016

kiyokawa-sake.co.jp/home

This distillery is built around a "farm to bottle" concept, which is no mean feat given the harsh winters in the area. Whisky production started in 2019. There are 4 washbacks made from Italian oak and 6 stainless steel ones as well as stills from Frilli in Italy. There is also equipment on site to make grain whisky.

Ikawa

Shizuoka, Shizuoka, founded in 2020

juzan.co.jp/contents/ikawadistillery/

At the moment, Ikawa is the highest whisky distillery in Japan. Located in a UNESCO Eco Park in the Southern Alps at an altitude of 1,200m, this is also one of the most remote distilleries in Japan. It's a four-hour drive from the centre of Shizuoka City. The distillery is owned by Juzan Co., Ltd. and the equipment includes four stainless steel washbacks and one pair of stills with slightly descending lyne arms. Barley (peated as well as un-peated) is imported from Scotland. For the maturation, bourbon and sherry wood is used, but the company also has ambitious plans to make its own barrels using wood types other than oak, harvested from the forests surrounding the distillery.

Kaikyo

Akashi, Hyogo, founded in 2017

akashisakebrewery.com/the-kaikyo-distillery

Kaikyo Distillery is located on the site of the Akashi Sake Brewery, established by the Yonezawa family, which has been brewing since 1856 and distilling (albeit not whisky) since 1918. To mark their first century of distilling, a new stillhouse was built to house Forsyths stills and the building was named The Kaikyo Distillery. Together with Torabhaig Distillery (on the Isle of Skye), The Borders Distillery and Mossburn Distillers & Blenders, Kaikyo Distillery is part of a family-owned Swedish investment company. There is a close reciprocal relationship between the distilleries in Scotland and the team at Kaikyo in Japan. The aim is to produce a light, fruity spirit that will age well. In the fall of 2022, a single wooden washback was added to the distillery kit.

Kamui Whisky K.K.

Rishiri, Hokkaido, founded in 2020

kamuiwhisky.com

Kamui Whisky was established by husband-and-wife entrepreneurs Casey Wahl and Miku Hirano. The location they chose couldn't be more remote: Rishiri Island off the northwestern tip of Hokkaido. It is equipped with two stills from Vendome in Louis-ville, Kentucky. Both are heated using steam jackets and cooled with miniature worm tubs. Production started in the fall of 2022 and the production is still very limited by necessity.

Kanosuke

Hioki, Kagoshima, founded in 2017

kanosuke-en.com

Kanosuke distillery is owned by Komasa Jozo, one of the leading shochu makers in Kagoshima prefecture. The idea to establish a whisky distillery was born in 2015. Yoshitsugu Komasa, who represents the fourth generation of the family, picked some vacant land next to three warehouses where the company's shochu is matured and had the necessary equipment installed in the summer of 2017: a 6,000 litre mash tun, 5 stainless steel washbacks and 3 pot stills (6,000, 3,000 and 1,600 litres respectively) all with wormtub condensers. In 2022, five additional stainless steel washbacks were installed. In September 2021, Diageo made an investment in the distillery through accelerator Distil Ventures. The first whisky was released in June 2021 and the most recent release was the peated Kanosuke 2023 Limited Edition in June 2023.

Karuizawa

Karuizawa, Nagano, founded in 2021

karuizawa-whisky.co.jp

Not to be confused with the legendary distillery of the same name that is long gone, this new distillery is the brainchild of Shigeru Totsuka, the 16th generation master distiller of Totsuka Sake Brewery. Totsuka acquired land in the town of Karuizawa and production started in December 2022. Master distiller is Yoshiyuki Nakazato who used to work at the original Karuizawa distillery. The pot stills are similar to the original stills, though slightly larger and sherry wood will play a key role in the maturation.

Kobe

Kobe, Hyogo, founded in 2015

kobedistill.official.ec

In 2021, trading company GrowStars decided to add a whisky-making facility to the existing alembic at "Michinoeki Kobe Fruit Flower Park Ozo" in Kobe. The alembic had been used for brandy-making in the past. The idea was to revive that but also add whisky production. A mash tun, two washbacks and a pair of pot stills were installed and whisky production began in the fall of 2022.

Komoro

Komoro, Nagano, founded in 2020

karuizawadistillers.com/en/

Komoro distillery is the brainchild of Koji Shimaoka, who worked in investment banking for over 20 years before moving into the hotel business in Karuizawa. Looking to bring back distilling to the Greater Karuizawa area, Shimaoka found the perfect site, in the city of Komoro. In 2020, he brought Ian Chang, formerly of Kavalan, on board as co-founding partner. There is a one ton mash tun, 5 stainless steel washbacks and 5 made from Oregon pine. Atypically, the spirit still is larger than the wash still (7.8kl and 5kl, resp.). This setup enables the low wines of two first distillations to be combined for one second distillation. The yearly capacity of the distillery is 500,000 litres of alcohol and the first spirit ran off the stills in June 2023. The spirit will be non-peated for the most part, but to honor Dr Jim Swan (Ian Chang's mentor), December will be set aside to make a mildly-peated whisky. The distillery is open to visitors and offers a variety of experiences.

Kuju

Taketa City, Oita, founded in 2021

kujudistillery.jp

The distillery is located at an altitude of 600m in the majestic Kuju Plateau. For owner Shoji Utoda it is the realization of a dream he has harboured since the early 2000s. In 2016, Utoda found a plot previously used by a sake brewery and in January 2021 the distillery got its license. The distillery is equipped with a 0.5 ton mash tun, five washbacks made of Douglas fir and two stills from Forsyth. Both peated (40-50ppm) and unpeated malt is used and most of the production is filled into ex-bourbon wood.

Kurayoshi

Kurayoshi, Tottori, founded in 2017

matsuiwhisky.com/en/distillery/

Kurayoshi first emerged on the Japanese whisky scene in 2015 as a brand rather than a distillery, with age-statement releases of 'Japanese pure malt whisky' at a time when age-statement Japanese whisky had become rare. The fact that Japanese whisky-makers don't swap stock made it easy for savvy consumers to figure out that the liquid in the bottles was imported in bulk from abroad. In 2017 they set up an actual distillery, but all of this happened away from the public eye. They started with three small Hoga alembic-type stills. In 2018, they added two larger stills and slowly started to let people into their distillery. Matsui Whisky is without a doubt the most widely-available Japanese craft whisky brand though it's not always clear what exactly the provenance of the liquid is.

Kyoto Miyako

Kyotamba-cho, Kyoto, founded in 2020

kyotoshuzo.com/en/distillery/

The distillery, owned by Kyoto Shuzo Co., is located in the Tamba highlands. All production takes place under one roof and the equipment includes four enamel-coated open tanks used as washbacks with a 60 hour fermentation and two pot stills with slightly descending lynearms. There is also a small alembic type still, used for the production of gin. The whisky products currently sold by the company appear to contain liquid sourced from abroad.

Maoi

Naganuma, Hokkaido, founded in 2008 (as a winery)

maoidistillery.com

Starting as a winery, a distillery (for both whisky and brandy) was added in 2021. Whisky production started in September 2022. The set-up includes a hand-stirred mash tun, two stainless steel washbacks and a hybrid still made by Forsyths with two columns used for grain whisky and brandy. The company uses both local barley and local peat.

Mars Shinshu

Miyada village, Nagano, founded in 1985

hombo.co.jp/visiting/shinshu/

Mars Shinshu was built at the peak of whisky consumption in Japan, but 7 years into what would turn out to be a 25-year long

decline, the doors were closed. The distillery was mothballed in 1992 and it wasn't until 2011 that the decision was made to fire up the stills again. In 2014, the old pot stills were replaced with brand new ones and in 2018, three Douglas fir washbacks were installed. As part of a massive 1.2 billion yen investment, 2019-2020 saw the construction of a new warehouse, new stainless steel washbacks and mashtun as well as a new visitor centre. In March 2021, locally grown barley was distilled. The most recent release was the 2023 edition of the Komagatake IPA Cask Finish.

Mars Tsunuki

Minami-Satsuma, Kagoshima, founded in 2016

hombo.co.jp/visiting/tsunuki/

Towards the end of 2015, Hombo Shuzo started setting up a second distillery in their homebase of Tsunuki in Kagoshima with the first distillation in October. The distillery is the playground of Tatsuro Kusano who learned the ropes at Mars Shinshu under distillery manager Koki Takehira. Some things are the same as there but there are marked differences too not least in the approach to making whisky including the use of specialty malts, various yeast types etc. The first single malt expression was launched in April 2020 and the most recent release was the Tsunuki 2023 Edition.

Nagahama

Nagahama, Shiga, founded in 2016

romanbeer.com/whisky/

Nagahama, one of the smallest distilleries in Japan, was set up in a record time of 7 months as an extension of Nagahama Roman Brewery. The distillery started production in November 2016. Mashing and fermentation takes place in the equipment used for beer making. For the rest of the process, a small 'still room' with three 1,000 litre Hoga alembic-type stills was created. The first widely available expression, The First Batch, appeared in late 2022.

Niigata Kameda

Niigata, Niigata, founded in 2019

niigata-distillery.com

Niigata Kameda is located in Kameda Industrial Park, close to JR

Komoro Distillery in Karuizawa began distilling in 2023

Niigata Station. This station is serviced by the bullet train so, from Tokyo, it's the shortest trip to a whisky distillery. The distillery is a side project of Otani, the biggest maker of inkan (personal seals) in Japan. The first distillation took place in February 2021. Most of the malted barley (both peated and non-peated) is imported from Scotland, but some local Niigata barley is used as well. A small, automated malting machine was purchased in 2022 and the plan going forward is to do the malting of local barley in-house. There is also equipment and plans to make grain whisky (rice-based) and rum (from Hokkaido beet sugar) in the future.

Niseko

Hokkaido, founded in 2019

niseko-distillery.com

Niseko Distillery is the brainchild of Jiro Nagumo, CEO of the sake producer Hakkaisan Brewery. The equipment includes a Buhler mill from Switzerland, a one ton full-lauter mash tun from Slovenia, three Douglas fir washbacks made in Japan and a pair of pot stills from Forsyths in Scotland - one 5,500 litre wash still and a 3,600 litre spirit still. There is also a 600 litre hybrid Holstein still for the production of gin. The first whisky distillation took place in March 2021 and the first whisky release is planned for 2024.

Nozawa Onsen

Shimotakai District, Nagano, founded in 2020

nozawaonsendistillery.jp/en/

The distillery is situated in Nozawa Onsen – a well-known tourist destination in Nagano prefecture – and whisky production began in January 2023. The head-distiller, Sam Yoneda, uses a mash cooker with direct steam injection and a crash-cooling jacket. It is used in conjunction with a mash filter. There are also stainless steel washbacks, a pair of lantern shaped pot stills and a gin still. It is currently the only Japanese craft whisky distillery using a mash filter, giving huge flexibility to develop unique flavour profiles.

Nukada

Naka, Ibaraki, founded in 2016

kodawari.cc

Nukada distillery was set up by Kiuchi Shuzo in a corner of their new Hitachino Nest brewhouse. In terms of output, it is the smallest

whisky distillery in Japan. The 1,000 litre hybrid still is used to make whisky as well gin. The production volume varies from year to year and is limited by the fact that the staff also distill beers and make some of the Kiuchi liqueurs.

Okayama

Okayama, Okayama, founded in 2011

whiskyokayama.com/english/

Miyashita Shuzo was founded as a sake brewery in 1915. In 1994, they became one of the pioneers of Japanese craft beer. In 2003, the company started distilling some of their hoppy beer in a stainless steel shochu still. Then, in 2011 they got a license to produce also malt whisky – at first in the shochu still and since 2015 in a copper hybrid still. Production is extremely limited (40 batches per year) and bottlings are rarely seen.

Ontake

Kagoshima, founded in 2019

nishi-shuzo.co.jp/ontake

Ontake Distillery was established by liquor producer Nishi Shuzo and is part of a golf course they own. The distillery is equipped with one mashtun, five stainless steel washbacks (fermentation time 5 days) and two pot stills. Production started in December 2019. For the time being, only non-peated malted barley is used. Most of the production is aged in oloroso butts but he distillery also uses pinot noir casks from their own winery in New Zealand.

Oriental Kanazawa

Kanazawa, Ishikawa, founded in 2016

orientalbrewing.com

Oriental Brewing, a craft brewer based in Kanazawa city, installed a hybrid still, three wooden washbacks and three repurposed enamel-coated steel sake tanks in summer 2022 and started distilling soon after. The aim is to launch the first whisky in 2025.

Osuzuyama

Koyu-gun, Miyazaki, founded in 1998 (whisky since 2019)

osuzuyama.co.jp/en/

Originally established as a shochu distillery. All ingredients are

The first release from Niseko Distillery is expected in 2024

sourced locally and the equipment includes 15 fermenters made of Obi-Sugi, a type of cedar tree. The barley is malted in-house using a propriety method called "box malting". A combination of stainless-steel shochu stills and a copper pot still is used. The most recent release in April 2023 was the Osuzu Malt Chestnut Barrel matured in casks partially made from Japanese chestnut wood.

Rokkosan

Kobe, Hyogo, founded in 2020

rokkosan-distillery.com

Rokkosan Distillery was established by Axas Co., Ltd on top of Mt Rokko, at an altitude of 800m. The distillery is tiny with only 40 batches per year but still offers tours to visitors. Malted barley (predominatly heavily peated) is milled off-site and brought to the distillery as grist. One mashtun and two stainless steel fermenters are used in conjunction with one Holstein still.

Saburomaru

Tonami, Toyama, founded in 1990

wakatsuru.co.jp/saburomaru/en/

Wakatsuru Shuzo started making whisky following the end of the Pacific War, but the company has been making sake since 1862. They focused on simpler whiskies but in 2016 they revitalized their distillery to produce malt whisky. A new mill and mashtun were installed in 2018. In 2019, the distillery started using a new pair of pot stills, the world's first cast copper pot stills also known as Zemon stills and in 2020, a single Douglas fir washback was added to the set-up followed by a second one in 2022. These are used for 24 hours after 4 days' fermentation in enamel tanks. The most recent expression was II The High Priestess.

Sakurao Distillery

Hatsukaichi, Hiroshima, founded in 2018

sakuraodistillery.com/en/sakurao/

Sakurao may be a new distillery, but the liquor company behind it is not. Chugoku Jozo was established in 1918 and incorporated in 1938. Their liquor portfolio comprises shochu, sake, mirin and various liqueurs. Chugoku Jozo started 'producing' whisky in 1938 and until the liquor-tax change of 1989, their field was 'budget' whisky. In 2003, they launched the Togouchi brand which

was made up of whisky imported from abroad. To mark the 100th anniversary of the company, a whisky distillery with a hybrid still to make grain whisky as well as gin was set up. Both peated (20ppm) and unpeated spirit is produced. Casks are matured on site as well as in disused tunnels. Sakurao is a rare instance of a Japanese craft distillery with two permanently available single malts on the market: Single Malt Sakurao and Single Malt Togouchi.

Setouchi

Kure, Horoshima, founded in 2020

setouchidistillery.com/en

Setouchi Distillery is the most recent project of Miyake Honten, a company that traces its history back to 1856 when it started producing mirin, shochu and later sake. In the late 1920s, its products became the official military-use sake aboard naval ships. The new whisky operation (starting 2021) is relatively small but in August 2022, a pot still was added to the exisiting hybrid still. The most recent release, in July 2023, was Newborn – Aged 1 Year.

Shindo

Asakura City, Fukuoka, founded in 2021

no website

Shindo Distillery was built by Shinozaki Co., Ltd, the famous barley shochu maker, Since the start many types of malted barley have been used but one month a year is reserved for heavily-peated (50ppm) production. Mashing takes place in a one ton semi-lauter tun and the distillery is also equipped with 5 stainless steel washbacks with water jackets and one pair of copper pot stills. The first product to come out of the distillery was Shindo New Make, released in September 2022.

Shizuoka

Shizuoka, Shizuoka, founded in 2015

shizuoka-distillery.jp

The distillery is owned by Gaia Flow founder Taiko Nakamura and started producing in February 2017. Initially there were 5 washbacks at the distillery: four made from Oregon pine and one made from Shizuoka cedar. In February 2018, three more cedar washbacks were installed. The stillhouse has 3 pot stills: one from

Nozawa Onsen - currently the only Japanese distillery using a mash filter

the old Karuizawa distillery and a new pair made by Forsyths in Scotland with the wash still being directly fired. The most recent release was Pot Still W 100% Japanese Barley First Edition which went on sale in May 2023.

Tamba

Tamba-Sasayama, Hyogo, founded in 2018

kizakura.co.jp/tamba/

Tamba Distillery is owned by Kizakura Co., a liquor producer founded in 1925 and their distillery is based in an inland basin surrounded by mountains on all sides and blessed with a subtropical climate. Since 2004, shochu has been produced but the owners felt the humid location was also ideal for making whisky. At first whisky was produced using a stainless steel still but in October 2021, two copper pots made by Forsyths were installed. Milling and mashing takes place off-site and both peated and un-peated barley is used. Fermentation takes place in one of two enamel-coated tanks of the type used in sake production. Three limited single malt expressions have been released so far: the inaugural Tamba 1st Edition, Tamba Bottled in 2022 2nd and Tamba Bottled in 2023 1st.

Yamaga

Yamaga, Kumamoto, founded in 2021

yamagadistillery.co.jp/?eng

Being the first distillery in Kumamoto, Yamaga is equipped with a one ton mash tun, five stainless steel washbacks and a pair of pot stills. For the maturation, a warehouse on site with mobile racks and a capacity of 3,300 barrels is used. Yamaga is one of few Japanese distilleries open to the public. The most recent release was Yamaga New Born, a non-peated distillate matured for 5-7 months.

Yasato

Ishioka, Ibaraki, founded in 2019

no website

The owners designed the distillery based on making a new type of whisky, using various kind of grains and different types of yeast. There's a four-roller mill, a 5,000 litre cereal cooker for step mashing and rice/buckwheat/corn cooking and a 6,000 litre lauter tun, four 12,000 litre stainless fermenters and four 6,000 litre wooden fermenters. There is also a 12,000 litre wash still and an 8,000 litre spirit still. The first distillation was in March 2020. The whisky is sold under the name Hinomaru and the most recent release (December 2022) was Hinomaru 2023 Celebration, a vatting aged in bourbon casks, sherry casks and red wine casks.

Yuza

Yuza, Yamagata, founded in 2018

yuza-disty.jp

Kinryu, the owners of the distillery, was founded in 1950 and was a joint venture funded by nine local sake producers, initially to make neutral spirit. Over time, they started making and selling shochu made in a continuous still. Overall consumption of shochu (as well as sake) has been on the decline for decades. To mitigate that, the company decided to start producing whisky and set up a brand new distillery in Yuza city. The first distillation took place in November 2018 and their third release appeared in May 2023.

Pakistan

Murree Brewery Ltd.

Rawalpindi, founded in 1860

www.murreebrewery.com

Started as a beer brewery, the assortment was later expanded to include whisky, gin, rum, vodka and brandy. The core range of single malt holds two expressions – Murree´s Classic 8 years old and Murree´s Millenium Reserve 12 years old. There is also a Murree´s Islay Reserve, Vintage Gold.

South Korea

Three Societies Distillery

Namyangju-si, Gyeonggi Province, founded in 2020

threesocieties.co.kr

With three distilleries having been built in the late 1980s and early 1990s and later closed, this is the first malt whisky distillery in modern times in South Korea. One of the three owners is Andrew Shand who used to work at Speyside distillery in Scotland and later Virginia distillery in USA. Located 40 kilometres east of Seoul, the distillery is equipped with a 5,000 litre wash still and a 3,000 litre spirit still – both from Forsyths and the capacity is one million litres of alcohol. There is also a 700 litre still for making gin, rye, bourbon and experimental spirits. To show the progression of their spirit, two malt spirits appeared in 2022 (13 months old The Tiger and 19 months old The Unicorn). The distillery´s first flagship whisky, Ki One, appeared in March 2023.

Three Societies Distillery in South Korea

Taiwan

Kavalan Distillery

Yuanshan, Yilan County, founded in 2005

www.kavalanwhisky.com/en

On the 11th of March 2006 at 3.30pm, the first spirit was produced at Kavalan distillery. This was celebrated in a major way a decade later when guests and journalists from all over the world were invited for the 10th anniversary. But it was not just to celebrate 10 years of whisky production but also to witness the recent expansion of the distillery which has made Kavalan one of the ten largest malt whisky distilleries in the world! This rapid development may even have surprised the founder, entrepreneur and business man Tien-Tsai Lee, and his son, the current CEO of the company Yu-Ting Lee. Early on, it was decided that expertise from Scotland was needed to get on the right track from the beginning. Dr. Jim Swan was consulted and he developed a strategy including production as well as the future maturation. Jim Swan passed away in early 2017.

The distillery lies in the north-eastern part of the country, in Yilan County, one hour's drive from Taipei. Following the expansion in 2016, the distillery is equipped with 5 mash tuns, 40 stainless steel washbacks with a 60-72 hour fermentation time and 10 pairs of lantern-shaped copper stills with descending lye pipes. The capacity of the wash stills is 12,000 litres and of the spirit stills 7,000 litres. Kavalan only uses a very narrow cut from the spirit run, leaving more foreshots and feints to accommodate a complex and rich flavour profile. The spirit vapours are cooled using shell and tube condensers, but because of the hot climate, subcoolers are also used.

On site, there are two five-story high warehouses and in September 2020 they broke ground for a third warehouse which, when completed October 2023, was larger than the two existing combined. The climate in this part of Taiwan is hot and humid and on the top floors of the warehouses the temperature can reach 42°C. Hence the angel's share is dramatic – no less than 10-12% is lost every year. At the moment, Kavalan are doing experiments aiming to reduce the angel's share to below 10%. The distillery has its own cooperage where the preparation of the STR (shave-toast-rechar) casks plays an important part for the final character of the whisky.

Since the first bottling of Kavalan was released in 2008, the range has been expanded and now holds 30 different expressions. In spring 2020, the core range was complemented by two bottlings being priced competitevely to act as an entry level to the rest of the range. One of them was launched already in 2018 and is now called Distillery Select No. 1 while the new expression is Distillery Select No. 2. Apart from them, the core range consists of Classic and an "upgraded" version of that called King Car Conductor. There is also the port finished Concertmaster which has been supplemented by Concertmaster Sherry. Finally there are Ex Bourbon and Oloroso Sherry, both bottled at 46% and Podium.

The range that first opened the world's eyes to Kavalan was Solist first introduced in 2009. Matured in different types of casks these are all bottled at cask strength and released in batches. The first two were Bourbon and Oloroso and have been followed by Fino, Vinho Barrique, Brandy, Amontillado, Manzanilla, PX, Moscatel and Port. Another two bottlings are exclusively sold at the distillery visitor centre; Distillery Reserve Rum Cask and Distillery Reserve Madeira Cask. The distillery has produced whisky from peated barley (10ppm) as well and the first time it was released was in autumn 2020 in a single cask, cask strength collection of four named "Kavalan Artists Series". Peated Malt had been matured in STR casks and the other three in the series were Puncheon, Virgin Oak and French Wine Cask. Recent limited releases include a bottling matured in ex-Bordeaux wine casks, launched in late 2019 to celebrate the 40th anniversary of the foundation of King Car Group. A limited collection appeared in June 2021 when three bottlings with exotic animals native to Taiwan pictured on the labels were launched and in November 2021 Triple Sherry cask was launched. This was the distillery's first attempt to release an expression matured in three different sherry casks; oloroso, PX and moscatel. Finally, a Master's Select exlusive to the travel retail market was launched in autumn 2023.

Whisky is, of course, the main product for Kavalan but production of gin is also carried out. The first release in a series of triple distil-led gins appeared in early 2019. In June 2020, the owners launched a "ready-to-drink" range called The Kavalan Bar Cocktail and since 2018 they are producing beer at a plant in Taoyuan. In May 2019, Kavalan opened their first designated 'Cask Strength Whisky Bar' in the busy Zhongshan District of Taipei. Recreating the inside of the distillery's warehouse, it was the only bar in the world to carry the full range of Kavalan whisky. Guests can order whiskies straight from the cask and the bar also uses special effects to illustrate the environmental impact on the flavour of the whisky. This was later followed by a second bar at the distillery in Yilan. The Kavalan Garden Bar dominates the second floor of the Spirits Castle.

Kavalan is being exported to more than 60 countries and apart from Taiwan, Europe and the US are the most important markets. There is an impressive visitor centre on site with no less than one million people coming to the distillery every year.

This gigantic third warehouse at Kavalan Distillery was opened in October 2023

Other distilleries in Taiwan

Nantou Distillery

Nantou City, Nantou County, founded in 1977
(whisky since 2008)

omarwhisky.com.tw

Located in the central east of Taiwan, Nantou distillery is a part of the state-owned manufacturer and distributor of cigarettes and alcohol in Taiwan – Taiwan Tobacco and Liquor Corporation (TTL). Between 1947 and 1968 it exercised a monopoly over all alcohol and tobacco products sold in Taiwan. It retained the monopolies until Taiwan's entry into the WTO in 2002.

There are seven distilleries and two breweries within the TTL group, but Nantou is the only with malt whisky production. The distillery is equipped with a 2,5 ton full lauter Huppmann mash tun and eight washbacks made of stainless steel with a fermentation time of 60-72 hours. There are two wash stills (9,000 and 5,000 litres) and two spirit stills (5,000 and 2,000 litres). The owners are currently looking to expand the distillery with more stills and warehouses. Malted barley is imported from Scotland and ex-sherry and ex-bourbon casks are used for maturation. Nantou distillery also produces a variety of fruit wines and the casks that have stored lychee wine and plum wine are then used to finish some of their whiskies. Initially the spirit from Nantou was all unpeated but in 2014 trials with peated malt brought in from Scotland were made.

The single malt is sold under the brand name Omar and in 2013, two cask strength single malt whiskies were launched – one from bourbon casks and the other from sherry casks. Three years later Sherry Cask and Bourbon Cask, bottled at 46%, were launched and the two now make up the distillery´s core range. Another range is called Liqueur Finish and bottled at cask strength they have all been finished in different wine or liqueur casks; plum, lychee, black queen wine and orange brandy. The Cask Strength range is represented by ex-bourbon, ex-sherry and peated ex-bourbon. Recent releases include a 12 year old finished for four years in PX sherry casks and number four in the Omar Harvest Series. In March 2023, a 13 year old single PX sherry cask expression was released - the oldest expression from the distillery so far. There is also a sub brand named Yushan, mainly for the European market, with one blended malt and three single malts - Sherry Cask, Bourbon Cask and Smoky.

Thailand

Red Bull Distillery

Tambon Nadee, Muang District, founded in 1988

thaibev.com

A large distillery producing a multitude of spirits and since at least ten years, also single malt whisky. It is owned by one of Asia´s top drinks producers, ThaiBev, controlled by the Thai billionaire Charoen Sirivadhanabhakdi and his family. There seems to be no single malt release from the distillery yet and the main seller when it comes to whisky is the Blend 285 which is made up from whiskies distilled in Thailand and Scotland.

Africa

South Africa

James Sedgwick Distillery

Wellington, Western Cape, founded in 1886 (whisky since 1990)

threeshipswhisky.co.za, bainswhisky.com

Distell Group Ltd. was formed in 2000 by a merger between Stellenbosch Farmers' Winery and Distillers Corporation, although the James Sedgwick Distillery was already established in 1886. The company produces a huge range of wines and spirits including the popular cream liqueur, Amarula Cream. James Sedgwick Distillery has been the home to South African whisky since 1990. The distillery has undergone a major expansion in the last years and is now equipped with one still with two columns for production of grain whisky, two pot stills for malt whisky and one still with five columns designated for neutral spirit. There are also two mash tuns and 16 washbacks. Grain whisky is distilled for nine months of the year, malt whisky for two months and one month is devoted to maintenance. Three new warehouses have been built and a total of seven warehouses now hold more than 150,000 casks. There is also a highly awarded visitor centre on site. In February 2022, a majority of Distell´s share holders accepted a take-over bid from Dutch brewer Heineken worth $2.4bn. Distell was also the owner of three Scottish distilleries since 2013; Bunnahabhain, Deanston and Tobermory. After the Heineken deal, these are now owned by CVH Spirits, a subsidiary of the investment company Remgro.

In Distell´s South African whisky portfolio, it is the Three Ships brand, introduced in 1977, that makes up for most of the sales. The range consists of two blends; Select and the 5 year old Premium Select, the latter being a blend of South African and Scotch whiskies. Furthermore, there is the 10 year old single malt which was launched for the first time in 2003. A new addition to the range in 2021 was the whisky.based spirit aperitif Mash Tun which is bottled at 24%. A range called the Master´s Collection was introduced in 2015 with the idea to annually launch something limited in volume and a South African first. Now into it's 7th year and following on from the 10 year old PX finish, a 15 year old Pinotage cask finish, an 8 year old lightly peated Oloroso cask finish, a 9 year old Fino cask finish and an 11 year old Shiraz cask finish there is the 6 year old Chenin Blanc finish. In 2023 the pinnacle of Three Ships whisky was reached when a 21 year old bottled at 51.8% was released! Apart from the Three Ships range, the distillery also produces South Africa´s first single grain, Bain´s Cape Mountain Whisky, where the core version is 5 years old. A limited 15 year old was released in 2019 and in 2021 a 21 year old which had been further matured in amontillado and manzanilla sherry casks appeared in travel retail.

Helden Distillery

Parys, Free State, founded in 2018

helden.co.za

The founder, Pieter van Helden, began his career as a producer of fruit brandies but soon moved on to focus on whisky. The range is focused on an African style, both in terms of the grains but also the wood used for maturation. Apart from a Helden Single Malt, a number of single malts spirits (not yet 3 years old) matured in wood such as hickory and cherry have been released.

Incendo Distillery

Hartbeespoort, North West, founded in 2017

incendo.co.za

Founded by Francois and Vonmari Joubert, the distillery produces a wide range of spirits; gin, rum, brandy, liqueur and whisky. Limited expressions of 3 year old single malt from barley as well as from other mashbills have been released under the name Lexicon.

South America

Argentina

La Alazana Distillery
Golondrinas, Patagonia, founded in 2011

laalazanawhisky.com

Located in the Patagonian Andes, this is the first malt whisky distillery in Argentina. The distillery is owned and run by Nestor Serenelli and his wife Lila. The owners are firm believers in the "terroir" concept where local barley, water and climate will be expressed in the flavour of the whisky. A new twist on "terroir" came in late 2022 when two casks of maturing whisky were brought to Marambio military base in the Antarctic to mature for another couple of years in extreme climate. The distillery is equipped with a lauter mash tun, four stainless steel 1,100 litre washbacks with a fermentation time of 100 hours and two stills. For the last three years, the owners have been growing and malting their own barley. Besides the Classic and Organic malt, they do a lightly peated malt named Haidd Merlys. The first, limited release was made in 2014 and in 2019 an 8 year old matured in a combination of ex-sherry and ex-bourbon was launched. The owner´s first 10 year old whisky was bottled in December 2021. In autumn 2023 an unexpected collaboration between Penderyn distillery in Wales and La Alazana resulted in a Welsh/Argentinian whisky!

Other distilleries in Argentina

Emilio Mignone y Cia
Luján, Buenos Aires province, founded in 2015

emyc.com.ar

Owned by brothers Carlos and Santiago Mignone, this became the second whisky distillery in Argentina. The first distillation was in November 2015 and the distillery is equipped with a 300 litre open mash tun, a 600 litre washback with a 72-96 hour fermentation and two stills, directly fired by natural gas. The distillery was expanded in 2022 to an annual capacity of 6,000 bottles. The distillery has four different editions; the EM&C Pampa Single Malt Classic matured in ex-bourbon barrels, released in 2019, the EM&C Pampa Single Malt Peated matured in PX sherry barrels, launched in 2020, the EM&C Pampa Single Malt Classic matured in ex-sherry barrels, released in July 2022 and, in September 2022, a new Peated edition that had been matured in ex-whisky casks in a location on the Atlantic coast.

Madoc Distillery
Dina Huapi, Rio Negro, founded in 2015

madocwhisky.com

The owner is one of the founders of the first Patagonian distillery, La Alazana. In 2015, he left the company and brought with him some of the equipment, as well as part of the maturing stock to build a new distillery in Dina Huapi. The existing equipment with a lauter mash tun, a washback and a copper pot still was complemented by a wash still and the first distillation took place in September 2016 and a single malt bottled at 40% has been released.

Brazil

Union Distillery
Veranópolis, founded in 1972

maltwhisky.com.br

The company was founded in 1948 to produce wine, before focusing on malt whisky production from 1972. In the 1980's, it invested in its production facilities including a co-operation with Morrison Bowmore Distillers. Most of the production is sold as bulk whisky, but the company has recently re-started to release their own products since 2019. Their Single Malt core range includes 'Pure Malt' (Wine Cask Finish; Virgin Oak Finish; the peated Turfado and the heavily peated Extra Turfado) as well as 'Autograph' limited releases and 'Vintage' releases, including the Vintage 2005, possibly the oldest single malt released in Latin America.

Lamas Destilaria
Matozinhos, founded in 2019

lamasdestilaria.com.br

Started by the Lamas brothers this is now managed by the second and third generation Lamas family members. The craft distillery produces a wide range of spirits, including single malt whisky. Lamas' single malt whisky core range includes: Plenus, Verus, Rarus, and the smokier Nimbus and Nimbus Robustus. They also produce a blended whisky named Canem and sometimes use Brazilian native woods for the maturation resulting in special releases such as the recent Putumuju (*Centrolobium robustum*).

Copper pot stills at Union Distillery, Brazil
Photo, Rafel Nardi

Nestor Serenelli brought two casks from La Alazana to the Antarctic

The Year
that was

Including the subsections:
Single malt hot spots | The big players
The big brands | New distilleries

In most parts of the world, 2022 was the year when the final restrictions due to the pandemic were lifted. But already the year before, the alcohol industry had experienced a significant recovery back from the disastrous 2020.

Global alcohol consumption increased also in 2022 (volumes up by 5%) but at a much slower rate. According to the IWSR we can expect a volume growth of 1% per annum 2022-2027 year on year and a value growth of 2%. The drivers in volume will be countries such as India, Mexico and Brazil while USA and China will drive the value.

Another company, Straits Research, presented different figures where they anticipated the global alcoholic drinks sector to grow at a compound annual growth rate of 2,5% between 2023 and 2031. The report pointed out Asia Pacific as a major growth hub due to the region´s large young adult population and the continued acceptance of western culture as well as the perception of drinking as a social and lesiure activity.

International air travel suffered great losses during the pandemic and, as a consequence of that, so did duty free sales. The sector hasn´t fully recovered yet and one reason for that is that the Chinese haven´t fully returned to their pre-covid pattern of travelling. It also seems clear that many producers will be prioritising value over volume.

In many countries, the pandemic also created a change in consumer behaviour that seems to be here to stay – consumption of more at home and at moderation. Premiumisation (drinking less but better) continues while rising inflation and higher interest rates, especially in Europe, affect brands in the standard and lower price tier.

If we look at the 2022 sales in different categories, global beer volumes grew by 3% while wine lost 5%. According to the IWSR spirits declined 2% in volume but if we exclude national spirits (the denominator for Asian spirits such as baijiu, soju, shochu and arrack) the category grew by 5%. Some of the main drivers were whisky (+8%), rum (+9%) and brandy (+6%). Cognac on the other hand lost 10% while vodka and especially gin seem to be on a long-term decline or at least saturated as categories.

One category that excels is agave based spirits (tequila, mezcal, raicilla etc). Global growth in 2022 was 13% and in USA tequila is set to overtake vodka in 2023 to become the industry leader. The hype of tequila as seen in USA and Mexico has started to become obvious also in the UK but it remains to be seen if it will continue at the same pace in other countries.

The aforementioned "national spirits" could be set up for an international break-through. The Chinese baijiu itself sells more volume in China than the combined volumes of whisky, vodka, gin and tequila worldwide. Domestic sales of baijiu is forecasted to reach $200 billion by 2024. A number of international spirits producers have invested in baijiu distilleries in China and what have been trickles of the spirit emerging into the rest of the world could soon evolve to more. The South Korean spirit soju, with the world's largest spirits producer Jinro as the main producer, also attracts an interest not least from the on-trade business in the rest of the world. Jinro itself sold 1.2 billion bottles in 2022.

The main trends going forward will to a large extent be influenced by the current economic concerns. The important consumer groups will consist of financially stable individuals with low debts rather than the "millennials", e-commerce will continue to be an important sales channel – although growing at a slower rate than a year ago – and moderation, both as a health and wellness concern but also driven by the economic situation, will continue to shape the industry.

The two main categories of whisky – Scotch and Bourbon – were close in terms of value in 2022. Both demonstrated sales of around $8 bn. In third place is Irish whiskey with $1.2 bn. In the past decade Irish whiskey has been the fastest grower but in 2022 value was up by 25% while Scotch grew by 37%.

It was a year of impressive growth for Scotch whisky in 2022. In the words of Mark Kent, Chief Executive of the Scotch Whisky Association; "During a year of significant economic headwinds and global supply chain disruption, the Scotch whisky industry continued to be an anchor of growth..."

Volumes of exported Scotch were up by 21%, reaching the equivalent of 1.67 billion bottles while values increased by an incredible 37%, coming in at £6.2 billion – the first time over £6 bn! According to the SWA the reasons for this were post-pandemic restocking, the return of global travel retail and premiumisation. At the same time Mark Kent highlighted potential threats in the near future such as inflation and increasing energy and business costs.

The volume of single malt Scotch still represents 10% of the total exports of Scotch while the value is 32% (slightly lower than 2021).

SINGLE MALT SCOTCH - EXPORT 2022

Value: +30.0% to £1.99bn
Volume: +30.1% to 180.3m bottles

BLENDED SCOTCH* - EXPORT 2022

Value: +40.6% to £4.13bn
Volume: +19.6% to 1.39bn bottles

TOTAL SCOTCH - EXPORT 2022

Value: +37% to £6.2bn
Volume: +21% to 1.67bn bottles

* incl. bottled and bulk blend, bottled and bulk blended malt and excl. grain

Overall, in 2022 exports in terms of value have fallen in 49 of 180 global markets but the decline often took place in very marginal markets. The year before, 43 of 188 global markets showed negative figures for value. The export statistics from the SWA is divided into eight regions and seven of them showed positive, often double digit, growth during 2022 in terms of both values and volumes. The only exception was Eastern Europe including Russia which isn't that surprising given the invasion of Ukraine and the following sanctions.

The European Union

The EU is still the largest market for Scotch whisky when it comes to volumes but it also shows every sign of being a mature market. Last year it represented 35% of the volumes and now it is down to 33%. In terms of values it was overtaken by Asia & Oceania in 2022 and now has a share of 26% (down from 30% since last year). The growth in both volumes and values since 2021 was 17%.

The European Union — Top 3

France	volumes	+16%	values	+26%
Germany	volumes	+48%	values	+36%
Spain	volumes	+39%	values	+46%

There is definitely no other market in the region that stands a chance of challenging France in the near future, regardless if it concerns values or volumes. In fact it has been the largest market for Scotch in terms of volumes for many decades. In 2022 however, India surpassed it when it came to volumes of imported Scotch even though France increased by 16%. This just goes to show what an impact India will have in the years to come. In all honesty, the category that gave India the first place was blended malt imported in bulk. France is still the largest importer of bottled Scotch whisky in terms of volumes.

In second place we find Germany beating Spain in terms of volumes by just a whisker. That meant they reclaimed the second place in the EU (which they lost in 2021). In terms of values (+36%) Germany firmed their position as number two. Spain is, however, closing in. They gained less in volume than Germany but more (+46%) in value. If we look just at single malts, the increase for Spain was 50% which may indicate a change of consumer behaviour. Historically malt whisky in the country has often been enjoyed young and not rarely together with Coca Cola.

Runner ups in the EU are Poland (single digit increase) and the Netherlands (double digits) while Latvia has lost 38% in volumes and 46% in values. The latter is not surprising as Latvia has been a hub for re-export to Russia for many years, a business obviously hampered due to the Russian invasion of the Ukraine and the following trade sanctions.

Asia and Oceania

Since 2022, Asia and Oceania is the world's largest region in terms of values with an increase of no less than 50% and a 45% rise in volume. It seems that it is just a matter of time (perhaps as soon as next year) before the region will be number one in the world in both values and volumes when it comes to import of Scotch. The major part of the increase this year can be attributed to larger sales to India but also to Singapore, Taiwan and, to a lesser degree, China.

Asia and Oceania — Top 3

India	volumes	+60%	values	+93%
Japan	volumes	+33%	values	+32%
Singapore	volumes	+32%	values	+50%

India is the largest market in the world for whisky but Scotch only accounts for 2% there. The producers have regarded India as one of the most important of the emerging markets for Scotch for two decades now. Success was minor in the beginning but year by year India has climbed the list. In 2022 it was time for the country to occupy the number one spot (held by France for many years) as the largest importer of Scotch in terms of volume, an increase of 60% since 2021. The main part of this is bulk whisky and in terms of single malt it's only number twelve. Regardless, this is most probably only the beginning of a profitable relationship between Scotland and India. Currently imported Scotch is banned with a 150% tax but negotiations between the UK and India have been going on for almost two decades. In the recent eighth round of discussions, the lowering of tariffs to 50% and even 30% have been discussed and hopefully a solution will be agreed upon where Scotch can grow its share of the whisky market in India from the current 2%. Some industry representatives say a duty relief could double the size of the Scotch whisky market in India in the next five years, increasing the value by £1 billion.

In second place we find Japan which is one of the largest importers of bulk Scotch (blends, blended malts and grain

The on-trade business (bars, pubs and restaurants) has become increasingly important for the whisky industry

whisky that hasn't been bottled) in the world. Due to a much softer legislation in Japan, this whisky is then blended with domestic spirit and often sold as Japanese whisky. But the country also ranks as the tenth most important market for single malt. The younger generations in Japan drink considerably less than their parents, which means less tax revenue for the government. Campaigning under the motto "Sake Viva!", launched in 2022, the government tries to encourage the young population to drink more to facilitate for the industry and increase tax revenues.

The third biggest market in 2022 for Scotch in Asia was Singapore with a double-digit rise in both volumes and values. It is in fact the third-most valuable market in the world (worth £316m). With a population of a mere 6 million the figures seem surprisingly high but Singapore is also the gateway to China for many companies in the industry and large volumes are re-exported from there. Last year's increase for Singapore was on the blended side (+36%) and to a lesser degree single malts (+16%).

The large increases in 2021 that lifted China to third place, weakened during 2022 and the country is now down to fourth place (although number three in terms of value). What is remarkable is the high share of single malt – no less than 70% of the total value, a figure that no other country in the world can match, not even Taiwan.

North America

Since 2020, when it was overtaken by Asia & Oceania, this is the third largest region in terms of values. In 2021 it lost its third place in volumes to Latin America and Caribbean. Together with The European Union and Sub-Saharan Africa, the region showed a weaker performance in 2022 (just like in 2021) with volumes up by 8% and values by 32%.

North America — Top 3

USA	volumes	+9%	values	+33%
Mexico	volumes	+2%	values	+22%
Canada	volumes	+15%	values	+32%

USA is by far the largest importer in the region with a 68% share of the volumes ad no less than 79% of the values. It is also by far the most important market for Scotch (especially single malt) in the world. Their value was almost as much as the combined value for France, Singapore and Taiwan (numbers 2-4 on the top list). The most sold type of whisky in the USA however is bourbon (270 million litres) followed by Canadian (175 million), Scotch (90 million) and Irish (55 million). Irish whiskey has enjoyed a strong momentum ahead in the past few years and it is not unlikely that the category could overtake Scotch in a few years from now. Scotch has for a long time enjoyed legal protection as a Geographical Indication (GI status) product in the USA. To strengthen the status even more, Scotch was also trademarked in USA in 2022.

Mexico, in second place, is of course mostly known as a tequila producer – a spirit category that has broke through the roof in the past five years. Surprisingly though, only one of the ten largest tequila producers is based in Mexico – Becle, owner of José Cuervo. On the other hand it is the largest of them all with almost 30% of the market. On the Scotch whisky side Mexico is a very important market, mainly for blends and the share of single malt is only 7%. The most sold Scotch by far is Buchanan's and the story behind its success is quite extraordinary. It has been featured in a number of so called *narcocorridos*, ballads that have been accused of glorifying drugs and especially the lifestyle of drug lords and criminal organisations.

Canada, finally, defended its 14th position from last year on the Scotch whisky global top list and if we focus on just single malt it is in place 7 with an increase in value by 25% compared to 2021.

Latin America and Carribean

This region continued the success from last year and in 2022 volumes were up by 18% while values soared, increasing by 66%. It is a region hugely dominated by blends and single malt only make up 3% of the total value. In fact the values of single malt export to Sweden in Europe (with ten million people) equals that of Latin America (670 million people). Historically Latin America and the Caribbean has been a volatile region for Scotch. The re-occurring economic downturns have seen consumers looking for less expensive alternatives, locally produced spirits such as *cachaca* in Brazil, *aguardiente* in Colombia and *pisco* in Bolivia and Peru. However there is a small but growing awareness about quality whisky and even a handful of malt whisky producers in Argentina, Brazil and Chile.

Latin America and Carribean — Top 3

Brazil	volumes	+14%	values	+64%
Panama	volumes	+107%	values	+165%
Colombia	volumes	+3%	values	+56%

The biggest market in terms of volume (39%) is Brazil with 21% of the region's value. The country is now the world's fourth largest importer of Scotch when it comes to volumes and number 13 if we look at values. This clearly indicates that the interest from the Brazilian consumers lies in blended whisky and single malt only makes up 1,5% of the value.

In second place we find Panama which by an incredible performance in 2022 made its way back to the Top 3 in the region. The single malt volumes are just a mere 1,5% of their total import but the value of single malt makes up 23% of the entire region. It is also the world's seventh biggest export market for Scotch in terms of values (the year before it came in at 18th place), and larger than Brazil. The trading conditions for Panama are special. The country has several economic zones with the Colon Free Trade Zone on the Atlantic side being the largest free-trade zone in the Western Hemisphere. This means that a substantial share of the Scotch imports are being distributed to other parts of Latin America and the Caribbean.

Number three in the region is Colombia, down from second place in 2021. While total numbers increased moderately during 2022, the value of imported single malts were up by no less than 82% to reach £7m which is three times as much as Brazil.

Sub-Saharan Africa

In terms of volumes, with an increase of just 5%, this region was the least impressive in 2022 with the exception of Eastern Europe (including Russia). Values though were up by 30% and if we focus on just single malts it was +40%.

Sub-Saharan Africa — Top 3

South Africa	volumes	+15%	values	+37%
Angola	volumes	+41%	values	+29%
Kenya	volumes	-42%	values	-24%

As usual, South Africa is the dominant market in the region and more so than last year. In 2022 it represented 51% of the values (48% in 2021) and 59% of the volumes (54%). The increase in 2022 was better than last year and its position on the global top list improved slightly. It is now number 10 in terms of volumes (number 12 in 2021) and 20 in terms of value (19).

The new number two was Angola where the improvement was all due to a substantial increase in bulk blend and bulk blended malt. All other categories were down. Last year's number two, Kenya, is now in third place with the only positive figures from 2022 coming from single and blended malt. Nigeria in fourth place is interesting as 68% of its imports are single malts compared to 21% of imports for South Africa.

Middle East and Northern Africa

The region performed well during 2022 with volumes up by 39% and values by 74% (which is best of all the regions). The top 3 markets (same as last year) are responsible for 72% of the volumes and 79% of the values of the region.

Middle East and Northern Africa — Top 3

UAE*	volumes	+45%	values	+86%
Israel	volumes	+26%	values	+36%
Iraq	volumes	+40%	values	+66%

* United Arab Emirates

A major part of the imports to the UAE are destined for duty free sales and with the travel market being restored following the pandemic, the impressive 86% increase in values was not surprising. In fact single malts were up by almost 100%. Israel, with knowledgeable consumers, not least thanks to successful local producers, continues to be a good market for single malt Scotch.

Western Europe exc EC

What used to be the smallest of the nine regions in terms of volumes is now the second smallest due to the sanctions against Russia (part of the Eastern Europe region). By its own merits however, the region increased 49% by values and 32% by volume during 2022. This was far better than the single digits increases during 2021.

Western Europe exc EC — Top 3

Turkey	volumes	+36%	values	+63%
Switzerland	volumes	+15%	values	+23%
Norway	volumes	+11%	values	+16%

There are only seven markets in the region and the top three tend to be the same. Turkey is by far the biggest, responsible for 81% of the total volumes and 72% of the values. It was also the country of the Top 3 that increased the most during 2022. The other two countries are far more biased towards single malts than Turkey. For Switzerland it was 58% of the total values and for Norway 52%. The corresponding figure for Turkey was 7%.

Eastern Europe

This is the smallest of all regions and consists of Russia and some of the surrounding countries including parts of the Balkans. States traditionally included in Eastern Europe but being members of the European Community are not included here. Since the Russian invasion of Ukraine in February 2022, the region has been difficult for the Scotch whisky producers to do business in, as well as for companies in every other industry. Trade sanctions against Russia were imposed in early 2022 but the inertia of implementing the ban and the fact that several companies continued, albeit on a smaller scale, to do business with the country has prevented the export figures in this presentation from being zero. The fact that the Russian government has been able to sidestep the boycott by allowing "parallel" or "grey" import from "friendly" countries is another story. The market left open by western producers of whisky has created an interest amongst Indian whisky producers, not least Allied Blenders and Distillers (owners of one of the best selling whiskies in the world, Officer's Choice) and in spring 2023 they entered the Russian market. In 2022 exports to the region declined by 41% in terms of volumes and 18% in values.

Eastern Europe — Top 3

Russia	volumes	-47%	values	-46%
Georgia	volumes	+85%	values	+84%
Ukraine	volumes	-30%	values	-26%

Russia is still the main market in the region even though volumes have declined by 47% since last year and values by 46%. In second place comes Georgia where not least an increase in values of single malt by 95% stands out. The main part of the Georgian import is re-directed to Russia. In third place is Ukraine with diminishing numbers in both volumes and values.

Single malt hot spots

I often get asked the question which countries have a preference for single malt Scotch so let's have a look. In these figures, I have focused on the Top 40 markets and selected the 10 nations with the largest single malt share.

Single malt share of Scotch whisky imports 2022

	Country	Volume	Value
1.	Taiwan	52%	63%
2.	China	41%	70%
3.	Canada	39%	58%
4.	Germany	29%	56%
5.	Sweden	27%	62%
6.	South Korea	24%	30%
7.	USA	21%	38%
8.	Israel	21%	32%
9.	Singapore	20%	31%
10.	Italy	20%	49%

If we instead take into account the number of people living in the respective countries, i. e. volume of single malt Scotch per capita, the ranking looks like this (and again we're talking about the Top 40 markets);

Largest single malt Scotch import per capita in 2022

1. Latvia
2. Singapore
3. Taiwan
4. Netherlands
5. France
6. Sweden
7. Germany
8. Australia
9. Israel
10. Canada

It is important to remember that both Singapore and Latvia serve as hubs for re-export to other markets.

The big players

Diageo

A solid report issued in the beginning of August for the 2023 fiscal year (ending 30 June 2023) from the world's largest spirits producer was preceded by a tragic message less than two months before that: the company's CEO since ten years back, Ivan Menezes, had died at the age of 63 from complications of stomach ulcer surgery. Menezes joined the company in 1997 when Diageo was formed through the merger of Guinness and Grand Metropolitan. As a global marketing director he was responsible for developing the "Keep Walking" campaign for Johnnie Walker in 1998 and during his ten years as CEO he strengthened Diego's number one position in the industry. He was set to retire on 30 June 2023 with Debra Crew succeeding him. Due to Menezes' sudden illness, Crew stepped in as CEO already at the end of May. Menezes was knighted in the 2023 New Year Honours for services to business and equality.

The full year report for 2022/2023 showed an increase in net sales of 10.7% to £17.1 bn despite volumes declining by 7%. The reason for that was strong organic growth, not least from Scotch and tequila, and favourable foreign exchange impacts. Operating profits grew by 5.1% to £4.6bn.

The company's biggest market, representing 39% of sales, is North America with a growth of 11% in the last year. Europe comes in second, representing 21% of sales and also with an increase of 11%. Third is Asia Pacific, 19% of the sales and, again, an increase of 11% in the last year. Here, a 4% decline in China due to remaining covid restrictions, was offset by a growth of 17% in India. Latin America and Carribean represent 11% of the sales with an increase of 18% last year while Africa (10% of sales) declined by 2%.

Looking at the different product categories, tequila (12% of net sales) continued to lead in terms of growth (+19%) with Don Julio and Casamigos (the world's two biggest tequila brands) as the main drivers. The growth is almost entirely located to the USA but the new CEO, Debra Crew, made it abundantly clear that the growth of Diageo until 2030 will in a major way be based on the expansion of tequila in other markets as well as premiumisation of the category in the same way they have done with Scotch.

Scotch, however, is still the company's most important

The CEO of Diageo for ten years, Ivan Menezes, passed away 7 June 2023 following a brief illness

category with 25% of total sales and a growth of 12% which was significantly lower than last year's 29%. The world's best selling Scotch, Johnnie Walker, grew by 15%. For the calendar year of 2022 that translated into 272 million bottles, an all time high. Other blends performing well were Buchanan's (+7%), Old Parr (+18%) and Black & White (+20%). The malt portfolio increased by 16%. The second largest category after Scotch is beer (15%) with an increase in sales by 9%. The growth was primarily driven by Guinness which in December 2022 became Britain's number one beer in bars and pubs for the first time.

On the acquisition side, it was an unusually slow year for Diageo. In November 2022 they took over the innovator and cult whiskey producer Balcones Distilling in Texas and in March 2023 they bought the super-premium Philippine rum Don Papa for €260m.

Pernod Ricard

The world's second largest spirits producer, Pernod Ricard, can look back at a job well done during the latest fiscal year, ending 30th June 2023. Their increase in sales were similar to the ones from Diageo (number one in the world) with a growth of 13% to €12.1 billion but in terms of increase in profits, Pernod Ricard was the winner. Profits from recurring operations were up by 11% to €3.35 billion. The percental increases for both sales and profits were, admittedly, larger the year before but these came from a decline the year before that due to the pandemic.

Of the three regions, Asia-Rest of the World (the largest market representing 42% of the sales) was the definitive star with a 17% increase led by Japan (+28%) and India (+27%) and with a solid performance also in South Korea (+19%) and Greater China (+7%). Europe grew 8% with Spain and Germany as the main markets. In the Americas, finally, sales grew with just 2%. There was also an overall

strong rebound for Travel Retail around the world.

Scotch whisky represents 34% of the company's sales and Chivas Brothers (the Scotch business of the company) reported an increase of 17%. Ballantines's and Chivas Regal (number two and three on the Top 10 list of Scotch) increased by 13% and 25% respectively. Notable growth markets for the two were India, Japan, Turkey, Spain and Travel Retail. The global number one Scotch single malt, The Glenlivet, grew by 9% with a strong performance in USA, Taiwan and India. Irish whiskey (which in this case means Jameson) represents 13% of the company's sales and grew by 11%. The Irish dominator sold 133 million bottles and is one of the 10 most sold whiskies in the world. Other important brands in the Pernod Ricard portfolio are Martell, Absolut, Malibu and Ricard.

Acquisitions or investments in other companies during the year include Codigo 1530 (tequila), Skrewball (flavoured whisky) and Ace Beverage Group (ready-to-drink products). Huge investments are also made in Scotland on the sustainability side of production and the capacity at both Aberlour and Miltonduff distilleries will be doubled within the next 2-3 years.

Edrington

Scott McCroskie, the CEO of Edrington was pleased when he commented on the financial year which ended 31 March 2023. "Our business has delivered another highly successful year, despite a range of external challenges." And it was indeed a good performance. Core revenue (sales) was up 22% from last year to £1.1bn, an increase which was less than last year's 45% but, for the first time in history, the company exceeded £1 billion. Profits before tax increased by 43% to £388m. Like last year, the growth in value outstripped the growth in volume which clearly shows that Edrington is very much focused on premium products, not least when it comes to Macallan but also Highland Park and Glenrothes which belong here. Recent ultra-premium releases for Macallan have been the James Bond Collection, the Red Collection and the Macallan M series.

The owners are usually reluctant to reveal sales volumes for specific brands but Macallan, the third biggest Scotch single malt is now close to breaking the 1 million case barrier. The reputation of Macallan single malt has been built on whisky matured in sherry casks. In spring 2023, Edrington took a step to secure sherry-seasoned casks for the future when they acquired a 50% stake in the sherry producer Grupo Estévez.

Other brands in the portfolio include Famous Grouse blended Scotch, the blended malt Naked Malt and Brugal rum. For many years, Edrington was not represented in the American whiskey category. In 2018, however, they bought a 35% share in Wyoming Whisky which was increased to 80% in 2023.

Edrington's principal shareholder is The Robertson Trust which has donated £343 million to charitable causes since 1961. Since 2020, the Japanese company Suntory owns 10% of Edrington as well as 25% of Macallan (a share they have held since 1989).

Gruppo Campari

The company presented a solid result for the fiscal year 2022 with net revenues increasing by 24% to €2.7bn while net profits went up by 17% to €333m.

The company's main brands are divided into three groups with Global Priorities representing 57% of the sales. Aperol is by far the most important brand and sales increased by 28% while Campari grew by 24%. In both cases the success is boosted by the interest in drinks such as Aperol Spritz and Negroni. The third biggest brand is Wild Turkey bourbon with sales going up by 21% mainly thanks to US, South Korea and Australia.

The second tier is Regional Priorities (25% of the sales) with brands such as Espolòn tequila, Crodino bitter, Cinzano and Glen Grant single malt. The latter grew by double digits being particularly successful in South Korea and in the global travel retail market. Local priorities (8%), finally, is mainly made up of ready-to-drink brands.

Since Bob Kunze-Concewitz took over as CEO 17 years ago, Campari have been diligent when it comes to

acquisitions of other companies and brands. No less than 40 deals have been signed by him and it is apparent that he does not intend to slow down. The most recent acquisitions are the aperitif brand Picon and Wilderness Trail Distillery bourbon. The US, where Campari Group only have a 2.5% share of the market, is viewed as having the highest potential for growth. But acquisitions are not stand-alone success factors, an increase in capacity is also necessary and a second Wild Turkey distillery is planned in Kentucky.

The existing strategy is summed up by Kunze-Concewitz; "To satisfy future demand, we are accelerating our investments in supply chain with the aim to double our overall production capacity in key aperitifs, bourbon and tequila categories."

Beam Suntory

When Suntory bought Beam in 2014 an entire new company was founded - Beam Suntory - which is now responsible for its parent company's (Suntory Holdings) spirits operations. The company recently moved the headquarter from Chicago to New York and in October 2023, Albert Baladi was succeeded as CEO by Greg Hughes.

Financial figures for Beam Suntory are not revealed in detail by Suntory Holdings but for 2022 net sales were up by 10.5% which represented a 24% growth versus the pre-pandemic year of 2019. Baladi's comments to the result was; "We delivered these results despite significant challenges including supply chain disruptions, record inflationary pressure, our withdrawal from Russia and restrictive covid policies in China."

Over the last few years, Jim Beam, the company's flagship brand, has grown at a slower rate than arch rival Jack Daniel's but is still the best selling bourbon in the world while Jack Daniel's (a Tennessee whiskey) is number one as the top American whiskey. Other bourbons include Maker's Mark (+11% in 2022) and Basil Hayden (+40%).

Beam Suntory is also the owner of a portfolio of Scotch single malts where Laphroaig takes the lead followed by Islay neighbour Bowmore. The other three are Auchentoshan, Ardmore and Glen Garioch. Substantial investments have been made over the last couple of years in all five distilleries, aiming at improving the quality rather than increasing the capacity. In August 2023 the company applied for planning permission to build a maturation facility outside Glasgow with space for half a million of casks. Furthermore, in the Scotch category is the Teacher's blend and in 2023 the company introduced a new blend – Ardray. In the Japanese whisky segment, the company's main brands are Yamazaki (celebrating its 100th anniversary this year), Hibiki, Suntory, The Chita and Hakushu and, finally, the company owns other well-known brands such as Canadian Club whisky, Courvoisier cognac, Sauza tequila and Pinnacle vodka.

Brown Forman

The company is on the Top 10 list of the world's largest spirits producers with Jack Daniel's – the biggest selling American whiskey in the world – as the megastar. In the latest financial year (ending 30 April 2023) net sales were up by 8% to $4.2bn while operating profits were down by

The James Bond Collection from Macallan

6% to $1.1bn. Reasons for the decrease were lower gross margin, higher non-cash impairment and expenses relating to the acquisition of Diplomático rum.

The ever growing Jack Daniel's family of brands showed an increase in sales of 4% and in autumn 2022 the anticipated premixed ready-to-drink Jack & Coke made its debut in Mexico. It came on sale in USA in March the following year and will now be rolled out globally. Premium bourbons such as Woodford Reserve and Old Forester showed strength, especially in the US, with double digit growth.

Brown Forman also has interests in tequila (El Jimador, the fourth largest in the world) and vodka (Finlandia, number 14 on the global sales list) but lacked a rum in the portfolio – at least until autumn 2022 when they announced they were buying Diplomático from Spain's Destillers United Group.

Brown Forman also owns distilleries in Scotland. In 2016 they bought BenRiach, GlenDronach (soon to be expanded) and Glenglassaugh (with a brand new product range). A year before, the company also entered the Irish whiskey scene when they took over Slane distillery in collaboration with the Conyngham family.

The big brands
Blended Scotch

The resilience of Scotch in spite of rising interest rates, inflation and an overall higher cost of living in many markets is clearly shown in the sales figures for the major Scotch blends. Only four of the Top 20 brands showed negative growth in 2022.

The number one, as it has been for more than half a century, was Johnnie Walker. Diageo's flagship brand showed an impressive growth of 18% to reach 272 million bottles which is an all time high. In the past few years the number of special and limited bottlings of Johnnie Walker has increased substantially and two years ago a brand home was opened in the centre of Edinburgh. In its second year (2022) it received 300,000 visitors!

Number two on the list, and no surprise there either, was Chivas Brothers-owned Ballantine's which increased sales by 6% to 110 million bottles. The prestige range of the brand did exceptionally well across Asian markets and global travel retail. The brand's latest collaboration (announced in June 2023) was commemorating the 50th anniversary of hip hop together with hip-hop legend RZA.

In third place there's been a shift since last year. Chivas Regal made an impressive climb to reach 62 million bottles with a 27% increase! In particular, the gains were achieved in emerging markets where the brand grew by 42%. Like Ballantine's (both brands owned by Pernod Ricard) Chivas Regal is also looking to the music scene to grow the brand, lately together with K-pop singer Lisa.

Last year's number three (and now in fourth place) is Grant's which grew by a mere 2% to reach 50 million bottles in 2022. The brand has slowly been decreasing in sales the past decade and during the same time the owners have created internal competition by introducing the blended malt Monkey Shoulder which is already selling 8 million bottles annually.

The number one Scotch in the UK with a market share of 27%, Famous Grouse, occupies fifth place with sales of 45 million bottles. Apart from the UK, the brand is also hugely popular in the Nordics and in Eastern Europe.

One of the biggest climbers in recent years, Black & White, is in sixth place with an increase in 2022 of 12% to 43 million bottles. This is the 13th consecutive year of growth for the brand which has become popular not least in Latin America and India. Dewar's occupies seventh place and with an increase of 25% it was together with Chivas Regal the biggest climber amongst the Top 20 Scotch blend in 2022. Total sales were 42 million bottles and around 12 million of them were sold in the important US market.

The second of the big Bacardi blends, Lawson's, was close behind as number 8 with sales of just over 40 million bottles and an increase of 3%. The brands' heavy exposure towards the Russian market is probably one explanation for the modest rise in sales. Number 9 is J&B with a sales increase of 4% in 2022. The 35 million bottles sold has not yet come up to pre-pandemic figures. Finally, in 10th place, we find William Peel owned by the French company Marie Brizard Wine & Spirits. Sales were 32 million bottles and the brand has been at that level for at least the past five years.

Single Malt Scotch

Single malts continue to be an integral part of the industry even though its share of total value for Scotch export has gone down from last year's 34% to 32%. The share of the volume is still around 11%. If we divide total values of exported Scotch single malts by the equivalent of bottles exported, we get £11.14 per bottle which is an increase of

The Glenlivet is the world´s best selling single malt

23% in the last five years. The corresponding calculation for exported Scotch blends and blended malts show an average exported price of £2.97 per bottle in 2022 and a decrease of 11% since 2017.

Let's look at last year's sales development for the Top 10 Scotch single malts;

For the second year in a row, The Glenlivet came in as the world's number one single malt. An increase by 13% resulted in slightly more than 20 million bottles sold. The prestige expressions of the brand are doing well in Asia and it is still, by far, the largest Scotch single malt in USA with close to 7 million bottles sold every year.

In second place is Glenfiddich, the brand which according to many initiated the world interest in malt whisky as early as in 1963. For many years it was way ahead of its competitors in terms of sales volume. In 2022, due to a 14% increase, the brand sold 19 million bottles. It used to be the number one single malt in the UK but that position was overtaken by Jura in 2020.

For the rest of the malts on the Top 10 list, there were no sales figures for 2022 available at the time of printing so what follows here is the position and figures from 2021; Macallan (10.8 million bottles), Glenmorangie (8.3 million), The Singleton (7.5 million), Balvenie (4.4 million), Talisker (4.3 million), Aberlour (3.9 million), Laphroaig (3.8 million) and Cardhu (3.5 million).

All Top 10 are the same as last year but places have shifted and some of the brands have excelled if one compares the 2021 sales to 2019 (the year before covid). Glenmorangie is up by 31%, The Singleton by 18%, Talisker by 32% and Aberlour by 39% (although still behind its best year which was 2016 with 4.3 million bottles sold). The brands in the Top 10 that have travelled in the opposite direction are Macallan, Balvenie, Laphroaig and Cardhu.

Lurking just behind the Top 10 are Glen Grant which has sold around 3 million bottles yearly in the past decade, Dalmore with 2.7 million bottles and showing a very strong increase in sales since 2016 and Bowmore (2.4 million bottles) being number two on Islay but definitely challenged on the global top list by Ardbeg, Glenfarclas and the rapidly increasing Jura.

Finally, let's take a look at the top whiskies in North America, India and Ireland.

In North America, Jack Daniel's is the undisputed leader. It is also the sixth most popular whisk(e)y in the world with 175 million bottles sold in 2022 which was a volume increase of 8%. In second place is the most sold bourbon in the world, Jim Beam. The exact number of sold bottles hasn't been communicated by the owners this year apart from a comment in the financial report saying "single digit growth". In 2021 the brand sold 131 million bottles. It is followed by the Canadian whisky Crown Royal (101 million, -7%) and two bourbons – Evan Williams (37 million, +-0%) and Maker's Mark. This brand is also owned by Beam Suntory and the situation is the same as with Jim Beam – no exact sales volume has been disclosed but the financial report for 2022 indicated an 11% growth for the brand in 2022 which might indicate sales of 35 million bottles.

In India, we find six of the ten most sold whiskies in the world even though they cannot be sold in the EU as whisky

since they are made from molasses rather than grain. The top 5 are McDowell's No. 1 (370 million bottles, +2%), Royal Stag (325 million bottles, +21%), Officer's Choice (298 million, +7%), Imperial Blue (288 million, -1%) and, probably, Haywards Fine (144 million bottles sold in 2021). In this case the owners have not disclosed the volumes for 2022. Official records say that Blenders Pride should be number five with 114 million bottles and an increase of 19%.

Finally we have Ireland where Jameson has dominated and in many ways defined the category for a very long time. In 2021 the brand occupied place 9 on the Top whiskies of the world selling 133 million bottles which was an increase by 16% compared to 2021. Number two is Tullamore Dew with 17 million bottles (-7%) and Bushmills comes in third with 12 million bottles.

New distilleries
Scotland

This part of the book deals with the embryonic distillery projects – those that haven't started producing yet. In those cases where neither funds have been secured nor planning permission has been granted, their stories are more about plans rather than what has taken place.

There has been a virtual explosion of new Scottish whisky distilleries since the new millenium. A total of 48 can be counted, with six of them starting production in 2022/2023. You can read more about 8 Doors, Dunphail, Moffat, Port Ellen, Port of Leith and Uile-bheist in the New Distilleries chapter, page 160-182.

The revival of whisky production in the Lowlands in the past 15 years - which is still ongoing - has been very much in the focus as well as the interest in building new distilleries on Islay. One location that is now getting more and more attention is Campbeltown. With around 25 distilleries operating in the early 1900s, only two (Springbank and Glen Scotia) survived and a third one, Glengyle was re-opened in 2004. There are now plans to build no less than three new distilleries.

Behind one of them, Dál Riata in the very heart of Campbeltown on Kinloch Road overlooking Campbeltown Loch, we find Iain Croucher and Ronnie Grant. A planning application was submitted to the local council in April 2022 and is still awaiting decision. With a capacity of 850,000 litres of alcohol, it will be equipped with a two ton semi-lauter mash tun, ten washbacks, a 10,000 litre wash still and a 7,200 litre spirit still.

At the same time as Dál Riata was announced, plans for a second distillery in the vicinity of Campbeltown were presented. The Dhurrie Farm north of the town will be converted from a dairy farm to a regenerative arable farm and a distillery named Machrihanish will be set up. The owners of Isle of Raasay Distillery, R&B Distillers, are behind the project and a planning application, that is still awaiting decision, was submitted in December 2022. The 360 degree view from the distillery (and not least the planned visitor centre bar) will be spectacular. Machrihanish will be equipped with a mash filter, six stainless steel washbacks with cooling jackets, two 6,250 litre wash stills and two 4,000 litre spirit stills. The spirit will mainly be matured in ex-sherry casks with a combination of American, Spanish and French oak. There are also plans for small maltings on site. Barley intended for the spirit will be grown in the surrounding fields. If everything goes according to plan, the distillery could be up and running in 2025.

The third new distillery in the Campbeltown area, and quite close to Machrihanish, was announced in June 2023. Brave New Spirits, an independent bottler established in 2020, submitted a planning application (approved in August 2023) for a distillery by the name of Witchburn, to be located between Campbeltown airport and Machrihanish village. Powered by renewable energy sources, the distillery will have an impressive capacity of 2 million litres and will be equipped with 16 washbacks and two pairs of stills. For distillery manager Brave New Spirits hired Andrew Nairn, a veteran in the industry with experience from Glenkinchie and Borders Distillery.

Over on Islay, Elixir Distillers, spearheaded by wellknown whisky dealer and collector Sukhinder Singh and his brother Rajbir, finally got the green light in April 2021 to their planning application for Portintruan Distillery. The distillery, managed by the experienced Georgie Crawford, will be situated just outside Port Ellen on the road to Laphroaig, Lagavulin and Ardbeg and in July 2022 the contractors started putting in the foundations. The hopes are set to begin production during 2024. Equipped with 14 washbacks (eight wooden and six stainless steel) and two pairs of stills with direct fired wash stills, the distillery will have the capacity to produce 1 million litres of pure alcohol. On site floor maltings will produce between 60 and 80% of the barley needs. Included in the project are 14 houses for families working at the distillery, a visitor centre and an education facility. There are also plans for a micro distillery with two pot stills and a column still for experimentation and, possibly, other spirits, not least rum. This part of the distillery will have a hammer mill and a mash filter.

While still on Islay, a planning application for ili Distillery, to be built on Gearach Farm south of Kilchoman and west of Port Charlotte, was approved in November 2022. Behind the project are Bertram Nesselrode (owner of Gearach Farm) and Scott McLellan, a local farmer. Their aim is to make the 200,000 litre distillery carbon neutral and entails a hydrogen plant, solar panels and a wind turbine.

Mackay Smith and Donald MacKenzie, known as the Islay Boys, have plans to move the Islay Ales Brewery to a new site east of Islay airport and at the same time add a rum- and whisky distillery. The plans for the Laggan Bay Distillery at Glenegedale were approved by the local council in June 2022 and shortly after that, it was announced that one of Scotland's largest spirits companies, Ian Macleod Distillers, were involved as well.

On the west coast of the Cowal Peninsula, the village Polphail was built in the 1970s to house workers on a planned oil rig construction plant nearby. The oil rig yard was never realised though and the houses that had already been built turned into a ghost town and were finally demolished in 2016. In 2017, Sandy Bulloch, the previous owner of Loch Lomond Distillery, bought the site with the aim of building a distillery named Portavadie. The planning application was approved by Argyll & Bute Council in 2018 but nothing happened. Recently the entire project (with a second approval in October 2022) was taken over by the Indian company Piccadily Agro Industries (known for their single malts Kamet and Indri) who have invested £15m in the site.

Independent bottler Compass Box submitted a planning application to the Highland Council in June 2023. Their plans are to build a distillery, blending centre, warehouses and a visitor centre in Inverlochy, Fort William just 500 metres north of Ben Nevis Distillery.

Down in the Borders, Mossburn Distillers, owner of Torabhaig distillery on Skye, are involved with two distilleries. One of them, the Reivers Distillery outside Melrose, has already started production. Equipped with pot stills as well as columns, they produce mainly rye and mixed grain

The founders of Kythe Distillery in Perthshire – Jonny McMillan, Aaron Chan and Angus MacRaild

The site for Cabrach Distillery lies beautifully in Speyside, 15 minutes south of Dufftown

spirits but genever and other spirits are also on the cards. This is a fairly small distillery with a capacity of 100,000 litres while their other distillery is of a much grander format: It will be built on the site of Jedforest Hotel near Jedburgh and will actually consist of two distilleries – one equipped with three pot stills and a capacity of 1.5 million litres and the other with five columns. The intention is to start with the building of warehouses needed for the company's other operations followed by the distillery. A possible production start will not take place until perhaps in 2025.

Another distillery in The Borders has been in R&B Distillers' plans for a long time by. Eventually, they went ahead and founded a distillery on Raasay and now plan to build yet another on the Kintyre peninsula. The company hasn't given up on The Borders though. Current aspirations include to build a micro grain distillery in Coldstream south west of Berwick-upon-Tweed and right on the border to England but this is probably 4-5 years into the future.

It's been a long time coming for Ardgowan Distillery in Inverkip 30 miles west of Glasgow. They received planning permission in 2017 and the owners hoped to start production in 2019. The timeline was later revised and a new application submitted. The founders secured a major investment of £7.2m from Austrian investor, Ronald Grain, who is the owner of the IT company Grain GmbH. In spring 2023 it was announced that the company had signed a £100m deal with one of Spain's oldest bodegas, Miguel Martin, to secure supply of high quality sherry casks.

Angus MacRaild and Jonny McMillan have been advocates of old-style whisky for more than a decade not least through their Old & Rare Whisky shows in collaboration with Sukhinder Singh. Since 2014 they have nurtured the idea of building a distillery of their own in line with their objectives and in April 2023 the plans were revealed for Kythe distillery on Hills of Bendlochy Farm in Perthshire just north of Coupar Angus. The distillery, due to start production in late 2024, will be equipped with a one tonne mash tun, 7 wooden washbacks, a wood-fired wash still and an electrically heated spirit still. The spirit will be condensed through worm tubs, heritage barley grown in the surroundings and proprietary yeast will be used and they also have plans to do floor malting in the future. Apart

from utilising old distilling techniques, an environmentally sustainable production, including regenerative farming, is very much in the focus. The owners are in no hurry to release the first whisky once the production has started. In the words of another of the new generation of distillers (Francis Cuthbert of Daftmill) "it's ready when it's ready".

Plans to open a combined brewery and whisky distillery in Loch Lomond National Park were revealed in spring 2020. The Glen Luss distillery is supposed to open up in the village of Luss which is on the A82 on the western shores of Loch Lomond. Planning permission was approved in February 2021 but apart from a sponsorship deal with Netball Scotland in November 2021 very little has happened (or, at least, has been communicated).

The third whisky distillery to open up in Glasgow in modern times is not far away. In 2017 independent bottler Douglas Laing announced that they had plans to build a distillery named Clutha on the banks of the river Clyde at Pacific Quay. The project also includes a bottling complex, a new corporate head office, a visitor centre, a whisky laboratory and an archive. The site for the future distillery was later moved to the west, to Hillingdon, where warehouses have already been built and a bottling hall is up and running. There is no set date for when the 250,000 litre distillery will be completed.

Campbell Meyer & Co own a 150,000 square ft bonded warehouse in East Kilbride, just south of Glasgow. In spring 2016, the company announced they harboured plans to add a distillery named Burnbrae as well. Little news has been shared since then but, according to the owners, the distillery could be up and running in 2023 and in June 2023 they were hiring staff for the distillery.

Up in Speyside, The Cabrach Trust is building a distillery in the village of Cabrach 15 minutes south of Dufftown. The old Inverharroch Farm is being converted to a distillery with renewable energy and local provenance of raw material in focus. Some of the barley will be grown on the farm. Beyond the distillery, complimentary actions have been taken forward by the Trust including riparian planting designed to nurture riverside wildlife corridors whilst increasing river shade which serves to reduce water temperatures for critical species such as Wild Atlantic Salmon. To date, more than 3,000 native, broadleaf trees have been planted with a further 1,200 willow saplings planted in April 2023. Equipped with a 0,5 ton mash tun, 6 wooden washbacks, a 2,500 litre wash still and a 1,800 litre spirit still, both attached to wormtubs, the distillery will have a capacity of 100,000 litres of pure alcohol. There will also be a unique 1,250 litre direct fired still cooled via a small, internal worm tub. The first distillation is planned for spring 2024.

Further to the west in Castletown near Dunnet, Martin and Claire Murray were granted planning permission in July 2022 to convert the historic Castletown Mill into a whisky distillery. Their company Dunnet Bay Distillers already produces gin and vodka and the £4m project would finance a whisky distillery with four washbacks and one pair of stills. In November 2022, two hundred casks of their future Stannergill single malt were offered to the public.

Out on Barra in the Western Isles, a gin distillery has been operating since 2017. It is the owners', Michael and Katie Morrison, intention to include also whisky production in a new distillery at Eoligarry. In December 2022 they received planning permission from the Comhairle nan Eilean Siar planning department. The capacity of the distillery will be 200,000 litres of alcohol, the equipment will come from Forsyths and once established it will become the most westerly whisky distillery in Scotland.

In the outer Hebrides, on the island of Benbecula (situated between North and South Uist), we find two distillery projects. Behind the one that is likely to open first is businessman Angus A Macmillan and his son Angus E. Their Uist Distilling Company secured almost £2m in July 2021 from Highlands and Islands Enterprise for a distillery near Gramsdale on Benbecula. The building of the distillery has started and it is possible it could be producing already in late 2023 or early 2024.

Meanwhile, Jonny Ingledew and Kate MacDonald opened a gin distillery on North Uist already in April 2019 and in July 2020 they bought the 18th century Nunton Steadings on Benbecula. They intend to open a designated whisky distillery within the next couple of years.

In 2020, the former Whyte & Mackay chief executive Michael Lunn (who passed away in 2023) announced plans to set up a new distillery, Wolfcraig, in Stirling. In 2021, the original location had been changed to Craigforth Campus in Stirling but the company's planning application was refused by the council. The decision was appealed but was rejected again in 2023. The founders, headed by Michael's son Jamie, are now looking at alternative locations.

In Easter Fearn on the Dornoch Firth, just a few miles west of Balblair, the Brooke family (proprietors of the estate since 1893) are looking at building a whisky distillery. The family submitted a planning application to the Highland Council in May 2022 which was approved in October for a distillery equipped with one mash tun, ten washbacks and two pairs of stills and with a capacity of one million litres.

In 2021, Speyside Distillers announced that their lease of the current distillery south of Kingussie would expire and that they were looking for a new site to build on. Rumours about the possible location travelled around but the facts appeared in May 2023 when a planning application was sent in to the council for a distillery near Laggan, some 40 km southwest of the current location. The location is fitting

to say the least as it is right next to river Spey. Compared to the current distillery, the new one will be substantially larger with 12 washbacks and two pairs of stills.

Finally, plans for Balmaud distillery outside Turiff, 10 kilometres south of Banff, were approved by Aberdeenshire council in September 2021 with the old Yonderton farm being converted to a distillery with more than 1 million litre capacity. Revised plans were submitted in July 2022 and these were finally approved in April 2023. Construction started in August and the owners (the Strachan family) hope to start production by middle of 2024. Distillery manager is Allan Findlay who previously managed Speyside Distillery.

Ireland & Northern Ireland

Few have failed to notice that Irish whiskey has made a magnificent come-back in the recent decades and the speed of opening up new distilleries shows no sign of losing momentum. There are currently 41 distilleries already operating (read more about them in the section Distilleries Around the Globe) and at least another 20 either being built or seeking funds for starting up.

In Laherdane, Co Mayo, Jude and Paul Davis together with Mark Quick been tirelessly working on the construction of their Nephin Distillery for quite some time now. The pandemic threw a spanner in the works when Italian engineers from the still manufacturer were prohibited to fly to Ireland to work on the instalment of the stills. On top of that, the Davis couple and their (now former) business partner Quick were involved in a legal dispute over several issues which was settled out of court in October 2022. In March 2023, the Davis couple announced they were looking for another investment of 1.1 million euros to complete the distillery.

The island co-op at Cape Clear, six kilometres off the Cork coast, received planning permission in August 2016 to build a €7m distillery on their island. Unfortunately, one of the major investors pulled out along the way and the owners initiated a Kickstarter campaign in spring 2019 in order to fund parts of the project. A year later a gin distillery was working. They've also obtained planning permission for a separate whiskey distillery to be built, but for the time being focus is on whisky distilled elsewhere and then maturing it on the island.

Gortinore Distillers, based in Waterford, launched their sourced, triple-distilled Natterjack Irish Whiskey in 2019. In late 2020 the owners were granted planning approval to build a whiskey distillery at the site of the Old Mill in Kilmacthomas. However in spring 2022 the company entered examinership (an insolvency process) as a result of the negative impacts of the covid pandemic. In August 2022 a group of American investors acquired the company to avoid liquidation. Natterjack as a brand is still very much alive but it remains to be seen if a distillery will be built.

Further to the west, in Cahersiveen, Co. Kerry, a company is transforming an old sock factory into a distillery called Skellig Six 18. The unusual name was inspired by the number of steps (618) to the top of Skellig Michael, an island situated 10 kilometres off the coast of Iveragh Peninsula. Currently, gin is produced but three copper stills have been ordered from Italy and the owners hope to start whisky production in 2023.

Killarney Brewing Company are starting up a distillery in late 2023 or early 2024

In Fossa, the Killarney Brewing Company are busy completing a distillery of quite some size. Beer production started in 2013 on a site in the centre of Killarney while the new brewery/distillery is situated by Lough Leane on the western outskirts of the town. The distillery will be equipped with three Italian 2,000 litre copper pot stills and while waiting for their first own whiskey, sourced whiskey has been released. The brewing part became operational in summer 2022 and the distillery will be commissioned during 2023.

Just a stone's throw away, in Aghadoe, Torc Brewing Company with Aidan Forde and John Keane are planning to build a craft distillery in an old coach house. They have been distilling at Killarney Distillery 12 kilometres to the north since 2020. For two years Killarney Brewing Company and Killarney Distillery have been involved in a legal dispute regarding the right to the name Killarney whiskey.

Still in Killarney, Wayward Irish Spirits have built a bonding facility at the Lakeview Estate where they blend and mature sourced whiskies (made from their own barley) under the brand names Wayward and Irish Liberator. The plan is to have a single estate grain to glass distillery on the site by 2024.

In Derrylavan, Co. Monaghan and just west of Dundalk, lies Old Carrick Mill Distillery. Gin has already been launched and production of triple distilled whiskey is in the pipeline. The stills are of own design and manufactured in China. A sourced whiskey, May Loag, is available.

An old mill in Ahascragh, Co. Galway has been converted into a whiskey and gin distillery by McAllister Distillers. Powered by renewable energy the distillery opened to the public in July 2023 and will probably be producing during autumn 2023. Sourced whiskey under the name Clan Colla and UAIS has already been released.

Another old mill, for restoration into a distillery and owned by Ciara and Harvey Appelbe, can be found at Ballymore Eustace, Co. Kildare. A planning application has been approved but a lot of work remains however as the buildings are nothing but ruins.

The Earl of Tyrone, Richard de la Poer Beresford, intends to build a distillery on his magnificent Curraghmore Estate in Portlaw, Co. Waterford. The barley will be grown on the estate and the distillery fitted into the 18th century hay barns. Currently new make spirit from Ardara distillery is sourced.

In Balbriggan, 40 kilometres north of Dublin, a distillery project of a major magnitude is growing. With the backup from loan-note specialist Invest 123, James McNally has plans to create a business-park which will include a distillery. The entire project is expected to cost €100m! The name of the distillery will be Harvest Lodge and the planning application that was submitted to the local council in late 2021 was approved in January 2023.

Finally, in Northern Ireland, there are a number of ongoing projects; Joe McGirr is the mastermind behind Boatyard Distillery in Enniskillen which began distilling in May 2016. The company has had some remarkable success with their gin and vodka and recently they secured £634,000 in funding to grow the business even further, not least in the US. The owners are also planning to launch a whiskey in the near future.

Michael McKeown, founder of Matt D'Arcy & Company, was granted planning permission in summer 2018 for a whiskey distillery in Newry in Co. Down. Around £7m was supposed to be invested in the distillery complete with a visitor centre. In March 2023 however, the plans were abandoned and the site was up for sale.

In Garrison, Co. Fermanagh, a couple of kilometres from the Irish border, work has begun on a £5m whiskey distillery where the financial backup comes from a group of investors based in London. Scott's distillery takes its name from the original owner of the farm on which the site is based – Hammy Scott. It looks as if the distillery could be producing in 2023.

There hasn't been a whiskey distillery in Belfast for many years but in summer 2023 Titanic Distillery opened in the old Thompson Dry Dock and now another one is on the go. Ten years ago it was announced that a distillery would be built in the old Crumlin Road Gaol jail and it was due to be completed by 2016. That never materialised and a group of American investors took over the £25m project which is now back on track. Three stills were installed in May 2023 and the owners hope to start production in October. Meanwhile a sourced whiskey is sold under the name McConnell's – a historic whiskey brand from Belfast.

A new distillery is underway in Lurgan, Co. Armagh. Lough Neagh Distillers already operate Spadetown brewery and are working on building a whiskey distillery as well but the covid pandemic has forced it to pause temporarily.

Independent
bottlers

Independent bottlers play an important role in the whisky business. With their innovative bottlings, they increase diversity. A new and brilliant book on the topic is David Stirk's *Independent Scotch – The History of Independent Bottlers* (ISBN 978-1-399-94553-0). The following are a selection of the major companies. Tasting notes have been prepared by Ian Wisnewski.

Gordon & MacPhail

gordonandmacphail.com

Established in 1895 the company is owned by the Urquhart family. Apart from being an independent bottler, there is also a legendary store in Elgin which is currently being moved from South Street to St Giles Centre in High Street while the old shop will be turned into a whisky experience venue. In 1993 they bought Benromach distillery and in summer 2022 they commissioned their second distillery, The Cairn close to Grantown-on-Spey. In July 2023 the owners surprised many consumers when they announced that they would stop purchasing stock for independent bottlings from 2024. One reason for the decision is that more and more producers want to release their own bottlings, resulting in less available new make to buy. Going forward, the company will focus more on their own brands but also reassured their customers that they have maturing casks in stock that will last for several decades of independent bottlings.

Gordon & MacPhail's part in establishing the interest in single malt Scotch before the vast majority of producers realised the potential, can not be overrated. Currently there are five distinctive ranges; Connoisseurs Choice consists of single malts bottled either at 43% or 46%. Over the years there have been more than 2,000 bottlings from almost 100 distilleries. Discovery is grouped under three flavour profiles – smoky, sherry and bourbon. Distillery Labels is a relic from a time when Gordon & MacPhail released more or less official bottlings for several producers. Private Collection features old single malts including bottlings from closed distilleries and in 2023 Glen Mhor 1973, Banff 1976 and Port Ellen 1981 were included. There was also a 1948 Glen Grant to commemorate the coronation of King Charles III. Generations, finally, comprises the oldest and rarest whiskies in stock, including Glenlivet 80 years old in September 2021 – at that time the oldest single malt ever bottled.

Glenrothes 11 year old Discovery, 43%
Nose: Coconut, creme brûlée, fruit cake, then malty, oak notes emerge and extend with espresso.
Palate: Silky mouthfeel yields creamy cappuccino, dark chocolate, sticky toffee pudding, chocolate brownie with chocolate sauce.

Ardmore 2000/2021 Distillery Label , 46%
Nose: Lightly toasted wafts, walnuts, extra virgin olive oil, oak and barbecue hints.
Palate: Ethereal mouthfeel, light creamy sweetness expands, vanilla leads to bread and butter pudding, then maltyness and wafting barbecue notes.

Berry Bros. & Rudd

bbrspirits.com

The world's oldest wine and spirit merchant, founded in 1698, celebrated their 325th anniversary in 2023! The famous address 3 St James's Street, where the company has been since the start, was in 2017 returned to its appearance of 35 years ago and is now a space for consultations and a new flagship store opened just around the corner in 63 Pall Mall. Berry Brothers had been offering their customers private bottlings of malt whisky for years, but it was not until 2002 that they launched Berry's Own Selection of single malts. Under the supervision of Doug McIvor and Rob Whitehead some

30 expressions are on offer every year. A new series called The Classic Range, including Sherry and Peated, was released in 2018. In 2021 the company launched a new communication campaign, "Since 1698", and at the same time the spirits range was revamped by way of the first bespoke spirits bottles in the company´s history including series such as Small Batch, Exceptional Casks and Perspective. The spring 2023 release comprised 8 expressions including the first independent bottling of Spirit of Yorkshire. In April 2023 Berry Bros acquired a minority stake in England´s largest whisky producer, Cotswolds Distillery. The company has also taken an interest in whisky from the Nordics and in autumn 2022 a second range, including a Nordic blended malt, was launched. The company is also working with other world whiskies including Paul John in India, Milk & Honey in Israel and Chichibu in Japan.

Wire Works 2018/2023, 60,9%
Nose: Waft of buttered toast, light smoke carries vanilla and citrus, camomile tea then rich honey.
Palate: Ultra-delicate softness with sweetness expanding impressively across the palate, plenty of creme caramel, apricots and hints of creme brûlée.

Ledaig 2009/2023 Oloroso, 53,5%
Nose: Hint of embers and struck match, olives in brine, sizzling bacon.
Palate: Rich mouthfeel and a composed structure, sweetness provides top notes with malt and oak adding underlying dryness, then butterscotch and ginger bread continue.

Signatory

signatoryusa.com

Founded in 1988 by Andrew and Brian Symington, Signatory Vintage Scotch Whisky lists at least 50 single malts at any one occasion. The most widely distributed range is Cask Strength Collection which recently featured a 16 year old Glenlivet, a 22 year old Benriach and a 25 year old Linkwood. In the same range some staggering single grains also appear such as a recent 31 year old Cambus from 1991. Another range is The Un-chill Filtered Collection bottled at 46%. Some of the latest bottlings released include Mortlach 15, Linkwood 10 and Teaninich 13 year old – all bottled in 2023. Andrew Symington bought Edradour Distillery from Pernod Ricard in 2002 and the entire operations, including Signatory, are now concentrated to the distillery in Perthshire.

Ian Macleod Distillers

ianmacleod.com

The company was founded in 1933 and is one of the largest independent family-owned companies within the spirits industry. Gin, rum, vodka and liqueurs, apart from whisky, are found within the range and they also own Glengoyne, Tamdhu and Rosebank distilleries. Their biggest seller is the blended whisky King Robert II while their single malt range includes The Chieftain´s where a Cigar Malt is a recurrent bottling. Macleod´s Regional Malts are single malts chosen to represent the 5 whisky regions in Scotland. There are two As We Get It single malt expressions – Highland and Islay. The Six Isles blended malt contains whisky from the majority of whisky-producing islands while one of the top sellers is the blended Scotch Isle of Skye available at 8, 12, 18, 21, 25 and 30 years old. Finally, Smokehead, a heavily, peated single malt from Islay introduced in 2006, has become a huge success. The range was revamped in 2018 and several new expressions have been released including Smokehead Tequila Cask Terminado in 2022. Since July 2021 it is also

available as an RTD (ready to drink) mixed with either cola or ginger/lime. In 2023, the company launched two malts exclusive to the travel retail market - The White Cask First-Fill Edition and Shieldaig American Oak Reserve.

Smokehead Tequila Terminado, 43%
Nose: Hints of grilled vegetables, olive oil, then vanilla, malty and wafting smoke.
Palate: Creamy texture opens up with creamy vanilla and growing sweetness, hints of cinnamon and clove, grilled peppers and umami.

Smokehead Twisted Shout, 43%
Nose: Malt, cereal notes with smoke, chocolate, and an edge of fresh hops.
Palate: Lightly creamy texture becomes sweet, rich and luscious with ripe fruit, pineapple, cappuccino, and a hint of hops adding edge and structure, with subtle underlying dryness.

Blackadder International

blackadder.com

Behind Blackadder is Robin Tucek together with his two children Michael and Hannah. Apart from Blackadder Raw Cask (bottled straight from the cask without any filtration at all), there are also a number of other ranges – Smoking Islay, Peat Reek, Peat Reek Embers, Statement and special bottlings of Amrut single malt. In recent years, three new brands have become increasingly popular; Black Snake which is a vatting of casks finished in a single sherry butt, Red Snake which are single cask malts, always from first fill ex-bourbon and Sherry Snake from first fill sherry casks. All bottlings from Blackadder are uncoloured and un chill-filtered and most of them are diluted to 43-46% but Raw Cask is always bottled at cask strength.

Murray McDavid

murray-mcdavid.com

The company was founded in 1996 by Mark Reynier, Simon Coughlin and Gordon Wright. In 2013 Murray McDavid was taken over by Aceo Ltd. and a year later they signed a lease for the warehouses at the closed Coleburn distillery for storing their own whiskies as well as stock belonging to clients. The bottlings are divided into six different ranges; Mission Gold (exceptionally rare whiskies bottled at cask strength), Benchmark (mature single malts bottled at 46%), Mystery Malt (single malts where the distillery is not revealed), Select Grain (single grains), The Vatting (vatted malts) and Crafted Blend (blended Scotch from their own blending). A seventh range, Cask Craft, was introduced in 2022, showcasing different wood finishes. Aceo also releases other whiskies under the name Coleburn and Parkmore.

Duncan Taylor

duncantaylor.com

Founded in Glasgow in 1938 as a cask broker and trading company. In 2002, the company was acquired by Euan Shand and operations were moved to Huntly. Duncan Taylor´s flagship brand is the blended Scotch Black Bull, a brand with a history going back to 1864. Black Bull was rebranded in 2009 by Duncan Taylor and the range consists of four core releases – Kyloe, an 8 year old, a 12 year old and a 21 year old. There are also limited versions such as 40 year old and the Peated Edition. Two excptionally old versions, 50 and 55 years old, were launched in 2023. The Black Bull brand is complimented by Smokin' which is a blend of peated Speyside, Islay and grain whisky from the Lowlands.

The portfolio also includes The Rarest (single cask, cask strength whiskies of great age from demolished distilleries), Dimensions (a collection of single malts and single grains aged up to 39 years), The Tantalus (a selection of whiskies all aged in their 40s), Battlehill (a range of single malts and single grains) and Rare Auld Grain (a selection of rare grain whiskies bottled at cask strength). The perhaps most popular range in recent years is The Octave. These are single malt whiskies matured for a further period in small, 60-70 litre ex-sherry octave casks. In 2019 The Octave Premium with substantially older whiskies, was introduced. Finally, the blended malt category is represented by Big Smoke, a young peated whisky available at 46% and 60%.

Black Bull 18 year old, 50%

Nose: Turkish Delight, floral hints, dried fruits, sherry overtones.

Palate: Long and intense with dark chocolate, herbal aromas and baked apple pie.

Black Bull 30 year old, 50%

Nose: Sugar coated almonds, rich fruit cake, orchard fruits, runny toffee.

Palate: Ripe citrus fruits, delicate floral notes, cloves, ginger and warm pastries.

Scotch Malt Whisky Society

smws.com

The Scotch Malt Whisky Society was founded in 1983 and was owned by Glenmorangie Co from 2003 until 2015 when it was taken over by a group of private investors and later, Artisanal Spirits Company became the owner. Since 2021 it is listed on the London Stock Exchange. The society has more than 35,000 members worldwide and apart from UK, there is a network of international branches and partner bars in 26 countries around the world. The idea from the very beginning was to buy casks of single malts from the producers and bottle them at cask strength without colouring or chill filtration. The Society has played a significant role for the interest in single cask Scotch that has exploded in recent decades. The labels do not reveal the name of the distillery. Instead there is a number but also a short description which will give you a clue to which distillery it is. Around 500 casks are bottled every year. The SMWS operates four venues with bars and member rooms in Edinburgh (Queen Street and Leith), London (Greville Street) and Glasgow (Bath Street) and also works with partner bars around the world. In recent years, the range has been expanded to also include single grain, whiskies from other countries as well as rum, gin, cognac and other spirits.

Compass Box Whisky Co

compassboxwhisky.com

John Glaser, founder and co-owner of the company, has a philosophy which is strongly influenced by meticulous selection of oak for the casks, clearly inspired by his time in the wine business. But he also has a lust for experimenting to test the limits, which was clearly shown when Spice Tree, matured in casks containing extra staves, was launched in 2005. Glaser and Compass Box are also advocating more transparency in the industry where the customer is given as much information as possible about the contents of the bottle. The company divides its ranges into a Signature Range and a Limited Range. Spice Tree (a blended malt), The Peat Monster

(a combination of peated Islay whiskies and Highland malts), Hedonism (a vatted grain whisky), The Story of the Spaniard (a blended malt partially matured in Spanish red wine casks) and the blended malt Orchard House are included in the former. In the Limited Range, whiskies are regularly replaced and at times only to resurface a couple of years later in new variations. Two of the latest expressions are two blends; Delos (with a third of the recipe coming from the demolished Imperial) and Ultramarine (an unusually complex recipe and bottled at 51%). There is also a cask strength version (56,7%) of Peat Monster. A special range is called Bespokes made up by collaborations with partners in the trade. The latest was Duality where part of the content was a single malt from Bimber distillery and the rest, a single malt Islay. Finally there are two regular blended Scotch, Artist's Blend and Glasgow Blend. In 2015 Bacardi acquired a minority share of Compass Box which they offloaded in spring 2022 when Cælum Capital Limited, a specialist investor focused on premium beverage businesses, took over a majority stake of the company.

Metropolis, 49%

Nose: Buttered toast with orange marmalade, enhanced by lemon freshness, vanilla emerges with cinnamon hints.

Palate: Lightly silky mouthfeel, subtle sweetness ushers in tangerines and juicy oranges, dry oak provides a base note with citrus fruitiness at the core.

Hedonism, 43%

Nose: Dark chocolate, vanilla, overtones of orange marmalade, porridge, molasses.

Palate: Lightly creamy mouthfeel, creme anglaise suffused with fruit, sweetness emerges garnished with richness, followed by dark chocolate, hints of tiramisu and spicy oak.

North Star Spirits

northstarspirits.com

Founded in 2016 by Iain Croucher who used to work for AD Rattray before deciding to go it alone. The latest releases in his single cask single malt range in 2023 included an 8 year old Glen Garioch oloroso finish, A Bruichladdich matured for 12 years in a sherry hogshead and a 29 year old blend. They have developed a Blended Malt range called Supersonic and continue to bottle sherry finished Caol Ila as CHAOS. In spring 2023 a new range named Periodical was introduced; 50 cl bottlings, presented at 50% abv and priced at £50. In early 2022 Croucher together with Ronnie Grant and other partners announced that they had the intention of building a new distillery in Campbeltown named Dál Riata. If everything goes according to plan the distillery could be opened some time in 2024.

Meadowside Blending

meadowsideblending.com

Donald Hart, a Keeper of the Quaich and co-founder of the well-known bottler Hart Brothers, runs this Glasgow company together with his son, Andrew. There are six sides to the business – blends sold under the name The Royal Thistle, single malts labelled The Maltman, single cask single grains under the label The Grainman, Vintage Cask Reserve featuring ultra rare bottlings, Vital Spark focusing on single malts with "a maritime twist" and, introduced in 2020, The Granary with blended grain whiskies.

Master of Malt

masterofmalt.com

Master of Malt is an online retailer of much more than just whisky, and as one of the most innovative spirits, wine and beer retailers in the UK, the company also produces their own independent bottlings of rum, gin and whisky, relaunched last year with over 100 new gems including closed distilleries like Caroni and Caperdonich, ancient single grain Scotches, cask-aged gin and more. They have also secured exclusive cask selections from brands like Glenfarclas, The Lakes Distillery, That Boutique-y Whisky Company and Darkness (tasting sample provided). The retailer also offers a "Pour & Sip" whisky subscription service, as well as a Blend Your Own option, a cask ownership programme, and has a pretty impressive gift finder to help with special occassions.

Willowbank 18 year old, 56,5%
Nose: Rich and distinct, toasted hints meld into oak then prunes, red fruit in syrup, glace cherries and muscovado sugar.
Palate: Lightly silky mouthfeel produces a medley of cherries, prunes, raisins, muscovado sugar, with glimpses of each ebbing and flowing.

Atom Brands

Atom Brands, part of the Atom Group which includes online retailer Master of Malt, Master of Malt Trade and the UK Distributor Maverick Drinks, is the producer of an ever-increasing number of innovative new brands as well as independently bottled whiskies, rums, gins and other spirits from around the world. Included in their portfolio is Drinks by the Dram, the creators of the booze-filled Advent calendars, tasting sets and 30ml dram samples, as well as Bathtub Gin, Rumbullion!, That Boutique-y Drinks Company, The Character of Islay Whisky Company, Darkness and the innovation "hits factory" behind Jaffa Cake Gin, Seaweed&, Burnt Ends and Atom Labs.

That Boutique-y Whisky Company

thatboutiqueywhiskycompany.com

Boutique-y celebrated it's 10th Birthday in 2022 with an incredible whisky lineup and an evolution of their category-leading label artwork aesthetic. Renowned for taking what's inside the bottle seriously but making everything that surrounds it over-the-top fun, 2023 has seen deadly animals on their Return to Oz series, collector baseball card labels for their USA Series, riffs on movie posters for it's Cinema Series, and a whole series dedicated to the World of Smoke. Each bottle adorned with graphic novel-style labels hand illustrated by Glasgow-based artist Emily Chappell comes in a box full of stickers (updated this year) and their podcasts, events and quarterly themed releases ceaselessly celebrate the silly as well as the cerebral joys of whisky.

Helsinki 6 year old rye, 51,3%%
Nose: Rich and direct, raisins, sticky toffee pudding, then oak, followed by more raisins and chocolate.
Palate: Elegant, lightly chewy mouthfeel, opens with big notes: raisins, cloves, toasted oak, cinnamon and muscovado sugar, gift-wrapped.

Darkness

darknesswhisky.com

Darkness is a collection of intensely sherried whiskies with the 8 year old in 2019 as the first expression. With six additional months of extra maturation in hand-coopered sherry cask octaves, whether it's the flagship 8 year old Speyside whisky or one of the Limited Edition Oloroso, PX, Palo Cortado or Moscatel finished releases, Darkness represents a unique proposition for the sherried whisky lover.

Blair Athol 15 year old, oloroso finish, 51,4%
Nose: Antique oak, floating lightly toasted notes, mango and pineapple, a dollop of honey.
Palate: Lightly creamy mouthfeel, abundant vanilla arrives, with mango and pineapple chunks at the edges, mid-way rich honey and toasted oak take centre stage.

Atom Labs

Innovation is at the heart of Atom Brands, and their rapid testing innovation arm "Atom Labs" is the perfect representation of this whether it is Wormtub, the Jaffa Cake range or Burnt Ends. Following the success of Seaweed & Aeons & Digging & Fire, the range widened to include a cask strength version, two sherry-matured Seaweed& versions (one at 40% and one at cask strength), about a dozen "mash-ups" as well as a 10 year old bourbon (Charcoal&) and 30yo single grain Scotch whisky (Butterscotch&).

Wormtub 10 year old sherry finish, 56,8%
Nose: Gingerbread, nutmeg,cinnamon, rich and rounded.
Palate: A very delicate texture delivers richness and nuances in waves of flavour: chocolate cake, prunes, raisins, treacle, dark chocolate, indulgent but composed.

The Whisky Agency

whisky-agency.de

The man behind this company is Carsten Ehrlich, to many whisky aficionados known as one of the founders of the annual Whisky Fair in Limburg, Germany. His experience from sourcing casks for limited Whisky Fair bottlings led him to start as an independent bottler under the name The Whisky Agency, a business that celebrated its 10th anniversary in 2018. There are several ranges including The Whisky Agency, The Perfect Dram and Specials with some unusual bottlings.

A Dewar Rattray Ltd

adrattray.com

The company was founded by Andrew Dewar Rattray in 1868. In 2004 the company was revived by Tim Morrison, previously of Morrison Bowmore Distillers and fourth generation descendent of Andrew Dewar, with a view to bottling single cask malts from different regions in Scotland. In 2011, the company opened A

Dewar Rattray´s Whisky Experience & Shop in Kirkoswald, South Ayrshire. Apart from having a large choice of whiskies for sale, there is a sample room, as well as a cask room.

One of the company´s best-sellers is a single malt named Stronachie which is actually sourced from Benrinnes. There are currently two expressions, a 10 year old and a 10 year old sherry finish. In 2011 a peated, blended malt, Cask Islay, became the first in a new series called Casks of Scotland. There are now three expressions available – Cask Islay Classic, Cask Orkney and Cask Speyside – in different versions. The AD Rattray´s Cask Collection, with four releases per year, is a range of single cask whiskies bottled at cask strength and without colouring or chill-filtration while Vintage Cask Collection contains rare and old single malts. In 2020 a new range of single cask whiskies, The Warehouse Collection, was introduced. Bottled at either cask strength or 46% these are a mixture of full or part casks, 'bin ends' and remnants from casks that have be re-racked. Finally there is the House Malts range, exlusively available in the shop (and on line).

Cask Islay Classic, 46%
Nose: Coffee and walnut cake, hints of roasted coffee beans and background wafting smoke.
Palate: Soft mouthfeel, tiramisu with espresso notes then muscovado sugar, while chocolate mousse and dark chocolate emerge.

Stronachie 10 year old, 43%
Nose: Fresh lemon juice, camomile tea, honey, hints of lime and orange.
Palate: Lightly velvety, luscious mouthfeel, then camomile tea, juicy lemon and lime, waves of vanilla and butterscotch.

Douglas Laing & Co
douglaslaing.com

Established in 1948 by Douglas Laing, this firm was run for many years by his two sons, Fred and Stewart. In 2013, the brothers decided to go their separate ways. Douglas Laing & Co is now run by Fred Laing and his daughter Cara. Douglas Laing has the following brands in their portfolio; Provenance (single casks bottled at 46%), Premier Barrel (single malts in ceramic decanters) and Old Particular, a range of single malts and grains. The latter has also been expanded with two brand extensions; XOP and XOP "The Black Series". A range named Double Barrel was recently re-branded and consists of expressions where just two single malts have been blended together.

A decade ago the company started a range that has become highly succesful. The first installment in the series that eventually was given the name Remarkable Regional Malts, was Scallywag – a blended malt influenced by sherried whiskies from Speyside. More versions have followed with the sherry matured Scallywag The Chocolate Edition #2 and Three Peaks Edition as some of the latest. Regional Malts has been expanded

over the years and now also includes Timorous Beastie from the Highlands with a no age statement and a 10 year old. Recent limited expressions include the Sherried Beast #2 and Port Edition. Rock Island is a blended malt combining whiskies from Islay, Arran, Orkney and Jura and can be bought without age statement, as a 10 year old, a Cask Strength and a Sherry Edition Recent limited releases include Rum Cask Edition and the 14 year old Sherry Edition. The Epicurean represents the Lowlands with a no age statement and a 12 year old as well as the recent, limited Amarone Edition and Glasgow Edition #2. The Gauldrons is made from Campbeltown malts with a sherry cask edition as the latest expression and the final regional whisky is Big Peat, a vatting of Islay malts. This was launched several years ago but was later included in the range. The core range is made up of a no age statement bottling and a 12 year old. Recent limited versions include Storm Edition, Beach BBQ Edition and the yearly Christmas Edition. A recent limited edition with malts from several regions was The Asia Moon Edition, finished in a combination of port, bourbon and sherry casks.

In July 2017, it was announced that Douglas Laing were also planning to build a distillery. Their chosen site in Glasgow is Hillingdon where warehouses have already been built and a bottling plant is up and running. The Clutha distillery will probably be ready in a couple of years. In 2019 the company bought Strathearn distillery west of Perth and have released a number of bottlings since.

The Gauldrons Sherry Cask Edition 50%
Nose: Toastyness, mango, passionfruit, underlying porridge.
Palate: Soft mouthfeel, juicy apples, pears, base notes of oak, with vanilla, nutmeg and dark chocolate above.

Rock Island 14 year old, 46,8%
Nose: Malty, toasty, oak, fruit cake and honey, then butterscotch.
Palate: Soft, mouth filling texture, vanilla, cappuccino, zesty lemon and juicy fruit, subtle sweetness with underlying shortbread and dryness.

Hunter Laing & Co
hunterlaing.com

This company was formed after the demerger between Fred and Stewart Laing in 2013 (see Douglas Laing). It is run by Stewart Laing and his two sons, Scott and Andrew. The Hunter Laing portfolio consists of the following ranges and brands; The Old Malt Cask (rare and old malts, bottled at 50%), The Old and Rare Selection (an exclusive range of old malts offered at cask strength), The Sovereign (a range of old and rare grain whiskies), Hepburn´s Choice (younger malts bottled at 46%) and The First Editions. The latter was created by Andrew Laing before Hunter Laing was formed and is now a substantial part of the portfolio. In 2019, Scarabus, a single malt from an undisclosed Islay distillery, was released as the first in a new range and there is also the Journey series (Islay, Highland, Campbeltown and Hebridean) with blended malts from four different regions in Scotland. Finally, a remarkable series by the name Eidolon was introduced in late 2020. It consisted of three extremely rare Port Ellen single malts. A second release appeared in February 2023.

In November 2018, Ardnahoe distillery was opened on the north-east coast of Islay near Bunnahabain. The distillery, with a capacity of making 1 million litres per year, was opened to the public in spring 2019. To celebrate their presence on the island, the company has since then released a number of old and rare Islay single malts, often in connection with the Feis Ile, under the name Kinship. In 2023 there were five Islay malts and one from Highland Park, aged from 18 to 33 years.

Kinship Laphroaig 25 year old, 54,2%
Nose: Shortbread with lemon tea, then gentle embers, orange marmalade, and pineapple chunks.
Palate: Delicate mouthfeel, sweetness opens rapidly with luscious lemon tart and pineapple chunks in syrup, lemon zest garnish, then creamy maltyness at the core.

Kinship Cao Ila 33 year old, 44,5%
Nose: Sea breeze with brine, vanilla custard, lemon tart and ripe brie.
Palate: Ultra-delicate mouthfeel, opens gradually with creamy vanilla, hint of ripe brie, garnished by fresh lemon juice and zest, cider and underlying oak.

Malts of Scotland

malts-of-scotland.com

A German bottler founded by Thomas Ewers in 2009. The backbone of the assortment is the Basic Line with three blended malts; Classic (18yo), Sherry (15yo) and Peat (10yo).Apart from other ranges of Scotch single malts, Ewers also has three ranges called Malts of Ireland, Malts of India and Whiskeys of America. At the moment he has released more than 200 bottlings and apart from a large number of single casks, there are two special series, Amazing Casks and Angel's Choice, both dedicated to very special and superior casks.

Wemyss Malts

wemyssmalts.com

Founded in 2005, Wemyss Malts is an independent, family-owned company run by brother and sister duo William and Isabella Wemyss, whose centuries-old family heritage is rooted in Fife, on Scotland's East Coast. In 2014 they also opened their own distillery, Kingsbarns, a few miles south of St Andrews. The company is mainly known for its range of blended malts of which there are three core expressions – The Hive, Spice King and Peat Chimney. These are available at 46% un chill-filtered and also in limited edition batch strength. A limited 12 year old Spice King Highland & Islay was also recently released. In autumn 2020 the entire range was rebranded including new packaging. In 2017 The Family Collection of blended malts was launched. The latest releases include Bohemian Blossom and Nectar Grove matured in madeira casks. Finally, there are two version of the blend Lord Elcho (NAS and 15 year old). Another side of the business involves single cask single malts. either bottled at 46% or occasionally at cask strength. All whiskies are un chill-filtered and without colouring. In 2019, Wemyss launched a brand new range called the Wemyss Malts Cask Club with exclusive bottlings for the members.

In 2021 the range from the owner's own Kingsbarns distillery was revamped and now consists of the 5 year old Balcomie and, launched in spring 2023, Doocot which has been matured in a combination of bourbon and STR red wine barriques. Limited releases include the new Bell Rock bottled at 61,1% and a range of single cask bottlings from a variety of cask types.

Kingsbarns Bell Rock, 61,1%
Nose: Rich and detailed, oak, honey, gingerbread, then chocolate, nutmeg and a dusting of cocoa powder.
Palate: Luscious mouthfeel, initial sweetness then an acceleration of gingerbread, vanilla, nutmeg, tiramisu and prunes.

Kingsbarns Doocot, 46%
Nose: Linseed, oak and malty hints form a core within a toffee apple.
Palate: Silky mouthfeel, opens with rich-sweet-lusciousness, apricots and peaches, then toffee, butterscotch and chocolate with underlying dryness.

Elixir Distillers

elixirdistillers.com

The company is owned by Sukhinder and Rajbir Singh, known by most for their three very well-stocked The Whisky Exchange shops in London as well as being the largest on-line retailer of Scotch whisky in the world. In the beginning of October every year, they are hosting the iconic The Whisky Show in London, one of the best whisky festivals in the world and for the last six years they have also been involved in the Old & Rare Show in Glasgow and London. Recently the retail part of their business was sold to Pernod Ricard. In 2002 they started as independent bottlers of malt whiskies operating under the brand name The Single Malts of Scotland. There are around 50 bottlings on offer at any time, either as single casks or as batches bottled at cask strength or at 46%.

In 2009 a new range of Islay single malts under the name Port Askaig was introduced. The current core range consists of 100° Proof, 110° Proof (exclusive to the USA) and an 8 year old. Over the years limited releases (some up to 45 years old) have occured with a 25 year old, exclusive to the USA, as one of the latest. Elements of Islay, a series of cask strength single malts in which all Islay distilleries are, or will be, represented was introduced one year before Port Askaig. The list of the product range is cleverly constructed with periodical tables in mind in which each distillery has a two-letter acronym followed by a batch number. There are blended malts in the range (Cask Edit, Bourbon Cask and Sherry Cask) but also single malts where the most recent bottlings include Lg_{12}, Ar_{11} and Cl_{14}. The company is at the moment building a whisky distillery on Islay on the outskirts of Port Ellen. Equipped with floor maltings and two pairs of stills, the goal is to have Portintruan Distillery opened during 2024. In 2022 they also bought Tormore Distillery in Speyside.

Port Askaig 25 year old, 45,8%
Nose: Shortbread and muesli, sea breeze and fresh lemon zest leading to lemon syllabub.
Palate: Lightly creamy mouthfeel, creaminess grows with vanilla and juicy lemon, becomes more luscious, complimented by subtle underlying dryness.

Elements of Islay Sherry Cask, 54,5%
Nose: Toasted notes, Christmas pudding, then tiramisu and gentle wafting smoke with embers beyond.
Palate: Silky mouthfeel, dried fruits become juicy, then toasted, barbecue notes grow accompanied by sweetness.

Single Cask Nation

singlecasknation.com

Initially Single Cask Nation was formed a a member's club but in 2017, the owners decided to also start selling through retailers in the USA and, later, Europe and Canada as well. Although the focus is on Scotch, Single Cask Nation has over the years released more and more bottlings from distilleries in other parts of the world, including expressions from Milk & Honey, Mackmyra, Paul John and Australian rye whisky from Backwoods Distilling.

The Ultimate Whisky Company

ultimatewhisky.com

Founded in 1994 by Han van Wees and his son Maurice, this Dutch independent bottler has until now bottled close to 1,000 single malts. All whiskies are un chill-filtered, without colouring and bottled at either 46% or cask strength. The van Wees family also operate one of the finest spirits shops in Europe – Van Wees Whisky World in Amersfoort – with i.a. more than 1,000 different whiskies including more than 500 single malts.

Svenska Eldvatten

eldvatten.se

Founded in 2011 and since the start, well over 100 single casks, bottled at cask strength, have been released. In their range of spirits they have aged tequila and rum and they have also launched their own rum, WeiRon, as well as gin and aquavit. Svenska Eldvatten are also importers to Sweden of whisky from Murray McDavid, AD Rattray, North Star Spirits, South Star Spirits, Sansibar, Hidden Spirits, Claxton's, Single Cask Nation and Spey Whisky.

The Vintage Malt Whisky Company

vintagemaltwhisky.com

Founded in 1992 the company supplys whisky to more than 35 countries. In 2022 they opened up a rum distillery in Port Ellen on Islay and recently their first bottlings, Geal Pure Single Rum followed by Peat Spiced, were released. The most famous brands in the whisky range are two single Islay malts called Finlaggan and The Ileach. The latter comes in two versions, bottled at 40% and 58%. The Finlaggan range consists of Old Reserve, Eilean Mor, Port Finish, Sherry Finish, Cask Strength (58%) and Red Wine Cask Matured. Other expressions include a wide range of single cask single malts under the name The Cooper's Choice.

Wm Cadenhead & Co

cadenhead.scot

A classic bottler established in 1842. The owners, J&A Mitchell, also own Springbank and Glengyle distilleries in Campbeltown. Their core range, Authentic Collection, is made up of single cask cask strength whiskies, exclusively sold in their own shops and on-line. Other collections are World Whiskies (single malts from non Scottish distillers), Closed Distilleries and Small Batch, a range which can be divided into three separate ranges; Single Cask, Small Batch Cask Strength and Small Batch 46%. The Creations range consists of small batch blends and blended malts and they also have their own ranges of gin and rum. In May 2023 Cadenheads opened up a Blending Lab in Campbeltown where customers can create their own blend to take home.

Adelphi Distillery

adelphidistillery.com

Founded in 1993 (celebrating its 30th anniversary this year) by Jamie Walker and named after a distillery which stopped making malt whisky in 1907, the company offers a range of single malts bottled at cask strength with new releases four times a year. There are also two recurrent brands, Fascadale and Liddesdale, where the single malt differs from batch to batch. In 2015, the first two bottlings of a new brand saw the light of day. Together with Fusion Whisky,

Adelphi launched The Glover – a unique vatting of single malt from the closed Japanese distillery Hanyu and two Scottish single malts, Longmorn and Glen Garioch. This has been followed by collaborations with Amrut in India, Starward in Australia, Zuidam in The Netherlands and High Coast in Sweden. The latest (The Glover 6) is a fusion between Ardnamurchan and Chichibu in Japan.

Since 2014, Adelphi is also making whisky in their own Ardnamurchan Distillery in Western Scotland. Since the opening, the owners regularly released malt spirit (less than 3 years old) and in October 2020 the first single malt whisky from the distillery was launched. Recent bottlings, in 2023, include the Sherry Cask Release (a combination of oloroso and PX casks) and the 6 year old Paul Lanois finished in champagne barriques.

Maclean's Nose, 46%

Nose: Poached plums meld into prunes, cherries in syrup.

Palate: Soft mouthfeel, immediate sweetness extends with richness and dryness, dried fruits move to poached fruits in syrup, and creamy chocolate truffles.

Ardnamurchan, 46,8%

Nose: Millefeuille evolves into creamy fruit trifle, with hints of nutmeg and cappuccino.

Palate: Lightly velvety mouthfeel, creamy vanilla, chocolate and orange marmalade, then sweetness peaks in conjunction with dry malt and juiciness.

Deerstalker Whisky Co

deerstalkerwhisky.com

Dating back to 1880, the Deerstalker brand was bought by Aberko Ltd in 1994. Currently there is one core single malt in the range, a 12 year old, and two blended malts - Peated Edition and Highland Edition. Limited Deerstalker single malts are released from time to time.

Morrison Distillers

morrisondistillers.com, carnmorwhisky.co.uk

Owned by a family with decades of experience in the Scotch whisky industry, the company's most famous range is Carn Mor single malt whiskies. Currently there are three series; Strictly Limited, usually bottled at 47,5%, Celebration of the Cask which are single casks bottled at cask strength and a new series named Family Reserve. Other ranges are Mac-Talla with Islay single malts and Old Perth blended malts. In 2017 the owners also opened a distillery of their own in Fife – Aberargie Distillery.

Sansibar Whisky

sansibar-whisky.com

The idea is to fill high quality single malts from Scotland and to market them in connection with the well known Sansibar restaurant on the island of Sylt in northern Germany. Around 60 bottlings are produced per year and the range also includes rum.

Dramfool

dramfool.com

Bruce Farquhar sources his whisky from private individuals as well as from brokers and has so far released around 100 different bottlings. In spring 2021 a new range was added - the Jim McEwan

Signature Collection where the different styles from Bruichladdich are represented. Together with Felipe Schrieberg from the Rhythm & Booze Project, Bruce released a 13 year old blended malt in July 2023.

Angel´s Nectar

angelsnectar.co.uk

Highfern Ltd fills and sells whisky under the name Angel´s Nectar. Current expressions include the blended malt Original, the single malt Oloroso Sherry cask Edition bottled at 46% which was recently followed by a version bottled 57,9%. There is also a new version of the Cairngorms 4th Edition Single malt. Highfern is also the UK importer for Langatun Swiss single malt.

The Single Cask Ltd

thesinglecask.co.uk

Ben Curtis was distributor for a number of Scottish distilleries in south-east Asia before he started as an independent bottler in Singapore in 2010. Since then he has moved back to the UK. The business has grown over the years and the brand is now sold in the UK, Europe and Asia. Some of the most recent expressions include a 27 year old Tobermory, a 29 year old Ledaig and a series of four single casks named Abstract Sensory Journey in collaboration with Whisky Studio. The company also acts as a broker selling casks with both newmake and maturing whisky.

Selected Malts

selectedmalts.se

A Swedish bottler and blender specialising in single malts from Scotland but also from Sweden. In 2019 they released their own blended malt, Zippin, and later they became distributors for GlenAllachie, James Eadie and Milk & Honey in Sweden. Recently the company has expanded the business into selling casks to private customers.

The Alistair Walker Whisky Co.

alistairwalkerwhisky.com

When Alistair Walker´s family sold BenRiach, GlenDronach and Glenglassaugh in 2016, he decided to start up as an independent bottler. The brand is called Infrequent Flyers and to date more than 100 different bottlings have been released. Batch 12, released in April 2023, included a 25 year old Bowmore from a PX hogshead, a 10 year old Craigellachie madeira finish and a 14 year old Teaninich rye finish.

Watt Whisky

wattwhisky.com

When Mark Watt left Cadenheads he decided to start a company of his own together with his wife Kate who has a background working for both Springbank and Glenfarclas. Their philosophy is to mainly bottle single malt Scotch (but also grains and rums) at cask strength and without colouring or chill filtration. In autumn 2020 Mark, together with his friend David Stirk, launched a range of its own named Electric Coo. The most recent releases from Watt Whisky include a Campbeltown Blended malt matured in rum barrels, a 22 year old, sherry matured Peated Highland and the blend A Tale of Two Cities made up of Campbeltown malt, Glasgow malt and North British grain

The Whisky Baron

thewhiskybaron.co.uk

Jake Sharpe began the business trading casks as an investment but eventually started to sell bottled single cask malt to private customers. The current range is divided into Rennaisance, Founder´s Collection and the Signature series. One of the latest releases was a triple distilled, 11 year old from the English Distillery in Norfolk, matured in a bourbon barrel.

Lady of the Glen

ladyoftheglen.com

Hannah Whisky Merchants was founded by Gregor Hannah in 2012 and is mainly known for their brand Lady of the Glen with bottlings of single malt and single grain Scotch. Around 40 casks are bottled per year and the latest releases, in May 2023, include a 10 year old oloroso finished Auchroisk, a 10 year old Benrinnes finished in tawny port and an unusual 10 year old Glen Spey finished in a Banyuls cask – all bottled at cask strength.

The Islay Boys

islayboys.com

Mackay Smith and Donald MacKenzie bought the Islay Ales Brewery in 2018. Soon after they started as whisky bottlers and at the moment their range consists of Bårelegs Islay single malt and Flatnöse blended malt and blended Scotch. In June 2022 their planning application for building Laggan Bay Distillery on Islay was approved with Ian Macleod Distillers being a partner in the project.

Asta Morris

asta-morris.be

Founded by former Malt Maniac Bert Bruyneel in 2009, the company started with whisky but has later also branched out into rum, cognac and calvados. Typically around 15 single malts are released yearly from young and affordable expressions to old and are bottlings. A special project for Bert is his NOG gin which has been matured in some of his used whisky casks and is bottled in batches.

James Eadie

jameseadie.co.uk

Founded by Rupert Patrick who is the great-great-grandson of James Eadie, a Scottish blender in the 1800s. With a long background in the Scotch whisky industry Rupert set up as a independent bottler specialising in small batch and single cask Scotch. He also managed to recreate Eadie´s blend from the early days when he launched Trade Mark X. Two of the most recent releases (in spring 2023) are a 24 year old Cameronbridge single grain finished in a marsala cask and a 27 year old from the same distillery finished in a madeira cask. Apart from whisky, the company also published an astonishing book in 2022 – The Distilleries of Great Britain and Ireland. It is a 630 page compilation of long since forgotten articles (and amazing photos) about 124 distilleries written in the 1920s.

Claxton´s Spirits

claxtonsspirits.com

A company with a bonded warehouse on the Dalswinton Estate just north of Dumfries. This facility allows them to have an impressive scheme of re-racking, finishing, blending and bottling - rather unusual for an independent bottler. Focus is on single malt or single grain Scotch bottled at cask strength. The range is divided into three series; Warehouse No. 1, Warehouse No. 8 and Exploration. The latest in Warehouse No. 1 are an 11 year old Inchgower from a first fill oloroso cask, a 15 year old PX Auchroisk and a 16 year old Cameronbridge single grain.

Brave New Spirits

bravenewspirits.com

A fairly new independent bottler and blender with their own warehouse in Glasgow. In a short period of time they have estabslished themselves as one of the more prolific companies in the industry. In what they themselves call the Party Department they work with volume brands, often designed for specific supermarkets and retailers. For the connoiseurs there are three ranges; Whisky of Voodo (small batch releases), Yellow Edition (traditional single barrel releases) and Cask Noir (single barrel releases from unusual and interesting casks). In May 2023 they also announced that they are going to build a distillery near Machrihanish airport north of Campbeltown.

Whisky
shops

AUSTRALIA
The Odd Whisky Coy
25 Anzac Ridge Road, Bridgewater,
SA, 5155
Phone: +61 (0)417 852 296
www.theoddwhiskycoy.com.au
On-line whisky specialist with an
impressive range. Agents for brands such
as Springbank and Berry Brothers.

World of Whisky
Shop G12, Cosmopolitan Centre
2-22 Knox Street, Double Bay NSW 2028
Phone: +61 (0)2 9363 4212
www.worldofwhisky.com.au
A whisky specialist with a wide range,
most of them single malts. The shop is also
organising and hosting regular tastings.

The Whisky Company
PO Box 2559, Seaford, VIC, 3198
Phone: +61 (0)434 438 617
www.thewhiskycompany.com.au
One of the largest on-line retailers of
single malt whisky in Australia with
around 800 products currently in stock.

My Bottle Shop
34D Fitzroy St., Marrickville, NSW, 2204
Phone: +61 (0)2 9516 3816
www.mybottleshop.com.au
More than 2,000 whiskies with some of
them being sourced directly from the
suppliers on demand. On-line only.

The Oak Barrel
152 Elizabeh St, Sydney, NSW, 2000
Phone: +61 (0)2 9264 3022
www.oakbarrel.com.au
They have a nice range of Scotch whiskies
but it is the range of Australian whiskies
that impresses the most. Wine, beer, cider
and other spirits as well.

Nicks Wine Merchants
10-12 Jackson Court, East Doncaster,
VIC, 3109
Phone: +61 (0)3 9848 1153
www.nicks.com.au
A supplier of all sorts of spirits and wines
and with an extraordinary range of whisky
- the largest in Australia - with more than
500 Australian whiskies in the range!

AUSTRIA
Potstill
Laudongasse 18, 1080 Wien
Phone: +43 (0)664 118 85 41
www.potstill.org
Austria's premier whisky shop since 1992
with over 1100 different single malts,
including some real rarities.

Whisky Wien
Hahngasse 17, 1190 Wien
Phone: +43 (0)677 622 476 40
www.whiskywien.at
The former Cadenhead whisky shop but
now with a new life.

Pinkernells Whisky Market
Alter Markt 1, 5020 Salzburg
Phone: +43 (0)662 84 53 05
www.pinkernells.at
More than 500 whiskies are on offer and
they are also importers of Maltbarn, The
Whisky Chamber and Jack Wiebers.

Hirschenbrunner Spirits
Zieglergasse 88-90/23, 1070 Wien
Phone: +43 699 1132 37 30
www.hirschenbrunner.com
A very well equipped store with more than
1,000 whiskies including many old and
rare bottlings. There is also a substantial
amount of other spirits in the range.

BELGIUM
Whiskycorner
Kraaistraat 16, 3530 Houthalen
Phone: +32 (0)89 386233
www.whiskycorner.be
A very large selection of single malts,
more than 2000 different. Also other
whiskies, calvados and grappas.

Huis Crombé
Doenaertstraat 20, 8510 Marke
Phone: +32 (0)56 21 19 87
www.crombewines.com
A wine retailer which also covers all kinds
of spirits. A large assortment of Scotch is
supplemented with whiskies from Japan,
the USA and Ireland to mention a few.

We Are Whisky
Avenue Rodolphe Gossia 33
1350 Orp-Jauche
Phone: +32 (0)471 134556
www.wearewhisky.com
On-line retailer with a range of more than
800 different whiskies. They also arrange
regular tastings every month.

Dram 242
Rijgerstraat 60, 9310 Moorsel
Phone: +32 (0)477 26 09 93
www.dram242.be
A wide range of whiskies. Apart from
the core official bottlings, they have
focused on rare, old expressions as well as
whiskies from small, independent bottlers.

CANADA
Kensington Wine Market
1257 Kensington Road NW
Calgary, Alberta T2N 3P8
Phone: +1 403 283 8000
www.kensingtonwinemarket.com
The shop has a very large range of
whiskies (more than 1500) as well as other
spirits and wines. More than 80 tastings in
the shop every year. Also the home of the
Scotch Malt Whisky Society in Canada.

World of Whisky
Unit 240, 333 5 Avenue SW
Calgary, Alberta T2P 3B6
Phone: +1 587 956 8511
www.coopwinespiritsbeer.com/stores/
world-of-whisky/
Specialising in whisky from all corners of
the world. Currently there are over 1100
different whiskies in the range including
some extremely rare ones from Scotland.

DENMARK
Whisky.dk
Vejstruprødvej 15
6093 Sjølund
Phone: +45 5210 6093
www.whisky.dk
Henrik Olsen and Ulrik Bertelsen are well-
known in Denmark for their whisky shows
but they also run an impressive spirits
shop with an emphasis on whisky but also
including an impressive stock of rums.

Juul´s Vin & Spiritus
Værnedamsvej 15
1819 Frederiksberg
Phone: +45 33 31 13 29

Lyngby Hovedgade 43
2800 Kongens Lyngby
Phone: +45 33 18 37 93
www.juuls.dk
A very large range of wines, fortified
wines and spirits with more than 1100
different whiskies (800 single malts).

Whisky Watcher
Kongensgade 69 F
5000 Odense C
Phone: +45 66 13 95 05
www.whiskywatcher.com
Whisky specialist with a very good range,
and also a Nice assortment of champagne,
cognac and rum. Arranges whisky and beer
tastings. On-line ordering.

ENGLAND

The Whisky Exchange
2 Bedford Street, Covent Garden
London WC2E 9HH
Phone: +44 (0)20 7100 0088

90-92 Great Portland Street, Fitzrovia
London W1W 7NT
Phone: +44 (0)20 7100 9888

88 Borough High Street, London Bridge
London SE1 1LL
Phone: +44 (0)20 7631 3888
www.thewhiskyexchange.com
An excellent whisky shop founded by
Sukhinder and Rajbir Singh who recently
sold it to Pernod Ricard. Started off as a
mail order business, run from a showroom
in Hanwell, but later opened up at
Vinopolis in downtown London. Moved
to a new and bigger location in Covent
Garden a couple of years ago and have
since then opened two more shops. The
assortment is huge with well over 1000
single malts to choose from. Some rarities
which can hardly be found anywhere else
are offered thanks to Singh's great interest
for antique whisky. There are also other
types of whisky and cognac, calvados,
rum etc.

The Whisky Shop
(See also Scotland, The Whisky Shop)
11 Coppergate Walk
York YO1 9NT
Phone: +44 (0)1904 640300
www.whiskyshop.com

7 Turl Street
Oxford OX1 3DQ
Phone: +44 (0)1865 202279

3 Swan Lane
Norwich NR2 1HZ
Phone: +44 (0)1603 618284

169 Piccadilly
London W1J 9EH
Phone: +44 (0)207 499 6649

Unit 7 Queens Head Passage
Paternoster
London EC4M 7DZ
Phone: +44 (0)207 329 5117

3 Exchange St
Manchester M2 7EE
Phone: +44 (0)161 832 6110

25 Chapel Street
Guildford GU1 3UL
Phone: +44 (0)1483 450900

Unit 9 Great Western Arcade
Birmingham B2 5HU
Phone: +44 (0)121 233 4416

64 East Street
Brighton BN1 1HQ
Phone: +44 (0)1273 327 962

3 Cheapside
Nottingham NG1 2HU
Phone: +44 (0)115 958 7080

9-10 High Street
Bath BA1 5AQ
Phone: +44 (0)1225 423 535

Unit 1/9 Red Mall,
Intu Metro Centre
Gateshead NE11 9YP
Phone: +44 (0)191 460 3777

Unit 210 Trentham Gardens
Stoke on Trent ST4 8AX
Phone: +44 (0)1782 644 483

36 Royal Arcade
Cardiff CF10 1AE
Phone: +44 (0)29 2213 0033

12-14 County Arcade, Victoria Quarter
Leeds LS1 6BN
Phone: +44 (0)113 430 0158

The largest specialist retailer of whiskies
in the UK with 22 outlets. A large product
range with over 1500 Scotch single
malt whiskies as well as other spirits,
accessories and books. They also run
The W Club, the leading whisky club in
the UK where the excellent Whiskeria
magazine is one of the member's benefits.
Shipping all over the world.

Berry Bros. & Rudd
63 Pall Mall, London SW1Y 5HZ
Phone: +44 (0)800 280 2440
www.bbrspirits.com
A legendary company dating back to
1698! One of the world's most reputable
wine shops but with an extensive and
exclusive selection of malt whiskies, some
of them bottled by Berry Bros. themselves.
The company is also known as as well
respected independent bottler of whiskies
and rums.

The Wright Wine & Whisky Company
The Old Smithy, Raikes Road, Skipton,
North Yorkshire BD23 1NP
Phone: +44 (0)1756 700886
www.wineandwhisky.co.uk
An eclectic selection of near to 1000
different whiskies. 'Tasting Cupboard' of
nearly 100 opened bottles for sampling
with regular hosted tasting evenings. Great
'Collector to Collector' selection of old
whiskies plus a fantastic choice of 1200+
wines, premium spirits and liqueurs.

Master of Malt
Unit 1, Ton Business Park, 2-8 Morley Rd.
Tonbridge, Kent, TN9 1RA
Phone: +44 (0)1892 888376
www.masterofmalt.com
Online retailer and independent bottler
with a very impressive range of more
than 2,500 whiskies, including over 2,000
Scotch whiskies and over 1,500 single
malts. In addition to whisky there is an
enormous selection of gins, rums, cognacs,
armagnacs, tequilas and more. The website
contains a wealth of information and news
about the distilleries and innovative personalised gift ideas. Drinks by the Dram
30ml samples of more than 3,300 different
whiskies are available also they also offer
the Dram Club monthly whisky subscription service, as well as a Blend Your Own
option, personalised whisky and has a gift
finder to help with special occassions.

Whiskys.co.uk
The Square, Stamford Bridge
York YO4 11AG
Phone: +44 (0)1759 371356
www.whiskys.co.uk
Good assortment with more than 600
different whiskies. Also a nice range
of armagnac, rum, calvados etc. The

owners also have another website, www.
whiskymerchants.co.uk with a huge
amount of information on just about every
whisky distillery in the world.

The Wee Dram
5 Portland Square, Bakewell
Derbyshire DE45 1HA
Phone: +44 (0)1629 812235
www.weedram.co.uk
Large range of Scotch single malts with
whiskies from other parts of the world and
a good range of whisky books. Run 'The
Wee Drammers Whisky Club' with seminars and tastings. In October they arrange
the yearly Wee Dram Fest whisky festival.

Hard To Find Whisky
1 Spencer Street, Birmingham B18 6DD
Phone: +44 (0)121 448 84 84
www.htfw.com
As the name says, this family owned shop
specialises in rare, collectable and new
releases of single malt whisky. The range
is astounding - more than 3,000 different
bottlings including more than 500 different
Macallan. World wide shipping.

Nickolls & Perks
37 Lower High Street, Stourbridge
West Midlands DY8 1TA
Phone: +44 (0)1384 394518
www.nickollsandperks.co.uk
Mostly known as wine merchants but
also has a huge range of whiskies with
1,900 different kinds including 1,300
single malts. They also organize Midlands
Whisky Festival, www.whiskyfest.co.uk

Gauntleys of Nottingham
4 High Street, Nottingham NG1 2ET
Phone: +44 (0)115 9110555
www.gauntleys.com
A fine wine merchant established in 1880.
The range of wines are among the best
in the UK. All kinds of spirits, not least
whisky, are taking up more and more
space and several rare malts can be found.

Hedonism Wines
3-7 Davies St., London W1K 3LD
Phone: +44 (020) 729 078 70
www.hedonism.co.uk
Located in the heart of London, this is a
temple for wine lovers but also with over
1,200 different whisky bottlings from
Scotland and the rest of the world.

The Lincoln Whisky Shop
87 Bailgate, Lincoln LN1 3AR
Phone: +44 (0)1522 537834
www.lincolnwhiskyshop.co.uk
Mainly specialising in whisky with more
than 300 different whiskies but also 500
spirits and liqueurs. Mailorder worldwide.

Milroys of Soho
3 Greek Street, London W1D 4NX
Phone: +44 (0)207 734 2277
www.milroys.co.uk
A classic whisky shop in Soho with a very
good range with over 700 malts and a wide
selection of whiskies from around the
world. Also a whisky bar within the shop.
Recently opened another whisky bar in
Spitalfields in East London.

Cadenhead's Whisky Shop
26 Chiltern Street, London W1U 7QF
Phone: +44 (0)20 7935 6999
www.whiskytastingroom.com
One in a chain of shops owned by
independent bottlers Cadenhead. Sells
Cadenhead's product range and c. 200
other whiskies. Regular tastings.

Drinkfinder
30 Fore Street, Constantine, Falmouth
Cornwall TR11 5AB
Phone: +44 (0)1326 340226
www.drinkfinder.co.uk
A full-range wine and spirits dealer with a
great selection of whiskies from the whole
world (of which more than 1,000 are
Scotch).Worldwide shipping.

House of Malt
48 Warwick Road, Carlisle CA1 1DN
Phone: +44 (0)1228 658 422
www.houseofmalt.co.uk
A wide selection of whiskies from
Scotland and the world as well as other
spirits and craft ales. Regular tasting
evenings and events.

The Vintage House
42 Old Compton Street
London W1D 4LR
Phone: +44 (0)20 7437 2592
www.vintagehouse.london
A huge range of 1400 kinds of malt
whisky, many of them rare. Supplementing this is also a selection of fine wines.

Whisky On-line
Units 1-3 Concorde House, Charnley
Road, Blackpool, Lancashire FY1 4PE
Phone: +44 (0)1253 620376
www.whisky-online.com
A good selection of whisky and also
cognac, rum, port etc. Specializes in rare
whiskies and hold regular auctions.

FRANCE
La Maison du Whisky
20 rue d'Anjou
75008 Paris
Phone: +33 (0)1 42 65 03 16

6 carrefour d l'Odéon
75006 Paris
Phone: +33 (0)1 46 34 70 20

(1 shop outside France)
The Pier at Robertson Quay
80 Mohamed Sultan Road, #01-10
Singapore 239013
Phone: +65 6733 0059
www.whisky.fr
France's largest whisky specialist with
over 1200 whiskies and also a number of
own-bottled single malts. La Maison du
Whisky acts as a EU distributor for many
whisky producers around the world. Also
run the Golden Promise whisky bar and
store in rue Tiquetonne in Paris.

The Whisky Shop
7 Place de la Madeleine, 75008 Paris
Phone: +33 (0)1 45 22 29 77
www.whiskyshop.fr
The large chain of whisky shops in the UK
has now opened up a store in Paris as well.

GERMANY
SCOMA
Am Bullhamm 17, 26441 Jever
Phone: +49 (0)4461 912237
www.scoma.de
Very large range of c 750 Scottish malts
and many from other countries. Holds
regular seminars and tastings. The
excellent, monthly whisky newsletter
SCOMA News is also produced.

The Whisky Store
Am Grundwassersee 4, 82402 Seeshaupt
Phone: +49 (0)8801 30 20 000
www.whisky.de
A very large range comprising c 1700
kinds of whisky of which 1100 are Scotch.
Also sells whisky liqueurs, books and
accessories. The website is a goldmine of
information, in particular the videos with
Horst and Ben Luening.

Whisky Market Cologne
Luxemburger Strasse 257, 50939 Köln
Phone: +49 (0)221-2831834
www.whisky-market.com
Good range of malt whiskies (c 350
different kinds) including Cadenhead's
bottlings. Other products include wine,
cognac and rum etc. Arranges recurring
tastings and also has an on-line shop.

Tara Spirits
Rindermarkt 16, 80331 München
Phone: +49 (0)89 26 51 18
store.tara-spirits.de
An excellent supplier of whiskies as well
as gin and rum. Also holds regular tastings.

Home of Malts
Hosegstieg 11, 22880 Wedel
Phone: +49 (0)4103 965 9695
www.homeofmalts.com
Large assortment with over 800 different
single malts as well as whiskies from
many other countries. Also a nice selection
of cognac, rum etc. On-line ordering.

Reifferscheid
Mainzer Strasse 186, 53179 Bonn
Phone: +49 (0)228 9 53 80 70
www.whisky-bonn.de
A well-stocked shop with a large range of
whiskies, wine, spirit, cigars and a deli-
catessen. They also have a wide range of
whiskies bottled especially for the shop.

Whisky-Doris
Germanenstrasse 38, 14612 Falkensee
Phone: +49 (0)3322-219784
www.whisky-doris.de
Large range of over 300 whiskies and also
sells own special bottlings. Orders via
email. Shipping also outside Germany.

Finlays Whisky Shop
Hohenzollernstr. 88, 80796 München
Phone: +49 (0)89 3270 979 145
www.finlayswhiskyshop.de
Whisky specialists with a large range of
over 700 whiskies and 300 rums. Also
importer of a number of Scottish brands.

Weinquelle
Lübeckerstrasse 145, 22087 Hamburg
Phone: +49 (0)40 300 672 950
Jacobsrade 65, 22962 Siek (showroom)
Phone: +49 (0)4107 908 900
www.weinquelle.com
An impressive selection of both wines and
spirits with over 1000 different whiskies of
which 850 are malt whiskies.

The Whisky-Corner
Reichertsfeld 2, 92278 Illschwang
Phone: +49 (0)9666-951213
www.whisky-corner.de
A small shop but large on mail order.
A very large assortment of over 2000
whiskies.

World Wide Spirits
Am Söterberg 12, 66620 Nonnweiler
Phone: +49 (0)6873 800 990
www.worldwidespirits.de
A nice range of more than 1,000 whiskies
with some rarities from the twenties. Also
large selection of other spirits.

WhiskyKoch
Weinbergstrasse 2, 64285 Darmstadt
Phone: +49 (0)6151 96 96 886
www.whiskykoch.de
A combination of a whisky shop and
restaurant. The shop has a nice selection
of single malts as well as other Scottish
products and the restaurant has specialised
in whisky dinners and tastings.

Kierzek
Weitlingstrasse 17, 10317 Berlin
Phone: +49 (0)30 525 11 08
www.kierzek-berlin.de
Over 600 different whiskies in stock. In
the product range 50 kinds of rum and 450
wines from all over the world are found
among other products.

Smoke & Whisky
Wittelsbacherstrasse 14, 82319 Starnberg
Phone: +49 (0)8151-368223
www.smokeandwhisky.shop
A specialist on whisky and cigars (they
even have a huge walk-in humidor). More
than 700 different whiskies and rums.

Whisky For Life
Fahrgasse 6, 60311 Frankfurt am Main
Phone: +49 (0)173-6602413
www.whiskyforlife.de
Good range of malt whiskies and other
spirits.

The Whisky Brothers
Glockengasse 8, 93047 Regensburg
Phone: +49 (0)941 99 22 44 15
www.the-whisky-brothers.de
A family run shop with more than 1000
whiskies and also a range of rum, gin etc.

HUNGARY
Whisky Shop Budapest
Veres Pálné utca 7., 1053 Budapest
Phone: +36 1 267-1588

Hadak útja 1., 1119 Budapest
Phone: +36 20 325 29 75
www.whiskynet.hu
www.whiskyshop.hu
Largest selection of whisky in Hungary.
More than 900 different whiskies from all
over the world as well as a large selection
of other fine spirits. Most of them can be
tasted in the GoodSpirit Whisky & Cocktail Bar which operates in the same venue.

IRELAND

Celtic Whiskey Shop
27-28 Dawson Street, Dublin 2
Phone: +353 (0)1 675 9744
www.celticwhiskeyshop.com
More than 900 kinds of Irish whiskeys but
also a good selection of Scotch, wines and
other spirits. World wide shipping.

ITALY

Whisky Shop
by Milano Whisky Festival
Via Cavaleri 6, Milano
Phone: +39 (0)2 48753039
www.whiskyshop.it
The team behind the excellent
Milano Whisky Festival also have an on-
line whiskyshop with almost 700 different
whiskies including several special festival
bottlings.

Whisky Antique S.R.L.
Via Giardini Sud, 41043 Formigine (MO)
Phone: +39 (0)59 574278
www.whiskyantique.com
Whisky enthusiast and collector Massimo
Righi owns this shop specialising in rare
and collectable spirits – not only whisky
but also cognac, rum, armagnac etc.

JAPAN

Liquor Mountain Co.,Ltd.
4F Kyoto Kowa Bldg.
82 Tachiurinishi-Machi,
Takakura-Nishiiru,
Shijyo-Dori, Shimogyo-Ku,
Kyoto, 600-8007
Phone: +81 (0)75 213 8880
www.likaman.co.jp
The company has more than 150 shops
specialising in spirits, beer and food.
Around 20 of them are designated whisky
shops under the name Whisky Kingdom
(although they have a full range of other
spirits) with a range of 500 different whiskies. The three foremost shops are;

Rakzan Sanjyo Onmae
1-8, HigashiGekko-cho, Nishinokyo,
Nakagyo-ku, Kyoto-shi
Kyoto
Phone: +81 (0)75-842-5123

Nagakute
2-105, Ichigahara, Nagakute-shi
Aichi
Phone: +81 (0)561-64-3081

Kabukicho 1chome
1-2-16, Kabuki-cho, Shinjuku-ku
Tokyo
Phone: +81 (0)3-5287-2080

THE NETHERLANDS

Whiskyslijterij De Koning
Hinthamereinde 41
5211 PM 's Hertogenbosch
Phone: +31 (0)73-6143547
www.whiskykoning.nl
An enormous assortment with more than
1400 kinds of whisky including
c 800 single malts. Arranges recurring
tastings.

Van Wees - Whiskyworld.nl
Leusderweg 260, 3817 KH Amersfoort
Phone: +31 (0)33-461 53 19
www.whiskyworld.nl
A very large range of 1000 whiskies
including over 500 single malts. Also have
their own range of bottlings (The Ultimate
Whisky Company). On-line ordering.

Wijnhandel van Zuylen
Loosduinse Hoofdplein 201
2553 CP Loosduinen (Den Haag)
Phone: +31 (0)70-397 1400
www.whiskyvanzuylen.nl
Excellent range of whiskies (circa 1100)
and wines. Email orders with shipping to
some ten European countries.

Wijnwinkel-Slijterij
Ton Overmars, Hoofddorpplein 11
1059 CV Amsterdam
Phone: +31 (0)20-615 71 42
www.tonovermars.nl
A very large assortment of wines, spirits
and beer which includes more than 400
single malts. Arranges recurring tastings.

Wijn & Whisky Schuur
Blankendalwei 4, 8629 EH Scharnegoutem
Phone: +31 (0)515-520706
www.wijnwhiskyschuur.nl
Large assortment with 1000 different
whiskies and a good range of other spirits
as well. Arranges recurring tastings.

Wine and Whisky Specialist van der
Boog - Passion for Whisky
Prinses Irenelaan 359-361
2285 GA Rijswijk
Phone: +31 70 - 394 00 85
www.passionforwhisky.com
A very good range of almost 700 malt
whiskies (as well as a wide range of other
spirits). World wide shipping.

NEW ZEALAND

Whisky Galore
834 Colombo Street, Christchurch 8013
Phone: +64 (0) 800 944 759
www.whiskygalore.co.nz
The best whisky shop in New Zealand with
750 different whiskies, approximately
400 which are single malts. There is also
online mail-order with shipping all over
the world except USA and Canada. Owned
by Michael Fraser Milne who became a
Master of the Quaich in 2019.

POLAND

George Ballantine´s
Krucza str 47 A, Warsaw
Phone: +48 22 625 48 32

Pulawska str 22, Warsaw
Phone: +48 22 542 86 22

Marynarska str 15, Warsaw
Phone: +48 22 395 51 60

Zygmunta Vogla str 62, Warsaw
Phone: +48 22 395 51 64
www.sklep-ballantines.pl
A huge range of single malts and apart
from whisky there is a full range of
spirits and wines from all over the world.
Recurrent tastings and organiser of
Whisky Live Warsaw.

Dom Whisky
Wejherowska 67, Reda
Phone: +48 691 760 000, shop
Phone: +48 691 930 000, mailorder
www.sklep-domwhisky.pl
On-line retailer with a shop in Reda and
another two in Wroclaw and Warsaw. A
very large range of whiskies and other
spirits. Organiser of a whisky festival in
Jastrzębia Góra.

SCOTLAND

Gordon & MacPhail
58 - 60 South Street, Elgin
121 High Street, Elgin
Moray IV30 1JY
Phone: +44 (0)1343 545110
www.gordonandmacphail.com
This legendary shop opened already in
1895 in Elgin. The owners are perhaps
the most well-known among independent
bottlers. The shop stocks around 1000
single malt whiskies and more than 600
wines. Tastings are arranged in the shop
and there are shipping services within
the UK and overseas. The shop attracts
visitors from all over the world and the
company also owns two whisky distilleries
- Benromach and The Cairn.

Royal Mile Whiskies
379 High Street, The Royal Mile
Edinburgh EH1 1PW
Phone: +44 (0)131 2253383
www.royalmilewhiskies.com
Royal Mile Whiskies is one of the most
well-known whisky retailers in the UK. It
was established in Edinburgh in 1991. The
whisky range is outstanding with many
difficult to find elsewhere. They have a
comprehensive site regarding information
on regions, distilleries, production, tasting
etc. Royal Mile Whiskies also arranges
'Whisky Fringe' in Edinburgh, a two-day
whisky festival which takes place annually
in mid August. On-line ordering with
worldwide shipping.

The Whisky Shop
(See also England, The Whisky Shop)
Unit L2-02 Buchanan Galleries
220 Buchanan Street
Glasgow G1 2GF
Phone: +44 (0)141 331 0022

17 Bridge Street
Inverness IV1 1HD
Phone: +44 (0)1463 710525

93 High Street
Fort William PH33 6DG
Phone: +44 (0)1397 706164

52 George Street
Oban PA34 5SD
Phone: +44 (0)1631 570896

Unit 23 Waverley Mall
Waverley Bridge, Edinburgh EH1 1BQ
Phone: +44 (0)131 558 7563

28 Victoria Street
Edinburgh EH1 2JW
Phone: +44 (0)131 225 4666

Unit 18, Multrees Walk
Edinburgh EH1 3DQ
Phone: +44 (0)7721 973 463

www.whiskyshop.com
The first shop opened in 1992 in Edinburgh and this is now the United Kingdom's largest specialist retailer of whiskies with 22 outlets (plus one in Paris). A large product range with over 700 kinds, including 400 malt whiskies and 140 miniature bottles, as well as accessories and books. The own range 'Glenkeir Treasures' is a special assortment of selected malt whiskies. The also run The W Club where the excellent Whiskeria magazine is one of the member´s benefits.

The Scotch Malt Whisky Society
(venues)
28 Queen Street, Edinburgh EH2 1JX
Phone: +44 (0)131 625 7484

87 Giles Street, Edinburgh EH6 6BZ
Phone: +44 (0)131 554 3451

38 Bath Street, Glasgow G2 1HG
Phone: +44 (0)141 739 8810

19 Greville Street, London EC1N 8SQ
Phone: +44 (0)20 7831 4447
www.smws.com
A legendary society with more than 35 000 members worldwide, specialised in own bottlings of single cask Scotch whisky, releasing between 150 and 200 bottlings every year. Recently, the Society has also started bottling whisky from other parts of the world as well as gin, rum, armagnac and other spirits. Operates four venues in the UK and cooperates with partner bars around the world.

Whiskies of Scotland
36 Gordon Street
Huntly AB54 8EQ
Phone: +44 (0) 1466 795 105
www.thespiritsembassy.com
Owned by independent bottler Duncan Taylor. In the assortment is of course the whole Duncan Taylor range but also a selection of their own single malt bottlings called Whiskies of Scotland. A total of 700 different expressions. Also an on-line shop with shipping worldwide.

The Whisky Shop Dufftown
1 Fife Street, Dufftown
Moray AB55 4AL
Phone: +44 (0)1340 821097
www.whiskyshopdufftown.com
Whisky specialist in Dufftown in the heart of Speyside, wellknown to many of the Speyside festival visitors. Over 600 whiskies and 50 gins. Arranges tastings as well as special events during the Festivals.

Cadenhead's Whisky Shop
30-32 Union Street
Campbeltown PA28 6JA
Phone: +44 (0)1586 551710
www.cadenhead.scot
Part of the chain of shops owned by independent bottlers Cadenhead. Sells Cadenhead's products and other whiskies with a good range of Springbank.

Cadenhead´s Whisky Shop
172 Canongate, Royal Mile
Edinburgh EH8 8DF
Phone: +44 (0)131 556 5864
www.cadenhead.scot

The oldest shop in the chain owned by Cadenhead. Sells Cadenhead's product range and a good selection of other whiskies and spirits. Recurrent tastings.

The Good Spirits Co. (3 shops)
23 Bath Street, Glasgow G2 1HW
Phone: +44 (0)141 258 8427

21 Clarence Drive
Hyndland, Glasgow G12 9QN
Phone: +44 (0)141 334 4312

(mainly wine and beer)
105 West Nile Street, Glasgow G1 2SD
Phone: +44 (0)141 332 4481
www.thegoodspiritsco.com
A specialist spirits store selling whisky, bourbon, rum, vodka, tequila, gin, cognac and armagnac, liqueurs and other spirits. They also stock quality champagne, fortified wines and cigars. There are more than 400 single malts in the range as well as whiskies from the rest of the world.

A.D. Rattray´s Whisky Experience & Whisky Shop
32 Main Road, Kirkoswald
Ayrshire KA19 8HY
Phone: +44 (0) 1655 760308
www.adrattray.com
Recently revamped, this is a combination of whisky shop, sample room and educational center owned by the independent bottler A D Rattray. A wide range of whiskies and tasting menus with different themes are also available.

Loch Fyne Whiskies
Main Street, Inveraray, Argyll PA32 8UD
Phone: +44 (0)149 930 2219

36 Cockburn St
Edinburgh EH1 1PB
Phone: +44 (0)131 226 2134
www.lochfynewhiskies.com
A legendary shop and with a second shop in Edinburgh since 2018. The range of malt whiskies is large and they have their own house blend, the prize-awarded Loch Fyne, as well as their 'The Loch Fyne Whisky Liqueur'.

The Carnegie Whisky Cellars
The Carnegie Courthouse, Castle Street
Dornoch IV25 3SD
Phone: +44 (0)1862 811791
www.carnegiewhiskycellars.co.uk
Opened in 2016, this shop has already become a destination for whisky enthusiasts. The interior of the shop is ravishing and the extensive range includes all the latest releases as well as rare and collectable bottles. International shipping.

Abbey Whisky
Dunfermline KY11 3BZ
Phone: +44 (0)800 051 7737
www.abbeywhisky.com
Family run online whisky shop specialising in exclusive, rare and old whiskies from Scotland and the world. Apart from a wide range of official and independent bottlings, Abbey Whisky also selects their own casks and bottle them under the name 'The Rare Casks' and 'The Secret Casks'.

The Scotch Whisky Experience
354 Castlehill, Royal Mile
Edinburgh EH1 2NE
Phone: +44 (0)131 220 0441
www.scotchwhiskyexperience.co.uk
The Scotch Whisky Experience is a must for whisky devotees visiting Edinburgh with an interactive visitor centre dedicated to the history of Scotch whisky. This five-star visitor attraction has an excellent whisky shop with almost 300 different whiskies in stock. Following an extensive refurbishment, a brand new and interactive shop has been opened.

Tyndrum Whisky
Tyndrum, Perthshire FK20 8RY
Phone: +44 (0)1301 702 084
www.tyndrumwhisky.com
The new name for Whisky Galore at The Green Welly Stop. It was established at a road junction between Glencoe and The Trossachs nearly 60 years ago. Well equipped with a nice range of Scottish single malts, grains and blends but also world whiskies and other spirits.

The Whisky Castle
6 Main Street, Tomintoul AB37 9EX
Phone: +44 (0)1807 580 213
www.whiskycastle.com
A legendary shop that specialises in single malts (more than 600) and single casks in particular. Also a range of whiskies bottled exclusively for The Whisky Castle.

Whiski Shop
4 North Bank Street
Edinburgh EH1 2LP
Phone: +44 (0)131 225 7224
www.whiskishop.com
www.whiskirooms.co.uk
A new concept located near Edinburgh Castle, combining a shop and tasting room combined with a bar and restaurant in 119 High Street. Also regular whisky tastings.

Robbie's Drams
3 Sandgate, Ayr, South Ayrshire KA7 1BG
Phone: +44 (0)1292 262 135
www.robbieswhiskymerchants.com
An extensive range of whiskies available both in store and from their on-line shop. Specialists in single cask bottlings, closed distillery bottlings, rare malts, limited edition whisky and a nice range of their own bottlings. Worldwide shipping.

The Whisky Barrel
Unit 3, Cupar, KY15 5JY
Phone: +44 (0)1334 655 499
www.thewhiskybarrel.com
Online specialist whisky shop based in Edinburgh. They stock over 3,000 single malt and blended whiskies including Scotch, Japanese, Irish, Indian, Swedish and their own casks.

Drinkmonger
100 Athol Road, Pitlochry PH16 5BL
Phone: +44 (0)1796 470133

11 Bruntsfield Place
Edinburgh EH10 4HN
Phone: +44 (0)131 229 2205
www.drinkmonger.com
Owned by Royal Mile Whiskies, the idea is to have a 50:50 split between wine and

specialist spirits with the addition of a cigar assortment. The whisky range is a good cross-section with some rarities and a focus on local distilleries.

Luvian's
93 Bonnygate, Cupar, Fife KY15 4LG
Phone: +44 (0)1334 654 820
66 Market Street, St Andrews
Fife KY16 9NU
Phone: +44 (0)1334 477 752
www.luvians.com
A legendary wine and whisky retailer owned by the three Luvian brothers with a very nice selection of more than 1,200 whiskies (600 single malts).

The Johnnie Walker Experience
145 Princes Street, Edinburgh EH2 4BL
Phone: +44 (0)131 376 9494
www.johnniewalker.com
Opened in 2021 this extraordinary five storey venue in the middle of Edinburgh is dedicated to the world's most sold whisky - Johnnie Walker. Tours and spectacular experiences can be booked and there are is a restaurant and a roof top bar. The shop on ground floor sells a variety of Johnnie Walker bottlings as well as a wide range of single malts from Diageo.

The Stillroom
Gleneagles Hotel
Auchterarder, Perthshire PH3 1NF
Phone: +44 (0) 1764 694 188
www.gleneagles.com
Located in the famous hotel, the shop has an excellent range of both rare and collectible whiskies as well as single malts from a large number of Scottish distilleries.

Robertsons of Pitlochry
44-46 Atholl Road, Pitlochry PH16 5BX
Phone: +44 (0) 1796 472011
www.robertsonsofpitlochry.co.uk
With new owner since 2013, the shop has grown to become one of Scotland's best. An extensive range of both whisky and gin is complemented by single malts bottled under their own label. There's also an excellent tasting room (The Bothy).

Robert Graham Ltd (3 shops)
194 Rose Street
Edinburgh EH2 4AZ
Phone: +44 (0)131 226 1874

111 West George Street
Glasgow G2 1QX
Phone: +44 (0)141 248 7283

9 Sussex Street, Cambridge CB1 1PA
Phone: +44 (0)1223 354 459
www.robertgraham1874.com
Established in 1874 this company specialises in Scotch whisky and cigars. A nice assortment of malt whiskies is complemented by an impressive range of cigars. They also bottle whiskies under their own label.

The Speyside Whisky Shop
110A High Street
Aberlour AB38 9NX
Phone: +44 (0) 1340 871260
www.thespeysidewhisky.com
Opened in 2018, the shop is situated in the very heart of Speyside, in Aberlour. The

owners specialise in highly collectable single malts from a variety of distilleries. Also a wide selection of craft gins.

Inverurie Whisky Shop
1 Burnside, Burn Lane,
Inverurie AB51 3RY
Phone: +44 (0)1467 622412
www.inveruriewhiskyshop.com
An excellent wine and spirits shop with a very large range of whiskies including their own bottlings. Arranges regular tastings as well as whisky tours. There is also a regular whisky chat on-line called "The Blether" where people from the industry are invited to share their views.

Highland Whisky Shop
23 Castle Street, Inverness IV2 3EP,
Phone: +44 (0)1463 592 055
www.highlandwhiskyshop.co.uk
A fairly new whisky shop right by the castle in Inverness. Close to 400 different whiskies as well as other spirits and there is also a bar where you can create your own tasting.

Whisky Please
24 Heather Avenue, Glasgow G61 3JE
Phone: +44 (0)781 806 1010
www.whiskyplease.co.uk
Online retailer of whiskies and other spirits. A very nice presentation of each distillery with a picture and text.

The Islay Whisky Shop
Shore Street, Bowmore, Islay PA43 7LB
Phone: +44 (0)1496 810 684
www.islaywhiskyshop.com
A must for any visitor to Islay, this shop has an impressive range of Islay whiskies, some of them very rare and limited.

Aberdeen Whisky Shop
474 Union Street, Aberdeen AB10 1TS
Phone: +44 (0)1224 647 433
www.aberdeenwhiskyshop.co.uk
A nice selection of whiskies but also other spirits. Free tastings in the shop every Saturday.

SOUTH AFRICA
WhiskyBrother (3 shops)
Shop 16 D Middle Mall,
Hyde Park Corner Shopping Centre,
Johannesburg
Phone: +27 (0)63 294 7285

Nicolway Mall (top level)
William Nicol Drive, Bryanston,
Johannesburg
Phone: +27 (0)81 081 8832

Bedford Centre (Inside mall, ground level)
Van Der Linde Road, Bedfordview,
Johannesburg
Phone: +27 (0)10 054 6007
www.whiskybrother.com
Three shops specialising in all things whisky - apart from 400 different bottlings they also sell glasses, books etc. Also sell whiskies bottled exclusively for the shop. Regular tastings and online shop. Also run a whisky bar in Johannesburg with more than 1,000 different whiskies to try. The owner, Marc Pendlebury, is also the organiser of The Only Whisky Show in Johannesburg and Cape Town.

SWITZERLAND
P. Ullrich AG
Schneidergasse 27
4051 Basel
Phone: +41 (0)61 338 90 91
Another two shops in Basel:
Laufenstrasse 16 and Unt. Rebgasse 18, one in Talacker 30 in Zürich and one in Kramgasse 45 in Bern.
www.ullrich.ch
A very large range of wines, spirits, beers, accessories and books. Over 800 kinds of whisky with almost 600 single malt. On-line ordering. Recently, they also founded a whisky club with regular tastings and offers. (www.whiskysinn.ch).

Eddie's Whiskies
Bahnhofstrasse/Dorfgasse 27
8810 Horgen
Phone: +41 (0)43 244 63 00
www.eddies.ch
A whisky specialist with more than 750 different whiskies in stock with emphasis on single malts (more than 500 different). Also arranges tastings.

UKRAINE
WINETIME
Mykoly Bazhana 1E
Kyiv 02068
Phone: +38 (0)44 338 08 88
www.winetime.ua
WINETIME is the largest specialized chain of wine, spirits and food shops in Ukraine. The company runs 31 stores in 14 regions of Ukraine. An impressive selection of spirits with over 1000 whiskies of which 600 are malt whiskies. On-line ordering. Also regular whisky tastings.

USA
Binny's Beverage Depot
5100 W. Dempster (Head Office)
Skokie, IL 60077
Phone:
Internet orders, 888-942-9463 (toll free)
www.binnys.com
A chain of no less than 45 stores in the Chicago area, covering everything within wine and spirits. Some of the stores also have a gourmet grocery, cheese shop and, for cigar lovers, a walk-in humidor. Also lots of regular events in the stores. The range is impressive with more than 2400 whisk(e)y including 600 single malt Scotch, 630 bourbons, 300 rye and more. Among other products more than 700 kinds of tequila and mezcal, 600 vodkas, 490 rums and 300 gins.

Statistics

The information on the following pages is based
on figures from Scotch Whisky Association (SWA), Drinks International
and directly from the producers.

The Top 30 Whiskies of the World

Sales figures for 2022 (units in million 9-litre cases)

McDowell´s No. 1 (Diageo/United Spirits), Indian whisky — 30,8
Royal Stag (Pernod Ricard), Indian whisky — 27,1
Officer´s Choice (Allied Blenders & Distillers), Indian whisky — 24,9
Imperial Blue (Pernod Ricard), Indian whisky — 24,0
Johnnie Walker (Diageo), Scotch whisky — 22,7
Jack Daniel´s (Brown-Forman), Tennessee whiskey — 14,6
Jameson (Pernod Ricard), Irish whiskey — 11,1
Blenders Pride (Pernod Ricard), Indian whisky — 9,5
Ballantine´s (Pernod Ricard), Scotch whisky — 9,2
8 PM (Radico Khaitan), Indian whisky — 9,1
Crown Royal (Diageo), Canadian whisky — 8,4
Royal Challenge (Diageo/United Spirits), Indian whisky — 7,2
Kakubin (Suntory), Japanese whisky — 6,1
Chivas Regal (Pernod Ricard), Scotch whisky — 5,2
Grant´s (Wm Grand & Sons), Scotch whisky — 4,2
Black & White (Diageo), Scotch whisky — 3,6
Dewar´s (Bacardi), Scotch whisky — 3,5
William Lawson´s (Bacardi), Scotch whisky — 3,5
Kanoka (Asahi Breweries), Japanese whisky — 3,5
Black Nikka Clear (Asahi Breweries), Japanese whisky — 3,3
Evan Williams (Heaven Hill), Bourbon — 3,1
Royal Green (ADS Spirits), Indian whisky — 3,1
Director´s Special (Diageo/United Spirits), Indian whisky — 3,0
J&B (Diageo), Scotch whisky — 2,9
Torys (Beam Suntory), Japanese whisky — 2,9
8 PM Premium Black (Radico Khaitan), Indian whisky — 2,8
William Peel (Marie Brizard), Scotch whisky — 2,7
White Horse (Diageo), Scotch whisky — 2,7
Label 5 (La Martiniquaise), Scotch whisky — 2,5
Buchanan´s (Diageo), Scotch whisky — 2,5

* For some brands that are usually on this list, the producers have chosen not to disclose sales figures for 2022.
These include Jim Beam, Bagpiper, Hayward´s Fine and Old Tavern.

Source: Drinks International, The Millionaires Club 2023

Global Exports of Scotch by Region 2022

Volume (litres of pure alcohol)			Value (£ Sterling)		
Region	000s of litres	Change in %	Region	000s of £	Change in %
Asia & Oceania	134 081	+45,2	Asia & Oceania	1 818 114	+50,1
Eastern Europe exc EU	7 988	-40,9	Eastern Europe exc EU	38 916	-17,7
European Union	157 623	+17,1	European Union	1 595 871	+17,1
Latin America & Carribean	67 083	+17,7	Latin America & Carribean	736 953	+66,2
Middle East & North Africa	16 461	+39,1	Middle East & North Africa	325 708	+73,8
North America	56 227	+7,6	North America	1 326 533	+32,0
Sub-Saharan Africa	18 225	+4,8	Sub-Saharan Africa	203 924	+29,6
Western Europe exc EU	10 841	+32,5	Western Europe exc EU	146 471	+49,1
Total	468 530	+21,0	Total	6 192 515	+37,2

Source: Scotch Whisky Association

Export of Scotch Whisky 2022

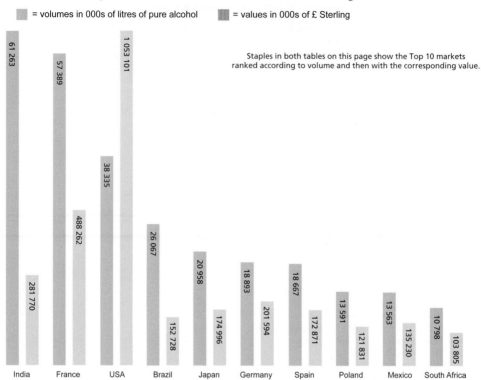

= volumes in 000s of litres of pure alcohol   = values in 000s of £ Sterling

Staples in both tables on this page show the Top 10 markets ranked according to volume and then with the corresponding value.

India: 61 263 | 281 770
France: 57 389 | 488 262
USA: 1 053 101 | 38 335
Brazil: 26 067 | 152 728
Japan: 20 958 | 174 996
Germany: 18 893 | 201 594
Spain: 18 667 | 172 871
Poland: 13 591 | 121 831
Mexico: 13 563 | 135 230
South Africa: 10 798 | 103 805

Source: Scotch Whisky Association

Export of Single Malt Scotch 2022

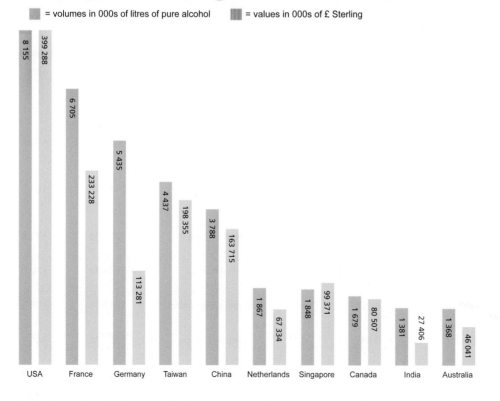

= volumes in 000s of litres of pure alcohol   = values in 000s of £ Sterling

USA: 8 155 | 399 288
France: 6 705 | 233 228
Germany: 5 435 | 113 281
Taiwan: 4 437 | 198 355
China: 3 788 | 163 715
Netherlands: 1 867 | 67 334
Singapore: 1 848 | 99 371
Canada: 1 679 | 80 507
India: 1 381 | 27 406
Australia: 1 368 | 46 041

Source: Scotch Whisky Association

Distillery Capacity
Litres of pure alcohol - Scottish, active distilleries only

Glenfiddich	21 000 000	Dalwhinnie	2 200 000	Burn O´Bennie	680 000
Glenlivet	21 000 000	Fettercairn	2 200 000	Kilchoman	650 000
Macallan	15 000 000	Bowmore	2 150 000	The Clydeside	620 000
Roseisle	12 500 000	Ben Nevis	2 000 000	Kingsbarns	600 000
Ailsa Bay	12 000 000	Bruichladdich	2 000 000	Annandale	500 000
Glen Ord	11 900 000	Glendronach	2 000 000	Ardnamurchan	500 000
Teaninich	10 200 000	Knockdhu	2 000 000	Glenturret	500 000
Dalmunach	10 000 000	Balblair	1 800 000	Royal Lochnagar	500 000
Glen Moray	8 500 000	Pulteney	1 700 000	Springbank	500 000
Glenmorangie	7 100 000	The Borders	1 600 000	Torabhaig	500 000
Balvenie	7 000 000	Bladnoch	1 500 000	Brew Dog	450 000
Caol Ila	6 500 000	Glen Garioch	1 500 000	Harris	400 000
Glen Grant	6 200 000	Glen Spey	1 500 000	Port of Leith	400 000
Dufftown	6 000 000	Knockando	1 400 000	Glasgow	365 000
Glen Keith	6 000 000	Glencadam	1 300 000	Jackton	300 000
Mannochmore	6 000 000	Scapa	1 300 000	Edradour	260 000
Auchroisk	5 900 000	Falkirk	1 200 000	Holyrood	250 000
Miltonduff	5 800 000	Lochranza	1 200 000	Lindores Abbey	225 000
Glenrothes	5 600 000	Tobermory	1 200 000	Isle of Raasay	220 000
Linkwood	5 600 000	Glenglassaugh	1 100 000	Arbikie	200 000
Dailuaine	5 200 000	Glengoyne	1 100 000	Dunphail	200 000
Glendullan	5 000 000	Ardnahoe	1 000 000	Lochlea	200 000
Loch Lomond	5 000 000	Ardross	1 000 000	8 Doors	150 000
Tomatin	5 000 000	The Cairn	1 000 000	Glen Wyvis	140 000
Ardmore	4 900 000	Rosebank	1 000 000	Strathearn	140 000
Clynelish	4 800 000	Oban	870 000	Wolfburn	135 000
Kininvie	4 800 000	Speyside	850 000	Ballindalloch	100 000
Tormore	4 800 000	Brora	800 000	Eden Mill	100 000
Dalmore	4 500 000	Glen Scotia	800 000	Ncn´ean	100 000
Longmorn	4 500 000	Aberargie	750 000	Daftmill	65 000
Speyburn	4 500 000	Glengyle	750 000	Abhainn Dearg	20 000
Royal Brackla	4 300 000	Lagg	750 000	Uile-bheist	20 000
Glenburgie	4 250 000	Port Ellen	750 000	Dornoch	12 000
Allt-a-Bhainne	4 200 000	Bonnington	720 000	Moffat	12 000
Braeval	4 200 000	Benromach	700 000		
Glentauchers	4 200 000				
Tamnavulin	4 200 000				
Craigellachie	4 100 000				
Glenallachie	4 000 000				
Inchdairnie	4 000 000				
Tamdhu	4 000 000				
Aberlour	3 800 000				
Mortlach	3 800 000				
Glenlossie	3 700 000				
Benrinnes	3 500 000				
Bunnahabhain	3 500 000				
Glenfarclas	3 500 000				
Talisker	3 500 000				
Aberfeldy	3 400 000				
Cardhu	3 400 000				
Macduff	3 400 000				
Laphroaig	3 300 000				
Tomintoul	3 300 000				
Aultmore	3 200 000				
Inchgower	3 200 000				
Deanston	3 000 000				
Lagavulin	3 000 000				
Tullibardine	3 000 000				
Balmenach	2 900 000				
Benriach	2 800 000				
Blair Athol	2 800 000				
Glen Elgin	2 700 000				
Strathmill	2 600 000				
Auchentoshan	2 500 000				
Glenkinchie	2 500 000				
Highland Park	2 500 000				
Jura	2 500 000				
Strathisla	2 450 000				
Ardbeg	2 400 000				
Cragganmore	2 200 000				

Summary of Malt Distillery Capacity by Owner

Owner (number of distilleries)	Litres of alcohol	% of Industry
Diageo (30)	124 520 000	29,1
Pernod Ricard (12)	71 700 000	16,7
William Grant (4)	44 800 000	10,5
Edrington Group (3)	23 100 000	5,4
Bacardi (John Dewar & Sons) (5)	18 400 000	4,3
Beam Suntory (5)	14 350 000	3,4
Emperador Inc (Whyte & Mackay) (4)	13 400 000	3,1
Pacific Spirits (Inver House) (5)	12 900 000	3,0
Moët Hennessy (Glenmorangie) (2)	9 500 000	2,2
La Martiniquaise (Glen Moray) (1)	8 500 000	2,0
CVH Spirits (Burn Stewart) (3)	7 700 000	1,8
Campari (Glen Grant) (1)	6 200 000	1,4
Ian Macleod Distillers (3)	6 100 000	1,4
Benriach Distillery Co (3)	5 900 000	1,4
Loch Lomond Group (2)	5 800 000	1,4
Tomatin Distillery Co (1)	5 000 000	1,2
Elixir Distillers (Tormore) (1)	4 800 000	1,1
Angus Dundee (2)	4 600 000	1,1
InchDairnie Distillery Ltd. (Inchdairnie) (1)	4 000 000	1,0
The Glenallachie Distillers (1)	4 000 000	1,0
J & G Grant (Glenfarclas) (1)	3 500 000	0,8
Picard (Tullibardine) (1)	3 000 000	0,7
Nikka (Ben Nevis Distillery) (1)	2 000 000	0,5
Rémy Cointreau (Bruichladdich) (1)	2 000 000	0,5
Isle of Arran Distillers (2)	1 950 000	0,5
Gordon & MacPhail (2)	1 700 000	< 0,5
The Three Stills Co. (The Borders) (1)	1 600 000	< 0,5
David Prior (Bladnoch) (1)	1 500 000	< 0,5
J & A Mitchell (2)	1 250 000	< 0,5
Stewart family (Falkirk) (1)	1 200 000	< 0,5
Hunter Laing (Ardnahoe) (1)	1 000 000	< 0,5
Others (36)	12 334 000	2,9
Total (139)	**428 304 000**	

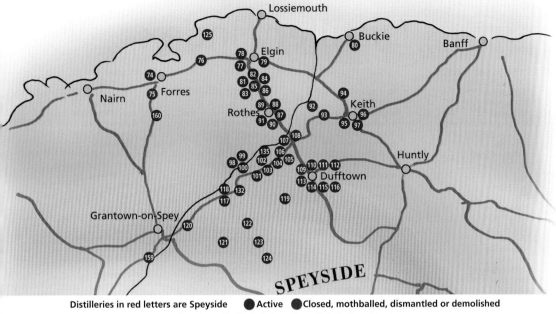

Lossiemouth · Buckie · Banff · Elgin · Forres · Nairn · Rothes · Keith · Huntly · Dufftown · Grantown-on-Spey

SPEYSIDE

Distilleries in red letters are Speyside ● Active ● Closed, mothballed, dismantled or demolished

c = Closed, m = Mothballed, dm = Dismantled, d = Demolished

164 8 Doors	45 Deanston	43 Kingsbarns	2 Highland Park	56 Ladyburn (dm)	110 Dufftown
148 Aberargie	144 Dornoch	114 Kininvie	3 Scapa	57 Bladnoch	111 Pittyvaich (d)
39 Aberfeldy	110 Dufftown	100 Knockando	4 Pulteney	58 Arran	112 Glenfiddich
106 Aberlour	160 Dunphail	21 Knockdhu	5 Brora	59 Springbank	113 Balvenie
127 Abhainn Dearg	136 Eden Mill	56 Ladyburn (dm)	6 Clynelish	60 Glengyle	114 Kininvie
126 Ailsa Bay	38 Edradour	63 Lagavulin	7 Balblair	61 Glen Scotia	115 Mortlach
119 Allt-a-Bhainne	154 Falkirk	150 Lagg	8 Glenmorangie	62 Ardbeg	116 Glendullan
128 Annandale	32 Fettercairn	64 Laphroaig	9 Ben Wyvis (c)	63 Lagavulin	117 Tormore
134 Arbikie	141 Glasgow	137 Lindores Abbey	10 Teaninich	64 Laphroaig	118 Cragganmore
62 Ardbeg	13 Glen Albyn (d)	79 Linkwood	11 Dalmore	65 Port Ellen	119 Allt-a-Bhainne
25 Ardmore	105 Glenallachie	48 Littlemill (d)	12 Glen Ord	66 Bowmore	120 Balmenach
147 Ardnahoe	76 Glenburgie	156 Lochlea	13 Glen Albyn (d)	67 Bruichladdich	121 Tomintoul
131 Ardnamurchan	34 Glencadam	46 Loch Lomond	14 Glen Mhor (d)	68 Kilchoman	122 Glenlivet
151 Ardross	23 Glendronach	36 Lochside (d)	15 Millburn (dm)	69 Caol Ila	123 Tamnavulin
58 Arran	116 Glendullan	143 Lone Wolf	16 Royal Brackla	70 Bunnahabhain	124 Braeval
49 Auchentoshan	85 Glen Elgin	84 Longmorn	17 Tomatin	71 Jura	125 Roseisle
92 Auchroisk	35 Glenesk (dm)	107 Macallan	18 Glenglassaugh	72 Tobermory	126 Ailsa Bay
94 Aultmore	101 Glenfarclas	20 Macduff	19 Banff (d)	73 Talisker	127 Abhainn Dearg
7 Balblair	112 Glenfiddich	81 Mannochmore	20 Macduff	74 Benromach	128 Annandale
132 Ballindalloch	52 Glen Flagler (d)	15 Millburn (dm)	21 Knockdhu	75 Dallas Dhu (c)	129 Wolfburn
120 Balmenach	24 Glen Garioch	77 Miltonduff	22 Glenugie (dm)	76 Glenburgie	130 Strathearn
113 Balvenie	18 Glenglassaugh	161 Moffat	23 Glendronach	77 Miltonduff	131 Ardnamurchan
19 Banff (d)	50 Glengoyne	115 Mortlach	24 Glen Garioch	78 Glen Moray	132 Ballindalloch
30 Ben Nevis	87 Glen Grant	145 Nc´nean	25 Ardmore	79 Linkwood	133 Inchdairnie
82 Benriach	60 Glengyle	33 North Port (d)	26 Speyside	80 Inchgower	134 Arbikie
104 Benrinnes	96 Glen Keith	40 Oban	27 Royal Lochnagar	81 Mannochmore	135 Dalmunach
74 Benromach	55 Glenkinchie	111 Pittyvaich (d)	28 Glenury Royal (d)	82 Benriach	136 Eden Mill
9 Ben Wyvis (c)	122 Glenlivet	65 Port Ellen	29 Dalwhinnie	83 Glenlossie	137 Lindores Abbey
57 Bladnoch	31 Glenlochy (d)	163 Port of Leith	30 Ben Nevis	84 Longmorn	138 Borders
37 Blair Athol	83 Glenlossie	4 Pulteney	31 Glenlochy (d)	85 Glen Elgin	139 Torabhaig
153 Bonnington	14 Glen Mhor (d)	53 Rosebank	32 Fettercairn	86 Coleburn (dm)	140 Harris
138 Borders	8 Glenmorangie	125 Roseisle	33 North Port (d)	87 Glen Grant	141 Glasgow
66 Bowmore	78 Glen Moray	16 Royal Brackla	34 Glencadam	88 Speyburn	142 Clydeside
124 Braeval	12 Glen Ord	27 Royal Lochnagar	35 Glenesk (dm)	89 Glenrothes	143 Lone Wolf
5 Brora	89 Glenrothes	54 St Magdalene (dm)	36 Lochside (d)	90 Caperdonich (c)	144 Dornoch
67 Bruichladdich	61 Glen Scotia	3 Scapa	37 Blair Athol	91 Glenspey	145 Nc´nean
70 Bunnahabhain	91 Glenspey	88 Speyburn	38 Edradour	92 Auchroisk	146 Isle of Raasay
155 Burn O´Bennie	93 Glentauchers	26 Speyside	39 Aberfeldy	93 Glentauchers	147 Ardnahoe
159 The Cairn	41 Glenturret	59 Springbank	40 Oban	94 Aultmore	148 Aberargie
69 Caol Ila	22 Glenugie (dm)	130 Strathearn	41 Glenturret	95 Strathmill	149 Glen Wyvis
90 Caperdonich (c)	28 Glenury Royal (d)	97 Strathisla	42 Daftmill	96 Glen Keith	150 Lagg
99 Cardhu	149 Glen Wyvis	95 Strathmill	43 Kingsbarns	97 Strathisla	151 Ardross
142 Clydeside	140 Harris	73 Talisker	44 Tullibardine	98 Tamdhu	152 Holyrood
6 Clynelish	2 Highland Park	98 Tamdhu	45 Deanston	99 Cardhu	153 Bonnington
86 Coleburn (dm)	152 Holyrood	123 Tamnavulin	46 Loch Lomond	100 Knockando	154 Falkirk
109 Convalmore (dm)	133 Inchdairnie	10 Teaninich	47 Inverleven (d)	101 Glenfarclas	155 Burn O´Bennie
118 Cragganmore	102 Imperial (d)	72 Tobermory	48 Littlemill (d)	102 Imperial (d)	156 Lochlea
108 Craigellachie	80 Inchgower	17 Tomatin	49 Auchentoshan	103 Dailuaine	157 Jackton
42 Daftmill	47 Inverleven (d)	121 Tomintoul	50 Glengoyne	104 Benrinnes	158 Toulvaddie
103 Dailuaine	146 Isle of Raasay	139 Torabhaig	51 Kinclaith (d)	105 Glenallachie	159 The Cairn
75 Dallas Dhu (c)	157 Jackton	117 Tormore	52 Glen Flagler (d)	106 Aberlour	160 Dunphail
11 Dalmore	71 Jura	158 Toulvaddie	53 Rosebank	107 Macallan	161 Moffat
135 Dalmunach	68 Kilchoman	44 Tullibardine	54 St Magdalene(dm)	108 Craigellachie	162 Uile-bheist
29 Dalwhinnie	51 Kinclaith (d)	162 Uile-bheist	55 Glenkinchie	109 Convalmore (dm)	163 Port of Leith
		129 Wolfburn			164 8 Doors

Distillery Index

Distillery Index

Distillery Index